Withhold Not Thine Hand

Withhold Not Thine Hand

SUNDAY EVENING SERMONS

AND

THURSDAY EVENING LECTURES

To which are added

SERMONS PREACHED ON SPECIAL OCCASIONS

WILLIAM JAY

SOLID GROUND CHRISTIAN BOOKS
BIRMINGHAM, ALABAMA USA

Solid Ground Christian Books
2090 Columbiana Rd, Suite 2000
Birmingham, AL 35216
205-443-0311
sgcb@charter.net
http://solid-ground-books.com

Withhold Not Thine Hand
SUNDAY EVENING SERMONS AND THURSDAY EVENING LECTURES

William Jay (1769-1853)

Taken from 1879 edition by R.D. Dickinson, London

Solid Ground Classic Reprints

First printing of new edition June 2005

Cover work by Borgo Design, Tuscaloosa, AL
Contact them at nelbrown@comcast.net

Special thanks to Ric Ergenbright for permission to use the image on the cover. Visit him at ricergenbright.org

ISBN: 1-932474-85-4

INTRODUCTION.

THE following brief sketch of Mr. JAY'S career, which appeared in the *Congregational Year Book* for 1855, will be new and interesting to many of the present generation of preachers :—

JAY, WILLIAM, Bath, was a native of Tisbury, Wiltshire. He was born May 8th, 1769. His father was a stone-cutter and mason, and intended his son to follow his steps, but God had otherwise designed. The lad was thoughtful, a lover of rural scenes, and industrious in his calling. He had few religious or educational advantages. A room was opened for preaching in his native village; he was one of the first attendants, with his white jacket and his tucked-up leather apron. Cornelius Winter preached there one Sabbath, and was struck with the appearance of a shrewd, intelligent-looking mason's boy among the little flock. At his next visit he inquired for "Billy Jay," and found him to be the lad he had formerly noticed. He proposed taking him to Marlborough for education, and to prepare him for the ministry. His consent was obtained, and the youthful mason soon became a popular preacher. The two names of Cornelius Winter and William Jay will ever be associated in the memory of the Church. Each was indebted to the other for his fame; without Winter's influence Jay would have been an obscure village mason; and without Jay the incomparable memoirs of Cornelius Winter would never have been written, and Winter's name would have been unknown beyond the limits of the narrow circle in which he moved.

The "boy preacher" was soon sought for in every direction. He settled for a year at Christian Malford, and then at the Hot Wells, Clifton, but was soon called to Bath, where he spent sixty-three years of his precious life in preaching the Gospel to successive generations of hearers, and to numbers of the noble and titled, who attended his chapel for the same reason that they went to see the other "lions" of the city. Numbers of these were, by the blessing of God, rescued from the illusions of folly and sin, and became decided followers of the Redeemer. Here, too, he penned his valuable and instructive writings, collected by himself in twelve volumes; to which have been added one or two posthumous works. When living, he was one of the most useful of God's servants; and, now dead, he yet speaketh.

He was, while in his teens, introduced to Surrey Chapel as a supply, and attracted thousands to that noble sanctuary. He preached there, annually, through a long succession of years. His visits to London, and his position at Bath—the seat and centre of fashion during the earlier part of the present century—introduced him to many distinguished characters, and with many of whom he formed friendships which lasted through life. The names of Wilberforce and Hannah More, of John Newton and John Ryland, of Rowland Hill and Richard Cecil, of Robert Hall and John Foster, were embalmed in his memory, and are memorialised by him in his "Autobiography and Reminiscences," just published, and from whence this notice is drawn.

His sun set in glory. He preached almost to the last; his popularity never waned, either in his own sphere or beyond it. He went down to the grave, prepared to rise amid the unclouded splendours of eternity. His character, his fame, his works, are so well known, and the notices, memoirs, funeral sermons, are so numerous—and, above all, his "Autobiography and Reminiscences" are so complete—that little further need be said, either for information or commendation.

His life is a study and a lesson for all who aspire to the ministry. His "Autobiography" is a reproduction of the sentiments, opinions, and advices he constantly repeated to such of his ministerial brethren as had the privilege of his acquaintance. His character was most estimable and lovely. Years neither made him sour nor garrulous. Though a patriarch among his brethren, he was kind, considerate, and encouraging. He sought to learn even from the youngest, as he was ever ready to instruct.

But death will come. "He died!" His sufferings were great at intervals, but patience did "her perfect work." He exclaimed, "The language of the publican did, does, and ever will befit me; and even down to my death must be my cry, 'God be merciful to me a sinner!' I do not murmur—allow me to groan; it seems to ease my pain. Objects most dear and attractive now fail to interest. O for a grateful heart! I have made some little stir in life; but now I am nothing. God seems to be saying, 'I can do without you.'"

His last distinct utterance was "Oh! none of you know what it is to die!" He sank gradually into death, and ascended to life on the morning of Tuesday, December 27, 1853, in the eighty-fifth year of his age, having been a preacher of the word during the long period of sixty-seven years. He rests from his labours, and "his works do follow him."

CONTENTS.

SERMONS PREACHED ON SUNDAY EVENINGS.

THURSDAY EVENING LECTURES.

X.

ASAPH'S CONCLUSION.

SERMONS PREACHED ON SPECIAL OCCASIONS.

I.

DELIVERED FROM THE PIT.

I waited patiently for the Lord; and He inclined unto me, and heard my cry. He brought me up, also, out of an horrible pit, out of the miry clay, and set my feet upon a rock, and established my goings. And He hath put a new song in my mouth, even praise unto our God: many shall see it and fear, and shall trust in the Lord.—PSALM xl., 1-3.

WE view religion under a threefold distinction. The first regards doctrine, the second regards practice, and the third regards experience. Some parts of Scripture are more appropriate to one, and some to another.

When we think of matters of experience we naturally turn to the Book of Psalms; for there David comes forward and lays open his various struggles and trials—the sources of his pleasure, and of his pain—of his fears and of his hopes, and we know his heart's bitterness and intermeddle with his joy.

It is a remark of good Matthew Henry, that sweetest of all commentators, that "it is impossible to read the Book of Psalms without being either inflamed or ashamed by the perusal." Let us not fear lest we should be ashamed of ourselves, for as Bishop Hall observes, "Our repenting days are always our best days"; and says the Saviour, "Blessed are they that mourn, for they shall be comforted." There is no prayer more becoming us than that of the publican, "God be merciful to me a sinner!" "He satisfieth the longing soul, and filleth the hungry soul with His goodness."

To come a little nearer to our text, observe, whatever feeling the perusal of the Scriptures may immediately produce in us, we know the ultimate end and aim of the whole; for says the Apostle, "Whatsoever things were written aforetime were written for our learning, that we through patience and comfort of the Scriptures might have hope." And with this corresponds the passage we have now read, "I waited patiently for the Lord; and He inclined unto me, and heard my cry. He brought me up also out of an horrible pit, out of the miry clay, and set my feet upon a rock, and established my goings. And he hath put a new song in my mouth, even praise unto our God: many shall see it, and fear, and shall trust in the Lord."

Now let us fill up the remainder of the time allowed for this service by considering four things: David's condition, his engagement, his success, and his profit under the dispensation.

I. DAVID'S CONDITION.

He was in "an horrible pit," and in the "miry clay."

We know not in what particular condition David was. So much the better; for did you know precisely what his condition was then, unless your condition happened to be the same, you would be ready to say that as yours does not correspond with it, you cannot look for the same support and consolation under it. But now none of you can say this, for you know not what it was; and so you see the Scripture is useful for what it conceals, as well as for what it reveals. Thus the shade on the dial aids in showing us the time as well as the shining of the sun.

All we know is this, that it was a destitute, a desolate, a dreary, and a dreadful condition. Observe the imagery, "a *horrible* pit," the bottom of it being "miry clay," where the poor prisoner would be sure to sink, and the very effort to draw one foot out would press the other the deeper down; and only think of him being there, not for an hour or a day, or a week, but for many weeks, ready to perish!

To what is this to be applied? It may be applied to a state of outward trial arising from the straits of poverty. It may be applied to worldly hopes and disappointments, to family bereavements, to sickness of body, to the persecution of enemies and the perfidy of friends. We may also apply it to the state of mind arising from doctrinal difficulties and perplexities, from doubts and fears arising from concern about Salvation, from the hidings of God's face, and from sore temptations.

The mind, when it is deprived of confidence and peace, falls into gloom, meditates terror, and takes apprehensions for realities.

Now, the case is much aggravated where there is a combination of these outward trials and these inward distresses. And such was David's case, as we see in a former Psalm, where he bemoans himself, saying, "My bones are vexed, my soul also is sore vexed; but Thou, O Lord, how long?"

Neither is it necessary that such a state of trial be derived entirely from your own personal experience. No, there are cases in which you as severely suffer relatively, as ever you do personally. Yes, there are cases in which the sympathiser feels more than even the afflicted themselves. The poor Syro-Phœnician woman came to our Saviour and said, "Jesus, Thou Son of David, have mercy on *me*; my daughter is grievously vexed with a devil."

Neither is it necessary that these trials, in order to constitute suffering like this, should be visible. A man's circumstances may appear very fair and agreeable; his business may be flourishing; his grounds may bring forth plentifully, and he may seem to have more than heart can wish. But oh, if you look into his heart, what anguish would you sometimes find there! If you could look into his mind, what mourning, lamentation, and woe would you see! And if the individual uttered his feelings, he would say, "The spirit of a man will sustain his infirmity; but a wounded spirit who can bear"? There have been thorns in the flesh too deeply incised to be perceptible, but they are not the less poignant and painful on this account, but even the more so.

Nor is it necessary that these trials should be real. No, the mind of man may be so constructed that he may become a prey to his own thoughts. One of these thoughts may be so gloomy as to sink him into despair, or hurry him into a state of frenzy or madness, so that his soul shall prefer death rather than life.

Now in the conclusion of this article (and we can afford no more time for the illustration of it), do not any of you complain and say, "Behold and see if there be any sorrow like unto *my* sorrow, wherewith the Lord hath afflicted me." You know not what others are called to endure. And do not invariably say when you meet with those grievances, "Why am I thus"? Hear David, "Oh that I had wings like a dove! for then would I flee away and be at rest." Yes, look at the man after God's own heart, the man who perhaps had more devotional religion than any individual before the incarnation of the Redeemer, the prophet of the Lord, the King of Israel, the sweet psalmist, there—see *him*, where is he? "*In a horrible pit and in the miry clay!*"

II. Observe his Engagement While There.

He says "I waited patiently for the Lord."

Nothing can be more interesting than to see a good man

calm and patient, while in a very distracted condition. To see a godly man in a state of deep affliction is calculated to awaken attention. Such a one is a witness for God. He has an opportunity afforded him of showing the reality, and efficiency, and excellency of the religion he professes. David therefore in this condition, you see, had recourse to God. Natural men apply to creatures in their affliction. When King Ahaz was in trouble, "he took away a portion out of the house of the Lord, and out of the house of the King, and of the Princes, and gave it unto the King of Assyria; but he helped him not. And in the time of his distress did he trespass yet more against the Lord." And "when Ephraim saw his sickness, and Judah saw his wound, then went Ephraim to the Assyrian, and sent to Jareb; yet he could not heal you or cure you of your wound." God complains of the Jews, because, saith He, "they turned not to Him that smiteth them." No, they turned to creatures; sometimes, indeed, mėn have employed the devil's devices, the opiates of infidelity, the dissipations of the world, or the bowl of intemperance. Why, a Christian had rather die at the feet of Jesus, saying "Carest Thou not that I perish"? than have recourse to such expedients as these.

Here the Psalmist waits for the mercy of the Lord, who is pitiful and gracious. So it was in the days of Hosea, "Come," said they, "and let us return unto the Lord; for He hath torn, and He will heal us; He hath smitten and He will bind us up. After two days will He revive us: in the third day He will raise us up, and we shall live in His sight." David therefore says, "I wait for the Lord, my soul doth wait, and in His Word do I hope;" and here he says, "I waited patiently for the Lord." Waiting includes not only seeking, but expecting; and waiting patiently for the Lord implies that God does not always immediately come to release and relieve His people when they think they most stand in need. No, He is not indeed slack concerning His promise, as some men count slackness; but when He does not come to our relief and assistance at the time we expect we feel disappointed. But He is not bound to observe our prescribed rules, and He must know in His infinite wisdom that we have very improperly fixed the times and the seasons for Him to display Himself. Depend upon it, in His own good time and way, He will listen to our prayer, and interpose for us. He hath said, "He that believeth shall not make haste." If the Lord appear to tarry long, we are to wait for Him. The husbandman does not go out and murmur at the clouds, or blame the weather;

he well knows that there must be a season between sowing and reaping, and that the various influences of nature, the rough and the smooth, the pleasing and frowning, all operate and combine to produce the final result; therefore he waiteth. "Behold" says James, "the husbandman waiteth for the precious fruit of the earth, and hath long patience for it, until he receive the early and latter rain. Be ye also patient."

Now it is very trying to flesh and blood to wait for God thus, especially under some circumstances. But let us even remember that we have no claim upon God. Think how long we kept Him waiting for us, how long He stood knocking at the door of our hearts, week after week, and month after month, before we rose up and opened unto Him.

Then it becomes us to exercise full confidence in God, and to feel assured that He will fulfil His promises; that His *delays* will be advantageous; and that His time is the best time, therefore it is said, "Blessed are all they that wait for Him." They are blessed, for they are preserved from more painful reflections others feel who disobey Him and who charge Him foolishly and unkindly before He explains Himself; and they are preserved from those sinful and improper expedients to extricate themselves from present difficulties and to obtain relief. This Abraham did, and so said of Sarah, "She is my sister." So with regard to the artifice of Rebekah respecting Jacob. Had they let God alone, so to speak, to bring about His purposes in His own time and way, how many stripes and how many storms they would have escaped! By nothing can we honour God more than by confiding in Him. "Them that honour me I will honour."

III. We have to Consider His Success.

"He inclined unto me, and heard my cry. He brought me up also out of an horrible pit, out of the miry clay, and set my feet upon a rock, and established my goings. And He hath put a new song in my mouth, even praise unto our God."

It includes *attention*. "He inclined unto me." He was not indifferent even while He was delaying. God says, "I have heard Ephraim bemoaning himself thus: Thou hast chastised me, and I was chastised as a bullock unaccustomed to the yoke: turn Thou me, and I shall be turned, for Thou art the Lord my God . . . therefore my bowels are troubled for him. I will surely have mercy upon him." O yes, God views you. He knows all your walking through the wilderness, and you may say with the Psalmist, "Thou hast considered my trouble; Thou hast known my soul in adversities." Job complains that he could find neither comment nor commentator with regard to the dispensation of Providence under which he was. "Behold," says he "I go forward, but He is not there; and backward, but I cannot perceive Him. On the left hand where He doth work, but I cannot behold Him. He hideth Himself on the right hand, that I cannot see Him. But He can see me, He knoweth the way that I take; when He hath tried me I shall come forth as gold."

It includes *audience*. Man may hear his fellow man put up a petition, and may disregard it; and instead of listening to his complaint, may turn a deaf ear to his request; but *hearing*, in the words before us, means attention, with the desire to answer. God renders the exercise beneficial to us; it solemnises the mind, and has a sanctifying effect upon the heart, so that we feel impressed while in the presence of God by a sense of His perfections and His glory.

But in answer, He brings seasonable supplies and relief. When Joshua prayed that the day might be longer, that he might finish the victory he had commenced, the sun stood still. And when Daniel sought the Lord his God, He heard and saved him in the lion's den. When the three Hebrew children prayed to the Lord in the burning fiery furnace, He interposed on their behalf. And when Elias prayed that there might be rain, not only did the prayer do him good, as all religious exercises will, but the prayer was answered, and the heavens gave rain upon the earth.

It includes *deliverance*. "He brought me up out of an horrible pit, out of the miry clay." What a release! What a change, so unlikely and unlooked for! a change so great that he could hardly realise it. He would feel somewhat like the Jews when God turned their captivity, they were like men that dreamed; as we may suppose Jacob felt when rescued from the hand of Esau; as Paul felt when rescued from the lion Nero, and many others recorded in the Scriptures: so may we suppose David felt, the Divine interposition was so manifest in all, "*He* brought me up also out of an horrible pit, out of the miry clay," according to the promise, "Call upon me in the day of trouble; I will deliver thee, and thou shalt glorify Me."

It includes *safety*. "He hath set my feet upon a rock," they were in the mire before, but they are now upon the rock of ages, and the Christian can say—

"He has fixed my standing more secure,
Than 'twas before I fell."

Adam fell, but this Man continueth ever, therefore they that belong to Him are safe and secure. "My sheep," says He, "hear my voice, and I know them, and they follow Me. And I give unto them eternal life; and they shall never perish, neither shall any man pluck them out of my hand." David says, "The Lord is my light and my salvation; whom shall I fear? the Lord is the strength of my life, of whom shall I be afraid." Yes, says the believer, "I know His promises, they are exceeding great and precious; I know that He hath made with me an everlasting covenant, ordered in all things and sure; and I know that His almighty arm is raised for my defence, and that I am kept by the power of God through faith unto salvation." Therefore his heart is established, trusting in the Lord.

Then it includes *progression.* "He hath established my goings." He has not placed me here in order to stand still, but to walk in His ways; not that I should be like a monument, but like a traveller; that my conduct should be distinguished from lying down in carnal repose; that going on my way I may grow stronger and stronger.

It includes, also, *gratitude* and *joy.* "He hath put a new song into my mouth, even praise unto our God." He hath furnished me with fresh matter and motive for praise, and therefore He shall have it. Not only will I praise the Lord at times, but His praise shall continually be in my mouth.

IV. We have to notice also the Usefulness of the Dispensation, for, says he, "many shall see it, and fear, and shall trust in the Lord."

Here you see *how* it was to be beneficial, *by being known.* "They shall see it;" that is, they shall be acquainted with it by the eye, or the ear, or by reading. Nothing can influence us unless it be known. The subjects of Divine grace will seize opportunities to speak to others, and say with David, "Come and hear, all ye that fear God, and I will declare what He hath done for my soul."

Observe the *nature* of the benefit. "Many shall see it and *fear.*" What was there in the dispensation to awaken fear? Why, was it not to show them that everything here is precarious? That while here we may be raised up, or cast down? But this is not the leading thought. The word in the original does not mean *dread,* but reverence combined with love. It is the reverence and respect which an inferior has towards a superior. It is also accompanied with *trust.* Such who possess it trust in the Lord, and are delivered from slavish fear of Him.

Observe the number referred to. "*Many* shall see it, and fear, and shall trust in the Lord." How many since then have heard and seen it from the Scriptures, from Christian conversation! And all shall see it in due time, for "the earth shall be filled with the knowledge of the glory of the Lord, as the waters cover the sea."

We conclude with two remarks. First, what God does for His people is always designed to have an influence upon others, and never terminates in ourselves.

Then, secondly, if the experience of others be so profitable, surely our own ought not to be less so. If we look back to those who have gone before us in former ages and feel induced to confide in God, how much more should we be by a review of the way in which He has led us, and in His making all paths mercy and truth, and be led to say with David, "Because Thou hast been my help, therefore in the shadow of Thy wings will I rejoice."

II.

THE HEART'S SECRETS.

(Preached on Sunday Evening, January 21st, 1844.)

The heart knoweth his own bitterness, and a stranger doth not intermeddle with his joy.—PROVERBS xiv. 10.

"ALL Scripture is given by inspiration of God, and is profitable for doctrine, for reproof, for correction, for instruction in righteousness; that the man of God may be perfect, thoroughly furnished unto all good works"; and in giving us the revelations of His will God "hath abounded towards us in all wisdom and prudence." The Proverbs contain many brief and sententious sayings, which embody much Evangelical truth. Who but "the God of all grace" speaks to us in this when He says, "Turn you at My reproof. Behold, I will pour out My spirit unto you; I will make known My words unto you"? Who but Wisdom—not wisdom personified, but Wisdom Incarnate—speaks to us here: "I love them that love Me; and those that seek Me early shall find Me"? "Blessed is the Man that heareth Me, watching daily at My gates, waiting at the posts of my door. For whoso findeth Me findeth life, and shall obtain favour of the Lord; but he that sinneth against Me wrongeth his own soul; all they that hate Me love death"? We are to take the Bible as a whole, and bring together its various parts to explain and supply each other; and then we may say, as the Apostle did in another case, "If the whole body were an eye, where were the hearing? If the whole were hearing, where were the smelling"? Revelation is designed, not only to form our creed, but to direct our conduct; not only to form our principles, but to regulate our lives. I wish, therefore, some professors of religion were obliged every morning in the week to "read, mark, learn, and inwardly digest" some of these proverbs, so that their good might not be evil-spoken of; for it is desirable now, as well as it was in the Apostle's days, that your serving Christ should not only be "acceptable to God, but approved of men."

But let us hasten to notice the proverb which we have chosen for our text: "The heart knoweth his own bitterness; and a stranger doth not intermeddle with his joy." This we consider two ways: First, generally in reference to men; and, secondly, particularly in reference to Christians.

I. Generally in Reference to Men.

"The heart knoweth his own bitterness, and a stranger doth not intermeddle with his joy."

It is no easy thing for us to know ourselves. Hence we are frequently induced to undertake services to which we are inadequate. But if it be difficult to know ourselves, it is much more difficult to know others. A heathen philosopher said, "Know thyself;" and the Apostle said, "Examine yourselves; prove your own selves." What strange effects would be produced if we knew some of our fellow-creatures! Surely in many cases, we should be tempted to exclaim, "All men are liars." Here we should see in one what passed for an instance of liberality, was only vainglory; and there, what passed for friendship, was only hypocrisy. And what would not the knowledge prevent? Some years ago I knew a good man and woman who were going to be married; but they passed three weeks previously together, in a common friend's house. This gave such an insight into each other's character, that they forbade the banns; and how many unions would be set aside by the fuller acquaintance of three weeks! Yet persons may live together long, and know but little of each other, as the character in some is wrapt up in very close folds, and it is only by particular events and circumstances that it is revealed; and sometimes those who are taken for very knowing ones are often deceived and taken in.

In nothing are we more likely to be mistaken than with regard to the sorrows and pleasures of our fellow-creatures.

Now, as to human sorrows, "The heart knoweth his own bitterness." We see persons in the midst of abundance, and whose "cup runneth over," yet we find that they are the subjects of grief which preys upon their very vitals. What is the reason of this? It may be some reproach under which they lie, and from which they cannot free themselves; or some desires which they cannot realise; or some affection or kindness which meets with no return. Some sufferers are forbidden by their connections and conditions in life to make known the cause of their distresses. The poor afflicted wife would only add to the hardships of her case, were she to tell the base treatment she endures from her brutal husband. The same may be said of others. Some are ashamed to make known the cause of their distress. Ahab falls sick and takes his bed, and is ashamed to own the reason; but it turns out that although he was a King, he is pining for a piece of garden ground belonging to Naboth. Haman goes home and cannot eat, and after enumerating all his possessions, says, "Yet all this availeth me nothing, so long as I see Mordecai sitting at the King's gate." In how many cases are the sufferings imaginary, though they are real enough to those that endure them! But who is prepared to speak upon this subject? How much have Cowper and others endured! Paul speaks of the "thorn in the flesh." This may not be visible, because of the depth of its incision, but the pain it produces is not the less poignant. Yes; there are real sufferers, though the cause of their sufferings may not be apparent to others. There are those who appear in company with a smile, and yet retire to weep. There are real mourners. O ye benefactors, remember this, and "visit the fatherless and the widows in their affliction." Yes; there are real mourners who feel they cannot make known their sorrows to the dearest relations on earth; but they can retire, and pour out their tears before God. "The heart knoweth his own bitterness."

Then again in regard to human happiness. How little do we know of this when we cast our eyes over society, we seem at a loss to conjecture what so much delights mankind in general; and there are those who turn the Scriptures into ridicule, and who are suprised to find many of their poor fellow-creatures very happy. Yea, happy in conditions which would render them miserable. You may have observed that a miser signifies a miserable man, and applies to a person who possesses much and enjoys nothing, for what pleasure can such a wretch feel in counting over his silver and his gold? And what gratifications can he feel in his sordid hoardings? And there is the joy of the epicure, and the joy of the sensualist, and there is the joy of the warrior. I hope you will never intermeddle with this joy; I hope you will become acquainted with that joy which is the "glory of man," and the joy of the Christian who carries out the counsel of his Lord, who says "Bless them that curse you, pray for them that despitefully use and persecute you; bless, and curse not."

II. Let us now proceed to consider this principle IN REFERENCE TO CHRISTIANS.

"The heart knoweth his own bitterness; and a stranger doth not intermeddle with his joy."

There is something in the Christian's joy and sorrow which is unknown to others. Religion has to do with the feelings. The sacred writers knew this; and you remember the language of one of our hymns—

> "True religion's more than notion,
> Something must be known and felt."

Again, there is a variety in the Christian's experience. He is the subject of both sorrow and joy. He is in a chequered state, amidst cloud and sunshine. What an emblem of the Christian's life is the bush burning with fire and not consumed; or a vessel tossed with winds and waves, weathering the storm, and yet entering into the desired haven. What a motto for the Christians is this: "We are troubled on every side, yet not distressed; cast down, but not destroyed; sorrowful, yet always rejoicing, as having nothing, but yet possessing all things." We see in the Christian now the conflicts of two armies, nature and grace, flesh and spirit. "The flesh lusteth against the spirit, and the spirit against the flesh, and these are contrary the one to the other, so that ye cannot do the things that ye would." We see this exemplified in the representations of Scripture. The subjects of divine grace are called those who "fear God," and those who "hope in His mercy." There are those among them who "return, and come to Zion with singing, and with everlasting joy upon their heads," and there are those who "come with weeping and supplication. These go out with weeping, bearing precious seed, and shall doubtless come again with joy, bringing their sheaves with them.

You should learn, therefore, in order to ascertain your religious character, not to judge of yourselves by one kind of feeling only. I have known some who have condemned themselves because they have so little joy, forgetting the language of Isaiah, that a man may obey the voice of his Maker, and yet "walk in darkness and have no light;" and that our Saviour says, "Blessed are they that mourn, for they shall be comforted." I have known others who have condemned themselves because they have had so little trial and affliction. This is not often the case. There are some who fancy they have only to march on without opposition, and when they come to actual fight they are discouraged. By the kindness of God they are allured on in the path of wisdom till they feel they cannot turn back; but at first they think they shall always enjoy themselves, and are apt to draw wrong conclusions. I heard of a pious woman, who soon after her conversion applied to Mr. Romaine. "I fear," said she, "I am not a pious woman, because I have had so little trial." "Oh," said he, "there is time enough yet for that, madam." And so indeed by the providence of God she found it. I have many stones in my garden, which are about the same as when I went there, but it is otherwise with the trees; and though these sometimes look dead and barren, yet they burst forth again, and are clothed with verdure. So the Christian should not sit still while here, but should go forth in "newness of life."

There is a peculiarity in the Christian's *sorrows.* "The heart knoweth his own bitterness." There is a peculiarity in the sorrow he feels for sin. The Apostle, therefore, says to the Corinthians, "I rejoice, not that ye were made sorry; but that ye sorrowed to repentance. For ye were made sorry after a godly manner. For godly sorrow worketh repentance to salvation, not to be repented of. For behold, the self-same thing that ye sorrowed after a godly sort, what carefulness it wrought in you; yea, what clearing of yourselves; yea, what indignation; yea, what revenge; yea, what vehement desire." So it is said in the promise: "I will pour upon the house of David, and upon the inhabitants of Jerusalem, the spirit of grace and of supplication, and they shall look on me whom they have pierced, and they shall mourn." How? "As one mourneth for his only son, and shall be in bitterness for him, as one that is in bitterness for his first-born." None can understand this but the sufferers themselves. I formerly thought I could enter a good deal into the feelings of parents, but when called to resign my beloved daughter, I found I had never known a parent's heart before; and those who have been pricked in the heart, alone could tell what true sorrow for sin is. Such alone can say with Job, "I abhor myself;" such know the heart's bitterness.

There is a bitterness also felt by the Christian through his remaining corruptions; there are some who suppose that the doctrines of Christianity lead to licentiousness; but if they knew all, instead of censuring the humble believer, they would behold him at the foot of the cross crying, "God be merciful to me a sinner!" bewailing himself for his iniquities, and mourning for infirmities which he can less excuse than others —such as coldness of affection in the things of God, wandering thoughts, questioning the divine faithfulness, kindness and care. The world knows them not, and therefore supposes that their belief of the permanency of the Saviour's regard towards them will lead them to give up their vigilance, whereas this assurance makes them more anxious to please Him, and make them pray the more, that "the words of their mouth and the meditation of their hearts" may be acceptable unto Him. Paul knew much of suffering; but in the history he has given us you never find him complain of any of his afflictions and trials, till he came here: "When I could do good, evil is present with me. O wretched man that I am! who shall deliver me from the body of this death?"

There is also a peculiarity in their creed. The world condemns them, and often calls them mopish and melancholy, ungrateful, and enthusiasts, while they themselves are often the cause of many of the tears they shed. Christians weep for them who never weep for themselves. "I have told you often," says the Apostle, "and now tell you even weeping, that they are the enemies of the cross of Christ." And says David, "I beheld the transgressors and was grieved: rivers of waters run down mine eyes, because they keep not Thy law." There are some, the Apostle observes, who not only commit sin themselves, but take pleasure in those that do. But nothing can be so opposed as this to the Christian disposition. "He rejoices not in iniquity, but rejoices in the truth." How does the Christian sorrow when he hears of the fall of professors! What joy have such occasioned in the enemy's camp! What a stumbling block do they prove to young inquirers, and how do they discourage the hearts and weaken the hands of God's ministers!

There is a peculiarity also in the Christian's sorrow under the hidings of God's countenance. Others cannot follow him here; but says David, "Thou didst hide Thy face, and I was troubled."

There is a peculiarity also in their sorrow with regard to death. I do not mean the experience of it; that is commonly blessed. "Mark the perfect man, and behold the upright, for the end of that man is peace." But in the apprehension of it. Not that this is the case with all, but the Apostle says that there are some who through fear of death are all their lifetime subject to bondage. There are some who can banish this from their minds, but the Christian cannot. He often asks himself, How shall I do in that conflict? How shall I pass the important hour of death?

> "Give me one kind assuring word,
> To sink my fears again;
> And cheerfully my soul shall wait
> Her three score years and ten."

Again, as there is a peculiarity in the believer's sorrows, for "the heart knoweth his own bitterness," so there is something in the believer's *joys* unknown to others; for "a stranger doth not intermeddle with his joy." Some suppose that the believer has nothing to do with joy. This was the opinion of Lord Chesterfield; "I hope," said he, "I shall never become converted, for I should be so miserable." He become a *Christian* and become miserable! Had he not found the world to be what the wise man describes it, "vanity and vexation of spirit?" Some of you have found it to be so. Oh, had he embraced Christianity, he would have found it infinitely superior to the world. We might appeal to the Scriptures for proof of this as well as to Christian experience. "Because when I called," says God, "when I spake, ye did not hear, but did evil before mine eyes, and did choose that wherein I delighted not: therefore, behold, my servants shall eat, but ye shall be hungry: behold, my servants shall drink, but ye shall be thirsty: behold, my servants shall rejoice, but ye shall be ashamed: behold, my servants shall sing for joy of heart, but ye shall cry for sorrow of heart, and shall howl for vexation of spirit." Ask those who have been in both conditions, who once served the world, and are now the servants of God—ask them what true godliness is, and whether the declaration be not true, "Her ways are ways of pleasantness, and all her paths are peace?" When Philip Henry preached from "His yoke is easy," he appealed to a Christian's experience; "Turn," said he, "to which of them you may, they will all agree that 'Her ways are ways of pleasantness,' and I," continued he, "will be a witness for one, for through grace I have been enabled to draw in this yoke between thirty and forty years, and have found it an easy yoke; I like my choice too well ever to think of a change."

"A stranger doth not intermeddle with his joy:" and O, what a joy is that which belongs to a real Christian! Peter therefore says, "It is unspeakable and full of glory." It is what the worldling cannot understand. There are "the comforts of the Holy Ghost;" there is the "joy in God through our Lord Jesus Christ;" and as Watts says—

> "Lord, how secure and blest are they,
> Who feel the joys of pardoned sin!
> Should storms of wrath shake earth and sea,
> Their minds have heaven and peace within."

Believers see that the dreadful breach between heaven and earth is filled up, and are filled with the "joys of salvation."

How unknown to others is the joy the believer feels under his affliction! What a strange injunction was that of the Apostle's, where he says, "Count it all joy when ye fall into divers temptations." How strange to hear the language of the Church: "Although the fig tree shall not blossom, neither shall fruit be in the vines; the labour of the olive shall fail, and the fields shall yield no meat; the flock shall be cut off from the fold, and there shall be no herd in the stalls: yet I will rejoice in the Lord, I will joy in the God of my salvation." Here, to the world, they are "men wondered at," and I hope you will make them wonder, Christians. There is nothing that is more honorable to the religion of Jesus than the manner in which you suffer affliction and losses, and trials and reproaches for Christ's sake. The people of the world can see your sufferings, but they cannot see your consolations. They can see how Providence comes and strips you of one support after another, but they do not see how "underneath are the everlasting arms." They cannot see, when creature comforts fail you, what a source of personal comfort you enjoy in the everlasting covenant, "ordered in all things and sure."

When they behold you giving up those things which seem essential to the very life of others, they think it "strange that you run not with them to the same excess of riot;" but you "have meat to eat which they know not of," you have "the hidden manna;" you have tasted of the grapes of Eshcol, and no longer want the onions and leeks of Egypt. They see not the pleasures you have, while they see you take up the cross. How marvellous to them is the language of the Apostle, "I take pleasure in infirmities, in reproaches, in necessities, in persecution, in distresses for Christ's sake, for when I am weak then am I strong." They are not acquainted with the love of Christ, and of its constraining influence, but; saith the Apostle. "The love of Christ constraineth us, because we thus judge, that if one died for all, then were all dead, and that He died for all, that they which live, should not henceforth live unto themselves, but unto Him which died for them and rose again. We know that it is the nature of love to make bitter thing sweet *and hard things easy.*

"A stranger doth not intermeddle with his joy" in regard to death. Death, to the unbeliever, is the king of terrors. Oh! say they, "how can a man be willing to leave all this delight and enjoyment?" But while the worldling says, "this is my grief and I must bear it," the Christian can say, "I desire to depart, and to be with Christ, which is far better."

"I could renounce my all below,
If my Creator bid;
Or run if I were called to go,
And die as Moses did."

They are able to say, "Yea, though I walk through the valley of the shadow of death, I will fear no evil." Yes, and how many thousands are there who *experience this joy in their departing hour!*

We make two remarks before we conclude:—

Though "a stranger doth not intermeddle with his joy," there are friends who can; there are those who have fellowship with Jesus, and truly their fellowship is with the Father and his Son Jesus Christ. There are those who have a general resemblance, and to whom the words are applicable, "As face answereth to face in a glass, so doth the heart of man to man." Therefore David said, "Come unto me, all ye that fear God, and I will declare what He hath done for my soul." "They that fear Thee will rejoice when they see me, because they have hoped in Thy truth." Yea, they even contribute to this joy, therefore "Comfort one another with these words."

Secondly, if their joy be so great now, what will it be above? Now this joy enters them, then they will "enter into the joy of their Lord." Now they have some drops from the fountain of blessedness, then they will enter into a fulness of their joy. Now their comforts vary, and their tears often flow: but then, "at God's right hand," they shall have "pleasures for evermore." But "Eye hath not seen, nor ear heard, neither have entered into the heart of man what things God hath prepared for them that love Him."

III.

THE FOUNDATION OF ZION.

(Preached on Sunday Evening, May 10th, 1846).

Therefore, thus saith the Lord God. Behold, I lay in Zion for a foundation a stone, a tried stone, a precious corner stone, a sure foundation; he that believeth shall not make haste.—ISAIAH xxviii. 16.

WHATEVER subordinate reference there is in these words to the Jews, who were surrounded with dangers, requiring divine interpositions, the principal reference is to the Messiah. It was in this way the prophets always endeavoured to comfort the Church even in outward troubles. "Oh," said they, "'twill be better soon; He is coming, and then the eyes of the blind shall be opened, and the ears of the deaf shall be unstopped. Then the lame man shall leap as an hart, and the tongue of the dumb sing." "For every battle of the warrior is with confused noise, and garments rolled in blood, but this shall be with burning and fuel of fire. For unto us a Child is born, unto us a Son is given, and the government shall be upon His shoulder; and His name shall be called Wonderful, Counsellor, the Mighty God, the Everlasting Father, the Prince of Peace." So says Zechariah, "Rejoice greatly, O daughter of Zion; shout, O daughter of Jerusalem: behold thy King cometh unto thee; He is just, and having salvation." Thus He was always regarded as "the Consolation of Israel." The Prophets therefore rise from the less to the greater thing, from the deliverance of the Jews to the deliverance of Christians: "God having provided some better thing for us, that they without us should not be made perfect." To which we may add, that every other explanation of the words before us would be poor, mean, and constrained, compared with the Evangelical import we have assigned to them. Hear what the Apostle of the Gentiles says: "As it is written." Where?

In our text. "Whosoever believeth on Him shall not be ashamed." You shall now hear the testimony of the Apostle to the circumcision: "Wherefore also it is contained in the Scripture, Behold, I lay in Zion a chief corner-stone, elect, precious: and he that believeth on Him shall not be confounded."

Observe the plan of our discourse: First, we have here the emblem of the Lord Jesus; secondly, His destination; thirdly, we see how well He fulfils His purpose; fourthly, the blessedness of those who make use of it; fifthly, the ushering in of the whole scene.

I. The Emblem of the Lord Jesus. "A stone."

Whether we consider Him as "a stone" for solidity—or for strength—or for duration, He is all these; for whatever changes may take place among men, with Him "there is no variableness nor shadow of turning."

Peter calls Him a "living stone." This seems strange. You have heard of the breathing canvas, of speaking or living marble; but if we should be afraid of so bold a figure, Peter was not. Stripping the metaphor, he means, He has life in Himself, and that He procures it and dispenses it to others. So Paul says, "When Christ, who is our life, shall appear, then shall we also appear with Him in glory." All metaphorical representations employed to hold Him forth fall infinitely short of His worth and glory.

> "Nor earth, nor sea, nor sun, nor stars,
> Nor heaven His full resemblance bears;
> His beauties we can never trace
> Till we behold Him face to face."

Owing to the imperfection of all imagery, the sacred writers multiply their metaphors, and attach to them attributes not naturally belonging to them; for, as Watts says,

> "Nature, to make His glories known,
> Must mingle colours not her own."

And all those images which express Him have some distinguished qualities. Thus He is not only said to be "a sun"—but "the Sun of Righteousness." He is not only called "a pearl"—but "the pearl of great price." He is not only spoken of as the Shepherd—but as "the good Shepherd," "the great Shepherd," "the chief Shepherd," "the Shepherd and Bishop of souls." If He be a "tree"—"He is the tree of life." If He be fair—"He is fairer than the children of men." If lovely

—"He is *altogether lovely.*" So here, He is not only "a stone" —but "a tried stone, a precious corner-stone."

He is "a *tried* stone." Nothing is much valued till it is tried; and you know how much counterfeit is discovered by trial; so, to preserve you from imposition, you try silver and gold. In your dangerous illness, you would send for one whose skill has been tried by his efficiency. Everything in regard to Him was tried in the days of His flesh. His wisdom was tried. He displayed in His figures and replies more than human knowledge, so that His apostles were induced to say, "Lord, Thou knowest all things." His meekness was tried; "When He was reviled, He reviled not again." His love was tried—toward us surely this was tried enough. Can we ever question it when we see Him in the manger, in the garden, or on the cross? when we see Him in the character of a Saviour, stooping to take our nature, that He might "redeem us from *all* iniquity, and purify unto Himself a peculiar people zealous of good works?"

He is also "a *precious* stone," infinitely precious is He to God the Father! who therefore says, "Behold my servant whom I uphold, mine elect, in whom my soul delighteth." He is precious to angels; He was seen of them on earth, and is adored by them in heaven. John beheld "and heard the voice of many angels round about the throne, and the beasts and the elders; and the number of them was ten thousand times ten thousand, and thousands of thousands, saying with a loud voice, Worthy is the Lamb that was slain to receive power, and riches, and wisdom, and strength, and honour, and glory, and blessing." Oh, how precious is He to Christians! "To you that believe He is precious," but how precious it is impossible for language to express. He is precious in every character; precious in every relation; precious, even in contemplation; precious in actual communion; precious in His atoning blood; precious in His justifying righteousness; precious in His ordinances; and precious in all the means of His grace. The world asks, "What is your beloved more than another beloved, that thou shouldst so charge us?" Ah, if they could see His glory as you do; if they could see His glory, "the glory as of the only begotten of the Father, full of grace and truth," then would they say, "Whither thou goest we will go, that we may see Him with you."

This is not all, for He is "a precious corner-stone." The "corner-stone" stands to unite, and is distinguishable by this; and we see what union and communion there is in Him, how like a corner-stone He unites in His person deity and manhood. We see united in Him the Old and the New Testament dispensation, the one looking back, the other looking forward; in Him they meet and harmonise; the one a type, the other a reality—the one a promise, the other an accomplishment—the one a prediction, the other a fulfilment. He unites Jews and Gentiles. "He is our peace," says the Apostle in this view; "He hath broken down the middle wall of partition between us"—"He is our peace, and through Him we both,"—both Jews and Gentiles—"have access by one spirit unto the Father."

This corner-stone not only harmonises, it is also fundamental. But this brings us to consider:

II. HIS DESTINATION. "Behold, I lay in Zion for a foundation."

He is everything to answer to the condition and exigencies of His people. If they are patients He is the Physician, bringing them health and cure. If they are sheep, He is the Shepherd, who feeds them, and leads them into green pastures. If they are His Church, or God's building, then, according to our text, He is the foundation.

Two things are to be remarked concerning this: first, *Who lays this foundation?* It is God. "Behold, I lay in Zion for a foundation." He who laid the foundation of the earth and the heavens could alone lay this. Then, as it implied His power, so it equally implied his goodness, that He would lay it, for He was under no obligation; we had no claim upon Him. "We were by nature the children of wrath even as others." He therefore accomplished this without our desert, yea, even without our desire, and ages before we had any being.

Secondly, *Where does He lay this foundation?* "Behold, I lay in *Zion*." This was accomplished literally. Jesus was a Jew. He was of the family of David. Zion often means Jerusalem, for being a very distinguished part of it, it is by a figure of speech often taken for the whole. There He died; there He rose again; there "He ascended up on high;" there, having received the promise of the Father, He sent forth the Spirit on the day of Pentecost. Now all this was spoken of by the prophets. Thus David said, "The Lord shall send forth the rod of His strength out of Zion: rule Thou in the midst of Thine enemies." Thus Isaiah says, "Come ye, and let us go up to the mountain of the Lord, to the house of the God of Jacob, and He will teach us of His ways, and we will walk in His paths; for out of *Zion* shall go forth the law, and the word of the Lord from Jerusalem." Yes, and "In this mountain," says our prophet again, "shall the Lord of Hosts make unto all people a feast of fat things, a feast of wines on the lees of fat things full of marrow, of wines on the lees well-refined."

III. Observe HOW WELL HE ANSWERS THE PURPOSE AND END. "A sure foundation."

This is the grand essential attribute of a good building, the very design is safety. The foundation ought to be sure in proportion to the value, grandeur, and the weight of the superstructure resting upon it. You would therefore look more after assurance of the safety of the foundation, if you are going to erect a hospital, than if you were going to erect a mere mud-wall cottage. Now observe, here, the salvation of a soul, what is it? One soul is more precious, according to "the Judge of all," than the whole world; therefore angels rejoice at the conversion cf a sinner; they see enough in this to draw forth their admiration; they know that this salvation by Christ, frees the sinner from all possible evil, and entitles him to all possible good, and that he is saved in the Lord with an everlasting salvation." Then think of the millions of the redeemed, the pressure of the salvation of every one of which bears entirely upon Him. He is "a sure foundation" for all. Some souls place their dependence upon something of their own, on their own works, or their own resolutions; verily, this is sand, and the building must fall before the winds and the waves. There are many things which might do for a superstructure that would not do for a foundation; nothing would do for this but the Divine Sacrifice, the righteousness and intercession of Christ. When a man is awakened to a sense of sin, of his guilt, depravity, danger and helplessness, he sees nothing of which he can lay hold, on which to build his hopes for eternity, and exclaims,

"Other refuge have I none,
Hangs my helpless soul on Thee."

He knows this will never give way, and believing he enters into rest, and feels a "peace passing all understanding." Are you afraid of relying upon Him? Do you question the accomplishment of your salvation in His due time? O, dismiss these fears. Behold, 'tis Jesus, bear hard upon Him; rely upon Him; "trust in the Lord for ever, for in the Lord Jehovah is everlasting strength."

IV. Observe THE BLESSEDNESS OF THOSE WHO MAKE USE OF IT. "He that believeth shall not make haste."

Here the prophet drops the imagery, otherwise he would have said, he that believeth shall never be mortified by seeing the work of his hands sink and fall. The Scriptures, brethren, are above human rules, and the Spirit of inspiration would not be indebted to human rhetoric, though it is frequently employed, and always honoured when it is thus employed. As the Scriptures drop it, let us do so.

"He that believeth shall not make haste." And what is it to believe? Believing is assent to the Scriptures, especially to "the record which God has given us of His Son." But it takes in more than common assent, or mental persuasion. It takes in consent, dependence, and application, so that the man from a deep conviction of his need, and belief of the Saviour's power and passion, goes to Him crying, "Lord, save, or I perish!" "God, be merciful to me a sinner!" Faith is not a mere inoperative principle; it always works, and always works towards *Him.* So it is always represented in its dealings with Him: it is a "looking to Him," a "hearing Him," a "receiving Him," and a "feeding upon Him." It is especially held forth by a coming to Him; that is, a believing on Him, as He Himself has explained it. "He that cometh to Me shall never hunger, he that believeth on Me shall never thirst," where the terms are used synonymously, and serve to explain each other. So if it be asked, what is coming to Christ? we answer, it is to believe in Him, and to deal with Him in the affairs of our souls.

Then it is said, "He that believeth on Him *shall not make haste.*" Now this declaration is not opposed to diligence; no, "the King's business requireth haste." "No," says David, "I thought on my ways, and turned my feet unto Thy testimonies; I made haste and delayed not to keep Thy commandments." This is what you should all do in religion. The Gospel takes you by the hand, and says, "Flee from the wrath to come." "Stay not in all the plain, escape to the mountain, lest thou be consumed." Hence you read of "fleeing for refuge"; of "flying as a cloud, and as doves to their windows"; and hence we read of "running the race set before you." "Draw me, we will run after thee."

But this is opposed to two things; first, to *impatience.* What but impatience led the Israelites to make a golden calf, when Moses delayed coming down from the mount. "Make us," say they, "gods to go before us; for as for this Moses, we wot not what is become of him." Turn to our Saviour's representation of the evil servant: "But and if that evil servant shall say in his heart, my lord delayeth his coming, and shall begin to beat the men-servants and the maidens, and to eat and drink, and be drunken, the lord of that servant will come in a day when he looketh not for him, and in an hour that he is not aware of, and shall cut him asunder, and appoint him his portion with the hypocrites; there shall be weeping and gnashing of teeth." You see it grew out of impatience. Hence men grasp at the present evil world, and lose the pleasures which are "unseen and eternal." But he that walks by faith will wait patiently on the Lord, and will enjoy the blessings here spoken of; for "blessed are all they that wait for Him." Though the Lord may apparently delay, the Christian will not draw hasty conclusions, and say, "Why should I wait for the Lord any longer?" but will "wait on the Lord, and He shall strengthen his heart." He will not have recourse in these delays to improper means to extricate himself. Beware, therefore, perpetually, lest you do anything rashly; remember David: "I said in my haste, all men are liars." But Nathan was not a liar; good Asaph was not a liar; those brave men who would not allow him to hazard his life on a particular occasion were not liars unto him. "I said in my haste, I am cut off from before Thine eyes," but this arose from his impatience; "nevertheless," he adds, "Thou heardest the voice of my supplication when I cried unto Thee."

Then it is opposed to *confusion.* When persons are overcome by fear and know not which way to escape, they are thrown into a hurry, especially if the enemy is behind them, and seems to be approaching their very heels. But God told His people that they should not go out of Babylon "with haste nor by flight; for the Lord will go before you, and the God of Israel shall be your reward." God would come and stand between them and their foes. The meaning is, they shall not be overcome by fear, nor driven hither and thither. "Therefore will not we fear, though the earth be removed, and though the mountains be carried into the midst of the sea." "The Lord is my light and my salvation; whom shall I fear? The Lord is the strength of my life; of whom shall I be afraid?"

Then they shall not be deceived in their expectations; their faith shall not fail; their very trials shall be found to their praise and honour; their dependence shall not give way; no, in the midst of their sufferings they can justify their choice. The religion of Paul made him a sufferer, and his enemies would banter, and say, "You are now a suffering man, soon you will be a dying man." "Very true," says the Apostle, "nevertheless I am not ashamed; for I know whom I have believed, and am persuaded that He is able to keep that which I have committed unto Him against that day. So will you find when "the tribes of the earth shall wail because of Him." His people will be able to lift up their heads with triumph. "They shall have confidence, and not be ashamed before Him at His coming."

V. Lastly. Observe THE USHERING IN OF THE WHOLE SCENE. "Behold,"

How many things engage your attention and your wonder, and fix your minds: but behold this in compliance with the command of God. "Behold" this, and compare it with man's working, and what a difference here! Observe human productions, then observe God's productions; the one defective, the other perfect; the one finite, the other infinite; the one capable of alteration and improvement; with regard to the other nothing can be added to or taken from. "Behold" it, and compare it with God's other works. God says, "I will that men should magnify the works that they behold." There are His works in nature. What pains will some take, and what expenses incur, to survey the rural scenery of valleys, and mountains, and woods, and lakes! But oh, turn your attention from the works of nature to the works of grace. "He has magnified His word above all His name." "Behold," says He, "I create new heavens and new earth, and the former shall not be remembered nor come into mind." Here you see the angels of God; they are good examples, proverbial for their wisdom. We, however, read never of their being naturalists or philosophers, but they drop around the *Cross* and "desire to look into these things." And, brethren, "herein is His love made manifest." Herein He hath "commended His love, that while we were yet sinners Christ died for us." Here you may behold Him in His highest glory. May you not be of those who "Behold and wonder and perish;" but let the command inspire you with gratitude and admiration, obedience and zeal.

As to you who have been strangers to this Saviour, "Seek ye the Lord while He may be found; Call upon Him while He is near." Seek after those spiritual blessings which He alone can bestow. "Hear, and your soul shall live."

IV.

OWLS AND DRAGONS.

(Preached on Sunday Evening, June 21st. 1846.)

The beasts of the field shall honour me, the dragons and the owls: because I give waters in the wilderness, and rivers in the desert to give drink to my people, my chosen.—ISAIAH xliii. 20.

THESE words were never intended to be literally understood; they refer symbolically to the calling of the Gentiles, and the blessed effects produced by the Gospel. "Behold I will do a new thing; now it shall spring forth. Shall ye not know it? I will even make a way in the wilderness, and rivers in the desert."

From the words of our text we are furnished with two things: First, an agency ascribed to metaphorical beings, "The beasts of the field shall honour me, the dragons and the owls." Secondly, a blessed change expressed: "Because I give waters in the wilderness, and rivers in the desert to give drink to my people, my chosen." But we shall reverse the order, and begin in the first place with

I. THE CHANGE EXPRESSED.

Here we may observe the previous state of the region itself, "a wilderness," "a desert;" that is, a state of danger, devoid of culture, destitute of resources. This is to be taken morally and spiritually, and then it represents, very imperfectly, too, the state of those destitute of the gospel of salvation.

There are some who think favourably of such a state. They tell us we need entertain no alarm for them; that they are in no danger; that their religion is good enough for them. What is their religion? Everything absurd, everything cruel is connected with it; vice is turned into virtue, and drunkenness and lewdness are enjoined as duties necessary to the acceptableness of their worship.

How differently do the Scriptures speak of their condition. They tell us they are far off from God; they are ready to perish; they are sitting in darkness; they are without Christ, being strangers to the commonwealth of Israel, without God, and without hope in the world. And this is not only the testimony of Scripture but also of their own writers; not only of their poets, but of their philosophers and historians. Yes, man is fallen away from God, he is gone astray from Him, and in this condition is become depraved and wretched, knowing nothing of His grace; tyrannized by ungodly lusts and passions, tormented by the evil One, oppressed by evils and trials, and all his life-time subject to bondage through fear of death.

Note, secondly, The gracious change expressed. "Because I give waters in the wilderness and rivers in the desert, to give drink to my people, my chosen."

The imagery here is beautiful, even to us, but it must have been much more so to persons living in a warm climate, and travelling in a parched and sandy desert; there to see waters springing up in the wilderness, and rivers flowing in the desert. What does this intend? What, but the Gospel, in its doctrines, its truths, its promises, its means of grace, its provisions in the "new and everlasting covenant," and the joys of God's salvation? So when the gospel is carried to the heathen, when it enters a dark village, when it reaches a barren and cheerless soul, then the words of our text are fulfilled, "because I give waters in the wilderness, and rivers in the desert."

We may notice two things here: First, the *value* of these supplies. They are expressed by water; water is essential to life; life cannot be sustained without it. It is necessary to purify and cleanse. It is necessary to fertilize and refresh. A tree planted by the river of water is a fine image of fruitfulness. Then it satisfies the longing soul. Therefore saith God by the prophet Isaiah, "When the poor and needy seek water, and there is none, and their tongue faileth for thirst, I the Lord will hear them, I the God of Israel will not forsake them. I will open rivers in high places, and fountains in the midst of the valleys; I will make the wilderness a pool of water, and the dry land springs of water."

But we remark not only the richness of these supplies, but the *fulness* too. Hagar was sent off with a bottle of water, which was soon spent, and she exclaimed, "Let me not see the death of the child." There are, you know, receptacles to hold water. Some of these are very spacious; these, however, are sometimes dried up, and we read of "wells without water." But here we have not only water, but waters; not rills, but rivers, and those "clear as crystal, proceeding out of the throne of God and of the Lamb." Rivers flowing from perennial springs, rivers of living waters, whose streams fail not, and which can afford contentment, even to the very soul. Therefore the Saviour said to the woman of Samaria, "Whoso drinketh of the water that I shall give him, shall never thirst; but the water that I shall give him shall be in him a well of water springing up to everlasting life." Does not this show us the abundance of God's mercy, and the exceeding riches of His grace to those who are guilty and unworthy? Does not this afford encouragement to your hope? Does not this tell you that you need not fear of partaking too largely, for God Himself says, "Open thy mouth wide, and I will fill it." "Ask, and receive, that your joy may be full." You may be discouraged from applying to a man who had but one spring, or one well of water, but he who hath rivers of water that run like the Thames through his domains, would he grudge you? Would he not say: Come as often as you please; partake as much as you will, and bring others with you? There is no room for envy here because of the abundance; there is enough and to spare, enough for you, enough for others, enough for all, enough for the whole world. Here is an infinite fulness from which all may "receive grace for grace."

II. Let us now observe, secondly, THE AGENCY ASCRIBED TO METAPHORICAL BEINGS. "The beasts of the field shall honour me, the dragons and the owls; because I give waters in the wilderness, and rivers in the desert."

God has made all things for Himself, and all His works praise Him. Some of these may seem to us misshapen and unsuitable, but they never appear so in the eyes of their Maker; some may be deemed useless and even injurious, but they have all their places and use; they are all worthy of His workmanship, who "doth all things well."

Let us consider the characters themselves. We have called them metaphorical beings, and these are represented metaphorically two ways. First generally: "Man," says the Psalmist, "being in honour abideth not, he is like the beasts that perish." "Vain man would be wise, though he be born like a wild ass's colt." Some have fallen below the beasts, for their instinct secures *them*, while boasted man's reason fails him in a thousand instances. Men are called rational beings, but it is oft times from their possession of reason, rather than their proper use of it. Paul called Nero a "lion." Our Saviour called Herod a "fox." John said of many of the Sadducees, "O generation of vipers." People sometimes say by way of reproach, "The man is as drunk as a pig;" they ought to ask the pig's pardon for the insult offered him. He is what God made him; but the drunkard is what the devil has made him.

Then they are called specifically "owls and dragons." We have a similar representation in the latter part of these prophecies: "They hatch cockatrice eggs, and weave the spider's web; he that eateth of their eggs dieth, and that which is crushed breaketh forth into a viper. Their webs shall not become garments, neither shall they cover themselves with their works; their works are works of iniquity, and the act of violence is in their hands. Their feet run to evil, and they make haste to shed innocent blood; their thoughts are thoughts of iniquity; wasting and destruction are in their path." Their employment is working iniquity, or pursuing trifles; and here, in our text, they are represented as foolish and furious, simple and subtle.

Let us notice them separately.

1. *Owls.* This taken in a large proportion of men who dislike sunshine, who search for their food in the shadow. Who are these "owls?" Why, foolish men. "O ye fools, when will ye be wise"? Who? Why, the simple. "How long, ye simple ones, will ye love simplicity?" Who? Why, those who "love vanity, and seek after leasing." How foolish are many, even in common things! How incapable of conversation or reasoning! But take them in Divine things—here they are "alienated from the life of God." "The God of this world hath blinded the minds of them which believe not, lest the light of the glorious gospel of Christ, who is the image of God, should shine unto them." Hence you see them preferring the baubles of a moment to "the pearl of great price," unable to see any form or comeliness in Him who is the fairest among ten thousand and the altogether lovely; seeking after the praise of men, and disregarding the praise of God; "rising early and sitting up late," to amass the gold that perisheth, while they overlook "the unsearchable riches of Christ;" seeking happiness in a world which Solomon, who had the best opportunities of making experiments and was disposed to employ them, declares, "Is all vanity, and vexation of spirit;" seeking pleasure in sins which are but for a season, and which are not only

short but always unsatisfying, leaving a stain upon the mind, and a sting upon the conscience. "Ye Owls," for so God calls you in His Word, we may not as creatures be able to convince you of your folly, but God will soon convince you. Everything here is precarious and uncertain; the lamp of life will soon be extinguished. You may soon be deprived of your health, or your property, or your beloved connections, and then, Jonah, where art thou? Death will soon convince you. "Though men may live fools," says Dr. Young, "yet fools they cannot die." Then where will you flee for help, and on whose arm will you lean for support? Eternity will soon convince you, and then the righteous will stand with great boldness before the Judgment-seat of Christ, when the wicked shall be driven away like chaff. Oh, what fools will you confess yourselves when you come there! What miseries will you then see you have brought upon yourselves, and which you might have prevented! An immensity and an eternity of happiness you might have enjoyed, but this you sacrificed for—what? The pleasures of sin, which were but for a moment.

II. But they are also called "*dragons*." Satan is the old dragon, and sinners are the younger. "Ye are of your father the devil, and the lusts of your father will ye do." Cain was one of this offspring. "He was of that wicked one, and slew his brother. And wherefore slew he him? Because his own works were evil, and his brother's righteous." Under this character we have the persecutor Saul; he was not only a blasphemer, but a persecutor, and injurious. "One sinner" says Solomon, "destroyeth much good." What evil does a professor of religion do, by his falls and miscarriages! What mischief to the cause of Christ! How does he occasion the way of truth to be evil spoken of, and the name of Jesus to be blasphemed! He thus becomes a stumbling block to the weak, and discourages the hearts of God's ministers. Let that sinner be a father, and see by his example and influence, if not by direct instruction, how much evil he causes! How does he expose himself to the charges God brought against the Jews in the days of Jeremiah! Look at Paine and Voltaire; I remember some years ago attending a young man in his dying hours, and all he said some time before he expired was, "Oh, Voltaire." This he repeatedly exclaimed.

Now let us notice the acts ascribed to these metaphorical beings. "The beasts of the field shall *honour* me." You see God does not leave the subjects of divine grace in the state in which He finds them, but always produces a change in them. He finds them in love with sin, and leaves them in love with holiness. He finds them "walking according to the course of this world, and following divers lusts and pleasures," but they are brought by His grace to follow hard after holiness. So that "instead of the thorn shall come up the fir-tree, and instead of the briar shall come up the myrtle tree, and it shall be to the Lord for a name, for an everlasting sign that shall not be cut off." These owls are made birds of paradise, these dragons lambs and doves. What is conversion unless it produces a character the very reverse of what it was? Thus it is, these owls and dragons shall honour God, and there are two ways in which these changed and reformed beings will do this: first, *passively;* as the work of His hands, they show forth what He is able to do, in displaying what He has actually done already. Therefore, He adds immediately after our text, "This people have I formed for myself, they shall show forth my praise." Therefore, says He, "they shall be called trees of righteousness, the planting of the Lord." Not only the planting, but the making of them to bear fruit, that He may be glorified. "Ye are God's husbandry," says Paul, "Ye are God building." In both these and in other representations of them, they hold forth the perfections of God, they show us His works, and display His mercy and grace. Secondly, they honour God *actively*. The sun has been glorifying God for thousands of years, but then it has been passively. He makes our morning, and our spring, and our summer, and fills the earth with plenty. This he does passively. It is the same with all the heavenly bodies; they are called God's servants, they serve Him with amazing regularity. Yea, "all His works praise Him," from the greatest to the least. But His people honour Him by their acknowledging what He has done for them; they *discard* their own praise, and give Him the glory, saying, "Not unto us, O Lord, not unto us, but unto Thy name give the glory." "By the grace of God I am what I am." They honour Him by confiding in Him, in all His attributes, in all His relations towards them, in all His great and precious promises. How finely as well as truly does Cowper express this!

"Retreat beneath His wings,
And in His grace confide,
This more exalts the King of Kings
Than all your works beside.

Persons never feel themselves so much honoured as when

implicitly confided in. Christians honour God by their willingness to make sacrifices for His cause, by their readiness to suffer for His sake, by denying themselves, by taking up their cross and following the Redeemer. Paul had such an intense regard for the Saviour that he made no scruple to say, "Yea, doubtless I count all things but loss for the excellency of the knowledge of Christ Jesus my lord."

To conclude: you find these beasts of the field, these "owls and dragons," were to honour God, *because* He produced "waters in the wilderness, and rivers in the desert." All God's doings demand praise; they are all wonderful; but He has "magnified His Word above all His name." All His works display His perfections, but some rise far above others. We ought to praise Him for the meat that perisheth, but how much more for the meat that endureth unto everlasting life! We ought to praise Him for the sun in nature, but how much more for "the Sun of Righteousness, which ariseth with healing in His wings!" "Blessed be ye," said the Saviour. Why were they so blessed? "For many prophets and righteous men have desired to see those things which ye see, and have not seen them." Christians, remember your destiny. God hath said, "I will place salvation in Zion for Israel my glory." You are to glorify God, you are charged with a portion of His honour; may you carry it unsullied down to the grave. You are destined to glorify Him; He looks to you for it; O may it be our concern while here, our desire and our study, that "whether we eat or drink, or whatever we do, to do all to His glory."

V.

THE FUTURE TRIUMPHS OF THE GOSPEL.

(Preached on Sunday Evening, March 24th, 1844). .

I have sworn by myself, the word is gone out of my mouth in righteousness, and shall not return, That unto me every knee shall bow, every tongue shall swear. Surely, shall one say, in the Lord have I righteousness and strength: even to Him shall men come; and all that are incensed against Him shall be ashamed.—ISAIAH xlv., 23, 24.

THE revelation of God's mercy is coeval with man's existence. It commenced in paradise. The first promise was contained in the threatening "And I will put enmity between thee and the woman, and between thy seed and her seed; it shall bruise thy head, and thou shalt bruise his heel." Here first bubbles up the water of life which was hereafter to fertilize so many nations; here first dawned that light, "which shineth more and more unto the perfect day."

The discoveries were enlarged from age to age. For this purpose a people were chosen and separated from the nations of the earth, to be the depositaries of the truth, and heirs of righteousness which is of faith. There was established a system of sacrifices which were "a shadow of good things to come." And there was appointed a succession of prophets whose office it was to proclaim the coming of the Messiah. We cannot be mistaken here. "Of which salvation" says Peter, "the prophets have enquired, and searched dilligently, who prophesied of the grace that should come unto you."

The testimony of Jesus, therefore, was the spirit of prophecy; "to Him gave all the prophets witness," though not all equally. Isaiah was "anointed with the oil of joy above his fellows;" he is called "the Evangelical prophet." Calamy calls him "the fifth Evangelist." Hear what God says by him in the preceding verse: "Look unto me, and be ye saved, all the ends of the earth; for I am God, and there is none else. I have sworn by myself, the word is gone out of my mouth in righteousness, and shall not return. That unto me every knee shall bow, every tongue shall swear. Surely, shall one say, in the Lord have I righteousness and strength; even to Him shall all men come, and all that are incensed against Him shall be ashamed."

These words announce, firstly, an universal subjection; secondly, the way in which it is to be exemplified; and thirdly, the consequences of refusing the overtures of mercy.

I. Universal subjection is implied in the expressions, "every knee shall bow, and every tongue shall swear"—in token of allegiance, of service, and of submission to His pleasure.

"I have sworn by myself." Here seems to be implied that God has a right to this subjection; and this right is peculiar and perfect; it is very superior to that of any master to a servant, or a sovereign to a subject, for God has an entire and absolute property in us all. Our very existence is owing to Him. If you will not acknowledge this, why are you beholden to Him? We breathe His air, eat at His table, and wear His apparel, and are daily living upon His bounty. O for shame! and not confess we are indebted to Him for all we possess and enjoy! If God were to call all creatures to Him, and say, "Take that thine is, and go thy way," what would you take? You would not take even yourself, but would relapse into non-existence. "For in Him we live and move and have our being."

This submission is not natural. "Unto me *shall* every knee bow, and every tongue *shall* swear." No, this was not the case once. Their previous condition was a state of alienation and rebellion. It is somewhat remarkable that every formulary of devotion recognises this principle. The Liturgy of the church is full of this mortifying doctrine, and it is lamentable that the pulpit should contradict the reading-desk. Who was it that said, "Out of the heart of man proceed evil thoughts, adulteries, fornications, murders, thefts, covetousness, wickedness, deceit, lasciviousness, an evil eye, blasphemy, pride, foolishness: all these evil things come from within and defile the man"? Why, it is the faithful and true Witness who said, "The heart is deceitful above all things." *He* said it who knows the heart, and is perfectly acquainted with all that is in man. Has not God always treated mankind as if they were depraved creatures? Have not His judgments always been abroad in the earth? What inflictions of His justice has He sent on individuals, families, and nations! Yes, "the whole creation travaileth and groaneth together until now." And has there not been a cause? What says all history, all observation on this subject? Is it not strange that such a wise man as Locke should speak of a child's mind as a sheet of unsoiled paper? Take the child in regard to evil. How is it that once seeing is enough to induce him to act? Then take him with regard to good. Here there must be, "line upon line, and precept upon precept." And why is not good, as easily imbibed as evil? You need not go to the child at all. Think of yourself. You complain of your memory. Does the tradesman forget the market? "Can a woman forget her sucking child, that she should not have compassion upon the son of her womb?" "Can a maid forget her ornaments? or a bride her attire?" Oh, there is memory enough in other things, only it is so slippery and treacherous in the things of God arising from a want of attention and congeniality. Consult your own experience. Have you not found yourselves prone to evil, to ingratitude, and to murmur at the will of God? And have not these evil propensities grown with your growth, and strengthened with your strength? If we were not prone to evil, why should we need so many checks to restrain us? Why need so many excitements, and why are these so often in vain? If we are not lost, why should we need a Saviour? If we were not enslaved, why should we need a Redeemer? If we were not defiled, why need washing from our sins? If we were not rebellious and unwilling to return, and bow to the will of God, why is it necessary that He should send His servants and His own Son to beseech us in His stead to be reconciled to God?

Thirdly. We are here reminded that this submission is to be general and universal: "Unto me every knee shall bow, and every tongue shall swear." This is often mentioned in Scripture. Accordingly you will find our Saviour in His parable observing that though Christianity was very small in its commencement its diffusion should be very wide. Again, "The kingdom of heaven is like unto leaven which a woman took and hid in three measures of meal till the whole was leavened." Also "The kingdom of heaven is like to a grain of mustard seed, which a man took and sowed in his field: which indeed is the least of all seeds: but when it is grown, it is the greatest among herbs, and becometh a tree, so that the birds of the air come and lodge in the branches thereof." Hitherto the progress of Christianity has been comparatively small and its success much confined. Down to this period, it has only been found in the experience of individuals, and sometimes in households. There is no country, or town, or village, where even the majority are as yet governed by it. But it is not to be so always. We read of a nation being born in a day; we read of "the nations of them that are saved"; we read that "He shall sprinkle many nations"; yea, "that all nations shall bow down before Him, all people shall serve Him;" that "the Lord shall be King in the whole earth," "and in that day there shall be one Lord and His name one." We need not therefore fear, whatever be the apprehensions of some, that better days are before us, better days than the world ever witnessed, when every valley shall be exalted, and every mountain and hill shall be made low.

And here observe, this subjection is certain and divinely ensured. How strong is the pledge He Himself has here given. "By myself have I sworn, the word has gone out of my mouth in righteousness and shall not return." And if it be a righteous thing for God to do He will do it. The word *righteousness* means faithfulness, and who ever could impeach His veracity? "And shall not return." His word has sometimes returned. "Yet forty days," said He to Jonah, "and Ninevah shall be overthrown;" but it was not, the word returned. God said to Jeremiah, "At what instant I shall speak concerning a nation, and concerning a kingdom, to pluck up, and to pull down, and to destroy it." These threatenings were conditional; for, says God, "If that nation, against whom I have pronounced, turn from their evil, I will repent of the evil that I thought to do unto them." But here the engagement is absolute: it is nothing less than an oath; "By myself have I sworn," says God. Why swear by Himself? Because He could swear by no greater. Why swear at all? Was it necessary to bind Himself down? No; but "an oath for confirmation is an end of all strife," "wherein God, willing therefore more abundantly to show unto the heirs of promise the immutability of His counsel, confirmed it by an oath: that by two immutable things"—for His *word* is as immutable as His oath,—"in which it was impossible for God to lie, we might have a strong consolation who have fled for refuge to lay hold upon the hope set before us in the Gospel."

II. Observe THE WAY IN WHICH THIS PREDICTION IS TO BE EXEMPLIFIED.

"Surely shall one say, In the Lord have I righteousness and strength; even to Him shall men come."

This shows us that universal homage is to be eventually paid to Him in His Son. For it is with God in Christ we have to do: therefore we read, that "the Father judgeth no man, but hath committed all judgment unto the Son." And how does Paul write to the Philippians? "God also hath highly exalted Him, and given Him a name which is above every name, that at the name of Jesus every knee should bow, of things in heaven and things in earth, and things under the earth, and that every tongue should confess that Jesus Christ is Lord, to the glory of God the Father." In the same way we are to understand the passage before us. This is the grand subjection here intended: and this is the most difficult of all subjections to be accomplished. Here it is most hard to bend every knee, and induce every tongue to confess. The apostle mentions this with regard to the Jews, "I bear them witness." says he, "that they have a zeal for God; but not according to knowledge. For they being ignorant of God's righteousness, and going about to establish their own righteousness, have not submitted themselves unto the righteousness of God."

This subjection is to be exemplified two ways. First, by *conviction.* The man feels that he is not his own, and will subscribe to the language of the Apostle, "In me, that is in my flesh, dwelleth no good thing." "Enter not into judgment with Thy servant, O Lord, for in Thy sight shall no flesh living be justified." To this conviction the man must be brought. How can righteousness come by the law, since the law demands perfect obedience, perfect in its extent, principle, and duration? "Cursed is every one that continueth not in all things written in the law of the Lord to do them." Are we driven to despair? No; there is a righteousness without the law. "The righteousness which is of faith, which is upon all them that believe."

He is equally brought to acknowledge that his "strength" is found in Him as well as his "righteousness." The Fall not only left him without righteousness, but without strength. Men are generally willing to confess their guilt; they cannot very well deny that they have not done the things which they ought; and that they are not what they should be, and that in some respects and degrees they stand in need of forgiveness; but they question not their power to become righteous, and therefore resolve that at a more favourable opportunity they will become so. Well, they make the trial, and the result is, that without God they can do nothing. They are willing now to take hold of His "strength" and look to Him for the sanctifying influences of His Holy Spirit, as well as for pardoning mercy through Christ; for the renovation of their natures, as well as the justification of their souls. When the sinner's eyes are first enlightened, the work of salvation is all important; he sees a thousand difficulties in his way far above his ability to remove; and he would lie down in utter despair but for the prospect and assurance (the mere probability of this would not be sufficient, but for the prospect and assurance) of effectual aid. Therefore the Saviour comes forward and meets him with a promise, "Fear thou not, for I am with thee; be not dismayed, for I am thy God." "My grace is sufficient for thee."

Hence also this is exemplified in a way of *application*: "Even to Him shall men come." And to whom should men go for help, but to Him in whom all power is to be found? To Him, therefore," said the dying Jacob, "shall the gathering of the people be." If there were but one well in the neighbourhood, all the inhabitants around would come to it for water. If there were only one refuge from a cruel and victorious enemy, to this would "the gathering of the people be." When the famine was in Egypt, and the inhabitants of the surrounding countries went to Pharoah, he said, "Go unto Joseph, he is in possession of the corn." So our Saviour says, "Every man that hath heard, and hath learnt of the Father, cometh unto me." For, my brethren, this is the grand thing. Do you ask, "What must I do to be saved?" Then we are authorised to proclaim, "Behold the Lamb of God which taketh away the sins of the world." "The blood of Jesus Christ His Son cleanseth us from all sin." And the preacher who does not return the same answer is nothing less than a betrayer and murderer of souls.

III. THE CONSEQUENCES OF REFUSING THE OVERTURES OF MERCY. "And all that are incensed against Him shall be ashamed."

It seems strange that such characters as these should be found: yet such is the case. David said, "Why do the heathen rage, and the people imagine a vain thing? The kings of the earth set themselves, and the rulers take counsel together, against the Lord, and against His anointed, saying, Let us break their bands asunder, and cast away their cords from us."

You are mistaken if you imagine that the world will be induced to love and admire your religion. It is said of the Saviour, "They hated Him without a cause." Yea, they hated Him for the very excellences He displayed. He said to the Jews, "The world loveth you, but Me it hateth." Heathen philosophers thought that if virtue appeared incarnate all the world would fall in love with her. It did appear, and went up and down our world: thirty-three years "the image of the invisible God" was seen "going about doing good," and what was the result? "He was in the world, and the world was made by Him, and the world knew Him not. He came to His own, and His own received Him not." They pursued Him with remorseless malice, and at length hung Him on a tree. This is what they would have done with God Himself, had it been possible. "You have both seen," said the Saviour, "and hate both Me and my Father." Men say unto God naturally, "Depart from us, we desire not the knowledge of Thy ways."

So if we go to sacred history, we may see how the Church of Christ was opposed from its earliest commencement. They employed every kind of persecution against the disciples and the cause of Christ. Did they welcome the gospel when it came? Yea, did they not in numerous instances oppose it? How did the Jews oppose the Son of God Himself! Yet they said, "If we had been in the days of our fathers, we would not have been partakers with them in the blood of the prophets," at the very time they were imbuing their hands in the blood of the Son of God.

Persons sometimes bring a serious charge against Infidels and Socinians, while they themselves exclaim in their hearts, "We will not have this man to reign over us!"

There are such to be found who are good neighbours, honest and benevolent, yet are not brought to deny themselves, and take up their cross, and confess that when they have done all, they have had no meritorious hand in the work of redemption, and are entitled to no share of the glory. But if you ever enter heaven, you must enter it in the same way and on the same terms with the chief of sinners. The elder brother in the parable said to his father, "I have never at any time transgressed thy command." "Well, then," says the father, "since you have always kept my commands, keep them now; go in and embrace thy brother, and share the pleasure with the family." No, he would rather have died. Here was his goodness, his boasted obedience in fulfilling his father's commands! Oh, there is a deal of opposition against the sovereignty and grace of God in every self-righteous character.

We must now pass from the conduct to the condition of the

persons referred to. "All that are incensed against Him shall be ashamed." "They shall make war with the Lamb, and the Lamb shall overcome them." No wonder, for "He is King of kings, and Lord of lords." Here is the doom of those who oppose the spread of the gospel. "For the nations and kingdoms that will not serve Thee shall perish." Blessed be God, persecution is not a national crime; we are allowed to co-operate in endeavouring to spread the gospel of Christ, and are bold to believe that He will send out His light and His truth principally from this country. But this will not screen you as individuals. No; whoever you are who are His enemies, He will say of you, "Bring them out, and slay them before My face." "*All*," whether high or low, the moral as well as the profligate. "*All* that are incensed against Him shall be ashamed." There may be many of those, but though hand join in hand, yet shall not the wicked go unpunished. The multitude therefore will not afford any alleviation to their misery. Thus "the way of transgressors is hard," even here, and leads down to the chambers of eternal death. But there is a Saviour able and willing to save the chief of sinners, and who will in no wise cast out any who come unto Him.

—"For sinners Jesus died;
None who pray shall be denied."

VI.

THE SEED OF ISRAEL.

(Preached on Sunday Evening, September 21st, 1845.)

In the Lord shall all the seed of Israel be justified, and shall glory.— ISAIAH xlv. 25.

YOU will remember that not long ago I preached on the two verses immediately preceding this verse, and that I then had occasion, in closing, briefly to refer to our text. In bringing it now more specially before your attention, I shall endeavour to ascertain, first, who are the heirs of this promise; secondly, what is the substance of this promise; and thirdly, what is the privilege here announced.

I. WHO ARE THE SUBJECTS OF THIS PROMISE?

"All the seed of Israel."

Israel means Jacob, and you know how he obtained the name; you know how he was knighted on the field of battle. He had to meet his incensed brother Esau, who came forth with a determination to slay him, accompanied by four hundred men. Jacob did all he could to produce a reconciliation. He sent him a present, and "a man's gift makes way for him," and "a soft answer turneth away wrath"; but when he had done all, he depended on God for success, and therefore said, "O Lord, I beseech Thee, deliver me from the hand of my brother, from the hand of Esau." "And Jacob was left alone, and there wrestled a man with him until the breaking of the day. And when he saw that he prevailed not against him, he touched the hollow of his thigh; and the hollow of Jacob's thigh was out of joint as he wrestled with him." Few would have continued wrestling upon one leg, but he did, and this gave rise to a proverbial expression, that "a wrestling Jacob will come off a prevailing Israel." "And he said unto him, What is thy name? And he said Jacob. And he said, thy name shall be called no more Jacob but Israel, that is, a prince of God, for as a prince hast thou power with God and with men, and hast prevailed."

"The seed of Israel" may be viewed under two aspects. First, as Jews, as being the natural descendants of Jacob. They always were very far from being the people of God, unless by a national alliance and covenant. We see them under Moses, under Joshua, and under the kings of Israel; we see them during the Babylonish captivity, and in the days of our Saviour. "He came to His own, and His own received Him not; but to as many as received Him, to them gave He power to become the sons of God"; "but with wicked hands they crucified and slew Him." Yet the twelve Apostles were Jews—the seventy disciples were Jews—the first churches, with few exceptions, were Jews; and the period will come when the veil shall be taken from their hearts. "They shall turn unto the Lord and look upon Him whom they have pierced." It is matter of dispute as to their return to their own country, but there is no dispute as to their return to Christianity; and so it is said, "Israel shall be saved in the Lord with an everlasting salvation."

But there is another aspect under which we may view Israel; and observe the distinction which the Saviour makes when speaking of Nathaniel: "Behold," says He, "an Israelite indeed, in whom there is no guile." In speaking of him as "an Israelite," He distinguishes him from other nations, and by calling him "an Israelite *indeed*," He distinguishes him from his own nation. You will also remember the language of the Apostle, where he says, "All are not Israel that are of Israel." All along there were some who were partakers of faith and humility. These were peculiarly the Israel of God, and the ground of their being so called, was not their natural relationship to Jacob, but their spiritual relationship; for from the beginning he was "not a Jew who was one outwardly, neither was that circumcision which was outward in the flesh: but he is a Jew which is one inwardly; and circumcision is that of the heart, in the spirit and not in the letter, whose praise is not of men, but of God." Therefore if your hearts are circumcised, if you are renewed in the spirit of your minds, though you are Gentiles by nature, you are "the Israel of God"; you are "the true circumcision, who worship God in the Spirit, who rejoice in Christ Jesus, and have no confidence in the flesh." "If ye are Christ's, then are ye Abraham's seed, and heirs according to the promise."

But who of this "seed of Israel" are entitled to the promise? Why, all of them. "In the Lord shall all the seed of Israel be justified and shall glory."

The expression seems to imply *number*. Though the righteous have always been few compared to the wicked around them, yet collectively considered, and when gathered out of all nations and tongues, they will be accounted "as a number which no man can number." We are told, therefore, that the Captain of their salvation is leading many sons unto glory. We are assured that He will "see of the travail of His soul and be satisfied," and no little will satisfy the benevolence of His heart, and lead Him to say, "enough are saved; more need not be redeemed; I am satisfied."

But if the expression does not imply number, it expressed *impartiality*. "As many as are led by the Spirit of God, they are the sons of God," whatever distinctions may prevail among them. "And in the Lord shall all the seed of Israel be justified, and shall glory"—the rich, the poor, the high, the low, the bond, the free, for there is no difference here as to country, condition or complexion. No, the salvation which Paul called "so great salvation," Jude calls "the common salvation," and all here are upon a level, as we are taught expressly in the Lord's Supper, where all eat the same bread, and drink the same wine, where there is no better wine for the rich than for the poor, for the master than for the servant, for the prince than for the peasant. All believers are "one in Christ Jesus." "All the seed of Israel" have one Father, they are all included in the same eternal purpose, all redeemed by the same precious blood, all justified by the same grace, all destined to the same "glory, honour, immortality, and eternal life." Therefore you should love them all and never be ashamed to hold communion with those with whom He holds communion. Children differ in age, in size, in strength, and in feature, but they form one and the same family. Before the time of harvest the wheat grows in various places, and is separated by hedges and by walls, but when it is reaped it is carried home, and gathered into the same garner, while no inquiry is made whether it grew in this enclosure or in that.

II. But we hasten to lay open, in the second place, THE SUBSTANCE OF THIS PROMISE.

"In the Lord shall all the seed of Israel be justified, and shall glory."

Observe the dignity of the Benefactor, the relation upon

which this blessedness is founded, and the nature of the privilege itself. Let us briefly review each of these, considering first, the dignity of the Benefactor. "*In the Lord* shall all the seed of Israel be justified and shall glory." Who is the person here spoken of? This is a very important inquiry, and the reason is, because of the name here given—"The Lord." Wherever you see this word in capitals in the Bible, you are apprized of the word Jehovah in the original. This name therefore is applied to Him; for it would be very easy to prove that He is the person spoken of in the preceding verse; that it is of Him it is said, "Surely shall one say, in the Lord have I righteousness and strength." Then it is declared that "all that are incensed against Him shall be ashamed." Why, then, you would make even Jesus Christ to be God? No, I do not make Him to be so; I find Him to be so. And it is necessary He should be so, for without this there could not be an all sufficiency of worth to expiate our offences; or of merit in His blood to obtain for us the dispensation of the Spirit, or of love in His heart, or of power in His arm. All through from the beginning to the end, we must be able to say, "My Lord and my God."

Observe, secondly, the relation upon which the blessedness depends: "*In* the Lord." Now, we find much of this is said in Scripture. In the preceding verse, it is written, "In the Lord have I righteousness and strength." Hence says the Apostle, "If any man be *in* Christ he is a new creature." Hence he says, "We are blessed with all spiritual blessings *in* Christ Jesus." And hence the expression of his own desire, "that I may win Christ and be found *in* Him." There is, therefore, an union between Him and all His people, a virtual, a visible, a vital union. A virtual, which existed before the world began; a vital, when they are enabled to receive and embrace Him by faith; and a visible one when they join His Church, and make a profession of His name. You will find this connection with Him is necessary. It shows us that He is not only the source of blessedness, but that in this state alone we can enjoy it; we can only be made partakers of it by being in Him. You know a refuge is a place of safety, you know you can only be secure by being in it. The ark preserved Noah and his family, but had they been out of it when the rain descended they would have perished along with the unbelieving world; but "the Lord shut him in," and therefore he was preserved. So must it be with regard to us. The branches, to use our Saviour's figure, draw the sap from the vine to render them fruitful. But you will observe that these are in the vine, and He remarks, "The branch *cannot* bear fruit of itself." Take the branch of a vine and place it as near as you please—yea, fasten it on by any external ligaments; there will be no vitality or fruit. "As the branch cannot bear fruit of itself, except it abide in the vine, no more can ye except ye abide in Me, for without [or separate from] Me ye can do nothing."

III. We observe THE PRIVILEGE.

This takes in two things. First it takes in *justification.* "In the Lord shall all the seed of Israel be justified." Does this mean they shall be justified from imputations and from slander? Yes, in a sense this may be implied, so that the Christian may say, "He is near to justify"; and when things are said of him falsely he may say with the Church, "He will bring forth my righteousness as the light, and my judgment as the noon-day: for my witness is in heaven and my record is on high." So Joseph's innocence, after a while, was made to appear; and so David, after a while, was cleared from all the calumnies raised by Saul and others. So shall it be with all God's people who have borne reproach for His sake. Their reputation may have been tarnished for a while, but there will be a resurrection of the enemies of the cross of Christ as well as of Christians by and by, and "then shall the righteous shine forth as the sun in the kingdom of their Father."

Now also there are many things in which they condemn themselves, while they read that "the soul that sinneth it shall die," and that "cursed is every one that continueth not in all things written in the law to do them." Yet they are justified. How is this? Why, "all that believe in Him are justified from all things from which they could not be justified by the law of Moses." "Being justified by faith we have peace with God." In what way? "Through our Lord Jesus Christ." He hath made Him to be sin for us who knew no sin, that we may be made the righteousness of God in Him? How was He made sin for us? By imputation only. Our sin was reckoned to Him, and He became responsible for the consequences. "He once suffered for sins, the Just for the unjust, that He might bring us to God." How are we made righteous before God? In the very same way. His righteousness is reckoned to us, and in consequence of it we are absolved and justified. You remember, Christian, you had a burden too heavy for you to bear, and you know how it was removed. Bunyan tells us how you came within sight of the Cross, and your load fell off, and rolled into the sepulchre. What is this but saying, "He was delivered for our offences, and raised again for our justification?" How far does this justification extend? The Apostle says, "There is no condemnation to them that are in Christ Jesus." And Jeremiah assures us, that "if their sins be sought for, they shall not be found." They have now obtained favour; they are now "accepted in the beloved," both as to their persons and their services, and are not only freed, by this justification, from the curse of the law, but invested with a title to everlasting life.

This is not all; but here is *exaltation* too. Not only shall "all the seed of Israel be justified," but they "shall glory." Poor, mean, and despised as they are, yet now the shout of a king is heard among them. Low, mopish, and melancholy, as they are considered by the world, yet David's representations of them is true: "Happy are the people who are in such a case; yea, happy is the people whose God is the Lord." "In His name shall they rejoice all the day, and in His favour shall they be exalted." In whom, though now they see Him not, yet they rejoice with joy unspeakable and full of glory. In Him they are "justified and shall glory." Glorying is the exaltation of joy. They are called upon to "rejoice evermore"—to "rejoice in the Lord always." There is enough in Him to draw it forth. But does not this seem to contradict the language of Scripture? "Where is boasting then?" says the Apostle. "It is excluded." But here we find it. "By what law is it excluded? By works;" that is, it is excluded by any works or worthiness of our own, but not absolutely. No, we can boast in another. No, says the Apostle, "He is made of God unto us, wisdom, righteousness, sanctification, and redemption." "Therefore let him that glorieth, glory in the Lord"—and he cannot glory too much while he glories in Him. Oh, there is indeed enough in Him to draw this forth, and to raise it much higher than it has ever been felt or expressed by us. "Oh," says the Christian, "Christ is my all and in all."

> "Jewels to thee are gaudy toys,
> And gold is sordid dust."

Oh, what a friend have I, "that sticketh closer than a brother," a friend that loveth at all times! Oh, what a guide have I! Though He may lead me in a way that I know not, and in paths that I have not known, yet will He make darkness light before me. Oh, what a shepherd have I! The Lord is my Shepherd, I shall not want; He maketh me to lie down in green pastures; He leadeth me beside the still waters: yea, though I walk through the valley of the shadow of death, I will fear no evil. Oh, what a portion have I! The Lord is my portion, saith my soul; therefore will I hope in Him. Oh, what a prospect have I! There is laid up for me a crown of righteousness, which the Lord, the righteous Judge, shall give unto me, and not unto me only, but unto all them that love His appearing. "Eye hath not seen, nor ear heard, neither have entered into the heart of man the things which God hath laid up for them that love Him." And what we glory in—what we love to think of—may we never be ashamed to own, to talk of, and to publish, that others may judge of our glorying in Him! And soon "He will come again to be glorified in His saints, and admired in all them that believe."

VII.

INSTRUCTION AND PEACE.

(Preached on Sunday Evening, January 11th, 1846.)

And all Thy children shall be taught of the Lord; and great shall be the peace of Thy children.—ISAIAH liv. 13.

GOD has always had a people for His name, and has always dealt with them by way of promise. "He also is faithful who hath promised." God could have done for His people all He means to do, without previously promising, but then how could faith be exercised? Then how could they have lived and rejoiced in the expectation, or how could they have pleaded with Him in prayer? Whereas they can now sue God in His own court, and can say, "Fulfil Thy word unto Thy servant, upon which Thou hast caused me to hope." The devil makes promises enough, but he never performs them; "and men of high degree are a lie, and men of low degree are vanity." "But the Lord is not a man that He should lie, nor the son of man that He should repent. "Hath He spoken, and will He not do it? hath He promised, and will He not make it good?" Dear brethren, He cannot deny Himself, He abideth faithful. Heaven and earth shall pass away, but His words shall not pass away. But while "all the promises of God are yea and amen in Christ Jesus," they are as valuable as they are true. They are "exceeding great and precious." "The Lord God is a sun and shield; the Lord will give grace and glory; no good thing will He withhold *from them that walk uprightly*."

Let us now descend from the promises at large, to notice one in our text: "All Thy children shall be taught of the Lord, and great shall be the peace of Thy children." We pause a moment to ask a question: to whom is this promise addressed. "*My* children"—the Churches' children. What Church? The Church of the living and true God, of "Jerusalem which is from above;" and which, as the apostle says, "is the mother of us all." God is the Father of His Church; believers are all His offspring. The Church is the mother which travails and brings them forth, and then by her ministers and ordinances brings "them up in the nurture and admonition of the Lord." Not a few have been her children in former times, taken in the aggregate, and she will be more fruitful in future, till the period arrives when "a nation shall be born in a day," and filled with surprise at her own increase, she will exclaim, "Who hath begotten me these? and who hath brought up these? these, where have they been?"

Let us consider the two blessings here referred to: instruction and peace; the kind and extensiveness of the one, and the nature and degree of the other.

I. THE INSTRUCTION spoken of in our text; "All Thy children shall be taught of the Lord."

All therefore need it. There is nothing of which men are prouder than knowledge. "Vain man would be wise, though man be born like a wild ass's colt." But in this respect he is inferior to the beasts that perish, for they show much consciousness and skill, specially in providing for themselves almost from their very birth. But man comes into the world destitute of all information; all his knowledge is external, and all drawn in through the senses; and as to spiritual knowledge, he is "alienated from the life of God, through the ignorance that is in him," because of the blindness that is in him. Want you an evidence of this blindness and ignorance? behold here is a Saviour, "fairer than the children of men and altogether lovely," but man's understanding is so darkened that he can see no "beauty that he should desire Him." Our Saviour said of the Jews, "They do always err in their hearts, and they have not known my ways;" and He said to His disciples, "Are ye yet without understanding?"

The knowledge referred to in our text is not the knowledge of astronomy, or of the languages, or of commerce, or of politics, or of natural philosophy. We do not undervalue these in their places, they are very useful. The community derives a thousand advantages from them. But all this knowledge appertains to the life that now is; as the apostle says, "Whether there be knowledge, it shall vanish away;" and it is a humiliating thought that the larger part of that knowledge which men acquire with so much difficulty, will be of no avail in another world. The great thing is to be wise for eternity.

This is the same, therefore, which Peter refers to when he says, "He hath called us out of darkness into His marvellous light." It is the same as that which the apostle prays for for the Ephesians, when he says, "That the God of our Lord Jesus Christ, the Father of glory, may give unto you the spirit of wisdom and revelation in the knowledge of Him, the eyes of your understanding being enlightened, that ye may know what is the hope of His calling, and what the riches of the glory of His inheritance in the saints." This is the knowledge of which he speaks in reference to himself, when he says, "Yea, doubtless, and I count all things but loss for the excellency of the knowledge of Christ Jesus my Lord."

Let us notice the Author of this knowledge. "All thy children shall be taught of the *Lord*." They are instructed in the hidden wisdom. All Christians have a divine Teacher, they are taught of the *Lord*. "Every good gift and every perfect gift cometh down from the Father of lights." Isaiah, speaking of the husbandman and his sowing, says, "His God doth instruct to discretion, and doth teach him." Hence the discoveries for which the children of men are distinguished. But He shines in the heart "to give the knowledge of His glory as it is in the face of Jesus Christ." It is here, brethren, we are to behold Him, and none teacheth like Him. None so *patient*, accommodating Himself to our weakness, teaching us as we are able to bear it; none so *effectual*, He gives the faculty as well as the lesson; none so *perfectly unerring*, for under His instruction, "a wayfaring man, though a fool, need not err therein." He gives spiritual understanding, of which we find much among the poor and unlearned, while men of condition, and the worldly wise are ignorant of it. The reason is, the one is naturally taught, while the other is Divinely instructed. But there is a vast difference between their present and future knowledge; now they know as children, then they shall know as men. Then "the light of the moon shall be as the light of the sun, and the light of the sun shall be sevenfold, as the light of seven days, in the day that the Lord bindeth up the breach of His people, and healeth the stroke of their wound."

The second thing is the extensiveness of it.

"*All* thy children shall be taught of the Lord." "Such honour have all the Saints."

They are all born from above; they are all born to wealth, for they possess "unsearchable riches;" they are all born to honour, the honour that cometh from above; they are nobles, and princes, and priests. God will not suffer any of His children to grow up savages. They are all "made meet for the inheritance of the saints of light." Though they are all taught of the Lord, they are not all *equally* taught; some have little knowledge, but though small in the degree, it is peculiar in its kind; it is spiritual, saving knowledge.

Are you the subjects of this Divine tuition? How are we to know it? We will only mention a plain but decisive proof, furnished by our Saviour. "Every man therefore that hath heard and learned of the Father *cometh unto me*." He goes to Christ, therefore, to deal with Him concerning the salvation of his soul. He goes to His cross, he goes to His throne, he goes to His house, and he finds in the Saviour "wisdom, and righteousness, sanctification, and redemption." One that has been divinely taught will be continually coming to Christ; so says the Apostle, "To whom *coming* as unto a living stone." And the promise is, "Him that cometh unto Me I will in no wise cast out."

II. We now pass to the second blessing, "PEACE." "And great shall be the peace of thy children."

The nature and degree of this we just glance at.

As to the blessing itself it is peace. Peace means prosperity. David says "Pray for the peace of Jerusalem, they shall prosper that love thee." "For my brethren and companions' sake I will now say, Peace be within thee." The Saviour says, "My peace I give unto you; not as the world give I unto you." Joseph said, "God shall give Pharaoh an answer of peace." Artaxerxes superscribes peace, and at such a time. And Jehovah Himself says, "This man shall be the peace." In all these instances it means welfare or prosperity, and in this sense "great shall be the peace of thy children." Yes, they are blessed, truly blessed. It is not every kind of knowledge that increases happiness; so far from it that Solomon says, "He that increaseth knowledge increases sorrow." But here "Blessed are the people that know the joyful sound; they shall walk, O Lord, in the light of Thy countenance." Yes, says Isaiah, "Say ye to the righteous, it shall be well with him." Happy are they who can use the language of David in the twenty-third Psalm, "The Lord is my Shepherd, I shall not want; He maketh me to lie down in green pastures; He leadeth me beside the still waters." The Apostle says, "Jesus came and preached peace to them which were afar off and to them which were nigh." and we read of "the gospel of peace." Jesus is called the "Prince of peace," and God is called "the God of peace." Here peace refers to holy tranquility of soul. Our Saviour said, "In the world ye shall have tribulation, but in Me ye shall have peace." He does not mean an abundance of good things. He said unto His disciples, "Peace I give unto you, my peace I give unto you," and it is here clearly intimated that this peace is connected with the results of divine teaching, for says our text "All the children shall be taught of the Lord, and great shall be the peace of thy children."

There is what is called a peace that results from ignorance, but it does not deserve the name; and therefore the prophet declares that "there is no peace for the wicked." No, it is all delusion; it is like the calm of a dead sea, or like that amazing stillness in the air, observed just before an earthquake. The Holy Spirit destroys this false peace, and makes way for, and enables us to embrace the gospel of peace. This peace of God in the soul will always be increased in proportion as the believer has clear and reverential views of divine things. When things are right, a knowledge of it is always satisfactory. If a man fears that his house is not built upon the rock, the examination of it may fill him with confidence. If he supposes his title to an estate is not valid when it is, then the search will fill him with satisfaction: so will it be with the believer in Jesus. The Apostle says, I "know whom I have believed, and that He is able to keep that which I have committed to Him against that day."

We notice briefly the *degree* of this blessing, having considered its nature. "Great shall be the peace of thy children." This is often referred to in Scripture. "*Great peace* have they that love Thy law, and nothing shall offend them." "Thou wilt keep him in perfect peace whose mind is stayed on Thee." "In His days shall the righteous flourish, and *abundance* of peace so long as the moon endureth."

In order that you may see the greatness of the peace of God's children, let us briefly view it in five stages.

First, see the relief it brings the conscience under a sense of pollution. When the law cries "Cursed is every one that continueth not in all things written in the law to do them," the man sees the curse ready to fall upon his head, and owns the righteousness of it; and what but the sight of the Cross can loosen the burden? But this can do it. So says the Apostle, "We joy in God through our Lord Jesus Christ, by whom we have received the atonement;" and "Being justified by faith, we have peace with God through our Lord Jesus Christ."

Secondly, view this peace under the afflictions of the righteous. I pity the man who has it not under his trials; he is apt to "charge God foolishly;" but, says the believer, "I know, O Lord, that Thy judgments are right, and that Thou in faithfulness hast afflicted me." "Athough the fig-tree shall not blossom, neither shall fruit be in the vines, the labour of the olive shall fail, and the fields shall yield no meat: the flock shall be cut off from the fold, and there shall be no herd in the stalls: yet I will rejoice in the Lord, I will joy in the God of my salvation."

Thirdly, view it in the hour of death. David did, and said, "Mark the perfect man, and behold the upright, for the end of that man is peace." We have seen enough, my brethren, to verify the language of our sweet singer:—

> "Jesus can make a dying bed
> Feel soft as downy pillows are,
> While on His breast I lay my head,
> And breathe my life out sweetly there."

Fourthly, view it in the last day, "Wherein the heavens being on fire shall be dissolved, and the elements shall melt with fervent heat; nevertheless we, according to His promise, look for new heavens and a new earth wherein dwelleth righteousnesss;" and then the child of God may lift up his head with joy, knowing that his redemption draweth nigh.

Lastly, you may see it in heaven. There he enters into peace, pure and lasting peace. Oh, who can describe it? Then the days of his mourning shall not be suspended only, but *ended*, and then the last tear, whatever occasioned it, shall be wiped away; well, then, may we exclaim with the prophet, in the words he employs after our text, "This is the heritage of the servants of the Lord, and their righteousness is of me, saith the Lord."

VIII.

AN IMPERATIVE COMMAND.

(Preached on Sunday Evening, January 18th, 1846.)

Turn.—EZEKIEL XXXIII. 2.

WHEN we take an address of this kind we must always expect to encounter an objection. It arises from professed orthodoxy; it seems specious, but is easily answered. If, say some, you believe the scriptural account concerning the depravity of human nature; if you believe that men are left without strength, that they are blind and dead, with what propriety can you call upon them to awake, to see and live? Because, my brethren, these things are spoken of morally, and not physically; because if the persons are blind, it is moral blindness; which consists with a rational mind which is capable of illumination, or otherwise we should no more address them than the beasts of the field. If they are dead, they are "dead in trespasses and sins," a death which consists with a rational life, which is capable of spiritual life, and without this we should no more think of addressing them than addressing the stones in the street. We call upon them to "be strong in the grace which is in Christ Jesus," for if they have no strength of their own, there is One near to them who says, "Take hold of My strength;" "Ask, and ye shall receive: seek, and ye shall find." In the beginning God called things which were not, and they appeared. Angels might have said, "Of what use is it to address nothing? nothing cannot hear." But nothing *did* hear. There was no light, but He said, "Let there be light, and there was light." Means are so far from excluding agency, that they always imply and require it, and means are not left to their own natural aptitude and tendency, but accompanied with His own presence and blessing. "So," says He, "shall my word be that goeth forth out of My mouth; it shall not return unto Me void."

One day our Lord was dining with a Pharisee, and there was a man that had a withered hand; Jesus said to him, "Stretch forth thy hand." How could he do this? but it was His command, and this rendered it possible, and the command conveyed the efficiency.

We could also appeal to authority. Here we find our prophet one day saw a valley of dry bones, and they were *exceedingly* dry. And the Lord said unto him, "Son of man, can these dry bones live?" And he answered very properly, "O Lord God, Thou knowest. Again He said unto me, Prophecy unto these bones, and say unto them, O ye dry bones, hear the word of the Lord." And what was his reply now? "Why, it is useless and absurd"? No. "So I prophesied as I was commanded: and as I prophesied, there was a noise, and behold a shaking, and the bones came together, bone to his bone. Then said he unto me, Prophecy unto the wind; prophecy, son of man, and say to the wind, Thus saith the Lord God: Come from the four winds, O breath, and breathe upon these slain, that they may live." Well, did he object now? No. "So I prophesied as He commanded me, and the breath came into them, and they lived, and stood up upon their feet, an exceeding great army."

When John saw the Sadducees coming to him, he said unto them, "O generation of vipers, who hath warned you to flee from the wrath to come? Bring forth, therefore, fruits meet for repentance." Peter said to Simon Magus, "Repent, therefore, of this thy wickedness, and pray God, if perhaps the thought of thine heart may be forgiven thee. Thou hast neither part nor lot in the matter: for thy heart is not right in the sight of God." Paul, although inspired, makes no scruple to say, "Awake, thou that sleepest, and arise from the dead, and Christ shall give thee light." Therefore, whatever difficulties attend this subject—and what subject is free from difficulties?—we have authority, reason, and Scripture on our side. We follow the example of the apostles, the example of Jesus, yea, of God Himself. 'Tis He who says this evening "*Turn.*"

And now we wish you to ask, and we will endeavour to answer, five questions. First, What are we to "turn" from? Secondly, What are we to "turn" to? Thirdly, How are we to "turn"? Fourthly, When are we to "turn"? And, Fifthly, Why are we to "turn"?

I. What are we to "turn" from?

We answer immediately, *sin.* It is the dishonour and destruction of our nature; the source of all the miseries of earth and hell. The Apostle could not find a name worse than its own to describe it by, and therefore says, "sin is exceeding sinful." Now we shall not attempt to enumerate particulars, otherwise we might say, Here is the sabbath-breaker, the swearer, who takes God's name in vain, and never opens his lips but to vent the abominations of his wicked heart. Here is the drunkard, yielding himself up to an insatiable appetite, which, like the horseleech, is continually saying "give, give." Here is the senualist, living in "chambering and wantonness, fulfilling the desires of the flesh and of the mind." Here is the liar, and the lover of a lie, who is to have his "portion in the lake which burneth with fire and brimstone." But where shall we go, if we follow this direction, and when shall we end?

You will observe, therefore, two things. First, you are to turn from all sins; not only from open sins, but from private ones; not only from gross sins, but from refined ones; not only from sins to which you have but little inclination, in your constitution or outward calling, but from your bosom sins, from your right eye sins, and your right-hand sins. Your right eyes must be plucked out, and your right hands be cut off. All sins are equally forbidden of God. He who said, "Do not commit adultery," said also, "Do not steal." He who said, "Thou shalt do no murder" said also, "Thou shalt not bear false witness against thy neighbour."

There are but few individuals who are *universally* wicked. Some sins are incompatible with others, not in their principles, but in their practice. Avarice is war with luxury. "Herod heard John gladly and did many things," but the charms of Herodias drew him back, and spoiled all those fair beginnings. It will be of little relief in hell to reflect that you resisted some sins, while you were overcome by others. The devil is free from some sins; the devil was never drunk in all his life. The same may be said with regard to other sins. And is this all you value yourself upon, to be only equal with him? All natural antipathies operate universally. The sheep feels an universal hatred to all wolves, not to one only, but to all, and flees from all. So it is with the real Christian. We must not only forsake some sins, but all sins. We must forsake sin, as sin.

The other thing we mention is, we must not only turn from all sin, but from the *love* of sin. Lot's wife left Sodom, but loved it still; therefore she looked back, and was turned into a pillar of salt. The Israelites did not march back into Egypt, but they turned back in their hearts. Some persons abstain from sins, but they wish they were allowed to live in them and enjoy them. But now take a real Christian: if you were to give him liberty to sin, it would be like placing before a man a piece of human flesh, and saying, "Sir, you may eat it if you like it." Could he like it? Why, every feeling would revolt from it. The people of the world think that the principles of Christ only lead to antinomianism; that the religion of the Cross is not friendly to good works. But sin is not only the Christian's avoidance, it is his aversion; he not only forsakes it, but is dead to it; and "how can they that are dead to sin live any longer therein?"

II. To what are we to turn? For negative religion is not sufficient of itself. You find the tree which yielded no fruit, though it bore no bad fruit, was cut down and cast into the fire. The man who hid his talent in the ground did not abuse it, but he is called "the unprofitable servant," and had his "portion with hypocrites and unbelievers, where there is weeping, and wailing, and gnashing of teeth." As you are to "deny all ungodliness and worldly lusts," so you are to "live soberly, godly, and righteously in this present evil world." As you are to avoid that which is evil, so you are to "cleave to that which is good;" and the language of God is, "Let the wicked forsake his ways, and the unrighteous man his thoughts, and let him return unto the Lord, and He will have mercy upon him; and to our God, for he will abundantly pardon."

The Law of God is positive as well as negative, and as there were two things which we observed *from* which you were to turn, so there are two things *to* which you are to turn; for as you are not to forsake some sins but all, so you are to turn to "all righteousness and true holiness." There *may* be imperfections, but there *must* be impartiality. You must be brought to say with David "I esteem all Thy commandments concerning all things to be right, and I hate every false way." Yes, we are therefore to repair, not only to the temple to pray, but also to enter our closets, for God has commanded it. We are not only to profess His truth, but, says the Apostle, "To do good and to communicate forget not: for with such sacrifices God is well pleased." As you are not to prescribe to God, so you are not to come and select and choose, but to throw down your will at His feet, saying, "Lord, what wilt Thou have me to do"? And as you are not only to turn from every sin, but forsake it, so you must not only turn to every duty, but *love* it. God commands, saying, "My Son, give me thine heart." If the heart be given Him, nothing will be withholden. If the heart be withholden, nothing will be accceptable to Him. "Blessed are the pure in heart, for they shall see God." "To them "His commands are grievous," because the love of God is shed abroad in the heart. Their actions correspond with inward principles and dispositions; these render them pleasant and delightful. Yes, the religion of Jesus will always be a yoke, but His people find it an easy one, like the yoke of marriage to that happy pair who daily bless God for the bondage. It is a burden, but always light, because of His grace and love; the burden of a pair of wings to a bird, which gives buoyancy, ascension, and the expanse of the skies.

III. You ask, HOW YOU ARE TO TURN. And here much depends upon the answer. For this purpose we refer you "to the law and to the testimony," for if we speak not according to this rule, it is because there is no light in us. Now, what is the subject of the Apostle's ministry? This will enable us to answer the inquiry. He tells us he preached "repentance towards God, and faith towards our Lord Jesus Christ." Verily here we have a full answer.

There must be repentance towards God, against whom all our sins have been committed, and who is the offended, injured law-giver, who could easily destroy us. "They shall come with weeping," for repentance is not confined to a single period, but pervades the Christian's life. "They shall look upon Him whom they have pierced, and mourn." There must be conviction before there is conversion. There must be a broken heart and a contrite spirit, and, blessed be His name, "A broken and a contrite heart, O Lord, Thou wilt not despise." There must be self-condemnation, self-abhorrence, self-renunciation; there must be a feeling of our spiritual diseases, or we shall never be induced to apply to the "Balm of Gilead," for "they that are whole need not a physician, but they that are sick."

But besides this, and in order to it, there must be faith, too, in our Lord Jesus Christ, the only hope of a sinner, the only mediator between God and man. Hence, in answer to the question of the jailer of Phillipi, "What must I do to be saved?" Paul and Silas answered, "Believe on the Lord Jesus Christ, and thou shalt be saved;" and the preacher who does not return the same answer to the same question is but a betrayer and a murderer of souls. We must therefore come in His name, plead His merits, make mention of His sacrifice only for acceptance in the sight of God; we are therefore not to build up a shelter of our own which cannot abide the storm, but to "flee for refuge to lay hold on the hope set before us." There is salvation in no other. Christ is the only way to the Father; "no man cometh unto the Father but by Him." What are men dreaming of? That holiness and good works are meritorious? But Christ is our only righteousness and strength. On Him we are to depend for sanctification as well as justification. Here men often begin at the wrong end. They begin at the sinner's conduct, instead of the sinner's condition. Of what purpose would it be to go to the dying bed of a sinner lecturing there how he may eat, drink, and take exercise? That he must work or he never will recover? He knows he never can do those unless he does recover. Here is the man sick and dying; send for a physician; apply the remedy; after which your admonition may be seasonable and proper.

IV. When are you to "turn"? Here the scripture says, *To-day*, if ye will hear His voice: "*now* is the accepted time; behold, *now* is the day of salvation." Life is the only opportunity. This is the seed time. Therefore, say the sacred Scriptures, "Seek ye the Lord while He may be found; call upon Him while He is near." Therefore, says the Saviour, "Strive to enter in at the strait gate, for many, I say unto you, shall seek to enter in and shall not be able." Why? because they will seek too late. "When once the master of the house has risen up, and hath shut the door, and ye begin to stand without, and to knock at the door, saying, Lord, Lord, open unto us; and He shall answer and say unto you, I know you not whence you are: then shall ye begin to say"—What? "Not know us? Why we were born in Thy house, we have eaten and drank in Thy presence, and Thou hast taught in our streets;" "but He shall profess unto them, I never knew you; Depart from me, ye workers of iniquity."

This, therefore, is your season, and your only season, and Oh! how short it is! "For what is your life? It is even a vapour which appeareth for a little time and then vanisheth away. A few more social entertainments, a few more walks, and "the place that now knows you will know you no more for ever." "Oh, that you were wise, that you understood this, that you considered your latter end!" Consider how near it may be. Life is uncertain, as well as short. Death never comes without a warrant, but it often comes without a warning. How many do you know in the circle of your acquaintance who have suddenly expired! While, therefore, you live, death does not linger, and when you feel your infirmities and the feebleness of your frame, the diseases and accidents to which you are exposed, it seems wonderful that you should live a day, or a week, or an hour.

Then there is what Young calls "a slow sudden death," the death of opportunities, and of your powers; you delay and delay till you are in a fever, till you are paralysed, till you are delirious, till you can only bring up the name of God in a consumption; then you send for your preacher to prepare skin and bones for eternity.

The Apostle speaks of the heart being hardened through "the deceitfulness of sin." When Felix heard Paul preach concerning the faith in Christ he trembled, but instead of cherishing this feeling, he said, "Go thy way for this time; when I have a more convenient season, I will send for thee." He saw Paul repeatedly after this, but said nothing concerning the faith in Christ. Oh no, the funeral of his convictions had taken place; he never felt again as he felt then. Conviction, if it be not assassinated, may be starved; and some of you starve your convictions, while others of you murder them.

A great deal has been said about the lapse of a day of grace. In a general way we may say, while there is life there is hope, and with our sweet singer:

> "And while the lamp holds out to burn,
> The vilest sinner may return."

And not only are there losses of opportunities, but there is the last offer of mercy somewhere; whether this is the last opportunity some of you will ever have, it is impossible for us to determine. But if you are sincere in seeking to know what you must do to be saved, He is able and willing to save you, whereas if you neglect the great salvation, He will say, "Because I called, and ye refused; I stretched out my hand, and no man regarded; therefore will I laugh at your calamity, and mock when your fear cometh." "He that being often reproved, hardeneth his neck, shall suddenly be destroyed and that without remedy."

We have but one more question to ask, WHY ARE WE TO "TURN"? Now, surely the command of God is a sufficient answer. Surely from His authority there is no appeal, and it should immediately determine us. He might have treated us with neglect, but He has been long-suffering towards you, "not willing that any should perish, but that all should come to repentance." And again this evening He says, by my mouth, "Turn." If you turn not you must die. "Turn, or Burn," was one of the quaint sayings in one of Baxter's most alarming works; yes, it is true you must "turn" or die. So says our text, "I have no pleasure in the death of the wicked: but that the wicked turn from his way and live: turn ye, turn ye, from your evil ways; for why will ye die, O house of Israel." And what is the death that will be the consequence of your not turning? Not annihilation, not the destruction of the powers of mind; such a death as this the wicked would hail as a privilege. No, but it is the death of your happiness, the death of your well-being, the death of your hopes. What dreadful images are held forth in the Scriptures of truth! Qualify them as you please, what a tremendous meaning do they convey! Oh, this is dreadful, and "none knoweth the power of His anger." If you turn, you shall *live*. This, again, is the language of God in another part of this prophecy, where he says, "For I have no pleasure in the death of him that dieth, saith the Lord God: wherefore turn yourselves, and live ye." Oh, how you value life! "Skin for skin, yea, all that a man hath will he give for his life." Yet this life is full of sorrow, for "Man is born to trouble as the sparks fly upward." Our days are "few and evil," and we spend them as a shadow. But there is the life of God in the soul, eternal, everlasting blessedness.

If you "turn," you will find *pardon*. What a privilege is this! your sins are numberless and aggravated; but oh, to hear Him say, "your sins and your iniquities I will remember no more!" "Blessed is the man whose transgression is forgiven, whose sin is covered." How blessed is he in his mercies, in his duties, and in his trials too!

If you "turn," you will find *liberty*. What a blessing is this! "He that commiteth sin is the servant of sin." What a black, wretched master he serves! what a bondage is the bondage of corruption! But if the "Son make you free, you shall be free indeed." O, what a glorious liberty is that of the sons of God!

If you "turn," you will find *peace.* "Being justified by faith, we have peace with God, through our Lord Jesus Christ." "Great peace have they that love Thy law, and nothing shall offend them."

In a word, if you "turn," *happiness* will be the result, and this is your being's end and aim. Who is happy? One day a man was singing "I am happy as a king." I wonder who believed him. Is a *king* likely to be happy? Was Haman happy, "whom the king delighted to honour?" No, he groaned. "All this availeth me nothing, so long as I see Mordecai sitting at the king's gate." But "blessed are the people who know the joyful sound; they shall walk, O Lord, in the light of Thy countenance." And if they are so blessed now, what will be their enjoyment above? for "eye hath not seen, nor ear heard, neither hath entered into the heart of man, the things which God hath prepared for them that love Him."

To conclude, I have had as short a text this evening as I could; you will, therefore, easily be able to remember it, and I hope you will remember it for good. But you must be reminded that something more is required than your remembrance of it. Yes, there are many whose judgments are well informed in Divine things, but who are forgetful of our Saviour's remark, "If ye *know* these things, happy are ye if ye *do* them;" who see and approve better things, but follow worse; who are clear in their heads, but whose hearts are not changed by Divine grace; who have God upon their lips, and the devil in their lives. We come to you in the name of the Lord of Hosts, but you often send us back to tell Him, that while we offer heaven, you are for hell. We study plainness, but you understand us not. Our message is a most serious one, but you hear it not. We exhibit before you the greatest things to attract your attention, the sweetest to allure you, and the most awful to alarm you. If the truth could convince you, you would soon be convinced. If Scripture, reason, and experience, your own, and that of others, could decide you, we should soon hear you exclaim, "Behold, I am vile." We should soon see you at the Saviour's feet, saying "Lord, save, or I perish." But since all these persuasions and addresses avail you nothing, we must leave you to death and to judgment, and to that dreadful fiat, "He that is righteous, let him be righteous still; and he which is filthy, let him be filthy still."

Your sins are now all recorded, and by-and-by you will hear them all read before angels and men. God keeps the book now, but He will then deliver it into your hands, and conscience will keep for ever.

"But as yet there is a hope ;
You may His mercy know ;
Though His hand is lifted up,
He still withholds the blow."

"'Twas for sinners Jesus died ;
Sinners, He invites to come.
None who seek shall be denied ;
He says 'there yet is room.'"

IX.

GOD'S RETRIBUTIVE JUSTICE.

What wilt thou say when He shall punish thee.—JEREMIAH xiii. 21.

It is questionable whether there be such a creature in the world as a speculative Atheist, one who denies the existence of a God. We naturally think it impossible for a person possessed of reason and common sense really to believe this: that there are creatures without a Creator—effects without a cause; the eye and ear *accidentally* so exactly adapted to their use and design. If there be such a monster to be found, I am persuaded he will be found in a Christian and not in a heathen land. How far God may give up to strong delusions, that they may believe a lie, those who have contemned the Revelation He has so graciously given us, it is impossible to tell. But we read of those whose minds He has blinded, and whose hearts He has hardened, and who daringly provoke Him to His face. There may be a professed Atheist; we now and then hear of one of these heroes in our own nation, who disbelieve the truths of Revelation, and glory in their shame. "The fool hath said in his heart, *there is* no God." The sentiment is better expressed without the words in Italics, "The fool hath said in his heart, No God! away with Him!" There is no one being stands so much in his way as God; who so much opposes his designs, and who gives him so much uneasiness; therefore there is no being he wishes so much to get rid of.

There may, perhaps, be persons in this large assembly who would go thousands of miles if they could meet with a demonstration to prove that there is no God to see them, or to judge them, so that they might walk after their own lusts. But whatever opinion we may entertain, there can be no doubt of His existence. There are evidences enough to prove that many live without God, regardless of His glory and His grace; who lie down and rise up, who go out and return, who begin and end all their enterprises without God being in their thoughts. Then there are some who admit the being of a God, but deny His providence. Some again admit His natural providence, that is, the providence by which He takes care of all things He has made; but they deny His *moral* providence, that is, the providence that regards man as man, and as a reasonable creature; the providence that connects happiness with obedience, and sin with misery. For though there may be no person present who would openly confess this, there may be such who secretly believe it—then it opens a fine door for licentiousness for them, and tends to tranquilize their guilty consciences. Therefore, says David, "The wicked through the pride of his countenance will not seek after God: God is not in all his thoughts . . . He hath said in his heart, I shall not be moved; for I shall never be in adversity." "He hath said in his heart, God hath forgotten; He hideth His face; He will never see it." But "wherefore doth the wicked condemn God?" "What wilt thou say when He shall punish thee?"

I. Let us endeavour to establish the doctrine that *retributive justice belongs to God.*

Hence anger, wrath, fury, and vengeance are applied to Him in the sacred Scriptures. All this language, you understand, is metaphorical, but then it is founded on reality. These terms are designed to express nothing like passion, but only principle. And what is principle? We discharge the old word vindictive, and substitute vindication. We see God determined to maintain rectitude and order in the universe. The case is, that there is no happiness without order; there is no order without government, without laws, and laws are nothing without sanctions and penalties; and we should always be concerned for the execution of these in the country where we live. "God is of purer eyes than to behold iniquity." His holiness is necessarily opposed to sin, and His righteousness necessarily requires the punishment of it. Without this it would be impossible for us to esteem or love Him. How could you esteem or love Him, if you thought He would act and feel towards a Howard as He would towards a Voltaire? Suppose you brought before a magistrate the destroyer of your substance, or the murderer of your child, and he should turn to him, and say "Go in peace, it does not concern me?" "Not concern *you*," you might say; "Why, are not you the minister of God? are you not to be a terror to evil-doers, and a praise to them that do well?" And "shall not the Judge of all the earth do right?" "Is there unrighteousness with God? How, then, shall He judge the world?"

Now you will observe that men do not naturally dislike their fellow-creatures who may act against others, but they dislike their conduct when it opposes themselves. This is another proof, if necessary, how much infidelity is founded on selfishness. But now hear what Moses said, [Take heed] "lest there should be among you man, or woman, or family, or tribe, whose heart turneth away this day from the Lord our God, to go and serve the gods of other nations; lest there should be among you a root that beareth gall and wormwood; and it come to pass, when he heareth the words of this curse, that he bless himself in his heart, saying, I shall have peace, though I walk in the imagination of mine heart, to add drunkenness to thirst: the Lord will not spare him, but then the anger of the Lord and His jealousy shall smoke against that man, and all the curses that are written in this book shall lie upon him, and the Lord shall blot out his name from under heaven."

II. This will lead us to *assail your hope of impunity from it.*

The first foundation of the sinner's hope is derivable from God's delay. It is a sad thing that we should do evil because God is good. Yet it is so. "Because sentence against an evil work is not executed speedily, therefore the heart of the sons of men is fully set in them to do evil." Yes, delay tends to weaken their convictions and reduce their fear; but it should not be so. What is the truth here? It is not from a want of ability that God spares sinners; but He has various purposes to accomplish by forbearing to execute His vengeance for a while. He may employ their instrumentality in a way of wrath or mercy, though they mean not so. Hear what Peter says: "The Lord is not slack concerning His promise, as some men count slackness; but is long-suffering to us-ward, not willing that any should perish, but that all should come to repentance." Therefore it is that He still continues you in being, that you may have space for repentance. Hear what the Saviour says, "Except ye repent, ye shall all likewise perish." And what saith the Scripture, "There is no work nor device, nor knowledge, nor wisdom, in the grave, whither thou goest." Therefore, "Behold, now is the accepted time; behold, now is the day of salvation."

The second cause of this hope is prosperity. This is often the case. You will find the hope of the wicked perplexed our prophet, and therefore he says, "Wherefore, O Lord, doth the way of the wicked prosper? wherefore are all they happy that deal very treacherously? Thou hast planted them, yea, they have taken root: they grow, yea, they bring forth fruit: Thou art near to their mouth, and far from their reins." You will find also how it confounded Asaph; he therefore tells us, "I was envious of the foolish, when I saw the prosperity of the wicked. For there are no bands in their death: but their strength is firm. They are not in trouble as other men; neither are they plagued like other men. Therefore pride compasseth them about as a chain; violence covereth them as a garment. Their eyes stand out with fatness, they have more than heart can wish. They are corrupt and speak wickedly concerning oppression: they speak loftily. They set their mouth against the heavens, and their tongue walketh through the earth." What wonder if they indulge themselves and are led to conclude, because they enjoy health, connections, business, and grounds that bring forth plentifully, that the riches of eternity belong also to them. But know you not that "the ox is fat for the day of slaughter"?

The third source of this hope is founded on the mercy of God. Now God forbid that we should limit the Holy One of Israel, or diminish His mercy. He is rich in mercy to all that call upon Him. He is abundant in mercy, and His tender-mercies are over all His works. But truth as well as poetry tells us that, "A God all mercy is a God unjust." God's attributes must all harmonize. He has revealed himself "a just God" as well as a Saviour; as the Just, as well as the Justifier of those who believe in Jesus.

III. We proceed to *press for an answer to the question*, "What wilt thou say, when He shall punish thee? I suppose I must furnish the answer. After reflecting upon the subject I can only think of three replies which you may make.

First wilt thou say, "I do not deserve this condemnation"? When a criminal enters a court he is pressed for an answer to guilty or not guilty, but this remains for the decision of the law.

In proportion as a man becomes holy, he always entertains a greater notion of the evil of sin. Angels also entertain greater notions of sin than saints, because they are holy beings. And God entertains much higher notions than angels do of holiness. We have heard of one who suffered much from a cancer in his eye; looking up, he addressed the God who made him, saying

"Why do I thus suffer? Have I ever done Thee any harm"? Few ever go to such a length as this; yet many seem to think that God is not an observer of all their ways, that He is not acquainted with their secret faults. But it is not so with the real penitent; he says, "Why should a living man complain, a man for the punishment of his sins? I will bear the indignation of the Lord, because I have sinned against Him." An awakened and convinced sinner never thinks of excusing himself; he always acknowledges himself to be worthy of condemnation. And this will be the case with all sinners hereafter, whatever self-vindication they may have now. Then every mouth will be stopped, and all become guilty before God. Then, as Hannah says, "The wicked shall be silent in darkness." You see this was the case with the man who had not on the wedding garment, when the king came in to see the guests, and said, "Friend, how came thou in hither not having on a wedding garment"? What did he say? Did he say, "I was too poor to purchase one"? or, "I had not skill enough to make one"? If he *could* have justified himself, he would have done so. But, we are told, he was speechless. "Then said the king to the servants, Bind him hand and foot, and take him away, and cast him into outer darkness; there shall be weeping and gnashing of teeth."

Wilt thou say, "I was not warned"? No, you will not be able to say that. You know that "the wrath of God has been revealed from heaven against all unrighteousness and ungodliness of men."

Not warned! Did not the Scriptures warn you? Did not you there read, "God will bring every work into judgment, with every secret thing, whether it be good, or whether it be evil."

Not warned! Did you never hear the preacher's voice, and does it not ring in your ears still, when he cried, "*Flee from the wrath to come.*"

Not warned! Did your parents never warn you with tears and prayers? Did your father never warn you when he said, "My son, if thou wilt be wise, my heart shall rejoice, even mine?" Did your mother never warn you when she said, "What my son? and what the son of my womb? and what the son of my vows?"

Not warned! Were you not warned by the flood upon the ungodly world? *Not warned!* were you not warned by all that befell the Jewish people for their sins after all the privileges by which God had distinguished them? *Not warned!* Did not death warn you? The death of your neighbour—the death of your brother? That sudden death that took away your acquaintance in a moment? *Not warned!* Did not sickness warn you? were you not seized with it and laid upon a bed of languishing, when eternity was drawn up to your view, and you said "I shall no more see the light?" What were your prayers and your resolves then? But the Lord re-coloured your cheeks, and renewed your strength, and said, "Return, ye children of men."

The present is not properly a state of decision, yet there is an obvious tendency in sin to produce misery. You have seen the liar after awhile losing all confidence. You have seen the drunkard clothed in rags. How the licentious have been filled with the sins of their youth, and have laid down with them in the dust! We are now in a mixed state, and there are many checks thrown in. But by-and-by there will be an awful decision, and the things which now let shall be taken out of the way. Sin then shall have full liberty to bring forth fruit unto death.

Once more, "What wilt thou say when He shall punish thee"? Wilt thou say that there was no way of escape? This was indeed the case as far as it depended on yourself. But there was hope in Israel concerning this thing, even concerning your salvation. There was balm in Gilead, there was a Physician there. You were left without strength, but there was One mighty to save; "Able to save to the uttermost all who come unto God by Him;" and was equally willing. There was salvation in no other, for there was, "none other name under heaven given among men, whereby we must be saved," but the name of Jesus; but in Him is plenteous redemption. In Him it pleased the Father that all fulness should dwell. No man could come to the Father but by Him. He is "the way, the truth, and the life." Was the way then closed against you? Rather were you not allowed, invited, and *commanded* a thousand times to enter it? Forsake the foolish, and live, that you may be blessed with all spiritual blessings in Christ Jesus. Where does the Scripture forbid you to come to be saved? Is it here? "Ho, every one that thirsteth, come ye to the waters, and he that hath no money; come ye, buy, and eat; yea, come, buy wine and milk without money and without price." "Whosoever will, let him take of the water of life freely."

Yes, we have known those who were depraved and wretched, renewed in the spirit of their minds; whose souls were once like the troubled sea, who are now in the blessed enjoyment of the Divine presence. They are now sustained under their trials, while others sink in the day of their adversity. They have found Him of whom Moses in the law and the prophets did write, who is the Hope of the hopeless, and the Friend of the friendless; and they are now saying, "Come thou with us, and we will do thee good; for the Lord hath spoken good concerning Israel."

My dear hearers take away the text with you—never forget to ask yourselves the question, "What shall I say when He shall punish me"? Never say that you do not deserve punishment, that you were never warned, that there was no way of escape. There is a way made known, but you turn away from it, and reject the counsel of God against yourself, and constrain the Saviour to say, "Ye will not come unto me that ye might have life."

Oh, what will be the destruction under the gospel, while you have turned away from Him that speaketh from heaven! For hast thou not procured this unto thyself? Such a thought, dear hearers, will be intolerable—that you have brought destruction upon yourselves; that you are suicides—spiritual suicides; that you have destroyed your own soul.

Well, if you will not answer the question, there are two others which we address to you, and conclude. The first is, can you *escape* this punishment? "How shall we escape if we neglect so great salvation"?

The second is, can you abide it? "Though they dig into hell," says God, "thence shall my hand find them; though they climb up into heaven, thence will I bring them down. Can thine heart endure, or can thy hands be strong in the days that I shall deal with thee." "Who among us can dwell with the devouring fire? Who among us can dwell with everlasting burning?" "It is a fearful thing to fall into the hands of the living God."

> "But as yet there still is room;
> You may His mercy know;
> Though His hand be lifted up,
> He still forbears the blow."

X

PLUCKED FROM THE BURNING.

(Preached on Sunday Evening, April 21st, 1844.)

Is not this a brand plucked out of the fire?—ZECHARIAH iii. 2.

Two Joshuas are spoken of in the sacred Scriptures. The first was concerned in settling the Israelites in Canaan after their deliverance from Egypt, the other in rebuilding their city after their return from Babylon. This is the one referred to in the words of our text. This is a part of the prophecy of Zechariah, "And He shewed me Joshua the High Priest standing before the Angel of the Lord, and Satan standing at his right hand to resist him." That is, either to hinder him in going on with his work, or condemn him for his sins; for he is the accuser of the brethren, and if ever they rise up and endeavour to carry on the cause of truth, he will be sure also to oppose. But their privilege is to have an advocate and helper, and He will not suffer His servant Joshua to be destroyed: He is near to justify him. "And the Lord said unto Satan, The Lord rebuke thee, O Satan, even the Lord that hath chosen Jerusalem rebuke thee," that is, restrain thy malignant rage; "Is not this a brand plucked out of the fire"? No wonder, therefore, that he shows some signs of the position in which he is found, like a piece of wood rescued from the flame, all black and smoky, but rather to be pitied than blamed for his infirmities and remains of inbred sin. Not delivered to be destroyed, but to be employed, and glorified.

What can we learn then from thence, but this, that a saved sinner shall never become a prey to Satan? He may employ the fraud of the serpent, or the fury of the lion, he may accuse or oppose, but if God be for us who can be against us? "Who shall lay anything to the charge of God's elect? It is God that justifieth."

We make no apology for such an application of this passage; there is scarcely an incident in the whole history of the Jews but is designed and adapted to be typical, and it is well to rise from the less to the greater, and soar away from things seen and temporal, to "things unseen and eternal." If a captive released from Babylon and restored to his own land is called to rejoice, how much more has that man occasion to triumph, who is turned from darkness to light, and from the power of Satan unto God; who hath received forgiveness of sins, and inheritance among them which are sanctified by faith that is in Christ Jesus?

Five remarks, therefore, we have to make:—

I. The first regards THE NATURAL STATE OF MAN AS A SINNER. He is a brand; this will remind us of three things concerning him.

First, *his worthlessness.* "Since thou wast precious in my sight, thou hast been honourable, and I have loved thee." "Of whom," says the Apostle, "the world was not worthy." "The righteous is more excellent than his neighbour"; but a man in his unconverted state is not as silver and gold. He is not a cedar in Lebanon, not a shrub, not a carved piece of timber, but as a brand plucked from the fire, and fit for nothing else.

There are some who will have it that we take pleasure in degrading human nature, but we deny this charge. We admire man as the workmanship of God; we allow that his physical and intellectual powers are capable of producing the noblest achievements and results; but this is not the question. What is he morally and spiritually? Hear the testimony of one who knew what was in man, and whose judgment was always according to truth: "From within, out of the heart of man, proceed evil thoughts, murders, adulteries, fornications, thefts, false witness, blasphemies." His nature is corrupt and his judgment perverted, his will rebellious, and his affections earthly, sensual, devilish. Why should such a representation as this be rejected? It is corroborated by all the Scriptures, all history, observation and experience. Without the admission of this fact it is impossible to prove the beauty, or feel the importance, or enjoy the blessings of the Gospel, "For they that are whole need not a physician, but they that are sick." "The full soul loatheth the honeycomb, but to the hungry soul every bitter thing is sweet."

Secondly, we are reminded of *the perilousness of his condition.*

The Epistle to the Hebrews refers to the operation of the Gospel, and speaks of the rain as the means of drawing forth vegetation according to the contents of the soil; "For the earth which drinketh in the rain that cometh oft upon it, and bringeth forth herbs meet for them by whom it is dressed, receiveth blessing from God. But that which beareth thorns and briars is rejected, and is nigh unto cursing; whose end is to be burned." Yes, this is the doom of the man who dies in an unregenerate state. His end is to be burned. Our text has the very same figure, only with this addition: that he is already in the fire, and is like a brand already kindled and partially consumed!

Thirdly, reminds us of another thing, namely, *the commencement of his destruction.* The hell of a sinner is already begun in this world, for "cursed is every one that continueth not in all things written in the law to do them." If he has no want of worldly possessions, yet in the midst of his sufficiency he is in straits, and over all he groans, and asks, "Who will shew me any good"? His passions and lusts tyrannize over him, and the devil leads him captive at his will, and you see him smoking along to certain destruction. Do you not remember when a boy writing that copy, "They that swim in sin shall sink in sorrow"? Bacon says, "Sin and sorrow are connected by an adamantine chain"; and though the present state is not properly a state of retribution, and many things now check the tendency of moral evil, yet that evil is apparent in a thousand instances, and so the "end of these things is death, and the way of transgressors is hard."

II. Our second remark is, THE DELIVERANCE HE EXPERIENCED IN THE DAY OF HIS CONVERSION. He is a man "plucked out of the fire," he is completely changed.

There are some who talk most of Divine grace, and who would have themselves as the only or chief advocates of it. Those would do well to remember that the best way in which we can magnify and glorify the grace of God is by showing what it can do for us; and in us, and by us, for grace is not a mere notion, but a divine reality; not a mere profession, but a powerful agency. If we appeal to the sacred writers we find, they never consider God as leaving the sinner as He finds him. He finds him in darkness, but He calls him into his marvellous light, He finds him in the bondage of corruption, but calls him "into the glorious liberty of the children of God."

He finds him, "dead in trespasses and sins," but He quickens him, and brings him out to "walk in nearness of life."

Conversion is a turning about, and it does turn man not only from profane to moral, but from carnal to spiritual, from earthly to heavenly things; from walking by sight, to walking by faith; and from being a man of this world, to become a stranger and pilgrim, declaring plainly that he is seeking a country.

He is not indeed at present entirely sanctified, but his sanctification is real and prevailing, and in due time he shall be presented faultless before the presence of His glory with exceeding joy. As his former state was in a measure and degree predictive of hell, so his present state, in a measure and degree is predictive of heaven. Heaven to him is not only future, but commenced already. Of whatever heaven consists, he is now a partaker. If it be the day, he has now the dawn. If hereafter he shall be privileged to see God as He is, he now sees Him, though it be through a glass darkly, and we may say in the fine language of Dr. Watts

> "The men of grace have found
> Glory begun below;
> Celestial fruit on earthly ground
> From faith and hope may grow.
>
> The hill of Zion yields
> A thousand sacred sweets;
> Before we reach the heavenly fields,
> Or tread the golden streets."

III. Our third remark regards THE MEANS BY WHICH THIS CHANGE IS ACCOMPLISHED.

Here you perceive that the salvation of a sinner is entirely of God: "for we are His workmanship;" "He works in us to will and to do of His good pleasure;" His people are formed for His praise; and so far are means from being inconsistent with this agency that they are necessarily employed and required. Paul plants, Apollos waters, but God giveth the increase. "So neither is he that plants anything, neither he that watereth, but God that giveth the increase."

You may remember the wise woman Tekoah who endeavoured to bring over David to countenance Absalom's return. Among other things, she said, "God doth devise means that His banished be not expelled from Him." Oh, what a history would it prove, if the various means God employs to bring souls to Himself were to be published. Some of you remember the gracious means that have been blessed to you. What brought the prodigal to that state of mind which made him return to his father? It was when brought to himself that he said, "In my father's house is bread enough and to spare, and I perish with hunger; I will arise and go to my father and will say unto him, Father, I have sinned against heaven, and before thee, and am no more worthy to be called thy son; make me as one of thy hired servants."

What so struck the three thousand who in one day were added to the church in Jerusalem? It was the preaching of the gospel; and in a general way we find that the dispensation of the word by preaching is the common expedient God employs. Faith cometh by hearing, and hearing by the word of God.

In the case of Zaccheus, curiosity induced him to climb up a tree; because he was short of stature and could not see on account of the crowd; he ran before and got up a tree, and the Saviour said unto him, "Zaccheus, make haste, and come down; for to-day I must abide at thy house." He only thought of seeing Jesus, but he was to enjoy Him and accommodate the Saviour of the world under His roof.

A book has sometimes been blessed of God to the awakening of the soul. How many have been converted by reading Baxter's "Call to the Unconverted," "Doddridge's Rise and Progress of Religion in the Soul, and "Harvey's Theron and Aspasio!" I have met with not a few in the course of my ministry. How many, too, have been brought to a concern about their soul by reading that excellent work, called "Alleine's Alarm"! Dr. Watts, poet as he was, said, "I would rather be the author of that book than produce the greatest work in the world."

The conversation of a friend has proved the happy means of conversion; sometimes a letter has been thus blest.

Servants have been thus blest to their masters when they have "adorned the doctrine of God their Saviour in all things." Wives have been the means of the conversion of their husbands, having been won by the conversation of the wives, "while they behold their chaste conversation coupled with fear."

God sometimes meets with His people "in a dream, in a vision of the night; when deep sleep falleth upon man." Where shall we stop? "Lo! all these things worketh God ofttimes with man, to bring back his soul from the pit, to be enlightened with the light of the living."

IV. Our fourth remark regards THE SURPRISE IT PRODUCES: "Is not this a brand plucked out of the fire"?

Who awakens this inquiry? In some persons the change produced is very strange and remarkable. We are reminded of the poor man born blind; the neighbours came round and said, "This is like him, but he said, I am he." He was the same man yet another. Thus, it is promised: "Instead of the thorn shall come up the fir tree, instead of the briar shall come up the myrtle tree; and it shall be to the Lord for a name, for an everlasting sign that shall not be cut off."

Hence it is said, "Their seed shall be known among the Gentiles, and their offspring among the people: all that see them shall acknowledge them, that they are the seed which the Lord hath blessed."

Here is Manasseh; he is the son of the excellent Hezekiah; he had a good training and a pious education, but "he did that which was evil in the sight of the Lord," and became an idolater. He had the image of Baal erected in the very temple of God, as if to insult Him to His face. He caused the streets of Jerusalem to run down with innocent blood. "Then the Lord brought upon him the captains of the hosts of the king of Assyria, which took Manasseh among the thorns, and bound him with fetters, and carried him to Babylon. And when he was in affliction, he besought the Lord his God, and humbled himself greatly before the God of his fathers. And prayed unto Him, and He was intreated of him, and heard his supplication, and brought him again to Jerusalem into his kingdom. Then Manasseh knew that the Lord He was God." "Is not this a brand plucked out of the fire"?

That tyrant, Saul of Tarsus, the first time we meet with him is at the stoning of Stephen, holding the raiment of those who stoned him. They did not proceed fast enough for this young fiery Saul, so said he, "Strip and stone him, and I will take care of your clothes." And we find him "haling men and women to prison, being exceedingly mad against them, compelling them to blaspheme, and persecuting them even unto strange cities;" and if he could have driven them to hell as easily as he could expel them from earth, he would have done it. So voracious and desperate was he, that even those who knew the grace of God in truth seemed entirely to despair of him, and when they heard that he preached the truth that once he despised, they were all afraid of him, and drew back as sheep at the approach of a wolf. There he is, down upon his knees; and he became a preacher and an Apostle, and laboured more abundantly than they all, and at last died a martyr. "Is not this a brand plucked out of the fire"?

The Apostle, addressing the Corinthians, says, "Know ye not that the unrighteous shall not inherit the kingdom of God? Be not deceived: neither fornicators, nor idolators, nor adulterers, nor effeminate, nor abusers of themselves with mankind, nor thieves, nor covetous, nor drunkards, nor revilers, nor extortioners, shall inherit the kingdom of God." "And such," adds he, "were some of *you*: but ye are washed, but ye are sanctified, but ye are justified, in the name of the Lord Jesus, and by the Spirit of God." Were not these "brands plucked out of the fire"?

And what was John Bunyan, whose soul was as black as his business, and whose name was proverbially used to menace their children? We find he became not only a Christian but a Minister, and, by the incomparable union of genius and truth, writing works which will render him known and useful to the end of time. "Is not this a brand plucked out of the fire"?

Some of you are acquainted with the history of the late Mr. Newton. He tells us that he so long, and so dreadfully, resisted his convictions, till at length his conscience upbraided him, and he became alarmed, lest he should be found with the devil and his angels. Only think what service he rendered and what he achieved. Was not this "a brand plucked out of the fire"?

The Apostle, in writing to the Ephesians, says, "Among whom also we all had our conversation in times past in the lusts of our flesh, fulfilling the desires of the flesh and of the mind: and were by nature the children of wrath even as others." Yes, says he, "We ourselves also were sometimes foolish, disobedient, deceived, serving divers lusts and pleasures, living in malice and envy, hateful and hating one another." It was after this that the loving-kindness of God our Saviour appeared and plucked them as brands from the burning.

And are there not thousands now living who are witnesses for God—witnesses to prove the freeness, the power, and the riches of His grace; are there none here this evening who were once swearers, drunkards, revilers, and despisers of all that is good, but whose hearts God hath touched? In others, though the change may not be equally striking, it is equally true. The Apostle to the Gentiles once thought he was innocent, at least comparatively so, for he trusted in himself that he was righteous, and despised others; but he was brought to say, "What things were gain to me, those I counted loss for

Christ," and to make mention of His righteousness only in whom alone he gloried. He formerly never bent his knee in prayer, or if he did, it was his task, but now it was his very element. He formerly disregarded the Sabbath, but now he calls it his delight, holy of the Lord, honourable. And here is one who cannot answer any minute and circumstantial questions as to the time, the manner, the place in which the means whereby the work has been accomplished, yet he has the reality, and can say, "One thing I know, that whereas I was blind, now I see." He can venture to go as far as this, though afraid to pronounce his conversion real, yet he will never come into condemnation, being passed from death unto life.

V. Our last remark is, WHAT OUGHT TO BE THE SENTIMENTS OF THOSE WHO HAVE EXPERIENCED THIS DELIVERANCE?

First, they ought to feel an emotion of *solemnity*, like a man saved from shipwreck, or taken out of a house that is on fire, whose remembrance thereof would not only be pleasingly but awfully affected. The Apostle speaks of those who are "preserved in Christ Jesus, and called." There is a preservation after calling, for we are, "kept by the power of God through faith unto salvation." There are few Christians but can mention some particular days in which they have been exposed, but they have been preserved from day to day and year to year.

Then, brethren, we should feel an emotion of *humility*. We should remember that once "we were without hope and without God in the world." It might be well "to look to the rock whence we were hewn, and to the hole of the pit whence we were digged." "Pride was not made for man." In some creatures it may appear well; I like to see a proud swan, or a proud horse. I love to stand by the sea-shore and remember the words, "Hitherto shalt thou come, but no further, and here shall thy *proud* waves be stayed." But, "pride was not made for man;" poor man, mortal man, "whose foundation is in the dust, and who is crushed before the moth," "who is of yesterday and knoweth nothing;" for sinful man defiled in every part; *righteous* man, if you please, but whose righteousness is not self-derived, or self-sustained, for by the grace of God he is what he is.

Such a person ought to feel an emotion of *gratitude*, saying with David, "Thou hast delivered my eyes from tears, and my feet from falling; I will shew forth all Thy praise."

Zacharias blesses God that being delivered out of the hands of his enemies he might serve Him without fear.

We ought to feel an emotion of *confidence*, reasoning from what God has done for us to what He will do; saying with Watts,—

> "Grace will complete what grace begins,
> To save from sorrow and from sins:
> The work that wisdom undertakes,
> Eternal mercy ne'er forsakes."

We ought to possess an emotion of *zeal*; if we are the subjects of grace it should be our concern to be the medium of it to others. Having been benefited ourselves, we should be anxious to prove a blessing to others. You are to go forth in the strength of the Lord God, and as you have opportunity, "others save with fear, pulling them out of the fire." Extend your concern to all who come within your reach, remembering however vicious or wretched your poor fellow creatures may be, the Saviour will in no wise cast them out if they come to Him.

XI.

THE SHEPHERD SMITTEN.

(Preached on Sunday Evening, February 25th, 1844.)

Awake, O sword, against my shepherd, and against the man that is my fellow, saith the Lord of hosts: smite the shepherd, and the sheep shall be scattered; and I will turn mine hand upon the little ones.—ZECHARIAH xiii. 7.

WHY does the Scripture speak so much of Christ as the Saviour of ruined sinners? Because He is not only the Author but the substance thereof. This is true of the Old Testament as well as the New. Take for instance the typical parts: the Refuge from the Avenger of blood; the manna,—the smitten rock,—the table of shew-bread,—every slaughtered bullock, and every bleeding lamb;—these were a shadow of good things to come, whilst the body is Christ. Or take the historical parts. We find Him also in these, we see Him sacrificed in Isaac; we see Him in the law given by Moses; as conqueror in Joshua; as the Prince of Peace in Solomon; in Jonah we see Him buried and rising again the third day. Or take the prophetical parts, sever Him from them, and the whole system would be as the casket without the jewel and the body without the soul: for "the testimony of Jesus," says the angel, "is the spirit of prophecy." "To Him gave all the prophets witness," some indeed more obscurely, others more clearly. All this you say is very general, but it shows us the propriety of our Saviour's admonition, "Search the Scriptures," meaning those of the Old Testament, "for they are they that testify of me." All this you see bears towards our subject, and yields at least an introduction to it.

Our text only knows "Jesus Christ and Him crucified." In the close of the preceding chapter we read, "I will pour npon the house of David, and upon the inhabitants of Jerusalem, the spirit of grace and supplications and they shall look upon Me whom they have pierced, and they shall mourn." Read the first verse of this chapter, "In that day there shall be a fountain opened to the house of David, and to the inhabitants of Jerusalem, for sin and for uncleanness." Then follow dark and mysterious sayings, which apparently do not belong to Christ; but in the passage which is to engage our attention this evening, the Sun of righteousness breaks forth from His hiding place, with healing beneath His wings "Awake, O sword, against my shepherd and against the man that is my fellow, saith the Lord of Hosts; smite the shepherd and the sheep shall be scattered: and I will turn mine hand upon the little ones." We have express authority for applying these words to Christ; we have His own declaration when He said to His disciples, "This night shall all ye be offended, for it is written," referring to our text, "I will smite the Shepherd and the sheep shall be scattered; and after I am risen from the dead, ye shall go before me into Galilee."

I. We have here THE CHARACTER OF CHRIST.

Was there ever such a character? He is held forth in three ways: by His *office*, He is called the Good Shepherd. As such, Isaiah prophesied of Him, saying, "He shall feed His flock like a shepherd." He shall discharge fully the pastoral relations and regulate His conduct by the condition of His charge. He is called the "*Good* Shepherd," the "*Great* Shepherd," the "*Chief* Shepherd," and the Shepherd and Bishop of souls. Here He is called by His relation to God, "*My* Shepherd," because I have ordained Him for this office; for all my people are entrusted to Him, and He shall deliver them all at last, not one missing.

He is held forth by His *humanity*, "*the Man*." He was truly a man; a body was prepared for Him; He had all the sinless dispositions and infirmities of our nature; He passed through all. The intellectual as well as the corporeal powers gradually unfolded themselves to maturity. "He grew and waxed strong in spirit, filled with wisdom; and the grace of God was upon Him." This was important, as may be inferred from the language of the Apostle, "Having therefore, brethren, boldness to enter into the holiest by the blood of Jesus, by a new and living way which He hath consecrated for us through the veil, that is to say His flesh." It is by His manhood we have all our union and intercourse with Him; without this, He could not have been our example, going before us in the path of obedience and suffering; could not have sympathized with us in our woes, nor gained our confidence; without this He could not have died for us, and rose again.

He is held forth by His *dignity;* not only "*the Man,*" but "the man that is my fellow," saith the Lord! If any ask what manner of expression is this, we will appeal to the words of the Holy Ghost by the Apostle when He said, "Who being in the form of God, thought it not robbery to be equal with God, but made Himself of no reputation, and took upon Him the form of a servant, and was made in the likeness of men." Hear again the language of John, "In the beginning was the Word, and the Word was with God, and the Word was God. The same was in the beginning with God. All things were made by Him; and without Him was not anything made, that was made." Hear what the Jews said when our Saviour declared that "My Father worketh hitherto and I work." "Therefore the Jews sought the more to kill Him, because He not only had broken the Sabbath, but said also that God was His Father, making Himself equal with God." And was He not so? Is the Father omnipotent? He is called "The mighty God." Is the Father omnipresent? "Lo!" says the Saviour, "I am with you always, even to the end of the world." "Where two or three are gathered together in my name, there am I in the midst of them." Is the Father omniscient? "He needed not that any should testify of man, for He knew what was in man." Is the Father unchangeable? "He is the same yesterday, to-day, and for ever." Is the Father worshipped? He is worshipped by the highest order of beings, in His lowest state of humiliation too, for "when He bringeth His first begotten into the world, He saith, And let all the angels of God worship Him;" and we are informed that this was accomplished. "I heard" says John, "the voice of many angels round about the throne, and the beasts, and the elders: and the number of them was ten thousand times ten thousand and thousands of thousands: saying with a loud voice, worthy is the Lamb that was slain, to receive power, and riches, and wisdom, and strength, and honour, and glory, and blessing."

II. Pass we on, secondly, to observe THE SUFFERINGS THE SAVIOUR ENDURED.

Notice first the *author* of these sufferings. It was God who said, "Awake, O sword, against my Shepherd." Men and devils were the instruments; but they could have had no power at all against Him, unless it had been given them from above; only they served His design. "He was delivered by the determinate counsel and foreknowledge of God," though it was by wicked hands "He was crucified and slain;" yea, "He spared not His own Son, but delivered Him up for us all." "Yet it pleased the Lord to bruise Him: He hath put Him to grief; when Thou shalt make His soul an offering for sin, He shall see His seed, He shall prolong His days, and the pleasure of the Lord shall prosper in His hand."

Observe again the *dreadfulness* of His sufferings. It is not a rod, but a sword! Ah, Christian, you often feel the rod of a Father, and sometimes apprehend something worse, and therefore exclaim, "Do not condemn me, show me wherefore Thou contendest with me!" But of this there is really no danger with regard to you, for "there is therefore now no condemnation to them who are in Christ Jesus." There is nothing keener in any of your sorrows than the rod; but *He* bore the whole curse for you. You will never feel the sword of the judge, but He felt it, and the sword you see is roused, "*Awake*, O sword! smite the Shepherd;" and what a blow was here! the consequence of which leads us to apply to Him the language of the weeping Church, "Behold and see, if there be any sorrow like unto my sorrow, which is done unto me, wherewith the Lord hath afflicted me in the day of His fierce anger." It was the hand of God that touched Him, and made Him "sore amazed;" it was owing to this that His "soul was exceedingly sorrowful even unto death." It was this that made Him "sweat as it were great drops of blood." It was this that led him to exclaim upon the cross, "My God, my God, why hast Thou forsaken me."

Consider again the *reason* of His suffering. Why was He to be thus smitten? What evil had He done? Yet they "did esteem Him stricken, smitten of God and afflicted." And He was so. But "He was wounded for our transgressions, He was bruised for our iniquities; the chastisement of our peace was upon Him, and with His stripes we are healed." Here the mystery is at an end. He addressed His Father, "If it be possible, let this cup pass from me!" but it could not be. If he had saved others, Himself He could not save. If sin was to be pardoned, sin must also be condemned; if the sinner must be saved, God must be glorified in the highest; His law must be magnified, and made honourable; He must appear in the face of the universe as a just God, as well as a Saviour. Oh, what a scene was here! You behold the love of the Saviour, that He should interpose for us, when He knew tha interposition must cost His blood. Behold the evil of sin, that could only be expiated by the sacrifice of the Son of God.

Behold the believer's security, for surely justice will never demand a second payment. "Who is he that condemneth? It is Christ that died." Behold the sinner's encouragement. Do you want pardon? "He has made peace by the blood of His cross." Do you want cleansing? "The blood of Jesus Christ cleanseth us from all sin."

III. Let us notice THE DISPERSION OF HIS DISCIPLES. "I will smite the Shepherd and the sheep shall be scattered."

During our Saviour's public ministry, He never wanted hearers. When the High Priest asked Him of His disciples and of His doctrine, Jesus answered him, "I spake openly to the world; I ever taught in the synagogue, and in the temple, whither the Jews always resort; and in secret have I said nothing." People flocked by multitudes to hear Him, some to entangle Him in His talk, others out of curiosity; many from selfishness, gaping after "the loaves and fishes." Such successively fell off from Him, like leaves in Autumn. One day a number of them withdrew; as they were leaving Him, our Saviour said to the twelve, "Will ye also go away? Now is the time for you; you can now go in company; with less shame, as crowds will accompany you." But Peter turned to Him and said, "Lord, to whom shall we go? Thou hast the words of eternal life." This was a noble reply, and they acted according to this for nearly two years afterwards, and then our Saviour said to them, "Ye are they that have continued with me in my temptations, and I appoint unto you a kingdom, as my Father hath appointed me." No sooner was He apprehended, no sooner was the Shepherd smitten than the sheep were scattered, and "*all* His disciples," we are told, "forsook Him and fled."

Oh, let His people learn from this fact not to be surprised if they should be left and forsaken by some in the time of trouble. There are people who love the garden well while it yields flowers and fruits, who never enter it in the winter; who use their friends as they do their nosegays, place them in their bosom while fresh and green, and fling them into the street when they wither! Or as builders do with the scaffolding, they use it while the building is erecting, and afterwards take it down and place it as much as possible out of sight. If you look through the Scriptures you will find much of this. Yea, you will find God saying, not only by His word but by His providence, "Cease ye from man whose breath is in His nostrils; for wherein is he to be accounted of?" You see this with regard to David, who was exiled by the rebellion and treason of his son Absalom; when he said, "For it was not an enemy that reproached me; then I could have borne it: neither was it he that hated me that did magnify himself against me; then I would have hid myself from him." Poor Job, under his other sufferings, said, "My brethren have dealt deceitfully as a brook, and as the stream of brooks that pass away." And Paul says to Timothy, "At my first answer no man stood with me, but all men forsook me," though they had come down when he was approaching Rome, "as far as Appii Forum and the three taverns," in order to introduce him to the metropolis of the world. "I pray God it may not be laid to their charge."

The desertion of our Saviour by his disciples was a great aggravation of His sufferings. In proof of this you have only to apply to those who have suffered. "To him that is afflicted," says Job, pity should be shewed "from his friend." "Have pity upon me, have pity upon me, O ye, my friends, for the hand of God hath touched me." You then naturally look to them for kindness, and use such language as this. And if they can afford you no real succour and relief, their very presence and sympathy will yield satisfaction. But how was it with your Lord and Saviour in His sufferings? Where are the multitudes whom He fed, that fine evening, on the grass? Where are all those whom He healed? "Where is the son of that poor widow, whom I raised to life? Lazarus, where art thou? My disciples, where are you?" Not one of them appears. "I looked," says the Saviour, "for some to take pity, and there was none, and for comforters, and I found none."

Here we see the imperfections that may be discovered in those who are born again; there is *nature* in them, as well as *grace.* See the disciples, they were overcome by the fear of man. But their panic was perfectly groundless; for when our Saviour was apprehended in the garden, before He surrendered He stipulated for their safety; and when He said to those who sought Him, "If ye seek me, let these (meaning His disciples) go their way," and it is remarkable that they never attempted to lay hold of one of them. When under peculiar obligations to their Saviour, He appealed to them as His disciples and informed them, "all ye shall be offended because of me this night." The period was very near, and they professed the strongest attachment, and the firmest adherence, saying they were ready to go with Him to prison and to death. So said *all* His disciples; but as for Peter, he said, "Though all men be offended; yet will I never be offended," and "though I should die with Thee, yet will I not deny thee." Yet before the cock crew twice he denied Him thrice and even with oaths and curses. "Lord, what is man? The best of men," says one, "are but men at the best." Let us therefore be diffident of ourselves and pray, "Lord, hold Thou me up and I shall be safe." Let us, instead of indulging in self-confidence, come daily "to the throne of grace, that we may obtain mercy and grace to help in every time of need."

"Let us beware of Peter's words,
Nor confidently say
I never will deny Thee, Lord,
But, grant I never may"

Oh, my brethren, we know little of ourselves till we are tried. Therefore God brings us into trying circumstances. We do not properly believe His testimony; therefore experience must come and teach us that without Him we can do nothing. 'Tis well for us to learn this by faith, not by feeling; but if I must learn it by experience, let me learn it by the falls of others.

IV. Consider THE SAVIOUR'S AGENCY ON THEIR BEHALF. "And I will turn mine hand upon the little ones."

His disciples, who were called "sheep" before, are here called "little ones." They were so in every sense of the word, few in number, and not entitled to any consideration by birth or rank in life. They were commonly fishermen; distinguished by no greatness, very little esteemed among men; the world knew them not. And if this was the case with others, what were they in their own eyes? Little enough, as less than nothing and vanity. His "hand" here means His gracious power and influence. We read of some in the Gospel of Luke, concerning whom it was said, "And the power of the Lord was present to heal them;" When Isaiah speaks of God delivering His people, he says, "He shall set His hand again the second time to the work." He shall again exert His power and influence on their behalf. "And I will turn mine hand upon the little ones." That is, He would employ His power and influence for *two* purposes:—

First, to *preserve* them. They were among enemies, they were "as lambs in the midst of wolves," and the only reason they were not devoured was because His hand was present to deliver them.

Secondly, to restore them from their falls. The interval of their declension seems to have been very brief. The Saviour turned, and looked upon Peter, "and immediately he remembered the words of Jesus, and went out and wept bitterly." On the day on which the Saviour rose from the dead, He joined two of the disciples as they went to Emmans; and in the evening of the same day, He appeared to them at Jerusalem in their distresses, and said "Peace be unto you." He called the week after for Thomas—poor Thomas—confirmed his trembling faith, and led him to say, "My Lord, and my God." He filled them all "with power from on high." On the day of Pentecost, He enlarged their views and shed abroad His love in their hearts. They went forth with a divine boldness, preaching Jesus and the resurrection, rejoicing that they were counted worthy to suffer for His sake. They could say, "Christ shall be magnified in my body, whether it be by life or by death."

Well, we see in conclusion with what propriety the Christian can take up the language of the Church in the days of Micah, and say, "When I sit in darkness, the Lord shall be a light unto me." Says David, "The steps of a good man are o dered by the Lord, and He delighteth in his way; *though* he fall, he shall not be utterly cast down, for the Lord upholdeth him with His hand." His people may for a while forget their best friend, but they cannot long forget Him. They will be induced to say, "I will return to my first husband, for then was it better with me than now." God will not cast away His people because of their infirmities; will not reject the wheat because of the chaff, but will separate the one from the other. He will not "break the bruised reed, nor quench the smoking flax." Christian, live then in this full confidence. Yes, "being confident," as the Apostle says, "that He who hath begun a good work in you, will carry it on until the day of Jesus Christ." Say with David, with holy assurance, "He will perfect that which concerneth me." "Thy mercy, O Lord, endureth for ever; forsake not the work of Thine own hands."

But again, let not this confidence lull you to sleep. Christian, your comforts should be cordials, not opiates. You find enough to encourage you under a sense of your infirmities; still, "be not high minded, but fear." "Blessed is the man that feareth always." "Watch and pray, that ye enter not into temptation."

Lastly, while you confide in Him, be concerned to resemble

Him. "Brethren, if a man be overtaken in a fault, ye which are spiritual restore such a one in the spirit of meekness; considering thyself lest thou also be tempted." "Ye that are strong, ought to bear the infirmities of the weak, and not to please yourselves." "Comfort the feeble minded, support the weak." Do not bring forward the high portions of the Gospel, nor talk of your attainments before those who are now oppressed. Give new milk to *babes;* feed them not with strong meat, much less with the *bones* of controversy. Despise not the day of small things. "Be ye followers of God as dear children." "Walk in love, and the God of peace shall be with you."

XII.

REST FOR THE WEARY.

(Preached on Sunday Evening, November 16th, 1845.)

Come unto me, all ye that labour and are heavy laden, and I will give you rest.—MATTHEW xi. 28.

WHILE the Pharisees were gathered round, the Saviour proposed the question to them, "What think ye of Christ?" The question is most important and interesting, for He is the centre in which the lines of revelation all unite and harmonize. Every truth of the Gospel has some relation to His grace or His glory, and our love to Him, and our dependence upon Him, will be governed by our apprehensions of His character, or His designs. Your growth in grace is combined with your knowledge of Christ; hence Paul exclaims, "Yea, doubtless, and I count all things but loss for the excellency of the knowledge of Christ Jesus my Lord." And hence He is so fully, and so frequently, described in the Scriptures of truth. If you go back to the Old Testament prophecies, by nothing is He so distinguished as by His tenderness to the poor, the distressed, the weak and the wretched. Shall we refer to His actions? "He Himself took our infirmities, and bare our sicknesses." We read of His having compassion on the multitude because they had now been with Him three days and had nothing to eat. And on another occasion, that He had compassion on the multitude because they were as sheep having no shepherd; that He had pity on the widow of Nain, and gave her back her son. He wept at the grave of Lazarus, and occasioned the exclamation of the Jews, "Behold, how He loved him!" Or shall we appeal to His words? Where shall we begin? "Let not your heart be troubled," said He, "neither let it be afraid." "Peace I leave with you, my peace I give unto you." "If any man thirst, let him come unto me and drink." Where shall we end? "Come unto me, all ye that labour and are heavy laden, and I will give you rest."

Here are three things which we have to explain and improve: A character, an invitation, and a promise.

I. A Character. All who "labour and are heavy laden." The representation is a figure of speech. The meaning is, all they who labour by being heavy laden; being heavy laden, they struggle to be free, and weary themselves by their vain endeavours to obtain freedom. But who are the persons to whom our Saviour here refers? Why, all those who can say with David, "Mine iniquities are increased; they are gone over my head; as a heavy burden they are too heavy for me." Affliction is a burden, some of you feel it to be so, and Christ comforts those who are cast down. He is therefore called "The Consolation of Israel," as well as "the Saviour thereof in the time of trouble." But then you know there are many who, though afflicted, feel no proper concern about their souls, and do not say with Micah, "I will look unto the Lord; I will wait for the God of my salvation; my God will hear me." They acknowledge readily enough that "here they have no continuing city;" but they are not like Bunyan's pilgrim, moving on for Immanuel's land and the shining city, who, though pressed down with the burden on his back, amidst the scoffing of enemies, and the entreaties of friends, put his finger in his ears as he ran across the field crying, "Life, life, eternal life."

There is a sense in which the Saviour's representation is true of all mankind. Let us take the character of those who mind earthly things, and seek for happiness and pleasure where they are not to be found. May we not address the words of Isaiah to such? "Wherefore do ye spend money for that which is not bread, and your labour for that which satisfieth not? Hearken diligently unto me, and eat ye that which is good, and let your soul delight itself in fatness." But are you happy? You may not be willing to own that you are unhappy; you may not be willing to own that you are disappointed when you do not succeed, and often when you do. Are you not often mortified by your fellow-creatures. One stands in the way of your profit, another refuses to bend to your humour, and you are led to complain of the weakness of your friend. Are you strangers to a wish that you had never been born? Do you not envy the animals who have no fear with regard to the future, and no regrets with regard to the past? Is not solitude irksome? and were it not for what you term the amusements of life, you would destroy yourself. Well, here is One able to comfort you in all your mortifications and sorrows. In Him you will find rest, "rest to your souls"—that rest "which the world cannot give."

Do any of you say, "Why, sir, you draw a very unfavourable representation of life. 'Tis true there are some vexed and wretched, but this is not the case with us. We are not unhappy; we have our heart's desire; our 'cup runneth over,' everything is so agreeable in our condition; we should be content to live here always." Is this case true? If it be true, you are in a worse state than the former, for by your own confession you declare that you are not among the number that the Saviour calls "weary and heavy laden." This is the case with some as it regards their souls; they say "they are rich, and increased in goods, and stand in need of nothing," whilst "they are poor and wretched and miserable and blind and naked." These also by their own confession declare that they are not among the number of the "weary and heavy laden."

Who, then, are they? The case is this: All men are sinners, but all are not sensible of their spiritual state. A load lies upon them all enough to sink them into perdition, but as yet they are not labouring by being "heavy laden" in the sense here referred to. Our text speaks of those who first feel the pressure of the burden, and then seek deliverance from it. They feel the pressure of a burden. They have "a wounded spirit," and who can bear this? Conscience acts the part of an unwelcome accuser, and of an unwelcome informer, who renews the remembrance of a multitude of things with all their aggravations, and conscience is regarded now as the voice of God. The man hears and trembles, the world loses its charms for him, companions no longer entertain, "he eateth ashes like bread, and mingles his drink with weeping,"—sleep sometimes departs from his eyelids, or if he sleeps, he is scared "with dreams, and terrified with visions." This is frequently a good beginning. Sin is now seen to be as pollution to the soul, and the man cries with Job, "Behold I am vile, therefore I abhor myself and repent in dust and ashes;" and with Paul, "O wretched man that I am." Therefore we read, "They shall loathe themselves for all their abominations," and the representation includes a desire for relief. You cannot suppose a man properly burdened with a sense of his sins, who does not pray, and earnestly pray to be delivered. He wishes to forsake his sins, and to part with all his iniquities; not only those to which he has no proneness in his constitution, but his bosom sins, so that with Ephraim he can say, "What have I any more to do with idols?" He is willing to cut off a right hand, or pluck out his right eye; to "mortify the deeds of the body," and to "crucify the flesh with its affections and lusts." In this case something may be done; the man's strength will not be to sit still. If a man were in a house that was on fire, and he knew it, flying would be unavoidable; and he also was pressed down with a heavy burden, he would endeavour to throw it off. Sometimes, indeed, the more an awakened soul strives against his corruption, the more it seems to increase; he cannot succeed in his efforts, yet dare not give them up, and this is very wearisome. Sometimes also he seeks salvation by the works of the law. But all his efforts are baffled again and again, and he finds himself in the fire, and wearying himself for every vanity. If in some favoured moments he seems to feel himself at liberty, he finds the triumph is short, and he is again in bondage, and now he knows what it is to "labour," being "heavy laden."

II. Let us pass on to consider THE INVITATION OF THE SAVIOUR. "Come unto me, all ye that labour and are heavy laden."

This is the invariable language of Christ in the gospel. We are all naturally without Christ, and all our misery arises from our distance. He would therefore bring us nearer to Himself; and at the last day He will use the same language, "*Come*, ye blessed of My Father, inherit the kingdom prepared for you from the foundation of the world."

But what is this? It cannot intend a local access. How many in the days of His flesh came to Him! some to entangle Him in His talk—some out of curiosity—some for the loaves and fishes. Thousands came and derived no benefit. Therefore said He to those standing near enough to Him, "Ye will not come unto me, that ye might have life;" so that He intended something more than corporeal access. He intended spiritual approach. But how is this possible? The heavens have received Him. "I am no more in the world," says He. But there is still access to Him. He hath said, "Where two or three are gathered together in My name, there am I in the midst of them," and "He is not far from everyone of us." Yea—

> "Wher'er we seek Him He is found,
> And every spot is holy ground."

As He said to His disciples previous to His ascension, "Go into Galilee, and there shall ye find Me;" and they went, and did see Him according to His promise; so He is engaged to be found of all those who seek Him in the way of His own appointment, of all those who really believe in His name.

Coming to Him is believing in Him; this He Himself has decided in His gracious promise, "He that cometh to me shall never hunger, he that believeth on Me shall never thirst." This may be explained a little by what took place in the days of His flesh. Those who came to Him felt their need, or they would not have come; they had some confidence in His power and readiness, or they would not have come to Him in this way. The degrees were very various. The centurion, for instance, had a full persuasion that if the Saviour spoke only one word his servant would be healed. The leper was more doubtful; he said, "Lord, if Thou wilt, Thou canst make me clean." But the father of the lunatic, because his faith was fainter, still said, "If Thou canst do anything, have compassion on us, and help us." This faith was mixed with much unbelief. This he felt, and therefore he cried out and said, with tears, "Lord, I believe; help Thou my unbelief."

Here are three things to be observed. One of the important lessons to be derived from our Saviour's representation of faith, or coming to Him, is that faith, real faith, is not a mere speculative notion, but the full admission of the record that God has given us of His Son; and this coming to Him operates upon the mind, upon the heart, and the life. And then it draws the man away from every refuge of lies to the only refuge set before him in the gospel, from every false foundation to the only foundation which God has laid in Him; it brings him to the Saviour, where he says, "I cast myself at Thy feet; Thou art made unto me wisdom, and righteousness, sanctification, and redemption. I am guilty; Thy blood alone can cleanse me. I am darkness itself; Thou alone can'st enlighten me, through Thy grace and strength alone I shall be able to subdue my corruptions. Lord, save or I perish. God be merciful to me a sinner!" This is that to which the Saviour refers, when He says "Come unto me, all ye that labour and are heavy laden."

And secondly, this representation of faith, that of coming to Him, teaches us that the only successful act of an awakened sinner is an address to Christ. "To whom can we go?" says Peter, when the Saviour said, "Will ye also go away?" "To whom can we go? Thou hast the words of eternal life." Can we go back to sin? that has destroyed us. Can we go to the world? that has deceived us. Can we go to heathen philosophers? their foolish hearts are darkened. Can we go to Moses? he will send us back to Christ, "for he wrote of Him." Can we go to the law? To convince and to condemn is all the law can do. Can we go to our own works and worthiness? "The bed is shorter than that a man can stretch himself on it; and the covering narrower than that he can wrap himself in it." Why, then, shall we go for relief to the general and absolute mercy of God? No, for the Spirit has now convinced the man of sin, and nothing can relieve his mind but a discovery of the Lamb of God which taketh away "the sin of the world;" the discovery of a scheme in which "Glory to God in the Highest," is combined with "peace on earth and good will to man," the discovery of a scheme which condemns sin in the flesh, while "righteousness and peace kiss each other." Therefore, says Our Saviour, "Come unto me, all ye that labour and are heavy laden."

And thirdly, we shall behold that though our case is desperate in itself, and with regard to every other mode of address, Christ is equal to our relief and deliverance. Nothing is too hard for Him. "It hath pleased the Father that in Him should all fulness dwell." For thus we are blessed with all spiritual blessings. Therefore says He, "Come unto me, all ye that labour and are heavy laden."

III. This brings us to the last part of our topic, THE PROMISE, "and I will give you rest."

This rest does not consist in carelessness. It is not the rest of the antinomian, or that which would give you a licence to sin. Here, believer, you will go before your preacher, and nothing can be more pleasing than for a minister to know that the experience of his hearers echoes back the doctrine that he preaches. Let us therefore enter a little farther into this.

"Come unto me all ye that labour and are heavy laden and I will give you rest"—"rest" from uneasiness, uncertainty, and doubt, and these are more likely to rise in cases of importance, and religion is infinitely important. Here we may obtain certainty. But an infidel can never acquire this, do what he will: he can never free himself from doubt and suspicion. There may be a God who observes my ways after all; there may be a moral providence; there may be an hereafter, and after death there may be a judgment. But a real Christian admits the certainty of all this, and he is no longer floundering in the mud and mire; he finds rocks for his feet. His mourning is now exchanged for comfort! This is rest of the understanding.

"Come unto me, all ye that labour and are heavy laden, and I will give you rest"—"rest" from all the accusations of guilt and the torments of fear. For He sees that God his Saviour has surely "borne his grief and carried his sorrow;" he finds himself to be "reconciled to God by the death of His Son." This is the meaning of the Apostle when he says, "Being justified by faith we have peace with God."

"Come unto me, all ye that labour and are heavy laden, and I will give you rest"—"rest" from the memory of a sinful passion. "The wicked are like the troubled sea that cannot rest, which continually casteth up mire and dirt." "There is no peace, saith my God, to the wicked." Sin is the worst kind of slavery, but henceforth the believer does not serve sin, though he finds a continual struggle and warfare. He is at rest from the bondage of corruption. Being upheld by God's free Spirit, he runs in the way of His commandments with enlargedness of heart.

"Come unto me, all ye that labour and are heavy laden, and I will give you rest"—"rest" from the anxieties that arise from our conditions in life. How miserable must that man be who sets his affections on things on the earth, seeing that his portion must be in perpetual danger. Whereas the believer has a treasure in heaven; he has a hope laid up for him in heaven; he has "an inheritence incorruptible, undefiled, and that fadeth not away" reserved in heaven for him. Therefore he has nothing to dread with regard to his main and principal treasure. Then also how miserable must that man be who is the sport of chance and accident, who knows nothing of a providence which is engaged to manage all his concerns! But the believer knows that his Father ordains "the bounds of his habitation;" that He measures out to him all his trials and all his comforts too. He knows that "all things work together for his good."

"Come unto me all ye that labour and are heavy laden, and I will give you rest"—"rest" from the troubles and temptations of time; this is the rest of eternity, "there remaineth a rest for the people of God." "Blessed are the dead that die in the Lord; yea, saith the Spirit, for they rest from their labours." They shall enter into peace. When? "Mark the perfect man, and behold the upright, for the *end* of that man is peace." No earlier? O yes, they "who believe do enter into rest;" they enjoy the earnests and foretastes of heaven.

We have endeavoured to apply this subject all through, and

yet there are some things which ought to be briefly noticed for the improvement of this. The first thing is an *inquiry*, Why does He invite those only who "are weary and heavy laden?" To which we say, Because they only will receive the invitation. "The full soul loatheth the honeycomb, but to the hungry soul every bitter thing is sweet." They too are more in danger of excluding themselves from it. But as Watts says,

> "No mortal has a just pretence
> To perish in despair."

The second thing is a *caution*. You are liable to be mistaken as to the nature of the rest you possess. "Come unto me all ye that labour and are heavy laden, and I will give you rest." So says sin—so says infidelity—so says the world—and so says the devil. He has often said this, for the strong man armed loves to keep his palace and his goods in peace.

The third thing is an *admonition*. Some of you have long made light of it. The Saviour, however, still addresses you, and says, "Come unto me;" but you know not how long He may continue to do this. We therefore say to you, "Seek ye the Lord while He may be found, call ye upon Him while He is near." Remember you must die, and to enter into another world before you are prepared would be an awful thing indeed. "He that hath the Son hath life, and he that hath not the Son hath not life, but the wrath of God abideth in him." Do you question whether He will receive you after His own invitation? Remember that "all the fitness He requireth, is to feel your need of Him." Do not say, therefore, you are too bad, or too guilty to go to Him; but because you *are* so guilty you must go. Do not say "I am pressed down with a consciousness of my sins, I cannot go;" but rather say, "I am so pressed down that I *must* go." Well and why should you not? He stands ready to save you. Why tarriest thou, therefore? As I look round this large congregation, I trust I see some who feel contrite in their hearts—some who are convinced of their sins; painful as is your experience, it is a very blessed state; for though the world thinks you are going out of your senses, though yourself think you are likely to be distracted or thrown into despair, God looks at you with pleasure, and says, "To that man will I look, who is of a humble and contrite spirit, and who trembleth at my word." Jesus calls you to Himself, and says He will give you rest.

Then some of you have this rest already. You "who believe do enter into rest," and are enabled to "rejoice in hope of the glory of God." What have you to complain of since He hath promised He will "give grace and glory, and will withhold no good things from them that walk uprightly?" Do you fear your trials? These are but for the moment, and your Saviour is coming soon "to be glorified in His saints, and to be admired in all them that believe." But surely you will not wait for that day before you admire Him. What a Saviour have you! How glorious is His Person! How excellent is His offices and grace! What boundless resources has He! What power in His arm, and what love in His heart! And can you help admiring Him now? The more you know of Him, the more you will admire Him, but be not satisfied with the admiration; imitate and love Him. He is placed before you as your example, and "let the same mind therefore be in you which was in Christ Jesus." Endeavour to afford rest to any around you, in your measure and degree. Be a little like Him who hath said, "Come unto me all ye that labour and are heavy laden, and I will give you rest." Thus may you "be followers of God as dear children."

XIII.

MERCY ON SEA AND LAND.

(Preached on Sunday Evening, September 13th, 1846.)

And Peter answered Him and said, Lord, if it be Thou, bid me come unto Thee on the water. And he said, Come. And when Peter was come down out of the ship, he walked on the water, to go to Jesus. But when he saw the wind boisterous, he was afraid; and beginning to sink, he cried, saying, Lord, save me. And immediately Jesus stretched forth His hand, and caught him, and said unto him, O thou of little faith, wherefore didst thou doubt? And when they were come into the ship, the wind ceased. Then they that were in the ship came and worshipped him, saying, Of a truth Thou art the Son of God.

And when they were gone over, they came into the land of Gennesaret. And when the men of that place had knowledge of Him, they sent out into all that country round about, and brought unto Him all that were diseased: and besought Him that they might only touch the hem of His garment: and as many as touched were made perfectly whole.—MATTHEW xiv. 28-36.

A STORM at sea is one of the sublimest spectacles in all nature; hence it frequently employs the painter's pencil and the poet's pen. What can be more beautiful than the representation of David?—"They that go down to the sea in ships, that do business in great waters: these see the works of the LORD, and His wonders in the deep. For He commandeth, and raiseth the stormy wind, which lifteth up the waves thereof. They mount up to the heaven, they go down again to the depths: their soul is melted because of trouble. They reel to and fro, and stagger like a drunken man, and are at their wits' end. Then they cry unto the LORD in their trouble, and He bringeth them out of their distresses. He maketh the storm a calm, so that the waves thereof are still. Then are they glad because they be quiet; so He bringeth them unto their desired haven."

Matthew has furnished us with two very fine sea-pieces. Both happened on the same lake—the lake of Galilee. In both our Lord's disciples were on board; in both they sailed at His command; in both they encountered a storm, and were filled with dismay. In the first our Saviour was with them, but He was asleep, and they went to Him, and awoke Him, saying, "Master, carest Thou not that we perish?" In the second He was absent; but He soon reached them, and, as we have read, He hushed their fears and delivered them from their danger. Then it was that Peter preferred the request which we find at the beginning of our text for this evening. Our text contains three parts. The first regards the request of Peter; the second, the interposition, of Christ; and the third the arrival of the company at the land whither they would.

I. The Request of Peter.

The biography of the Scripture is very brief, but impartial and discriminating. Whenever Peter is introduced, he appears before us in his own character—that is, with a sanguine complexion and strong passions: with a mind ardent and bold, he discovered more zeal than prudence, speaking first, and reflecting afterwards. Such men as these have their importance in the state and in the church. It is not good for such to be alone. Brandy requires water. You always find John therefore accompanying Peter. Peter could animate John and John could temper Peter. The disadvantage of such a disposition as Peters is this, that it always renders the possessor liable to err on the side of doing too much, and to get into difficulties and embarrassments. This was the case with Peter in a measure in the instance before us, for as soon as Our Saviour said, "Be not afraid, it is I," Peter answered him and said, "Lord, if it be Thou, bid me come unto Thee on the water."

There was affection in this. It reminds us of another instance, when our Saviour appears to several of His disciples at the lake of Tiberius. The disciple whom Jesus loved said unto Peter, "It is the Lord." Now, when Peter heard that it was Jesus, he girt his fisher's coat about him and cast himself into the sea to go to Jesus. Love longs to be near the object of its affection. As soon as he saw the Saviour he wished to fly into His arms, but surely there was no need of such a proposal. We are not to be afraid of our trials, but we are not to seek after them. We are to take up our cross when it is in our way, but we are not to go out of our road in search of difficulties and dangers. We see, therefore, a very great difference between the first and second era of Christianity. What

God commands He will enable us to do, and He will accept. With regard to other things, He will say "Who hath required this at your hands?" and He abhors will-worship.

The apostle exhorts the Colossians, "Beware lest any man spoils you through philosophy and vain deceit, after the tradition of men, after the rudiments of the world, and not after Christ." Our Lord told His disciples that when they were persecuted in one city they should flee into another; but soon after this you will find persons longing for persecution, anxious to become martyrs. Then followed the doctrine of "forbidding to marry, and commanding to abstain from meats, which God hath created to be received with thanksgiving of them which believe and know the truth. "For every creature of God is good, and nothing to be refused if it be received with thanksgiving."

But while Peter here shows his imperfection, he also shows his wisdom in requiring our Lord's command and authority; he would not come down till he was bidden. "Lord, if it be Thou, bid me come unto Thee on the water." "And Jesus said, Come." Here was a trial of Peter's faith and love. And when Peter heard this he immediately went down to Jesus on the water. Paul speaks of great things that faith has performed, and great things it can suffer; it can enable us to enter a lion's den, and face a fiery furnace. Here we find that it could lead a man to slip down the side of a ship, and stand upon the bare water, and walk thereon. But how long does this continue? Why, till he saw that the wind was boisterous, then he was afraid. What a sudden change! and such changes are common in the experience of believers. What transitions are there in a day, or even in an hour, from light to darkness, from liberty to bondage, from joy to sadness! We never continue in one state long. But what was it that produced this change? Oh, it was looking to the storm, and not to Jesus. Had he done the latter, he would not have thus trembled. "Moses endured as seeing Him that is invisible." "Abraham believed, and it was accounted unto him for righteousness." And how did he act? He did not consider the difficulties which stood in the way of the accomplishment of the divine assurance. "He staggered not through unbelief, being fully persuaded that He who had promised was able also to perform."

While he thus trembled, he cried out, "Lord, save me." This is a proper prayer to be used by us. To whom, in any of our afflictions, should we repair for succour but to "Him who is the hope of Israel, and the Saviour thereof in the time of trouble." Oh, beware of looking elsewhere for succour, and beware of the rope, of the river, of the razor, or of the cup. Beware of worldly dissipation, and have recourse to Him who is the burden-bearer, who says, "Come unto me all ye that labour and are heavy laden, and I will give you rest."

'Tis well to observe to what our thoughts and desires first turn when we come into trouble and difficulty. Afflictions are designed to bring us to Him by way of prayer. "I will go," says the chastised backholder, "and return unto my first love." "In their affiiction they will seek me early." But Asa in his sickness sought to physicians, and not to God. And the prophet Hosea tells us that "when Ephraim saw his sickness, and Judah his wound, then went Ephraim to the Assyrian, and sent to King Jareb," who could not heal them, nor cure them of their wound.

No sooner does Peter ask for help, than he obtains it; and did God ever refuse any who sought Him? Is He not always more ready to hear, than we are to ask for His aid? Is there a Christian here who has not had instances of the truth of the promise, "Before they call I will answer, and while they are yet speaking I will hear"?

But while He gives Peter His hand, and helps him too, He also administers to him a gentle reproof, "O thou of little faith, wherefore didst thou doubt"? "Did I not call you to come? Was I not by your side? Should I sink, and be no longer able to sustain you?" "As many as I love I rebuke and chasten." This doubting does not refer to his interest in eternal life, but to his sinking into the water, yet it will apply to the concerns of the soul and eternity. It will be well for us when we doubt, to reflect upon the truth of God, as well as upon His kindness, and to pray earnestly to Him, that our faith may be strengthened and our hearts established.

Though He reproved Peter, yet He heard him and helped him, and so He did the father of the child "who cried out with tears," "Lord, I believe; help Thou my unbelief." He was compelled to say, "O faithless generation! how long shall I be with you? how long shall I suffer you"? But He adds, "Bring him unto me, and He restored him to his father."

II. Observe Our Saviour's Interposition. "When they were come into the ship the wind ceased. Then they that were in the ship came and worshipped Him, saying, of a truth thou art the Son of God."

You see He came into the ship, teaching us that when ordinary resources are sufficient we are not to be looking after extraordinary means and expedients. We see he did not enter the ship alone; we read, "When *they* were come into the ship, the wind ceased." Peter came with him. He might have said, "Why, this is what you wished; here you desired to come, and here you shall remain." But He would not deal with him according to his desert, but allowed him to enter along with Him. You may be sure now that Peter was delighted with the permission to enter the ship. "And as soon as they were come into the ship the wind ceased." It was not before the storm had done its appointed work: it had tried the Apostles, it had tried Peter, and now it was to proclaim the Saviour's power. We may apply this also to the concerns of the soul. When faith enters the soul, however stormy its condition before, it becomes a calm. "By believing we enter into rest." "Being justified by faith we have peace with God through Our Lord Jesus Christ." "Yea, we joy in God through Our Lord Jesus Christ."

Observe the effects of this interposition: they were two. First, the confirmation of their faith; they now said, "Thou art the Son of God." They knew this before but could not say so with fresh evidence and confidence; the thing was as true before, but their belief of it was increased and established. Then, secondly, it drew forth their adoration. "They worshipped Him, saying, Of a truth Thou art the Son of God," and Christians will be employed again and again in this blessed work; but when they leave this present world their prayers will be turned into praise.

III. Observe The Arrival of the Company at the Land. They had all this time only rowed about four miles, but now, says John, in the chapter we read at the commencement, and which contains another account of the event, "They gladly received Him into the ship, and immediately the ship was at the land whither they went." What seems to be miraculous was this: the wind now ceased, and they now could advance with greater rapidity and could use their oars to advantage, and enjoyed the smiles and blessing of His company, so that the distance seemed short, and the time passed rapidly away, and they were at the land before they were aware of it. Though time is always the same, for an hour always consists of sixty minutes, yet pain will seem to lengthen it, and "hope deferred maketh the heart sick." On the other hand, when we are with agreeable associates, time seems to pass insensibly away. How soon an hour is gone, when we enjoy the instructions and conversation of an esteemed friend. Ah, Christians, your voyage cannot be long if His presence is enjoyed by you; it will pass off speedily, and in a little while, "He that shall come will come, and will not tarry," you will reach that blessed shore, where there will be no more storms and tempests.

But now see how they were treated when they came on shore. Our Lord met with very different treatment in different places. Among the Gadarenes, you remember, although He healed many, instead of thanking Him for it, they came in a body and besought Him that He would depart out of their coasts, and He took His leave, never to return again. But here they received Him with surprise, joy and gratitude, and seemed disposed to improve the privilege. At first they were not aware of the treasure the vessel had brought them, "but when the men of that place had knowledge of Him, they sent out into all that country round about, and brought unto Him all that were diseased."

Two important remarks arise from hence. First, *the necessity of knowledge in order to our making use of Christ.* Hence you should be concerned to increase your own acquaintance with Him. The way to grow in grace, is to grow in the knowledge of Christ. Hence we should be concerned for the spread of that knowledge, and continually praying, "Send out Thy light and Thy truth, that Thy way may be known upon earth," "By His knowledge," says God, "my righteous servant shall justify many." We read in the Scripture, that "we are justified by faith;" but as the apostle says, "How can they believe on Him of whom they have not heard"?

The second remark is, *when we know Him we should be concerned to bring others to Him.* This was the case here: "they sent out into all that country round about, and brought unto Him all that were diseased." This was wise and kind; this was loving their neighbour as themselves; this was rendering the knowledge of Him social as well as personal. There are many ways in which we may do this, as teaching the ignorant, furnishing them with the Scriptures, inviting them to hear the Word, while we allure them by our own tempers and lives, and to do this is unquestionably our duty. We admire those who relieve the body, and who clothe the naked, but, after all, charity to the soul is the very soul of charity. Remember the case of the lepers of Samaria when they had found great spoil: "they said one to another, We do not well: this day is a day of good tidings, and we hold our peace: if we tarry till the morning light, some mischief will come upon us: now therefore come, that we may go and tell the king's household." Do you follow their example, and the example also of the first Christians, who said, "That which we have seen and heard declare we unto you, that ye also may have fellowship with us: and truly our fellowship is with the Father, and with His Son Jesus Christ." Thus as soon as Andrew had found the Saviour, he brought his brother unto Him; and as soon as Philip had found Christ, "he findeth Nathaniel, and saith unto him, we have found Him of whom Moses in the law and the prophets did write, Jesus of Nazareth, the Son of Joseph." And the woman of Samaria endeavoured to bring her fellow-citizens to Him.

We will now only observe the manner in which they applied to Him. First, it was *importunately:* "they besought Him." And it was *humbly,* "that they might only touch the hem of His garment." They were afraid of being too familiar, He being so pure and undefiled, and they being so sinful and polluted; He so glorious, and they so mean. A sense of their unworthiness made them keep their distance; they would not venture to shake hands with Him; they would not touch His body at all. "They besought Him that they might only touch the hem of His garment." So it was with the woman of Galilee; "she came and stood behind Him, and cried unto Him, Have mercy on me." Thus it was here, and this showed the greatness of their faith: they believed, not only in His teaching, but even in their touching the hem of His garment.

Then consider the result of the application; "as many as touched Him were made perfectly whole." The efficiency was universal in its extent. Some of these diseases were inveterate, and they had made many applications elsewhere, but now "as many as touched Him were made perfectly whole." Secondly, it was powerful in its degree; they were perfectly healed. Christ never does His work by halves; He never shows Himself unable to finish what He has begun. Thirdly, it was sudden in the operation. Other physicians required a long time, and in some cases, very long. The best means are frequently slow in their operations, and require to be often repeated, and the applicant is only gradually healed. But here all was done in a moment. Yet behold, it was all silent in its influence; He said nothing, and did nothing, but virtue came out of Him. The rose does not make a noise, or speak a word, yet it perfumes the air. The kingdom of God comes in power; yet it comes not with observation. What a change did this people experience! The blind received their sight, the deaf heard, and the sick are healed. This change must soon have been apparent to their neighbours, who rejoiced on their behalf. And so, if you have been with with Jesus and have learnt of Him, others will take knowledge of it.

Men and brethren, the grand thing is for you to feel your need of this Saviour. "They that are whole need not a physician, but they that are sick." If you feel your real condition, you know you must be healed, or perish for ever. Then remember, there is "balm in Gilead, there is a physician there." There is the same Saviour who restored all those afflicted creatures, and He is "the same yesterday, and to-day, and for ever." Can we touch Him then? Oh, yes; by faith we can not only make an application to Him, but an application of Him, and claim all the blessings He has to bestow. And may any of us repair to Him? Oh, yes; who is excluded? "Whosoever will, let him take of the water of life freely." And shall we be made perfectly holy? Not at once, indeed, but in due time. "He will perfect that which concerneth us," and will bring us to Immanuel's land, where we shall hunger no more, neither thirst any more, and where the inhabitants shall no more say I am sick. "Now the God of hope fill you with all joy and peace in believing, that ye may abound in hope through the power of the Holy Ghost."

XIV.

THE FRIEND OF SINNERS.

Preached on Sunday Evening, May 18th, 1845.

This man receiveth sinners.—LUKE XV. 2.

WHAT character and conduct was ever so perfect as the Saviour's? Yet He did not escape the look of envy or the tongue of slander. "He went about doing good," yet His motives were impugned, and He had to endure the contradictions of sinners against Himself. "Marvel not," said He to His disciples, "if the world hate you; it hated me before it hated you." "If ye were of the world, the world would love its own, but because ye are not of the world, but I have chosen you out of the world, therefore the world hateth you." "Remember the word that I said unto you, the servant is not greater than his Lord. If they have persecuted me, they will persecute you also." Why, every thing foul was laid to His charge. He was a Samaritan—He had a devil—He was accused of sedition and blasphemy—He was a glutton and a wine bibber, a friend of "publicans and sinners." Our text is a reflection of the same kind; "This man receiveth sinners." The charge arises from the malice of their hearts, but it was a specious appearance; there is much in the common proverb, "Shew me a man's company, and I will shew you the man." "Then drew near unto Him all the publicans and sinners for to hear Him. And the Pharisees and Scribes murmured, saying, This man receiveth sinners and eateth with them." Our Lord does not deny the fact, and there was truth in the declaration, not, as they would insinuate, that He would encourage them in their sin, but because "He came to seek and to save that which was lost." He was among them as a physician, not for His pleasure but for their profit. "Never man spake as this man." "And He spake this parable unto them saying,

What man of you having an hundred sheep, if he lose one of them doth not leave the ninety and nine in the wilderness, and go after that which is lost, until he find it? And when he hath found it he layeth it on his shoulders rejoicing. And when he cometh home, he calleth together his friends and neighbours, saying unto them, Rejoice with me: for I have found my sheep which was lost. I say unto you, that likewise joy shall be in heaven over one sinner that repenteth, more than over ninety and nine just persons that need no repentance." Our Saviour then was as a shepherd endeavouring to restore a strayed sheep or lamb. "This man receiveth sinners" not because He delighteth in sin, but because He delighteth in mercy. "He receiveth sinners" not because He needs them, but because He knows they need *Him*, and without Him they are undone for ever.

Let us glance at His Character, and secondly, at his Conduct.

I. Let us glance at HIS CHARACTER. "This man."

Under this appellation, it becomes us both to distinguish and to dignify Him; for you will observe, though He is *really* a man, He is not a man only. A man appeared to Jacob, and wrestled till the dawning of the day, and blessed him. It was "this man." A man came to Joshua and said, "As captain of the host of the Lord am I now come." It was "this man." Isaiah said, "A man shall be as a hiding place from the wind, and a covert from the tempest, as rivers of waters in a dry place, and as the shadow of a great rock in a weary land." It was "this man." Micah said, "This man shall be the peace." It was "this man." Zechariah said, "Behold the man, whose name is the Branch." It was "this man." And God said, "Awake, O sword, against my Shepherd and against the man that is my fellow." It was "this man." For "this man" was absolutely without a parallel. In His Birth He stood distinguished from all the human race beside. At the birth of whatever being did the heavens assume a new star? And here also the angels appeared to the shepherds: and a multitude of the heavenly host sang "Peace on earth, goodwill towards men." Wise men came from the east to worship Him. The spirit of prophecy again descends, and the power of miracles is again displayed when the Holy Child Jesus is born. In Him was no original corruption, "He did no sin, neither was guile found in his mouth." The prince of this world found nothing in Him." He fulfilled all righteousness. "He was the image of the invisible God, the first born of every creature, the brightness of His glory and the express image of His person." Angels are indeed sinless, but "this man" was made so much better than the angels, as He hath by inheritance obtained a more excellent name than they. For unto which of the angels said He at any time, "Thou art my son, this day have I begotten thee. And again, I will be to Him a Father, and He shall be to me a son. And again, when He bringeth in the first begotten into the world, He saith, And let all the angels of God worship Him." And of the angels He saith, "Who maketh His angels spirits, and His ministers a flame of fire; but unto the Son He saith, Thy throne, O God, is for ever and ever." "In Him dwelleth all the fulness of the Godhead bodily."

I wish you to notice, that without admitting the Deity and humanity of the Son of God, it would be impossible to explain the divinity of attributes and actions ascribed to Him in the Scriptures, for you will there find that many things are spoken of Him, some referring to His humanity, and others to His divinity, but both of the same person. We might refer to two or three passages only. "A virgin shall conceive and bear a Son, and they shall call His name Immanuel, which being interpreted is, God with us." "Unto us a Child is born, unto us a Son is given, and the Government shall be upon His shoulders, and His name shall be called Wonderful, Counsellor, the Mighty God, the everlasting Father, the Prince of peace." He was born in Bethlehem, and yet is the Maker of all things. It was prophesied concerning Him, "Thou Bethlehem Ephratah, though thou be little among the thousands of Judah, yet out of thee shall He come forth unto me that is to be ruler in Israel; whose goings forth have been from of old, from everlasting." And says the sacred historian, "We beheld His glory, the glory as of the only begotten of the Father full of grace and truth." If it be said that His humanity is much more mentioned than His divinity in the New Testament, we see that our principal concern lies in that nature which He voluntarily assumed, for unless He had been made like unto us, He could not be our surety; He could not go before us in the paths of obedience and suffering. Without this He could not from experience sympathise with us in our woes, have gained our confidence, and given His life a ransom for us, or put away sin by the sacrifice of Himself. Therefore, says the Apostle, "Because the children were partakers of flesh and blood He also Himself took part of the same." "For He verily took not on Him the nature of angels, but the seed of Abraham. Wherefore in all things it behoved Him to be made like unto His brethren, that He might be a faithful high priest in things pertaining to God, to make reconciliation for the sins of the people." These, brethren, are the true sayings of God, and without the admission of this doctrine we find nothing in the Gospel to meet our state as sinners. Then it is a doctrine according to Godliness. It purifies the heart by faith. Deny it, neglect it, or conceal it, and Christ will be a poor, empty Saviour to you, and you will be a poor, empty professor of His name. But Oh to be able to say with Dr. Watts,

> "While Jews on their own law rely,
> And Greeks of wisdom boast,
> I love the Incarnate mystery
> And there I fix my trust."

II. We proceed to consider HIS CONDUCT IN RECEIVING SINNERS. "This man receiveth sinners."

Here let us make three remarks. Whom does He receive? When does He receive them? and for what purpose?

First, Whom does He receive? Sinners. And all have sinned. "There is none righteous, no, not one." All have the same depraved nature, and "who can bring a clean thing out of an uuclean? Are all these equally wicked? A thousand things will diversify the degree and kinds of human guilt; therefore the Church says, in her confessions, "All we, like sheep, have gone astray; we have turned every one to his own way." Some are far more amiable, some are more moral than others. All this is to be commended as far as it goes; but as to spiritual capacity to enjoy or serve God in time or eternity, all are naturally on a level; therefore our Saviour said, "Ye must be born again." He does not speak this of a particular individual, but "Except a man"—that is all men, or every man—"be born again, he cannot see the kingdom of God." "If any man," says the apostle—you see he applies it universally—"If any man be in Christ he is a new creature; old things are passed away; behold all things are become new."

But now, though He receives sinners, He receives *convinced* sinners only. Let me explain, or this will be misunderstood and perverted. Though what we first said be true, it is not received by all. Men, so far from acknowledging the truth of it, say, "We are rich, and increased with goods, and stand in need of nothing," while indeed "they are poor, and blind and naked." Now, while this is the case, Christ can profit them nothing. And indeed they will have nothing to do with Him. No, till they are sick, they will not apply to the physician; till they are sensible of their danger, they will not be disposed to fly and "lay hold on the hope set before them;" till they feel their need, they will not be disposed to beg at the footstool of mercy; till they feel that they are sinners, and in the condition the Gospel supposes them to be, He cannot receive them. Not from any want of disposition on His part, but from want of disposition on their part. It is not necessary to recommend you to Him; He stands in need of no recommendation; but it is necessary to recommend Him to you. However poor, and needy, and wherever they may be, He receives all such that come unto Him, unless you can find any exception in such language as this: "Come unto me, and be ye saved, all the ends of the earth." "Ho, every one that thirsteth; come ye to the waters." Or here, "Whoever will, let him take the water of life freely." "Him that cometh unto me I will in no wise cast out." Whatever exceptions, therefore, any of you find, they are not found in the Book of God. There is, "no difference between the Jew and the Greek, for the same Lord is rich unto all them that call upon Him in truth."

In acts of grace amongst men there are commonly limitations. The ringleaders generally are executed; their escape is deemed incompatible with the safety of the State. But hear Paul: "This is a faithful saying and worthy of all acceptation, that Christ Jesus came into the world to save sinners, of whom I am chief." I am the ringleader, and have been so in all the persecutions against the saints, "yet I obtained mercy." For what purpose? That it might be concealed? No, but, "that in me first Jesus Christ might shew forth all longsuffering, for a pattern to them which should hereafter believe on Him to life everlasting." He receives great sinners—sinners without exception. "Come now and let us reason together, saith the Lord; though your sins be as scarlet, they shall be as snow, though they be red like crimson they shall be as wool." See what He has done. Manassah, proverbial for his wickedness, was saved. His very murderers are pardoned and sanctified. Read the Epistle to the Corinthians for a catalogue of sinners, concerning which we may say, the devil could neither have made them nor wished them worse than they were; "Yet" says he, "such were some of you, but ye are washed, but ye are sanctified, but ye are justified in the name of the Lord Jesus, and by the Spirit of our God."

Can an old sinner, then, be received by Him? Such a one is in an awful condition indeed; but there have been some saved even at the eleventh hour. And can backsliding sinners be saved? Those who have "tasted that the Lord is gracious," and been made to see and feel what an evil and bitter thing it is to sin against God? Oh, yes. Hear the exhortation and the promise! "O Israel return unto the Lord thy God; for thou hast fallen by thine iniquity. Take with you words, and turn to the Lord: say unto Him, Take away all iniquity, and receive me graciously . . . . . I will heal their backsliding, I will love them freely: for mine anger is turned away from him."

Secondly, let us enquire *when* He receiveth sinners? When Isaiah says, "Seek ye the Lord while He may be found," it clearly supposes that there are cases in which He is *not* to be found; and God Himself shews us that His patience will not last for ever; that His longsuffering has its bounds; that His pity is not weakness; that Jesus is not only "The Lamb of God," but also "The Lion of the Tribe of Judah." Yes, says He, and how awful is the representation ! "Then shall they call upon Me, and I will not answer; they shall seek me early, but shall not find Me. For that they hated knowledge and did not choose the fear of the Lord; they would none of My counsel; they despised all my reproof: therefore shall they eat of the fruit of their own way, and be filled with their own devices." "Now," says the Apostle—mark the emphasis—"*Now* is the accepted time," that is, the time in which persons may obtain acceptance. "He receiveth sinners" in time, not in eternity, and Oh, the vast difference between time and eternity; the one is the reign of grace, the other is the wages of sin; the one is a state of trial, the other a state of retribution; the one is a period for sowing, the other is the time for reaping. As says the Apostle, "Be not deceived; God is not mocked, for whatsoever a man soweth, that shall he also reap. He that soweth to the flesh shall of the flesh reap corruption. He that soweth to the Spirit, shall of the Spirit reap life everlasting." But in every age of the world "He receiveth sinners," and what an immense multitude must He have received during the patriarchal age, under the law and the prophets, and especially under the Gospel dispensation! How many must He receive, and will He receive in the future ages of the Church, when "a nation shall be born in a day;" when "He shall sprinkle many nations;" when "all nations shall be blessed in Him."

"He receiveth sinners" in every period of human life. God says, "My Spirit shall not always strive with man;" and it is certain there are favourable opportunities which may never return.

When Felix heard Paul reasoning "of righteousness, temperance, and a judgment to come," he trembled; but instead of cherishing his convictions, he sends the Apostle off, saying, "Go thy way for this time; when I have a more convenient season I will call for thee." He saw the Apostle several times afterwards, and heard him speak of the faith in Christ, but we read no more of his conviction; this seems to have ceased for ever. But in a general way, enough is said to encourage all; so that we may take up the words of Watts,

"While the Lamp holds out to burn,
The vilest sinner may return."

Beware then of sinking into despair; I believe it has destroyed more than presumption has. Despair paralyses the soul, and blocks up the way of life; yea, it locks the door, and flings the key into the bottomless pit. "We are saved by hope." Blessed are they who are enabled to exercise "hope in God, and faith in our Lord Jesus Christ."

Thirdly, let us observe *for what purpose "He receiveth sinners."* He receives them, not that they may remain as they are, but that He may make them what they must be, before they are eternally happy. The change wrought in them is variously set forth in the Scriptures of truth. Sometimes the reference is to the body, from its various disorders; then it is said "The eyes of the blind shall be opened, and the ears of the deaf shall be unstopped: Then shall the lame man leap as an hart, and the tongue of the dumb sing, for in the wilderness shall waters break out, and streams in the desert." Sometimes to the culture of the earth, and then "the wilderness and the solitary place shall be glad for them, and the desert shall rejoice and blossom as the rose." Then "they shall go out with joy and be led forth with peace; the mountains and the hills shall break forth into singing, and all the trees of the field shall clap their hands. Instead of the thorn shall come up the fir tree, and instead of the briar shall come up the myrtle tree; and it shall be to the Lord for a name, for an everlasting sign that shall not be cut off."

"He receiveth them" to *absolve* them, for "In Him they

have redemption through His blood." "By Him all who believe are justified. Oh, what can a man do in order to be delivered from this burden which is too heavy for him to bear? He need do nothing, he can do nothing, but come to Jesus who will deliver him from it. But this we must do; this deliverance we must obtain. How otherwise could he run in the way of God's commandments with enlargedness of heart, or "go on his way rejoicing"? Come, therefore, believer, and hear Him say, "Thy sins which are many are all forgiven thee." "Blessed is the man whose transgressions are forgiven, whose sin is covered! Blessed is the man unto whom the Lord imputeth not iniquity."

He also "receiveth sinners" to *sanctify* them. "He gave Himself for us, that He might redeem us from all iniquity," "to sanctify unto Himself a peculiar people, zealous of good works." "If I wash thee not," said he to Peter, "thou hast no part with me." Heaven itself would be no heaven to you while you are in an unregenerated state. To suppose that you could go to heaven while you love sin and walk "according to the course of this world" is contrary to common sense, and is blasphemy against every chapter of this holy Book, for "the unrighteous shall not inherit the kingdom of God." "If any man have not the Spirit of Christ, he is none of His." It is very true that "there is no condemnation to them that are in Christ Jesus," but then they "walk not after the flesh, but after the Spirit." "The water that I shall give him shall be in him a well of water springing up into everlasting life."

He "receiveth sinners" to *teach* them. "Come," says He, "sit at my feet and hear my words, and I will make you wise, wise unto salvation." "In Him are hid all the treasures of wisdom and knowledge." "Learn of me," says He, "for I am meek and lowly in heart, I will come down to your comprehension, I will teach you as you are able to bear it; I will not upbraid you with your ignorance, but will repeat my lessons and will give you line upon line, and precept upon precept." And none teacheth like Him; He can give not only the lesson but the faculty of learning it. He can make the blind to see, the deaf to hear, the dead to arise.

And He "receiveth sinners" to *protect* them. May a poor weak, feeble creature, surrounded by enemies subtle and strong—which are not the less dangerous because they are invisible—may such an one trust in His name? He may. He says to him as David said to Abiather, "Abide thou with me; fear not, for he that seeketh my life seeketh thy life: but with me thou shalt be in safeguard." Oh, yes, He is the stronghold in the day of trouble, flee to Him therefore to lay hold upon the hope set before you in the Gospel, and you will be perfectly safe in the midst of danger.

> "More happy but not more secure
> The glorified spirits in Heaven."

Lastly, He receiveth sinners to *glorify* them. He will give them a victory over death and the grave, and bring them nearer the throne than even the angels. He will confess them before His Father and before His angels and an assembled world; He will say, "Come, ye blessed of my Father; inherit the kingdom prepared for you from the foundation of the world." "Well done, good and faithful servant, thou hast been faithful over a few things, I will make thee ruler over many things; enter thou into the joy of thy Lord."

Well, what is the use we are to make of this truth?

You see, first, *how worthy He is of our admiration and praise.* Survey His majesty and then reflect upon His condescension. See Him who was in the form of God taking upon Himself the form of a servant. Behold "the grace of our Lord Jesus Christ, that though He was rich, yet for our sakes He became poor, that we through His poverty might be rich," and who died that you might live. Among men love always commences from some real or supposed excellence in the object. The apostle therefore says, "Scarcely for a righteous man will one die; yet peradventure for a good man some would even dare to die. But God commendeth His love towards us, in that while we were yet sinners Christ died for us." We were not worthy of the least of all His mercies. Our desert was on the other side, we deserved that His wrath should come upon us to the uttermost, as children of disobedience. But He not only spared us, but invited us to come to Him, showing Himself willing to receive us, and to bless us with all spiritual blessings in Christ Jesus. What are all human benefactors compared to Him? The liberality of a Thornton and a benevolence of a Howard are but as a drop to the ocean in comparison of His.

Then, secondly, *what think you of the baseness of His enemies?* "These should make war with the Lamb, and the Lamb should overcome them, for He is King of kings and Lord of lords." Not only may we rank among His enemies such men as Herod, Belshazzar, and Pharoah, but all who neglected to seek His favour, all who opposed Him. Yea, the Saviour hath said, "He that is not for me, is against me; and he who gathereth not with me, scattereth abroad." When we consider His greatness and goodness combined, and reflect upon what He has done and suffered, upon what He is now doing and ready to do, is it not surprising that we should not love Him more and serve Him better than we do? How shall we escape if we neglect so great salvation? "If any man love not our Lord Jesus Christ, let him be anathema maranatha." And no doubt greater condemnation will be experienced from the rejection of the Gospel, than from the transgression of the law.

Then, thirdly, *Here is encouragement for all.* In coming to God we need a mediator, but not in coming to Christ; we may come immediately to Him. If you were required to render yourself more worthy previously to coming to Him, this might well discourage you. But you must come as a sinner, as guilty, and as unworthy of His notice. Come, as polluted, to the fountain opened for sin and uncleanness, to Him who can cleanse your spotted souls from crimes of deepest dye. Come ye who are exposed to the wrath of God, and shelter yourselves in Him, and then rejoice in the declaration, "There is no condemnation to them who are in Christ Jesus, who walk not after the flesh, but after the spirit."

Lastly, "*Be ye followers of Christ as dear children.*" "Condescend to men of low estate; rejoice with those who do rejoice, and weep with those that weep." Like Him, be the friend of sinners. Sinners are the greatest subjects of your compassion. May you hate their sins, but love their souls! Pray for them. Do not treat them as the Pharisees of old did, with contempt, and insolence, who said, Come not near me, I am holier than thou. Do not avoid intercourse with them, if duty or kindness call you, for otherwise you only run into danger, and you are to watch and pray that you enter not into temptation. You are always to remember that there is a difference between the Saviour and you in this respect. He had nothing inflammable in Him, but as you have so much tinder, the neighbourhood of sparks will always be dangerous to you. But if duty and kindness call you, stand not aloof, employ what influence you can for their good; follow His bright example who went about doing good, and know that "he who converteth a sinner from the error of his way shall save a soul from death, and shall hide a multitude of sins."

XV.

THE FATHER'S LOVE FOR THE SON.

(Preached on Sunday Evening, June 28th, 1846.)

The Father loveth the Son, and hath given all things into His hand.—JOHN iii 35.

THESE are the words of John; not the Apostle, but John the forerunner of the Messiah. John was a very distinguished character; he was prophesied of five hundred years before he was born. After a long seclusion from the world, and a holy training, he appeared in the wilderness of Judæa, crying out "Repent ye, for the kingdom of heaven is at hand." He not only announced the coming of Christ, but had the honour of introducing Him personally to the people, saying, "Behold the Lamb of God which taketh away the sins of the world." He had also the honour of baptizing Him. But John was good as he was great. We can hardly find an instance of humility, of self-denial, and of pure zeal that would exceed his. The disciples of John, seeing the Saviour rise into respectability and popularity, grew jealous of Him, and therefore with long faces came and said unto Him, "Rabbi, he that was with thee beyond Jordan, to whom thou barest witness, behold, the same baptizeth, and all men come to him." But what was a source of grief to them, was a source of pure joy to him." "I am glad of it," John answered; "A man can receive nothing, except it be given him from heaven. He must increase, but I must decrease." And then, not only speaking of grandeur, but whence it is derived, he says, "He that cometh from above, is above all . . . and what He hath seen and heard, that He testifieth, and no man receiveth His testimony. He that receiveth this testimony hath set to his seal that God is true. For He whom God hath sent speaketh the words of God: for God giveth not the Spirit by measure unto Him." "The Father loveth the Son, and hath given all things into His hand."

Two things, therefore, appear to come before us. The love of the Father, this is the first: "The Father loveth the Son." And secondly, the riches of the Son: "and hath given all things into His hand."

I. We consider THE LOVE OF THE FATHER.

I think it may be necessary to observe four things with regard to this love.

First, its *object*. "God is good to all, and His tender mercies are over all His works." "The eyes of all wait upon Him, He openeth His hand and satisfieth the desire of every living thing." Thus He regards all men, and provides for their support. There is also in God a love of benevolence; this regards man as a fallen creature, at once "miserable and blind and naked." The love of God appears in His redemption, pardon, and sanctification. There is in God also a love of complacency; thus He regards man as a changed and renewed creature, "for what fellowship hath light with darkness? And how can two walk together except they be agreed." But God loves regenerate men, and beholds them with approbation and delight; "He takes pleasure in them that fear Him, in those that hope in His mercy." He loves angels as holy beings that never offended, who always "do His will, hearkening to the voice of His word." Thus He loves the Son, only in a higher and infinitely greater degree; for it is impossible for words to express, or imagination to conceive, the satisfaction He takes in the Son of His love.

Observe, secondly, the *grounds* of this love. One of these is *likeness*. There is a degree of resemblance in every Christian; therefore Christians are said to be partakers of the divine nature, and to "be renewed in the image of Him that created them, in righteousness and true holiness." But how much depravity is there in the holiest man upon earth! This is indeed their burden; this makes them moan and groan, saying' "O wretched man that I am!" But in the Son there is nothing of this. The prince of this world came, but found nothing in Him. If you would know what God is, go and behold Him in the person of His Son, "who is the brightness of the Father's glory, and the express image of His person."

Another of these grounds is *obedience to His will*. Hence in the eighth chapter of this Gospel, He says, "He that sent me is with me; the Father hath not left me alone, for I do always those things which please Him." Yea, this obedience was cheerful. He could say, "My meat is to do the will of my Father which is in heaven, and to finish His work." He could say, "I delight to do Thy will, O God; yea, thy law is within my heart." This obedience was invariably exercised, even when it required Him to be "a man of sorrows, and acquainted with grief," to bear "the contradiction of sinners against Himself;" to agonize in the garden, and to bleed upon the cross. "Arise," said He, "let us go hence," that is, to suffer and to die. "Father," said He, "if it be possible, let this cup pass from me: nevertheless not my will, but Thine be done." He could therefore say as He approached the end of life, with regard to every moment of His existence, with regard to every word, action, thought, or imagination of heart, "Father I have glorified Thee on the earth; I have finished the work which Thou gavest me to do."

Another ground of His love was *the sacrifice He made of Himself for sinners.* He therefore says, "Therefore doth my Father love me, because I lay down my life for the sheep." Does the Father love the Son because of this? How, then does the Father Himself love sinners, when He loved the Saviour for dying for them! There are some who seem to think the Father had no love towards a guilty world till the Saviour produced and procured it, not considering that "all things are of God," who hath reconciled the world unto Himself by the death of His Son; that "He hath made Him to be sin for us, who knew no sin, that we might be made the righteousness of God in Him;" that He hath called us with an holy calling; that "He justifies us freely by His grace; through the redemption which is in Christ Jesus." God takes pleasure in those of you who feed the hungry, who clothe the naked, who relieve the distressed, and who teach the ignorant, and He has told us that those "who turn many to righteousness shall shine as the stars for ever and ever." What, then, must be His love for His Son, the Ransomer of the world! What must be His love to Him, for all the millions He has redeemed and justified, sanctified, and saved!

"The Father loveth the Son." Consider, thirdly, the *evidence* of this love. The evidence of it turns upon His expressions; we often lay no stress upon these, as used by many, for they are not always to be depended upon. Judas, when he betrayed the Saviour, said, "Hail, Master; and kissed Him."

David said, "their words are smoother than oil, yet are they drawn swords." But God's language is true and righteous altogether. Therefore says He, "Behold my servant, whom I uphold; mine elect, in whom my soul delightest." At His baptism there was a voice saying, "This is my beloved Son in whom I am well pleased," and in the Transfiguration again there was a voice saying the same thing. Paul speaks of our "being delivered from the power of darkness, and translated into the kingdom of His dear Son." "Who was the only-begotten of the Father, full of grace and truth."

The evidence turns upon His reference to Him in all the arrangements He made previous to His birth. Was there a succession of prophets raised up from the first? "To Him gave all the prophets witness," and the testimony of Jesus was the spirit of prophecy. Were millions of sacrifices instituted? It was to prefigure Him. There was not a slaughtered bullock, nor a slain lamb, nor a loaf of shewbread, nor a particle of manna, nor a drop of water from the rock, but was intended to hold Him forth. Were there civil or sacred revolutions in states and churches? It was all for Him. "I will overturn, overturn, overturn, till He shall come whose right it is." "I will shake the heavens, and the earth, and the sea, and the dry land; and I will shake all nations, and the desire of all nations shall come; and I will fill His house with glory." Therefore the period of His incarnation is called "the fulness of time."

The evidence turns upon the personal honours that were shown Him when He was upon earth. God made a star in the east to go before the eastern Magi, till it went and stood over where the young child was. The angel of God appeared to the shepherds, and said, "Behold, I bring you good tidings which shall be to all people," "and the multitude of the heavenly host praised God, saying, Glory to God in the Highest, peace on earth and good-will to men." He dies, the heavens seem clothed in sackcloth; the sun hid his face; the earth shook and trembled; the rocks rent; the graves opened, and many of those who were dead appeared. He rises, and behold a God. "There was a great earthquake," the angel of the Lord again appeared, terrified the Roman guard, and said unto the women, "Fear not ye; for I know that ye seek Jesus which was crucified. He is not here: for He is risen, as He said. Come see the place where the Lord lay."

The evidence turns upon the exaltation to which He was advanced after death. You read, not only of the sufferings of

Christ, but of the glory that should follow, and who can describe, who can conceive what this is? There were conquerors before Him, but what victor ever spoiled principalities and powers? But this ruler triumphed over them on the cross. There have been many raised from degradation to splendour and eminence. God chose David from following the sheep "to feed Jacob His people, and Israel His inheritance." But in regard to Jesus, we behold a babe lying in a manger; we see "a man of sorrows and acquainted with grief;" we view Him expiring on the cross between two thieves, and the next thing we see is His ascending "up far above all heavens that He may fill all things;" and it is the will of God "That all men should honour the Son, even as they honour the Father which hath sent Him."

The evidence appears also in the appointment concerning Him in our worship, namely, that we should always, if we would be heard, pray in His name and for His sake. This looks like honour done Him indeed. What a proof of the King's regard would it be, for him to say to any, when they applied to him, "Remind me of such and such an one, and you shall receive; or let him plead for you, for I cannot, and will not refuse you anything that he may desire for you." So God said to the erring friends of Job, "My servant Job shall pray for you, for him will I accept." And the promise is, "Whatsoever ye shall ask the Father in my name, He will do it." And, O Christians, you have often addressed His throne; be more importunate in future. "Hitherto," said the Saviour, "ye have asked nothing in my name; ask and ye shall receive, that your joy may be full."

Let us now observe the use we should make of this love; for if the Father loveth the Son, let us love Him also, and so be followers of Him as dear children. Do you hate sin, and all sin? Do you love the ways of God? Do you love Him whom He delights to honour above all things in the universe? Does the Father see so much to love in Him, and do you see nothing to admire? How blind must you be, if you see "no form or comeliness in Him who is the altogether lovely!" What says the Apostle? "If any man love not the Lord Jesus Christ, let him be anathema, maranatha." Who, you say, does not love Him? Who *does?* If you love Him, you will resemble Him, you will be concerned to honour Him.

Then again, let us seek an union with Him, and we shall share in the same love. And what are we that we should be loved of God? Paul said, "that I may be found in Him." He knew that if he were found in Him, he should be accepted of God; that he should stand in the same relationship with Christ; that he should be a child of God, and if a child then an heir, an heir of God, and a joint-heir with Christ. Hence Our Saviour in His intercessory prayer says, "That the love wherewith Thou hast loved me may be in them, and I in them."

II. Let us consider THE RICHES OF HIS SON. "And hath given all things into His hands." Love is always generous; it delights to favour its object. But here is a love that makes its object a present of the universe. "Herein is love." How far does this universality extend? There are two other passages of Scripture which may throw light upon it, and it is well for us to compare spiritual things with spiritual. One is the language of the Saviour, where He says, "All power is given me in heaven and in earth." The other is the language of the Apostle, who says that "God raised Him up from the dead and gave Him glory." And again, "He raised Him from the dead, and set Him at His own right hand in the heavenly places, far above all principality and power and might and dominion."

We are accustomed to a twofold distinction, and to speak of nature and providence, grace and glory. Now, though these approximate to each other, yet they are distinct enough to furnish us with separate remarks.

"He hath given all things into His hand," all things in nature. This is much more true of the second Adam than of the first. "Thou madest Him to have dominion over the works of Thy hands; Thou hast put all things under His feet: all sheep and oxen, yea, and the beasts of the field; the fowl of the air, and the fish of the sea, and whatsoever passeth through the paths of the seas." It is said, "In His days shall the righteous flourish." And whose is the silver and the gold, and the cattle upon a thousand hills? "Why, the world is His, and the fulness thereof." He removeth Kings and setteth up Kings; yea, "He is the King of Kings, and Lord of Lords." All things are subservient to His designs. "He doeth all things after the counsel of His own will, and He is head over all things to His Church. The dispensation of the Spirit is His, and all spiritual blessings come to us through Him.

Now, what is the conclusion that should be drawn from this subject? Let us resign our spirits and all we possess into His hands. The Apostle says of the Corinthians, "They gave themselves unto the Lord." Where could they be so safe? Paul had done this; he knew that would be safe which he had committed unto Him against that day. You should resign yourselves into His hands, to glorify Him; and you should be willing for Him to choose your inheritance for you,—

"Pleased with all the Lord provides;
Weaned from all the world besides."

Then, let those who love the Lord rejoice in the prosperity of His cause. Love sympathizes with its object, weeping when it weeps, and rejoicing when it rejoices. You will therefore weep as you view the Saviour suffering, and hear Him blasphemed by sinners, and will rejoice to see the reproach rolled away from Him.

How able is He to fulfil His promise! How able to deliver you, and to make all things work together for your good! Why then will you faint or fear? He who has all things in His hand careth for you, and will never suffer you to want any good thing.

Finally, let those tremble who are His enemies. "The nations and the kingdoms that will not serve Me," saith God, "shall perish." "Bring hither my enemies that would not that I should reign over them, and slay them before my face." "These shall make war with the Lamb, but the Lamb shall overcome them, for He is King of Kings and Lord of Lords." Resistance, therefore, is vain, but submission is not. "Kiss the Son, lest He be angry, and ye perish from the way when His wrath is kindled but a little. Blessed are all they that put their trust in Him."

XVI.

THE BELIEVER'S DELIVERANCE FROM DEATH.

(Preached on Sunday Evening, May 17th, 1846.)

He that believeth in me, though he were dead, yet shall he live.—JOHN xi. 25.

THESE are the words of our Lord addressed to Martha on a memorable occasion. Jesus loved her brother Lazarus, yet suffered him to be sick, and when informed of his sickness, instead of hastening immediately to his relief, or at least to sympathise with his afflicted sisters, He remained still in the same place where He was. At length, Jesus determined on going to Bethany, telling His disciples plainly that Lazarus was dead, adding, "I am glad for your sakes that I was not there, to the intent that ye might believe; nevertheless let us go unto him." Go unto a dead man, pay him a visit! "Then when Jesus came, He found that he had lain in the grave four days already. Now Bethany was nigh unto Jerusalem about fifteen furlongs off: and many of the Jews came to Martha and Mary, to comfort them concerning their brother. Then Martha, as soon as she heard that Jesus was coming, went and met Him; but Mary sat still in the house. Then said Martha unto Jesus, "Lord, if Thou hadst been here, my brother had not died." This was a kind of reflection upon our Saviour for His absence, or His late arrival. But Martha had faith as well as infirmity. Hear her confidence in His power with God. "But I know, that even now, whatsoever Thou wilt ask of God, God will give it Thee." "Jesus saith unto her, Thy brother shall rise again." Martha said unto Him, I know that he shall rise again in the resurrection at the last day. Jesus said unto her, "I am the resurrection and the life: he that believeth in me, though he were dead, yet shall he live." "Hereafter, when all the dead shall rise, they will rise because I shall be there, and I am here now, the same personage, the same yesterday, to-day, and for ever, and what I shall do then I can do now."

We have here to review, to improve, and to explain three things: *A character*, "He that believeth in me;" *A supposition*, "though he were dead;" *A privilege*, "Yet shall he live."

I. A CHARACTER. "He that believeth in me."

The subjects of divine grace are frequently and variously described by the sacred writers, to show us who are the heirs of promise, and to enable us to compare their character with our own. Happy will it be for us if, after examination, we find that we are of the same species; that we are walking in the same way, though we may not be able to walk the same pace! They are called "righteous," "pure in heart," "spiritually minded;" they reckon themselves to be "dead indeed unto sin, but alive unto righteousness." But more commonly you find them characterised as "believers." "The multitude of them that believed were of one heart and of one mind." We are not of them that draw back unto perdition, but of them that believe to the saving of the soul." "That in me first Jesus Christ might shew forth all longsuffering, for a pattern to them that should hereafter believe on Him to life everlasting."

But it would be endless to quote all the passages used to set forth Christians under this character. We would therefore only observe that by a figure of speech faith is often used in Scripture for the whole of Christianity. Thus it expresses the whole by a part, but then it is a very essential part, and a very distinguishing part. This is the case with regard to faith, for there is nothing so important, nothing so influential. Faith takes the lead of everything in religion. Whatever may be the branches, this is the root. Whatever be the streams, this is the fountain. "Without faith it is impossible to please God." Without faith, the Scripture, true as it is in itself, would be a mere nonentity. There are indeed threatenings, but how could they alarm us, unless we believed them? There are promises, but how can they encourage us without faith? How can the Word profit us unless it be mixed with faith? It worketh indeed effectually, but it is in them that believe. We are "justified by faith." "We walk by faith." "By faith we overcome the world." So we read of "the good fight of faith;" of "the trial of our faith;" our "work of faith."

But faith, we observe, has peculiarly to do with the Lord Jesus. Therefore He says, "he that believeth *on* me." I believe Paul, I believe Peter, but I do not believe *on* or *in* either of them; yet says John, "He that believeth on the Son hath everlasting life;" and says our Saviour, "He that believeth on me shall never come into condemnation."

The Scriptures never hold forth faith in the nakedness of metaphysical abstraction, but clothe it with attributes and actions. In order that we may know what faith is, they tell us what faith does. So faith has peculiarly to do with Christ. The Christian believes that Jesus is the only Mediator between God and man, that there is salvation in no other; that He is "the Lord our Righteousness;" that as He is Mighty to save, so He is willing. This is not only his credence and opinion, but his conviction. Then he gives his consent, as well as his assent, to the way and manner of salvation. "The devils believe, and tremble." In the days of His flesh, they said, "We know Thee, who Thou art, the Holy One of God." Here was assent, but not consent; for they said "let us alone." In his epistle to the Romans the apostle says, "with the heart, man believeth unto righteousness." "Oh," says the Sandemanian, whose faith is mere assent, "the heart here intends the understanding." Why, then, did not the Apostle use the word understanding? Surely he had reason to employ the word heart. He here feels a complacency and delight; this is the case with every believer; he not only submits to the thing from necessity, though this is true, for there is no other way, but if there were a thousand other ways, he would turn his back upon them all, and say, "that I may be found in Him, not having mine own righteousness, which is of the law, but the righteousness which is of Christ by faith." "That I may know Him, and the power of His resurrection, and the fellowship of His sufferings, being made conformable unto his death." There is another thing which will necessarily result from the former, for, if I am persuaded that He is the only Saviour, in whom is plenteous redemption, and if I love His salvation, the nature of it, as it is holy, and the manner of it, as it is free and gracious, I shall repair to Him. Faith accordingly is represented by various actions, but all these terminate in Him. Sometimes it is the action of the eye; then believing is seeing, for we look unto Jesus. Sometimes the action is derived from the hand, and then believing is receiving: so we are said to "receive Christ Jesus the Lord." Sometimes the action is derived from the mouth; then faith in Him is eating, to use the language of Scripture, but it is the flesh of the Son of God, and thus His "flesh is meat indeed, and His blood is drink indeed." Sometimes the action is derived from the foot; then believing is coming to Him; "he that cometh to me, I will in no wise cast out." Verily, then, faith is the movement of a soul entirely to Christ, to deal with Him alone in all the concerns of our salvation. "Lord, I am a lost creature, perishing and helpless, but my hope is in Thee; save, Lord, or I perish; God be merciful to me a sinner, and by Thy Spirit lead me into all truth. Be Thou my Prophet, Priest, and King; be Thou my Shepherd, tell me where thou makest thy flock to rest at noon." Christ is now their foundation, their rest, their all to their soul; and, brethren, this is the application we make to Him, not only at the commencement of our Christian course, but all through life; therefore the Apostle Peter says, "To whom *coming* as unto a living stone." Coming to Him, in death, as well as life.

II. Let us pass from the *character*, to notice secondly THE SUPPOSITION. "He that believeth in me, though he were dead."

What is it to die? This is a question to which no answer can be obtained from experience, for, as Blair says, "none ever returned to blab the secret out." When we die there is an exclusion of all the things below the sun. It is a breaking up of the ties that unite husband and wife, parent and child, brother and sister, and the reducing us to new affinities, where we say "to corruption, Thou art my father: to the worm, Thou art my mother and my sister." It is a weakening our strength in the way, the consuming our beauty as the moth, and the wasting and decaying of that fine piece of divine workmanship, the human frame; so that however endeared before our connection may be, we are compelled to say, "Bury my dead out of my sight." It is an entrance and introduction into another world, called "the world to come."

"He that believeth on me, though he were *dead*." The supposition here is not to question the thing, but to affirm it. "It is appointed," says the Apostle, "unto men once to die." It is commonly quoted, "unto *all*," but *all* is not in the text. Yet "who is he that liveth and shall not see death?" The young? But the young die as well as the old. The rich? But the rich die as well as the poor. The righteous? But the righteous die as well as the wicked. Solomon therefore says, "there is one event with regard to the righteous and to the wicked."

And you will observe, that there is not only one event, as to the reality, but also as to the circumstances connected with death. So you see the righteous may die from home as well as the wicked. The righteous may die suddenly as well as the wicked. The righteous may die by accident, or by fever, or by dropsy, or by violence, as well as the wicked.

"He that believeth on me, though he were *dead*;" and he may die, he will die, he must die as well as others, but he will not die *like* others. Here is the distinction. Solomon remarks this, and says, "The wicked is driven away in his wickedness, but the righteous hath hope in his death." Even Balaam could make this distinction, and therefore said, "How goodly are thy tents, O Jacob! and thy tabernacles, O Israel! Let me die the death of the righteous." Since Christ redeemed us from the curse of the law, being made a curse for us, some may be ready to wonder that He does not exempt His people from death. So He does, as to the penalty of it, for "there is no condemnation to them that are in Christ Jesus." So He does, if not as to the *stroke*, yet as to the sting. "O death, where is thy sting?" The sting of death is sin, but

> "If sin be pardoned, I'm secure,
> Death hath no sting beside;
> The law gave sin its damning power,
> But Christ, my ransom, died."

So He does, as to experience. He said to His hearers, "If any man keep my sayings, he shall never see death." *Not he!* He is indeed mortal; but when death comes to him, it comes so changed, so beautified, so beautifying, that he shall never see death. No, he shall "sleep in Jesus," he shall "go home," he shall "depart to be with Christ, which is far better." Therefore "to die," says the Apostle, "is gain." But tongue cannot express, nor the imagination conceive, what believers gain by dying.

III. Pass we, therefore, from the Character and the Supposition to THE PRIVILEGE. "He that believeth on me, though he were dead, yet *shall he live*." And so he would, if he did not die. Death is not the extinction of existence, but only the termination of one mode of it, and the commencement of another. 'Tis the transition from a mortal to an immortal state of action; from a state of probation to a state of retribution. For when the dust returns to the earth as it was, "the spirit goes to God which gave it." After death is the judgment. When a man commits suicide, you are accustomed to say, "such a one has destroyed himself." This is very improper language: he has not destroyed himself; he cannot destroy himself; he may take the pistol and blow his body to pieces—so the house is destroyed; where is the inhabitant? In the grasp of God's mighty hand, and placed before His Tribunal. No, you cannot shake off existence. You may render it either a blessing or a curse, but you cannot terminate it. You may seek death, but death shall fly from you.

Then our Saviour must have intended something more than a continuance in existence. He refers to the *privilege* of existence. So says the Apostle, "Absent from the body, present with the Lord." "The body is dead, because of sin, but the spirit is life because of righteousness."

Our Saviour here does not refer to the intermediate state, but to the resurrection life; this is obvious from the whole connection. "Jesus saith unto her, thy brother shall rise again. Martha saith unto Him, I know that he shall rise again in the resurrection at the last day. Jesus saith unto her, I am the resurrection, and the life; he that believeth in me, though he were dead, yet shall he live;" he shall come to life, and live again as to his body. And will not others? Yes, they will thus rise, the wicked as well as the righteous. He does not, therefore, refer to the resurrection as being an universal event merely, but obviously as being a spiritual privilege. There will be, indeed, a resurrection of the body, both of the wicked and the righteous, "for all that are in their graves shall hear His voice, and shall come forth," "but some to the resurrection of life, and some to the resurrection of damnation." Is this a privilege? Some will rise to everlasting contempt. Will this be a privilege? What does the Apostle mean when he says, "If by any means I might attain unto the resurrection of the dead," but the blissful resurrection? What means David when he says, "I shall be satisfied, when I awake in Thy likeness?" What means Paul when he says, "The Lord, the Righteous Judge, shall give unto me a crown of glory in that day?" And what means our Saviour when He says, "They shall be recompensed at the resurrection of the just?" Thus, "though he were dead, yet shall he live."

He shall live embodied, as before, and as originally created. But his body will be improved, infinitely improved. "It is sown in corruption, it is raised in incorruption: it is sown in dishonour, it is raised in glory: it is sown in weakness, it is raised in power: it is sown a natural body, it is raised a spiritual body. Howbeit that was not first which is spiritual, but that which is natural; and afterward that which is spiritual. The first man is of the earth, earthy; the second man is the Lord from heaven. As is the earthy, such are they also that are earthy: and as is the heavenly, such are they also that are heavenly. And as we have borne the image of the earthy, we shall also bear the image of the heavenly." And this is the model of the Christian's spiritual body, for "we look for the Saviour, the Lord Jesus Christ, who shall change our vile body, and fashion it like unto His own glorious body." Thus "he that believeth in me, though he were dead, yet shall he live." Oh, how superior will that life be to that which he now possesses! How superior *locally!* for though heaven is *more* than a place, it is nothing *less* than a place. Our Saviour says, "I go to prepare a place for you." What a place must that be, which He is gone to prepare; which is to display the munificence of His fulness, and in which He is to dwell with them for ever! How superior *socially!* How few companions have we now! How intermixed is our state, how defective our connections! But then all will be wise, and good—patriarchs, prophets, apostles, and martyrs—all the best servants of God, and benefactors of man. How superior as to *enjoyment!* Here, every comfort has its cross; every pleasure has its pain. Nothing there shall be seen but joy and gladness, nothing heard but the voice of melody; for "when that which is perfect is come then that which is in part shall be done away." How superior as to *duration!* "Here we have no continuing city." "All, all on earth is shadow." But there, the laurels on the brow shall never wither. There the dwelling shall be "a house not made with hands." There the inheritance is eternal. There the Kingdom is everlasting. "But who is this that darkens counsel by words without knowledge?" We are expressly told that, "Eye hath not seen, nor ear heard, neither have entered into the heart of man the things which God hath prepared for them that love Him." No, we have no image proper enough to express it; no medium through which adequately to describe it; no powers to bear the disclosure; the lustre would be too much for the eye, the melody too much for the ear; our poor weak frames would break down under that "exceeding weight of glory."

Finally, How happy are they who believe in Christ! They can never be in a desperate state, let their state be what it will.

"Though they fall, they shall not be utterly cast down, for the Lord upholdeth them with His hand." Though the bush burn, it shall not be consumed. They can say in the language of triumph, "We are troubled on every side, yet not in despair; persecuted, but not forsaken; cast down, but not destroyed." Yea, though they *die*, yet shall they live. Let a worldly man be deprived of worldly enjoyments, and he cries with Micah, "They have taken away my gods, and what have I more?" But strip a Christian of this world's goods, and though he feels, yet he knows in himself that he has "in heaven a better and an enduring substance." Place him upon a bed of sickness, God comforts him there, and makes all his bed in his sickness. Throw him into prison, and he will with Paul and Silas sing praises to God, even at midnight. Follow him to the valley of the shadow of death; his Shepherd is with him there: "His rod, and His staff, they comfort him." Lay him in the grave; but says he, "He shall deliver my soul from the power of the grave." "Blessed are the people that are in such a case; yea, blessed are the people whose God is the Lord."

But in conclusion let me ask the question, "Dost thou believe on the Son of God?" This inquiry is important. Probably some of you will treat it with contempt and scorn. I hope, however, it will awaken a concern in your bosoms. And I think I hear some one say: "Oh, that I knew I was a believer in Christ, and could rejoice in hope of His glory. Lord, show me a token for good!" Now I would just give you two tokens. One is, if a concern about your soul produces much apprehension and anxiety; for this is not in you naturally. Bishop Hall says: "Though smoke is not fire, yet there is no fire without smoke; and though doubts, and fears, and anxiety, are not faith, yet they are the effects of it." Another token is, that if you believe in Him, He surely will be very endeared to your souls, for "to them that believe He is precious." How precious it is impossible to say: but to such He is "fairer than the children of men, yea, He is altogether lovely."

XVII.

ENSAMPLES RECORDED FOR OUR LEARNING.

(Preached on Sunday Evening, September 8th, 1844.)

Moreover, brethren, I would not that ye should be ignorant, how that all our fathers were under the cloud, and all passed through the sea; and were all baptized unto Moses in the cloud and in the sea; and did all eat the same spiritual meat; and did all drink the same spiritual drink; for they drank of that spiritual Rock that followed them: that Rock was Christ.—1 CORINTHIANS x. 1-4.

THE Apostle Paul was a man eminently wise, and would not that others should be ignorant. He therefore exhorts those to whom he wrote to prove all things and to hold fast that which is good. He would have you wise to that which is good, but simple concerning evil. He says, "In malice be ye children, but in understanding be ye men. I speak as unto wise men. For the soul to be without knowledge it is not good." It is like a ship without a compass, or a house without windows, or the body without mind. "Knowledge is power." For this maxim Lord Bacon has been much admired; but Solomon expressed the same sentiment ages before Bacon's cradle was made. Yea, he said more; he said, "Wisdom is *better* than strength." But it may be improperly as well as properly employed. We may injure, as well as benefit. We may diffuse error, as well as truth. We must always be careful, therefore, as to the subjects of our knowledge. To be ignorant of some things is a real privilege; and we may be safely ignorant of others. But there are some things which it is most desirable for us to know; which it is most important and most necessary for us to know. The very chief of these is to know Christ, whom to know is life eternal. And I hope there are not a few here this evening who can say with the Apostle Paul, "Yea, doubtless, and I count all things but loss for the excellence of the knowledge of Christ Jesus my Lord. Then there are many other things subordinate but which it is desirable should be known. Thus the Apostle would not have the Corinthians to be ignorant how that all their fathers were under the cloud; and all passed through the sea; "and were all baptized unto Moses in the cloud and in the sea, and did all eat the same spiritual meat, and did all drink the same spiritual drink, for they drank of that spiritual Rock that followed them, and that Rock was Christ."

Let us, then, advance two inquiries upon this text. The first is, *What* is it he would have them to know? And the second is, *Why* he would have them to know it.

I. *What is it he would have them to know?* "I would not that ye should be ignorant, how that all our fathers were under the cloud"—under the direction of which you are aware; under the direction of the fiery, cloudy pillar, which attended the Jews in all their journeys, the design of which was threefold:—

First, it was to be a *symbol of the Divine presence.* It was very desirable and necessary for them to know that God was with them and nigh to them in all that they would call upon Him for. And they had only to open their eyes at any time in order to see it. This phenomenon was clearly discernible by all; and its miraculous character could not be denied or questioned.

Secondly, it was to be a *defence.* It was therefore a pillar of fire by night, to lick up the unwholesome damps, and to cheer them in the darkness; while it was to be a pillar of cloud by day, like a large umbrella spreading over the whole camp to screen it from the scorching rays of the sun. This furnished David with his fine allusion when he said, "The sun shall not smite thee by day, nor the moon by night. The Lord shall preserve thee from all evil; He shall preserve thy soul."

Thirdly, it was to be their *conductor.* Thus the Psalmist says, "In the daytime also He led them with a cloud, and all the night with a light by fire." They had no map, and no road, and much depended upon their movements. This was not left to chance, nor to their own choice. As the cloud arose, they arose; as this turned to the right hand or to the left, they turned. As this rested, they rested. Sometimes it led them to a pleasant spot; sometimes to a trying station. Sometimes it continued for a week, or a month, or a year, and sometimes even more than a year. Thus it is said, God led them about,

He instructed them, He kept them as the apple of His eye. Thus He led them by a right way to a city of habitation; thus showing that He is to His people a suitable and all-sufficient relief. He affords them His special presence; He defends them from all harm; He guides them by His counsel, and will afterward receive them to glory. He will make darkness light before them, and crooked things straight; these things will He do unto them and not forsake them.

Another thing the Apostle would have them acquainted with was a marvellous salvation. "I would not that ye should be ignorant, how that all our fathers were under the cloud, and *all passed through the sea*, and were all baptized unto Moses in the cloud and in the sea." Observe, when the Jews left Egypt they soon got into a perilous condition. There were mountains on each side of them: if they turned back they would have had to encounter Pharoah with his armed host; if they moved on, the Red Sea was before them. In these trying circumstances, the people as usual began to murmur against Moses. "Because," said they, "there were no graves in Egypt, hast thou taken us away to die in the wilderness? Wherefore hast thou dealt thus with us, to carry us forth out of Egypt? Is not this the word that we did tell thee in Egypt, saying, let us alone that we may serve the Egyptians? For it had been better for us to serve the Egyptians, than that we should die in the wilderness." Moses felt a supernatural impulse, and said unto the people, "Fear ye not; stand still, and see the salvation of the Lord, which He will show you to-day: for the Egyptians whom ye have seen to-day, ye shall see them again no more for ever. The Lord shall fight for you, and ye shall hold your peace." But this assurance did not prevent him from calling upon God in this extremity; he had therefore recourse to prayer, and prayer is not to prevent action: therefore said God, "Wherefore criest thou unto Me? Speak unto the children of Israel that they go forward. But lift thou up thy rod, and stretch out thine hand over the sea to divide it, and the children of Israel shall go on dry ground through the midst of the sea." And we find that Moses did so, and the Lord caused the sea to go back by a strong east wind all that night, and made the sea dry land, and the waters were divided, "And the children of Israel went into the midst of the sea upon the dry ground; and the waters were a wall unto them on their right hand and on their left."

We may take three views of this passage. First, we may

view it as a *supernatural transaction.* I need not tell you what attempts have been made to set aside the miracle by our silly infidels, who would wish to make it appear that Moses availed himself of the knowledge he had of the ebbing of the tide. But did not the Egyptians know as well as Moses? But the thing is nowhere spoken of as gradual; but the waters suddenly subsided, and stood up as a wall on their right hand and on their left. It required strong faith in Moses and in the people to induce them to go forward, for how awful would it have been if the liquid walls should give way while they were in the midst of the sea, when they must have met with instant death! The Apostle therefore says, "By faith they passed through the Red Sea as by dry land; which the Egyptians, assaying to do, were drowned." For without full confidence in God they would not have taken a single step.

Secondly, we may view it as *an expression of Almighty power.* "Once have I heard this, yea, twice, that power belongeth unto God." It belonged to Him originally. Infinite power is His. There is no power but of God. He is the great Creator of all things, and He upholdeth all things. Once there was no earth and no sun: He spake and it was done; He commanded, and it stood fast. Sun, moon, and stars were by Him called into existence. He said, Let there be light; and there was light. And yet these "horns coming out of His hand," according to the Prophet, are only "the hidings of His power." And says Job, "These are parts of His ways; but how little a portion is heard of Him? but the thunder of His power who can understand?"

Thirdly, we may view it as *a seasonable deliverance in distress.* And this is the use the Church afterward frequently made of it when in danger. They said, "Awake, awake, put on strength, O arm of the Lord; awake as in the ancient days, in the generations of old. Art thou not it that hath cut Rahab and wounded the dragon? Art thou not it which hath dried the sea, the waters of the great deep; that hath made the depths of the sea a way for the ransomed to pass over?" Thus they were shown that nothing is too hard for the Lord; that He can always find a way for escape, or can make one; that our extremity is often His opportunity; and when all hope is taken away, He appears and secures undying glory to Himself.

II. Having seen what the Apostle would have the Corinthians to know, let us inquire

Secondly, *Why he would have them know it.* We cannot well be mistaken here, if we abide by the Apostle's own declaration, "I would not that ye should be ignorant, how that all our fathers were under the cloud, and all passed through the sea, and were all baptized unto Moses in the cloud and in the sea. And did all eat the same spiritual meat, and did all drink the same spiritual drink, for they drank of that spiritual Rock that followed them, and that *Rock was Christ.*"

The Apostle calls this meat and this drink "spiritual," by reason of their use and application; because they were typical of spiritual food; not because there was anything spiritual inherent in them, but because they were consecrated to the glory of God.

"But with many of them God was not well pleased, for they were overthrown in the wilderness. Now, these things were our examples, to the intent we should not lust after evil things as they also lusted. Neither be ye idolators, as were some of them; as it is written, the people sat down to eat and drink and rose up to play. Neither let us commit fornication, as some of them committed, and fell in one day three-and-twenty thousand. Neither let us tempt Christ, as some of them also tempted, and were destroyed of serpents. Neither murmur ye, as some of them also murmured and were destroyed of the destroyer." We see that notwithstanding all those means, and marvels, and miracles, with which they were favoured and distinguished, they lusted after evil things; they worshipped the calf; they committed fornication; they tempted Christ, and murmured against God. "Now all these things happened unto them for examples; and they are written for our admonition, upon whom the ends of the world are come. Wherefore, let him that thinketh he standeth take heed lest he fall."

Wherefore, as I perceive, he would not have them to be ignorant of this for four reasons:

First, *to show how ineffectual are the most powerful instrumentality and the most suitable means without the grace of God.* The rich man, in pleading for his brethren, said, "Let one go to them from the dead and they will repent, lest they also come to this place of torment;" but the answer was, "If they hear not Moses and the prophets, neither will they be persuaded though one rose from the dead." And how vain is it (as some do) to plead for the personal appearance of Christ to precede the conversion and return of the Jews, because, says one, "they are so inpenitent and unbelieving that nothing less will convert them!" Why, had they not miracles enough in Egypt? You know how our Saviour addressed them while upon earth. "You have seen Me," says He, "opening the eyes of the blind, unstopping the ears of the deaf, and raising the dead to life; you have seen Me moving about as the image of God; and what is the consequence? You have seen and hated both Me and my Father, and yet ye will not come unto Me." Let none look for extraordinary appearances, and entertain vain hopes, if their hearts are not made to yield by the ordinary instrumentalities employed by God. And in the diligent use of all the means of grace, let us learn to depend upon the influences of the Holy Spirit of God for their efficiency, seeing that Paul may plant, and Apollos may water, but God giveth the increase. Yea, persons may not only be witnesses of miracles, but they may be the subjects of miracles, and yet receive no saving change. Of the ten Lepers that were healed nine of them remained unconverted; *one* only returned to give glory to God. Yea, persons may not only have been witnesses of miracles, and subjects of miracles, but performers of them too, and still remain alienated from the life of God. Therefore our Saviour says, "Many will come unto Me in that day, saying, Lord, Lord, have we not prophesied in Thy name? and in Thy name have cast out devils? and in Thy name done many wonderful works? And then will I profess unto them, I never knew you; depart from me, ye that work iniquity." Have you never heard of robbers under the gallows? Have you never read an account of the earthquake that swallowed up Lisbon? It consisted of three successive shocks, and some little time only elapsed between each of them; yet during these little intervals some were running about for plunder, and even putting down their hands into the crevices of the earth, picking the pockets of those who were ingulfed below; and while some of these were thus committing sin, they also were hurried into the presence of Jehovah by another fearful shock.

Secondly, our text *should keep you from supposing that you stand in the Divine favour because of outward privileges.* You may possess a heritage of your own; you may have more than heart can wish of this world's goods; you may be blessed with affluence in regard to temporal blessings, and yet not be blessed with all spiritual blessings in Christ. You may be the children of pious parents—this is a great advantage—but the rich man in hell called Abraham, "Father." And our Saviour said to the Jews, "Many shall come from the east and the west, and shall sit down with Abraham, Isaac, and Jacob in the kingdom of heaven; *but the children of the kingdom* shall be cast out into outer darkness; *there shall be weeping and gnashing of teeth.*" You may have been baptized in your infancy, but this did not make you the children of God, or constitute you the heirs of glory. Yea, you may be immersed when you come to years of discretion, if ever you come to that age, and yet not be baptized unto Christ. Simon Magus was thus baptized, and yet was "in the gall of bitterness, and in the bond of iniquity." And how awful is the state of some who, though they have put on Jesus by public profession of His name, and have been baptized in the name of Christ, yet plainly show by their lives that their hearts are not right in the sight of God. Such do dishonour to the cause they have espoused, and God will surely visit them with His displeasure. What says God by the prophet Jeremiah? "Behold the days come, saith the Lord, that I will punish all them that are circumcised with the uncircumcised: Egypt, and Judah, and Edom, and the children of Ammon and Moab, and all that are in the utmost corners, that dwell in the wilderness, for all these nations are uncircumcised, and all the house of Israel are uncircumcised in the heart." Yea, they will be more punished upon this very ground. "Hear this word that the Lord hath spoken against you, O children of Israel, against the whole family which I brought up from the land of Egypt, saying, You only have I known of all the families of the earth, therefore will I punish you for all your iniquities."

Thirdly, our text *should keep you from concluding that you are in favour with God because you are indulged with providential mercies.* You may succeed in business; so did the man whose grounds brought forth plentifully, and who said to his soul, "Thou hast much goods laid up for many years; take thine ease, eat, drink, and be merry." So you may have a fixed and long share of health, and live without much trouble, while some of God's dear servants are made to possess months of vanity, and wearisome nights are appointed to them. "All things," says Solomon, "come alike to all; there is one event to the righteous and to the wicked. No man knoweth either love or hatred," that is, the love or hatred of God, "by all that is before him." His love or His anger cannot be known from any outward dispensation. It is not to be gathered from the book of Providence, but only from the book of God; and is to be judged of rather by your carriage toward God than by the estimation men in general may form of you.

Lastly, *partial and temporary religious impressions do not prove that you are in a state of salvation.* Israel at the Red Sea sang God's praises, but they soon forgot His works. At Horeb they said, "All that the Lord hath spoken we will do," but they worshipped the calf before Moses descended from the hill. The Apostle Peter speaks of some having escaped the pollutions of the world, but whose after conduct was worse than the beginning. "When He slew them," says the Psalmist, "then they sought Him; and they returned and inquired early after God." "They poured out a prayer when His chastening hand was upon them." It is the same with men now. When upon the bed of sickness, they acknowledge their guilt and pray to God and promise future amendment, but as soon as God says, "Return, ye children of men," they return again to folly. You may have another heart and not a new one. You may turn from error to orthodoxy, and not turn to the living and true God. Ephraim was a pleasant child, yet his goodness was as the morning cloud and the early dew which soon passeth away. "Let us, therefore, fear, lest a promise being left us of entering into His rest, any of you should seem to come short of it." Let us examine ourselves whether we be in the faith, let us prove ourselves and invite Divine scrutiny, and say, "Search me, O God, and know mine heart, prove me and know my ways; and see if there be any evil way in me, and lead me in the way everlasting." And may the grace of our Lord Jesus Christ, the love of God the Father, the communion and fellowship of the Holy Spirit, be with you and remain with you always. Amen.

XVIII.

OUR STATION AND OUR DUTY.

Do all things without murmurings and disputings: that ye may be blameless and harmless, the sons of God, without rebuke, in the midst of a crooked and perverse nation, among whom ye shine as lights in the world: holding forth the word of life.—PHILIPPIANS ii. 14, 15.

The Church at Philippi was formed by the Apostle Paul. Through his instrumentality a people were gathered from the world and formed into a Christian Church. After the Apostle left them, he continued to cherish the liveliest interest in this Church, and while at Rome he wrote them this instructive letter. Some imagine that the immediate cause of his writing this Epistle was to communicate to the temporal support of the poor saints belonging to this Church. But there are many passages in this Epistle in which we cannot but see the Apostle's anxiety for their *spiritual* prosperity. "God is my record," says he, "how greatly I long after you all in the bowels of Jesus Christ. And this I pray, that your love may abound yet more and more in knowledge and in all judgment."

He goes on in the same strain, and in this second chapter he says, "Fulfil ye my joy, that ye be likeminded, having the same love, being of one accord, of one mind, Let nothing be done through strife or vainglory; but in lowliness of mind let each esteem other better than themselves."

The words of our text also give expression to the same feeling. He was anxiously solicitous for their continual prosperity and usefulness, and union. We would invite your attention, first, to the Christian's station. The Church of Christ is placed as a light in the world. Secondly, to the Christian's duty: to shine. The Apostle says, "Holding forth the word of life; the sons of God, without rebuke."

I. We direct your attention to the CHRISTIAN'S STATION. The Church of Christ is placed as a light in the world.

The character of the world, as given in our text, is "crooked and perverse." The words here so translated convey an idea of moral obliquity. It is probable the primary reference was to the heathen by whom the Philippian Church was surrounded; but it describes the condition of unconverted men everywhere. It comprises everything that is in opposition to divine rectitude. We read that God made man upright—upright both in act and principle; but while God made man such, he himself wrought out many inventions. The Word of God is ever directing our attention to this state of things, as it now exists in our world, "All we like sheep have gone astray." "There is none righteous, no, not one."

Looking at the state of the world generally, I inquire what do the heathen know about God? What do they know of the spirituality of the Divine precepts—of the sanctity and extent of the Divine law—of the method of obtaining remission of sins through a Mediator—or what do they know of the certainty of the world to come? But look at home, and what does man know of God's purpose to save him only through a Mediator? We are aware this is part of the creed most men have in this professedly Christian country, but if it is a portion of light that has got into their intellect, it has not got into the heart, for they practically deny it. There are multitudes who seek to work out a plan of salvation of their own. They acknowledge that things are corrupt in this world; all, or nearly all, seem to admit that though things are not as they ought to be, yet imagine that by their own efforts they can set things right.

We fully admit that science and civilization have their use. These have done a great work, and probably are destined to do a great work in the world; but if you take science and civilization, and put them in the place of the sacred volume, you make them stand out of place. They must be servants of Revelation; apart from the cross they become useless. They must stand in the rear of Revelation, and never seek equality therewith. Some eighteen hundred years ago, they attempted in classic Greece what has been attempted at various periods and in various places since, to set crooked hearts, and crooked persons, and crooked things straight in this world; but they have always failed, as always human appliances must fail, when they neglect to acknowledge the pre-eminent importance of the Word of God.

The Apostle, in his Epistle to the Romans, has acknowledged this failure. "Professing themselves to be wise," says he, "they became fools, and changed the glory of the incorruptible God into an image made like to corruptible man, and to birds, and four-footed beasts, and creeping things. Wherefore God also gave them up to uncleanness through the lusts of their own hearts, to dishonour their own bodies between themselves: who changed the truth of God into a lie, and worshipped and served the creature more than the Creator." This is the necessary result. So far as the Gospel has spread and its renewing power felt in this world—wherever there is genuine Christianity, according to the extent thereof—it has purified the heart, the Church, and the community. What a different state of things exist there to what is observed elsewhere! Some tell us that Christianity has failed in this world, but they judge from what men call Christianity; and a vast amount of that which is designated Christian is not God's Christianity. It has no affinity with the Word of God; it is man's Christianity, the invention of the human mind, and that has failed. But God's Christianity has never failed, and never can fail; and when it shall have a world-wide support, when its mighty influences are felt everywhere, things will be put straight, and not till then. There is a great deal that is crooked as yet. Though we have reached the nineteenth century of the Christian era, and the Gospel has been so widely circulated, how much remains that does not lie even with the Divine rule of rectitude! If you inquire where, look at India, China, and Africa. But why go so far? Look at the nations of Europe. But why should we extend our observations so far as that? Look at this country, the most Christian, probably, upon the face of the earth. Are things straight here? Look at your own city, and you perhaps have been favoured more than any other city. Look at your own congregation.* You have had a great light for more than sixty years; it has but just passed away, and with your pre-eminent privileges are all things set right? Is there nothing crooked in your creed or in your lives? Are you bringing all to the test of this revealed standard? I fear not. In so far as you have trifled with your pre-eminent privileges, what responsibility rests upon you! All is crooked in every heart where sin has dominion, and crooked it will be until you have obtained justification by Jesus Christ, and sanctification by His Holy Spirit. These, brethren, are foundation doctrines, and though you may attempt to reform the exterior, and we would have you abate

*There is nothing in the M.S. to indicate where this sermon was preached.

no effort in that direction, there is no evangelical remedy but that which infinite Wisdom has provided. Man has got a number of outward applications, and they may be excellent in their kind, but they commence at the wrong place. God's remedy gets into the very centre of the man, and works outwardly; and you must possess that remedy before things will be put right. All is crooked, is perverse, till then. Seek to be justified by His grace, and to be sanctified by His spirit, and you shall be made holy and happy in God.

The character of the world is further displayed in the text by the word "perverse." More than three thousand years ago Moses, describing the same class of persons, said, "They have corrupted themselves, their spot is not the spot of His children; they are a crooked and perverse generation." A perverse generation is a nation that has departed from God's truth, and gone opposite to God's way. "They have corrupted themselves," may be said of mankind at large. What perverse ways are formed, and what perverse things are said, how contrary to God's revealed will! Even in this nineteenth century of the Christian era there is much that is perverse on every side. There are many who say there is no God; there are others that set aside the Divinity and atonement of the Lord Jesus Christ; and there are others who attempt to deny the Divine inspiration of the Scriptures.

We have a strange combination of perverse things raised against God's truth in the present day. There is Romanism, and infidelity, and that which by a strange perversion is called rationalism. This existed in classic Greece, and when the apostle Paul took the Gospel to them, they said they would try it by the same rules by which they tested any scheme of philosophy brought to them, and if it did not abide that test they would reject it.

These are among the perverse things which characterize the present generation. Such is the world in its apostasy from God, and it is in the midst of this morally corrupt and perverse generation that the Lord of heaven has placed His Church which is to shine as a light in the world. It is supposed that the word here translated light is borrowed from the flame which is constantly kept up at night in a light-house, to prevent ships from dashing against rocks in the darkness. Doddridge paraphrases the words "Shine as elevated lights." Dr. Bloomfield thinks that the allusion is to the heavenly luminaries which give light to the world. The plain truth, however, taught here is, that the God of heaven has placed a light in this world, and there are those who are enlightened and saved, and illuminated by His Word and Spirit, and these are to shine as lights in the world, "Let your light so shine before men, that they may see your good works, and glorify your Father which is in heaven." This is a dark night that is on the world of the ungodly; they are tossed about on the wild and wintry waters, and many a fatal wreck has taken place, and souls, immortal souls, are irrecoverably lost. God in His infinite mercy has provided a harbour; that harbour is Christ: the way into this harbour is narrow, and on either side are many dangers; but He has placed by this harbour a pillar—a light-house, shall I call it, that is the Church. It is the only permanent thing existing in this world, and the gates of hell shall not prevail against it, but it remains firm and secure. And God has placed a light upon this pillar, His own blessed Word, and He has charged His Church with His Word, that they should shine forth as lights in the world. They are to display the beauty of truth and righteousness, and show forth their influence on every side.

II. This brings us, secondly, to observe THE CHRISTIAN'S DUTY, to shine as a light in the world. The Apostle says, "among whom ye shine as lights in the world." If you will look at the marginal references of your Bibles, you will find that it is written there in the imperative mood, not "among whom ye shine," but "shine ye." Ye, if ye are His people, shine!

Now, there cannot well be a mistake as to who are God's people, and who constitute His Church in this world. He owns no Church as His that is not illumined by His Spirit; and no individual as His child, who is not converted by His grace, and who has not in him the incorruptible seed which liveth and abideth for ever. "If we say that we have fellowship with Him, and walk in darkness, we lie, and do not the truth."

We are to show forth the word of life; that is our mission. Oh, what a bright light is God's blessed Word in this world! Oh, what a luminary it is to light pilgrims through this wilderness to the heavenly Canaan! Life and immortality are brought to light by it. The path to God—the path to heaven and to happiness—is made plain thereby. Here we are told how and where we may obtain pardon, purity, and everlasting life, and we cannot learn these truths anywhere else. There is no other light that illumines life and immortality but the blessed, everlasting Gospel.

"Shine ye as lights in the world." It is the business of the Church, both minister and people, to hold forth the word of life, and nothing else. We must accept of no snbstitute; we are not to add thereto or take therefrom, but to take it as God has given it to us—to hold forth the word of life. The Apostle Paul said, "Woe is me if I preach not the *gospel.*" He might have preached, but if he had not preached the gospel, this woe would have rested upon him, and he was inspired by God to pronounce a curse on all who preach, but do not preach the everlasting gospel. "Though we, or an angel from heaven, preach any other gospel than that which we have preached unto you, let him be accursed." Yes, Paul, though an inspired Apostle, was not at liberty to depart from the text; he had important work, and he must mind that work. And we are similarly charged, every one of us; not only the pastor in the pulpit, but the people in the pews also; not in the house of God only, but everwhere; not on the Sabbath merely, but on every day of the week. We are to hold forth the word of life — to show its power on our own hearts and lives, and how it regulates every part of our conduct, so that our conversation and deportment in the world, in the family, and in the Church, should be one uniform act of holding forth the word of life. The Apostle Paul held it forth, not as the conclusion of Grecian philosophy—that would not do; not as the interpreter of Rabbinical learning—that would not do in the place of the gospel. He had one great object, which was to guide men to heaven and eternal life.

Is it not an atrocious crime to hold out a false light to the weather-beaten mariner when death rides upon the sea, and to allure such to certain destruction—is that a crime? What language shall we use to describe the wickedness of holding forth a false light to poor sinners who are candidates for immortality, and about to enter upon a vast unknown? Oh, let us rather direct such to Jesus, the Rock of Ages, that in Him they may be safe for ever.

Be ye reflectors of that light with which ye are favoured, and become more conversant with the Word of life, and never read it or hear it without invoking the aid of the eternal Spirit that you may be guided into all truth. Hold it forth in a pure creed, and hold it forth in a holy life. There are many who will not read your Bible, but let them read it in your lives and conversation, and you may profit them through that medium under God's blessing when you cannot do it in any other way.

Remember, too, that it is the business of the Church of

Christ to disseminate truth to the utmost. Every Church is a missionary Church, its province is to evangelize its own neighbourhood, and to send the everlasting gospel to every part of the earth. But to do this constantly and effectually, we must shine in our own several spheres of action, that others seeing our "good works may glorify our Father which is in heaven."

Your time forbids our entering upon the other portion of the text, more than close with a remark or two.

The Apostle tells us that our duty is to "do all things without murmurings and disputings." How oft have murmurings and disputings weakened the graces of the Christian Church, and obscured the light of Divine truth. Let us never envy a brother because he is more favoured than ourselves. When any disputes arise about who shall be esteemed the greatest, let the words of the Lord Jesus be remembered, "Whosoever will be great among you, let him be your servant."

Again, the Apostle adds, in our text, "that ye may be blameless and harmless;" not only do no injury to any, but so far as possible avoid raising the suspicion, "avoiding the very appearance of evil."

Great consistency also should mark the Church of God, "That ye may be the sons of God, without rebuke." "*Without rebuke*," so that if they speak evil of you, it may be falsely, for Christ's sake; that the severest censurer may be able to find no fault with you. Brethren, let us aim at this. Let us not only seek to get to heaven, but to get there without a blot or a stain upon our Christian character. Let us be on our guard lest we disgrace our Christian profession. Let us aim to be like Demetrius of old, to have a good report of all men, and of the truth itself.

And now, dear friends, are you enlightened by the heavenly light of which we have spoken? The world is corrupt. We want a mighty influence to bear upon it—that is, the spirit and the truth of God in His Church. It is not the Church itself that can save man. Christ must do that. No Church can do it; no creed can do it; not even an angel can do it; but Christ can, and your business is to hold forth Christ—Christ's mighty power—Christ's glorious person—Christ's perfect righteousness—Christ's complete atonement. Tell men the grand truth that, "God so loved the world that He gave His only begotten Son, that whosoever believeth in Him should not perish, but have everlasting life." Walk in this light; let it shine clearly upon you; and may you reflect it brightly upon others; "Holding forth the word of life."

XIX.

THE GOD OF PEACE.

(Preached on Sunday Evening, July 20th, 1845.)

Those things which ye have both learned, and received, and heard, and seen in me, do; and the God of peace shall be with you.—PHILIPPIANS iv. 9.

HERE are two things—an example and a promise. The example was the Apostle Paul, the writer of this Epistle. He was not one of those who said and did not. I have read of a minister who preached so well and lived so ill, that it was proverbially said, "when he was out of the pulpit, it were a pity he should ever go in; and when in, it were a pity he should ever go out." And I one day heard of a preacher who wantonly boasted that be was the best preacher in the nation, for, said he, "I teach my people both negatively and positively: by my doctrine I teach what they should do, and by my conduct what they should not do." But who loves to take meat, however good in itself, out of a leprous hand? "Be ye therefore clean," says Isaiah, "that bear the vessels of the Lord." And, asketh Paul, "Thou that teacheth another, teachest thou not thyself? Thou that preachest a man should not steal, dost thou steal? Thou that sayest a man should not commit adultery, dost thou commit adultery? Thou that abhorrest evils, dost thou commit sacrilege? Thou that makest thy boast of the law, through breaking the law, dishonourest thou God?" Jesus, we are told, began both to "do and to teach:" so should it be with every minister: so should it be with every master of a family, who is no less than a minister of God in his own household.

No one was more humble than Paul. He knew by the grace of God he was what he was; and yet a consciousness must he have had of his own sincerity and Christian disposition, to be able to say, "Be ye followers of me. Those things which ye have both learned, and received, and heard, and seen in me, do; and the God of peace shall be with you." We are not, however, going to enlarge upon the practice here but the promise, unless indeed as we see the one to be the condition of the other; unless as there is an indispensable connection, so that the one cannot be claimed without the others. Some of our Lutheran divines used the word "condition," but never would have done so if they had foreseen how it would be abused; for in process of time it has come to signify meritorious dependence, as if man could procure and purchase the blessings of salvation. Now, in this conclusion there is a gross error subversive of all the graces of the gospel. "If ye know," says the Saviour, "happy are ye if ye do them;" and says David, "In keeping His commandments there is great reward."

What then does the promise contain? It contains two things: God's character, and God's presence. It contains first, God's character: "The God of peace." Secondly, God's presence: "shall be with you."

I. GOD'S CHARACTER: "The God of peace."

This is one of the names, and titles by which He chooses to be known. It is found in several places, though I believe it never occurs anywhere but in the Epistles of St. Paul. Each of the sacred writers has some favourite phraseology and some peculiar term of his own. This does not detract from Inspiration: they thought as men, but the Spirit of God presided over their minds, to keep them from error and furnish them with matter, which they were allowed to express in their own manner. For instance, it is only John who calls The Saviour "The Word." The term "antichrist" is only found in his writings, and also the solemn asseveration which is so frequently employed by him, "verily, verily."

The name here given to God implies His being the *Author* of peace and lover of concord. Among men and Christians, oh, how valuable and precious is this, whether we view peace in a family, or in the Church, or in a neighbourhood, or in a nation! "Behold how good and how pleasant it is for brethren to dwell together in unity!" Therefore "depart from evil, and do good; seek peace, and pursue it." "Follow peace with all men, and if it be possible, as much as lieth in you, live peaceably with all men."

Dr. Cotton Mather, of New England, had attached to his Church a few individuals called a "Society of Peace and Concord," the office of whose members was to hinder and heal any breaches among friends, fellow-members of the Church. I daresay they had enough to do, but "blessed are the peacemakers, for they shall be called the children of God." The God of peace is their Father by adoption and by regeneration. At the revival of religion in America, President Edwards tells us that one Sunday morning, after he had finished his sermon at the Church, he saw two females remaining in the chapel at a remote distance from each other, as if from joint consent. He went and inquired the reason, and found that these individuals had previously lived in strife and animosity; and now feeling the power of religion, and being impressed with the importance of keeping the unity of the Spirit in the bond of peace, they had alike resolved they would not leave the place till they were reconciled to each other in the presence of God.

> "The spirit, like a graceful dove,
> Flies from the realms of noise and strife."

This Spirit, instead of inspiring us to hatred and malice, and all uncharitableness, will always induce us to esteem all who bear the image of the Saviour; to pray with the Apostle, "Grace be with all those who love our Lord Jesus Christ in sincerity;" and so resemble Him who stretched forth His hand to His disciples, and said, "Behold My mother and My brethren, for whosoever doeth the will of My Father which is in heaven, the same is My brother, and sister, and mother."

"The God of peace." Though this title implies nothing less than His being the Author of peace and lover of concord among men and Christians, the main thing is referred to by the Apostle in the Epistle to the Hebrews, where he says, "Now the God of peace, who brought again from the dead our Lord Jesus, that Great Shepherd of the sheep, through the blood of the everlasting covenant, make you perfect in every good work, to do His will, working in you that which is well pleasing in His sight, through Jesus Christ." It has, therefore, to do with the whole scheme of redemption. Let us enter a little into this.

God became the enemy of man as soon as man, by sin, became at enmity with Him. It could not be otherwise, How holiness such as His could not but hate the offender; how justice such as His could not but punish the guilty—this is the wonder of wonders. Though the offended Sovereign could as righteously, as easily, destroy the transgressors, His thoughts to them are thoughts of peace and love. And while He required an atonement, He Himself furnished it, and provided Himself with a Lamb for a burnt-offering. So we read of God being in Christ, "reconciling the world unto Himself, not imputing their trespasses unto them, and hath committed unto us," says the Apostle, "the word of reconciliation. Now, then, we are ambassadors for Christ, as though God did beseech you by us, we pray you, in Christ's stead, be ye reconciled to God. For He hath made Him to be sin for us, Who knew no sin, that we might be made the righteousness of God in Him." Thus God can save without the violation of any of His attributes. Yea, sin is condemned while it is pardoned. The law, instead of being trampled under foot, is magnified and made honourable. "Mercy and truth have met together, righteousness and peace have embraced each other." "Glory to God in the highest" is combined with "Peace on earth and goodwill toward men."

Persons talk of making their peace towards God. Why, our peace has already been made, by the atonement of the Son of God. If any professions, or almsgiving, or prayers, or vows, could have made peace, the world would never have witnessed the sacrifice of His dear Son, and it never would have pleased the Lord to bruise Him, and put Him to grief, and make His soul an offering for sin.

I remember, some years ago, a citizen of no mean city. He was poor but pious: he had met with a dreadful and fearful accident, and in consequence was conveyed to the hospital. The Chaplain was sent for, who immediately addressed him, saying, "My friend, I find that you have but a little time to be here. Therefore you had better make your peace with God without delay." "O sir," said he, "that is done already." "I am glad to hear it," was the reply, "but when?" "O sir," said he, "as long ago as when Christ died and made peace by the blood of His cross;" adding, with a smile, while the perspiration ran down his cheeks from the pain, "it is this, sir, that sustains me, and makes me think of death with confidence and pleasure."

To return, how wretched this state of the sinner is! Who has not tasted, as he passed through life, the bitterness of discord, and who has not felt the value of friendship? But to make a proper estimate of the blessings of reconciliation you must know the wrath to which we are exposed as sinners. "It is a fearful thing to fall into the hands of a living God." If the wrath of a king is as the roaring of a lion, what must be the wrath of Him who is King of Kings and Lord of Lords? "Who knoweth the power of His anger?" But "being justified by faith, we have peace with God, through our Lord Jesus Christ, through whom we have also received the atonement."

Peace of conscience flows from peace with God. One of these arises in the same proportion as does the other; and God can produce this in the very depth of spiritual distress and can plant the olive branch of peace in the very bosom of despair. He can also recall this peace when it has fled. And where is the Christian who has not sometimes said with Cowper:—

"Where is the blessedness I knew
When first I saw the Lord?
Where is the soul's refreshing view
Of Jesus and His word?

What peaceful hours I then enjoyed!
How sweet their memory still!
But they have left an aching void
The world can never fill."

Have you backslidden from the way of God? "Return, ye backslidden children," saith the Lord; "I will heal your backslidings, and love you freely." Go and cast yourself at His feet, and He will speak peace unto your soul; but return not again unto folly.

Oh, what will heaven be? When the Christian dies, he enters into peace. What peace, brethren, is that? Everlasting and unmingled peace and enjoyment. "There remaineth a rest for the people of God." There all will be peace; all will be quietness and assurance for ever. Nothing will be seen there but gladness, nothing heard but thanksgiving and the voice of melody. And from whom is it to come, but from Him? "The wages of sin is death, but the gift of God is eternal life through Jesus Christ our Lord."

II. Look now also at THE PROMISE, "the God of peace shall be with you."

This promise we will take four ways.

The first will distinguish it from the *omnipresence* of God, for God is everywhere; His eyes are in every place beholding the evil and the good. "Whither shall I go from Thy Spirit, and whither shall I flee from Thy presence? If I ascend up unto heaven, Thou art there: if I make my bed in hell, behold, Thou art there. If I take the wings of the morning, and dwell in the uttermost part of the sea, even there shall Thy hand lead me, and Thy right hand hold me. If I say, Surely the darkness shall cover me; even the night shall be light about me. Yea, the darkness hideth not from Thee; but the night shineth as the day: the darkness and the light are both alike to Thee."

Do you imagine that nothing more is intended here by His presence than the perfection of His nature? When His name is spoken of promise, it intends something saving and spiritual. "The Lord is nigh unto all them that call upon Him, to all them who call upon Him in truth." It is to them He has said, "I will not leave thee, nor forsake thee."

The second view will connect His presence with His *condescension and grace.* If you know what you are and what He is, you may exclaim with Job, "What is man, that Thou shouldest magnify him? and that Thou shouldest set thine heart upon him? and that Thou shouldest visit him every morning, and try him every moment?" If you consider the heavens the work of God's fingers, the moon and the stars which He hath ordained, well may you exclaim with David, "Lord what is man that Thou art mindful of him? Or the son of man, that Thou shouldest visit him?" If you believe the heaven of heavens cannot hold Him, you may well wonder with Solomon, and say, "Will God in very deed dwell with man upon earth?" If a nobleman or a king were seen walking with a peasant, giving him his arm, entering his cottage, and showing him many marks of kindness, you would be disposed to think that he was very meek and lowly in heart. But there is some proportion between a prince and a peasant, while there is an infinite disproportion between a creature and God.

"In vain might lofty princes try
Such condescension to perform;
The worms were never raised so high
Above their fellow-creature worm."

But we see not only His condescension but His *grace.* We are not only unworthy of the least of His mercies, but we are all *ill*-deserving and *hell*-deserving sinners. We are children of disobedience, and therefore "children of wrath, even as others." Hence Moses says, "Wherein shall it be known that

I and Thy people have found grace in Thy sight? Is it not in that thou goest with us? So shall we be separated, I and Thy people, from all the people that are upon the face of the earth."

The third view shows us the *importance* of the privilege We read of exceeding great and precious promises. And surely this must be one of them, "The God of peace shall be with you." And what does this contain? rather, what does it *not* contain? What is heaven, but the enjoyment of the presence of God? In His presence is fulness of joy; at His right hand are pleasures for evermore. What is the consummation of all blessedness? "The Tabernacle of God is with men, and He will dwell with them, and they shall be His people, and God Himself shall be with them and be their God."

"The God of peace shall be with you"—to *guide* you. The way of man is not in himself. "It is not in man that walketh to direct his steps," and yet how much depends upon every false course, upon every false step, you take! But you have an infallible God to guide and direct you in all your ways. This God is your God for ever and ever; He will be your guide even unto death.

"The God of peace shall be with you"—He will not only be your sun, but your shield. He will be your *protector* amidst the assaults of your enemies. "Greater is He who is with you than he who is in the world; if He is for you, who can be against you?"

"The God of peace shall be with you"—to *aid you*; to help you in your journey; to aid you to walk and to aid you to work. His strength shall be made perfect in your weakness. This is His promise: "Fear thou not; for I am with thee: be not dismayed; for I am thy God; I will strengthen thee; yea, I will help thee; yea, I will uphold thee with the right hand of My righteousness."

"The God of peace shall be with you"—to *comfort* you. "Trials must and will befall." "In the world ye shall have tribulation." But, says God, "when thou passest through the waters, I will be with thee; and through the floods, they shall not overflow thee: when thou passest through the fire, thou shalt not be burnt, neither shall the flames kindle upon thee." Bolingbroke said, in his affliction, "I find my philosophy fail me now." Did the prophet's philosophy fail him, when he looked around and saw everything bare? Oh, no! "Although," said he, "the fig tree shall not blossom, neither shall fruit be in the vines; the labour of the olive shall fail, and the fields shall yield no meat; the flock shall be cut off from the fold, and there shall be no herd in the stall: *yet* I will rejoice in the Lord, I will joy in the God of my salvation." Did Spilsbury's philosophy fail him? He had suffered for conscience sake; had been deprived of his living; had been in prison and released; and, when apprehended a second time and about to be conveyed to prison, seeing his wife and another weeping around him, he said to them, "Weep not for me, I am not afraid of going to prison; I *found God with me there the first time.*" Yes, God is "the God of comfort," and "as the sufferings of Christ abound in us, so our consolation also aboundeth by Christ."

The fourth view connects it with His *veracity*. The greater the promise is, the more desirous is one likely to feel whether it can be depended upon; especially when we consider the character of many of our fellow-creatures; when we consider that "men of low degree are vanity, and men of high degree are a lie: to be laid in the balance, they are lighter than vanity." "Confidence," says Solomon, "in an unfaithful man is like a broken tooth or a foot out of joint," which will not only be found useless, but very painful too. But how is it with regard to God. "All the promises of God in Him"—in Christ—"are yea, and in Him Amen, unto the glory of God by us." Even Balaam could say, "the Lord is not a man, that He should lie; neither the son of man, that He should repent. Hath He said, and shall He not do it? or Hath He spoken, and shall He not make it good?" Men may fail from fulfilling their engagements from many causes. They may forget, they may change their mind, or they may lose their ability to perform them. But neither of these will apply to God. Forgetfulness cannot enter a mind of infinite understanding; with Him is no variableness or shadow of turning; and with the Lord Jehovah is everlasting strength.

To conclude, may you encourage yourself by this promise in the text! May you be enabled to realize it, to apply it to your case! You know not what a day may bring forth. You know not what adversity may befall you. You may lose your health; you may lose beloved relations, or friends, and the minister you are accustomed to hear from time to time, but the Lord liveth and the God of peace shall be with you. Believe—will not this suffice? Who would murmur and complain, saying, "I have only the God of peace with me?" What said Asaph? "Whom have I in heaven but Thee? and there is none upon earth that I desire besides Thee." What think you of Luther's expression: "If I have Thee, I care not about heaven or earth?" This is like his boldness of manner, notwithstanding threats and persecutions. But as bold and more sublime is the language of Doddridge:—

"If Thou, my Jesus, still be nigh,
Cheerful I live and joyful die;
Secure, when earthly comforts flee,
To find ten thousand worlds in Thee."

Walk so as to please Him. Grieve not His Holy Spirit, so as to induce Him to hide His face from you. If you do, you will walk mournfully. But walk in faith, and then you will walk in comfort, and in the joy of the Holy Ghost.

He will be with you as long as you are here, but in a little time you will be with *Him*. He is now with you in the wilderness, but you will soon be with Him in the land of Canaan, in a land flowing with milk and honey. "I am happy now," said a dying saint, lately, "and am going from a less degree of happiness to a greater." Blessed are the people who are in such a state. Yea, happy is that people whose God is the Lord. "Remember me, O Lord, with the favour Thou bearest unto Thy people; Oh, visit me with Thy salvation, that I may see the good of Thy chosen; that I may rejoice in the gladness of Thy nation, that I may glory with Thine inheritance." Amen.

XX.

THE GREAT SALVATION.

(Preached on Sunday Evening, December 28th, 1845.)

And we have seen and do testify that the Father sent the Son to be the Saviour of the world.—1 JOHN iv. 14.

THIS, brethren, is a very plain text, but a very important one, and we may transfer to it the attributes which the Apostle has ascribed to a similar passage, where he says, "It is a faithful saying." What is common report but falsehood? What is a great part of history but fabulous? What are the promises of men but lies? "I said in my heart, all men are liars." But this is a "faithful saying;" it is a true saying, it is truth itself, and it will not deceive you. All that is important must be true, but all that is true may not be important. But here the importance equals the truth; therefore it is not only a "faithful saying, but worthy of all acceptation;" and worthy the acceptation of all, whether rich or poor, or high or low—of prince or peasant. It is worthy of all acceptation, worthy of all your desires, of all your hopes, of all your joys, of all your affections, of all your expectations. It is worthy of all your thanksgivings and praises which can be experienced and called forth in embracing it. "He," therefore, "who hath ears to hear, let him hear," for "we have seen and do testify that the Father sent the Son to be the Saviour of the world." Now we are not going to draw several doctrines from these words, or to treat them textually even, but in a way of inference, and there are six things which naturally and necessarily result from them.

I. The first inference is this: If the "Father sent the Son to be the Saviour of the world," *then was the world in a lost state.* "God made man upright, but he sought out many inventions." "By one man sin came into the world, and death by sin, so that death passed upon all men, for that all hath sinned." Adam begot a son in his own likeness, and the earth was soon filled with wickedness. We read that "every imagination of the thoughts of their hearts was only evil continually," and the "flood came and took them all away," except the few who were preserved in the ark: from these afterwards the earth was replenished. But David tells us that when God looked down again upon the children of men, He said, "They are all gone out of the way; they are all become filthy; there is none that doeth good, no, not one." This was the testimony of the Apostle in his Epistle to the Romans, in which he proved that both Jews and Gentiles were all under sin, and both guilty before God. Thus, as sinners, all are condemned, for "cursed is everyone that continueth not in all things that are written in the law to do them;" and "the soul that sinneth, it shall die." Thus all were sinners, and all depraved, and as such are strangers to peace, the vassals of corruption, tyrannized over by these passions, "serving divers lusts and pleasures," and ready to perish. And what is that perdition to which they are exposed? It is expressed by various images employed by the sacred writers, anyone of which is so dreadful as to be enough to drive any man out of his senses or out of his sins; compared with which all the sufferings of life, all the horrors of conscience, and all the rage of despair, are only the beginning of sorrows.

Now, can this state of human nature be denied? Let men turn their thoughts inward and examine their own experience. Surely every man is conscious that he has a tendency to evil, to malice, to pride and ingratitude; and when he examines himself, he cannot fix upon a period when he began to feel these evil tendencies; the reason is, they are collateral; they grow with his growth, and strengthen with his strength. Now, if there were a tree which was known to bring forth only bad fruit, in every age, in every climate, and in every soil, and under every kind of cultivation, should we hesitate to consider it a bad tree, for every tree is known by its fruit? And what has man been always, and what has man been everywhere, in all stations, and under all circumstances? What is the testimony of all history? Observe the most polished and cultivated state of society. Regard it according to the declarations of historians and travellers. Take their religion, and oh, how evil and licentious is their worship! Why, among them vices were not only not forbidden, they were encouraged and enjoined; gluttony, drunkenness, and lewdness, were even made parts and acts of their devotion. We are frequently censured for defaming human nature. But who is it that asks, "Who can bring a clean thing out of an unclean?" Who said, "the heart is deceitful above all things and desperately wicked; who can know it?" Who was it that testified, "For from within, out of the heart, proceed evil thoughts, adulteries, fornications, murders, thefts, covetousness, wickedness, deceit, lasciviousness, an evil eye, blasphemy, pride, foolishness: all these evil things come from within and defile the man." And who is it that says also, "We are of God, and the whole world lieth in wickedness?" Such, then, is the state of human nature. If it were otherwise, if we were not sick and dying, why send for the physician? If we were not in bondage, why need a Redeemer? If we were not lost and undone, what need have we of a Saviour? If therefore it be true that "the Father sent the Son to be the Saviour of the world," it is equally true that the world was in a lost state.

II. The second inference is this: If the "Father sent the Son to be the Saviour of the world" then *their salvation is a matter of importance.* God does not trifle with you, my hearers: His aim and His end always justified, and more than justifies, His actions and His doings. We should not indeed think very highly of this salvation, if we were to judge of it by the lives of men. They are alive to their temporal welfare, to the safety of their property; as to their bodies they show anxiety enough, they are willing to make any sacrifice to escape from floods and flames, from the dagger of the assassin and pestilential distempers; they are grateful when a disorder is removed, and when they are snatched from the borders of the grave; but they do not value the salvation of which our text speaks, because it is a spiritual salvation, and a holy salvation; it regards those evils which they neither feel nor fear. Hence they make light of it. They make sacrifices as to their farm and their merchandize, for their worldly aggrandisement, for their vanishing honours, and for the pleasures of sin which are but for a season; but were we to judge of the salvation of which we are speaking by the endeavours of many of you to obtain it, we should consider it as a thing of nought. Yet how will you view it by-and-by? How will you view it in a dying hour? and when you stand before the judgment-seat of Christ? And how would you view it immediately, if now you were convinced of sin, and if now you perceived the wrath of God ready to fall upon you as the children of disobedience? Would not your cry be then—not, "What shall I eat, or what shall I drink?" but—"What shall I do to be saved? How shall I come before the Lord? or bow myself before the Most High God?" What did the Apostle think of it? He calls it "so great salvation"—so unspeakably, so inconceivably great. It is a salvation for the soul, a salvation for eternity, a salvation rescuing us from all evil, and conferring upon us all possible good. What do the spirits above think of it, as every moment they are crying, "Unto Him that loved us, and washed us from our sins in His own blood, and hath made us kings and priests unto God His Father, unto Him be glory and dominion for ever and ever. Amen?" What do the angels in glory think of it? Do they not "desire to look into these things," and come to the Church to learn "the manifold wisdom of God"? Do they not rejoice over every sinner that repenteth? What said the angels to the shepherds? "Behold, we bring you good tidings of great joy, which shall be to all peoples, for unto you is born this day in the city of David a Saviour, which is Christ the Lord." And what was the subject of the praises of the multitude of the heavenly host? They came down, saying, "Glory to God in the highest, and on earth peace, goodwill toward men."

But again we repair to our inference. We behold the worth of salvation from the importance God Himself has attached to it. He cannot err; He could not have been mistaken; He knew the value of souls, and the misery to which we were exposed as sinners; He knew the full meaning of the terms "everlasting punishment" and "life eternal." And it is here you must study the subject, in the manger and upon the cross, while you behold "God manifest in the flesh." "Because the children were partakers of flesh and blood, He also took part of the same, that through death He might destroy him that had the power of death." Follow the Saviour through His history, see Him descending from the throne to the cross, and ascending from the cross to the throne, and "ask now of the days that are past, which were before thee, since the day that God created man upon the earth, and ask from the one side of heaven unto the other, whether there hath been any such thing as this great thing is, or hath been heard like it."

III. The third inference is this: If the "Father sent the Son to be the Saviour of the world," then *this salvation is no easy achievement.* No, my brethren, the scheme involved in it difficulties which He alone could remove. We deduce this from His wisdom and His perfections. Let us explain a little.

Men often degrade themselves by the means they employ to accomplish their purposes. Sometimes they employ unsuitable means, and thus become laughing stocks; and sometimes they employ inadequate men and thus fail in their enterprise; and sometimes they employ more means than is necessary, and then they shew their ignorance. What would you think of a man who would put himself to great expense in constructing a machine to crush a fly? or who would employ a thousand hands when one was enough? But if you were to see a skilful builder, and one in whose judgment you could confide, bringing together a vast number of workmen, and an immensity of materials, you would infer that an extensive work was to be going on, and one that was neither trifling nor easy. My brethren, we have defective notions of sin, and defective notions of the holiness and the righteousness of God, and therefore are not aware of the difficulties found in the way of our recovery; but God was perfectly aquainted with them, and He does nothing in vain. What he does, He Himself deems necessary, and His judgment is always "according to truth." What then has He done whose understanding is infinite, and who is liable to no error? He delivered the Jews from the land of Egypt, "with a strong hand, and a stretched-out arm." He often saved them from their enemies; He brought them back from the Babylonish captivity, and restored them to their religious privileges. But behold a new thing in the earth and something surpassing every previous dispensation. "Behold the Word was made flesh and dwelt among us." "A body was prepared for Him, and He suffered, He died, and He rose again, and He now sitteth on the right hand of God, as a Prince and a Saviour, to give repentance to Israel and remission of sins." For 4,000 years prophets predicted Him, sacrifices prefigured Him, and saints expected Him. And, brethren, what do we again infer from this? We are never so liable to err as when we come forward and determine what God should do, or what He should not do, in particular cases. But if God Himself comes forward, shewing us that He was under a kind of necessity—we use His own language—to do so and so, surely it becomes us to acquiesce; and has He not told us that "it *became* Him, by whom are all things, to make the Captain of their salvation perfect through suffering." Has He not told us that Christ ought to suffer these things, and to enter into His glory? That "it behoved Him in all things to be made like unto His brethren, that He might be a merciful and faithful high priest in things pertaining to God, to make reconciliation for the sins of the people?" And we may well suppose that if the mercies of God could have been exercised to the human race without this, and in harmony with His truth and justice, and righteousness, that the world would never have witnessed the incarnation and sufferings of His own Son.

IV. The fourth inference is this: If the "Father sent the Son to be the Saviour of the world," then *what compassion must have filled the bosom of Him who sent Him!* Ah, my brethren, the Apostle is beforehand with us here. It is from hence he says, "In this was manifested the love of God towards men, because that God sent His only begotten Son into the world, that we might live through Him." And "herein," says he, as if it appeared in nothing else, "herein is love, not that we loved God, but that He loved us, and sent His Son to be the propitiation for our sins." This is, indeed, the most transcendent instance of it, for observe the motive that influenced Him in doing so. He was not compelled to do this; He was not actuated by our desert; His love was not drawn forth by our desire; for, says He, "I was found of them that sought Me not; I was made manifest to them that asked not after Me." Then consider the messenger He sent. It was not a man; it was not an angel, but the Lord of angels; it was not a servant, but a Son—the Son of His love, and His only begotten Son. "For God so loved the world that He gave His only begotten Son, that whosoever believeth on Him should not perish, but have everlasting life." Then consider the condition to which this errand of love and mercy reduced Him, so that He appeared in the deepest abasement, and became "a man of sorrows and acquainted with grief." Then you may consider the purpose He had in view. The Son of God might have come down with a rod in His hand to destroy men's lives, for the human race deserved His displeasure; but though He could righteously have "sent His Son into the world to condemn the world," He did not do so, "but that the world through Him might be saved." Then reflect also on the multitude of the partakers of the benefit. "Are there few that shall be saved?" Why, the Saviour "shall see of the travail of His soul and shall be satisfied." And would a few satisfy the benevolence of His heart, and lead Him to say to the Father, "Stop Thine hand! there are enough; I am perfectly satisfied; save no more?" But the Apostle tells us, in the second chapter of Hebrews, "We see Jesus, who was made a little lower than the angels for the suffering of death, crowned with glory and honour; that He, by the grace of God, should taste death for every man." The Apostle tells us, that "He is the propitiation for our sins, and not for ours only, but also for the sins of the whole world."

The Fifth inference is this: If "the Father sent the Son to be the Saviour of the world," then *there is full encouragement for every desponding sinner.* What a difference is made in the mind of a man by a little clear and sound conviction! Before, it was hardly possible to induce him to fear; now, it is equally difficult to induce him to hope when he thinks of the guilt of his transgressions, of the pollution of them, and of their number, and when he thinks of their heinousness in the sight of God, he finds it hard to believe that God can be pacified towards him; and it is difficult to satisfy him that if he returns toGod, God will come forth and "receive him graciously, and love him freely." What, then, is the consolation he meets with while in such a condition? Is all the encouragement he can obtain a mere venture, that the Lord "may turn, and repent, and leave a blessing behind Him, that he perish not?" Is this all the encouragement he can derive from Him who hath declared that he has "no pleasure in the death of the wicked;" from Him who "waits to be grievous:" who never refused any who applied to Him for mercy? "He who spared not His own Son, but delivered Him up for us all, how shall He not freely give us all things?" Will He be displeased if you approach Him through this Saviour, when you apply to Him for the very purpose for which He sent His Son? while you beseech Him that you may be made partakers of His salvation? *No,* it is the pleasure of the Lord prospering in the Redeemer's hands. *No,* "He will rejoice over you with joy."

VI. The Sixth inference is: If "the Father ent His Son to be the Saviour of the world," *what are we to think of those who will not come to Him that they may have life?* Let us reflect upon their condition, and view it on two grounds. First, the helplessness of their condition: for "there is salvation in no other" but through Him who "was despised and rejected of men." No man can come unto the Father but by Him. What is the consequence? They need no decree, no threatening of God to cause them to perish; it results from the nature of the thing; for if there be only one remedy for the sick and disordered, and they refuse this, why they must perish. There was only one ark of old, therefore all who refused this were destroyed by the flood. There was only one sacrifice for sin, and if this be renounced "there remaineth no more sacrifice for sins but a certain fearful looking for of judgment and fiery indignation, which shall devour the adversaries."

Then look at it in the greatness of their guilt. Their ruin lies principally in their contempt of this salvation—their contempt of such an infinite Benefactor, and of the infinite provisions of mercy which He has made. O, how do they disobey the greatest of all His commands, for "this is His commandment, that we believe on the name of the only begotten Son of God." How do they rob Him of His rightful glory, the glory of His grace! How do they frustrate the grace of God, and make Christ to have died in vain! They cannot, therefore, come off with impunity. *Impossible.* How shall we escape if we "neglect so great salvation?" "He that despised Moses' law died without mercy under two or three witnesses. "Of how much sorer punishment"—what of dying without mercy? Yes, "Of how much sorer punishment, suppose ye, shall he be thought worthy who hath trodden under foot the Son of God, and hath counted the blood of the covenant wherewith he was sanctified an unholy thing, and hath done despite unto the Spirit of grace." So that if any of you should perish under the gospel, you will have double destruction. The law will deal with you first, then the gospel. You will have one destruction from the law you have transgressed, and another from the gospel you have rejected. Your misery, therefore, will be a *death unto death.* I am often ready to ask, What must angels think of the human race when they look down upon us? when they view us despising this salvation? Surely there is nothing like this in other cases amongst men. Who ever heard of a condemned criminal in prison, who was expecting execution, yet refused pardon sent by the King, by his prime minister, sent by his own son? And yet this is the case with many. "God hath committed unto us the ministry of reconciliation." "Yes, we are ambassadors for Christ; as though God did beseech you, we pray you in Christ's stead, be ye reconciled to God."

Yes, "we are workers together with God, and beseech you that ye receive not His grace in vain." But arise, "the Father hath sent His Son to be the Saviour of the world." *Go and embrace Him*, with the language of the Church, "Lo, this is our God: we have waited for Him, and He will save us; this is the Lord, we have waited for Him, we will be glad and rejoice in His salvation."

THURSDAY EVENING ADDRESSES.

I

JOSHUA'S FINAL CHARGE.

(Delivered on Thursday Evening, June 20th, 1844.)

And Joshua said unto all the people, Behold, this stone shall be a witness unto us; for it hath heard all the words of the Lord which He spake unto us: it shall be therefore a witness unto you, lest ye deny your God. —JOSHUA xxiv. 27.

THE lives of the generality of mankind pass unobserved and unknown from the cradle to the tomb. When gone, their history is summed-up in two little articles; on such a day they were born, and on such a day they died. Some begin their career late in life, and have few opportunities of usefulness; others begin early and continue their course long, improving as well as persevering in the path, like "the light that shineth more and more unto the perfect day." Such a one was Joshua; he had doubtless his imperfections, but none are laid to his charge in the sacred writings. He was trained up from his youth under the care of Moses; he joined not with the multitude when they made the golden calf. He stood alone with Caleb when the spies returned from searching Canaan and brought up a false report. Though he knew he was to succeed Moses, and finish the work he commenced, he was not weary or impatient when he saw others promoted, but left it to Providence to determine the time and manner of his elevation. A man is always best formed for commanding by obeying, and a good behaviour in a lower and private condition is always the best pledge of properly filling a higher station.

A Christian will be concerned to live as long as he breathes. Yes, he will be anxious to be useful even beyond the grave. Joshua is characterised by the influence of his example, and by his benevolence and dying advice. Joshua was now about to go the way of all the earth. He calls the elders of Israel together and tells them the great things that God had done for their fathers; and then urges them to serve Him fully. To this they agreed, and said to Joshua, "The Lord our God will we serve, and His voice will we obey." Joshua knew human nature; how many good impressions die away; how many clear convictions are uninfluential; how desirable it is to carry out such convictions as soon as possible. Consequently, you see, Joshua made a covenant. "And Joshua said unto all the people, Behold, this stone shall be a witness unto us; for it hath heard all the words of the Lord which He spake unto us."

This is a very strong figure, making a stone conscious, but it renders the thing more impressive—it shall be therefore a witness unto you, lest ye deny your God.

Let us glance, then, at three things: First, God's relation to His people; Secondly, Their Duty; and Thirdly, Their preservation from religious declension.

I. God's Relation to His People.

He is the Lord their God. To the Jews He was so nationally; therefore He is often called the God of Israel. There is a sense in which this will apply to a Christian country. He is the true and living God; He has given to us a revelation of His will, and all generally profess to be His people. But, alas! thousands live with a heart estranged from Him. We must therefore consider this subject more personally, and as to the partakers of Divine grace. The case is this: God loves them, and they love Him; He chooses them, and they choose Him; He rejoices in them as His inheritance, and says, "They are My people;" while they bless Him, and say, "He is the Lord our God."

All this you see is mutual; this is acknowledged; but the question is, Whether He begins with us, or we begin with Him. That is, whether our choosing Him is the occasion of His choosing us, and so of the rest. "Oh," say some of you, "this is of little importance;" but it is of very great importance, for upon this depends the question whether we or God can claim the praise: whether we thank ourselves, or say, "By the grace of God I am what I am;" "Not I, but the grace of God which is in me;" "Not unto us, not unto us, but unto Thy name be all the glory." What, then, say the Scriptures on this point? "We love Him, because He first loved us." It is to no purpose whether the Apostle refers to God's love as the motive or the producer; in both senses it is true, and therefore His love is previous to ours; our love flows from it. The one is the spring, the other is the stream. "I have loved thee with an everlasting love, therefore with loving-kindness have I drawn thee." His people are chosen from the beginning "through sanctification of the Spirit, and belief of the truth."

This we may consider as a standard by which to judge of the privileges of Christians; for what honour and happiness must there be if the Lord is their God! The gods of the heathen were made of silver and gold, the work of men's hands, and, of course, could not know the desires of those who prayed unto them, or arise to save such. But our God is in the heavens; He hath done whatsoever it hath pleased Him, and He is able to do for His people "exceeding abundantly above all that we ask or think." Therefore Moses said to the Jews, "What nation is there so great?" Not that *they* were so powerful and many; they had no secular arm to protect them; they had no trade for employment, no schools for their sons; they had on the same clothes they wore out of Egypt; they had not provision sufficient to maintain them a single day, and yet says he, "What nation is there so great?" Yes, but hear what he adds: "Who hath God so nigh unto them, as the Lord our God is in all things that we call on Him for?" Yes, the Eternal God was their refuge, and under them was the everlasting arms. "Happy art thou, O, Israel; who is like unto Thee? a people saved by the Lord, the shield of Thy help, and who is the sword of Thy excellency! and thy enemies shall be found liars unto Thee; and Thou shalt tread upon their high places."

This is equally to be viewed as a standard whereby to judge of the rule of duty; for if God is *your* God, what manner of persons ought ye to be in all holy conversation and godliness, always "walking worthy of Him who hath called us to His kingdom and glory!" Therefore, says the Church in the days of Micah, "For all people will walk, every one in the name of his god, and we will walk in the name of the Lord our God for ever and ever."

This brings us to notice—

Their Duty. They were not to "deny" their God, which here means to disown. This is the meaning of our Saviour when he says, "He that denieth me before men shall be denied before the angels of God;" and "Whosoever shall confess me before men, him shall the Son of Man confess before the angels of God."

There is a total denying of God which belongs to the wicked; to those who say, "Depart from us; we desire not the knowledge of Thy ways;" and "Cause the Holy One of Israel to cease from before us." But there is a partial denying of Him; and this may be chargeable even on good men. Therefore, the law of the house is, "If his children forsake my law and walk not in my commandments, then will I visit their transgressions with the rod, and their iniquity with stripes." He forgives their iniquity, but takes vengeance of their inventions.

There are two ways in which God's people may deny Him. One is verbally. Your tongues are the Lord's as well as your hearts, and you are required to confess with the mouth, as well as believe with the heart. By your speech are you distinguished from the brutes. Your tongues should be employed for God. Would you be dumb for Him who has done so much for you? Shall the things of this world set your tongues in motion, and not the things of God? "A good man out of the good treasure of his heart speaketh;" yet some of you can sit in the company of the ungodly, as men in whose mouths there is no reproach, afraid or ashamed to speak for His name and cause, whereas you ought to say with David, "I will speak of Thy testimonies also before kings, and will not be ashamed." Doddridge says:

> "Is there a lamb in all Thy flock
> I would disdain to feed?
> Is there a foe before whose face
> I fear Thy cause to plead?"

But God may be denied actually as well as verbally. Actions, you are accustomed to say, speak louder than words. So they do. You deny Him first in proportion as you say by your temper and lives that you have not His word abiding in you. You deny Him when it is not your chief concern to glorify Him with your bodies and spirits, which are His. You deny Him as your Lord when you serve other masters, and cause Him to say, "Why call me Lord, Lord, and do not the things which I say?" You deny Him as your portion when you search for happiness elsewhere, instead of in His fear and presence; when instead of praying, "Lord lift Thou up the light of Thy countenance upon me," you are joining so far with the fools in saying, "Who will show us any good?" You deny Him as your Teacher, when you lean to your own understanding, or depend on human authority instead of the teaching of His Spirit, who is willing to lead you into all truth. You deny Him as your Saviour when you go about to establish your own righteousness. You also deny God when you disown not only what He has done *for* you, but what He does *in* you. You should be very cautious how you draw conclusions in favour of your own character and state; but you may draw them, and you are commanded to examine yourselves, to prove your own selves whether or not Christ be in you; and though it becomes us as Christians to be humble, it equally becomes us to be thankful. But how can you be thankful, if you deny what He has done for your soul? And how can you speak of it to His praise and as encouragement to others? You should take care not to deny what God wrought in you. If you cannot admit that it is day, do not disown that it is dawn. If you cannot see the full corn in the ear, do not deny the blade, for who hath despised the day of small things? It is well if you have light enough to see your darkness; it is well if you have feeling enough to be sensible of the hardness of your heart; it is well if you have religion enough to hate yourselves for your ingratitude, and this cometh from Him that calleth you.

III. Consider THE MEANS OF PRESERVING THEM FROM RELIGIOUS DECLENSION. "It shall be a witness unto you."

Before we enter upon this we will notice briefly two or three things.

First, *be sensible of your danger.* If you think there is no danger, it shows how far you are advanced, and how near you are already to a precipice. For as Solomon says, "Pride goeth before destruction, and a haughty spirit before a fall." "Blessed is the man that feareth always." It shows how little you are acquainted with your own hearts. How many have there been who have far surpassed you in attainments and grace, and yet have been surprised and overcome! Look to Peter for a single instance, who says, "Though all men should deny Thee, yet will not I; and though I should die with Thee, yet will I not deny Thee." He spake this sincerely, according to his feelings then; but he had too much self-confidence. He knew not his own weakness and danger, but the Saviour did, and therefore forewarned and admonished him. But Peter deemed the warning unnecessary, and what was the consequence? He denied Him with oaths and curses. Therefore,

"Beware of Peter's words,
Nor confidently say,
I never will deny Thee, Lord;
But grant I never may."

Where was Peter when he denied Him? Why, with the rabble, warming himself by the fire. Ah, what have some suffered by a few evil companions at a warm fireside? especially in a public-house! We are to "watch and pray, lest we enter into temptation."

We remark further, Christian, *if you deny Him, He does not deny you.* He owns you for His, bearing witness with your spirit that you are "the children of God." He owns you in *prayer.* He says, "When they call, I will answer." He owns you in *ordinances.* He gives you communion with Him then, and enables you to say, "This is none other than the house of God, and the gate of heaven." He owns you in *providences.* Sometimes you may be at a distance from outward means: remember faithful Abraham, how God blessed him so as to render him the envy of all the surrounding nations. Those who fear God shall be blessed with faithful Abraham. "The eyes of the Lord run to and fro in the earth, to show Himself strong in the behalf of them whose heart is perfect towards Him." How does God own you in tribulation! "No chastening for the present seemeth to be joyous, but grievous; nevertheless afterward it yieldeth the peaceable fruit of righteousness. If ye endure chastening, God dealeth with you as with sons; for what son is he whom the father chasteneth not?" He will own you in death, and this induced Baalam to say, "Let me die the death of the righteous." He will own you in the last day, before an assembled world, and will say, "Well done, good and faithful servant; Come, ye blessed of My Father, inherit the kingdom prepared for you."

Remember *you are always under observation.* Be admonished, therefore, to say with David, "Make Thy paths straight before my face." God will not deny you in your retired walks, but you will not be happy there if God is not in all your thoughts. He will not deny you in your closets. God will be with you in your private devotions, in your praying in your families, and for your fellow Christians and Church members. The sanctuary of God will be a witness of your conduct. The table of the Lord will be a witness. God Himself will be a witness. But time forbids us to enlarge. May the Lord add His blessing to what has been said. Amen.

II.

A GOOD MAN MISUNDERSTOOD.

(Delivered on Thursday Evening, July 11th, 1844).

"*Behold, thou hast instructed many, and thou hast strengthened the weak hands. Thy words have upholden him that was falling, and thou hast strengthened the feeble knees. But now it is come upon thee, and thou faintest; it toucheth thee, and thou art troubled.*"—JOB iv. 3-5

WE read of Job's true friends who came every one from his own place, for they had made an appointment together to come to mourn with him and to comfort him. "A friend loveth at all times, and a brother is born for adversity." Yet how often has it been, while relying upon creatures, you have found them "broken cisterns which can hold no water," or broken reeds "which have not only deceived your hopes, but pierced you through with many sorrows!" Not Scripture only, but all observation and all experience in every period says, "Cease ye from man, whose breath is in his nostrils, for wherein is he to be accounted of?" The three friends of Job, instead of easing his complaint, were all "physicians of no value;" and instead of relieving his distresses, "miserable comforters were they all." They poured oil upon his head indeed, but it was the oil of vitriol. Here one pretends to say he can keep silence no longer. He cries, "Who can withhold himself from speaking?" and addressed him in the words of our text, in which we have both commendation and censure; the one altogether true, and the other altogether false. But you will observe the commendation was not intended to soften the censure, but to enhance it. It is no unusual thing for persons to kiss when they are going to betray; like the long African serpent which licks and slobbers the victim he is going to swallow.

From the words of our text we consider, first, WHAT ELIPHAZ SAYS OF JOB'S REAL CONDUCT. This was highly commendable and exemplary. "Behold thou hast instructed many, and thou hast strengthened the weak hands. Thy words have upholden him that was falling, and thou hast strengthened the feeble knees."

Job was a great man, *very* great, as you see in the first chapter. But this greatness did not raise him above the claims of duty, yea, it made him the more sensible of them. There are many who are blessed above others, who are only public scandals and disgraces. The more God does for them, the more they do against God; like vapours and exhalations, which only serve to eclipse the sun that draws them up. There are many called 'Right Honourables,' that ought to be called 'Right Horribles;' who render irreligion and vice current by the stamp of their influence and example. They are God's stewards, but not faithful to the trust; who seek to lay up for themselves what ought to be expended upon others. There are some who think it beneath them to regard their inferiors. But real goodness is the truest greatness, and real dignity is always condescending. It condescends to men of low estate. Job was a good man; and never from the beginning of the world to this hour was a good man to be met with who was useless. He who has the grace of God, has always a disposition to be useful; and we will add, he has also a capacity to be useful. He is in a happy measure qualified to glorify God; and serve his generation by his prayers, by the influence of his example, and by his life and lips.

We may remark here, that there were two ways in which Job exerted himself. First, by way of *instruction.* He had taught many; not a few, but *many.* When the ark was brought to Jerusalem, and placed for a season at Zion, David, you remember, offered burnt-offerings and peace-offerings before the Lord, he blessed also the people in the name of the Lord of Hosts, and then returned to bless his household. God says of Abraham, "I know him, that he will command his children and his household after him, that they shall keep the way of the Lord." Joshua said, "As for me and my house, we will serve the Lord." We may be sure then that Job did not overlook the instruction of his servants. He could say, "If I did despise the cause of my man-servant, or of my maid-servant when they contended with me, what then shall I do when God riseth up? and when He visiteth what shall I answer Him?" So then we are sure he would not neglect to instruct them. And he was so careful of his sons whenever they attended a festival in each other's house, that he always retired to pray, and offer a sacrifice for them, saying, "Lest my sons have sinned and cursed God in their hearts." Would he then neglect their instruction? Indeed here "He who provided not for his own hath denied the faith, and is worse than an infidel." It is false zeal that works abroad, and does nothing at home; that flames in the world, but goes out in dreadful darkness between God and the soul. But charity, which is allowed to *begin* at home, does not end there. So in regard to religion. First there is a personal, then family and domestic, then social and public solicitude. Job had instructed many—the poor, the young, and the old. We cannot determine the degree of knowledge he possessed, but we may be sure he was willing to communicate what he had received from God for this purpose, and in this he would be guided by his own convictions; for he has said, "Behold the fear of the Lord, that is wisdom, and to depart from evil is understanding."

There is none but has opportunities of instructing others. Though he may not have many, yet he has some, if he is willing to avail himself of them. For a word fitly spoken, how good it is! What did the woman of Samaria accomplish by the invitation, "Come, see a man that told me all things that ever I did; is not this the Christ?" In our day you have many opportunities of instructing others. You may send forth the Gospel, distribute religious tracts, teach the poor children in the Sunday-school.

> "O 'tis a glorious privilege to save,
> And he who scorns it is himself a slave."

Secondly, remark, Job exerted himself by way of *consoling*. "Thou hast strengthened the feeble knees." This language is metaphorical: it takes the members of the body and transfers them to the mind. For it is well known how depression makes the hands hang down and the knees to tremble; and where are the hands that never hang down or the knees that never tremble? The inference is, the effect of sympathy upon the mind. "Thy *words* have upholden him that was falling, and thou hast strengthened the feeble knees"—not exclusively—as if he had done nothing by actions. Job was not one of those who said, "Go in peace, be ye warmed and be ye clothed, notwithstanding ye give them not the things necessary for the body." He did not live in word only, but in deed and in truth. But how much is accomplished by words properly applied! How does the Gospel comfort us by the good news it brings under perplexing providences, under worldly cares, under bereaving dispensations, under bodily distresses, diseases, and infirmities. How does it support the wounded spirit, when overpowered by a sense of unworthiness and guilt, and when borne down by doubts and fears and spiritual conflicts. In this state God sometimes gives His people the tongue of the learned, and enables them to comfort others in their tribulations, with the comfort wherewith they themselves were comforted of God.

II. Observe WHAT IS SAID OF HIS ALLEGED INCONSISTENCIES. "But now it is come upon thee, and thou fainteth; it toucheth thee, and thou art troubled."

Job little imagined that he should stand in need of the consolation he had given to others. "Then I said I shall die in my nest, and I shall multiply my days as the sand." But how was it? He exclaims, "I was not in safety, neither had I rest, neither was I quiet, yet trouble came." You should always keep this in mind: the condition you see a fellow-creature in may be an emblem of your own very soon; you should say, "My neighbour has been bereaved of his child, and I may shortly be called to resign mine; I may soon lose my health, like my friend, and be made to possess months of vanity, and wearisome nights may be appointed me." Everything here is in perpetual change. Upon this, Solomon enforces charity. "Give a portion to seven, and also to eight, for thou knowest not what evil shall be upon the earth;" as much as to say, it may soon be your turn. So the Apostle to the Hebrews, "Remember them that are in bonds, as bound with them: and them which suffer adversity, as being yourselves also in the body;" and in writing to the Galatians, "Brethren, if a man be overtaken in a fault, ye which are spiritual restore such a one in the spirit of meekness, considering thyself lest thou also be tempted."

The charge here insinuated was not true in regard to Job; and it was not kind, candid or just in Eliphaz to speak of him thus. It is true Job did use some improper expressions in the paroxysm of his distress: he even cursed the day in which he was born, but then how did he receive the tidings of his successive calamities? What disposition had he displayed when he arose and rent his mantle, and shaved his head, and fell down upon the ground and worshipped, and said, "Naked came I out of my mother's womb, and naked shall I return thither: the Lord gave, and the Lord hath taken away; blessed be the name of the [Lord. In all this Job sinned not noi charged God foolishly." Why did not Eliphaz remember the answer he gave to his wife when she bid him curse God and die! You know Job replied, "What! shall we receive good at the Lord's hands, and shall we not receive evil?" Is a man to be judged of by a single action, or by a course of actions? Would an artist paint a man pallid with fear, or red with anger, because he once saw him so, instead of taking him according to his usual hue or complexion? O you cruel Eliphaz! Think of poor Job, of the greatness of his suffering, and the torture of his poor mind; "you have heard of the patience of Job, and have seen the end of the Lord; that the Lord is very pitiful, and of tender mercy." "Oh!" said David, "Let me fall into the hands of God, and not into the hands of man." You need not wonder that Job should say, "O that I knew where I might find Him, that I might come even to His seat! I would order my cause before Him, and fill my mouth with arguments." "Will He plead against me with His great power? No, but He would put strength in me." "Oh, let me be tried by Him who knoweth my frame, who remembers I am but dust!" "He knoweth the way that I take, though I may be unable to explain things to the satisfaction of those around me; but when I am tried, I shall come forth as gold." If Eliphaz was a good man, he was a very imperfect one, and I think a very unkind one.

The case here supposed does sometimes take place; there are persons to whom these words may be properly applied, "Behold, thou hast instructed many, and thou hast strengthened the feeble knees, thy words have upholden him that was falling, and thou hast strengthened the weak hands. But now it is come upon thee and thou faintest; it toucheth thee and thou art troubled." There are cases in which this happens really rather than blamably. There are some of God's people who cannot receive the comfort they communicate to others. This was the case with Cowper; he would go and encourage others, but could not take the comfort he administered. This might arise from some morbid affection in the physical system, and this in a degree may be the case with others who may be led to view things through a gloomy channel, and while they give comfort to others, refuse it themselves.

How much did Mr. Newton dread the consequences arising from the loss of his wife; he thought persons would naturally say, "You might find it easy to comfort others in their bereavements and trials, but how will you carry it out when you are called to suffer?" But by earnest prayer to God he was enabled to bear up with composure under this heavy trial, and even to preach her funeral sermon himself. Indeed, I heard him preach while she lay unburied.

The venerable and excellent Mr. Geard, of Hitchin, who was the esteemed Baptist minister there for about sixty years, for nearly three years during this period, though he preached the most consoling sermons which greatly encouraged others, yet he laboured under the most distressing apprehensions respecting the safety of his state towards God, not being able to realise his interest in the salvation which is in Christ Jesus; though after this, to the close of his very lengthened ministry, he was able to rejoice in the Lord and joy in the God of his salvation. And often, brethren, has the declaration been verified, "Weeping may endure for a night, but joy cometh in the morning."

III.

GOD'S KNOWLEDGE OF OUR LIFE.

(Delivered on Thursday Evening, May 27th, 1847.)

"*But He knoweth the way that I take.*"—JOB xxiii. 10.

THESE are the words of Job, and they may be taken two ways, according to the meaning of the word "know." This knowledge sometimes signifies approbation, sometimes intelligence. Yes, it sometimes signifies approbation, or complacency: "Know them that are over you in the Lord, and esteem them very highly in love for their work's sake;" "If a man love God the same is known of Him;" "The Lord knoweth the way of the righteous." In all these passages the word "know" signifies approbation; and it is what a Christian is so concerned to ascertain with regard to God. Hence the prayer of David, "Let the words of my mouth, and the meditation of my heart be acceptable in Thy sight, O Lord, my strength and my Redeemer!" Hence Paul says, "We labour that whether present or absent we may be accepted of Him." Acceptance, then, does not mean the acceptance of justification, but of approbation. But to ascertain this is no easy thing. Christians, under a sense of their unworthiness, of the imperfection of their performances, and the sins of their holy things, over which they blush and mourn, are often ready to say, "Can these services be approved of by God?" Yes, they "are accepted in the Beloved." All is presented and performed by the Saviour's mediation, and thus their sacrifices are "acceptable to God by Jesus Christ." They are also the work of His own Spirit, and however defective their services, they proceed from a principle of love flowing from the heart; and "the Lord looketh at the heart," and "where there is first a willing mind, it is accepted according to that a man hath, and not according to that he hath not." And oh, the happiness arising from this persuasion! "I am approved of God." This puts more joy into the Christian's heart than the worldling knows when his corn and wine increase. "Let them curse," says he; "but bless Thou! One smile of Thine will be enough to weigh down all the frowns of the universe." We read that Enoch was translated that he should not see death; for "before his translation he had this testimony that he pleased God." You are not to look for an extraordinary testimony like that which Enoch had; but He does not now suffer His people to pray in vain—"Say unto my soul I am thy salvation. Shew me a token for good, that I may be glad and rejoice in Thee," for He does this in various seasons and ways. "He takes pleasure in them that fear Him, in them that hope in His mercy." Their alms are as "an odour of a sweet smell;" their prayers are His delight; and He says, "Let Me see thy countenance, let Me hear thy voice, for sweet is thy voice, and thy countenance is comely."

But this word, in its more simple and common meaning, signifies intelligence. "He knoweth the way that I take;" that is, He is acquainted, entirely acquainted, with it. Let us then consider this reflection four ways. First, as true; secondly, as awful; thirdly, as encouraging; and, fourthly, as delightful. It is *true* with regard to all; awful with regard to the wicked; it is encouraging with regard to the penitent; delightful with regard to the believer.

I. Let us consider this as TRUE, true with regard to all. Omniscience is a perfection of the Divine nature. Even Deism admits this. There are wise men in the world, and there are angels much wiser than men, yet there are many things of which angels are ignorant; still they know much more than when they were created, and according to Peter, they are desirous of knowing more, especially of "the sufferings of Christ and the glory that should follow;" "which things," says he, "the angels desire to look into." But God is Omniscient. "His understanding is infinite." He knows all things, past, present, and future. Men know not what others may do, they know not what they themselves may do, it depends on circumstances over which they have no control. New occurrences lead to new views and determinations. But He knows all things—He knows all that the most changeable and wavering beings would accomplish or even wish. "All things," says Paul, "are naked and opened unto the eyes of Him with whom we have to do." All things are manifest in His sight. We know much less of persons than we may think, even with regard to those who appear to you the most intimate and unreserved, till the trial comes which developes the character, but He knows all; all their passions, all their actions, and their springs of action. "I, the Lord, search the heart; I try the reins of the children of men." "His eyes are in every place, beholding the evil and the good."

This doctrine needs no confirmation with regard to those who believe the revelation God has given us of Himself. But were we disposed to mention any arguments with regard to others, we should refer to conscience. Does not conscience bear testimony in your bosoms? Have you never been reproached, have you never been condemned by it when you have committed sins which no fellow-creature knew? But from whence did this fear arise? From an alarm within that God would remember.

We could also refer them to God's creation of all things, for surely He who made us cannot be ignorant of the being He has made. David, therefore, addressed some in his day thus: "Understand, ye brutish among the people, and ye fools, when will ye be wise? He that planted the ear, shall He not hear; He that formed the eye, shall he not see?"

We might also refer to the spirituality of His law. Human laws regard conduct only. Men can only infer the intention from the act, so that where there is no act in transgression the man cannot be condemned; but it is otherwise here. The commands of God comprehend the intention as well as the action, the disposition as well as the behaviour. A lascivious look, according to our Lord, is adultery, and groundless anger is murder. God's commands take cognisance of our thoughts. He must, therefore, as Law-giver, be acquainted with them. Would a Law-giver ever issue laws the infringement of which he would be unable to determine? If God did not know men, their intentions and designs, how could He judge the world? How could He judge the Jew who had the law, and the Gentile who was without the law? How could He determine between the servant who was to be beaten with many stripes, and the servant who was to be beaten with few? This, therefore, is a true reflection, "He knoweth the way that I take." It is true with regard to all. But—

II. We observe that it is AN AWFUL REFLECTION—Awful with regard to the wicked. What emboldens them to sin, but the hope of concealment? What says Job in the following chapter? "The eye also of the adulterer waiteth for the twilight, saying, No eye shall see me, and disguiseth his face. In the dark they dig through houses, which they had marked for themselves in the daytime; they know not the light. For the morning is to them even as the shadow of death; if one know them they are in the terrors of the shadow of death." The very presence of a child will restrain from the commission of many a sin. But what secrecy can there be here? He knows the way of man. "For the ways of man are before the eyes of the Lord, and He pondereth all his goings." "There is no darkness nor shadow of death where the workers of iniquity may hide themselves: Hell is naked before Him, and destruction hath no covering."

It is an awful reflection, because as He knows it He may make it known. In vain did Achan endeavour to conceal his sin, it was discovered to his own destruction. All things are under the direction and control and providence of God.

It is awful, because He abhors all sin, and records all to bring it into judgment with every secret thing. It is awful, because you cannot elude His research and His penetration. "Though they dig into hell," He says, "thence shall mine hand take them; though they climb up to heaven, thence will I bring them down."

There is something very irksome in this consideration to the men of the world. The wicked wish to banish this reflection from their minds, instead of cherishing it. "He knoweth the way that I take." There are two ways by which men may endeavour to get rid of it. One is by infidelity, by not believing it, which renders it a nonentity; and the other is by diversion. The thing will arise up in the mind, but it is possible by company, by business, and amusement, to drive it far away, so that the man for the time is no more influenced by it, but is as though it was absolutely denied. But does He hear all I speak? Does He see all I do? Does He witness all I imagine? He does, and how often do you indulge much more iniquity within than you ever commit without, so that if your hearts were suspended where your foreheads are, you would be ashamed to go out of your houses, or to mingle with company. Men love to be free, not only from restraint, but also from observation. How intolerable would you feel it to be always under the eye of one whom you disliked, who was always listening to what you said and who would mark down all you did, even in your most retired actions! Such is God to the natural man. Men wish to live without Him. How painful therefore for them to know that He is always near them, and noting down all they say. And how gladly would they avoid it! But ah, they know this is impossible.

There is one case in which it is peculiarly awful—that is, when the wicked assume religious professions and pretensions; when they act as if they belonged to God, while their souls are in the world. "What is the hope of the hypocrite when God taketh away his soul?"

> "God is a Spirit, just and wise,
> He sees our inmost mind;
> In vain to heaven we lift our eyes,
> And leave our souls behind."

"I know the blasphemy of them that say they are Jews and are not, but are of the synagogue of Satan." "Be not deceived, God is not mocked." You may impose upon your fellow-creatures, you may impose upon your fellow-members, you may impose upon your minister, but you cannot impose upon God. This, therefore, is an awful reflection, awful with regard to the wicked, "Thou, God, seest me."

> "O may this thought possess my breast,
> Where'er I roam, where'er I rest;
> Nor let my weaker passions dare
> Consent to sin, for God is there."

III. It is ENCOURAGING.—Encouraging to penitents. There is a difference between secret joy and secret sorrow. Secret joy is very powerful and very manifestative, it often will break forth and make itself known to others. But secret sorrow seeks solitude. "He sitteth alone and keepeth silence, he layeth his hand upon his mouth, if so be there may be hope." The convinced sinner, like the stricken deer, leaves the herd, and he is found much alone, and little do those around him, little do his immediate friends and relations, know what is passing in his mind; little do they know his conflicts and fears, but the Lord observes him: He sees the tear that drops upon his Bible. When he has entered his closet and shut the door, the Lord seeth him. Nathaniel had many imperfections, but our Saviour seeing him said, "Behold an Israelite, indeed, in whom is no guile." His heart was divinely touched; he was fond of retirement, and had retired to meditate and pray, little suspecting that through the thick boughs of the figtree any would discover him. But says the

Saviour, "When thou wast under the figtree I saw thee." Oh! said Nathaniel, in consequence of this, "Thou art the King of Israel, Thou art the Son of God." And said the Saviour, "Thou shalt see greater things than these." Ephraim also had retired to give vent to his distresses, and God heard him, and heard the language of his heart; it is probable he did not use these very words, but says God, "I have heard him bemoaning himself thus: Thou hast chastised me and I was chastised as a bullock unaccustomed to the yoke; turn thou me, and I shall be turned; for thou art the Lord my God. Surely after that I was turned I repented; and after that I was instructed I smote upon my thigh; I was ashamed, yea, even confounded, because I did bear the reproach of my youth." God could bear it no longer. "Is Ephraim my dear son? is he a pleasant child? for since I spake against him, I do earnestly remember him still." "Yes," says He, "to that man will I look, even to him that is poor"—that is, poor in spirit, who has a sense of his being a fallen creature, and of his possessing no worthiness of his own; who knows that if he be saved, it must be by grace; that if he be fed and clothed, it must be by charity, and that he must live upon alms. "To that man will I look who is humble and of a contrite spirit and who trembleth at my word." Yea, more than this, He has promised not only to look to this man, but "He that inhabiteth eternity, whose name is Holy, who dwelleth in the high and holy place," dwells also with the contrite and the humble. Be this ever remembered, and it will serve to show that this reflection is encouraging—encouraging to the penitent. "He knoweth the way that I take."

Lastly, It is DELIGHTFUL—delightful to the believer. He possesses not a self-righteous persuasion that God will see nothing in him that is amiss. Alas, he sees much in himself which induces him to say with Job, "Behold I am vile, I repent in dust and ashes." But the principle upon which the believer rejoices is, that God Himself will see nothing wrong in him but what he himself desires to see rectified, and he knows that God can do this, and deliver him from it. Why, then, should you wish to conceal anything from Him? If you call in a physician, would it be wise to hide from him any part of your complaint? The more perfectly he knows your constitution and your case the better. So in regard to the believer.

There are five instances to which we might refer. The first is in regard to his remaining corruptions. These he wishes to be acquainted with. How else can he be humbled? How else can he watch against them? How else can he pray for their pardon? But who can make this known but God? Who can understand his errors? Who else can hear his prayer, "Search me, O God, try my reins and my heart?"

The second is under misrepresentations and mistakes. You should never despise the opinions of your fellow-creatures: "A good name is rather to be chosen than great riches." Reputation is to be valued as a means of usefulness, but there are cases in which we must act independently and throw ourselves upon the candour of others. You may not be able to make out your justification to some of your fellow-creatures, or even to some of your fellow-Christians; yet you may be able to say with Job, "My witness is in heaven, and my record is on high." Yet you may say with David, when charged with being an ambitious youth, who wished to rise from his privacy into public notice, "Lord, my heart is not haughty, nor my eyes lofty, neither do I exercise myself in matters too high for me."

It is a delightful reflection in trial and distress, "He knoweth the way that I take;" "He knows my soul in adversity." If I am oppressed, He knows where the burden wrings. He knows my anxiety lest in suffering I should dishonour His holy name. It affords me a delightful thought that He who has afflicted me knows when to afflict—in what part to afflict—how long to afflict—and when to deliver me from it.

Then also it is a delightful reflection under perplexing dispensations of Providence. These are often very trying. This was the case with Job here in connection with our text. "Behold," says he, "I go forward, but He is not there; and backward, but I cannot perceive Him; on the left hand where He doth work, but I cannot behold Him; He hideth Himself on the right hand, that I cannot see Him! But He can see me, though I cannot see Him. He knoweth the way that I take." If you are travelling, it is not necessary that you should know the way, if you are under a guide that does; and this is the case with regard to you. Therefore, says God, I will bring the blind by a way that they know not; I will lead them in paths which they have not known; I will make darkness light before them, and crooked things straight; these things will I do unto them, and not forsake them."

Finally, it is a delightful reflection with regard to any movement in life, any change in connection, any removal of station, and a thousand other things in which Christians should act with circumspection, being concerned that "whatever they do, to do all to the glory of God." But sometimes how are they embarrassed. In some cases they know not the way they are to take, yet they know that "the way of man is not in himself to direct his steps." But he knows one way he is to take. "Trust in the Lord with all thine heart, and lean not to thine own understanding. In all thy ways acknowledge Him, and He shall direct thy steps." "This God is our God for ever and ever. He will be our guide even unto death." Beyond this we shall be in no danger. "Blessed are the people who are in such a case. Yea, blessed are the people whose God is the Lord." This, therefore, is a delightful reflection with regard to the believer, "He knoweth the way that I take."

IV.

TRUST AND LOVE.

(Delivered on Thursday Evening, April 13th, 1848.)

"*I will love Thee, O Lord, my strength. The Lord is my rock, and my fortress, and my deliverer; my God, my strength, in whom I will trust; my buckler, and the horn of my salvation, and my high tower.*" —PSALM xviii. 1, 2.

THERE are three modes of speaking in regard to God: there is a speaking for God, there is a speaking of God, and there is a speaking to God. There is a speaking *for* God; and it becomes us to espouse His cause, to defend His truth, and to commend His people, as we have opportunity, and not, in the presence of His enemies, to sit, as David says, "as those in whose mouths there is no reproof." Then there is a speaking *of* God. And oh, how pleasing and profitable is it to speak of His word, of His works, of His ways, of His dealings in Providence, and of His gracious dealings towards His people, saying with the psalmist, "Come and hear, all ye that fear God, and I will declare what He hath done for my soul;" and with the Church, "I will mention the loving-kindness of the Lord and the praises of the Lord, according to all that the Lord hath bestowed upon us, and the great goodness towards the house of Israel which He hath bestowed upon them, according to His mercies and according to the multitude of His loving-kindnesses." And there is a speaking *to* God. And this is a much better evidence of the sincerity of your love to God than either of the former. There are many who speak *of* God, yea many who speak *for* God, who yet never speak *to* Him. There is an awful silence between God and their souls. But if a man can return and place himself as in the Divine presence, and under those eyes, which are as a flame of fire, and look up to God, saying, "Lord, I have loved the habitation of Thy house and the place where Thine honour dwelleth; I will love Thee O Lord, my strength; the Lord is my rock, my fortress, and my deliverer; my God, my strength, in whom I will trust; my buckler, and the horn of my salvation, and my high tower," then you may be assured that you are "an Israelite, indeed, in whom is no guile." I fear there are some here this evening who have never said anything like this to God; I dare not hope better things of you; but there are some, there are I trust many here who, though sensible of a thousand imperfections, can still look up, and say, "Lord, Thou knowest all things; Thou knowest that I love Thee." So it was with David, whose words we have been reading. Here we have David's love to God, and David's views of God, but let us leave the order of the words, and consider the order of the thing, and note—

I. What David says for God.

He views Him as his own, and views Him under various allusions, all of which are very striking, and very interesting. Let us see therefore how he claims Him, and what he calls Him. He calls Him his—his by appropriation.

He calls Him his by appropriation, and nine times he repeats this appropriation: my Strength—my Rock—My Fortress—my Deliverer—my God—my Strength—my Buckler—my Salvation, and my High Tower." Now this is true with regard to all the partakers of divine grace, but all the partakers of divine grace cannot express this with an unwavering tongue, and an untrembling heart. Many of them feel doubts and fears concerning this, but they all desire and seek after this, therefore their prayer is, "Say unto my soul, I am thy salvation." Oh, what a blessed thing is the attainment, and assurance of this; and this is attainable.

> "When I can say my God is mine,
> When I can feel His glories shine,
> I tread the world beneath my feet,
> And all that earth calls good or great."

But observe here what he calls God: "His Strength—his Rock—his Fortress—his Deliverer—his God—his Buckler—his Salvation, and his High Tower." All these representations are acknowledged to be figures, but then they are figures founded in realities, and the substance will always be verified, and even exceed the similes themselves: they show at once what God is to His people; and tha tin His perfection,—in His covenant engagements—in His promises—in His providence and in His grace, there is an all-sufficiency adequate to relieve all their wants, to accomplish all their hopes, and to fulfil all their desires. Yea, God hath promised to "do for them exceeding abundantly above all that they can ask or think."

But how are these figures to be explained? Are we to explain them distinctively? No, some of them are hardly distinguishable; they run into each other; they seem to be a tautology, a repetition. They are so—they were designed to be so. They show us the force of the subject, and that in contemplation the author was overpowered with it. He could not be silent on the one hand, and could not do justice to it on the other. He therefore breaks forth with a kind of tautology and repetition. "The Lord is my rock and my fortress, and my deliverer; my God, my strength, in whom I will trust; my buckler, and the horn of my salvation, and my high tower." We have a similar instance to this in the Book of Revelation, for John says, "Worthy is the Lamb that was slain to receive power, and riches, and wisdom, and strength, and honour, and glory and blessing."

Some of these qualities cannot be distinguished from others; they were not intended to be so. The design was to show the importance of the thing, and even those glorious beings which are spoken of as being proverbial for their knowledge were overpowered with the thing, and could not do justice to the subject; therefore they broke forth in holy confusion, "Worthy is the Lamb that was slain to receive power, and riches, and wisdom, and strength, and honour, and glory, and blessing;" that is, every excellence is possessed by Him, and every praise is due to Him.

If we could distinguish these various articles from each other, the time of this brief exercise would not allow of our attempting it; we had better therefore fix upon one of them. And suppose we take the first, where he says, "I will love Thee, O Lord, my *strength*." What a feeble creature is man of himself! View him when he is born, how unable is he to take care of himself, and he has wants and necessities he is unable to relieve; therefore if he lives, others must take the charge of him. He grows in stature, he walks and exercises his senses, he sees, he hears, he feels, he observes and searches; and when we consider the frailty of his body, of the multitude of the organs of which it is constituted, the derangement of any one of which might occasion the destruction of the whole, and which we could not prevent, we see how entirely dependent we are on the providence of God, and the Christian will be induced to say with David, "Thou didst make me hope while I was upon my mother's breast," and with Watts,

"And from my mother's painful hour,
I am entirely Thine."

As he grows up, will he have then reason to glory in his strength? "Is his strength the strength of stones? or is his flesh of brass?" The weather may disconcert him, or an accident lay him aside; a cold may chill him, or disease may hasten his death; a fever may burn his brain, or a dropsy may drown his breath. But who brings him back from the borders of the grave? and braces up his nerves, and renews his strength like the eagle's? O, where is the man that has not in passing through life often raised an Ebenezer, saying, "Having obtained help of the Lord we continue to this day"?

But David regards God as the source of his *spiritual* strength. He is the strength of the believer's soul, of his principles, of his graces, of his convictions, and of his resolutions. Man, by the fall, was left without strength, as well as without righteousness. I have always found it more easy to convince men of their guilt, than of their weakness. They can hardly forbear to own that they have done that which they ought not to have done, and have neglected to do that which they ought to have done, though they do not like to say, or if they say it, they do not feel the truth of it. "There is no health in us." Therefore they conclude that they are *able* to render themselves religious whenever they choose, and resolve to do it at some future period. But the trial soon convinces them of the contrary, and they then feel that it is impossible to repent, believe, and obey of ourselves; and this conviction brings them, where we ought always to be, upon our knees, sensible, not only of our guilt, but of our inability, and praying that God would "work in us to will and to do of His good pleasure."

> "Man's wisdom is to seek
> His strength in God alone,
> And e'en an angel would be weak
> That trusted in his own."

The Christian, from a sense of his own insufficiency, feels that he cannot go farther than God leads him, or stand longer than God holds him: therefore he prays, "Hold Thou me up, and I shall be safe."

We cannot enlarge here, but must just observe that God's strength is without bounds and without limitation. We can do nothing without the help of God. "He speaks, and it is done; He commands, and it is made sure." "With Him is the residue of the Spirit;" and we "can do all things through Him that strengthens us."

We may observe also, that God can really communicate

strength. We can administer medicine to the sick, or lift him up, or lead him along, but we cannot impart strength to him. But "He giveth power to the faint, and to him that hath no might He increaseth strength." "Even the youths shall faint and be weary, and the young men shall utterly fail; but they that wait upon the Lord shall renew their strength; they shall mount up with wings as eagles; they shall run and not be weary; and they shall walk and not faint."

We may observe also, that His strength is made perfect in the weakness of His people. From the beginning of the world, they have been a large number taking them altogether, and all of them have been insufficient of themselves to do anything, even to think a good thought. Whence then comes their insufficiency, and what has rendered them so efficient? What has enabled them to defy their adversaries, and to glorify God their Heavenly Father? Who enabled Enoch to walk with God? and Noah to preach to the men of his generation? and Moses to choose affliction with the people of God rather than the pleasures of sin for a season? Who enabled Abraham to offer up his son, his only son, whom he loved? Who enabled Joseph to maintain reputation? and the three Hebrew children to brave the fiery furnace? All the goodness, and the excellency which have been displayed since the beginning of the world, came from Him whom David calls his strength.

II. Observe DAVID'S LOVE OF GOD. "I will *love* Thee, O Lord, my strength." Paul says, "Hope maketh not ashamed, because the love of God is shed abroad in the heart by the Holy Ghost given unto us." He there shows us the origin, and the author of this love to God, viz., the Holy Spirit; He it is that removes the blindness from our souls and the hardness from our hearts. We live in the Spirit, and walk in the Spirit, and without His influence no man ever really loved God. He may have loved an imaginary being. If men can persuade themselves that God is altogether such an one as themselves; if they can believe that God does not hate sin, and will not punish them for their iniquities, they may; but will it allow them (as Latimer says) "to dance with the devil all day, to sup with the Saviour at night, and to be for ever with the Lord?" They may love this idol of the brain, but not the God of the Scriptures. No, to love such a character we must be made partakers of His holiness, for

> "None but the soul that feels His grace,
> Can triumph in His holiness."

But the Spirit's influences are rational, and the Christian can give a reason of the hope that is in him. He loves Him for what He is in Himself, as well as what He is towards His creatures. Some have vainly talked of the dark side of the Deity, but the Scripture tells us, "In Him is no darkness at all;" and the Christian rejoices in this, that "He is righteous in all His ways, and holy in all His works." The Christian does not wish to bring his God down to his imperfect ideas, but to rise to His excellency, and to be "changed into the same image from glory to glory, as by the Spirit of the Lord." He loves Him for what He does—for what He does for others, for he is told to love others as himself; for what He has done for them in their trials and distresses. Who would not feel a regard for benefactors of the human race on account of what they have done for others? And the Christian loves God upon the same principle. He loves Him for having saved Manassah, Saul of Tarsus, and the Corinthians; he loves Him for saving his friends, yea, and for saving his enemies. That individual must be a selfish wretch who does not feel a regard for a Howard or a Thornton for what they have done for others, but he must be a much more ungrateful creature if he does not love them for what he has done for himself; if they have visited him at the peril of their lives, and relieved him from time to time. So, brethren, it is here; "We love Him, because He first loved us." "I love the Lord," says David. Why? Not only for what He is in Himself—for this I love Him; but "I love the Lord because He hath heard my voice and my supplications." And will you not love Him on the same account? Hath He not heard your voice and your supplication? and will you not resolve to "call upon Him as long as you live?" The believer loves God as his Creator and Preserver, and for all the blessings of the life that now is, but above all, for His inestimable love in the redemption of the world by our Lord Jesus Christ. And can you help loving Him who has forgiven you all trespasses? who hath renewed you in the spirit of your mind? who has preserved you from so many dangers, and who is also engaged to bless you for ever? For we observe that the Christian loves God for what He hath promised to do also. Thus said David, "Who am I, O Lord God? and what is my house, that Thou hast brought me hitherto? And this was yet a small thing in thy sight, O Lord God, but Thou hast spoken also of thy servant's house for a great while to come. Is this the manner of man, O Lord God?" Thus may the Christian express himself, and rejoice that God has engaged to guide him with His counsel, to supply all his need, to make all things work together for his good, to receive his soul at death, in the resurrection to recompense him; and the Saviour has said, "Where I am, there shall he be also." "I will love Thee, O Lord, my strength."

But now how does the Christian love Him? He loves Him *supremely*, for you do not love God *at all* unless you love Him *above all*. God is the King in Zion and He is the Husband of His Church. In Him are majesty and mercy combined, and He has no rivalry of claim, or competition of affection. 'Tis true the Christian does not love God perfectly, but he desires to do so, and to love Him with all his heart and soul and strength. There is no one whose favour he so much prizes, no one whose presence he so much wishes to enjoy, whose excellence he so much desires to resemble. Is not this a proof of affection? "But oh," says the Christian, "I fear I do not love Him." But whence comes this fear? Does not this show the bias of the mind? "Oh," says the Christian, "that I knew I was accepted in the Beloved!" Whence comes this concern? Is not this an evidence, not only of the reality, but of the supremacy of this affection? Then, he loves Him *sincerely*—not like Judas who gave the Saviour the lip only; not like those who draw near to Him "with their mouth and with their lips do honour Him, while their heart is far from Him;" not like those of whom Ezekiel speaks, when he says, "They come unto Thee, as the people come, and they sit before Thee as my people, and they hear Thy words, but they will not do them, for with their mouth they show much love, but their heart goeth after their covetousness." No, since the love of God has been shed abroad in their hearts, they love to keep His commandments, and His commandments are not grievous. This love brings us to His footstool, and leads us to ask, "Lord, what wilt Thou have me to do?" "Speak, Lord, for Thy servant heareth." Then this love is constant in its exercise. It can never be destroyed. There may be some emotions excited by external circumstances in the minds of the unregenerate, but these will die away with the occasions that produced them. Not so with the love of Christ, nothing can separate us from this; and the Saviour says, "The water that I shall give him shall be in him a well of water springing up to everlasting life." True grace at first is small, but like the precious grain, there is seen "first the blade, then the corn, then the full corn in the ear." And "the path of the just is as the shining light, which shineth more and more unto the perfect day."

V.

THE PRACTICE AND THE PRIVILEGE OF THE GODLY.

(Delivered on Thursday Evening, April 10th, 1851.)

"*For this shall everyone that is godly pray unto Thee in a time when Thou mayest be found: surely in the floods of great waters they shall not come nigh unto him.*"—PSALM xxxii. 6.

"As in water face answereth to face, so does the heart of man to man." From his own experience David concludes what would be the disposition and pursuit of those who should come after him, in all the future conditions of the Church. "For this shall everyone that is godly pray unto Thee in a time when Thou mayest be found." Many have supposed that David after his transgression felt no remorse till Nathan came to him and said, "Thou art the man;" but this is a mistake. His sin was ever before him, and his conscience was filled with anguish and horror; but he was unwilling to humble himself as a sinner before God, and condemn himself as a criminal before men, and this only served to aggravate his torture. At length the coal which was concealed in his bosom burnt its way through, and at last being no longer able to endure, he resolved to make a free, full, and open confession, and then he obtained relief. Hear him! "When I kept silence, my bones waxed old through my roaring all the day long. For day and night Thy hand was heavy upon me; my moisture is turned into the drought of summer. I acknowledged my sin unto Thee and mine iniquity have I not hid. I said, I will confess my transgression unto the Lord, and Thou forgavest the iniquity of my sin. For *this* shall everyone that is godly pray unto Thee in a time when thou mayest be found: surely in the floods of great waters they shall not come nigh unto him."

There are three things here to be briefly noticed: the persons, the practice, and the privilege.

I. The PERSONS. "The godly."

If there were no such persons as these, the language would be futile and absurd; but there always have been such; there always will be. There are such in this world which lieth in the wicked one, and we have reason to hope the number is increasing; and the Lord add to His people, however so many there be, a thousandfold. Many of these may be poor and needy, and afflicted, and they may be overlooked by the world and despised, but they are the most significant characters upon earth; of them the world is not worthy. They are of importance; they are "the chariots of Israel, and the horsemen thereof." They have power with God, and can prevail. And how does He express himself with regard to them? "Since thou hast been precious in my sight, thou hast been honourable and I have loved thee."

"And therefore," says David, "the Lord hath set apart him that is godly for Himself."

But, now, who are they? They are those who *know* God. It has been said by the Church of Rome, "Ignorance is the mother of devotion;" and if they mean of *their* devotion, it would be true enough. For surely nothing but ignorance would lead them to believe the mummeries and false miracles which they profess to believe. But it is not the mother of our devotion. We do not worship an unknown God. "We know whom we worship." An old writer says, "God never works in a dark shop; He always strikes a light when He goes to work; and gives the light of the knowledge of the glory of God as it shines in the face of Jesus Christ." The truth he is taught makes the believer feel so that he is able to give a reason of the hope that is in him. Though there are many things he remains ignorant of, he is taught the knowledge of Him whom to know is life eternal.

They also *fear* Him and *love* Him. I mention these together because the one involves the other; yea, in reality this fear and this love are the very same. The love of God is the fear of God, and the fear of God is the love of God. You will observe that love does not operate precisely in the same manner towards a superior as it does towards an inferior, but shows itself in a way of reverence, submission, and obedience. It may, therefore, seem paradoxical to some, but it is true, that the more you love God the more you will fear Him; the more you will fear to offend Him; the more you will dread to grieve His Holy Spirit; the more you will endeavour to please Him; and the more you will be found upon your knees, praying, "Let the words of my mouth and the meditation of my heart be acceptable in Thy sight, O Lord, my strength and my Redeemer."

They also *resemble* Him. They are partakers of God—they are partakers of His holiness; they are partakers of the divine nature, that is, by likeness and imitation. They are obedient children, not fashioning themselves according to their former lusts in their ignorance, but as He that has called them is holy, so are they holy in all manner of conversation. They are followers of God as dear children, and in their measure and degree are pure as He is pure. They make His word their rule, and the only rule of their conduct; they make His honour the aim, and the only aim of their lives; and whether they eat or drink, or whatever they do, they do all to the glory of God. They acknowledge Him in all their ways. Says the Apostle, "We have not received the spirit of the world, but the Spirit which is of God, that we may know the things which are freely given unto us of God." The ungodly receive the spirit of the world, and so are made partakers of it; they are transformed into its nature: on the other hand, the godly receive the Spirit which is of God, and this changes them into the same likeness from glory to glory; this transforms them from earth to heaven, from a carnal to a spiritual mind. Then they are new creatures; old things having passed away, all things having become new. So much for the persons.

II. Observe THE PRACTICE. "For this shall everyone that is godly pray unto Thee in a time when Thou mayest be heard." And here notice four things.

First, you see what is their course: "For this shall every one that is godly *pray* unto Thee." They are all praying characters: this characterizes them all. This is the generation of them that seek Him. By this are they described from the beginning of their religious course, and through the whole of their future life. They cannot live without it, any more than without their daily food. They consider it their honour, their duty, and their privilege. They know the command of God is, to "pray without ceasing." "Be instant in prayer." They know the determinations of God who hath said, "For this will I be enquired of by the house of Israel, to do it for them;" and they know that He has a right to determine the way in which He will communicate His favours, since they have no claim upon Him; and they know that He is the only Judge of the way which will most materially conduce to His glory and their welfare. And as they know it is the only way of success, so they know it is the *sure* way of success. They know His character is a God hearing and answering prayer; that He has never said to the seed of Jacob, "Seek ye me in vain;" but they know also that He has said "Their heart shall live that seek God." "Seek, and ye shall find."

Then you observe, secondly, the *Object*. "For *this* shall every one that is godly pray unto Thee." For what? They have numberless wants. They want wisdom, they want strength, they want peace and joy. But the reference seems here to forgiveness. Forgiveness is an inestimable blessing. Reflecting upon this, David is constrained to exclaim in the preceding verses, "Blessed is he whose transgression is forgiven, whose sin is covered. Blessed is the man to whom the Lord imputeth not iniquity, and in whose spirit there is no guile." Such a man "is truly blessed; he is blessed because his happiness is ensured." Forgiveness is a blessing that takes away the sting of death; it removes the curse of affliction. Without this blessing a man would be miserable in a palace; and in the possession of it he would be happy in the confines of a prison. This forgiveness ensures for him assistance in all duties, sweetens his temporal comforts, and brightens all his future prospects. This is the blessing which they implore.

Observe, thirdly, the *Universality* of the prayer. "For this shall *every one* that is godly pray unto Thee." This shows us that they all need it, every one. "For this shall every one pray unto Thee"—whatever be his advancement or progress in religion, he needs to pray, and feels that he needs it. What advances had Paul made in the divine life! and yet he says, "I have not yet attained, neither am already perfect." Solomon says, "There is not a just man on earth who liveth and sinneth not;" and says James, "In many things we offend all." And our Saviour admonishes us to pray for daily pardon as well as for daily food. The people of God while here are sanctified only in part: this humbles them before God. Then there is a law in their members warring against the law of their minds, so that when they would do good evil is present with them, and induces them to exclaim, "O wretched man that I am! who shall deliver me from the body of this death?" and this makes them long for heaven, where

> "Sin their worst enemy before,
> Shall vex their eyes and ears no more."

Observe, lastly, *When* they pray. "For this shall every one that is godly pray unto thee *in a time when Thou mayest be found,*" for there is a time when He is *not* to be found; and therefore says Isaiah, "Seek ye the Lord while He may be found; call ye upon Him while He is near."

Now, what is this time in which He is to be found? In one sense it takes in the whole length of the dispensation of the Gospel. The Apostle says, "Now is the accepted time; now is the day of salvation." In another view it takes in the whole length of life. Beyond this there is no work, nor knowledge, or device, or wisdom; that is, so as to affect their state or character after death. It has been questioned by some whether this time of audience—the day of life and the day of grace—are equal. Some very rash things have been said of persons surviving the day of grace, in the case of Francis Spiro and others who were driven out of their senses. In a general way we may say, "While there's life there's hope; and as Watts expresses it—

> "While the lamp holds out to burn,
> The vilest sinner may return."

But we would not make the awful trial whether the day of grace is as long as the day of life. Remember God has said, "My Spirit shall not always strive with man." Remember He has said, "He that being often reproved hardeneth his neck, shall suddenly be destroyed, and that without remedy." "Because I have called and ye have refused; I have stretched out my hand and no man regarded; but ye have set at naught all my counsel, and would none of my reproofs: I also will laugh at your calamity; I will mock when your fear cometh."

When Felix was reproved by Paul, he turned and felt as he never felt before or after; but instead of cherishing the impression, he attempted to drive it off, therefore he said to Paul, "Go thy way for this time; when I have a more convenient season I will call for thee." That convenient season came, for he had several interviews with Paul afterwards, and heard him speak of faith in Christ, but the feeling was gone, the conviction was gone for ever! Beware, therefore, how you trifle with conviction. Whenever you feel an inclination to pray, be sure it is a time in which you may be heard; for it is God that produces in you this excitement. It is God that urges you to pray, and He would not trifle with you; He would not mock you; He would not excite in you these desires that you may return to Him, saying, "Take away all iniquity, and receive me graciously," unless He intended to hear and answer you.

III. The Privilege. "Surely in the floods of great waters they shall not come nigh unto him."

The language is figurative. "Floods of great waters" mean great sufferings and afflictions. We often find the representation combined with fire. "We went," says the Church, "through fire and through water, but Thou broughtest us out into a wealthy place."

But do these great waters never come near the people of God? Did they not come near Joseph when he was in the pit, and in the prison? Did they not come near Job when he was stript of all he had? Did they not come near Jeremiah when he was cast into the dungeon? Did they not come near David when he said, "All Thy waves and Thy billows are gone over me"? What becomes, then, of the assurance, "Surely in the great waters they shall not come nigh him"? The language of Scripture is bold, and often requires considerable qualifications.

What is the assurance here? We know that no trial or affliction can come near the people of God without the knowledge, the arrangement, and permission of God. Sometimes He guards them naturally in cases of public calamity from evil; sometimes the interposition is remarkable, and so that a man shall say, "Verily there is a reward for the righteous: verily there is a God that judgeth in the earth." He is always able to screen His people; and He punishes His enemies at the same time and under the same dispensation. Thus it was in the deluge when Noah was preserved. Thus it was with Lot, when Sodom and Gomorrah was destroyed; and with the Israelites in the land of Egypt, who were free from all the plagues inflicted upon the Egyptians. So Peter says, "The Lord knoweth how to deliver the godly out of temptation, and to reserve the wicked unto the day of punishment." But then further you will observe that if He does not keep them from the suffering, He keeps them from injury in the suffering; so that it does not really come like a calamity, and with the Apostle they can say, "We are troubled on every side, yet not distressed; we are perplexed, but not in despair; persecuted, but not forsaken; cast down, but not destroyed"—like a man in a ship in the midst of deep waters; but they do not come near him so as to destroy, though they are not far off. Thus they find as their sufferings abound, their consolations abound also.

Then all will go into a state of destruction. "The heavens and the earth shall pass away, and all the works that are in them shall be burnt up ; " yet the Christian shall stand erect and secure amidst the destroying elements :

> "When desolation like a flood,
> O'er the proud sinner rolls ;
> They find a refuge in their God,
> And He defends their souls."

And even in the universal catastrophe will find a new heaven and new earth wherein dwelleth righteousness.

Two conclusions therefore arise from all this.

One is, the ungodly and the prayerless shall tremble. They have no security in life or in death. " The wicked are like the troubled sea, when it cannot rest, whose waters cast up mire and dirt. There is no peace, saith my God, to the wicked."

The other is, that the godly and the prayerful shall be courageous and cheerful. You may, Christians, be opposed, but you can say with David, " The Lord is my light and my salvation, whom shall I fear? the Lord is the strength of my life ; of whom shall I be afraid? You know not what a day may bring forth, but you know that all times are in His hand. You know not what you may lose or suffer, but you know that all the ways of the Lord are mercy and truth to them that fear Him, and that all things work together for good to them that love Him.

VI.

THE FAVOUR OF GOD.

(Delivered on Thursday Evening, February 25th, 1847.)

"*By this I know that Thou favourest me, because mine enemy doth not triumph over me. And as for me, Thou upholdest me in mine integrity, and settest me before Thy face for ever. Blessed be the Lord God of Israel from everlasting, and to everlasting. Amen, and Amen.*"—PSALM xli. 11-13.

So then David had an enemy. Yes, however amiable, however wise, however pious, he had an enemy. And who has not? "Woe unto you, when all men shall speak well of you," said the Saviour. The righteous have no reason to fear, for they are always taught in the Scriptures to reckon upon being evil-spoken of and persecuted. Some are ready to suppose that this is owing to the falls and miscarriages of professors themselves. There *are* those through whom "the way of truth is evil-spoken of," and who "cause the worthy name by which they are called to be blasphemed." "What glory is it, if when ye be buffetted for your faults, ye take it patiently?" "Let no man," says Peter, "suffer as a murderer, or as a thief, or as an evil-doer, or as a busybody in other men's matters." But, my brethren, could we remove everything that is improper and disagreeable from the character of Christians, religion would not be beloved by the world. No, look at the Saviour Himself. Was He chargeable with any impropriety? Yet, was He admired? Was He approved of? "Marvel not," says the Saviour, "if the world hate you. It hated me before it hated you. If ye were of the world, the world would love his own, but because ye are not of the world, even as I am not of the world, therefore the world hateth you."

David's enemy here was Ahitophel. You see this in the preceding words, "Yea, mine own familiar friend in whom I trusted, who did eat of my bread, hath lifted up his heel against me." David had been sadly distressed by him, and how he felt the disappointment is obvious from the fifty-fifth psalm: "For it was not an enemy that reproached me; then I could have borne it; neither was it he that hated me that did magnify himself against me: then I would have hid myself from him; but it was thou, a man, mine equal, my guide and mine acquaintance. We took sweet counsel together, and walked unto the house of God in company." "A brother is born for adversity," but the season in which Ahitophel abandoned David was the time of Absalom's rebellion, and when he was exiled from his palace. It is thus worldly friends regard their connections, as men treat their gardens; walking in them in summer, and forsaking them in winter; or as persons use their nosegays, putting them in their bosoms while they are fresh and green, and flinging them into the street when they wither. Thus builders by their scaffolding raise their edifice, then take it down and lay it aside.

But David says, "Thou, O Lord, be merciful to me and raise me up, that I may requite them." If this breathes anything like vengeance, we do not commend it; but it is the prophet who speaks rather than the man; and David expresses his expectation rather than his desire. But it was lawful for David to pray for his own deliverance, therefore he said, "O Lord, turn the counsel of Ahitophel into foolishness;" and no sooner was the prayer offered, than it was answered, and He turned "the counsel of Ahitophel into foolishness."

We should learn here to put our confidence in Him who has all events at His disposal, and all hearts under His control. He can make "the wrath of men to praise Him, and the remainder of wrath He can restrain." You see this wily sycophant, stung with mortification at having his counsel despised and lampooned, rises early in the morning, saddles his ass, puts his house in order, and hangs himself. Suicide is commonly the effect of derangement. Indeed it seems hardly credible that a man could commit such an act while in the possession of his senses, or while he has the least doubt upon his mind as to future retribution. But something has often struck my mind here, namely, that self-destruction does not commonly arise from infidelity or insanity, but from an overpowering impression which seizes and absorbs the soul, so that, for the time, it is incapable of reflection; and I remember having this opinion confirmed by the late Dr. Haweis, a physician, and Founder of the Humane Society in this country.

There is another thing also: God, when provoked, may give up men to "strong delusions, that they may believe a lie."

Satan entered into Judas; he then immediately went out, and God withdrew from him His restraining grace. Therefore he was his own no longer: he had no longer any free-will of his own. How many mere professors of religion have acted thus! We have three instances in the Scriptures of those who committed self-destruction, and all of them were pretenders to sanctity—Saul, Ahitophel, and Judas.

David did not rejoice in the suicide of Ahitophel. But he was allowed to see how God had answered prayer, by wonderful and "terrible things in righteousness," and to observe the divine interposition on his behalf in which he was made to rejoice with trembling. "Thou hast," said he, "delivered my soul from death, my eyes from tears, and my feet from falling." "By this I know that Thou favourest me, because mine enemy doth not triumph over me."

Let us notice the language of our text a little more; in regard to the spiritual experience of David and of ourselves, remarking three things.

First, his confidence, where we observe the subject itself, *God's favour.* "God is good to all, and His tender mercies are over all His works." But David in another psalm speaks of the favour He bears to His people especially. This is what Jacob intended when he said, "The good-will of Him that dwelt in the bush." This is the grand thing for us to experience. "Many," says Solomon, "will seek the favour of a prince." But how few succeed, and when they do, what do they gain? "Vanity and vexation of Spirit." Why do you not seek His favour "Whose favour is life"? Here you would be sure of success; and when obtained, your "soul shall be satisfied as with marrow and fatness," and you would have occasion to rejoice and be glad all your days. Here you would have something that would soften all your sorrows, and sweeten all your enjoyments; that would abide with you under all the changes of life, and would accompany you through the valley of the shadow of death.

Secondly, *his persuasion of this.* "By this I *know* that Thou favourest me;" and you may know it too, or how could you rejoice in it? How could you be thankful for it? How could the design of the Scriptures be answered, which "are written to you that believe in the name of the only-begotten Son of God, that you may have life through His name"? Or how could the "Spirit bear witness with your spirits that you are the children of God"?

Remark, thirdly, *the Performance of it.* "By this I know that Thou favourest me, because mine enemy doth not triumph over me." "All things," says Solomon, "come alike to all. There is one event to the righteous and to the wicked." "No man," says he, "knoweth either love or hatred"—that is, the love or hatred of God, "by all that is before him." The wicked man may have health, and success in his business, and agreeable connections, while a good man may have afflictions; and "many are the afflictions of the righteous." Lazarus here had his evil things, while the rich man had his good things. But soon the one was comforted, and the other was tormented; for eternity rectifies all this. But to know that you are favoured of God as David did, to know that you are one with Him in union and communion, this is a blessing to be desired. Then you will have something better than those outward things which equally befall the righteous and the wicked. Oh, to know that He has answered your prayer, when you have cried "Lord, say unto my soul, I am thy salvation!" 'Tis a token for good if you are convinced of sin, of your guilt and pollution, so as to abhor yourselves and repent in dust and ashes, so as to "hunger and thirst after righteousness." It is a good sign to have God's own Spirit, as a Spirit of grace and supplication to fear Him, to hope in His mercy: for "the Lord taketh pleasure in them that fear Him, in them that hope in His mercy." It is a token for good when you cleave to Him with purpose of heart, when you are willing to follow the Lamb whithersoever He goeth. Thus may you hope to "stand in the evil day, and having done all to stand;" and thus may you say with David, "By this I know that Thou favourest me." Are there not some here that can say the same, who have been long in the wilderness—long in a world lying in wickedness,—where you have been exposed to the enemy of souls "who goeth about seeking whom he may devour," of whose "devices you are not ignorant?" You have frequently said, "I shall one day perish by the hand of Saul." How then is it that you have not perished? How then is it that the enemy has not triumphed over you? Is it from want of any power, or of wisdom, or of malice in the foe? Or is it owing to your own strength, and skill, and caution? "By *Thee*," said David, "have I run through a troop, by *Thee* have I leapt over a wall." So can every Christian say, "By the grace of God I am what I am." He has holden me up, therefore I am safe. He keeps me by His power "through faith unto salvation." "He is able to keep me from falling, and to present me faultless before the presence of His glory with exceeding joy." And He who has kept me hitherto will never leave me, nor forsake me.

"And as for me, Thou upholdest me in my integrity, and settest me before Thy face for ever." What does this acknowledgment include? Does it refer to a particular instance, or to a whole course of life? "God requires truth in the inward parts," and it is well to be able to say, not with fleshly wisdom, but by the grace of God, we have had our conversation in the world. David calls this *his* integrity, not because he was the author of it, but because he was the subject of it. He knew that God was the source of every excellence, and even of every moral virtue, and He knew as He was the Author, so He is the sustainer and the upholder thereof; that it was owing to His influences he was able to stand; and that he could stand no longer than God upheld him, and could walk no further than God led him. Thus, brethren, is it with all the subjects of divine grace.

"Thou upholdest me in mine integrity, and settest me before Thy face for ever." What does this include? It is a very solemn and useful consideration, that when this is realised by the Christian it has a most powerful influence upon the whole of his temper and pursuits. So said Hagar, "Thou God seest me." Therefore God said to Abraham, "Walk before me, and be thou perfect:" as if he should say, "The way to be perfect," that is, the way to attain consistency and advancement in the Divine life, "is to remember that you are always before me." He sees you if you draw back, or if you look back; He sees you if you turn aside, or if you stand still.

But here it is spoken of not so much as a motive as a privilege, and a blessed privilege it is to be always in the view of your heavenly Friend. No human parent can always have his child in sight: he must sometimes be engaged in business, sometimes asleep, sometimes absent, and then his child is out of his sight. But it is not the case here. If Joseph had been always near his father, his brethren would never have injured him, for he would have cried, and his father would have heard; but, poor lad, it was when out of his father's sight his brethren evil entreated him. Christians, "the Keeper of Israel never slumbers nor sleeps." "All your desire is before Him, and your groaning is not hid from Him." "He knows all your walking through this great wilderness." He knows all the thorns and briers and snakes that are therein. Nothing can befall you without His knowledge, nothing but He has a full view of. You are ever in His sight, and He will guard you, and make "all things work together for your good."

Observe, lastly, His ascription of praise. "Blessed be the Lord God of Israel, from everlasting, and to everlasting. Amen, and amen." Oh, I love to see fervour in religion, zeal for God. I love for people to hear in hearing, and to pray in praying, and to sing in praising. What is zeal without knowledge? Wildfire. And what is knowledge without zeal? It is mere moonshine. Both these should be combined in the experience and practice of a Christian. "The spirit of judgment is the spirit of burning," as Isaiah expresses it, and they should always go together. Oh, Christians, if you are affected by petty instances of kindness shown you by your fellow creatures, what ought to be your gratitude to an Infinite Benefactor! How ought you to bow at His feet, saying, "Lord, what wilt Thou have me to do!" Oh, how do Seraphims burn with desire to do His will! Your fervour should be very superior to this in your religious concerns.

> "Never did angels taste above
> Redeeming grace and dying love."

Yet how is it with us?

> "Hosanna's language on our tongues,
> And our devotion dies."

Christians, heaven is your home, and there praise is to be your business and blessedness for ever. The more you feel of this spirit, and the more you abound in this practice, surely the better is it. Surely you should awake, and say, "Bless the Lord, O my soul, and all that is within me, bless His holy name."

> "If there be passions in my soul,
> And passions, Lord, there be,
> Let them be all at Thy control,
> My Saviour, all for Thee."

And Oh, how should you be concerned not only to show forth His praises with your lips, but in your lives, by giving up yourselves to His service and walking before Him all the days of your life.

VII.

DAVID'S POSITION AND PURPOSES.

(Delivered on Thursday Evening, January 21st, 1847.)

"*But I am like a green olive tree in the house of God; I trust in the mercy of God for ever and ever. I will praise Thee for ever, because Thou hast done it: and I will wait on Thy name; for it is good before Thy saints.*"—Psalm lii. 8-9.

THE words of our text plainly refer to something going before, and the title of the psalm will explain this. "To the Chief Musician, Maschil; a psalm of David, when Doeg, the Edomite, came and told Saul, and said unto him, David is come to the House of Ahimelech." You are acquainted with the narrative, as contained in the twenty-second chapter of the first book of Samuel. We are aware of the malicious persecutions of this man, the dreadful consequences in the destruction of "four score and five persons who did wear a linen ephod," and of the extreme jeopardy to which David was exposed. Thus he speaks of it; and his language shows us much of the workings of his mind. "Lo! this is the man that made not God his strength; but trusted in the abundance of his riches, and strengthened himself in his wickedness."

Let us now observe what David says of himself. "But I am like a green olive tree in the house of God; I trust in the mercy of God for ever and ever." But is not this egotism, boasting? By no means. When the Pharisee in the temple said, "Lord, I thank thee I am not as other men are," this arose from the spirit of self-applause, and self-satisfaction; but a good man knows "that by the grace of God" he is what he is, and has what he has. In acknowledgments such as these, therefore, he only glorifies God in himself, God being the author, he being only the subject of this workmanship. Here two things may be generally observed. The one is, that a good man may have a consciousness and full persuasion of his spiritual condition without presumption, and he may address others without vanity, saying, "Come unto me, all ye that fear God, and I will tell you what he hath done for my soul." "O taste and see that the Lord is good, blessed is the man that trusteth in Him." Let us now briefly consider, first, What he is; secondly, What he does; and, thirdly, What he purposes.

I. Let us observe WHAT HE IS. "But I am like a green olive tree in the house of God." It is needless to observe that the language is metaphorical. But the force of the passage takes in several things: for instance, an olive tree is the most lovely and attractive thing in nature, and a partaker of divine grace is beautified with salvation, and appears in the beauties of holiness. He wears a comely garment, which his God and Redeemer puts upon him.

It takes in also *verdure*. An "olive tree" is an evergreen; and the graces of God's Holy Spirit are never-dying graces. The work that God has commenced shall endure for ever. While "the outward man perisheth, the inward man is renewed day by day."

It takes in *fertility*. This was noticed in the parable in the Book of Judges, when "the trees went forth to anoint a king over them, and they said unto the olive tree, Reign over us. But the olive tree said unto them, Should I leave my fatness wherewith by me they honour God and man?" So the Apostle speaks of the fatness of the olive tree in his epistle to the Romans. "And in me," says God, "is thy fruit found." But there it is found; there must be fruit where there is divine grace. There are the fruits of the Spirit, which are "love, joy, peace, long-suffering, gentleness, goodness, faith, meekness, temperance, against such there is no law;" and Christians are filled with "the fruits of righteousness which are, by Jesus Christ, to the praise and glory of God." "Herein," said the Saviour, "is my Father glorified, that ye bear much fruit; so shall ye be my disciples."

We have here also, not only his resemblance, but his situation. "I am like a green olive tree in the house of God." None of us are there, originally or naturally. Isaiah shows us by whom and for what purpose we are placed there. "For," says God, "they shall be called trees of righteousness, the planting of the Lord that He may be glorified." Our text shows us how David loved this abode, and elsewhere he shows how continuously he would repair to it. "I will dwell in the house of the Lord for ever;" and addressing God he says, "Blessed is the man whom thou choosest, and causest to approach unto Thee, that he may dwell in Thy courts." "They shall be abundantly satisfied with the fatness of Thy house, and Thou shalt make them drink of the river of Thy pleasures, for with Thee is the fountain of life; and in Thy light shall we see light." When David says, "I am like a green olive tree in the house of God," he plainly intimates that he was *what* he was by being *where* he was, in a large measure and degree, and that his produce arises from his position. "I am like a green olive tree in the house of God," for there he was nurtured—there he was brought up—there he was trained—there he was defended. He enlarges upon this in another psalm, where he says, "the righteous shall flourish like the palm-tree, he shall grow like a cedar in Lebanon." But where? "Those that be planted in the house of the Lord, shall flourish in the courts of our God. They shall still bring forth fruit in old age, they shall be fat and flourishing; to show that the Lord is upright. He is my rock, and there is no unrighteousness in Him." Those who can neglect the Sabbath, who can turn their backs upon the sanctuary, upon the preaching of the Word, and upon our social and devotional exercises, must not look for soul-prosperity, for much of the life of godliness is combined with these. "The soul of the diligent shall be made fat." Therefore says the promise, "They that wait on the Lord shall renew their strength; they shall mount up on wings as eagles; they shall run, and not be weary; and they shall walk, and not faint." "Blessed is the man that feareth me, watching daily at my gates, waiting at the posts of my doors." "For whoso findeth me, findeth life, and shall obtain favour of the Lord." "But he that sinneth against me wrongeth his own soul; all they that hate me love death." I have more than once told you that a painted fire can be kept in without fuel, but a real one cannot. This will require additions from time to time, and excitement too.

II. WHAT HE DOES. "I trust in the mercy of God for ever and ever." Man is an indigent creature, therefore necessarily a dependant one; for, not being able to secure himself, he must go abroad for relief; and as creatures stand next to us, we begin by relying on them; and it is ofttimes by a very painful discipline that we are brought to say with David, "Now, Lord, what wait I for? my hope is in *Thee*." Man fell originally by losing his confidence in God, and he is to be restored alone by recovering it; therefore so much stress is perpetually laid upon this, and God has done so much to regain our confidence. The whole of the Scriptures are written, "that we, through patience and comfort, might have hope." So it is said of our Saviour, "God raised Him up from the dead, and gave Him glory, that our faith and hope might be in God." Thus we profess confidence "by the faith of Him." And Oh, how does He deserve and justify our confidence, when we view Him in the Son of His love, "through whom He has made with us an everlasting covenant, ordered in all things and sure," in whom all the promises are "yea and amen to the glory of God by us!" We may trust in man to our ruin, but whoso trusteth in the Lord "shall never be confounded." We may place reliance on man's engagements, and they may fail. "But the Lord is not a man that He should lie, nor the son of man that he should repent: hath He said, and shall He not do it? or hath He spoken and shall He not make it good?"

This trust is not only divine, but *durable.* "I trust in the mercy of God for ever and ever." That which is Divine will be durable, and that which comes from God will surely lead to Him; and thus, says the Apostle, "are we made partakers of grace, if we hold fast the confidence and the rejoicing of the hope firm unto the end." Accordingly it is said, "Trust ye in the Lord for ever, for in the Lord is everlasting strength;" "Trust in Him at all times, ye people; pour out your hearts before Him."

There are two cases in which it is not very easy to trust God.

The one is in adversity, when sense sees everything to be against us. Thus Jacob said, "All these things are against me." Oh, then it is not easy to look up and say with Job, "Though He slay me, yet will I trust in Him;" or with the Church, "Although the fig-tree shall not blossom, neither shall fruit be in the vines; the labour of the olive shall fail, and the fields shall yield no meat; the flock shall be cut off from the fold, and there shall be no herd in the stall; yet I will rejoice in the Lord, I will joy in the God of my salvation."

The other is in cases of prosperity. Here persons are mistaken. You sometimes hear them saying, but they are vain words, "Ah, when you are sitting in your elbow chair, or lying at ease upon your sofa, when business flourishes, when health is enjoyed, and when you are surrounded with agreeable connections, it is easy enough to trust in Him." Indeed it is not; for then is the danger of departing from Him—of making flesh your own arm—of forgetting that "this is not our rest," and of mistaking the way for our home. But where there is Divine grace, if there be a failing in the exercise, there will not be in the principle; this is immortal. "The water," says the Saviour, "that I shall give him, shall be in him a well of water, springing up unto everlasting life." And here is something very fine, and worthy of observation; for though He says, "I am like a green olive-tree in the house of God," he does not say, "I trust in myself," but "I trust in God;" he does not say, "I trust in my own merit," but "I trust in His mercy." Thus you began, Christians, and you can say with our admired Cowper,

> "Since the dear hour that brought me to Thy feet,
> And plucked up all my follies by the root,
> I never trusted in an arm but Thine,
> Nor hoped, but in Thy righteousness divine."

And do you feel less need of hoping in this mercy now, Christian, than when you began? When you examine yourselves after your Sabbath exercises, or after your holy communion with Him, fall you not upon your knees, saying, "Enter not into judgment with Thy servant, O Lord, for in Thy sight shall no flesh living be justified"? Do you ever get beyond this? Do you ever wish to get beyond it? When we have done all, we must say "we are unprofitable servants." According to Jude, we are to be "looking for the mercy of God through our Lord Jesus Christ unto eternal life." Can you not say with Halyburton, that you hope to die with the words of the publican in your mouth, "God be merciful to me a sinner"? and to expect salvation not as a profitable servant, but as a pardoned sinner? And said another, "Here goes one who sought and found mercy." And said Wesley,

> "I the chief of sinners am,
> But Jesus died for me."

III. One thing more, and that is, HIS PURPOSE. "I will praise Thee for ever because Thou hast done it; and I will wait on Thy name; for it is good before Thy saints."

Doubtless he made this resolve, not in his own strength; for all our resolutions and our vows, arising from self-dependence, will be sure to fail us, and prove a curse. Therefore

> "Retreat beneath His wings,
> And in His grace confide,
> This more exalts the King of kings,
> Than all our works beside."

> "Man's wisdom is to seek
> God's strength and grace alone;
> But e'en an angel would be weak
> That trusted in his own."

Though we can be "strong in the grace that is in Christ Jesus," "strong in the Lord and the power of His might," it is through this alone that we can "do valiantly."

He resolves to live a life of praise. "I will praise Thee for ever, because Thou hast done it." Done what? He does not tell us. But how much had he probably on his mind; how much had he that was good and excellent, that he would connect with God! "He has made me, and redeemed me, and called me by His grace; he has preserved me from my adversaries, aided me in all my duties, been with me in all my tribulations." Thus you see, he was willing to ascribe whatever he possessed, and whatever he did, to God as the Author: he was determined to "give Him the glory due unto His name;" and resolved that no creature should rob Him of any of His praise. You see, therefore, how much David abounded in this work; how he called upon his soul, and all that was within him, to "bless and praise His holy name;" how he embargoed his thoughts, saying, "Bless the Lord, O my soul, and forget not all His benefits;" how he called upon others, exclaiming, "Let us exalt His name together." How lamentable it is that we resemble him so little in this! Oh, dwell therefore more on your own unworthiness, for in proportion as you feel self-abasement God will be exalted in your minds. Mark the instances of His goodness, for "whoso is wise, and will observe these things, even he shall understand the loving-kindness of the Lord."

He would also live a life of prayer. "And I will wait on Thy name; for it is good before Thy saints." There are two ways of waiting in regard to God. There is a waiting *for* God, and this regards hope and expectation; it implies an expectation of His coming to deliver us from earth, or to answer our prayers, or to bestow some particular blessing upon us. And as God's time for doing this is always the best time, therefore 'tis said, "Blessed are all they that wait for Him." "It is good for a man that he both hope and quietly wait for the salvation of the Lord." Here, Christians, this waiting is very necessary, to keep us from despondency, in His apparent, not real delays; to keep us from saying with the unbelieving nobleman, "Why should I wait for the Lord any longer?"—to keep us from murmuring and repining, and employing unhallowed expedients to forward our plans, and accomplish our hopes.

Then there is also a waiting *upon* God. This is what is here intended; it regards our readiness to serve Him, and this is peculiarly done in the means of grace, in the ordinances of religion, and in our private and public worship. Therefore it is said, "Wait on the Lord, and keep His way." "Be of good courage, and He shall strengthen your heart; wait, I say, on the Lord." But the exercise is also of a general nature, and is not to be confined to a particular service. No, it is to regard the whole life; it implies a holding ourselves entirely at His disposal, receiving His orders, and asking continually, "Lord, what wilt Thou have me to do?" Therefore David says, not only "will I wait on Thee in Thy house, and in the closet," but "On Thee do I wait all the day," for it is good, not only for myself, but others would value it too. Therefore he resolved the more, "for it is good before Thy saints," or the holy ones. The people of God are chiefly to be regarded; their judgment, their approbation and their applause, should be far more to us than that of the vain world. Therefore says David, "I will wait on Thy name, for it is good before Thy saints." "They are children of the light and of the day;" they know divine things by experience. Let us examine ourselves with regard to them. Whom, then, do you value and esteem most among your fellow-creatures. Can you say

"Let others choose the sons of mirth,
To give a relish to their wine:
I love the men of heavenly birth,
Whose hopes and wishes are divine."

With whom do you walk? "He that walketh with wise men shall be wise, but a companion of fools shall be destroyed." With whom do you delight to associate? Can you say with David, in regard to the saints, "They are the excellent of the earth, in whom is all my delight"? Whom are you following? "Be ye followers of God as dear children;" and "be followers of those who through faith and patience inherit the promises." "Go forth by the footsteps of the flock;" and let your continual prayer be, "Look Thou upon me, and be merciful unto me, as Thou used to do unto those that love Thy name."

VIII.

THE SOUL SATISFIED.

(Delivered on Thursday Evening, October 1st, 1846.)

"*My soul shall be satisfied as with marrow and fatness; and my mouth shall praise Thee with joyful lips: when I remember Thee upon my bed, and meditate on Thee in the night watches.*—PSALM lxiii. 5, 6,

"As in water face answereth to face, so is the heart of man to man." It is so as to sin, for there is a general conformity of disposition in sinners. It is so as to grace, for there is a general resemblance of disposition in the righteous. And you need not wonder at this, when you consider their origin and their destination; for all true believers are born from above, and bound for eternity. Their way is the way everlasting, and the influences under which they live are derived from the agency of the Holy Ghost, and they are "all one in Christ Jesus." Hence we see the propriety of the sacred writers recording so much of the history and experience of those who lived in ages and countries remote from our own. Thus we are able to compare ourselves with them, and find we belong to the same species, though we may not be of equal stature; and thus we find by experience the truth of the Apostle's remark, "Whatsoever things were written aforetime were written for our learning, that we through patience and comfort of the Scriptures might have hope." Thus we value the psalm before us, and the text we have now read. Examine it, and you will observe first, a happy state; secondly, the means auxiliary to it; thirdly, the circumstances under which it is indulged; and, fourthly, the assurance of the fact.

I. Observe here A HAPPY STATE.

It includes soul-satisfaction and joyful praise. Satisfaction is the ease and contentment of the spirit. It is what all men are seeking after, but who finds it? And where is it found? It is not in the world. It is not to be found anywhere apart from the blessed God. Here is the hope, here is the strength of the soul and its portion for ever. Here you find this satisfaction, and a believer can say, " My soul shall be satisfied as with the marrow and the fatness ;" not with ordinary food, but " with marrow and fatness." For an explanation here we may refer you to the usages of the East. The expressions are metaphorically used for the richness of the provision. So Isaiah says, " And in this mountain shall the Lord of Hosts make unto all people a feast of fat things, a feast of wines on the lees, of fat things full of marrow, of wines on the lees well refined." So David says again, "They shall be abundantly satisfied with the fatness of Thy house ; and Thou shalt make them drink of the river of Thy pleasures," intimating that the fare the Lord provides for His people is not only nourishing, but very rich and expensive, and very delicious. No food, however, would afford satisfaction to those who have no appetite. "The full soul loatheth a honeycomb; but to the hungry soul every bitter thing is sweet." How much more sweet would marrow and fatness be ! Here we find Our Lord saying, " Blessed are they that do hunger and thirst after righteousness, for they shall be filled." They will be filled completely hereafter. They are filled in a blessed degree now. Yes, this is the case with all the Lord's people. " His favour is life, and His loving kindness is better than life." O satisfy us early with Thy mercy, that we may rejoice and be glad all our days." " My people shall be satisfied with my goodness, saith the Lord." They experience satisfaction in a blessed degree in their temporal concerns and enjoyments. They may indeed be poor, but having food and raiment, they learn therewith to be content. They now principally seek those things which are above, and are willing to leave all other things to the care of their heavenly Father. They now stand in another relation than once they did to the earth : they are now only "strangers and pilgrims," and judge of themselves not by what they have in the way, but what is in reserve for them at home. While in this condition, faith often whispers to them, if they are disposed to complain,

" Cease, pilgrim, cease !
Man wants but little here below,
Nor wants that little long."

"Seek ye first the kingdom of God," and all other "things shall be *added* unto you."

It includes also joyful praise. "And my mouth shall praise

Thee with joyful lips." This naturally arises from the former, for when the "soul is satisfied as with marrow and fatness," when it enjoys the comforts of religion, it is not easy to repress the expression of them; they will break forth in utterance, and the man will say, "Come and hear, all ye that fear God, and I will declare what He hath done for my soul." "My soul shall make her boast in the Lord; the humble shall hear thereof and be glad. I sought the Lord and He heard me, and delivered me out of all my fears." "O magnify the Lord with me, and let us exalt His name together."

It is lamentable that there should be so little of this praise on earth. It will be the employment and enjoyment of the blessed. "Blessed are they that dwell in Thy courts above; they will be still praising Thee." Christians must begin this worship below; they are learning now; they are practising now, though in a very imperfect manner, "The song of Moses and the Lamb." But if you would be more excited to "praise Him with joyful lips," there are three things you must regard. First, you must seek after a sense of your unworthiness; in proportion as people are humble, they will be grateful. Then you must endeavour to ascertain your interest in this Saviour. Then you must remember the instances of God's goodness to you. This brings us to the next branch of our subject—

II. THE MEANS AUXILIARY TO THIS HAPPY STATE.—Divine remembrance and divine meditation. "When I remember Thee upon my bed, and meditate upon Thee in the night watches."

These have a relation to each other. Remembrance is necessary to the exercise of meditation, and meditation is necessary to the act of remembering. Let us glance at these.

First he says, "My soul shall be satisfied as with marrow and fatness, when I *remember* Thee upon my bed." Though God surrounds us; though "He is not far from every one of us," though "in Him we live, and move, and have our being," natural men are represented as living "without God, and without hope in the world." They lie down and rise up; they go forth and return; they plan, and perform their enterprises, "and God is not in all their thoughts," any more than if He had no existence; nor do they implore His guidance, assistance, and blessing. Oh, if men had God always with them, how differently would they feel and act! "But of the Rock that begat them, they are unmindful; they have *forgotten* the God that formed them." And the best of you, I suppose, have sad memories, at least as to divine things; you can more easily remember your fellow-creatures, your relations, and your children, than you do God. How often do you forget Him who created and redeemed you, and who is the Author of all your mercies!

How little also do we meditate on Him; but the Psalmist meditated on Him "in the night watches." He did not mean a mere recollection of Him, but such a recollection as would be accompanied with corresponding actions and feelings. This is the meaning of the exhortation addressed to the young, "Remember now thy Creator in the days of thy youth." We cannot meditate without remembering; we may remember without meditating. When we meditate on Him as well as remember Him, we retain Him in our minds. The Apostle makes use of this expression when he says, "They did not like to retain God in their thoughts." This is the case with men under the influence of sin and of the world. If they have now and then a recollection of Him, they endeavour to banish it, instead of meditating upon it. And is it not so with regard to the lives of many? Their minds are void of thought with regard to religion; they love reading and hearing, but they do not love thinking. I fear many of you do not endeavour to think for yourselves, and taste the sweetness of your own thoughts. Surely you never can be at a loss for subjects on which to meditate while you have God for your remembrance—His works and His ways; His providence and His grace; His various characters and relations, as our God and Guard, our Father and Friend, our all and all. Oh, what subjects for meditation do we find here!

III. Let us observe THE CIRCUMSTANCES IN WHICH THIS STATE IS INDULGED. They are two; the one referring to place, the other to time. "My soul shall be satisfied as with marrow and fatness, when I remember Thee upon my bed, and meditate upon Thee in the night watches."

One regards, you see, the *place*: "When I remember Thee upon my bed." He had addressed others with regard to this. "Commune with your own heart upon your bed, and be still;" and had said, "Let the saints shout aloud upon their beds."

There were three beds he would have them to shout upon; and on which he could enjoy communion with God. There was the bed of natural refreshment, when as Dr. Watts says,

"And when I rest my weary head,
From cares and business free,
'Tis sweet conversing on my bed,
With my own soul and Thee."

Or if it should be the reverse, you find him saying in another place,

> "Amidst the wakeful hours of night,
> When busy cares afflict my head,
> One thought of Thee brings new delights,
> And adds refreshment to my bed."

And have you not, Christian, experienced this, while you have been thankful for your beds of natural refreshment?

Then also there are sick bed. These may be very painful, yet on them you may enjoy rest to your soul, according to the promise, "I will comfort thee upon the bed of languishing;" and thousands have found the promise true.

Then also there is the dying bed. Yes, this has often been found to be "none other than the House of God." For as Watts says again—

> "Jesus can make a dying bed
> Feel soft as downy pillows are,
> While on His breast I lean my head,
> And breathe my life out sweetly there."

The other regards *time*: "And meditate upon Thee in the night watches." Here the question is, whether David refers to this in a way of choice, as being a period freed from noise and distraction, affording therefore more solitude and retirement. Who has not read Hervey's meditations on the starry heavens? Who has not admired Young's "Night Thoughts?" Who has not employed some of the night to purposes other than sleep and repose? He seems to refer to this season as a season of necessity, as if he should say "When thou holdest my eyes waking, and I am unable to see, blessed be Thy name, I am able to think, and how precious are Thy thoughts unto me, O God! How great is the sum of them! When I am awake I am still with Thee." It is obvious how much he approved of nocturnal hours for meditation. How often does he refer to it. "My reins also instruct me in the right season." "At midnight will I rise and give thanks unto Thee."

IV. Lastly, let us observe THE CONFIDENCE WITH WHICH HE SPEAKS OF THE THINGS WHICH HE EXPECTS. "My soul *shall* be satisfied." But how could he be sure of this? Why, he would make it his endeavour; he would make it his concern; he would avoid whatever would impede, and would pursue whatever would promote it. The religion of the Bible fills the believer with holy, humble confidence. David knew this would be the case from the promises of God: he knew that God had said, "Draw near to me, and I will draw near to you." He could be sure of this from his past experience, for he had never sought God in vain, but had always found Him to be a very present help in trouble. He knew that though we often fail as to God he does not fail as to us; and that He hath promised that He will never leave us nor forsake us.

In conclusion one thing is to be observed, which is, how mistaken they are who suppose that religion is adverse to happiness; happiness as to this world, whatever they may allow as to another. But does this accord with reason? All will acknowledge that God is able to make a person happy, and is it reason to suppose that He will allow those who oppose Him to be more happy than those who love and serve Him? Does this accord with the Scriptures of truth, which are a joyful sound to the believer? Does it accord with this: "Her ways are ways of pleasantness, and all her paths are peace"? Does it accord with the experience of those who have made the trial? For some of you have not, but there are others there who first made trial of the world and afterwards of the religion of Jesus: they can make the comparison; they will tell you they were strangers to real happiness and real peace so long as they were strangers to the "Consolation of Israel." The happiness of the Christian is so supreme that it is independent of place and of time. David had seen the goings of his God and his king in the sanctuary; and Paul and Silas could sing praises to God at midnight. The question is, How do you feel habitually towards the blessed God? not only in His own House, but in your own houses; not only in a storm, but in a calm; not only on the Sabbath, but on other days; not only in good company, but with David when alone, and when no eye sees you, and no ear hears you but His? Can you make the language of our text your own? Be induced, therefore, no longer to seek the living among the dead, and ask "Who will show us any good;" but pray with the few, "Lord, lift Thou up the light of Thy countenance upon us: this will put more joy and gladness into our hearts than when their corn and their wine increase."

IX.

THE RIGHT USE OF PAST MERCIES.

(Delivered on Thursday Evening, December 23rd, 1843.)

"*Because Thou hast been my help, therefore in the shadow of Thy wings will I rejoice.*"—PSALM lxiii. 7.

THERE are three things for us to consider and improve. The first is, David's experience; the second is, David's resolution; and the third is, the connection between these. "Consider what I say, and the Lord give thee understanding in all things."

I. Consider DAVID'S EXPERIENCE. He says unto God, "Thou hast been my help."

Christians *need* help. When we consider what they have to forsake, and what they have to discharge with regard to themselves, their fellow-creatures, and to God Himself, there is enough to discourage them. But the God they serve is not like the Egyptian taskmasters, requiring them to make brick without straw. If of themselves they are not sufficient to think anything as of themselves, their sufficiency is of God. Observe how Paul speaks in this view: "I can bear any change of moral climate; I can rise without being elevated, and descend without murmuring; I can bear and can improve sickness; I have learned in whatever state I am therewith to be content. I know both how to be abased and how to abound. Everywhere and in all things I am instructed both to be full and to be hungry, both to abound and to suffer need." But this is not all. He adds, "I can do all things through Christ which strengtheneth me." What duty is there in which the Christian does not need divine aid? Is it prayer? O, what darkness and dulness, what a want of fervour would there be without this! You would long ago have discontinued the exercise—but for what? The apostle tells us. "The Spirit also helpeth our infirmities; for we know not what we should pray for as we ought; but the Spirit itself maketh intercession for us with groanings which cannot be uttered. And He that searcheth the hearts, knoweth what is the mind of the Spirit, because He maketh intercession for the saints according to the will of God." Never therefore, Christian, be discouraged, whatever duty comes before you. You are not left to yourselves, "For He hath said, I will never leave thee, nor forsake thee." Therefore you should say, "I will go in the strength of the Lord God." Abraham was able even to offer up his own son, and Moses was able to endure as "seeing Him who is invisible."

Secondly, they *have* help. Many there be that say of the Christian, "There is no help for him in God," but this is false. There *is* help for him in God. When he thinks of his foes, how numerous, how malicious, how wise, and how powerful they be; when he considers these enemies who so far surpass him, and then thinks of himself, verily there is enough to discourage him if he is to engage in the warfare alone. But then he is not alone; what says God to him? "When thou passest through the waters, I will be with thee; and through the rivers, they shall not overflow thee. When thou walkest through the fire, thou shalt not be burnt; neither shall the flame kindle upon thee." "Fear not, for I am with thee." Look to me! Greater is He that is for thee, than he that is in the world. "Fear not, thou worm Jacob, and ye men of Israel: I will help thee, saith the Lord, and My Redeemer the Holy One of Israel." You remember the case of the Israelites. They stood in need of help when the Philistines, who were then perhaps the best soldiers on the face of the earth, were approaching them. "But Samuel cried unto the Lord for Israel, and the Lord heard him, and the Philistines were smitten before Israel. And Samuel took a stone and set it before Mizpeh and them, and called the name of it Ebenezer, saying, Hitherto the Lord hath helped us." Perhaps there is not a Christian here this evening but who has at some seasons been ready to say, "I shall one day perish by the hand of my enemies." But you have not perished. And why is this? Because in the name of the Lord you set up your banners; and you can say to the praise of His glory, "By Thee I have run through a troop; and by my God have I leaped over a wall. Had not the Lord been on our side, we should have perished. If it had not been the Lord who was on our side, then the waters had overwhelmed us, the stream had gone over our soul." Learn, brethren, whenever you perceive an enemy not to go forth against him alone. Go and tell the Captain of your salvation, and ask Him to accompany you, and He will teach your hands to war, and your fingers to fight.

Thirdly, observe the *kind* of help they have. It is help from God. "Because Thou hast been my help, therefore in the shadow of Thy wings will I rejoice."

And what says the Church? "God is our refuge and strength, a very present help in trouble: God will help us." Mark this. Men may have help at a distance, and yet may be overcome and destroyed before it comes. But this cannot be the case with the Christian. He has help at all times. "God shall help, and that right early"—not so early as you expect, perhaps, or so early as you wish. He will help you "right early;" at the very time His infinite wisdom sees best. Such is the help the Lord affords His people.

He helps them in a way of *defence.* He helped Lot from the overthrow of Sodom; and Paul from assassination, when forty Jews had sworn to slay him, and watched for him night and day. But their plot was discovered and frustrated. How constant is His preventing mercy!

He helps them also in a way of *support.* They are not exempt from afflictions, but they are prevented from sinking under them. "If thou faintest in the day of adversity thy strength is small;" but obtaining help from God, you faint not. Worldly people wonder how it is the Christian bears so much. The reason is, they see the load of suffering, but do not see underneath the everlasting arms; if they did, they would not be so surprised. Christians sometimes wonder at themselves; they have been amazed at the composure and patience with which they have been enabled to bear losses and trials, at the thought of which their hearts sink within them. To what do they attribute this? The language of David will explain. "In the day that I cried, Thou answeredst me and strengthened me with strength in my soul." Thus He helped the martyrs, so that they were enabled to glory in tribulation, and to glory in the Saviour under the most violent persecution.

He helps by *preserving.* It is a great mercy to be kept from that to which a suffering state is so liable, namely, from hard thoughts of God. Hence Job, under his suffering, is mentioned as a moral wonder. "In all this," it is said, "Job sinned not, nor charged God foolishly." The Church could make this appeal: "Our heart is not turned back, neither have our steps declined from Thy way, though Thou hast sore broken us in the place of dragons, and covered us with the shadow of death." It is owing to this you have been enabled to glorify God in the fires, and to bear a testimony to the truth and excellency of the religion you profess. And under the sufferings of His people, how often has the Lord accomplished their deliverance, when they could see no way of escape! and how often has He turned the shadow of death into the morning!

II. See DAVID'S RESOLUTION. "Under the shadow of Thy wings will I rejoice." The shadow of God's wings is a very favourite expression of David's. Thus he says, "How excellent is Thy loving kindness, O God! Therefore the children of men put their trust under the shadow of Thy wings." "He shall cover thee with His feathers, and under His wings shalt thou trust." "In the shadow of Thy wings will I make my refuge, until these calamities be overpast." "Keep me as the apple of the eye; hide me with the shadow of Thy wings." God has no wings, but a hen has. The image seems poor when applied to the Supreme Being. But Christ has employed it, and said, "How often would I have gathered thy children together as a hen gathereth her chickens under her wings." God has no wings, but He has Perfections. He has made "a covenant ordered in all things and sure." He has made "exceeding great and precious promises." O, what security is here! O, what a hiding place from the wind have we! what a covert from the tempest! what "a shadow of a great rock in a weary land!"

But you will observe that this affords not only security but comfort, which also leads us to consider the tenderness of God as well as His power. Then observe the use David makes of it. "Under the shadow of Thy wings I will rejoice." He does not only know it, and acknowledges it, but makes use of it. A refuge is nothing unless it be entered. But observe the nature of the use David makes of it. He does not say "Under the shadow of Thy wings will I hide," or "Under the shadow of Thy wings will I trust." I wish persons would always quote Scripture accurately: God's language is always better than our own. But he says, "Under the shadow of Thy wings will I rejoice"—feeling complacency there, feeling satisfaction there, feeling confidence there; and a peace passing all understanding there. "In the shadow of Thy wings will I rejoice. I will rejoice and sing, and loud enough to be heard by others, that they may judge of the favourableness of the situation in which I am, that it may be the means of alluring them also to come." "O, taste and see that the Lord is good: blessed is the man that trusteth in Him."

III. See HOW THE ONE OF THESE BEARS UPON THE OTHER. "Because Thou hast been my help; *therefore* in the shadow of thy wings will I rejoice." The religion of the Bible is a reasonable service, and, as the Apostle Peter says, the Christian is able to give a reason of the hope that is in him. See what David does as an illustration of it, when he was going to engage with the Philistines. Thus he emboldened himself: "The Lord hath delivered me out of the paw of the lion, and out of the paw of the bear. He will deliver me out of the hand of this Philistine." You have heard how Asaph reasoned: "Will the Lord cast off for ever, and will He be favourable no more?" And he asks several more questions; but, says he, "This is my infirmity; and how am I to remedy it? I will remember the days of the years of the right hand of the Most High. I will remember the works of the Lord; surely I will remember Thy wonders of old. I will meditate also of all Thy works, and talk of Thy doings." He thus encouraged himself in the Lord his God. He is the same: what, therefore, He hath done, He will do. Man's inclinations and abilities may change, but with Him there is no variableness nor shadow of turning. He therefore has recorded this method himself, in order that we may draw encouragement from the past. Therefore our Lord said to the disciples when they had only one loaf in the ship, "When I brake the five loaves among two thousand, how many baskets of fragments took ye up?" And so God says in the days of Micah, "O, my people, remember now what Balak, King of Moab, counselled, and what Baalam son of Beor answered him from Shittim unto Gilgal, that ye may know the righteousness of the Lord." Thus should we call to mind the past goodness of the Lord, and feel assured that He will perform His promise. God has designed that His dispensations towards us for a season should afford future encouragement; He intended that they should not only relieve present exigencies, but give hope as to the future. And surely, Christians, you should call to mind experiences of this nature for your encouragement.

Now as to some of you, perhaps you have never applied to God in all your life. We pity your condition, but would admonish you to "seek the Lord while He may be found, and to call upon Him while He is near." "Behold, now is the accepted time; behold now is the day of salvation." The Saviour says, "Whosoever will, let him come unto me; and him that cometh unto me I will in no wise cast out."

But observe, the Christian has an encouragement derived from past experience. A beggar loves to go where he has never been repulsed. A Christian should never yield to despondency; he should exercise hope and confidence; and one way by which you may obtain this is to call to mind, not only God's word, but God's works. Remember what He has done for others; and still more remember what He has done for yourselves. This will enable you to go on your way rejoicing, and to say with David, "Surely goodness and mercy shall follow me all the days of my life." "Because Thou hast been my help, therefore in the shadow of Thy wings will I rejoice."

> "His love in times past forbids me to think,
> He'll leave me at last in sorrow to think;
> Each sweet Ebenezer I have in review
> Confirms His good pleasure to bring me quite through."

X.

ASAPH'S CONCLUSION.

(Delivered on Monday evening, April 8th, 1850.)

"*Truly God is good to Israel, even to such as are of a clean heart.*"—PSALM lxxiii. 1.

THE Book of Psalms is a treasury of spiritual experience. O what pleasure arises from its perusal! "O how often has the harp of the son of Jesse driven away the evil spirit from me, and kindled my thoughts and desires afresh," may the Christian say. What a psalm is this before us, one of the most interesting and sweet, especially the close of it! The Psalmist appears to have been in a state of perplexity, as we see in the following verses. But he comes to this conclusion, after he had weighed the matter, "Truly God is good to Israel, even to such as are of a clean heart"—notwithstanding all appearances to the contrary, and all the difficulties that lay in the way.

By Israel here, we understand the people of Israel. The name was given to Jacob when he wrestled with God and prevailed, and it was afterwards given to his natural posterity, and is now applied to his spiritual posterity. Christians are called "The Israel of God" and "Israelites indeed." "For he is not a Jew who is one outwardly, neither is that circumcision which is outward in the flesh, but he is a Jew who is one inwardly, and circumcision is that of the heart; in the spirit and not in the letter, whose praise is not of men but of God." "And they that are of faith are blessed with faithful Abraham." "If ye be Christ's, then are ye Abraham's seed, and heirs according to the promise." God has always had a seed to serve Him. If you desire to know who they are, we have a Book in which their characters are recorded. Do you wish to know whether your names are written among the living in Jerusalem? There we read, "Blessed are the pure in heart, for they shall see God;" "The Lord taketh pleasure in them that fear Him, in them that hope in His mercy." The Israel of God are distinguished not by outward condition, or by profession, but they are described as having a clean heart.

You say, perhaps, "I find my heart is vile enough when I look into it, and I am ready to exclaim with Job, 'Behold, I am vile!' and cry out with the leper, 'Unclean! unclean!' wherefore I abhor myself and repent in dust and ashes." Well, let us see whether this be not consistent with your consolation. If I should discourage you I should offend against the generation of His children, and should oppose the declarations of God; for "There is not a just man upon earth that liveth, and sinneth not;" "In many things we offend all." And the Saviour teaches us to pray for daily pardon, as well as for daily bread. According to this, who can say "I have a clean heart"? The Apostle, who was so far advanced in the divine life, said, "I have not yet attained, neither am I already perfect;" and who dare say, "I have already attained, and am already perfect"?

But the case is this: after all the concession we make, God's people do differ from others. They differ as much as darkness differs from light, or wheat from the tares. Instead of the thorn we see the fir-tree; instead of the brier, the myrtle tree. 'Tis He makes them differ. "This people have I formed for myself; they shall show forth my praise." There is in them a peculiar principle, such as is never found in others, such as once was not found in them. They are now made partakers of His holiness, as the Apostle says. They are now made partakers of that blessed promise, "I will put my Spirit within them." In this they principally differ. They "delight in the law of God after the inward man;" they rejoice at the holiness of God, and with David give thanks at the remembrance of His holiness, and

> "None but the saints who feel His grace,
> Can triumph in His holiness."

But he can. "He hungers and thirsts after righteousness; he esteems the saints as the excellent of the earth; he takes pleasure in holy exercises—in drawing near to God, and in holding intercourse with the Holy Ghost; he loves Christ not only as a Saviour, but also as a King; he loves the closet as well as the sanctuary; as to heaven, he desires it not only as a place and state of happiness,—that is natural,—but he desires it as a state and place of holiness,—that is supernatural. If a

Q

Christian mourns for sin, if he can say with the Apostle, "O wretched man that I am! who shall deliver me from the body of this death?" If he delights in the law of the Lord, and while he feels a law in his members warring against the law of his mind, so that he cannot do the things that he would; he finds that while the flesh is weak, the spirit is willing, if he may take encouragement; for He who hath begun the good work will perform and perfect it. I hope when you look at this representation, you can do it with satisfaction and comfort.

"Truly God is good to Israel, even to such as are of a clean heart." Good, not to them exclusively; "He is good to all, and His tender mercies are over all His works." There is nothing in the creation but needs His goodness. He feeds the fowls of the air, and the young lions when they cry. The eyes of all wait upon Him, and He giveth them their meat in due season. He openeth His hand and supplieth the wants of every living thing. He teaches the little spider to weave its web. He hears the young ravens when they cry. "Behold," says the Saviour, "the fowls of the air; they sow not, neither do they reap, nor gather into barns; yet your heavenly Father feedeth them; are ye not much better than they? And why take ye thought for raiment? Consider the lilies of the field, how they grow; they toil not, neither do they spin, and yet I say unto you, that even Solomon in all his glory was not arrayed like one of these. Wherefore, if God so clothe the grass of the field, which to-day is and to-morrow is cast into the oven, shall He not much more clothe you, O ye of little faith?" and will He not feed and provide for you? But we are sinners against Him, we have entered into alliance with His foes, and deserve His displeasure; but how excellent is His loving-kindness, so that the children of men are allowed to put their trust under the shadow of His wings! "He makes His sun to rise on the evil and on the good, and sendeth rain on the just and on the unjust." Though sinners live without Him in the world, yet they are indebted to Him for all they enjoy, and for the very breath by which they blaspheme His name.

"He makes the saint and sinner prove
The *common* blessings of His love;
But the wide difference that remains
Is endless joys or endless pains."

"Truly God is good to Israel." "He is good, and ready to forgive, and plenteous in mercy to all them that call upon

Him;" and all His people do call upon Him. David said, "Because He hath inclined His ear unto me, therefore will I call upon Him as long as I live." And again he prays, "Remember me, O Lord, with the favour which Thou bearest unto Thy people: O visit me with Thy salvation."

If we are of the Israel of God, we shall earnestly desire the blessings they enjoy. These are blessings spiritual in their nature, which afford them joy and satisfaction now, which abide with them in all the changes of life, which accompany them through the valley of the shadow of death, which stand by them when they appear at the judgment-seat of Christ, and shall be theirs for ever; blessings which appertain to the soul and eternity. It is thus that "God is good to Israel, even to such as are of a clean heart." He has redeemed them by the blood of Christ; He has justified them by His righteousness; He has forgiven them all their sins; He has brought them into favour and communion with Himself, so that their "fellowship is with the Father and His Son Jesus Christ." And as for their future blessedness, "Eye hath not seen, nor ear heard, neither have entered into the heart of man, the things that God hath prepared for them that love Him." But they are not strangers to blessedness even here. Heaven enters them before they enter heaven: they have here foretastes of the glory to be revealed. O, the blessedness of those who know the joyful sound! "They walk in the light of God's countenance; in His name they rejoice all the day, and in His favour shall they be exalted." Do you know anything of this experience? As to other instances of His goodness, you will soon be called to leave them. You brought nothing into the world with you, and it is certain you can carry nothing out. Whatever you possess here of a worldly nature, it will leave you when death brings you to the edge of the grave; but if you are the Israel of God, you will rejoice in hope of His glory, whatever trials and difficulties you may meet with. Asaph, after he had surveyed the dealings of God, came to the conclusion that, "Truly, God is good to Israel." He is good to them, however the world may behave towards them. "The world knoweth them not," as it knew Him not. They are not to look for better fare than He met with. He said, "Marvel not if the world hate you; ye know that it hated me before it hated you. If ye were of the world, the world would love his own; but because ye are not of the world, therefore the world hateth you." Blessed be God, their *hands* are tied, but the carnal mind is not; this, therefore, will mani-

Q 2

fest itself against them. The world never will do justice to real Christians. But beware if they speak evil of you, it be not for unrighteousness, but for truth's sake, and heaven will soon make amends for all. One smile from God will more than make amends for all the frowns of the world. "His favour is life, and His loving-kindness is better than life." Do not judge of yourselves by what men think of you, but by what God thinks of you; and having His approbation and His commendation, you are happy, or ought to be.

"Truly God is good to Israel, even to such as are of a clean heart." "I do not believe it," say the ungodly. Therefore they say unto God, "Depart from us, for we desire not the knowledge of Thy ways; What is the Almighty, that we should serve Him? And what profit shall we have if we pray unto Him?" ah, but they do not know what a spring you have. They see your sorrows, but not your source of support; they see your burdens, but not the everlasting arms that sustain you. But God's people themselves can scarcely believe it sometimes. Zion sometimes said, "The Lord hath forsaken me; my God hath forgotten me." Christians often draw conclusions that they have no part or lot in the matter, and have not the root of the matter in them; but sometimes before they depart hence, they have been brought to see that they have charged God foolishly; and this, when they come to see their mistake and to rectify their error, furnishes them matter for mourning and lamentation, and they are then enabled to trust Him more fully. Jonah said, "Yet will I look again toward Thy holy temple," and acknowledge that "Salvation is of the Lord;" and David said, "I am cut off from before Thine eyes, nevertheless Thou heardest the voice of my supplications when I cried unto Thee." So Jeremiah was puzzled, and said, "Righteous art Thou, O Lord, when I plead with Thee; yet let me talk with Thee of Thy judgments. Wherefore doth the way of the wicked prosper? Wherefore are all they happy that deal very treacherously?" So here Asaph says, "Truly God is good to Israel, even to such as are of a clean heart. But as for me, my feet were almost gone, my steps had well nigh slipped. Why? I was envious at the foolish, when I saw the prosperity of the wicked. . . . When I came to know this"—the prosperous lives and untroubled deaths of evil doers—"it was too painful for me (for I had no satisfactory explanation) until I went into the sanctuary of God; then understood I their end," and this served to explain all. And we must have recourse to the same expedient. We must look forward to the end which furnishes all and explains all. Then all that is now dark will be made light, all that is disorderly will be arranged, and you will be able to see and to explain that "God is a rock; His work is perfect, and all His ways are judgment. A God of truth and without iniquity, just and right is He." We may not be able to reconcile many things now, still we must confide in the truth of God's word, and He hath said all His ways are mercy. He hath said, "All things work together for good to them that love God," and we must remember that He cannot deny Himself. Even here, Christians, if you observe these things, you shall understand the loving kindness of the Lord. And how many have been able to say, "It is good for me that I have been afflicted," and to see that God does not afflict you for His pleasure, but that you may be partakers of His holiness!

Oh, that you would think much and dwell much upon His goodness. Remember He is good, even in His chastenings towards you. Dwell upon His goodness in nature, and upon His goodness in providence; above all upon His goodness in the redemption of the world by our Lord Jesus Christ, and in His goodness towards Israel, even towards those who are of a clean heart. And while you admire His goodness, seek to imitate Him. "As you have opportunity, do good unto all men, especially to those who are of the household of faith." Remember He is the Saviour of all men, but especially of those who believe. There is a peculiar love He shews towards them, and to these you are more especially to exercise benevolence and kindness. And seek to be kindly affectioned one to another in brotherly love. "Be ye therefore followers of God as dear children; and walk in love, as Christ also hath loved us, and hath given Himself for us, an offering and a sacrifice to God for a sweet-smelling savour."

XI.

SONGS IN THE NIGHT.

(Delivered on Monday Evening, October 14th, 1850.)

"*I call to remembrance my song in the night.*"—PSALM lxvii. 6.

THIS psalm is a psalm of Asaph. And who was Asaph? He was leader of a band of singers appointed to praise the Lord in the order of their courses. But he was not only a musician, but a poet; and if in his compositions he has expressed his own views and feelings, he was as pious as he was poetical. This you know is not at all times the case. Gifts and grace do not always combine, as you see in the character of Balaam who had an enlightened understanding and a corrupt heart. You cannot therefore always infer what an author is by his works, as we see in the case of Bacon and others. Dryden wrote some beautiful lines in support of revealed religion. Who has not been affected by reading Burns' "Cottar's Saturday Night"? You may learn truth even from an enemy. I remember hearing Mr. Moore once saying in company, "You may judge of God's estimation of talent in two things: First, from the rareness of its bestowment, for if it were so valuable and useful as some suppose, it would be more general, for God renders things common and general in proportion as they are useful and necessary. The other is the character of those who commonly possess it." Good Mr. Ryland I remember saying something to this effect, when some persons were speaking in favour of a man of great talent, but who was not a good character: "I would rather be without talent if I have not piety; it always does more evil than good if it be not sanctified." The Apostle says, "Covet earnestly the best gifts; and yet I show unto you a more excellent way." As if he should say, "Covet earnestly the best graces," Faith, Hope, Charity; these three; "but the greatest of these is charity." What says Our Lord when referring to some who had talent enough? "Many shall say unto me in that day saying, Lord, Lord, open to us; have we not eaten and drunk in Thy presence and in Thy name cast out devils, and done many wonderful works? Then will I profess unto them I never knew you; depart from me, all ye workers of iniquity." "Not every one that saith unto me, Lord, Lord, shall enter the kingdom of heaven, but he that doeth the will of my Father which is in heaven." But talents are sometimes sanctified. Milton, who possessed so sublime a genius, dedicated himself to the service and glory of God. Dear Cowper sang—

> "O happy day that fixed my choice
> On Thee, my Saviour and my God;
> Well may this glowing heart rejoice,
> And tell its raptures all abroad."

And you know how exemplary was the sweet psalmist in our British Israel; how he pointed to heaven and led the way. Doubtless, too, this was the case with Asaph. His language expresses his own views and feelings, but it expresses also the views and feelings of others, and I believe the views and feelings of some who are present here this evening.

"In the day of my trouble," says he, "I sought the Lord; my sore ran in the night and ceased not." What sore? Never were words so strangely rendered, says Patrick; and Scott and Clark tell us that literally rendered they would be, "My hand expanded and was lifted up in prayer, and ceased not to be continued in this action." He did not feel their weakness as Moses did and therefore required to be held up. "And ceased not in the night;" that is, he was engaged in this exercise all the night. "My soul refused to be comforted." This was very wrong. "I remembered God and was troubled: I complained and my spirit was overwhelmed." Then you see in what a sad condition he was. "Thou holdest mine eyes waking; I am so troubled that I cannot speak," that is, he could neither shut his eyes nor open his mouth. What a condition was this to be in! "Thou holdest mine eyes waking; I am so troubled that I cannot speak." But was it always so? *No.* "I have considered the days of old, the years of ancient times." "I have thought of what Thou didst for Abraham, and of what Thou didst for Isaac, and of what Thou didst for Jacob, and of what Thou hast done in the days of old"—yea, and in nights also. "I call to remembrance my song in the night."

What, then, have gracious people nights of darkness? and nights of trouble and sorrow? Yes. So had Asaph, and "many are the afflictions of the righteous." This may appear strange to some, and it appears strange even to some good men ; and they have been ready to ask, "If I am His, why am I thus?" when they are thus *because* they are His. "Surely," you are perhaps ready to say at times, "surely, if the Lord loves us, He would have kept us. Surely a man would have kept his friend or his child from all suffering if he could. God could have saved us from suffering by a single volition, if He chose. Why, then, did He not?" But as Cowper says,

> "The path of sorrow, and that path alone.
> Leads to the Land where sorrow is unknown ;
> No traveller e'er reached that blest abode
> That found not thorns and briers on the road."

This is a truth as well as good poetry. But if we were to leave the case for reason to determine, I dare say she would decide that the favourites of heaven would be more privileged upon earth, and saved from those troubles and trials which others endure. But "God's thoughts are not our thoughts, neither are His ways our ways." No ! therefore says Solomon, "He that spareth the rod hateth the child, but he that loveth him chasteneth him betimes." There is something analogous here, and which should confirm us in our views of the dispensations of Divine Providence. Thus we know that severity is sometimes evidential of affection, while negligence and indifference are proofs of the want of it. God therefore says, "As many as I love, I rebuke and chasten." "If ye be without chastisement, whereof all are partakers, then are ye bastards and not sons." So you may remember my telling you of Luther, who in a state of suffering cried out,

> "Strike on, Lord, strike on ; for now
> I know I am Thy child."

Various are the things which produce the nights of darkness and distress of Christians. They have their share of the common evils of human nature. Some are afflicted in regard to their health. Some of you perhaps enjoy such an abundance and continuance of this invaluable blessing that you know not how to sympathise with those who are deprived of it, and with those who are made to possess months of vanity and have wearisome nights appointed to them. You see how many of God's servants mentioned in Scripture were sick, as Lazarus, of whom his sisters said to the Saviour, "Lord, he whom Thou lovest is sick."

Sometimes, too, they are afflicted in their outward condition, that is, in their worldly circumstances; and they are allowed to feel this. Indeed, our trials will never do us any good unless they are felt. The Apostle says, "No affliction for the present seemeth to be joyous, but grievous; nevertheless afterward it yieldeth the peaceable fruit of righteousness unto them that are exercised thereby." But if they are insensible under them, and despise the chastening of the Lord, they will derive no benefit from it, and they may provoke God to lay a heavier affliction upon them. Thus you may have seen a child smitten by his father, who has said, "I don't mind that." "Then," says the father, "you *shall* mind;" so he immediately applies the scourge more severely than before. Christians are allowed to feel their trials. How many have I known in my time reduced from affluence to dependence, and when this has been the case they have evinced that grace which has verified the promise, "As thy day so shall thy strength be."

Sometimes also they suffer relatively, and they may suffer more relatively than even the personal sufferers do. Perhaps you are all more or less aware of this. Indeed, all through life in proportion to our affections will be our afflictions, and we suffer more from our connections than from our enemies.

Then when they are not outward, when they are not bodily they may be mental, they may be spiritual. Sometimes these are combined, and then the case is very sad. This was the case with David. "My bones are vexed, my soul also is sore vexed, but thou, O Lord, how long?" No affliction is to be compared to this, when both the body and the mind suffer together.

I was one evening at the Lock Chapel, in London, hearing a clergyman preach, who said he had just come from the dying bed of a professor of religion, who told him that he did not know that he ever had any affliction in all his life. "I began to wonder at this, while I thought of the Apostles words, 'Whom the Lord loveth He correcteth, and chasteneth every son whom He receiveth:' but when he opened the case of his experience, and mentioned the doubts and the fears, the terrors and the agonies, through which his soul had been led, I did not wonder so much that he escaped all outward trouble."

We little know what some persons suffer. There are some thorns in the flesh driven in so deep that you connot see them, but the anguish is not the less poignant. Some have complaints and distresses which they can hardly divulge to others, and the heart only knoweth its own bitterness.

Then sometimes God hides His face from His people, and then it is no wonder they should be led to say with David, "Thou didst hide Thy face and I was troubled."

So you see they have their nights of darkness and sorrow: "I call to remembrance my song in the night." The nights may be long and they may be dark, *very* dark, and yet many songs have been heard in them. God has promised the enjoyment of His presence and blessing. When Christians are entering into trouble, they may look fcr it, and their friends may look for it on their behalf. Yes, says the God of all grace, "When thou passeth through the waters, I will be with thee, and through the floods, they shall not overflow thee; when thou passeth through the fire, thou shalt not be burnt, neither shall the flames kindle upon thee." Why, says the dear Saviour, "In the world ye shall have tribulation, but in me ye shall have peace." "Peace I leave with you, my peace I give unto you, not as the world giveth, give I unto you; let not your heart be troubled, neither let it be afraid." "Be of good comfort: I have overcome the world. Ye now have sorrow, but your sorrow shall be turned into joy: and your joy no man taketh from you." "I will not leave you comfortless," or as it is in the margin, "I will not leave you *orphans*." "You must depend upon my presence, and my care." Now these assurances are not like the devil's promises, or like man's, which by the way are much like his; so that you can place no dependence upon them, and you are ready to say, "All men are liars." But "all the promises of God in Christ Jesus are yea, and in Him amen, unto the glory of God by us." Depending upon the promises of men is like standing upon cracking ice, one is afraid of being engulfed; but relying upon the promises of Jehovah is like standing upon the earth, which comparatively liveth for ever. Yea, we have something firmer than the earth, for this shall pass away, but His Word shall not pass away; His promises shall be fulfilled.

See how the words before us have been exemplified. Sometimes they have been exemplified even literally. Christians have songs in the night. You see this literally fulfilled in the case of Paul and Silas. They were scourged, and while they were suffering from the scourge, they were thrust into the inner prison, and their feet were made fast in the stocks. But at midnight they not only prayed—that was natural enough—but also sang praises to God, and with so loud a tone, and with such energy, that the prisoners heard them. Their sad condition did not prevent their joy in God.

So Jacob, when he fled from his brother Esau: he came as far as to Padan-aram, where [he paused, for it was night, when the beasts of the forest break forth and seek for their prey, therefore he deemed it proper to go no further. But what a condition to be in! Here was a night, literally and metaphorically too. But what a song was he furnished with! so that in the morning when he awoke, he found,—looking round upon the briers and thorns,—he was not *in* heaven, yet that he was near to the gate. "Surely this is none other than the house of God, and this is the gate of heaven." He little expected this—to have such a visit—to see such a ladder reaching from earth to heaven, and God above addressing him in such a way as to remove all his fears and confirm all his hopes.

Again, think of Paul in the hurricane, when neither sun nor star was seen for many days, and when all hopes of being saved seemed entirely taken away. In this condition an angel is sent to him. Now, could an angel find him, think you, in the darkness of the night? Yes; darkness is as nothing to them, nor is distance. An angel soon found him, and presently the Apostle said to the crew, "Be of good cheer, for there shall be no loss of any man's life among you, but of the ship. For there stood by me this night the angel of God whose I am and whom I serve." So then it seems to have been the angel of the Covenant, saying, "Fear not, Paul; thou must be brought before Cæsar, and lo, God hath given thee all them that sail with thee."

And unto how many has the Lord appeared in the time of trial and distress! Their sufferings have abounded, but the consolations have superabounded. They have had their nights, but they have had their songs; and their songs even in their nights.

You remember Lord Bolingbroke under his sufferings: surely they were severe, but one day he asked God, "What business He had to put him to such pain?" and said he, a little before he died, "I find my philosophy fail me now in my affliction." But the philosophy of the Church did not fail her under her distresses, when she said, "Although the figtree shall not blossom, neither shall fruit be in the vines; the labour of the olive shall fail, and the fields shall yield no meat; the flock shall be cut off from the fold, and there shall be no herd in the stalls: yet will I rejoice in the Lord, I will joy in the God of my salvation." Lady Hervey's religion did not fail her in the evil day, for when told that her two and only sons were drowned, she raised her hands and impressively exclaimed, "Well, I see, O Lord, Thou art determined to have all my heart, and I am determined Thou *shalt* have it."

So you see that though God's people have sorrows they have songs. What do they sing about? In a general way the Scripture expresses them by two references. "They sing the song of Moses the servant of God and the song of the Lamb," which does not refer so much to heaven as to the Church even on earth. Their song is taken from Providence and from Grace, so that they derive materials for their song from both these. No wonder they derive it from the latter—from salvation by grace; from the contrivance of the plan of redemption; from the way in which it is applied to the soul; from the way in which the believer holds on his course under Divine agency; from the first-fruits, the pledges, the earnests of the glory that is to be revealed. Oh, what a delightful subject for reflection and praise and joy is here! How many a Christian has sung this song in his affliction! How precious has God's Word been to him under his trials! More precious than gold and silver, sweeter also than honey and the honeycomb.

Then Providence also has furnished them with a song. How much is there here to excite the joy and praise of Christians! David therefore says, "I will sing of mercy and judgment; unto Thee, O Lord, will I sing." "I will sing," as an old author calls it, "of my sweet mercies and of my bitter mercies." Both of them properly considered will furnish matter of joy and praise. Nothing here is casual, all is arranged by the God of all grace; all is foreseen and dispensed by Him. Sometimes His dispensations perplex you. Sometimes for a while you may be required to walk by faith, and not by sight, and to trust God in the dark. But I don't think He commonly requires His people to remain long in the dark; He soon throws some light upon their path. What He does they know not now, but they are brought to see afterwards, even here, so that they perceive wisdom in what seemed perplexing, and kindness in what seemed the reverse. Job was in a maze and no light was thrown upon his path for a considerable season, but he exclaimed, "He knoweth the way that I take: when He hath tried me, I shall come forth as gold;" and how soon did the dispensation begin to open and explain itself! "Oh," says the Christian, "I now see why I was visited with that sore trial, for the world was obtaining an undue influence over me." The Apostle Paul could say, "I know why I suffered from that thorn in the flesh, and why the messenger from Satan was sent to visit me, for I was in danger of being exalted above measure. I was not aware of it, but He who watched over me knew me better than I knew myself. I was not exalted above measure, but was in danger of it, and therefore there was given unto me a thorn in the flesh, the messenger of Satan to buffet me."

So David said, "It is good for me that I have been afflicted, for before I was afflicted I went astray, but now I have kept Thy word;" that is, "I grew too corpulent; He bled me, and I recovered."

So will it be with regard to many of the troubles and distresses of God's children. After a while, they will be able to see the reasonableness of them. They will not therefore say as in the phophecies of Jeremiah, "This is my grief, and I must bear it:" but with their Divine Lord, "The cup which my Father hath given me, shall I not drink it?" It is a high attainment, but it is a possible one, for a Christian not only to submit, not only to acquiesce with the will of God, and say "He hath done all things well," but in everything to give thanks, knowing what is the will of God in Christ Jesus concerning us; even in our sanctification.

"I call to remembrance my song in the night." Nothing affects us longer there; it is remembered. Therefore, says Paul in the Corinthians, "I declare unto you the gospel which I preached unto you, which also ye have received, and wherein ye stand; by which, also, ye are saved, if ye keep in memory what I preached unto you, unless ye have believed in vain." Therefore, he says again, You should "give the more earnest heed to the things which are spoken, lest at any time you let them slip." If you do, they can no longer influence you. Memory, therefore, is of great importance. But grace is most valuable. Grace can make a heart-memory where a head-memory is wanting. There may be a speculative memory without a practical; but there cannot be a practical without a speculative.

You should call God's goodness to remembrance, in order to excite your gratitude. You know you are backward enough here, but David says, "Bless the Lord, O my soul; and all that is within me, bless His holy name; bless the Lord, O my soul, and forget not all His benefits." Oh, it was this bad memory that produced the ingratitude of the Jews. Thus Moses said to them, "Of the Rock that begat thee thou art unmindful, and hast forgotten God that formed thee." Hence they were so little impressed and excited with a sense of the mercies of the Lord. You should often retire, and make them go backwards and forwards before the eye of your mind; and while you are musing, the fire will burn, and you will be induced to praise and bless God's holy name.

You should also call to remembrance your song in the night, to encourage and to establish your confidence in the Redeemer. Thus, when you come into fresh difficulties, you may be able to say, "Well, I have been here before, and the Lord did not abandon or neglect me, but brought me safely through; and He who has delivered, doth deliver, and we trust that He will yet deliver. It was thus with David, when going to engage in his encounter with Goliath. He would not have been so ready to gapple with so formidable a foe if he had not remembered that the Lord had delivered him from the lion, and from the bear. But, says he, "The Lord who delivered me out of the paw of the lion, and out of the paw of the bear"—for they had both of them got their paw upon his breast—"will deliver me out of the hands of this Philistine."

Why did the disciples complain or despond because they had only one loaf in the boat? Says the Saviour, "Do ye not remember? When I brake the five loaves among five thousand, how many baskets full of fragments took ye up? They say unto Him, Twelve. And when the seven among four thousand, how many baskets full of fragments took ye up? And they said, Seven." Oh, they had forgotten this, or they would have been able to place more implicit trust and confidence in Him.

Thus may it be with you. This is the experience of all true Christians at times; they have hardly anything for the present to live upon. When this is the case, you must imitate the bees and the ants, and go and live upon what you have picked up in sunny weather, and call these things to remembrance. Thus did the psalmist. "O my God, my soul is cast down within me: therefore will I remember Thee from the land of Jordan, and of the Hermonites, from the Hill Mizar." And while thus engaged, they have been able to say,

"His love in times past forbids me to think
He'll leave me at last in trouble to sink:
Each sweet Ebenezer I have in review
Confirms His good pleasure to help me quite through."

There is another reason why you should call your song to remembrance, which is, that you may encourage and comfort others. You are not to regard yourselves as unconnected individuals, for you are connected with others, and especially with your fellow-Christians. You are to comfort them, and to comfort them with those comforts wherewith you yourselves are comforted of God. You will be poor comforters if you can tell nothing of your own experience; but in this respect most of you are furnished with a word in season. To those who are afflicted, tell how you have been called to suffer affliction, and how under it the Lord enabled you to sing, and to sing on your way out of it. Tell them to take courage, for the Saviour will be with His people in their affliction. You know who hath said, "Fear thou not, for I am with thee; be not dismayed, for I am thy God; I will strengthen thee, yea, I will uphold thee with the right hand of my righteousness." "I will be with him in trouble, and will deliver him, and honour him." Now all this turns upon experience. Oh! I love Christian experience. I don't like all that is *called* experience. I don't like fanaticism and enthusiasm. But genuine religion is always known by the godly practice that will follow. When this is the case, we cannot speak too highly of it. As Mr. Hart says—

> "True religion's more than notion,
> Something must be known and felt."

You see what a chequered scene the Christian has while here. Erskine calls it heaven and hell by turns. We see the church of Christ like a bush burning but not consumed; a vessel tossed and not sunk;" "troubled on every side, but not distressed; perplexed, but not in despair; cast down, but not destroyed." And thus it is the believer is prepared and sweetened for the inheritance of the saints in light.

O, Christians, you should be looking forward to that period, and sing with Dr. Watts,

> "There is a land of pure delight
> Where saints immortal reign,
> *Infinite day excludes the night*,
> And pleasures banish pain."

Ah, there is no night there! No! Christians, your nights are all here, there is no night there. You will have no song in the night there, but you will have songs enough in the day. There is everlasting day. For "Thy sun shall no more go down; neither shall thy moon withdraw itself; for the Lord shall be thine everlasting light, and the days of thy mourning shall be ended."

XII.

THE SOUL'S REST.

(Delivered on Thursday Evening, November 7th, 1844.)

"*Return unto thy rest, O my soul; for the Lord hath dealt bountifully with thee.*"—PSALM cxvi. 7.

VERILY, brethren, our obligations to the Scriptures of Truth are immense. This blessed Book, "given by inspiration of God, is profitable for doctrine, for reproof, for correction, for instruction in righteousness; that the man of God may be perfect, thoroughly furnished unto all good works." One of the peculiar advantages we enjoy is this: we have so much of the history and experience of good men of old, enabling us to compare ourselves with them. If we consider them as travellers, here we find the way-marks which they cast up, showing us where they once were, and where we now are. If we consider them as sheep, we can "go forth by the footsteps of the flock," and are told where they fed, and where they rested at noon. Blessed be God for the relation we have of David's experience. How often have we taken sweet counsel with him! How often have we known his heart's bitterness, and have "intermeddled with his joy"! How often have we prayed with him, "Show me a token for good"! and, "Say unto my soul, I am thy salvation"! And with him reproved our despondency, saying, "Why art thou cast down, O my soul? and why art thou disquieted within me? Hope thou in God, for I shall yet praise Him for the help of His countenance." And how often, also, have we endeavoured to check our wandering thoughts and our roving affections in the words we have now read: "Return unto thy rest, O my soul, for the Lord hath dealt bountifully with thee!" Now these words contain the character of God, as the rest of the soul. They imply a possibility of our departing from Him. They contain a resolution to return, and also a motive to influence it. Here are the four articles upon which we intend to enlarge.

I. These words contain THE CHARACTER AS GOD AS THE REST OF THE SOUL. "Return unto Thy rest, O my soul."

That which concerns the soul is the main thing. "What shall I eat, and what shall I drink, and wherewithal shall I be clothed?" This regards the animal. Where is the man? Where is reason? Where is conscience? Where is immortality? Where is the soul? The soul is the man. The soul is spiritual in its nature, and eternal in its duration. The soul has its appropriate good, as well as the body, and this is God Himself. Man's body has its supplies and indulgences, suited to its nature, and so has the soul. It would be absurd to think of satisfying the body with books and thoughts; and it would be equally absurd to think of the soul's living on things derived from silver and gold. All these are unsuited to the nature of the soul: and, therefore, they cannot meet its wants and desires, they cannot satisfy it. Man has a soul which is made for eternity, and capable of knowing, of resembling, and enjoying God, and of union and communion with Him; and whatever he seeks after to supply His place will issue in disappointment. Whatever else the man acquires, some void will still urge him to cry, "Who will show me any good?" But this is not the case with the Lord's people. God is their portion, and He is their rest. Some may think that this is enthusiasm; but he that believeth on the Son of God hath the witness in himself. He has made the trial, and knows that all an immortal being can want is to be found in God. Yes, he has made the trial, and knows the truth of the declaration of our Lord, "He that cometh unto me shall never hunger; he that believeth on me shall never thirst." He has found satisfaction, which is only to be derived from union with the Saviour. Now, take him in any condition; take him in prosperity. or in adversity, and you will find that "God is the strength of his heart, and his portion for ever." Has he been called to sustain losses? has he been reduced in circumstances? has he been exercised with various afflictions? he is not miserable; he is not in despair. He *had* been had he made these things his rest; and in the loss of them would have exclaimed, "They have taken away my gods, and what have I more!" But now he encourages "himself in the Lord his God." Now he can say, "Although the fig-tree shall not blossom; neither shall fruit be in the vines, the labour of the olives shall fail, and the fields shall yield no meat; the flock shall be cut off from the fold, and there shall be no herd in the stalls." Why, it seems all gone! "*Yet* I will rejoice in the

Lord, I will joy in the God of my salvation." While he uses and enjoys these things, he passes by them as his portion, and says with David, "The Lord is the portion of mine inheritance and of my cup: Thou maintainest my lot. The lines are fallen unto me in pleasant places; yea, I have a goodly heritage." And while he has connections here, he can say with Doctor Watts:—

> "To Thee we owe our life and health,
> And friends and safe abode;
> Thanks to Thy name for meaner things,
> But these are not my God."

> "Give what Thou wilt, without Thee we are poor;
> And with Thee rich, take what Thou wilt away."

And this is the case with them all. They differ in their experience, and in the degree of their graces, but not as to their choice. They all choose God as the rest of their souls.

II. It is possible for us to depart from Him. Otherwise there would be no need of *returning* to Him. Solomon tells us, "There is not a just man upon earth that liveth and sinneth not;" and James says, "In many things we offend all." If we look into the Scriptures, we shall find a record of some bad falls in God's most distinguished servants. Thus we find that Abraham's faith failed him; that Moses spake unadvisedly with his lips; and that Job cursed the day in which he was born. And to which of the saints will you turn, in order to find one free of infirmities? Where there is no backsliding in life, there is backsliding in heart. Who, on examination of himself, but discovers a thousand infirmities? David, after his grievous fall, implored Divine preservation; and need we not say with him, "Quicken Thou me, according to Thy word"? We are liable to fall, and, if God's people were not even *prone* to backslide, God would never have said, as he did concerning the Jews, "Take heed, brethren, lest there be in any of you an evil heart of unbelief, in departing from the living God." Is not all sin a departure from God? Do we not depart from Him when we forget His benefits? or when, having succeeded in any concern, we "sacrifice to our own net, and burn incense to our own drag," as if by these "our portion had been made fat, and our meat plenteous"? Have we not departed from God when we have yielded to earthly attachments, giving that to the creature which is due only to the Creator; who is "God over all blessed for evermore"? Do we not depart from Him when we lean upon a broken reed; or on an arm of flesh? To whom did John say, "Little children, keep yourselves from idols"? Oh, how many idols have we all! Persons may make idols of their children, of their friends, of their relations, of their ministers, or even of the ordinances of God; they may repair to these ordinances regardless of God, and use them as if there was merit in anything they could do, and without having recourse by prayer to Him, who, while Paul plants and Apollos waters, can alone give the increase.

Then we have—

III. An exhortation to return. "Return unto thy rest, O my soul." Let us learn, dear brethren, that the departure of a child of God from Him is never total or final. His soul is like the compass, where, indeed, the needle may turn from its direction, but it cannot continue; it will tremble back again, and turn to the north. So it is with the true Christian. This is therefore in unison with the declarations of Scripture, where it is said, "The righteous shall hold on his way, and he that hath clean hands shall wax stronger and stronger." "A good man's steps are ordered by the Lord: though he fall, he shall not be utterly cast down, for the Lord upholdeth him by His hand." And you will find this is secured by various engagements. "I will not," says God by Jeremiah, "turn away from doing them good." But may they not turn away from Him? No, says God, "I will put my fear in their hearts, and they shall not depart from me," that is, totally and finally. The Apostle says, "Being born not of corruptible seed but of incorruptible, which liveth and abideth for ever." "Whoever," says John, "is born of God, cannot commit sin," that is, he cannot sin as others do, he cannot sin habitually, and with the full bias of his mind, "for His seed remaineth in him, and he cannot sin because he is born of God." Now you see how this is exemplified in Peter. Peter trusted in his own strength, and denied his Lord after all the admonitions given to him. But the Saviour said, "I have prayed for thee that thy faith fail not." Was His prayer accomplished? It was. His faith did not fail, that is, it did not fail as to its fixed principles, though it did fail as to its momentary exercise; accordingly, "the Saviour turned and looked upon Peter" and the look broke his poor heart, and hiding his face in his mantle he hurried out "and wept bitterly." There is always something in the experience of a regenerate man to check every evil propensity. Jonah said, "I am cast out of Thy sight, yet I will look again towards Thy holy temple." Asaph said, "This is my infirmity, but I will remember the years of the right hand of the Most High." How finely does David express this: "My soul is gone astray like a lost sheep: seek Thy servant, for I do not forget Thy law."

IV. Consider THE MOTIVE BY WHICH THE EXHORTATION IS ENFORCED.

"Return unto thy rest, O my soul, for the Lord hath dealt bountifully with thee."

Now it is not with the fact itself that we have here to do, but with the use David makes of it. "The Lord," says he, "preserveth the simple; I was brought low, and He helped me." Yes, David, you may say so; He gave you many a favour, and enriched you with many a gift, and raised you from being a shepherd to the throne; these are blessings which David acknowledges, but these were not all the blessings which he received at the hand of God. He had still higher favours, but these so far from being peculiar to him, are common to all believers in all ages of the world. Ah, Christians, sensible of your unworthiness, you will readily acknowledge that you are "less than the least of all God's mercies." The air you breathe in, is a mercy; the food you eat, is a mercy; the sleep you enjoy, is a mercy; your ease from pain, is a mercy. But hear what the Apostle says: "Herein is love, not that we loved God, but that He loved us, and sent His Son to be the propitiation for our sins." O what infinite bounty is here! that He would not spare His own Son, but delivered Him up for us all, and with Him also freely gave us all things. Ah, Christian, through Him He has forgiven you all trespasses, and not only changed your relative condition, but also your very nature, and He has put His laws in your mind and written them in your heart. O what Sabbaths has He given you! how often have you heard with pleasure His holy word, and often at His table too you have found the fruit of the tree of life sweet to your taste. But notice, with the use that David makes of this resolution, his desire is, that his soul should be brought back to God his rest, and nothing conduces so much to this as the Christian's experience. When a mere professor of religion is thrown off from his forms and exercises, he has nothing of this to restrain him when going astray, and nothing of it to excite him to return after he has gone astray.

He knows nothing of the sweetness and blessedness of wisdom's ways and of communion with God. The real Christian has experienced this, and what is the consequence? He is brought to say with Job, "O that it were with me as in months past, as in the days when God preserved me! when His candle shined upon my head, and when by His light I walked through darkness; when the secret of God was upon my tabernacle, and when the Almighty was yet with me." After awhile he is enabled to say with the church in Hosea, "I will go and return to my first husband, for then was it better with me than now." Thus David here says, "Return unto thy rest, O my soul; for the Lord hath dealt bountifully with thee." Is this thy kindness to thy friend—thy best, thy Almighty Friend, who has blessed thee with all spiritual blessings in heavenly places in Christ Jesus? Hast thou not found anything in His loving-kindness to keep thee to Himself? Has He not in exchange for a land of darkness given thee light in thy dwelling? and for a barren wilderness given thee to feed in the green pastures of His word? and what joy hast thou found in the world compared to the joys of His salvation? Can you not say,—

"Why should my foolish passions rove?
Where can such sweetness be,
As I have tasted in Thy love,
As I have found in Thee?

"What peaceful hours I then enjoyed!
How sweet their mem'ry still!
But now I feel an aching void
The world can never fill.

"Return, O holy dove, return,
Sweet messenger of rest;
I hate the sins that made Thee mourn,
And drove Thee from my breast."

But you must not only desire *Him* to return to you in a way of consolation, you must return to Him in a way of duty. You must therefore summon your soul to say with holy resolution,

"The dearest idol I have known,
Whate'er that idol be,
Help me to tear it from Thy throne;
And worship only Thee."

You may learn from hence to walk with holy caution and circumspection, to "watch and pray lest you enter into temptation," and lest you depart from the living God. For as Bishop Hall says, "A Christian never falls but to the breaking of his bones; and never gets up again but to the breaking of his heart."

Then learn that the full enjoyment of this rest is reserved for hereafter. There will be no departure from Him. How little of God now do we see! How many interruptions do we find! But, Christian, you are going home, and then in the most blessed sense will you say, "Return unto thy rest, O my soul; for the Lord hath dealt bountifully with thee." Now go and enjoy perfect and uninterrupted blessedness.

What shall we say to those who have no desire after God? What a state of moral disorder must you be in, to say "Depart from us, we desire not the knowledge of Thy ways." And if you reject Him now, will it not be righteous in God to reject you, and to say as He did to the Jews, "Israel would none of me, therefore I gave them up"? Yet by the prophet Isaiah He says, "O that thou hadst hearkened to my commandments! Then had thy peace been as a river, and thy righteousness as the waves of the sea."

XIII.

WAITING UPON GOD.

(Delivered on Thursday Evening, November 28th, 1844.)

"*My soul waiteth for the Lord more than they that watch for the morning: I say, more than they that watch for the morning. Let Israel hope in the Lord: for with the Lord there is mercy, and with Him is plenteous redemption. And He shall redeem Israel from all his iniquities.*"—PSALM cxxx. 6-8.

THOUGH the Jews lived under a dispensation abounding with carnal ordinances, some of them were far from being carnal men. The Apostle, while writing to the Hebrews, considered them worthy of Christian invitation and therefore said, "Be not slothful, but followers of those who through faith and patience inherit the promises." And such an one was David. Read only the Psalm before us,—and is there a Christian here this evening who has not said, "Out of the depths have I cried unto Thee, O Lord! Lord, hear my voice; let Thine ears be attentive to the voice of my supplications. If Thou, Lord, shouldest mark iniquity, O Lord who should stand? But there is forgiveness with Thee, that Thou mayest be feared. I wait for the Lord, my soul doth wait, and in His word do I hope." Is there a Christian here this evening, who cannot and will not say, "My soul waiteth for the Lord more than they that watch for the morning: I say more than they that watch for the morning. Let Israel hope in the Lord: for with the Lord there is mercy, and with Him is plenteous redemption. And He shall redeem Israel from all his iniquities."

Let us now hasten to consider the three things contained in the text: I. David's experience; II. His admonition; and III. the relation which these have to each other.

I. Let us consider DAVID'S EXPERIENCE. It is thus expressed: "My soul waiteth for the Lord more than they that watch for the morning: I say, more than they that watch for the morning." You will perceive the word "waiteth" is in italics; a proof that it is not in the original, but according to the excellency of our translation, it is supplied, and supplied well as appears from the verses immediately preceding. "I wait for the Lord, my soul doth wait, and in His word do I hope. My soul waiteth for the Lord more than they that watch for the morning: I say more than they that watch for the morning."

Now this is not the language of any in *Heaven*. They have waited for the Lord, but they now behold His face in righteousness and are satisfied, because they have awaked up in His likeness. It is not the language of any in *Hell*. Oh, how they seek to escape the reach of His hand and the sight of His eye! "Oh," say they, "to find a place where God is not!" It is not the language of many upon earth.

"Broad is the way that leads to death,
And thousands walk together there;
While Wisdom shows a narrower path,
With here and there a traveller."

And says David, "There be many that say, Who will show me any good?" Here and there you will find one of those praying with him, "Lord, lift Thou up the light of Thy countenance upon me, and that shall put more joy and gladness into my heart than in the time that their corn and wine increase." Yea, the language is in a measure peculiar to some even among believers. Believers all indeed desire to enjoy more of it; but this language more properly belongs to awakened souls—to mourners in Zion—to those who are complaining, "When I would do good, evil is present with me. O wretched man that I am! who shall deliver me from the body of this death?"

But what does this language itself contain? "My soul waiteth for the Lord." This waiting surely implies *the renunciation of every other dependance*, and our making God the strength of our heart and our portion for ever: so that we shall be able to say with the Psalmist, "My soul, wait thou only upon God; for my expectation is from Him."

We are all naturally indigent and therefore dependant creatures, and of course unable to succour and to defend ourselves. We look abroad, and as the world and creatures stand next, we always begin by leaning upon them, and what is the consequence? Very frequently a painful disappointment, or a series of disappointments to recall us from such reliances, and to induce us to say, "Therefore will I look unto the Lord; I will wait for the God of my salvation; my God will hear me." "And now Lord what wait I for? my hope is in Thee." It is well if brought to this, if when our lamps are extinguished we are illumined by the Sun of Righteousness; if, when our cisterns are dashed to pieces and can hold no water, we are led in search of the Fountain of living waters.

You well remember how Israel was censured for their dependance upon Assyria, which like placing dependance upon a broken reed, not only failed as to their hope, but "pierced them through with many sorrows." Yet by this very means they were weaned from all creature confidence. "And it shall come to pass in that day, that the remnant of Israel, and such as are escaped of the house of Jacob, shall no more again stay upon him that smote them; but shall stay upon the Lord, the Holy One of Israel in truth."

And as to spiritual things, oh, how many expedients are tried before you have recourse to the "balm in Gilead" and to the "Physician" there! How many shelters are attempted to be built up before you fly for refuge to the only hope set before you in the Gospel! Oh, how long and how earnestly do you go about to establish your own righteousness before you go to the dear Saviour, saying, "In the Lord have I righteousness and strength. I will go in the strength of the Lord God, I will make mention of His righteousness only."

This waiting upon God includes *desire.* "In the way of Thy judgments," says the Church, "we have waited for Thee." "The desire of our soul is to Thee and to the remembrance of Thy name." "My soul," says David, "panteth for God, for the living God; when shall I come and appear before God? My soul followeth hard after God,"—to possess His fear, to wear His lovely image, to be engaged in His service and for His glory. These longings after God are naturally expressed in prayer, which is now no longer the language of the lip but the expression of the heart; and it attracts the Divine notice itself. Thus the Saviour said of Saul after his conversion, "Behold, he prayeth!"

Waiting upon God takes in *expectation.* The degrees of this vary from "full assurance of hope" down to probability, and in some cases possibility. But if a man entirely despairs, he will forbear the exercise, and say with the unbelieving nobleman, "Why should I wait for the Lord any longer?" There is always, therefore, in the lowest state some degree of hope; there is a ray of hope thrown across the darkness of life to show that we are not in perdition itself; there is some plank laid hold of to keep the head above water till the deliverer comes to our relief. The soul, therefore, ventures and says, "I will go in unto the King, and if I perish, I perish!" But did any ever perish at His feet? Have any ever sought Him and been rejected? And have you not His own declaration, "Him that cometh unto me, I will in no wise cast out"?

That this waiting upon God takes in desire and expectation is so obvious as to require no proof of illustration. He is a God of judgment and arranges all things by infinite wisdom, and therefore blessed are all they that wait for Him, and that in patience possess their souls. This waiting upon God keeps the mind calm and composed, which otherwise would experience nothing but irritation. This preserves us for the time from drawing any hard and unfavourable conclusion; this secures us from delivering ourselves by any unhallowed means, such as Rebecca for instance employed in order to ensure the accomplishment of the promise to Jacob. On the other hand we are told that, "He who believeth maketh not haste;" and Jeremiah says, "It is a good thing that a man both hope and quietly wait for the salvation of the Lord."

But though it is the Christian's duty to wait for the Lord, it is not always a very easy thing, especially when it is exercised in the midst of trying dispensations without and a depressing experience within.

> "You seem forsaken and alone,
> You hear the lions roar;
> And every door is shut but one,
> And that is mercy's door."

But you would not find it easy to exercise patience, and be very calm and easy at the door at which you knocked, if you saw a great lion drawing near you and ready to devour. Oh, when in trouble and distress, how slow the time moves on, it seems to pass over us with leaden wings! An hour seems almost a day, and a day almost a week, and hope deferred maketh the heart sick. But in this case the believer remembers that God is under no obligation to hear, to succour, and to deliver him at all, and he remembers how long God had to wait for him, and that God's time is always the best time, and that we cannot eventually wait in vain however long, we may be called upon to wait; for "Blessed are all they that wait for Him," and "none of them that wait for me," says He, "shall be ashamed."

Finally this waiting upon God includes *diligence in the use of the means which He has ordained.* We are to wait to receive His orders, that we may serve Him in His own appointed way. This is the promise, "Blessed is the man that heareth me, watching daily at my gates, waiting at the posts of my doors." This is the assurance, "They that wait upon the Lord shall renew their strength; they shall mount up on wings as eagles; they shall run, and not be weary; they shall walk, and not faint." This is the rule of the Divine procedure, "Draw nigh to God, and He will draw nigh to you."

Now having considered the *nature* of this experience, namely, his waiting for the Lord, let us glance at the *degree* of it. For, says David, "I not only wait but my soul waiteth for the Lord more than they that watch for the morning: I say *more than they that watch for the morning.*"

You will observe that feelings produced by genuine religion are always very powerful and distinguishable. Then prayer is "crying out for the living God." Then our desires are expressed by a hungering and thirsting after righteousness. Then repentance is a loathing and abhorring ourselves. Then sorrow for sin is mourning for an only son, and a being in bitterness as for the loss of a first-born. Then the joy is joy unspeakable and full of glory, and the peace is a peace which passeth all understanding. The zeal in the various exercises of the Divine life is nothing less than striving to enter in at the strait gate, running the race set before us, fighting the good fight of faith, and taking the kingdom of heaven by violence. Surely all this is much more than some imagine; surely all this is much more than that easy soft compliance that requires no exertion, that demands no sacrifice, that allows of worldly conformities and indulgences. I have told you more than once, that though you may go asleep on your way to hell, there must be a continual struggle and contention all the way to the kingdom of heaven; and that it is by patient continuance in well doing we may expect ultimately to enjoy glory, honour, immortality, and eternal life.

Observe further, the *import of the figure*: "more than they that watch for the morning: I say more than they that watch for the morning." And who are they? No one is mentioned here; so much the better, because we may bring forward in our minds all characters that will furnish an example. Think of a watchman in a cold and inclement night as he cries the hour and longs for the day. Perhaps the immediate reference is to the guards that watched around the Temple. Or, we might think of a traveller in a wilderness, ignorant of his way. The night approaches, he has no one to guide his movements, while he hears the wild beasts roaring abroad. Dr. Watts beautifully expresses it—

"Just as the guards that keep the night,
Long for the morning skies;
Watch the first beams of breaking light,
And meet them with their eyes."

Then again,—

"As the benighted pilgrims wait,
And long and wish for breaking day,
So waits my soul before Thy gate;
When will my God His face display?"

Only think now of Paul and his companions, after being about fourteen nights in the hurricane, casting four anchors and wishing for the day as every wave beat over the ship! Only think of the Eastern sufferer "made to posess months of vanity," and saying, "Wearisome nights are appointed to me. When I lie down I say, When shall I arise, and the night be gone? And I am full of tossings to and fro unto the dawning of the day."

Perhaps there are persons here this evening who have realized in their own experience every one of these images—(you know the brevity we assign to this service, and I see our time is nearly gone, I therefore must leave the remainder for another opportunity)—but we would not conclude without noticing a little more the metaphor here employed. We would not overlook its *comparison* or its *contrast*. Both these are worthy of our notice.

Observe two things with regard to those who "watch for the morning" and "wait for the Lord." *The first is*, that those who wait for the Lord *are as sure of success* as they that watch. The one is as fixed and certain in grace, as the other is in nature, for God has promised it, and what He hath promised He is able also and faithful to perform. He hath said, "Ask and it shall be given you; seek and ye shall find; knock and it shall be opened unto you." He never said to the seed of Jacob, "Seek ye me in vain." Hence David says, "I waited patiently for the Lord, and He inclined unto me and heard my cry. He brought me up also out of a horrible pit, out of the miry clay, and set my feet upon a rock and established my goings." He required him to wait, and to wait patiently, but not without success;—"and He hath put a new song in my mouth, even praise unto our God; many shall see it and fear and shall trust in the Lord."

The second is, that the morning in regard to your mind *will far surpass* that of the natural morning; and will be far more beneficial. God's appearances on the behalf of His people, and the manifestation of Himself to them, will produce a better and more glorious day. As Watts has most beautifully expressed it—

"So waits my soul to see Thy grace,
And more intent than they;
Meets the first opening of Thy face,
And finds a brighter day!

Well, but when will this day arrive? There are two periods, my brethren, when those who wait upon God will find a glorious and blessed day.

One is partly here. When our Lord spake of manifesting Himself to His disciples, some of them said, "Lord how is it that Thou wilt manifest Thyself unto us, and not unto the world?" He can always do this. How often has He done it on the behalf of his people now here!

"The Lord can change the darkest skies,
Can give us day for night;
Make sacred floods of sorrow rise
To rivers of delight."

This manifestation of God here—the morning he brings you *here*—is not to be undervalued. Oh, what an answer to prayer! Oh, what a support in tribulation! Oh, what a comfort of the Holy Ghost is it! Oh, how reviving, how refreshing, how satisfying to the soul, when weeping has endured for the night and joy has come in the morning!

But it will be perfectly accomplished hereafter. Oh, what a morning will *that* be, believer, when you wake up in God's likeness! A morning unmingled with a cloud, and never followed by a night! No, *no*. "For there shall be no night there. There, your sun shall no more go down, nor your moon withdraw itself, for the Lord shall be your everlasting light, and the days of your mourning shall be ended."

XIV.

REDEMPTION FOR ISRAEL.

(Delivered on Thursday Evening, December 5th, 1844.)

"*Let Israel hope in the Lord: for with the Lord there is mercy, and with Him is plenteous redemption. And He shall redeem Israel from all his iniquities.*"—PSALM cxxx. 7, 8.

SOME of you will remember that I read these words, with the sixth verse, as a text last Thursday evening, and after an introduction which turned upon the spirituality of some of those who lived under the Jewish dispensation, and which led the Author of the Hebrews to consider them worthy of Christian imitation, we applied this peculiarly to David; remarking, with regard to the Psalm before us, how easily every Christian can make the language of it his own, for where is the Christian who has not often said, "Out of the depths have I cried unto Thee, O Lord! Lord, hear my voice; let Thine ears be attentive to the voice of my supplication. If Thou, Lord, shouldest mark iniquity, O Lord, who shall stand? But there is forgiveness with Thee, that Thou mayest be feared. I wait for the Lord, my soul doth wait, and in His word do I hope"! Then come on the words we have again read. You remember we engaged to consider from them three things. First, David's *experience:* "My soul waiteth for the Lord, more than they that wait for the morning: I say more than they that wait for the morning." Secondly, his *admonition:* "Let Israel hope in the Lord, for with the Lord there is mercy, and with Him is plenteous redemption. And He shall redeem Israel from all his iniquities." And thirdly, the *relation which these have to each other*, his experience and admonition. He begins with himself and ends with Israel.

The first of these we have considered, both as to the *nature* of his experience, waiting for the Lord, and the *degree* of it, waiting more for Him than they that watch for the morning. But we had not time then to consider the second and third:

we will therefore attempt to fill up the remainder of the hour in contemplation upon these, and approach the second division of our subject, namely, HIS EXHORTATION. "Let Israel hope in the Lord, for with the Lord there is mercy, and with Him is plenteous redemption. And He shall redeem Israel from all his iniquities."

The admonition here is an exhortation with regard to hope. Hope regards good things only. You may expect evil, but you can only hope for good. So hope is distinguished from expectation. Hope regards something future. That which is seen and enjoyed is not hope. For what a man seeth that it is in his possession, why should he yet hope for it? It regards something attainable. No man can hope for that which he believes impossible to be obtained.

Let us now enter a little into this admonition, and two things may be regarded in it, namely, the persons addressed, and the encouragement afforded them.

With regard to the first, *the persons addressed*: "Let *Israel* hope in the Lord:" not Israel according to the flesh, but Israel according to promise. All along, they were not all Israel which were of Israel. Always he was not a Jew that was one outwardly; neither is that circumcision which is outward in the flesh;" but he is a Jew which is one inwardly; and circumcision is that of the heart, in the spirit, and not in the letter; whose praise is not of men but of God." In the seventy-third Psalm, Asaph says, "Truly God is good to Israel, even to such as are of a clean heart." Here the latter part is explanatory of the former. The Israel of God have a love to holiness which leads them to oppose sin, and to seek after purity and sanctification.

Observe the distinction of our Lord with regard to Nathaniel: "Behold an Israelite indeed, in whom is no guile." By calling him "an Israelite indeed," He distinguishes him from his own countrymen, and by adding "in whom is no guile," He distinguishes him from his own nature. And so says the Apostle Paul in writing to the Philippians, "We are the circumcision who worship God in the Spirit, and rejoice in Christ Jesus, and have no confidence in the flesh."

This admonition being addressed to *them* reminds us of three things:—

First, that even the Israel of God need exhortation and encouragement. Though their principles are heavenly, yet their souls often cleave to the dust, and they are often constrained to pray, "Quicken Thou me, according to Thy word." Though alive they are not always lively. Though always entitled to joy, and joy unspeakable, they are not always rejoicing. Young converts may rather wonder at this, while for a time they are walking in the comforts of the Holy Ghost. Isaiah says, "They shall go out with joy, and be led forth with peace." So our translation; but Bishop Louth has it, "And be led *on* with peace." And this is a very proper representation of Christians generally. "They shall go out with joy, and be led on with peace." That fervour which may result from novelty may subside into tranquility, aud we shall have no reason to complain if we go out with *joy*, we are led on with *peace*. Peace is far superior in the whole to joy. There are experiences awaiting them for which they are not yet prepared. They have concealed from them, for the time, the number of forces of their enemies, and therefore conclude that they have them not. God affords them at first some peculiar consolations to induce them to go on, till they consider that they have gone too far to think of ever going back in their course. We are reminded also of their duty to hope much. Let "Israel hope in the Lord." They are said to be saved by hope and to rejoice in hope. In the storms of life this hope is an anchor of the soul. It is an helmet, says the apostle, to put on the head, to secure it in the day of battle. It is equally a sanctifier. Whatever some may think, it has a powerful, practical influence in the Christian's course, and, therefore, John says, "He that hath this hope in him purifieth himself, even as He is pure." Paul therefore prays for the Romans, that they may be filled with all peace and joy in believing, and that they may "abound in hope by the power of the Holy Ghost," and tells them that the design of the Scriptures from beginning to end is this, to produce and sustain the Christian's hope, that "whatsoever things were written aforetime were written for our learning, that we, through patience and comfort of the Scriptures, might have hope." And so Peter tells the Christians scattered abroad, that this is the ultimate design of the mediation of the Saviour in His death and resurrection. "God raised Him from the dead, and gave Him glory, that your faith and hope might be in God."

Then also it reminds you that they are peculiarly authorized to indulge this hope. Others are not forbidden to hope. None are excluded by the Gospel but those who choose to exclude themselves. All should remember that "God waiteth to be gracious, and is exalted to have mercy," that "He is long-suffering to us-ward, not willing that any should perish, but that all should come to repentance."

But, then, some are in a state of union and communion with Him already. He is the Father and the Friend of some, and they are His by covenant engagements. In a word, theirs are the promises of grace in the Scripture; promises suited to all their circumstances, and they may go and plead them before God, and say, "Do as Thou hast said." Those who are the heirs of grace, who answer to the character referred to, may call them their own. Thus our Saviour says, "Blessed are the poor in spirit, for theirs is the kingdom of heaven: Blessed are they that mourn, for they shall be comforted: Blessed are they which do hunger and thirst after righteousness, for they shall be filled." "They that wait upon the Lord shall renew their strength; they shall mount up with wings as eagles; they shall run, and not be weary; they shall walk, and not faint."

III. Pass we from the persons addressed in the exhortation to THE ENCOURAGEMENTS AFFORDED THEM.

These are four:—

First, "Let Israel hope in the Lord, for with the Lord there is *mercy.*" There can be no hope in Him till we discover this, and till we believe this. Without this every view of God will be tremendous. His wisdom, His power, His omniscience, His omnipotence, will all be dreadful, unless we can discern that with the Lord there is mercy. But, blessed be His name—it is not difficult to discover this. Judgment is His strange work. It is remarkable that when He comes forth, according to Isaiah, "to punish the inhabitants of the world for their iniquity," He comes *out of His place,* and then He *goes back and resumes the mercy-seat.*

We read in the Scriptures that He is "abundant in mercy"; that He is "rich in mercy to all that call upon Him;" that "He delighteth in mercy;" that "He is the Father of mercies." Does the father of the prodigal represent Him? Unquestionably. Can you doubt, then, that with the Lord there is mercy? "When he was yet a great way off, his father saw him, and had compassion and ran, and fell on his neck, and kissed him. Henry, the sweetest of Commentators, says: "Here were eyes of mercy, he spies him though a great way off; feet of mercy, he ran to meet him; arms of mercy, he fell on his neck; lips of mercy, he kissed him Here were words of mercy: he said, 'Bring forth the best robe and put it on him; and put a ring on his hand, and shoes on his feet.' Here were actions of mercy: 'Bring hither the fatted calf, and kill it; and let us eat, and be merry; for this my son was dead, and is alive again; he was lost, and is found.'"

Secondly, "Let Israel hope in the Lord, for with the Lord there is mercy, and with Him is plenteous *redemption.*" This is the grand thing, and if this be not provided for we are all undone; without this there is no foundation for our hope. But it is provided for. "He remembered us in our low estate, for His mercy endureth for ever." "He spared not His own son, but gave Him up for us all." "He sent His only-begotten son into the world, that we might live through Him." The purpose, the accomplishment, and the application of this redemption were all His own. He redeemed us with a price unspeakable, that of His own Son's most precious blood. "He made Him to be sin,"—that is, a sin offering "for us, who knew no sin, that we might be made the righteousness of God in Him,"—that is, that we might be made righteous before God through Him.

This redemption is "*plenteous.*" There is infinite value in the blood that redeemed us, and therefore called by the Apostle the blood of God. If only one sinner in our world needed to be saved, the same Mediator would have been necessary. But what was necessary for one was necessary, and more than necessary, for all. The righteousness of Adam in Paradise, the righteousness of Gabriel above, is nothing compared to the righteousness which is of God by faith; which justifies the sinner and gives him a title to heaven; through which the believer is not only justified, but, as David says, is "*exalted;*" and therefore he makes mention of this righteousness only. There are some who think their case desperate; but it is not so. There is hope in Israel concerning this thing. "With Him is *plenteous* redemption." His blood cleanseth from all sin. He is mighty to save, able also to save to the uttermost all who come unto God by Him.

The third encouragement is, the *certainty* of this redemption. "Let Israel hope in the Lord, for with the Lord there is mercy, and with Him is plenteous redemption; and He *shall* redeem Israel from all his iniquities." "The Lord is not a man that He should lie, nor the Son of man that he should repent. Hath He said, and shall He not do it; hath He spoken, and shall He not make it good?" God has bound Himself. We could not have bound Him. His counsels are full of faithfulness and truth. He has determined that His people shall finally be saved. His word is surer than the Earth and the Heavens: for Heaven and Earth shall pass away, but His word shall not pass away. His word is faithfulness and truth.

Then consider the *completeness* of this deliverance. "Let Israel hope in the Lord, for with the Lord there is mercy, and with Him is plenteous redemption; and He shall redeem Israel from *all* his iniquities:"—from the guilt, the power, the pollution, the remains of sin, and from its effects. At death, the soul is removed into His immediate presence, and presented faultless before the presence of His glory with exceeding joy; and in the resurrection the body is made partaker of the blessedness, being raised up and fashioned like unto Christ's glorious body, and the believer shall enter into the joy of his Lord.

Now, we have seen David's experience in regard to the nature and the degree of it. You have also seen his admonition in regard to the subjects and the grounds of it. You have seen also *there is a relation between them.* We must not overlook or forget this, as it is a matter of great importance. We have seen here that David begins with himself, and ends with the Israel. We have seen that there is also a relation between personal and social religion; and we see the manner in which they operate; the one preceding, and the other following. Yes, personal religion must precede social. Without personal religion, social religion will always be partial and defective. A man who has no real regard to his own personal salvation is not very likely to feel a regard for the souls of others.

Truth is truth, and should be regarded from whatever quarter it comes, but in moral and religious concerns the character of the admonisher should never be forgotten. What is given may be good in itself, but you are loth to take it out of a filthy and leprous hand; and all the endeavours of some to produce reformation are only like arrows bounding back from an impenetrable shield, with the question, "Thou that teachest another, teachest thou not thyself? Thou that preachest man should not steal, dost thou steal? Thou that sayest a man should not commit adultery, dost thou commit adultery?" But, then, though personal religion should precede social, social religion should always follow personal; and will, in some measure and degree. You will not only be blessed, but prove blessings; and you will in some blessed degree serve your generation according to the will of God. Having tasted that the Lord is gracious, you will follow the example of David, and say, "O taste and see that the Lord is good; blessed is He that trusteth in Him;" or, like the first Christians, you will say, "That which we have seen and heard, declare we unto you, that ye also may have fellowship with us; and truly our fellowship is with the Father and with His Son, Jesus Christ."

And not only does experience of Divine things excite a man to this, but it also qualifies him for it. It comes with more efficiency from him. What comes from the heart is most likely to reach the heart. Such can speak with more confidence, for he has the witness in himself. He can speak with more tenderness, as he can speak from experience; and God often brings His people into outward disrespect, and exercises them with inward trials, that He may give them the tongue of the learned, that they may know how to speak a word in season to him that is weary.

Well, you see there are some whom you should consider your best friends: they are the godly. The godly walk with God; they have power with God.

If you had a long and trying journey in prospect, and a multitude of persons surrounded you, you would prize those most who had been the way and could give you the information required; you would be willing to part with the rest to be alone with them. So we read of some who take hold of the skirt of him who is a Jew, saying, "We will go with you, for we perceive that God is with you;" and it is God you want. "Happy art thou, O Israel; who is like unto thee, O people, saved by the Lord, the shield of thy excellency? And thine enemies shall be subdued unto thee, and thou shalt tread upon their high places." "Remember me, O Lord, with the favour which Thou bearest to Thy people. O visit me with Thy salvation, that I may see the good of Thy chosen, that I may rejoice in the gladness of Thy nation, that I may glory with Thine inheritance." Amen.

XV.

THE WAY OF GOOD MEN.

(Delivered on Monday Evening, September 16th, 1851.)

"*That thou mayest walk in the way of good men.*"—PROVERBS ii. 20.

SOLOMON is here admonishing his son, and the purpose of his admonition is this: to dissuade him from the way of evil men, and to encourage him to walk in the way of good men. "When wisdom entereth into thine heart, and knowledge is pleasant unto thy soul, discretion shall preserve thee, understanding shall keep thee, to deliver thee from the way of the evil man, from the man who speaketh froward things; who leave the paths of uprightness, to walk in the ways of darkness; who rejoice to do evil, and delight in the frowardness of the wicked; whose ways are crooked, and they froward in their paths; to deliver thee from the strange woman, even from the stranger which flattereth with her words, which forsaketh the guide of her youth, and forgetteth the covenant of her God. For her house inclineth to death, and her paths unto the dead. None that go unto her return again, neither take they hold of the paths of life." Then come the words, I will not say of our text, for I am not now preaching, I am only talking upon these occasions. Now if we take in the twelfth to the twentieth verse as we have just quoted, we shall see that Solomon opens before his son two ways—the way of evil, and the way of goodness; the way of the flesh, and the way of the Spirit; the way of life, and the way of death. And we may add what our Saviour Himself said concerning these two ways: "Enter ye in at the strait gate: for wide is the gate, and broad is the way, which leadeth to destruction, and many there be which go in thereat: because strait is the gate, and narrow is the way, which leadeth unto life; and few there be that find it."

We may observe two things with regard to these two ways. The one is, that all mankind without exception are walking in the one or in the other of these. They who are not walking in the way of good men, are walking in the way of evil men. There is no neutrality here. We walk either after the flesh or after the Spirit. We either mind the things of the flesh or of the Spirit. And, "to be carnally minded is death, but to be spiritually minded is life and peace." "We cannot serve two masters, for either we shall love the one and hate the other, or else we shall cleave to the one and despise the other; we cannot serve God and mammon." If we love the world, the love of the Father is not in us.

And the other is: It is not enough for us to avoid walking in the way of evil men; we must walk in the way of good men. Religion is not made up of negatives. We must not only cease to do evil, we must learn to do well. We must not only deny ungodliness and worldly lusts; but we must live soberly, righteously, and godly in the present world. Religion is positive as well as negative; that is, it commands as well as forbids. Omissions, therefore, are as criminal as transgressions. Indeed, they are transgressions. Why, the disobedience of the servant appears as much in his refusing to do what his master enjoins, as in doing what he forbids. The tree that brought forth no fruit, if it yielded no bad, was cut down and cast into the fire. The servant that hid his talent in the earth did no harm with it, if he did no good; but it is said, "Cast ye the *unprofitable* servant into outer darkness, there shall be weeping and gnashing of teeth." Be not satisfied, therefore, with negative religion, if I may so express it. What is it if you never swear, if you do not pray? What if you never worship and serve the creature, if you do not worship the Creator? What if you do not *oppress* the poor, if you do not relieve them?

Where do you find the good men referred to in the words before us? Who are they, since the Saviour has said, "There is none good but one, that is God"? He only is essentially good, universally and infinitely good. But if there were not some good men to be found even in such a world as this, the various references in the Word of God would be futile and absurd. There are persons who like perpetually to dwell upon the representations of the people of God which are relative, and which turn upon their privileges, such as "chosen," "pardoned," "justified," "redeemed," "preserved," and so on. But they do not like those representations which are personal, and which regard their character, such as "humble," "spiritual," "godly," "good." I have known many who object especially to the term "good." But we find it in the Word, and that is enough for us. We find it in the Old Testament. "Do good to them that are good." "The Lord shall be with the good." And again, "A good man leaveth an inheritance to his children's children." In the New Testament, Barnabas is called "a good man." We read of the lovers of good men. Our Lord Jesus was not backward to use the word; thus He said, "A good man out of the good treasure of his heart."

We might here just remark that there are none who are absolutely good. Says the apostle, "the Scripture hath concluded all under sin," both Jews and Gentiles. For there is no difference. All have descended from the same fallen original. "And who can bring a clean thing out of an unclean? Not one." Men are naturally not in different states, but in different degrees of the same state. They are all fallen, guilty, and depraved. They are all going astray, but each turns aside to his own way. Alas! there are none who are completely, who are perfectly good.

There are some, indeed, who have pretended to it, and some who have viewed themselves as such. What are we to do here? Mr. Wesley says, But some will ask me, Are you perfect? "No," says he, "far from it. But I have met with persons entitled to credence and integrity, who have assured me that they have lived so long without sin, and that for a considerable time they have not had a sinful thought." How is this?

In a general way we suppose the most holy persons are the most humble. "I am sure," says Newton, "if an angel were sent down from heaven to find out the most advanced Christian, he would fix upon the man who had the most exalted sentiments of the Saviour, and the most abased views of himself." If ever a man could say he was perfect, I think the Apostle Paul was that man. But Paul, with all his attainments and advancements, says, "I have not attained." I am not already perfect, though I am seeking after it. "Forgetting those things which are behind, and reaching forth to those which are before, I press towards the mark for the prize of the high calling of God in Christ Jesus." Yet he is the man who says, "When I would do good, evil is present with me. For I delight in the law of God after the inward man; but I see another law in my members, warring against the law of my mind, and bringing me into captivity to the law of sin which is in my members. O, wretched man that I am, who shall deliver me from the body of this death?"

But now, not to speak negatively in such a case, but to speak positively, we see there are none who are good by nature, but there are some made so by grace. For they are God's workmanship, and are created in Christ Jesus. Though they are not perfectly good, there is a difference between them and others and their former selves, so in them there has been a fulfilment of the promise that "instead of the thorn shall come up the fir-tree, and instead of the brier the myrtle-tree; and it shall be to the Lord for a name, and for an everlasting praise that shall not be cut off." They were by nature far off, but are now made nigh. They were once darkness, but are now light in the Lord. They are not now perfectly good, but there is that about them sufficient to entitle them to the character. Thus we denominate a person wise, not because he never says or does any weak or foolish thing, but because his conduct and conversation are habitually and eminently distinguished by wisdom. Thus we call a man healthy, not because he knows not what ailment means, but because he is generally well, has a good appetite, a good flow of spirits, and his hands are equal to perform an enterprise. So we denominate persons in religion as righteous and godly, and as good, though at present they are not free from imperfection. But even this will be the case in due time, and it will not be long ere this is the case. Yes, they will soon be presented faultless before the presence of God with exceeding joy, without spot or wrinkle or any such thing.

"Sin, their worst enemy before,
Shall vex their eyes and ears no more;
Their inward foes shall all be slain,
Nor Satan break their peace again."

"Then shall they see, and hear, and know
All they desired or wished below;
And every power find sweet employ
In that eternal world of joy.

In due time the Lord will perfect that which concerneth you: your sanctification will be perfect as your justification is already; for "He who hath begun a good work in you will perform it to the day of Jesus Christ."

Again, What are we to do with these "good" people? Are we to admire them only? No, we are also to follow them. We are to be followers of those who, through faith and patience, now inherit the promises. We are to go forth by the footsteps of the flock. We are to seek for the good old way, and walk therein. I dislike innovations in religion. We are to look for no more here than is to be found in our Bible. There are many new wines now; but when I have tasted them, I have said, "The old is better." Those give the best evidence of being "good" who walk with God and are bound for glory.

There is a particular way in which these persons go; let us try and find it out if we can, that we may walk in it.

It is the way of self-degradation and deep humility, where the lofty looks of man are humbled, and the haughtiness of men is bowed down, and the Lord alone is exalted. We call this *conviction.* The degree of terror or of anguish of spirit is various. These distresses for sin are among the order of means by which God has designed to bring us to Christ, and to lead us to submit to the righteousness of Christ. And if you are truly convinced of sin, you have had terrors enough to bring you to the feet of the Saviour, and to make you willing to be saved by Christ alone. All, as we said, have not the same degree or kind of conviction. We cannot suppose that Lydia was so alarmed as was the jailor. Nor was Dr. Watts, and Janeway, and others, as was Bunyan and Bradford: yet there never was a true disciple of Christ but was deeply abased and humbled before God. Job says, "Behold, I *am vile*;" and Isaiah says, "Woe is me! for I am undone, because I am a man of unclean lips, and I dwell in the midst of a people of unclean lips: for mine eyes have seen the King, the Lord of Hosts." Peter said to Jesus, "Depart from me, for I am a sinful man, O Lord;" and the Apostle Paul said, "I am less than the least of all saints."

There is also the way of *repentance.* They all mourn over sin, and they all look upon Him whom they have pierced, and mourn for it. They all loathe themselves for their transgressions. They all turn to God with purpose of heart, and are concerned to walk in newness of life.

There is nothing in this repentance servile—there is nothing in it legal. Some speak of it as legal: but the law has nothing to do with repentance. The law does not bestow repentance; it does not allow of repentance; but says, "The soul that sinneth, it shall die." It is therefore evangelical repentance. God allows a space for it, and the Saviour is exalted to give it. He said, "Blessed are they that mourn, for they shall be comforted." The Christian's best days are his weeping days. He never has more holy joy than when he abhors himself, and repents in dust and ashes. And he can say with Cowper—

"It is enough, my all in all,
At Thy dear feet to lie;
Thou wilt not lower let me fall,
And none can higher fly."

So, also, the way they walk in is the way of *faith.* "To them that believe He is precious." They all think highly of Christ, and speak highly of Christ. They hold Him forth as "altogether lovely," as "fairer than the children of men." They turn away from every refuge of lies, and flee for refuge to lay hold of the hope set before them. They abandon every false foundation and build alone upon the foundation laid in Zion.

It is the way with them all to renounce self-confidence and self-glorying, and to say, "In the Lord have I righteousness and strength." They "worship God in the spirit, rejoice in Christ Jesus, and have no confidence in the flesh." So also, this is said in the Scriptures to be "the way of *holiness;*" "the way of *truth;*" "the way of *righteousness*," &c.; for this is a very general term. We may observe good men moving in them all. We may observe their particular goings, and watch them.

Observe these men, see whither they are going. You will find them going to the *cross.* There they go frequently; yea, constantly. It is the way with them all. You will hear each of them saying—

"Nothing in my hand I bring;
Simply to Thy cross I cling."

"Sweet the moments, rich in blessing,
Which before the cross I spend."

"Here it is I find my heaven,
While upon the Lamb I gaze."

"God forbid that I should glory save in the cross of our Lord Jesus Christ, by whom the world is crucified unto me and I unto the world."

Whither, again, are they going? Look at them. They are going to the *throne.* This is the way with them all. "A glorious high throne is the place of their sanctuary." Behold, they pray. They can no more live without praying than they can without breathing. And they not only pray, but they take delight in approaching the throne of grace. Each of them can say, "It is good for me to draw near to God."

Follow them again. Whither are they going? You see they

are all going to the *sanctuary*. They are glad when it is said to them, "Let us go up to the house of the Lord." It is the way with them all. Each of them can say, "Lord, I have loved the habitation of Thy house, and the place where Thine honour dwelleth." "One thing have I desired of the Lord, that will I seek after; that I may dwell in the house of the Lord all the days of my life, to behold the beauty of the Lord, and to inquire in His temple."

Again follow these people, see whither they are going. They are going to God's *Word*, to kneel before this and say, "Speak, Lord, for Thy servant heareth." "I will hear what God the Lord shall speak." It is the way with them all. "To the law and to the testimony." "We will search the Scriptures," say they; "in them we have eternal life, and they are they which testify of Christ." Here is the authority by which alone they would be bound. They have always, therefore, been fond of their Bibles. There is nothing they seek more to be able to realize than the exhortation of the wise man, when speaking of this Book: "Bind them continually upon thine heart, and tie them about thy neck. When thou goest it shall lead thee; when thou speakest, it shall keep thee; and when thou wakest, it shall talk with thee." Oh, what a blessed companion it will be!

Again follow them, whither are they going? They are going to *keep holy-day*. This is the way with them all. They call the Sabbath a delight, the holy of the Lord, honorable. It is the best day of the week with them; the day in which, by waiting upon God, they lay up a store of instruction, comfort, and strength for the remainder of the week, for all its duties and for all its trials.

Now this is a little of the way of good men, so that you may know how to follow them, and to walk in it. Solomon would not have enjoined this upon his son, unless he saw there were advantages to be obtained by it. Hence I observe, first, that if you walk in this way you will have a good *Guide*. You need a Conductor, and much depends upon it. Hear God say, I will lead you, I will direct you, I will guide you with mine eye.

You need a *Guard*. You cannot keep yourselves. But here you will be kept by the mighty power of God through faith unto salvation, and you shall walk in your way safely. "Thou shalt tread upon the lion and adder, the young lion and the dragon shalt thou trample under feet;" for He is with you Who is "mighty to save."

> "A thousand savage beasts of prey
> Around the forest roam,
> But Judah's Lion guards the way,
> And takes the travellers home."

If you walk in this way, you will have good *supplies.* You shall want no good thing. Bread shall be given you, and water shall be sure. "My God shall supply all your needs according to His riches in glory by Christ Jesus."

If you walk in this way you shall have good *privileges and dignities.* You will be the sons and daughters of the Lord God Almighty. Angels will all be ministering spirits, seeing they are sent forth to minister to those who are the heirs of salvation.

And if you walk in this way you shall have a good *end.* Says Henry, "That is well that ends well." It is the end that crowns all; and this will be complete salvation of your souls. Whatever disadvantages may attend religion in any part of its progress; whatever privations any who walk in this way may experience; yet it has always this to recommend it: it will soon deliver us from all our temptations and sorrows; and while we have our fruit unto holiness, our end will be everlasting life.

What can I say more? There are some present who have been a good while in this way of good men: that is a great mercy. Well, Mason, you old disciple, what say you of this way? You have been long in it. "Oh," you say, "it is the most excellent way. I have had my trials, yet still I can recommend it." What said Matthew Henry when he was dying? "I have found a life of communion with God the happiest life in the world!" You aged Christian, cannot you bear your testimony to this, notwithstanding your trials? Have you not found the ways of wisdom to be ways of pleasantness, and all her paths peace? Have you not found that faith, and love, and hope, can produce a thousand blessings here—"before you reach the heavenly fields, or walk the golden streets"? You complain of yourself, and you do well; but I am sure of this: you do not complain of your Lord and Master, whatever you may be called upon to endure or suffer for His sake. You are all ready to say, "Thou hast dealt well with Thy servant, O Lord."

But be not satisfied by walking in this way yourself. You should be ashamed to go to heaven alone, without seeking to bring others along with you. You should say, as Moses did to his relations: "We are journeying to the place concerning which the Lord hath said, I will give it you. Come thou with us, and we will do thee good, for the Lord hath spoken good concerning Israel."

Are there any here who have not trodden this path as yet? Oh, that you may be induced from this time to walk in it. You young people, you cannot enter it too soon. Your entering it will be attended with a thousand advantages. "I love them that love me, and those that seek me early shall find me." So shall all who seek. But there must be a meaning in the promise. They shall find Him peculiarly and in such a way as others cannot. They will escape many evils and temptations they would otherwise be liable to fall into; and they will enjoy that delight in God in their youth which others know nothing of. And if your progress in this way is cut off, and you are called home, early death will be early glory. And if you continue in it till old age and grey hairs, He will say, "I remember thee, the kindness of thy youth, the love of thine espousals when thou wentest after me in the wilderness, in a land that was not sown. Israel was holiness unto the Lord, and the first-fruits of his increase." He will never leave you, nor forsake you, but will finally bring you into His more immediate presence, where is fulness of joy, and pleasures for evermore.

XVI.

RICHES AND RIGHTEOUSNESS.

(Delivered on Thursday Evening, February 4th, 1847.)

"*He that trusteth in his riches shall fall: but the righteous shall flourish as a branch.*—PROVERBS xi. 28.

THERE are some expositors who question whether there is anything evangelical in the Book of Proverbs: but does not God here promise to pour out His Spirit upon them that turn to Him? and is not our Lord here represented as saying, "I love them that love Me, and those that seek Me early shall find Me"? "Now, therefore, hearken unto Me, O ye children, for blessed are they that keep My ways." The Scriptures are "the whole counsel of God," made up of various parts, and what is omitted in one place is furnished in another; and then "*all* Scripture is given by inspiration of God, and is profitable for doctrine, for reproof, for correction, for instruction in righteousnesss; that the man of God may be perfect, thoroughly furnished unto all good works." The professors of religion require, not only to be instructed and admonished as to their faith in Christ, but also as to their walk and conversation, both as regards God and as regards their fellow-creatures, in all their relations and connections in life. In matters of practice and prudence general declamation will do but little good; here we require detail, and instances, and exemplifications; here also we derive advantage from contrasts and oppositions, such as the language of our text: "He that trusteth in his riches shall fall: but the righteous shall flourish as a branch."

The opposition is not naturally nor easily made out. We shall therefore offer a few brief remarks on this antithesis, which, we hope, will not be unedifying. Here we find, then, riches and righteousness placed over against each other, with an intimation that they are rarely found in one and the same character. Our Saviour said, "How hardly shall they that have riches enter into the kingdom of God! It is easier for a camel to go through the eye of a needle than for a rich man to enter the kingdom of Heaven." "But with God all things are possible," and we now and then see such a moral wonder. It ought also to be observed, that the danger here arises, not from the possession, but from the abuse of them. It is not said, "no man can have God and mammon;" meaning by "mammon" only wealth; but "no man can *serve* God and mammon." Therefore our Lord qualified the expression by saying again to His disciples, "How hardly can they that *trust* in riches enter the kingdom of God." It is not, therefore, having silver and gold, but it is making "gold their hope, and fine gold their confidence;" thus becoming idolaters. You see also how prone are men—for men are all naturally seeking after happiness—how prone are men to forget the Saviour's declaration, "A man's life consisteth not in the abundance of the things which he possesseth." How many are there who value them intemperately, who pursue them and confidently rely upon them, as if they were their portion! Therefore Paul says, "Charge them that are rich in this world, that they be not high-minded nor *trust* in uncertain riches, but in the living God, who giveth us richly all things to enjoy."

Observe the danger connected with this false confidence. "He that trusteth in his riches shall fall." Fall into what? Into difficulties, and embarrassments, and disappointments. How frequently is this the case! For riches certainly "make themselves wings; they fly away as an eagle towards heaven." "Therefore lay not up for yourselves treasures upon earth, where moth and rust corrupt, and where thieves break through and steal; but lay up for yourselves treasures in heaven, where neither moth nor rust doth corrupt, and where thieves do not break through nor steal."

But more than this, they "fall" into sin; they "fall" into hell. The Jewish Rabbis tell us that when a covetous man dies, the angels sing his soul down to hell, with these words: "Lo, this is he that made not God his hope, but trusted in the abundance of his riches." We do not believe a word of this, but we *do* believe that "he who trusteth in riches" leans over "the bottomless pit," upon a "bruised reed;" we do believe him who said, "He that maketh haste to be rich shall not be innocent;" we do believe the Apostle when he says, "They that will be rich, fall into temptation and a snare, and into many foolish and hurtful lusts, which drown men in destruction and perdition. For the love of money is the root of all evil; which, while some coveted after, they have erred from the faith, and pierced themselves through with many sorrows."

The Apostle seems to refer to two classes of persons. First, those to whom the love of money is supreme and paramount. These we compare to men in a vessel overloaded, which sinks to rise no more; he therefore says they are "*drowned* in destruction and perdition." He then refers to others, in whom a degree of this evil prevails: and he compares them to travellers, who, as they go along the road, see some inviting fruit, surrounded by thorns and briers; they therefore turn aside, and they "pierce themselves" in getting at it, and they "pierce themselves" in getting back from it. "These," says the apostle, "pierce themselves through with many sorrows." Pray you, therefore, with David, "Incline my heart unto Thy testimonies, and not to covetousness." Mind the apostle's expression: "Let your conversation be without covetousness, and be content with such things as ye have; for He hath said, I will never leave thee, nor forsake thee;" and oh, brethren, if He is with you, having Him you have all. If a child is satisfied while he travels with his father, though he may have very little in his purse, and says, "My father is here, and he will provide for me as he goes along," how much more should it be so with you! May you seek after the "true riches," "durable riches," and "unsearchable riches," for these you cannot unduly estimate: here your desires cannot be too excessive; here your trust will not be disappointed; for while "he that trusts in his riches shall fall," the righteous shall flourish "as a branch."

But who can claim this privilege? and what does this import? "The righteous shall flourish as a branch." The Scriptures tell us "there is none righteous, no, not one." "The Scripture includes all under sin." There are different degrees in the state, but all men are in this state. "All we like sheep have gone astray." All spring from a corrupt original, but, blessed be God! there are some who are made righteous, made so by grace: they are "justified from all things, through the obedience of Christ," and are thus made relatively righteous. They are also sanctified, and "renewed in the spirit of their minds," and thus are they made personally righteous, old things having passed away, and all things having become new. . . It will be readily allowed that this sanctification—this personal sanctification—is not at present perfect, but then it is real! The man has those principles and those dispositions which are of Divine origin; and though they are opposed, they shall completely and finally prevail. Even now the owner has them to such a degree as to give his character a distinction. Thus we call a man healthy, not to intimate that he never feels any aches or pains; and we call a man wise, not to intimate that he is never chargeable with folly or mistake, but that they are distinguished by these qualities. So with regard to the righteous: he has distinguishable features; he has righteous views, righteous desires, righteous feelings, righteous actions, and a righteous life. What says David of such characters as these? "He is like a tree planted by the rivers of water." And what says Solomon? "The righteous shall flourish as a branch."

It was while I sat under the bough of a tree in a garden last summer that these words first occurred to me, which, however, I had forgotten till last evening, and now feel that I cannot do anything like justice to them. But let us observe four things:—

"The righteous shall flourish as a branch;" that is, *dependently.* The branch lives in the tree, the sap of which sustains it, and makes it fruitful; and if it were to be cut off from it, it would soon wither and die. Does not this remind you of our Saviour's words, "Abide in Me, and I in you; as the branch cannot bear fruit of itself, except it abide in the vine, no more can ye, except ye abide in Me. For without Me"—or, as the margin reads, "separate from Me"—"ye can do nothing." He is the tree, His people are the branches; the branches are sustained by the tree. This is an important truth, whether you believe it or not; but the grand thing is to believe it—to realize it by faith, and in our experience; then we may say with Paul, "When I am weak, then am I strong;" that is, "when I am weak in myself, then am I strong in the Saviour." If ever you feel a disposition to rely on your own wisdom, on the force of your own resolutions, or upon your profession of *your* love to Christ, call to remembrance the case of Peter, and—

> "Beware of Peter's words, nor confidently say,
> I never will deny Thee, Lord; but grant I never *may.*
> Man's wisdom is to seek his strength in God alone,
> And e'en an angel would be weak, that trusted in his own."

"The righteous shall flourish as a branch;" that is, *progres-*

sively. In the first instance, a branch is a germ, hardly perceptible; then it becomes a small shoot; for a time it is scarcely able to sustain the least weight; but in time it increases in strength and firmness and can bear a man. Now, there are some who tell us—but who told them?—that there is no such thing as growth in grace. What! can a man have no more knowledge, or patience, or courage than he had at first? Do we not read that "the righteous shall wax stronger and stronger;" that the saints are "renewed day by day;" that they are "changed into the same image from glory by glory, as by the Spirit of the Lord?" Does not every representation of them in Scripture import and express this? Are they not said to "grow up as calves of the stall"? Is it not said that "the path of the just is as the shining light, that shineth more and more unto the perfect day;" that they produce "first the blade, then the ear, then the full corn in the ear"? It is true, this growth is not always rapid; nothing is produced in immediate perfection in nature. Here we have the evidence of analogy; but with small beginnings things are brought forward gradually to maturity, and things are slower in their growth in proportion to their worth and excellence. The growth of the oak is slower than that of the osier or of the bramble-bush. I would rather "flourish as a branch" than grow up as a mushroom. We are not fond of these instantaneous operations. This branch partakes of a variety, and is influenced by the seasons. Thus, during the winter it seems dead, but it is not; it is indeed leafless, but it is not lifeless. Life is indeed concealed, but it is down in its root, and at the return of spring it will revive again, and at autumn will produce fruit. This, brethren, is the case, notwithstanding all the changes produced, in regard to every believer in Jesus.

"The righteous shall flourish as a branch;" that is, *gracefully*, or beautifully. Take an instance. Take the branch of "the apple-tree among the trees of the wood." View it in its season: its green leaves issue forth, its lovely blossoms appear, and at length its fruits begin to redden and ripen, and ask to be gathered in. Thus they even adorn the tree that upholds them; the tree enlivens them, and they adorn the tree. Thus we read, "Thy people shall be willing in the day of Thy power, in the beauties of holiness." Thus we read, "He will beautify the meek with salvation." Thus we find, they not only pursue things that are honest and pure, but "whatsoever things are lovely and of good report." They were to pursue and practice these, and make it their concern to "adorn the doctrine of God, their Saviour, in all things."

"The righteous shall flourish as a branch;" that is, *fruitfully*. A tree indeed bears the branch, but it is the branch that bears the fruit. Thus it is here: they are "filled with the fruits of righteousness, which are by Jesus Christ to the praise and glory of God." "They bring forth fruit." What fruit? "The fruit of the Spirit," such as "love, joy, peace, long-suffering, gentleness, goodness, faith, meekness, temperance." Thus Isaiah says, "They shall be called trees of righteousness, the planting of the Lord, that He may be glorified." How glorified? By their leaves? No; but by their fruit. "Herein," said the Saviour, "is my Father glorified, that ye bear much fruit."

Where, professors of religion, where is your fruit? You have leaves enough, but where is your fruit? Where is "your work of faith, and labour of love, and patience of hope in our Lord Jesus Christ"? "They that be planted in the house of the Lord shall flourish in the courts of our God. They shall bring forth fruit in old age, they shall be fat and flourishing; to show that the Lord is upright. He is my rock, and there is no unrighteousness in Him." If they flourish in His courts below, how much more will they flourish in His courts above when "that which is perfect is come, and that which is in part shall be done away," and they shall "be presented faultless before the presence of His glory with exceeding joy!"

XVII.

QUIETNESS OF MIND.

(Delivered on Thursday Evening, January 15th, 1846.)

"*Commit thy works unto the Lord, and thy thoughts shall be established.*"—PROVERBS xvi. 3.

DUTY should be coupled with reason, and enforced by motives. God Himself deals with us in this way. He speaks more like a friend than a sovereign. He counsels, rather than commands. He condescends to explain the admonitions He gives, shewing us the principle upon which they are founded, and the advantages which will arise from observance of them. This He does in the words I have now read: "Commit thy works unto the Lord, and thy thoughts shall be established." The words naturally divide themselves, and lead us to consider a duty enjoined and a privilege ensured.

I. We are here led to consider A DUTY ENJOINED. "Commit thy works unto the Lord."

Our works here take in all our enjoyments and intercourse, our civil as well as our religious affairs. We are active creatures; and from our nature and conditions in life we have many things to do; we have not only various, but numberless exertions and employments, and they are full, as Solomon says, of labour. So that we are reminded of the original malediction pronounced on Adam: "Cursed is the ground for thy sake; in sorrow shalt thou eat of it all the days of thy life; thorns also and thistles shall it bring forth to thee; and thou shalt eat the herb of the field; in the sweat of thy face shalt thou eat bread, till thou return unto the ground: for out of it wast thou taken; for dust thou art, and unto dust thou shalt return."

But what are we to do with all these works of ours? Are we to neglect them? Are we to leave them to chance? Shall we leave a vessel to the winds and the waves? Would it not be better to have a helm and a compass, a pilot and a port?

Can we manage these works ourselves? No. Shall we repair to others? To whom shall we repair? To man? "Wherein is he to be accounted of?" "Men of low degree are vanity, and men of high degree are a lie." "Commit thy works unto the LORD!" He is fully qualified to manage all. "Commit thy way unto the Lord, and He shall direct thy paths." He is perfectly qualified for this transfer. Trust Him now for everything you can need or desire. As to your fellow-creatures, many of them are too weak to afford aid. Some are too busy to attend to you, others are too proud, and deem themselves above it, but He is always able, and ever nigh. "He wings an angel, and guides a sparrow." "Even the hairs of your head are all numbered." Well may we say with David, "Lord, what is man that Thou art mindful of Him? or the son of man that Thou visitest Him?" But nothing is more true, for He is continually mindful of us, and invites and commands us to "cast all our care upon Him."

How is this to be performed? In what way are we to "commit our works unto the Lord"?

First, we are to "commit our works unto the Lord" in a way of *communication* or information. Is it necessary then to inform God? In one sense it is not, for "His understanding is infinite;" "nothing can be hid from Him." But in another sense it is, for though He knows all things, He will be informed by us. He knows our sins and the aggravations of them far better than we do, still he requires us not only to confess our sins and spread before Him all our wants, but "in everything by prayer and supplication with thanksgiving to make known our requests to Him." Therefore we are to conceal nothing from Him. As Hezekiah did, we are to go to Him. When he received the blasphemous letter he went up and spread it before the Lord; he did this probably before he divulged the thing to any of his ministers. What did poor John's disciples do? They took up the body and buried it, and went and told Jesus. So let it be with us. He is our Friend. He takes an interest in all our affairs; hide nothing from Him, but say with David, "All my desire is before Thee, and my groaning is not hid from Thee." Where there is true friendship, there is always candour, freedom, and openness. If you were to conceal your difficulties and trials from your bosom friend, he would feel pained, if he were not offended; he would consider this a proof of suspicion rather than confidence.

Secondly, "Commit thy works unto the Lord" in a way of

inquiry, to know whether He approves of them, or whether He condemns. With regard to some works, it is not necessary to ask counsel of God, for you must know that He disapproves of them. If, for instance, you deceive you neighbour, or ruin his reputation, or desire to get money for the sake of money, or that you may retire by-and-by, to live an idle life, you may know that He disapproves of all this, and therefore your consulting Him would only be hypocrisy and mockery. But there are many things which are doubtful; concerning these it is necessary to know the pleasure of God. Perhaps the formation of some intimate connection, or an important opening for business, or it may be the removal of a residence, and many other things. A Christian cannot feel otherwise than reluctant to proceed till he has sought to know the will of God; he cannot move with pleasure till he sees the cloudy pillar move. He goės to God, and says, "What wilt Thou have me to do? Here I am; shew me the way wherein Thou wouldst have me go, and the thing Thou wouldst have me do." How much depends upon a single wrong step! The consequences may give a new complexion and direction to the whole of your future character and life. But who is infallible? "The way of man is not in himself; it is not in man that walketh to direct his steps." You must therefore go to God. "In all thy ways acknowledge Him, and He shall direct thy paths." A Christian cannot feel himself at liberty to engage in any enterprise without His approbation. "Whatever I may possess, or however I may succeed, all will be embittered," says he, if "I have an apprehension that I displease Him. I cannot dispense with His will and pleasure. If I walk contrary to Him, how can I expect but that He will walk contrary to me? But He has done so much for me, and promised to do so much more, that I should be the vilest and most ungrateful wretch, if I can proceed without asking counsel of Him. Lord, what wilt Thou have me to do? Speak, Lord, for Thy servant heareth."

Thirdly, "Commit thy works unto the Lord" in a way of *application* for assistance. "Acknowledge Him in all your ways; depend entirely upon Him for success; follow His direction; without Him you can do nothing. Not that you are to be enthusiastic; not that you are to neglect the use of means under a notion of relying upon God. God requires the use of means. Divine aid is promised to afford assistance to our weakness, and not to encourage our sloth. Therefore says the apostle, "Work out your own salvation with fear and trembling, for it is God that worketh in you to will and to do of His good pleasure."

We have a fine exemplification of this in Jacob. He met his brother Esau, who, he was afraid, was determined to murder him; he sends forward a present, for, as Solomon says, "A man's gift maketh way for him;" he delivers a soft answer; he divides his company; but then he *retires to pray.* So when we employ all the means to afford success, even then we must commit all to God, and say, "O God, I beseech Thee send now prosperity;" and if we do thus act we shall find Him able to do so for us "exceeding abundantly above all that we can ask or think."

Fourthly, "Commit thy works unto the Lord" by way of *submission* and resignation, referring the issues entirely to Himself. Say, the Lord shall chose our inheritance for us. Lord, succeed or disappoint us according as Thou seest it shall be for Thy honour and our advantage. Thus did David when his son exiled him from his throne: "Here I am! do with me as seemeth to Thee good." This is what James enjoins: "Go to, now, ye that say, to-morrow we will go into such a city, and continue there a year, and buy and sell, and get gain; whereas ye know not what shall be on the morrow. For what is your life? It is even a vapour, that appeareth for a little time and then vanisheth away. For that ye ought to say, if the Lord will, we shall live and do this or that. But now ye rejoice in your boastings; all such rejoicing is evil."

So much for the first part; now let us attend—

II. To THE PRIVILEGE. "And thy thoughts shall be established."

To explain this, it will be necessary to ask what we are to understand by our thoughts being established. We are to understand by "the thoughts" the schemes and purposes connected with these works. Then their being "established" means, their being accomplished, their being prospered. This is the thing you desire when you engage in any enterprise. This is what Moses prayed for, when he said, "Let Thy work appear unto Thy servants, and Thy glory unto their children; and let the beauty of the Lord our God be upon us, and establish Thou the work of our hands, yea, the work of our hands establish Thou it." This also accords with the promise in the thirty-seventh Psalm: "Commit thy way unto the Lord; trust also in Him, and He shall bring it to pass." You cannot imagine that God has absolutely engaged to render all your enterprises prosperous and successful, but only those which are good in themselves and beneficial to you. If the thing we desire is not for our good, it is kind in Him to oppose it; but if we "commit our way unto the Lord," we may be assured of this, that if it be for our welfare He will succeed it.

Then the establishment of the "thought," means the composing of our minds, and freeing them from perturbation. I need not tell you how many anxieties your various exertions and undertakings naturally produce, for they breed in your works, as worms in rotten wood. Sometimes you can say with David, "In the multitude of my thoughts within me;" there is a "multitude" turmoiling the mind at once, and conflicting there. You know what excitements and apprehensions often arise from your undertakings and exertions, but how is the mind to be calm and established here? You know how it was with Hannah. She was afflicted, and had a particular object in view, but when she had poured out her soul before the Lord she went her way, and her countenance was no more sad. If you honour God, He will honour you; if you seek Him, He will answer you; if you commit your way unto Him, He will soothe and compose your minds. This is the way to gain a tranquillity and establishment of soul which nothing else can produce. Oh, may you get this establishment in your minds! Remember the admonition of Our Lord: "Let not your heart be troubled, neither let it be afraid."

But remember, that *all* peace and satisfaction of mind with regard to your successes and doings is not of God. Sometimes it arises from infidelity, sometimes from worldly-mindedness, and sometimes from spiritual indolence. But the satisfaction here spoken of is that firmness of mind which frees the Christian from anxiety and turmoil, and which arises from the performance of duties, and complacency in the divine will. God will then compose the mind, and enable you by believing to enter into rest. This rest may well arise from your having committed your way unto the Lord. "I am in good hands now," may the Christian say, "for I have entrusted all my concerns unto God; I hope to receive eternal life from Him, and it would be shameful in me not to trust Him for present supplies. God, my God, doth all things well: the Lord is my helper, I will not fear what man can do unto me." A good man after he had been much exercised with a very trying dispensation, which occasioned him many a prayer and many a sigh, but in which ultimately he succeeded, said: "O, what peace and consolation I have felt in that text! I am that proverb alive."

"Commit thy works unto the Lord, and thy thoughts shall be established." O, what a happy man would the Christian be, if he lived up to his high privilege! How mistaken are the men of the world! They consider religion a gloomy thing; but none are so free from gloom, none so cheerful, so thankful; there are none whose thoughts are so established, whose minds are so composed, as those who are enabled to commit their all to God. Others "rise early and sit up late, and eat the bread of sorrows;" they are fretful when they meet with untoward events and are unsuccessful in their enterprises. But ah! "when *He* giveth peace, who then shall give trouble?" The Christian gives up all his concerns to God. He casts his burden on the Lord, and is sustained." He is not afraid of evil tidings, seeing his heart is fixed trusting in the Lord." Then the words of Isaiah are accomplished: "Thou wilt keep him in perfect peace whose mind is stayed on thee." That is the meaning of the privilege in our text, "Commit thy works unto the Lord, and thy thoughts shall be established."

XVIII.

THE KING'S FRIENDSHIP.

(Delivered on Thursday Evening, March 12th, 1846.)

"*He that loveth pureness of heart, for the grace of his lips* [*or having gracious lips*], *the king shall be his friend.*"—PROVERBS xxii. 11.

KINGS may be considered two ways: as they are, and as they ought to be. Thus the sacred writers often speak of them. It will be desirable to bear this distinction in mind while we are endeavouring to explain the words we have now read. Kings as well as their subjects have their prejudices and their failings. These frequently appear in the improper choice they make of their ministers, and of their favourites; but if a king be wise and good, he will be concerned for the happiness of his people, and will take care to be surrounded only by men of approved ability and tried integrity. Hence the language of Solomon in our text, "He that loveth pureness of heart, and hath grace in his lips, the king shall be his friend."

Kings are only men, and they have their friends as well as others to whom they can unbend and unbosom themselves. Hushai was "David's friend." I dare say he was much envied. Such intimacy as he enjoyed has always been regarded as a peculiar honour and advantage, and is thus spoken of in proportion to the greatness and goodness of the king by whom it has been granted.

My brethren, there is another king, one Jesus, whose dominion is an everlasting dominion, whose kingdom is not of this world, who is the blessed and only Potentate, King of kings and Lord of lords. His goodness is as boundless as His greatness. He said in the days of His flesh to a company of poor fishermen, "Ye are my friends, if ye do whatsoever I command you;" and this is as true of you as of them, if you obey Him, for such honour have all the saints.

To Him therefore we shall apply these words. We do not mean to intimate that this is the spiritual meaning thereof. There is no spiritual meaning in them. There are no expositors so bad as those who give that sense to Scripture it never had; who are always converting its facts into figures, and its figures into facts; till at last some seem to think that there is no fixed meaning in Revelation. It is time these were driven off the stage. But we must consider these words as an accommodation, while we are led from them to consider what is clearly revealed in the Word of God; and so I would preach from them as from the apple-tree among the trees of the wood, or as from the rising sun, or the descending showers. We may regard the text as a kind of image or metaphor holding forth two things, a character and a privilege.

I. A CHARACTER. "He that hath pureness of heart and grace in his lips." This is the character. You see it comprehends two things; the one regards the heart, the other the lips—the purity of the one and the grace of the other. This will be found a very fine representation of the disciples of our Lord.

"He that hath pureness of heart;" that is, a lover of pureness. Hence the language of the Saviour in one of the beatitudes: "Blessed are the pure in heart, for they shall see God."

But some of you are ready to say, "I see nothing beside evil in my heart." It is well you do see this: you did not always see this. This is a token for good. But now you see it as it is held forth in Scripture, and by natural light, too, as "deceitful above all things and desperately wicked." You think that you are strangers to this part of the character; you fear you have no purity of heart; but do you not *love* purity? O yes, you do; and it is surprising what evil you now see in sin when you view it in connection with the cross of Christ. O how odious and vile you feel yourself to be! What will become of me? say you; I am unprepared for communion with His saints, to associate with holy angels, for fellowship with the Father, who is holy in all His ways, and of purer eyes than to behold iniquity. Woe is me! Unclean! unclean! is my exclamation, behold I am vile; wherefore I abhor myself, and repent in dust and ashes." Yet you say, you behold a dignity and beauty in holiness; you can "give thanks at the remembrance of God's holiness." Yes, you do love purity of heart, and you approach "the fountain opened for sin and uncleanness." Hence you apply to that "blood which cleanseth from all sin," and hence you are induced continually to cry, "Create in me a clean heart, O God, and renew a right spirit within me." You are distressed that you make such little progress in your divine course that you cannot do the things that you would, and under your grief and burden exclaim, "O wretched man that I am." Hence heaven appears desirable not only as a state and place of happiness, but of holiness too, where you shall not "only see His face, but never, never sin."

The other is, "the grace of his lips." The lips will not do without the heart; but when speech flows from inward principles and dispositions, it is valuable. Our Saviour tells us that "a good man out of the good treasure of his heart bringeth forth good things."

Need I tell you what a stress is laid upon the grace of speech in Scripture? "For in many things we offend all. If any man offend not in word, the same is a perfect man, and able also to bridle the whole body." "If any man among you seem to be religious, and bridleth not his tongue, but deceiveth his own heart, this man's religion is vain." Hence the Apostle's admonition to the Ephesians, "Let all bitterness and wrath, and anger, and clamour, and evil speaking, be put away from you, with all malice: and be ye kind one to another, tender-hearted, forgiving one another, even as God for Christ's sake hath forgiven you." And again, "Let no corrupt communication proceed out of your mouth, but that which is good to the use of edifying, that it may minister grace unto the hearers." And again, "Neither filthiness, nor foolish talking, nor jesting, which are not convenient, but rather giving of thanks." "Let your speech be always with grace, seasoned with salt."

The grace of the lips is an extensive subject. It takes in humility when we speak of ourselves, charity when we speak of our fellow-creatures, and piety when we speak of God. But our time forbids enlargement here, we must therefore leave this for your own meditation and proceed to consider—

II. THE PRIVILEGE combined with this character. "He that loveth pureness of heart, having gracious lips, the King shall be his friend."

It was asked by Ahasuerus, when he wished to shew favour to Mordecai, "What shall be done unto the man whom the king delighteth to honour?" You know what followed. Our Saviour makes no parade with His friendship. "The same events that befall others, befall Christians also; in this respect all things come alike to all. He does not advance them to the high places of the earth. The world knoweth them not; it knew Him not." Yet His friendship is sincere and glorious. It is principally reserved for another world. Their blessedness is future. "Eye hath not seen, nor ear heard, neither have entered into the heart of man the things which God hath prepared for them that love Him." "But this we know"—and this is knowing no little—"this we know, that when He shall appear, we shall be like Him, for we shall see Him as He is." And it is a very striking remark of the Apostle's wherein he says, "He is not ashamed to be called their God, for He hath prepared for them a city;" as much as to say, that God would be ashamed to stand in the universe in the relation He has assumed, if He did nothing more for them than He does now in this vale of tears, and in this body of death, under all their various moral and natural imperfections. But He does not withhold proofs of His regard even now; therefore David says, "O how great is Thy goodness which Thou hast laid up for them that fear Thee,"—and he adds—"which Thou hast *wrought* for those that trust in Thee before the sons of men."

We may specify a few instances in which God's friendship is exercised, and in which He shows himself to be the friend of the godly.

The first we shall mention is His *revealing Himself* familiarly. The Saviour therefore says, "I will manifest myself unto them." This induced Judas (not Iscariot) to say unto Him, "Lord, how is it that Thou wilt manifest Thyself unto us, and not unto the world?" So He said to His disciples, "Henceforth I call you not servants, for the servant knoweth not what his Lord doeth, but I have called you friends; for all things that I have heard of my Father, I have made known unto you." You ought to be good masters, but if you are wise you do not make your servants your counsellors, lest they should become your controllers also. Servants should know their master's orders, for they are required to obey without having a reason given for everything they do. But as to real friends nothing is concealed. So "the secret of the Lord is with them that fear Him, and He will show them His covenant." "The meek will He guide in judgment, and the meek will He teach His way." "The natural man knoweth not the things of the Spirit of God, neither can he know them, because they are spiritually discerned. But he that is spiritual judgeth all things, yet he himself is judged of no man;" and he has "an unction from the Holy One, and knoweth all things."

Another proof of friendship is observable in *reproving.* "Faithful are the wounds of a friend," while "the kisses of an enemy are deceitful." So says the Saviour, "As many as I love, I rebuke and chasten; be zealous therefore and repent." While others are addicted to their various idols or vices, He says, "They are joined to idols; let them alone;" but He never will say so of His people. If they go astray, He will hedge up their way with thorns, so that if they are determined to persevere, they will "pierce themselves through with many sorrows," in order that they may be brought to a holy resolution, and induced to say, "I will go and return to my first husband, for then was it better with me than now." Know you not that forbearance is sometimes indicative of indifference, while severity is a proof of love? Does not Solomon say, "He that spareth the rod hateth the child; but he that loveth him chasteneth him betimes"? If you saw a person advancing towards a precipice while walking in his sleep, or lost in meditation, would it be right to let him pass on and be dashed to pieces, or to rush forward and prevent his fall by breaking his reverie and spoiling his musing?

There is another instance which the King gives of His friendship: that is, *by affording advice.* Hence Solomon says, "Ointment and perfume rejoice the heart; so doth the sweetness of a man's friend by hearty counsel." The Saviour says, "Counsel is mine and sound wisdom." He gives you counsel in the time of your conversion and in after periods, in times of perplexity and darkness. You sometimes feel your loneliness and the need there is of another head as well as your own. There are perplexities enough to break down a single understanding. There arise circumstances relative to business, the removal of your situation, in regard to your condition in life, or the formation of some connection in which before your minds may appear an almost equal balance, and you are unable to decide; how delightful in such circumstances to go and fetch in the judgment of another, who is capable of directing and admonishing you! And, brethren, does your Friend fail in this? Is His counsel not sufficient? His counsel is not only safe, but *free.* A man may buy counsel, and sometimes pay very dear for *bad* advice. It is not so here, all the Saviour requires of you is that you should follow His counsel, and nothing else.

Then this friendship is distinguished by another trait: that is, by *sympathy.* By sympathy "shall the king be his friend." This was peculiarly the case with our Lord at the grave of Lazarus. When He saw Mary and her sister Margaret weeping, "He groaned in His spirit and was troubled." Yea, "Jesus wept." So says the Apostle, "We have not a High Priest who cannot be touched with the feelings of our infirmities, but One who was tempted in all points as we are, yet without sin."

O, here is the peculiar advantage of having such a friend as Jesus is; one who, having rejoiced with us while we rejoiced, will weep while we weep, so that thought touches thought, and sentiment touches sentiment, and by the union and association of feeling the distress of one mind is drained into another and is lessened.

But then there is *assistance:* and this is the last proof we name of the friendship of the King. He does not live in word and in tongue, but in deed and in truth. There are some who, when addressed, say, "Be ye warmed, and be ye clothed," notwithstanding they give them not those things that are necessary. This may arise sometimes, not from illiberality, but from inability; the ear is not heavy that it cannot hear, but the hand is shortened that it cannot aid. But it is otherwise with the Lord Jesus. Nothing is too hard for Him. "He is able to do exceeding abundantly above what we ask or think." He is all-wise to direct, almighty to succour; able to make all things, however adverse, work together for good. Jonathan was a friend to David and took off his own raiment to give to him; but "you know the grace of our Lord Jesus Christ, how though He was rich, yet for our sakes he became poor, that we through His poverty might be rich." *He* is a friend born for adversity; He will afford you aid when you most need it. "In all your afflictions, He is afflicted." Are you on the bed of languishing, He will lay underneath you His everlasting arms. *He* will help you when all other helpers fail. He will be with you in the valley of the shadow of death. He will be your friend in the day of judgment. How limited is the help of man; but *His* friendship stretches into eternity, and produces blessings which never end. "Permanency adds bliss to bliss." "A friend loveth at all times." "He is the same yesterday, to-day, and for ever," not only in His being but in His affection. How intense is His friendship! Other friends will bear no comparison with this friend. As the heavens are higher than the earth, so is His friendship higher than theirs.

Is this King your friend? Examine yourselves, and judge not by dreams, or sudden impulses, but by the expressions of the Lord Himself. Here you have His holy Oracles: compare your hopes and fears, your joys and sorrows, your inclinations and dispositions, with the experience of those herein described as heirs of the promises. Are you poor in spirit? Do you "hunger and thirst after righteousness"? Is the Saviour precious to you? and do you "esteem the words of His mouth more than your necessary food?"

Do you not need His friendship? Can you do without it? What can you do in the day of trouble? What in a dying hour? What in the day of final account? What is the friendship of the world? "Cease ye from man, whose breath is in his nostrils, for wherein is he to be accounted." Have you not learned from facts as well as from assertions that creatures are empty cisterns? That they are as bruised reeds, upon which if you lean, they will not only break but pierce you through with many sorrows? Sometimes you may have endeavoured to secure the favour of an individual, but you have found it like penetrating marble or brass, and after much time and attention you may have been only smiled upon, and perhaps only smiled *at!* Neither have you been known by them in the day of distress and trouble. O turn this desire into another direction, and seek an interest in the friendship of this King; then will you find love for love, and friendship for friendship. He loved you and gave Himself for you; seek Him and He will relieve all your distresses. He is now peculiarly known by His expression, "Come unto me;" but hereafter He will say, "Depart ye," to those who are His enemies. But He never uses this language now. Now He says, "Him that cometh unto me I will in no wise cast out." Remember, too, if He is not your friend, He will be your enemy; and He will say, "As for these mine enemies who would not that I should reign over them, bring hither and slay them before me." O, what an enemy will he prove! "Whoever hardened himself against Him and prospered?" Where there is a probability, or even possibility, it may be worth while in some cases to risk an encounter; but who, unless he be a fool or a madman, would undertake to wage war with an enemy by whom he was *sure* to be defeated? O sinner, surely this is your case. "They shall make war with the Lamb, and the Lamb shall overcome them." There is no doubt of it, for "He is King of kings and Lord of lords." Yea, everything, from an insect to an archangel, would be ready to avenge Him of His enemies. But there is no need of this; for as His creatures you are "crushed before the moth." But "He is the hope of Israel, the Saviour thereof in the time of trouble."

Christian, you cannot be called a friendless person; no, you have something in hand, but more in hope; something in life, but more in death; something in time, but more for eternity. You have an Almighty friend; and one, too —

> "Whose heart is made of tenderness,
> Whose bowels melt with love."

Envy not others if they have a few toys and trifles which you have not. The King is your friend. This is a privilege they enjoy not. Make use of this in every emergency. Sink not under any of your trials and afflictions while you can look up and call this friend your own.

See to it, that you employ your interest at Court in speaking a word for others. "The effectual fervent prayer of a righteous man availeth much." Job prayed for his friends in his affliction, and the Lord heard him. May you pray for one another, and the Lord will bless you also. Amen.

XIX.

A HAPPY CONVERSION.

(Delivered on Thursday Evening, May 1st, 1845.)

"*And it shall come to pass in that day, that the remnant of Israel, and such as are escaped of the house of Jacob, shall no more again stay upon him that smote them; but shall stay upon the Lord, the Holy One of Israel, in truth.*—ISAIAH x. 20.

THE History of the Jews is very instructive and useful, especially when we bring it home to our own experience, and remember that the Apostle says, "Now all these things happened unto them for ensamples, and they are written for our admonition, upon whom the ends of the world are come." They were a fair specimen of our common nature, and we have no reason to believe that we should have been better than they if we had been placed in the same condition. And in the persual of their narrative—

> "Here as in a glass we see
> How fickle, and how false are we."

Were they ungrateful? Are not we? Were they impatient? Are not we? Were they unbelieving? Are not we? Were they prone to creature and vain confidence? Are not we? What says our text? "It shall come to pass in that day, that the remnant of Israel, and such as are escaped of the house of Jacob, shall no more again stay upon him that smote them." These words will apply to a spiritual as well as to a natural Israel.

They were indeed forbidden to go down to Egypt and to trust in chariots, but they paid a practical disregard to the prohibition; hear therefore the language of the prophet. "For thus saith the Lord, the Holy One of Israel: In returning and rest shall ye be saved; in quietness and confidence shall be your strength, and ye would not. But ye said, No; for we will flee upon horses; therefore shall ye flee; and we will ride upon the swift; therefore shall they that pursue you be swift. One thousand shall flee at the rebuke of one; at the rebuke of five shall ye flee; till ye be left as a beacon upon the top of a mountain, and as an ensign on a hill." So their dependence gave way from time to time, till they were led to say, "Asshur shall not save us, we will not ride upon horses, neither will we say any more to the work of our hands, Ye are our own gods, for in Thee the fatherless findeth mercy." "Truly in vain is salvation hoped for from the hills and from the multitude of mountains! Truly in the Lord our God is the salvation of Israel." But we are not going to stop with the Jews; how often has the language of the text been exemplified in the experience of God's people in all ages! Now to see this, let us consider, first, what is said of their former error; secondly, what is said of their renewed experience; and thirdly, what is said of the reality of their change.

I. Let us consider WHAT IS SAID OF THEIR FORMER ERROR; For when we read that they shall "no more again stay upon him that smote them," it surely implies that they had done this before, and this is what we mean by their former error. Yes, they had stayed upon another, and they were to be delivered and recovered from this, and "no more to stay upon him that smote them, but upon the Lord, the Holy One of Israel, in truth."

Three things are here implied and expressed.

First, *they had exercised an improper dependance.* To this we are all naturally prone; we are indigent creatures, naturally dependent; and finding many exigences which we cannot relieve, we naturally look out of ourselves, endeavouring to lay hold of some external assistance, and lay hold of that which is nearest. This is the creature, or something seen and temporal. Paul speaks of some things which he had considered as "gain;" that is, he had gloried in, and depended upon them, though afterwards he tells us, "these I counted loss for Christ;" for he was led to see, that instead of their being advantageous to him, as he supposed, they had been a real injury, because they drew him away from Christ, "the chief among ten thousand, and the altogether lovely." Oh, how often do creatures keep us from the Creator, "God over all, blessed for ever." How well does John say, even to professed Christians, "Little children, keep yourselves from idols." How many of these we might enumerate! Whatever transfers our heart from God to the creature, whatever draws away our affections from the Saviour, is an idol.

Again, *their dependance had been disappointed.* Yes, that upon which they had stayed themselves, smote them; it not only failed them, but pressed them. Therefore Jeremiah says, "Thus saith the Lord, Cursed be the man that trusteth in man, and maketh flesh his arm, and whose heart departeth from the Lord. For he shall be like the heath in the desert, and shall not see when good cometh; but shall inhabit the parched places in the wilderness, in a salt land and not inhabited." This creature confidence brings a curse upon us in two ways. It smites those who repose on it, first, by the very nature of the things on which we stay ourselves, for they are all vain and unsatisfying. When a philosopher was asked, "What his hope had done for him?" he said, "It has been but as a waking dream." Solomon, referring, to riches, says, "They set their heart upon that which is not, for riches make to themselves wings and fly away." What are creatures? "Men of low degree are vanity, and men of high degree are a lie." Therefore, says Isaiah, "Cease ye from man whose breath is in his nostrils, for wherein is he to be accounted of?" Secondly, by divine rebukes. Sin always brings sorrow along with it, and the law of God's house is this: "Hast thou not procured this unto thyself, in that thou hast forsaken the Lord thy God, when He led thee by the way? Thine own wickedness shall correct thee; and thy backslidings shall reprove thee; know therefore and see that it is an evil thing and bitter that thou hast forsaken the Lord thy God, and that My fear is not in thee, saith the Lord God of Hosts." Jonah's gourd did not last long. What do we read? "God prepared a worm when the morning rose the next day, and it smote the gourd that it withered." Your children are mortal; they may be removed in divine correction if you make idols of them. So it is with anything else.

Again, we here see *their folly was to be corrected by their sovereign.* "And it shall come to pass in that day, that the remnant of Israel, and such as are escaped of the house of Jacob, shall no more again stay upon him that smote them; but shall stay upon the Lord, the Holy One of Israel;" that is, they shall learn wisdom by the things which they suffer, and keep away from the fire which scorched them and which might have consumed them. This is not always the case. We know thousands who acknowledge that here they "have no continuing city," yet keep company with the worldlings; and that "the way of transgressors is hard," yet show no disposition to get out of that way. Yea, though continually disappointed in their efforts, they seek happiness by unholy means, till the lamp of life is extinguished and an end is put to their career. Oh, how many instances are there where disappointments have been vain: that is, they have produced in mankind no moral effect. Thus Isaiah says, "The people turneth not to Him that smiteth them, neither do they seek the Lord of Hosts." Thus Jeremiah says, "O Lord, Thou hast stricken them, but they have not grieved; Thou hast consumed them, but they have refused to receive correction; they have made their faces harder than a rock, they have refused to return." What a number of articles does the prophet Amos mention with regard to suffering being useless! "Hear this word, O ye children of Israel, saith the Lord God. I have given you cleanness of teeth in all your cities, and want of bread in all your places: yet have ye not returned unto me, saith the Lord. And also I have withholden the rain from you, when there were yet three months to the harvest; and I caused it to rain upon one city, and caused it not to rain upon another city; one piece was rained upon and the piece whereupon it rained not withered. . . . . I have smitten you with blasting and mildew; when your gardens and your vineyards and your fig-trees and your olive-trees increased, the palmerworm devoured them; yet have ye not returned unto me, saith the Lord. I have sent among you the pestilence after the manner of Egypt: your young men have I slain with the sword, and have taken away your houses; and I have made the stink of your camps to come up unto your nostrils; yet have ye not returned unto me, saith the Lord. I have overthrown some of you, as God overthrew Sodom and Gomorrah, and ye were as a firebrand plucked out of the burning; *yet ye have not returned unto me, saith the Lord.*" Here we see the depravity of human nature in rendering inefficacious all these divine chastisements, and when this is the case there is a danger of one of these two things: either that God in anger will throw down the rod, saying, "Ephraim is joined to his idols, let him alone;" or that He will fulfil His own threatenings. "If ye walk contrary unto me, and will not hearken unto me, I will bring seven times more plagues upon you, according to your sins;" "and if ye will not be reformed by me by these things, but will walk contrary unto me, then will I also walk contrary unto you and will punish you yet seven times for your sins."

My brethren, "God does not grieve or afflict willingly the children of men." He has a mercful design in all your crosses and trials and afflictions. He hath said, "By this shall the iniquity of Jacob be purged, and this is all the fruit to take away his sin." His design is to lead us to say with David, "It is good for me that I have been afflicted;" and when these dispensations are thus sanctified, the man in unison with our text will say, "What have I any more to do with idols? I have suffered enough from them; they have all smitten me; and now, Lord, what wait I for? My hope is in Thee." Thus the prodigal was starved back. "He began to be in want"—and it was a blessed want that led him to think of his father's home, and resolved him to return. You have no reason to complain if, when your earthly props have been taken away, you have been induced to take fresh hold of God.

II. Let us consider WHAT IS SAID OF THEIR RENEWED EXPERIENCE: "but shall stay upon the Lord, the Holy One of Israel." We have only time to glance at three views of it.

First, it is *enlightened*. Confidence is the offspring both of ignorance and wisdom; but the one is the confidence of a fool, the other the confidence of a wise man, for who but a fool would pass over a deep river upon a plank before he had ascertained whether the wood were rotten or sound? Who would entrust a precious deposit to a stranger, or to a suspicious character? Paul did not, and therefore said, "I know whom I have believed, and that He is able to keep that which I have committed unto Him against that day." Therefore said David, "They that know Thy name will put their trust in Thee." This accords with every part of religion, for whatever the world may think of it, it is a most "reasonable service." A Christian could not have stayed upon God without a discovery of His character; he could not have stayed upon such a Being whom he had offended unless He had given him an assurance that He was willing to receive him graciously. But this has been the case. God has given us a revelation of Himself in which He says, "Take hold of My strength, and ye shall make peace with Me." God's power, His wisdom, His faithfulness, His truth, and even His holiness and righteousness, all become vouchers to encourage and confirm our confidence in Him.

Secondly, this confidence is very *extensive*; how extensive may be inferred from the language of David, "Trust in Him at all times, ye people;" and from the admonition of Isaiah, "Trust in the Lord for ever, for in the Lord is everlasting strength." This confidence reaches to all the events that can awaken our anxiety. It pervades every condition in which we can be found; it regards all that appertains to life and godliness, not only grace, but glory; it has a respect, not only to our journey's end, but also to the way. The first and grand thing for which we have to trust God is eternal life: the glorification of the soul at death, and of the body at the resurrection. This to the humble believer seems too much to hope for from a Being he has so often offended. "But this is the record, that God has given unto us eternal life, and this life is in His Son." When we are brought to trust in Him for this, surely we shall trust in Him for everything else. One might imagine this would be easy, but it is very difficult to trust Him with all our concerns; yet there are moments in which the Christian is enabled to do this, and when reflecting upon His care in providence, he can say, "I can trust in Him for everything."

"Our cares, we give you to the wind,
And shake you off like dust;
Well may we trust our all with Him
With whom our souls we trust."

Thirdly, it is a *blessed* confidence. Solomon says, "The fear of man bringeth a snare, but whoso putteth his trust in the Lord shall be safe." So David says, "They that trust in the Lord shall be as Mount Zion, which cannot be moved, but abideth for ever." That is, the man has now a rock to rest on, not a bed of sand; he has now a fountain of living waters, and drinks no longer at the broken cistern. Nor is this all; for says Isaiah, "Thou wilt keep him in perfect peace whose mind is stayed on Thee, because he trusteth in Thee." What a life does he now live! "Blessed is the man," says Jeremiah, "that trusteth in the Lord, and whose hope the Lord is. For he shall be as a tree planted by the waters, and that spreadeth out her roots by the river, and shall not see when heat cometh, but her leaf shall be green; and shall not be careful in the day of drought, neither shall cease from yielding fruit."

III. Let us consider THE REALITY OF THEIR CHANGE. "They shall stay upon the Lord, the Holy One of Israel, in truth." Ah! this is the thing: "He requireth truth in the inward parts." Everything is counterfeited, and there is a special imitation of every moral excellence, and of every Christian grace. When it is said that they "shall stay upon the Lord, the Holy One of Israel, in truth," there is an intimation that this shall not be the case. This confidence therefore is distinguishable from two things.

First, they "shall stay upon the Lord," *in distinction from mere pretensions.* There are those who profess to know God, but in works deny Him. It seems strange that persons should act the hypocrite here, for what do they gain? "What is the hope of the hypocrite, when God taketh away his soul?" If they impose upon themselves, they cannot impose upon God, who "is greater than their heart, and knoweth all things."

Secondly, they "shall stay upon the Lord," *in distinction from imaginary confidence.* Persons may not endeavour to deceive others, yet they may deceive themselves. Thus Solomon says, "There is a generation that is pure in their own eyes, and yet is not washed from their filthiness." While this is entirely the case with regard to some, it is so in a degree with regard to others. An instance of this we have in our Lord's disciples; for after He had made a fuller discovery of Himself, He asked them, "Do ye now believe?" You say so, and you think so, but fancy is not reality; you may be mistaken, but I have a better knowledge of you than you have of yourselves. You say you may believe. "Behold the hour cometh, yea, is now come, when ye shall be scattered every man to his own, and shall leave Me alone; and yet I am not alone, because the Father is with me." And how was it with these disciples? A few hours after this, as the Saviour predicted, "they all forsook Him and fled." Lord, what is man? You see what a difference there is between this trusting in the Lord in truth, and our imagining that this is the case, or supposing that we do this. Therefore—

"Beware of Peter's word,
Nor confidently say,
I never will deny Thee, Lord,
But grant I never may."

XX.

THE DUTY OF GLADNESS.

(Delivered on Thursday Evening, March 3rd, 1846.)

"*Cry out and shout, thou inhabitant of Zion: for great is the Holy One of Israel in the midst of thee.*"—ISAIAH XII. 6.

Two things are here observable. First, *the person addressed*, the "inhabitant of Zion." Zion was the name of a high mound situated upon a bed of rock enclosed within the walls of Jerusalem, and making the finest and strongest part thereof. There David's palace was; therefore it was frequently called "the city of David." There was first the Tabernacle, then the Temple, "whither the tribes went up, the tribes of the Lord, unto the testimony of Israel, to give thanks unto the name of the Lord;" and concerning which God said, "This is My rest for ever; here will I dwell, for I have desired it. I will abundantly bless her provision; I will satisfy her poor with bread. I will also clothe her priests with salvation; and her saints shall shout aloud for joy. There will I make the horn of David to bud: I have ordained a lamp for mine anointed. His enemies will I clothe with shame; but upon himself shall his crown flourish."

If we look through the literal description to the spiritual glory discernible, we shall soon see that it was typical of a higher state, and a shadow of good things to come. I hardly need remind you that by a figure of speech Zion is used in the New Testament as significant of the Church of the living God. Witness only the language of the Apostle to the believing Hebrews: "Ye are not come unto the mount that might be touched, and that burned with fire, nor unto blackness and darkness and tempest, and the sound of trumpet, and the voice of words; which voice they that heard entreated that the word should not be spoken to them any more: for they could not endure that which was commanded. And if so much as a beast touch the mountain, it shall be stoned or thrust through with a dart: and so terrible was the sight that Moses said," as he was going up, "I exceedingly fear and quake; but ye are come unto mount Sion, and unto the city of the living God, the heavenly Jerusalem." "The inhabitant of Zion," therefore, in the language of the evangelical Prophet means, one who is no longer a stranger and foreigner, but a fellow-citizen with the saints and of the household of God.

The second thing observable here, is *the admonition given.* "Cry out and shout, thou inhabitant of Zion; for great is the Holy One of Israel in the midst of thee."

Let us fill up the remainder of the time allotted to this service in considering the *truth* upon which the admonition is founded, and the *exhortation* which it enjoins. Consider what I say, and the Lord give you understanding in all things.

I. THE TRUTH UPON WHICH THE ADMONITION IS FOUNDED. We consider this as including God's chararacter, His greatness, and His residence.

First, it takes in His *character.* "The Holy One of Israel." This is a very distinguishable attribute of the Divine nature. You remember in the vision of the prophet Isaiah, He was adored under this representation by the Seraphim and Cherubim, who "cried one to another saying, Holy, holy, holy is the Lord of hosts: the whole earth is full of His glory." We are told that "He is righteous in all His ways and holy in all His works." Had we time to contemplate Him as the Creator, Lawgiver, Governor, and Saviour, we should see how fully this excellency is always possessed and displayed by Him, and say with Mary, "Holy is His name," or with Hannah, "There is none holy as the Lord." But, though holiness is God's beauty, and though we are told that He is glorious in holiness, yet as Dr. Watts expresses it—

"None but the soul that feels His grace,
Can triumph in His holiness;"

the attribute that since the Fall has rendered God so unlovely to His apostate and depraved creatures. There is nothing the sinner views with so much dislike and dread, because it condemns him in his favourite trust. Therefore God represents men as putting their actions and passions into language, and how dreadful is their language when this is the case! Thus He represents them as saying, "Cause the Holy One of Israel to cease from before us."

What enmity the world naturally has to the perfections of God appears obvious from the practice of the Heathen. Among the beings they deify, they never deify one for holiness, but only for something which gratified their vile propensities; or at best for something they deemed valuable and useful in the concerns of life. They deified Esculapias for his skill in curing diseases; and Bacchus for the use of the grape; and Vulcan for the use of the forge; and Hercules for the destruction of beasts and monsters; and so of the rest. So natural men now may value their fellow creatures for their generosity, and learning, and wealth, and power, but they do not value them for their holiness. Christians, you know this was the case once with you. You despised the righteous, because of the quality of holiness in which they resembled God in their measure and degree. But it is otherwise with you now. You now delight to view His image in His creatures. Now you love a holy God. Now you can comply with the admonition of David, "Sing, O ye saints of His, and give thanks at the remembrance of His holiness." Some of you may feel that you have nothing to fear from this attribute. It smiles upon you. Yes, you may say, "I rejoice in the thought that He is the Holy One; for as He is holy, I hope He will make me a partaker of that holiness which He loves, and destroy in me that sin which He so much hates." Then, Christian, combine this character of God with all His engagements. He has spoken in His holiness, and will assuredly fulfil all that He has promised: "The Lord is not a man that He should lie, nor the Son of man that He should repent. Hath He said, and will He not do it? hath He promised and will He not make it good?" "He cannot deny Himself."

It takes in, secondly, His *greatness*. "*Great* is the Holy One of Israel in the midst of thee." His greatness is unsearchable. All things before Him are as nothing, less than nothing, and vanity. Great in *duration*. Only think of a Being who is from everlasting to everlasting—with whom a thousand years are as one day. Great in *wisdom*. He knoweth all things—all things present, all things past, and all things future; nothing can be hid from Him. Great in *power*. While some are mighty, He is Almighty. He is the Creator of all things and upholdeth all things by the word of His power. Great in *dominion and resources*. "The silver and the gold are His, and the cattle upon a thousand hills. The world is His and the fulness thereof. The sea is His, and He made it, and His hands formed the dry land. His throne is in the heavens, and

His kingdom ruleth over all!" Why, all this greatness would render Him more dreadful if He were your enemy: but, Christians, He is your Friend and your Father! Can your Friend be too great? Can your Father be too mighty? Can He have too much power and dominion who is merciful and gracious, long-suffering and full of compassion? It is this thought in connection with such a Being which is the source of our relief and satisfaction. All that is great in God is laid under a contribution to advance our welfare and happiness, if we belong to Him. It is so in regard to His *duration.* "The eternal God is our Refuge, and underneath are the everlasting arms." It is so in regard to His *wisdom.* "Thou shalt guide me with Thy counsel," may the believer say; "This God is our God for ever and ever, He will be our guide even unto death." It is so in regard to His *power.* "The Lord will give strength unto His people, the Lord will bless His people with peace." As He is over all, so He is rich unto all who call upon Him, and can supply all your need according to His riches in glory by Christ Jesus.

It takes in, thirdly, His *residence.* "Great is the Holy One of Israel *in the midst of thee.*" It is the name by which the Church is called, *Jehovah Shammah.* So we read in the last verse in Ezekiel, "and the name of the city from that day shall be, THE LORD IS THERE."

But is He not *everywhere*? Does He not fill heaven and earth? Where can we flee from His presence? and whither can we go from His Spirit?

Observe when God's presence is spoken of in a way of promise as privilege, it is to be distinguished from the perfection of His nature, or what we call His Omnipresence; for it has then in it something peculiarly beneficial and saving. Thus we read, "The Lord is nigh unto them that are of a broken heart, and loveth such as be of a contrite spirit." He is indeed everywhere, but not everywhere in the same way and manner. He is in heaven as He is not upon the earth. He is in the Church as He is not in the world. He is with His people as He is not with others. Let us for a moment glance at the speciality and peculiarity of the case.

There are *three* ways in which he may be said to be in the midst of His people. First, *universally.* For they all form one Church, and only one, comprehending all those who love, serve, and fear Him—all the subjects of His grace of every age and country, of every condition and denomination. He has said, "Lo, I am with you always, even unto the end of the world."

Secondly, He is with them *socially.* That is, in their assemblies, in the institutions of religion, in the exercises of religious worship, and in the means of grace, according to His promise, "In all places where I record my name, I will come unto you and will bless you." "*Where*"—let it be where it will. "Where two or three are gathered together in my name, there am I in the midst of them." It was this that so endeared the house of God to David, and that induced him to say, "I have loved the habitation of Thy house, and the place where Thine honour dwelleth." His people in all ages have seen His goings there, and the goings of their God and King in the sanctuary. And, Christians, you can also bear your testimony. There you have seen His face; there you have heard His voice; there you have tasted that the Lord is gracious, and found Him to be a very present help in trouble. By waiting upon Him you have renewed your strength, and said from time to time, "A day or an hour in Thy courts is better than a thousand. I had rather be a door-keeper in the house of my God than dwell in the tents of wickedness."

Thirdly, He is with them *individually.* He is in the very recesses of their souls by His own Spirit. For saith the Saviour to His disciples, "He dwelleth with you, and shall be in you." Accordingly, God in the New Covenant hath said, "I will put my law in their inward parts, and write it in their hearts;" and again, "I will put my Spirit within you, and cause you to walk in my statutes, and ye shall keep my judgments to do them." Thus He is in them by His Spirit for all the purposes of the religious life, action, and enjoyments. Therefore all religious dispositions are called "the fruits of the Spirit," because they are not derived from our depraved natures, but from His operation producing and sustaining them.

How often does God speak of being in us! For instance, in that fine text, "God is love; he that dwelleth in love dwelleth in God, and God in him." This is no fiction, but an important truth. Therefore, says John, "Hereby we know that He abideth in us, by the Spirit which He hath given us." So David says, "That Thy name is near Thy wondrous works declare;" that is, he inferred God's agency from His operations, and His presence from His agency. Thus He is in all His people, working in them to will and to do of His own good pleasure.

The Jews are said to have tempted God by asking, "Is the Lord among us or not?" It was very improper for them to ask this after that God had delivered them from Egypt, poured down manna from heaven, fetched water out of the rock, and led them through the wilderness by a pillar of cloud by day and a pillar of fire by night, to show them the way; it was very improper for them to ask, Is the Lord among us or not?

Christians are sometimes led to form sad conclusions that the Lord has not been with them, yet at the very time they have experienced things which none could experience unless the Lord had been with them and on their side. They have been brought to behold more clearly the way of salvation by Christ, to hate sin more, and desire more holiness, to hunger and thirst after righteousness, and have felt a desire above all things to win Christ and be found in Him. From whence comes this? from nature, or from grace? from our depraved selves, or from the Spirit of the living God?

As the Lord is thus in the midst of His people, you should be concerned to be connected with them, and to be their associates. Indeed this will be the case if you are divinely wrought upon. You will then be induced to ask, "Tell me, O Thou whom my soul loveth, where Thou feedest, where Thou makest Thy flock to rest at noon? For why should I be as one that turneth aside by the flocks of Thy companions?" You will then let go the sons and daughters of vanity and vice readily enough, and run and "take hold of the skirt of him that is a Jew, saying, We will go with you, for we perceive that God is with you." It is God we now want, and cannot be satisfied without.

May you who are blessed with this privilege be filled with adoring views of God's condescension! Think of His condescending love, and then exclaim with David, "Lord, what is man that Thou art mindful of him? or the son of man, that Thou visitest him?" Or with Solomon, "Will God in very deed dwell with man upon the earth?" An answer to which—for it is as true as it is wonderful—you find in Isaiah's prophecy: "Thus saith the high and lofty One that inhabiteth eternity, whose name is Holy: I dwell in the high and holy place, with him also who is of a contrite and humble spirit, to revive the spirit of the humble, and to revive the heart of the contrite ones."

This leads us to notice—

II. The exhortation enjoined. "Cry out and shout, thou inhabitant of Zion, *for* great is the Holy One of Israel in the midst of thee." What is here required cannot be merely the exclamation, separate from suitable dispositions and sentiments, as is the case with some. "There are some religious people who resemble trunk-makers, their work being more noisy than solid." Persons may cry out and shout or make any other noise, while there is nothing in the state of their minds and hearts corresponding with it; and on the other hand, there may be much felt where little is expressed. There may be "a joyful noise," as David has it, "unto God," which He, and He alone, can hear. On the other hand, "Out of the abundance of the heart the mouth speaketh," and the lips are seldom closed when the passions are in action. John tells us he heard the angels "saying with a *loud* voice, Worthy is the Lamb that was slain!" We have no objection to a little stir in religion. It awakens attention, but is hardly to be found in many cases. The conversion of a sinner, like the turning of a bell, can hardly be done without some noise. We suppose there was a little of this noise and stir, as in the Gospel, when the blind man was restored to sight. Some say, "Is this he?" Others say, "He is like him;" but *he* says, "I am he." Another, and yet the same; a new creature; old things being passed away, and all things having become new.

This admonition, "Cry out and shout, thou inhabitant of Zion," teaches us two things. The first is, that as religion has to do with the feelings, so it is very absurd and ignorant to place it in external forms and cheap moralities in which the heart has no share. "My son," says God, "Give me thine heart." Take the Gospel. What is it? Not a decision of Parliament, or the termination of a debate which may have no effect on our welfare. It brings us glad tidings of great joy. It is infinitely important, it is eternally interesting to us. It is our life. It is all our salvation, and should be all our desire. Therefore we should receive it is a faithful saying, and worthy of all acceptation. We should receive it as a dying man would receive a remedy; or as a condemned criminal would hail a reprieve. We should receive it with feelings superior to those with which we receive anything else.

Some would here urge the charge of enthusiasm. Enthusiasm is sometimes used in a *good* sense: then it insures the energy of genius. And it is generally supposed, and justly so, that without a degree of this no man is likely to succeed in any line of business or profession. But how often, alas, when applied to religious concerns, is the possessor of it viewed by the world as having a weak mind or a diseased imagination! Yet here is a subject which rises infinitely above all others in interest and importance, and demands all the energies of the soul; and renders Dr. Young's words the words of truth and soberness:—

> "On such a theme t'were impious to be calm:
> Passion is reason; transport, temper here."

Yes, religion calls for not only feeling and sentiment, but the highest degrees of feeling and sentiment. If the subject be sorrow, we are to "look upon Him whom we have pierced, and mourn." How? "As one that mourneth for his only son; and be in biterness, as one that is in bitterness for the loss of his first-born." Or if it be desire, it is nothing less than hungering and thirsting after righteousness. If it be hope, it is "abounding in hope," it is the "full assurance of hope." If it be peace, it is a peace passing all understanding. If it be joy, it is a "joy which is unspeakable and full of glory." Or if it be excitement, it is "CRY OUT AND SHOUT, thou inhabitant of Zion, for great is the Holy One of Israel in the midst of thee."

The other is, as this exhortation requires, feeling. So it teaches us that religion is not only animated, but rational; that there is a foundation made to excite and to justify all this; that it is really wisdom, and justified in all the saints. It is a "reasonable service," and a Christian is able to give a "reason of the hope that is in him"; and so does our prophet. Hear him again: "Cry out and shout, thou inhabitant of Zion." *Why*? "For great is the Holy One of Israel in the midst of thee." This is enough. This more than justified him; for from hence the Church can infer *safety*. "God is in the midst of her, she shall not be moved." From hence she can infer *honour*: and says God, "I will be a wall of fire round about her, and the glory in the midst of thee." From hence she may infer *assistance*: for she is called to the discharge of various duties far above her own strength. But the Lord is with her, and says, "Fear thou not, for I am with thee; be not dismayed, for I am thy God; I will strengthen thee, yea, I will help thee; yea, I will uphold thee with the right hand of My righteousness." And from hence also she may infer *consolation*. If in distress, He is with her who is the God of all comfort, and who sympathises with her in all her afflictions. If distressed or bereaved she can yet say with her Saviour, "I may be left alone, yet I am not alone, because the Father is with me."

Thus, God is with His people here, and this is *grace*: soon they shall be with Him in heaven, and that is *glory*. So shall they ever be with the Lord. "In His presence is fulness of joy; at His right hand are pleasures for evermore." "Wherefore comfort one another with these words."

"O Thou, by long experience tried,
Near whom no grief can long abide;
All scenes alike engaging prove,
When we can realize Thy love.

I can be calm, and free from care,
On any shore since God is there:
Where'er I dwell, I'm still with Thee,
In heaven, in earth, or on the sea.

While place we seek, or place we shun,
The soul finds happiness in none;
But with a God whose grace I know,
'Tis equal joy to stay or go.

Could I be cast where Thou art not,
That were indeed a dreadful lot;
But regions more forlorn I call,
Secure of finding THEE IN ALL."

XXI.

THE ORDAINER OF PEACE.

(Delivered on Thursday Evening, November 12th, 1846.)

"*Lord, Thou wilt ordain peace for us: for Thou also hast wrought all our works in us.*"—ISAIAH XXVI. 12.

SOME texts are of a more doctrinal complexion, and some of a more practical; but the passage before us is experimental. Experience when properly considered implies doctrine, and produces practice; and unless it be preceded by the one, and followed by the other, it is nothing better than delusion. You will bear me witness, and my own conscience assures me, that I am never afraid of speaking freely on either of these through a dread of being charged with antinomianism by one class of hearers, or of being charged with legality by another; but I confess that I love those texts which lead into the region of experience, especially on these week-evening lectures, and in these brief exercises. Although experience is misrepresented by some, and ridiculed by others, there is much truth in the language of Hart—

> "True religion's more than notion,
> Something must be known and felt."

Let us plunge into the subject, considering three things. The first regards the Christian's present condition; the second, his future expectations; the third, the dependance of one of these upon the other.

I. Let us observe THE CHRISTIAN'S PRESENT CONDITION, observing four things:—

"*Thou* hast wrought all our works in us." How fully does the Apostle confirm this when he says, "It is God that worketh in you both to will and to do of His good pleasure." And again, "By grace are ye saved through faith . . . . for we are His workmanship, created in Christ Jesus unto good works, which God hath before ordained that we should walk in them." It cannot be otherwise, for "who can bring a clean thing out of an unclean?" Not one. The stream cannot be better than the fountain. The effect cannot be superior to the cause. Our Saviour hath said, "That which is of the flesh is flesh," and, however modified, will be flesh only; and "that which is of the Spirit is spirit." You will find that everything is ascribed to the agency of the Spirit. We are said to be "born of the Spirit," to "live in the Spirit," and to "walk in the Spirit." All the fruits of righteousness are called "the fruit of the Spirit," and all the comforts which Christians enjoy are called "the comforts of the Holy Ghost."

Secondly, as the operation is divine, so is it internal in its effects: "Thou hast wrought all our works *in* us." There are many things God has done for us which we should not overlook; many things in His kind and tender providence, for "goodness and mercy have followed us all our days." There has been indeed less of miracle, but not less of mercy, in God's providing for us, than in His feeding the Jews in the wilderness with manna. We have been also from our birth up encompassed with danger, "but having obtained help of the Lord we continue to this day." There are some of you who realize the promises: "I will bring the blind by a way they knew not; I will lead them in paths they have not known: I will make darkness light before them, and crooked things straight. These things will I do unto them, and not forsake them." But the greatest of all God's works for you, Christians, is redemption by the blood of the cross. This was accomplished long ago. When dying, our Saviour said, "It is finished." Yes, it was then finished, and nothing can now be added to it; but you are mistaken if you suppose that His work *for* you is to supercede His work *in* you. If your sins are not subdued as well as pardoned; if you are not "renewed in the spirit of your mind," as well as "justified by faith;" you never will be able to serve and enjoy God. Unless you have a meetness for heaven, as well as a title for it, you never will be able to enjoy its pleasures, or perform its employments. You will not be at home there. Our Saviour speaks of something internal when He says, "The water that I shall give him shall be in him a well of water springing up into eternal life," and the promise of the new covenant shews something to be done in us. "A new heart also will I give you, and a new spirit will I put within you; and I will take away the stony heart out of your flesh, and I will give you a heart of flesh." David felt his need of this, and therefore not only prayed, "Blot out all mine iniquities," but also "Create in me a clean heart, O God, and renew a right spirit within me." And this was the case with the church here.

Observe, thirdly, the operation is *manifold* in its influence. They do not say "our work," but "our works," and "*all* our works." Thou hast wrought all our works in us." It is not a single exertion that will bring a soul from all the ruins of the fall to glory. How much is there by this agency to be done in the man! Conscience is to be awakened, purified, and pacified; the understanding is to be enlightened; the judgment is to be informed; the will is to be subdued; the affections to be spiritualized; the world is to be dethroned in the heart, and holy principles implanted there. God's law is to be put into our minds, and written upon the table of our hearts, and how much is the man, by divine grace, to be enabled to do! He is to believe, to fear, to hope, to mourn, to rejoice. O how many good thoughts and feelings and desires are produced in a Christian in one year, in one month, yea, in one week, or one day! We read of God's putting His hand the second time to the work; a *second* time! His hand must be put a thousand times before the work will be entirely accomplished. Paul tells us that "He who hath begun a good work in you will perform it until the day of Jesus Christ." What an agency is here! what a continued act of a performing God, from the hour of the first conviction of sin to the resurrection of the body unto eternal life!

Lastly, it is *acknowledged.* They speak without doubt and without hesitation: "Thou also *hast* wrought all our works in us." The Christian finds no difficulty in owning and acknowledging that what he is, he is by the grace of God; but the question with him is, whether he *is* anything; not whether God has done the work, but whether the work *is* done. Well, whatever difficulty attends it, it is possible to ascertain this; and the Lord's people have been able to acknowledge the one as well as the other. We should be concerned to know this, and able to express ourselves as the Church here does. We should be concerned not only to be humbled, and humility well becomes us, but to be thankful, and gratitude becomes us equally; but we cannot bless God for doing what he never has done; we cannot thank Him for bestowing upon us what we believe He never has bestowed. It is therefore desirable that we should come to a conclusion; and John says, "These things have I written unto you that believe, that ye may *know* that ye have eternal life, and that ye may believe"—still more—"on the name of the Son of God." The Christian therefore cannot leave these things in a state of indecision, but will be often upon his knees, crying, "Shew me a token for good."

II. We have THEIR FUTURE EXPECTATION. "Lord, Thou wilt ordain peace for us." We may notice here the appointment and the blessing.

To ordain is an act of authority and power. You may wish a thing and promise a thing, but a king ordains, and what he ordains is supported by all the resources of the realm, and will be accomplished. But God is King of the whole earth. "He is King of kings, and Lord of lords." Who can reverse *His* appointment. "I will work," says He, "and who shall let it?" "My counsel shall stand and I will do all my pleasure." He hath said that "the seed of the woman should bruise the serpent's head," and accordingly Jesus "spoiled principalites and powers, triumphing over them;" He "blotted out the handwriting of ordinances that was against us, which was contrary unto us, and took it out of the way, nailing it to His cross." "In the beginning," Moses tells us, "God ordained the heavenly bodies for signs and for seasons;" and what does David say in reference to this? "For ever, O Lord, Thy word is settled in heaven. Thy faithfulness is unto all generations: Thou hast established the earth and it abideth. They continue this day according to Thine ordinances: for all are Thy servants." He ordained them for this purpose. The power to ordain is remarkably ascribed to His people. Job says, "Thou shalt call upon Him, and He shall hear thee; thou shalt also decree a thing and it shall come to pass." A Christian, *he* decree a thing, "and it shall come to pass"? This can only be spoken of as they are the people of God; as they are, so to speak, partakers of Him, and are instruments of promoting His views and His designs. Coming into His measures, they are sure of success, and when His will becomes yours, your will must be accomplished.

Having seen the security, let us ask what the blessing is that He will ordain? It is "peace." "Behold," says David, "how good and pleasant it is for brethren to dwell together in unity!" Oh, how valuable is peace! Peace in a nation, in a church, in a family! Solomon says, "Better is a dinner of herbs where love is, than a stalled ox and hatred therewith."

Peace *temporal*—this God ordains for His people, as far as He sees it will be good for them. Thus it is said, "When a man's ways please the Lord, He maketh even his enemies to be at peace with him." You see this in the cases of Jacob and Esau, and we have other instances in Scripture. Solomon tells us, "The king's heart is in the hand of the Lord, as the rivers of water; He turneth it whithersoever He will;" can turn it without changing it, just as a husbandman can give the stream a new direction while the stream is the same in quality. We see much of this in God's government; we see how God can change men, without renewing them. *Spiritual* peace is also here implied. What is a fine mansion? What is wealth and friendship? and what is everything agreeable here, while there is discord and tumult within? "The spirit of a man will sustain his infirmity: but a wounded spirit who can bear?" On the other hand it matters not what trouble a man may be in if he has this peace; he may be "cast down, but he is not destroyed." It is not the water outside the vessel, if it be as wide as the Atlantic, that will sink it, but that which gets within. Jesus said unto His disciples, "Peace I leave with you, my peace I give unto you: not as the world giveth, give I unto you." This can be enjoyed in the midst of trouble. "In the world ye shall have tribulation: but be of good cheer, I have overcome the world. These things I have spoken unto you, that in me ye might have peace." "This Man *is* the peace, when the Assyrian cometh into the land," and in proportion as by faith you realize your connection with Him you will feel a "peace passing all understanding."

This peace in the experience of Christians often fluctuates. It has various degrees. Some have comparatively little of it, arising immediately from constitutional malady, from ignorance, or as a correction for sin, but it commonly increases in death. It is compared therefore to a river, which meanders and fertilizes as it goes, but becomes wider and deeper as it approximates to the sea; so the peace of God's people generally increases as they get nearer eternity. God calls upon us to witness this. "Mark the perfect man, and behold the upright: for the end of that man is peace"—peace in the exit, peace in the departure. This is commonly the case, for this peace is ordained for His people, principally and perfectly in heaven. It is then "the wicked cease from troubling and the weary are at rest." "There remaineth a rest for the people of God"—the rest of the sabbath, after the toils of the week;

the rest of Canaan after the marches, the thorns and briers of the wilderness; the rest of the soldier after a painful warfare; the rest of the mariner after the waves and the wind: "then are they glad because they are quiet; so He bringeth them to the desired haven."

III. You have seen the Christian's present condition, and future expectations, but you are reminded, thirdly, of THE DEPENDANCE OF ONE OF THESE UPON THE OTHER. Let us see how the experience of the one authorises the expectation of the other. "Thou wilt ordain peace for us: for thou hast wrought all our works in us."

Be it remembered, that the ground of our confidence is the Word of God, and not forms and feelings.

There are two sources of relief derived from this quarter.

The first is derived from the experience of others, of those who have gone before us. "Our fathers trusted in Thee; they trusted, and Thou didst deliver them. They cried unto Thee, and were delivered; they trusted in Thee, and were not confounded." This is encouraging. Therefore says the Church in the latter part of Isaiah's prophecies, "Awake, awake, put on strength, O arm of the Lord; awake, as in the ancient days, in the generations of old. Art not thou it that hath cut Rahab, and wounded the dragon? Art not thou it which hath dried the sea, the waters of the great deep; that hath made the depths of the sea a way for the ransomed to pass over?"

The other is, their own experience: this comes nearer, and is more encouraging still. An old writer says, "Former experiences are so many cordials, which faith keeps in her cupboard against the Christian's fainting-fits." And looking into the Scripture you will see how continually the people of God are rejoicing in this. Thus it was with Asaph; he complains of his infirmity. "But I will remember," says he, "the years of the right hand of the Most High. I will remember the works of the Lord; surely I will remember thy wonders of old." "O my God," exclaims David, "my soul is cast down within me: therefore will I remember Thee from the land of Jordan, and of the Hermonites, from the hill Mizar"—some little hill where he had experienced delivering mercy. So he begins the hundred and sixteenth psalm: "I love the Lord, because He hath heard my voice and my supplications. Because He hath inclined His ear unto me, therefore will I call upon Him as long as I live." It is easy to explain this, for God is "the same yesterday, to-day, and for ever." When a friend has always been kind, we think it base and unworthy not to suppose that he is ready to succour and help. But here we have the advantage: man may be weak and unable to help, but God is Almighty; men may change their mind, but "with Him is no shadow of turning." They may forget, but says God, "I will not forget thee." Therefore, Christians, let this establish your faith and hope in God. "It is a good thing for the heart to be established." Your religion allows of certainty, you should therefore endeavour to obtain it; certainty as to principle, certainty as to privileges, and certainty as to your own interest in them. You should remember what God has done; view it as a pledge, a beginning, an earnest, a foretaste of what He will do. Oh, if He *has* been with you He will never leave you, nor forsake you. If He *has* been working in you He will ordain everything for your welfare. Has He not shown you the evil of sin, the beauty of holiness, and the preciousness of a Saviour? If He had a mind to destroy you, would He have shown you such things as these?

Then this should preclude presumption. Those who are destitute of divine grace may have something like peace, but what peace is it? The peace of an antinomian—this is a devil's dream. The peace of the hypocrite—this is "a lie in his right hand." The peace of the Pharisee—this is a spider's web, curiously wrought, but easily destroyed. "There is no peace saith my God to the wicked," no peace whatever. "But there is hope in Israel concerning this thing." O seek peace and grace; and seek grace that you may have this peace, and you will become the subjects of it, for "Whoso asketh receiveth."

XXII.

THE ROUGH WIND STAYED.

(Delivered on Thursday Evening, September 18th, 1844).

"*Hath He smitten him, as He smote those that smote him? or is he slain according to the slaughter of them that are slain by Him? In measure, when it shooteth forth, Thou wilt debate with it: He stayeth His rough wind in the day of the east wind. By this therefore shall the iniquity of Jacob be purged; and this is all the fruit to take away his sin; when He maketh all the stones of the altar as chalkstones that are beaten in sunder, the groves and images shall not stand up.*"—ISAIAH xxvii. 7-9.

THE people of God are here spoken of as an afflicted people, and this supposition is well founded. Is it strange that a child should be corrected? or a vine pruned? or that a field should be ploughed? or that an ox should be proved? "Many are the afflictions of the righteous." "Whom the Lord loveth He chasteneth, and scourgeth every son whom He receiveth." Well, but if they are sufferers, *how* do they suffer? The text presents two views of them: the first regards their alleviation, the second their design.

I. THEIR ALLEVIATION. "Hath He smitten him, as He smote those that smote him? or is he slain according to the slaughter of them that are slain by Him? In measure, when it shooteth forth, Thou wilt debate with it: He stayeth His rough wind in the day of the east wind." They shall be tempered.

This is exemplified in two ways.

First, *They shall escape the severer afflictions of others.* "Hath He smitten him, as He smote those that smote him? or is he slain according to the slaughter of them that are slain by Him?" That is, He does not deal with them as with their enemies. He distresses their enemies, He only chastises them. He deals with their enemies in wrath, with them only in mercy. They only feel the rod of a father, while their enemies feel the sword of a judge. Now this is true of Israel of old. He did not deal with them as with their adversaries.

Amalekite He utterly destroyed. The Assyrians and Babylonians He completely vanquished, and the places that once knew them knew them no more, whereas the Jews are preserved even to this day. Thus we read the language of God by Jeremiah: "In those days, saith the Lord, I will not make a full end of you; but I will correct thee in measure, and will not leave thee altogether unpunished." "Behold, the eyes of the Lord God are upon the sinful kingdom, and I will destroy it from off the face of the earth; saving that I will not utterly destroy the house of Jacob, saith the Lord. For lo, I will command, and I will sift the house of Israel among all nations, like as corn is sifted in a sieve, yet shall not the least grain fall upon the earth." How often has God exempted His people from those calamities which have overwhelmed others! You see this in the case of Noah, in the case of Lot, and in the case of the Israelites with regard to the plagues of Egypt. "For the Lord knoweth how to deliver the godly," while He reserves the ungodly to be punished. Others have no hiding-place, but God is "their refuge and strength, a very present help in trouble." Others have nothing to support them in their sorrows, but God's everlasting arms are underneath these. Others say "they have taken away my gods, and what have I more?" These can say, "Although the fig-tree shall not blossom, neither shall fruit be in the vines; the labour of the olive shall fail, and the fields shall yield no meat; the flock shall be cut off from the fold, and there shall be no herd in the stalls; yet I will rejoice in the Lord, I will joy in the God of my salvation."

You should learn, therefore, from hence to compare your condition with others, especially with the wicked; you should say, "O what a mercy I am not like them in my sorrows, without hope, and without God in the world."

Observe, secondly, *their afflictions are moderate.* "In measure, when it shooteth forth, Thou wilt debate with it. He stayeth His rough wind in the day of the east wind." That is, He will chide and check it, saying, "Hither thou shalt come, but no further." The east wind is sharp and piercing, and you all know if it were rough it would be withering too: but He stays its fierceness, even when He does not change the quarter whence it comes. "He stayeth His rough wind in the day of the east wind." This shews us that all your troubles are under the divine control, and it gives us such a view as will meet the desire of every afflicted believer. Who does not deserve correction? and who does not say with Jeremiah, "O Lord, correct me, but with judgment" (that is, with moderation): "not in Thine anger, lest Thou bring me to nothing"? An ungrateful mind always looks at the dark side, while a grateful mind looks at the bright side. The believer says, "'tis bad, but it might have been worse."

Numerous are the *alleviations* God affords His people in their trouble, sometimes from the shortness of their afflictions, for says God, "I will not afflict for ever." Sometimes the alleviation is founded in the things in which they are afflicted. You have been deprived of affluence, but not support. One parent has been taken, the other has been spared to you. "Joseph is not, and Simeon is not," but Benjamin is left. You have been greatly afflicted; you might have been dead. You are become helpless, but you might have been enduring anguish and torture.

Observe also their *counterbalances*. You are tried in one child, you are equally comforted and indulged in another. Your substance has been reduced, but your health has been improved; and improved, perhaps, by the very efforts you have been compelled to make. You have less outward, but you have more inward, joy. If you have tribulation, you have been enabled to glory in it; and as the sufferings of Christ have abounded, so your consolations have abounded by Christ, and you have had strength equal to your day. If you saw a man groaning under a heavy load, and you could give him strength to bear it, this would be equal to your taking the burden. Now this is the case with God. He has said, "As thy day so shall thy strength be." Latimer and Ridley suffered together at Oxford. When confined to the stake they were near enough to shake hands. "Give me your hand," said Latimer, adding, "my brother, God will either resist the violence of the flames, or give us strength to abide them;" and then he said in the sweetest strains, "God is faithful, and He will not suffer us to be tempted above that we are able." Another saint, in writing to his friend, said, "Do not pray that I may be kept from pain, but pray that God may increase my patience, that in patience I may possess my soul." God sometimes gives you increasing views of your own unworthiness. Perhaps you have been ready to murmur and repine; but when God gives you enlarged views of what you are and what you deserve, then instead of wondering that your trials are so many, you will wonder that they are so few. Instead of wondering that they are so great, you will wonder that they are so small; for when a sense of sin lies heavy upon your conscience, trouble will always lie light. "Why should a living man complain? a man for the punishment of his sins?" "I will bear," says the church, "the indignation of the Lord, because I have sinned against Him." Aaron held his peace, after both his sons had been slain, for he had been,—what? He had been engaged in making a golden calf. It did not become him to murmur and complain after this. If you have clearer and brighter prospects of the glory that is to be revealed in you, you have a counterbalance; therefore says the Apostle, "For our light affliction, which is but for a moment, worketh out for us a far more exceeding and eternal weight of glory; while we look not at the things which are seen, but at the things which are not seen; for the things which are seen are temporal, but the things which are not seen are eternal."

II. Let us pass on to consider THEIR DESIGN; and here you will consider the general expression, and the particular reason of the thing.

Consider first the general expression of the text: "By this therefore shall the iniquity of Jacob be purged; and this is all the fruit to take away his sin." In this sense we are to understand this language as referring, not to meritoriousness, but efficiency; it is thus, and thus alone, that the blood of Jesus Christ taketh away sin. You read that the martyrs "washed their robes," not in their own blood, though they shed it so plentifully. Neither do afflictions possess any efficacy in themselves. In how many instances do they leave persons even worse than they were before; but though they cannot sanctify sufficiently, yet they do instrumentally; they are means used by the Spirit of God. How oft does He employ them to effect His gracious purposes. This was the case with the prodigal: he began to be in want, and then he resolved to return to his father. This was the case with Manassah: in his affliction he sought the Lord. Where is the Christian who cannot say with David, "It is good for me that I have been afflicted, for before I was afflicted I went astray, but now I have kept Thy word"? These trials serve as incitements when you become insensible and indifferent to Divine things. "In their afflictions," says God, "they will seek me early." Thus it was with the Church in the days of Hosea. They were wandering after their lovers; God seemed determined to prevent it. Thus He says, "Behold I will hedge up her way with thorns, and make a wall that she shall not find her paths; and she shall follow after her lovers, but she shall not overtake them," and after her efforts to get through the one, or over the other, she will return and say, "I will go and return to my first husband, for then was it better with me than now." "O that it were with me," says the Christian, "as in months past!" "Let us search and try our ways, and turn again to the Lord."

It fares with God's afflicted people as it did once with persons in this country who had the falling sickness. If they slept, they died. To keep them continually awake, they were smitten with a rosemary bush, and the patient cried, "Let me sleep, you will kill me;" but by this smarting they were kept alive. So is it with God's people now. God's rod is like Jonathan's, it has honey at the end; yea, it is "like Aaron's rod that blossomed and bore fruit; so that though no chastening for the present seemeth to be joyous, but grievous, nevertheless afterward it yieldeth the peaceable fruits of righteousness to them that are exercised thereby."

Secondly, observe the particular illustration. "When HE maketh all the stones of the altar as chalkstones that are beaten in sunder, the groves and images shall not stand up." It will be easy to explain this. Let me refer you to the address of Moses to the Jews with regard to the idols of other nations: "Ye shall overthrow their altars, and break their pillars, and burn their groves with fire; and ye shall hew down the graven images of their gods, and destroy the names of them out of that place." What they were required to do to the idols of others, these people were to do with regard to their own; that is, they were to abandon them; not only to abandon, but to destroy them. To shew the reality and intensity of their repentance, they would even crush them to pieces and beat them to powder as Moses did the golden calf. This was so with regard to the Jews as a people. They were effectually cured of idolatry by their seventy years captivity in Babylon. Ephraim said, "What have I any more to do with idols?" and says John to the Christians, admonishing them, "Little children, keep yourselves from idols." Ah, there are many idols, and these idols have been the ground of God's quarrels with you, and of the most trying dispensations. Happy is the man who is brought to say with our Cowper—

"The dearest idol I have known,
Whate'er that idol be,
Help me to bear it from Thy throne,
And worship only Thee."

Our discourse has been on the subject of afflictions: can it ever be unseasonable? Is not man "born to trouble"? and if you are exempt now, are you not continually exposed? and will you not remember the language of Solomon,—"Truly the light is sweet, and a pleasant thing it is for the eyes to behold the sun; but if a man live many years, and rejoice in them all, yet let him remember the days of darkness, for they shall be many; all that cometh is vanity"? You know the common proverb, "What can't be cured must be endured." I want you to go on further than this. I want you to have enlightened and sanctifying views of this subject: I want you to see enough to lead you to exclaim with Job, "Though HE slay me, yet will I trust in Him." "It is the Lord, let Him do what seemeth Him good." Do you not see enough in your afflictions, and of their alleviations, to see that God designs them for your benefit? O ye sons and daughters of affliction, cannot you bless God that though called to suffer, God moderates your afflictions, and that He intends that you should be purged thereby? Natural man is only concerned to obtain deliverance from them, but the real Christian desires that when God hath tried him, he may "come forth as gold;" and he wishes for deliverance only in God's time and in His way. Affliction in Scripture is compared to a prison, and when God puts us there we are not to get out of the window or over the wall, but must cry with David, "Bring my soul out of prison, that I may praise Thy name." "The righteous shall compass me about, for Thou shalt deal bountifully with me."

Here is another reference to be drawn from this point of our subject. You see what, as a sufferer, you should be concerned for. It is that the *end* may be accomplished; it is not only lamentable, but awful, to come out of afflictions as you go in. Indeed you cannot; but you will come out of the furnace nearer God, or farther from Him—more hardened, or more softened. When food fails, you have recourse to medicine; and when medicine fails, the case begins to look hopeless. You pity a fellow-creature when he has suffered a painful operation: perhaps he has had to sustain the loss of a limb, or been excoriated with the stone, but his sufferings after all are but short. But how awful to think of a man after having been deprived of health, of his substance, his friends and connections, after all these losses for him to be lost for ever! Pray therefore this may not be your case. Pray that your iniquity may be purged, and that your affliction may be the fruit to take away your sin, that it may destroy all the idolatry of your heart; this is the way to obtain a blessing. "Blessed is the man that endureth temptations; for when he is tried he shall receive the crown of life which the Lord hath promised to them that love Him."

XXIII.

WAITING UPON GOD.

(Delivered on Thursday Evening, April 3rd, 1845.)

"*And therefore will the Lord wait, that He may be gracious unto you; and therefore will He be exalted, that He may have mercy upon you: for the Lord is a God of judgment: blessed are all they that wait for Him.*"—ISAIAH XXX. 18.

HERE you see God waiting, and man waiting: God waiting to give, man waiting to receive; God waiting from condescension; man waiting from necessity.

I. We consider, first, THE CHARACTER OF GOD: "The Lord is a God of judgment."

Judgment here means what we understand by prudence, which is wisdom applied to knowledge. We therefore read that "by Him actions are weighed." He sees all things in their causes and in their issues, however remote or contingent. Observe His own challenge, "Who hath directed the Spirit of the Lord, or being His counsellor, hath taught Him? With whom took He counsel, and who instructed Him, and taught Him in the path of judgment, and taught Him knowledge; and showed to Him the way way of understanding?"

The judgment of God in the Scriptures is also associated with justice and righteousness. We therefore read that "Justice and judgment are the habitation of His throne," even when "clouds and darkness are round about Him." It is connected also with this power of God. Thus Eliphaz says, "He is wise in heart, mighty in strength." So Job says, "Thou canst do everything, no thought can be withholden from Thee." And it is also connected with the satisfaction and comfort of His people. This renders it so interesting. "Hast thou not known, hast thou not heard, that the everlasting God, the Lord, the Creator of the ends of the earth fainteth not, neither is weary? there is no searching of His understanding; His understanding is infinite." Let us, therefore, never charge Him foolishly, but let us feel persuaded that God is a rock, that "His work is perfect, and that no unrighteousness is in Him." O Christians, what a consolation is it for you to know that you are not only preserved by an Almighty arm, but guided also by unerring wisdom; that "the eyes of the Lord run to and fro throughout the whole earth, to show Himself strong on the behalf of them whose heart is perfect towards Him."

"He is a God of judgment," therefore able to teach His family, and they are all trained up in the knowledge and fear of the Lord. All the children of the Church shall be taught of the Lord; for none teacheth like Him.

And as "He is a God of judgment," He knows how to correct. Jeremiah therefore prays, "O Lord, correct me, but in judgment; not in Thine anger, lest Thou bring me to nothing." When He employs a rod, He never errs as to the time, the manner, or the continuance of it. He knows all your dangers; He knows all your walking through this great wilderness; He knows your souls in adversity, and He is able, if you refer it to Him, to choose your inheritance for you. You know not what is best for you in this vain life which you spend as a shadow, but He does, for He sees the end from the beginning. He can distinguish between your wants and your wishes. You frequently confound these. He times His blessings. He knows the fittest and most beneficial opportunity for doing you good; He is always ready with His blessing, if you are ripe for it, only He will not suffer a child to stretch forth his hand to gather the fruit before it be ripe, but will keep it till it has a finer appearance, more delicious taste, and possesses a more nutritious quality.

II. God's appearances on account of His people are sometimes delayed. This is clearly implied. "Blessed are all they that wait for Him."

"The Lord is not slack concerning His promise as some men count slackness." There is never any delay with regard to His purposes and His counsels. He has a time, a *set* time to favour Zion; and as He is never a moment before the time, so He is never too late. "God shall help us, and that right early"—not only early, but "*right early.*" But without any authority from Him, and ignorant of His designs, we appoint seasons for His work and His coming, and when He does not appear according to our expectations then we think He delays, and "hope deferred maketh the heart sick." We all know that momenst when we are expecting something of importance, and which seems exceeding desirable, pass away very slowly. So the believer sometimes finds it. Thus we hear him exclaim, "O Lord, how long?" "Make haste, O Lord, to deliver me; lighten my eyes, lest I sleep the sleep of death."

God does not always immediately appear on behalf of His people, in four instances.

First, *In answer to prayer*, and this is often very perplexing. We read, "He is a God hearing prayer." He derives His name from it, and says, "Before they call, I will answer; and while they are yet speaking, I will hear." Yet says the man, "He keeps me at the door; He hears me not, or He will not open; and when He has opened it, He frowns and shuts it again and shuts out my prayer." That is, it *seems* so to the man. How was it with the Syro-Phenœcian woman who came to Our Lord on her daughter's behalf? At first He answered her not a word; then, in answer to her persistent prayer, He said, "It is not meet to take the children's bread, and cast it to dogs," seeming to reject her. And yet what said He immediately upon her continued importunity? "O woman, great is thy faith; be it unto thee even as thou wilt."

Secondly, God does not always immediately appear on behalf of His people *in relieving them in their afflictions.* These are sometimes various and very oppressive. When the disciples were in a great storm at sea, He showed no concern for them. He was asleep in a ship, and they said, "Lord, carest Thou not that we perish?" Does God sleep? "He that keepeth Israel neither slumbereth nor sleepeth." No, but He apparently disregards His people; that is, He does not immediately exert Himself for their deliverance. How was it with Joseph? He was thrown into a pit, and sold to the Ishmaelites; he was imprisoned and fettered, and for twenty-four years there seemed to be no accomplishment of the prophetical dreams with which he was favoured. God did not, you see, soon appear for him, and this is frequently the case. "The clouds return after the rain," and the storm seems to increase instead of subsiding.

Thirdly, God does not always immediately appear on behalf of His people *in explaining Himself with regard to their afflictions.* Therefore says Job, "Shew me wherefore Thou contendest with me." But this He does not always do immediately. "His way is in the sea, and His path in the great waters, and His footsteps are not known." Verily, He is a God that hideth Himself, though He is the God of Israel, the Saviour. So it was with poor Job. "Behold," said he, "I go forward, but He is not there; and backward, but I cannot perceive Him; on the left hand where He doth work, but I cannot behold Him: He hideth Himself on the right hand, that I cannot see Him." But this was his satisfaction: "But He knoweth the way that I take; when He hath tried me, I shall come forth as gold."

Fourthly, God does not always immediately appear *in affording the joys of His salvation, and the comfort of the Holy Ghost.* Hence they may suffer for a length of time from doubts and apprehensions. Hence they resemble the Jews whose souls were discouraged because of the way. They are discouraged from a sense of guilt, and the remains of corruption; and though they have "seen the King in His beauty" they can hardly venture to call Him *their* Lord, and *their* God; and though they have seen the land of Canaan, yet it seems to them very far off.

These are the instances in which God, in His appearances on behalf of His people, may seem to delay.

III. We proceed therefore to consider thirdly, YOUR DUTY IN THE MEANTIME. It is to *wait* for Him.

Wherein does this consist? It is not so much to be viewed in a single action as in the whole frame of the soul. It appears in four things. First, in *calmness of mind*, in opposition to hurry and haste, for you always find people when in difficulties and dangers liable to confusion and haste, if they have not confidence in God. "He that believeth shall not make haste." No, he will not rush from one quarter to another, and run from one creature dependance to another in quest of deliverance; his strength will be to sit still. This is exemplified in the foregoing verses: "For thus saith the Lord God; the Holy One of Israel: in returning and rest shall ye be saved, in quietness and in confidence shall be your strength: and ye would not. But ye said, No; for we will flee upon horses; therefore shall ye flee: and, We will ride upon the swift; therefore shall they that pursue you be swift. One thousand shall flee at the rebuke of one; at the rebuke of five shall ye flee, till ye be left as a beacon upon the top of a mountain, and as an ensign upon a hill." In opposition to this, the man will feel a composedness of mind, as David did, who said, "I was dumb; I opened not my mouth, because Thou didst it." And as Aaron, who, under his immense affliction, instead of complaining, raging, and running from creature to creature, held his peace. There will be a degree of this calmness of mind.

Secondly, this implies *attention*, in opposition to indolence and indifference. Though the believer is tranquil and calm, he is not regardless of the mind and will of God. He says with David, "I wait for the Lord, my soul doth wait, and in His word do I hope. My soul waiteth for the Lord more than they that watch for the morning; I say, more than they that watch for the morning." So says the Church, "I will stand upon my watch-tower." "I will stand there, looking to see if God is passing by, hearkening to what He has to communicate, otherwise I may lose the opportunity of seeing Him." Various are the means He may employ, and therefore let us say, "Behold as the eyes of servants look unto the hand of their masters, and as the eyes of a maiden unto the hand of her mistress, so our eyes wait upon the Lord our God, until that He have mercy upon us."

This takes in *patience*. The enemy of our souls knoweth our frame, and takes advantage of our weakness. Because Moses stayed so long in the Mount, the people made a golden calf and danced before it. So Rebecca—she was peculiarly attached to Jacob, and knew that he should have the blessing, but by a crooked policy and unhallowed means she must take it out of the Lord's hands. So trouble is called a prison. David says, "Bring my soul out of prison, that I may praise Thy name." You are not to force open the door or the window; if you do, you will be confined more firmly than before; but you must stay there till God lets you out. When He is walking by, you may look through the bars, and say, "O Lord, come to my succour; bring my soul out of prison." All this is wise and well, but "in patience" you are to "possess your souls." "By patient continuing in well-doing" you are to "seek for glory, honour, immortality, and eternal life." You are not to be "weary in well-doing, for in due season you shall reap if you faint not."

Again, this implies *expectation*, in opposition to despondency. This is the very essence of waiting upon God. If this is not in exercise, you will not hold out long, but will be ready to say with the unbelieving nobleman, "Why should I wait for the Lord any longer?"

IV. Consider, lastly, THE BLESSEDNESS THAT WILL ATTEND THE EXERCISE OF WAITING FOR HIM. "Blessed are all they that wait for Him."

The work itself is blessed: therefore says Jeremiah, "It is good for a man that he hath hope and quietly wait for the salvation of the Lord." Your happiness depends not so much upon outward things as upon the state of your own mind. If you are quiet from the fear of evil, your soul dwells at ease; your mind is kept in perfect peace, being stayed upon Him. You are like Noah in the Ark, all peace within, while the floods are rolling around; or as the Apostle says, "We are troubled on every side, but not in despair."

"Blessed," secondly, because it will prevent matter for bitter reflection. How miserable are you when you have been led to censure a kind friend, or have entertained some hard unworthy thoughts of him, and afterwards have seen that you were mistaken. So will it be, so often has it been with Christians here; they say, "I lament that I should have been so foolish and so wicked in judging my Lord and Saviour. Why did I not honour him with my entire confidence? O that I had stayed longer before I had judged Him. How it grieves *me* now, that I have grieved the Holy Spirit."

Thirdly, they are blessed, because His coming will amply recompense their waiting. How does the absence of a friend endear his presence! How does the night endear the morning! How does the winter make us hail the spring! And when God comes to us, when He appears, what once appeared wrong will be seen to be right in all His dispensations.

"Jesus, on Thee our hope relies,
To lead us on to Thine abode,
Assured our rest will make amends
For all our toil upon the road."

"Blessed are all they that wait for Him," because they will not, cannot, wait in vain. No, the vision is for an appointed time; though it tarry, wait for it. "They that sow in tears shall reap in joy." "Be patient therefore, brethren, for the coming of the Lord draweth nigh;" and if ever Satan assaults you, repel the temptation with this declaration, "Yet a little while and He that will come shall come, and will not tarry." Then turn inward and say, "Why art thou cast down, O my soul? and why art thou disquieted within me? Hope in God, who is the health of my countenance and my God."

XXIV.

THE CITY OF OUR SOLEMNITIES.

(Delivered on Thursday Evening, December 10th, 1846.)

"*Look upon Zion, the city of our solemnities.*"—ISAIAH xxxiii. 20.

"BE not conformed to this world," says the Apostle. The world has always been immensely the larger portion of the human race, but we are persuaded this will not always be the case; for said Our Saviour, "I, if I be lifted up will draw all men to me:" and when, without a figure, it may be said, "Behold the world is gone after Him," we shall then, brethren, have to change even the language of Scripture, and to say, "Strait is the way, and narrow is the gate that leadeth unto *death*, and few there be that find it." The Lord hasten it in His time! When "a nation shall be born in a day;" when "all kings shall fall down before Him, and all nations shall serve Him!" But down to the present hour, the saints have been spoken of individually rather than collectively; and their numbers comparatively have been small. Our Saviour is still addressing these, and saying, "Fear not, little flock." Yet He never left himself without witness. He has always had people for His name, however poor and despised they may be. What says Zechariah? "These are men wondered at." What says Solomon? "The righteous is more excellent than his neighbour." What says Paul? "Of such the world is not worthy." And how does God, the Judge of all, speak of them? "Since thou hast been precious in My sight, thou hast been honourable, and I have loved thee." Now to them the prophecy before us applies, for whatever partial accomplishment took place in the experience of the Jews after their return from Babylon to their own country, the very strength of the language compels us to look further.

"Look upon Him, the city of our solemnities." Let us observe the object of contemplation, and the contemplation of the object; and this is all the division of our subject.

I. The object of contemplation. "Look upon Zion." You know what Zion was literally considered; it is hardly necessary to add, that it is symbolical of the residence of the Living God. To mention one instance, let me refer you to the language of the Apostle in writing to the Hebrews, where he says, "Ye are come unto Mount Zion, the city of the living God." In all proper types, two things are to be looked for, resemblance and pre-eminence; and here we have truth, for as to *pre-eminence*, how superior is the Church to the hill of Zion! What was Judaism compared with Christianity? One was the dawn, the other the day. One was infancy, the other the manhood of the Church. The one a series of ceremonies and shadows, the other the substance: "God having provided some better things for us that they without us should not be made perfect." Yet you may see a *resemblance*, a strong and striking resemblance. Was Zion beautiful? She was "beautiful for situation, the joy of the whole earth." Had God chosen her? He had. We read: "The Lord hath chosen Zion, He hath desired it for His habitation." Was the foundation thereof strong? Was it the place of the divine residence? Was the tabernacle fixed there? Did the temple stand there? Did God say, "This is my rest for ever: here will I dwell; for I have desired it. I will abundantly bless her provision: I will satisfy her poor with bread. I will also clothe her priests with salvation: and her saints shall shout aloud for joy. There will I make the horn of David to bud: I have ordained a lamp for mine anointed. His enemies will I clothe with shame: but upon himself shall his crown flourish"? What is it by all this that you are reminded of? Of the Church of the living God; adored with comeliness, chosen for the habitation of the Deity, impregnable in its defence, the place where God maintains His ordinances, where He dispenses His influence and the blessings of salvation.

Then it is called, "the city of our solemnities;" and was so called because it was the place of their holy convocations. There the Jews attended, at their three grand annual festivals. This was divinely appointed. "Thrice in the year," says God, "shall all your males appear before me at Jerusalem." Unbelief and selfishness would be ready to murmur at this command, and say, "How can that be? When all our males are drawn from the extremities of the land, it will lie open to the incursions of our adversaries, who are watchful for every opportunity to injure us; and what will become of our wives and children and substance?" Hear how God meets them:

"I will cast out the nations before thee, and enlarge thy borders: neither shall any man desire thy land, when thou shalt go up to appear before the Lord thy God thrice in the year." They shall not even wish for the thing. As the king in history said to the prime minister, so says God to us: "You mind my affairs, and I will mind yours." Oh, the God we serve is able to overrule persons by His providence, when He does not change them spiritually by His grace. Oh, let us put all our concerns into His hand, for "when a man's ways please the Lord, He maketh even His enemies to be at peace with him." There is a striking reference in the eighty-fourth psalm to their travelling up to attend these festivals. "Blessed is the man whose strength is in Thee; in whose heart are the ways of them. Who passing through the valley of Baca make it a well; the rain also filleth the pools. They go from strength to strength, every one of them in Zion appeareth before God." David says, "Our feet shall stand within thy gates, O Jerusalem," referring to these festivals. "Jerusalem is builded as a city that is compact together: whither the tribes go up, the tribes of the Lord, unto the testimony of Israel, to give thanks unto the name of the Lord. For there are set thrones of Judgment, the thrones of the House of David."

We read in the prophecies of Zephaniah of those "who are sorrowful for the solemn assembly." "The solemn assembly" is where religious services are solemnly performed, where the Scriptures are solemnly read, where the Gospel is solemnly preached, where prayers are solemnly offered, and where communion of saints is solemnly administered. But the word "solemnities" in Scripture refers much more frequently to what is festive than to what is serious, and Christians have their spiritual festivites to attend upon as well as the Jews had. What is the Gospel but a festivity? According to the language of our prophet, "In this mountain shall the Lord of Hosts make unto all people a feast of fat things, a feast of wines on the lees, of fat things full of marrow, of wines on the lees well refined." What is the Lord's Supper but a festivity, a domestic feast, where the household of faith partake and rejoice together? Wherefore saith the Apostle, "Christ our Passover is sacrificed for us." Therefore says he, "Let us keep the feast, not with old leaven, neither with the leaven of malice and wickedness; but with the unleavened bread of sincerity and truth."

Though the word "solemnities" with us signifies what is serious rather than what is sacred, this was not the original meaning, neither was it so used in Scripture nor in our text. It must be admitted indeed that the things that are sacred should be things that are serious; they are not to be trifled with. Religious concerns are important and solemn; they regard God, the soul, and eternity; and require a serious frame of mind when we are engaged in them, as nothing is more likely to conduce to our improvement by them than this state of mind. Therefore says David, "God is greatly to be feared in the assembly of the saints, and to be held in reverence of all them that are about Him." Therefore Paul requires us to "have grace, whereby we may serve God acceptably, with reverence and godly fear." "How dreadful is this place! This is none other but the house of God, and this is the gate of heaven!" Yea, and the gate of *hell* too; when there is one that goes to heaven from the House of God, how many are there who go from thence to hell! And the Gospel itself is to them "the savour of death unto death."

II. Having noticed the object of contemplation, let us consider THE CONTEMPLATION OF THE OBJECT. "Look upon Zion, the city of our solemnities."

To whom is this addressed? Does the prophet address the worldlings? or awaken penitents or believers? or God Himself? We may take them all in here.

First, we consider him as addressing the worldling. To them He speaks, and says, "Look upon Zion, the city of our solemnities." This should be a look of conviction. "See," you should say to them, "how far superior are our enjoyments to things of time and sense. Is there anything like satisfaction in any of your pursuits and successes? Are you not while "observing lying vanities, forsaking your own mercies"? And have you not found, as Job says, that "in the midst of your sufficiency you are in straits"? Have you not found, in the midst of your enjoyment, a cold and aching void which leads you still to ask, "Who will show us any good?"

There are persons, and you know many of them, who have been delivered from their evil passions and affections; and, possessing a confidence in God, they enjoy a peace with God "passing all understanding." They can "rejoice in hope of the glory of God." Are not these persons worthy of your belief? Why do you think they are not? Why do you think they endeavour to impose upon you? They tell you they never knew anything of real liberty till Christ had made them free; they were strangers to real pleasure as long as they were strangers to Him. O turn, therefore, from a world that is full of vanity; forsake the foolish and live, and go in the way everlasting." Drop the sons of vanity, and run and "take hold of the skirt of him that is a Jew," saying, "We will go with you; for we have heard that God is with you." Moses did so, and "chose rather to suffer affliction with the people of God than to enjoy the pleasures of sin for a season; esteeming the reproach of Christ greater riches than the treasures in Egypt." David did so. He came down from his throne, and praying by the humblest subject of divine grace, he said, "Remember me, O Lord, with the favour that thou bearest unto Thy people: O visit me with Thy salvation; that I may see the good of Thy chosen, that I may rejoice in the gladness of Thy nation, that I may glory with Thine inheritance."

He addressed this to the awakened penitents. To them He said, "Look upon Zion, the city of our solemnities:" and *this* should be a look of encouragement. Zion has long fixed my gaze, long have I admired her, and desired her condition. "How goodly are thy tents, O Jacob, and thy tabernacles, O Israel! Who can count the dust of Jacob, and the number of the fourth part of Israel? Let me die the death of the righteous, and let my last end be like his!" Do you say, "O that I were a companion of all them that fear Thee!" and "no longer a stranger and foreigner"? Well, look here, see not only their privileges, but remember how they obtained them. "They were once children of wrath, even as others;" and destitute of all spiritual blessings: but now hear them saying, "We, who were sometime far off, are made nigh by the blood of Christ;" "By the grace of God we are what we are." The door by which they entered is open still; and the inmates, so far from wishing to engross the blessings to themselves are saying, "Come in thou blessed of the Lord, why standest thou without?" They are saying, "Come with us, and we will do thee good: for the Lord hath spoken good concerning Israel." Yes, they will rejoice when they see you, because you have hoped in the truth. This is their aim, and what they make known. "That which we have heard and seen," say they, "declare we unto you, that ye also may have fellowship with us: and truly our fellowship is with the Father and with His Son Jesus Christ."

Thirdly, He addresses this to believers themselves, and says,

"Look upon Zion, the city of our solemnities," and say with David, "They are the excellent of the earth, in whom is all my delight." Look with a look of gratitude, and "learn in whatsoever state you are therewith to be content." Why should you envy the rank of others? You have a much more noble descent, you have much greater treasures, even "unsearchable riches;" you have much better enjoyments, and can say—

> "The hill of Zion yields
> A thousand sacred sweets,
> Before we reach the heavenly fields,
> Or walk the golden streets."

Why should you murmur and complain because some things are withholden from you? Many things are given to you which are withholden from them, and infinitely superior too. What is their portion compared with yours? or their rock, compared to your Rock, even if you are under the rebukes of Providence, though these may produce an unfavourable conclusion in your minds, for "Zion said, My God hath forsaken me, and my Lord hath forgotten me. Can a woman forget her sucking child, that she should not have compassion on the son of her womb? yea, they may forget, yet will I not forget thee." Look with a look of glory, and say with Isaiah, "I will greatly rejoice in the Lord, my soul shall be joyful in my God; for He hath clothed me with the garments of salvation." Look with a look of zeal. Remember the language of David, "Pray for the peace of Jerusalem; they shall prosper that love thee." See what is to be done with regard to this church of the living God, and what you can do in the condition and sphere in which you are placed, and then comply with the admonition of the psalmist, and exclaim, "Let mount Zion rejoice, let the daughters of Judah be glad because of Thy judgments. Walk about Zion, and go round about her: tell the towers thereof. Mark ye well her bulwarks, consider her palaces; that ye may tell it to the generation following. For this God is our God for ever and ever: He will be our guide even unto death." And, oh, if you are struck now, when you look upon Zion in its present excellencies and attainments, what will it be when you view it in its final and finished state; when what is here spoken of shall be accomplished: "Thy sun shall no more go down; neither shall thy moon withdraw itself: for the Lord shall be thine everlasting light, and the days of thy mourning shall be ended"? when what John says shall be fulfilled: "And I John saw the holy city, new Jerusalem, coming down from God out of heaven, prepared as a bride adorned for her husband. And I heard a great voice out of heaven saying, Behold, the tabernacle of God is with men, and He will dwell with them, and they shall be His people, and God Himself shall be with them, and be their God. And God shall wipe away all tears from their eyes; and there shall be no more death, neither sorrow, nor crying, neither shall there be any more pain: for the former things are passed away"?

Lastly, he says to God Himself, "Look upon Zion, the city of our solemnities." This is similar to what we find in one of the psalms: "Lord, look down from heaven; behold and visit the vine." The same thing under another image is here enjoined by the prophet: "Give Him no rest, till He establish, and till He make Jerusalem a praise in the earth." David says, "Pray for the peace of Jerusalem;" praying that God would look upon Zion, that He would heal its breaches and divisions, that He would enlarge its borders, that He would lengthen her cords and strengthen her stakes, that she may break forth, on the right hand and on the left; then shall the church go forth, "clear as the sun, fair as the moon, and terrible as an army with banners."

XXV.

THE SALVATION OF ISRAEL.

(Delivered on Thursday Evening, July 9th, 1846.)

"*But Israel shall be saved in the Lord.*"—ISAIAH xlv. 17.

OUR divines of former years, "of whom the world was not worthy," were, among other things, noted for drawing distinctive characters in their sermons, and addressing them separately, always having, as they said, a word for saints and sinners. Let this be called formal if you will; it has the sanction of God's authority, who says to His ministers, "Say ye to the righteous that it shall be well with him; for they shall eat of the fruit of their doings. Woe to the wicked, it shall be ill with him; for the reward of his deeds shall be given him." And it can plead also inspired example. Says Paul, "He that soweth to the flesh, shall of the flesh reap corruption; but he that soweth to the Spirit, shall of the Spirit reap life everlasting." Says Solomon, "The wicked is driven away in his wickedness; but the righteous hath hope in his death." And so in the words which I have now read: "They," says Isaiah, "shall be ashamed; and also confounded; they shall go to confusion together that are makers of idols. But Israel shall be saved in the Lord."

I wished to have noticed the whole of this combined passage, but I perceive it will lead us to trespass too long on the time allotted for this service, and therefore I confine your attention exclusively to the latter part; calling upon you to observe the heirs of promise, the blessing announced, the manner in which it is to be realised, and the assurance of the possession.

Let us consider THE HEIRS OF PROMISE. "Israel."

The word Israel may be noticed three ways. First, *personally*. The name belonged originally to Jacob. You are informed how he obtained it, and in what place. It was by his wrestling with the angel, and his not letting him go till he had blessed him. Then the angel immediately knighted him in the field: "Thy name shall no more be called Jacob; and he blessed him there."

We may also notice it *nationally*; for Jacob had many children; and they multiplied into a numberless people, and were called by his new name. They were a peculiar nation, distinguished by numerous dispensations and ordinances. They were the depositaries of divine truth, and "heirs of the righteousness which is of faith." To them was committed the oracles of God. "To whom pertaineth the adoption, and the glory, and the covenants, and the giving of the law, and the service of God, and the promises; whose are the fathers, and of whom as concerning the flesh Christ came." And there is a day coming when these from being Israelites after the flesh, will become "Israelites indeed, in whom is no guile;" and the veil will be taken from their eyes, and they shall turn unto the Lord. For we are persuaded of their conversion, though we are by no means convinced of their return to their own country, and, as we have seen in some recent instances, they seem to begin to give up their own expectation and desire.

Then we may notice it *spiritually*. Thus Gentiles are included as well as Jews in "the Israel of God," for says the Apostle, "He is not a Jew that is one outwardly: neither is that circumcision which is outward in the flesh. But he is a Jew, which is one inwardly: and circumcision is that of the heart, in the spirit and not in the letter, whose praise is not of men, but of God." And again, "We are of the true circumcision:" we are the people whom the Jews typified, "who worship God in the Spirit," and so on. If we are "Christ's, then are we Abraham's seed and heirs according to the promise." This is "the Israel of God" here spoken of.

II. Let us refer to THE BLESSING ANNOUNCED. "But Israel shall be saved in the Lord."

The state unto which these Christians are brought by divine grace is frequently called in Scripture, "Salvation;" because it is not a condition wherein they are preserved and in which they were before, but a condition into which they enter, in consequence of a deliverance being accomplished in them so that they are saved from numberless evils to which they were exposed. Many of the evils from which we are saved in passing through this vale of tears arise from the passions of unreasonable men. How are we saved from floods and flames, from accidents and diseases! These are not to be overlooked. Many of these salvations have we experienced. There are many more of these than we are aware of, the discovery of which in yonder world of light will awaken our praise and our wonder too. "But our God," as David says, "is a God of salvation, to whom belongs the issues from death"—spiritual death, and death eternal. This is the salvation which is called "His salvation," and in which Hannah resolved to rejoice. "I will rejoice in His salvation." It was a glorious salvation which God wrought for Israel when He delivered them from the house of bondage with an outstretched arm. It was a glorious salvation when He rescued them from the yoke of Babylon, and restored them to their own land. But here is a salvation which excelleth both. Here is a salvation which the Apostle calls "so great salvation"—so inexpressible, so inconceivably great; freeing us from all evil, conferring upon us all possible good, advancing us to a state of blessedness and glory superior to Adam's condition in paradise, or to angels in heaven.

Hence you will observe the quality attached to it. It is "an everlasting salvation."

"Permanency," says Young, "adds bliss to bliss." You know that duration is essential to your happiness. The more you value a blessing, the more do you wish its continuance; and the apprehension of its destruction or loss would be enough to embitter a cup of nectar, or to turn hope into despair. There is no ground for this here; persons have been raised up from sickness, and have fallen into a worse disease; indeed every recovery is only a reprieve; the sentence is still suspended over the convalescent, "Dust thou art, and unto dust shalt thou return." People have been freed from tyranny, but they have been conquered and oppressed more than before. How often were the Jews saved from the hands of their enemies, and again brought into bondage where they have suffered more than before. But this is inapplicable to "the true Israel;" they will never be destroyed. "The God of grace will bruise Satan under your feet shortly." "Sin shall not have dominion over you, for ye are not under the law, but under grace." Yes, the enemies which you see to-day, you will see them no more for ever. Some of you have had much to do with tears, and many tears have been wiped away, but soon, Christians, "all tears will be wiped away." You have had much to do with sorrow; still the days of your mourning shall be ended. Now you enjoy at times communion with your God, but soon you will be "for ever with the Lord." Everything here is changeable and ready to vanish away; you have only a life-interest in anything you now possess; as our admired Cowper says finely, "Our pleasures are short-lived." How soon may "riches make to themselves wings and fly away"! And how soon may you be deprived of health and "made to possess months of vanity"! How soon may you be induced to exclaim with Heman, "Lover and friend hast Thou put far from me, and my acquaintance into darkness"! But everything pertaining to the salvation here spoken of is lasting, everlasting. Here the house is "a building of God, eternal in the heavens." Here the "inheritance is incorruptible, undefiled, and fadeth not away;" "it is reserved in heaven for you." Here is "the everlasting kingdom of our Lord and Saviour."

There are advantages derivable from this salvation even now. We are said to be saved, justified, and renewed even now, amidst all our afflictions and imperfections. "Now are we the sons of God, and it doth not yet appear what we shall be." Whatever advantages we derive from this salvation in time will issue in a far more glorious and blessed state in eternity; and it is in reference to this that we are principally to view this salvation, "for when that which is perfect is come, then that which is in part shall be done away."

III. Let us observe HOW THIS SALVATION IS REALIZED. "In the Lord." That is, the salvation is in Him, and they are in Him who are partakers of it, for both these must be admitted into the idea in order to do justice to the phrase. He is the source and author of this salvation; therefore they are saved in Him.

The greatness and difficulty of the work may be judged of by the means used for the accomplishment of it. Your views of the heinousness of sin, your views of the holiness of God, and of the nature and claims of His law are all defective, so that you do not form adequate views of His greatness and your own sinfulness. But what did angels think when they saw "The Lord of life and glory" come down to assume our nature, and become a man to bear our sins? For "He was delivered for our offences, and raised again for our justification." What did they think when they saw Him descending from the throne to the cross? and then reascending from the cross to the throne? All this was necessary for the accomplishment of our salvation; "for it became Him, for whom are all things and by whom are all things, in bringing many sons unto glory, to make the Captain of their salvation perfect through suffering." This, therefore, is the source of your salvation. It is in *Him* that we have redemption. "This is the record, that God hath given unto us eternal life, and this life is in His Son." The Apostle therefore exclaims, "I know whom I have believed, and that He is able to keep that which I have committed to Him against that day." There is, says the divine testimony, salvation in no other. Therefore, trying to find the salvation anywhere but in the Lord will not only be found vain but criminal, because it is opposed to the divine pleasure and appointment. It is disobedience to the command, "Believe on the Lord Jesus Christ, and thou shalt be saved." It is robbing Him of His highest glory; it is frustrating His grace, and making Christ dead in vain.

But this is not all we are reminded of. When Isaiah says, "But Israel shall be saved in the Lord," he means not only to lead us to consider the Author and the source, but also the medium. He means not only to inform us that this blessing is to be found in Him, but that the partakers are to be found in Him too; or otherwise it is impossible to enjoy it; no more than any could enjoy a refuge without being in it: a man must be in it in order to benefit by it. There was security *in* the ark; Noah and his family were in safety there, while all beside perished. Not only are these blessings in Christ, but we must be in Him in order to realize them. It is thus "we are blessed with all spiritual blessings in Christ Jesus," not only because the blessings are in Him, but are partaken of by us, in consequence of our union to Him; and this extends to the exercise of grace in the soul. There is sap, you know, in the vine, but how does the branch partake of it? Only by being in the vine. Though the sap is in the vine, the branches must be there too. So the Saviour says, "As the branch cannot bear fruit of itself, except it abide in the vine, so no more can ye, except ye abide in me." "For without me"—or as it is better in the margin —"separate from me ye can do nothing."

II. Consider THE ASSURANCE OF THE BLESSING. What can you desire more than the engagement of a God that cannot lie? Who is it that has said in so many words, in a sense not requiring philosophy to determine, "Israel shall be saved in the Lord." Notwithstanding their fears, and they are many, He says, "I will strengthen thee; yea, I will help thee; yea, I will uphold thee with the right hand of my righteousness." *They* say with David, "I shall one day perish;" but *He* says, "They shall *never* perish, neither shall any man pluck them out of My hand," notwithstanding all the efforts their adversaries may make to destroy them. Their enemies are numerous andskilful, and powerful, and have been successful, for they have cast down many mighty, yea, many strong men have been slain by them; yea, peers, scholars, philosophers, and many professors of religion too. "But *Israel* shall be saved." "In all these things they are more than conquerors, through Him that hath loved them." The Apostle therefore says with regard to the Philippians, "We are confident of this very thing, that He who hath begun a good work in you will perform it unto the day of Jesus Christ." When a man is the workman, it is impossible to infer the confirmation. How often does a man expose himself to reproach, and lead those that pass by to say, "This man began to build, and was not able to finish." But the hands of Zerubbabel have laid the foundation of this house; His hands shall also finish it, and "the headstone shall be brought forth, shoutings, Grace, grace unto it." "The pleasure of the Lord shall prosper in His hand." And you may be assured that His counsel shall stand, and He will do all His pleasure. This we may safely infer from the love of His heart, and the power of His arm, for He is able to do above what we are able to ask or think; so that we may fully conclude that "Israel shall be saved in the Lord with an everlasting salvation." Sometimes Christians can realize it; their *state* is always safe, and they sometimes feel safe as to their apprehension. Then they can say with David, "The Lord is my light and my salvation; of whom shall I be afraid? the Lord is the strength of my life; whom shall I fear? Though an host should encamp against me, I will not fear; though war rise up against me, in this will I be confident." If we are Christians, we shall always feel this more or less, as we are enabled to exercise faith in God.

"O for a strong, a lasting faith,
To credit what my Saviour saith!
To embrace the message of His Son,
And call the joys of heaven my own."

What can you desire more? You should value His promise as Christians, for His promise cannot fail for evermore. Man's promises, when you depend upon them, will plunge you into confusion and distress; "but the Lord is not a man that He should lie; nor the son of man, that He should repent. Hath He said, and will He not do it? Hath He spoken, and will

He not make it good?" Heaven and earth may pass away, but His Word will never pass away.

"His very word of grace is strong
  As that which built the skies;
The voice that rolls the stars along
  Speaks all the promises.

He said, 'Let the wide heaven be spread,'
  And heaven was stretched abroad;
'Abram, I'll be thy God,' He said,
  And He was Abram's God.

Oh, might I hear Thine heavenly tongue
  But whisper, Thou art mine;
Those gentle words should raise my song
  To notes almost divine.

How would my leaping heart rejoice,
  And think my heaven secure;
I trust the all-creating voice,
  And faith desires no more."

XXVI.

THE NEARNESS OF OUR VINDICATOR.

(Delivered on Thursday Evening, June 18th, 1846.)

"*He is near that justifieth me.*"—ISAIAH l. 8.

IN this brief exercise, let us consider these words, first, as THE LANGUAGE OF CHRIST TO HIS FATHER.

We scruple not to say that these words immediately refer to Him. "The testimony of Jesus is the spirit of prophecy." But though "to Him gave all the prophets witness," Isaiah prophesied more of Him than the rest—more fully, more explicitly, more clearly—concerning "the sufferings of Christ, and the glory that should follow." He therefore has been called the evangelical prophet.

Let us verify our application, and turn to the fourth verse. "The Lord God hath given me the tongue of the learned, that I should know how to speak a word in season to him that is weary." Here He is referred to as the prophet of His Church, and if we go forward to His history, and attend to His preaching, we shall see the truth of David's language: "Grace is poured into His lips." Nor shall we be surprised that all His hearers wondered at the gracious words that proceeded out of His mouth: "Blessed are they that mourn, for they shall be comforted. Blessed are the meek, for they shall inherit the earth. Blessed are they that are persecuted for righteousness sake, for theirs is the kingdom of heaven." "Come unto me all ye that are weary and heavy laden, and I will give you rest." Here is "the tongue of the learned." Here is "a word in season to him that is weary." But those who teach well must discriminate. "He wakeneth morning by morning, He wakeneth mine ear to hear as the learned." The wisest are always the most attentive to instruction. "Teach a wise man," says Solomon, "and he will be yet wiser." So after being referred to as a Teacher, He is regarded as a Sufferer. "The

Lord God hath opened mine ear, and I was not rebellious, neither turned away back." "I gave My back to the smiters, and My cheeks to them that plucked off the hair: I hid not my face from shame and spitting." "I gave My back to the smiters:" this refers to their scourging Him. "And My cheeks to them that plucked off the hair." This is an incident which we do not meet with in the Gospels. But you will remember that the Gospels were not designed to convey all that befell the Saviour, nor the larger part of it. "I hid not my face from shame and spitting." This degradation is recorded by the Evangelists, which goes to prove the minuteness and accuracy of the prophecy. Well, for whom was all this suffering? You will see when you are led to "mourn for Him whom you have pierced."

We talk of our suffering for Him. What have any of you yet endured for His dear sake who gave His back to the smiters, and His cheeks to them that plucked off the hair, and who hid not His face from shame and spitting; who for you "was a man of sorrows and acquainted with grief"? Why, Paul valued the very fellowship of His sufferings; and "Oh," said one of the martyrs at the time of persecution, "Oh, that I was honoured to suffer thus for Christ!" referring to whipping, which none at that time had to endure; but soon after the infamous Bishop Bonner whipped several of the martyrs with his own hand!

Well, He expresses His courage and His confidence. "For the Lord God will help Me; therefore shall I not be confounded; therefore have I set my face like a flint, and I know that I shall not be ashamed." Then, in the words which we first read, we have the ground of His confidence: "He is near that justifieth Me." He therefore said to the Jews, "He that sent Me is with Me." "The Father hath not left Me alone, for I do always those things that please the Father." His various miracles evince this, according to Nicodemus, who said, "No man can do these miracles that Thou doest except God be with Him."

He was forsaken, indeed, by those who were His professed adherents, and how He felt this is obvious from His language: "I looked and there was none to help; and I wondered that there was none to uphold." But hear how He expressed Himself to His disciples, who had said, "Now we know Thou camest forth from God." Jesus answered them, "Do ye now believe? Behold the hour cometh, yea, is now come, that ye shall be scattered, every man to his own, and shall leave me alone, and yet I am not alone, because the Father is with me." But did He not exclaim upon the cross, "My God, my God, why hast Thou forsaken me?" He did, but He there referred to His outward sufferings, to His being given up for a season to the power of darkness; for you see even then He confided in Him. He calls Him *His* God twice, and committed His Spirit to His hands; yea, He could say, "He is near that justifieth me."

"Great is the mystery of Godliness. God was manifest in the flesh, justified in the Spirit." What means this justification in the Spirit? Why, as regards the imputation He lay under, and the various charges of His enemies, they considered Him as "smitten of God and afflicted." They represented Him as an impostor, and every evil they could think of was laid to His charge. He was put to death under the charge of blasphemy and sedition. But He was declared to be "the Son of God with power," by His resurrection from the dead. Thus every reproach was rolled away, and because He had been "obedient unto death, even the death of the Cross, God highly exalted Him, and gave Him a name which is above every name." Yes, said Peter at Jerusalem, "He hath made this same Jesus, whom ye crucified, both Lord and Christ." And this is the meaning of Our Saviour's words, where He says, in reference to the Holy Ghost, "He shall convince the world of righteousness, because I go to my Father, and ye see Me no more." "He shall admit Me into His glorious presence, as a proof that I have finished the work that He gave Me to do."

II. We consider these words as THE LANGUAGE OF CHRISTIANS TO CHRIST. They may say, "He is near that justifieth me." There is an union, a federal, a vital, an everlasting union, and there is a resemblance between Christ and His people. What is said of the one may be said of the other, only with this difference, that there is a supremacy on His side. In all things he has the pre-eminence; and yet you find a sameness. He is called "The Son of God," and says John, "Beloved, now are we the Sons of God." He is called "The Heir," and they are "heirs of God, and joint-heirs with Christ." "I am," said He "the light of the world;" and says He, "Ye are the light of the world." Light is the same as to quality, whether it be found in the sun or in a candle.

Christians may express themselves with confidence in regard to His presence, and say, "He is near that justifieth Me." His presence, indeed, fills heaven and earth, and "He is not far from us;" but you must distinguish what we call His omnipresence from His presence when it is spoken of in a way of privilege or promise. Here reference is made to His peculiar—to His special—to His gracious presence. Thus Moses prayed, "If Thy presence go not with me, carry me not up hence." "Fear thou not," says God, "for I am with thee." "The upright shall dwell in His presence." This shows us the amazing condescension of God. Well may Solomon exclaim, "Will God in very deed dwell with man upon the earth?" Yes, but this argues His patience, for you would soon drive an angel from you; he could not bear with your manners; but it is otherwise with God, "He is long-suffering to usward," and hath said, "I will never leave thee nor forsake thee." This, brethren, is the happiness of His people. "He is nigh unto all those who are of a broken heart, and saveth such as are of a contrite spirit." He is near to protect them from their enemies; near to sustain them in affliction. "He is a very present help in trouble," and says to them, "When thou passest through the waters, I will be with thee." He is near to help them in every duty. Hence Paul could say, when he stood before Nero, and when all his friends had forsaken him, "Nevertheless the Lord stood by me." He was with Daniel in the lion's den. He was with the three Hebrew children in the fiery furnace. He is near His people to hear their cry, and to answer their prayers, and therefore says Moses, "What nation is there who hath God so nigh to them, as the Lord Our God is, in all things that we call upon Him for." Oh, what blessedness, Christian, is connected with this! He is near unto you wherever you are, and in whatever condition you may be found. He is at your right hand so that you need not be moved, and you may say with Watts:

"If Thou, my Jesus, still be nigh,
Cheerful I live, and joyful die;
Secure when earthly comforts flee,
To find ten thousand worlds in Thee."

He also justifies you. "He is near that justifieth me."

Consider this as to their state. When the Saviour says, "He is near that justifieth Me," and when the Christian says, "He is near that justifieth me," observe this difference: God justified His Son as innocent, for "He did no sin, neither was guile found in His mouth." When "the prince of this world came, he found nothing in Him" to condemn. "But how can man be just with God?" "It is God that justifieth." He is the Being against whom our sin is committed; therefore unless He justifies us we must be condemned, whoever justifies us.

But how? The question may be divided into five parts. He justifies us originally; that is, regardless of all works of our own. He justifies us liberally, or freely, as the Apostle tells us: "Being justified *freely* by His grace." He justifies us meritoriously; that is, through "the redemption which is in Christ Jesus." "He bore our sins in His own body, on the tree." "He was delivered for our offences, and raised again for our justification." "He once suffered for sin, the just for the unjust, that He might bring us unto God." He justifies us instrumentally, by faith as opposed to works. "Being justified by faith, we have peace with God through Our Lord Jesus Christ." They are justified *evidentially.* Thus Abraham's faith justified him in the sight of others; and how publicly will God's people be justified at last, when the Saviour will say to those on His right hand, "Come, ye blessed of My Father, inherit the kingdom prepared for you from the foundation of the world."

We pass on to consider more fully the sense in which the prophet uses the words as applicable to the believer. This regards the aspersion of their character, or the imputation of charges under which they may lie from others. It is necessary to avoid two extremes. We should seek to stand fair in the eyes of others. Some say, "I don't care what others think of me;" but you *ought* to care. Your reputation is an instrument of usefulness, and a good name is better than gold and silver. In your passage through life there may be various instances in which you may have acted in the most conscientious manner, when your conduct may appear doubtful in the sight of others, and men are so liable to judge of another's conduct; but the Saviour hath said, "judge not," and as we cannot penetrate the heart, surely we ought not to judge. Then there is an equal disposition in man to evil speaking, and to be evil spoken of is one of the characteristics of those who follow the Redeemer; and the sufferings the Christian endures for Christ are called "the reproach of Christ." There is Paul under misrepresentation from the Corinthians, to which he refers when he says, "But with me it is a very small thing that I should be judged of you, or of man's judgment," and "Our rejoicing is this, the testimony of our conscience that in simplicity and godly sincerity, not with fleshly wisdom, but by the grace of God, we have had our conversation in the world, and more abundantly to you-ward." And we might refer to Joseph, whose innocence was brought to light in so remarkable a manner; and to David, who, though accused by Saul, yet could turn to God and say, "Lord, my heart is not haughty, nor mine eyes lofty, neither do I exercise myself in things too high for me."

Let us here learn the blessedness of those who are reconciled to God by the death of His Son, and who, having been renewed in the spirit of their minds, now walk in "newness of life." "He is near that justifies them" continually. And we may remark that God is near the sinner to condemn him. You cannot escape from His presence—from His eye—or from His hand. How can you escape if you "neglect so great salvation"? "He is near" to observe you continually, to record all you do, to bring every thought into judgment with every secret thing; and if you continue to despise Him He will be near to punish you. At the same time He calls upon you to return, and declares that "He will receive you graciously and love you freely." If you humble yourselves at the foot of the cross, and say, "Other lords have had dominion over us, but henceforth will we be called by Thy name," He will be near you now to defend and to bless, and you shall dwell for ever near Him, where in His presence is fullness of joy, and at His right hand where there are pleasures for ever.

XXVII.

HEAR!

(Delivered on Thursday Evening, April 16th, 1878.)

"*Hear, and your soul shall live.*"—ISAIAH lv. 3.

MAN is a fallen, guilty, depraved, perishing creature. This is implied in all the doctrines of the Gospel, and confirmed by all history, observation, and experience. His deliverance from this state is called a "great salvation." I hope you all admit this truth. There are some who believe it who may abuse it; and it is abused when it is employed to prevent our using means to alarm the careless, and to convert the sinner from the error of his ways. God Himself requires us to use means. Therefore the Scriptures say, "Draw near to me, and I will draw near to you." He Himself uses them. He addresses men as *rational* creatures; He informs, He expostulates, He argues, He pleads, He persuades; He employs hope, and fear, promises and threatenings; He sets before men a blessing and a curse, life and death, and commands them to choose the good, and refuse the evil. So our evangelical prophet, in His name, and under the inspiration of His Spirit, calls upon us to employ the means that God has appointed, and says, "Ho, every one that thirsteth, come ye to the waters, and he that hath no money; come ye, buy and eat; yea, come, buy wine and milk, without money and without price." If it be said that the persons thus addressed were spiritually athirst, we deny it; they were indeed spiritually blind; therefore the prophet says, "Wherefore do ye spend money for that which is not bread? and your labour for that which satisfieth not?"

Our text contains two things: a requisition and a privilege. "Hear," this is the requisition; "and your souls shall live;" this is the privilege. Sin entered the world by the ear, and grace enters by the same medium. Man was lost by hearkening to the voice of his worst enemy, and he is saved by hearkening to the voice of his best friend. "Faith cometh by hearing, and hearing by the word of God."

I. Now attend to THE REQUISITION. It is expresssd in one word, "Hear"; but how much does this word comprehend! In order to understand it, it will be necessary to ask and answer *three* questions.

First, *Whom should we hear?*

It is God Himself. He not only demands, but deserves always to be heard; whether we consider the greatness of His power, or the relation in which He stands to us. We should exclaim with the Jews, but with a better spirit, "all that the Lord commanded us, we will do," for He is our Father; and should not a father be heard? He is our Master, and should not a master be heard? He is our Sovereign, and should not a sovereign be heard? He is our Benefactor, and should not a benefactor be heard? You should also remember, that all He says is true and important. That cannot be important which is not true, but that may be true which is not important. Here, however, we always find them combined. His message is "a faithful saying, and worthy of all acceptation." He never deceives, He never trifles with us. His words are spirit, and they are truth.

Secondly, *How does God speak?*

He does not speak to us in a voice from heaven, or in dreams and visions, "as He spake in times past to the fathers by the holy prophets." Yet He speaks, and He really speaks to us. In how many ways are you able to convey your sentiments to others! The pressure of a finger may awaken rapture; the glance of an eye can say, "I love you." By a few strokes on paper, you may tell your meaning in Paris, or New York, or in China. Now, brethren, can He who gives us such powers of communication, be at a loss Himself, if He deigns to inform us! Impossible. We may reason with David, "He that planted the ear, shall not He hear? He that formed the eye, shall not He see? He that chastiseth the heathen, shall not He correct? He that teacheth man knowledge, shall not He know?"

He speaks by His works of creation. "The heavens declare the glory of God, and the firmament sheweth His handy work. Day unto day uttereth speech, and night unto night sheweth knowledge. There is no speech nor language where their voice is not heard." "All His works praise Him," by proclaiming His wisdom, power, and goodness.

He speaks to us by the dispensations of His providence. This is the meaning of Micah, when he says, "Hear ye the rod, and who hath appointed it." Ah! by these dispensations He can speak home, and to the purpose. David knew this, and therefore said, "It was good for me that I was afflicted; before I was afflicted I went astray; but now have I kept Thy word."

Conscience is God speaking in man; sometimes in whispers, and sometimes in thunders. Some of you have found it no easy thing to commence an evil course; for at your very entrance upon it, conscience has said, "Forbear, for the end of these things is death." "Her steps take hold on hell," but still you proceed. Then the admonitioner becomes the reprover, and the reprover the accuser. Better a thousand times would it have been for you never to have had a conscience, than thus to have done "despite to the Spirit of grace."

The Scriptures are above everything else as God speaking to us. They are the words which the Holy Ghost speaketh. They are all written by the inspiration of God, and are "profitable for doctrine, for reproof, for correction, for instruction in righteousness." Whenever you read the Scriptures, imagine that God addresses you.

Then also He speaks to us by the mouth of His servants, who "warn every man, and teach every man in all wisdom that they may present every man perfect in Christ Jesus." "These men shew unto you the way of salvation." They call upon you to exercise repentance towards God, and faith in our Lord Jesus Christ; to "behold the Lamb of God, that taketh away the sins of the world."

Thirdly, *How are we to hear?*

You are to hear with *attention*. This is something very different from coming to the house of God to spend an idle hour, or to let your mind like the fool's eye wander to the ends of the earth. There are some who reckon the preacher their enemy because he tells them the truth. But Job could say, "I have esteemed the words of His mouth more than my necessary food." And David could say, "O how love I Thy word!" and describing a good man, he says, "It is his meditation day and night."

You should hear with *application*. Say, "I will hear what God the Lord will say concerning me." There are some who hear for others. They resemble Peter, who said, "Lord, and what shall this man do?" It would be much better for you to say with Saul of Tarsus, "Lord, what wilt Thou have *me* to do?" Those who hear for others often misapply the word, and suffer self to escape. "You gave it well," said a person to me one day, "to Mrs. such-a-one." "Oh," I answered, "I intended that for *yourself*." But so it often is. Whatever comes before you, brethren, you should look after your own interest in it. If it be a promise, you should enquire, "Is it intended for me?" If a reproof, "Do I fall under it?" If a consolation, "Does it encourage me?"

You are also to hear *practically*. Hearing is not religion, as some people imagine; but one of the means of becoming religious. "If ye know these things," said the Saviour, "happy are ye if ye do them." It was not a bad reply of a poor woman when asked if the sermon was done, who said, "No, it is not yet practised." Our Saviour said, "Blessed are they who hear the Word of God and keep it." You should hear the Word, and then go and preach it over again; and reduce it to practice.

Above all, you should hear the Word of God *prayerfully*. You must pray over it because "the excellency of the power is of God, and not of men." "Paul may plant, and Apollos may water, but God giveth the increase." Hearing of a remedy may be necessary to your availing yourself of it, but hearing of it without applying it will never cure your disease. Hearing of a refuge will never secure you, unless you enter it. We could, if time permitted, exemplify it by our Saviour's comparison at the close of His sermon on the Mount. "Therefore, whosoever heareth these sayings of mine, and *doeth them*, I will liken him unto a wise man which built his house on a rock."

II. We must now pass from the requisition to THE PRIVILEGE. "Hear, and your soul shall live."

The privilege has four attributes. Let us just glance at them.

The first is *spiritual*. "Hear, and your *soul* shall live." I fear this is no recommendation to some. They have no more regard for their souls than as if they had none. "They are men of the world, who have their portion in this life." They have all their portion upon the earth. Like the horse-leech, they fasten upon everything fleshly. All their concern regards the outer man; to get money and spend it; to dress and adorn the body; to nurse it in sickness and pamper it in health, is all the concern of thousands: they never enquire, "How can my soul be saved?" Sometimes they die as they live. They send for the physician to prescribe for them, and for the lawyer to make their will, and arrange the time and manner of their funeral; but utter not a word about their souls, but die as though they had none. One is ready to exclaim in such a dying room, Where is your immortal spirit going? Is your soul saved? A man in a proper frame of mind would say, "Oh, it is of little importance what becomes of my poor body, if its remains are consumed in the fire, or carried down by the flood, or devoured by worms, so that my soul be saved in the day of the Lord Jesus." "The soul is the standard of the man," and he is the blessed man who is receiving what Peter calls "the end" of his faith, even the salvation of his soul; and who with the Apostle can say, "Blessed be the God and Father of our Lord Jesus Christ, who hath blessed us with all spiritual blessings in heavenly places in Christ."

Secondly, it is *vital*. It regards life. Life, whatever subtle thing it is, and however incapable of definition, is the most precious and valued boon in the world; because it is the foundation of all possessions, of all enjoyments, of all actions, and of all improvements. Solomon therefore says, "A living dog is better than a dead lion;" and Satan, though the father of lies, for once spake true, and said, "Skin for skin, all that a man hath will he give for his life." What is this poor life which we spend as a shadow? "We dwell in houses of clay, whose foundation is in the dust, which is crushed before the moth." It is full of "vanity and vexation of spirit." Still the Christian's life is worthy of the name. It is preparatory to a life of infinite honour, of freedom, of glory, and of blessedness. "In His presence is fulness of joy, and at His right hand are pleasures for evermore." How often in the Scriptures is it called "eternal life," over which the shadow of death shall not even flit! An eternal life, begun here, now enjoyed in the "peace passing all understanding!" But who can describe what this life will be hereafter! for "Eye hath not seen, ear hath not heard, neither have entered into the heart of man, the things which God hath prepared for them that love Him." "It doth not yet appear what we shall be, but we know that "when He shall appear we shall be like Him, for we shall see Him as He is."

Thirdly, it is *ensured*; there is no uncertainty in the case. "Hear, and your souls *shall* live." This, brethren, is the promise of a God that cannot lie, the promise of Him who is a God of truth, just and right is He. When you have to deal with men, absolute confidence would be nothing less than folly. "Surely," says David, "men of low degree are vanity, and men of high degree are a lie: to be laid in the balance, they are altogether lighter than vanity." And says his son, "Confidence in an unfaithful man in time of trouble is like a broken tooth, and a foot out of joint," which is not only unprofitable, but painful and vexatious. So it is with men.

> "Sure as on creatures we depend,
> Our hopes in disappointment end."

They will be found like "broken cisterns" or like "bruised reeds;" but God is a rock." Even Balaam could bear this testimony. He says, "God is not a man that He should lie, nor the son of man that He should repent. Hath He said, and shall He not do it? or hath He spoken, and shall He not make it good?" Men may fail in fulfilling their promises through forgetfulness, or a change of mind, or by sheer depravity, or a shameful dishonesty and falsehood; but with God "there is no variableness neither shadow of turning." "I the Lord change not, therefore ye sons of Jacob are not consumed."

Fourthly, this privilege is *personal.* "Hear and *your* soul shall live." Whose soul? The souls of those who hear; and *all* of *them* of whatever nation or condition they may be. "Hear," ye *aged* sinners, "and your souls shall live," though God could righteously reject you, after despising Him for so many years; but even at the eleventh hour He waiteth that He may be gracious unto you, and says, "Seek ye the Lord while He may be found." "Hear," ye *young*, "and your souls shall live," and you shall enjoy a thousand pleasures and advantages which are not to be found in religion if you embrace it not in early life; you shall know the fulness of that promise, "They that seek me early shall find me;" and if you die early —and oh, how many do die in early life! how many of our roses and lilies are nipt in the bud!—His grace will be sufficient for you; and if you live, God will sanctify to you every trial, and will say unto you, "I remember thee, the kindness of thy youth, the love of thine espousals," and you shall be able to look back on a life spent to His glory. "Hear," ye *rich*, "and your souls shall live," and your prosperity shall not destroy you. "Hear," ye *poor*, and your souls shall live," and you shall be "rich in faith." Yea, all who love the Saviour, whether rich or poor, ignorant or learned; all here form one family, for they are "all one in Christ Jesus." "He never said to the seed of Jacob, seek ye me in vain." God might have treated us with severity, but He exercises forbearance. He might have treated us with contempt, but "He remembered us in our low estate," and without our desert, and without our desire, devised" means whereby His banished ones should not be expelled from Him." And He has made all this known, and by a thousand means is arousing your attention, and inducing us to seek the things that belong to our peace before they be hid from our eyes. He is always saying, "Come unto Me;" "Hear, and your souls shall live."

We see also, the perverseness and folly of men who are insensible to all this. "God," says Elihu, "speaks once, yea twice, yet man perceiveth it not." He often resembles Pharoah, exclaiming, "Who is the Lord, that I should obey Him?" He may not speak the same words, but actions speak louder than words, and by these he says unto God, "Depart from me, I desire not the knowledge of Thy ways." All other creatures hear God when He speaks. The sun hears Him, and "knoweth his going down;" and even the restless sea hears Him when He says, "Hither shalt thou come and no farther, and here shall thy proud waves be stayed." Comets never deviate from their prescribed course, and "fire and hail, snow and vapours, and stormy winds fulfil His word." There are only two classes of beings in all God's universe that disobey His voice: devils and wicked men: and those who share in their disobedience, will share in their punishment. Thus God will be constrained to say, "Depart, ye cursed: I never knew you." The reverse therefore of our text is true: if you hear not, your souls shall die; and oh, what is it for a soul to die? It is not annihilation—not the extinction of its being, but of its well-being; its exclusion from God, the Fountain of Life. It is called "the second death," which is more dreadful than the first. O, "how shall we escape if we neglect so great salvation?" "See that ye refuse not Him that speaketh. For if they escaped not who refused him that spoke on earth, much more shall not we escape, if we turn away from Him that speaketh from heaven."

XXVIII.

THE LORD'S FLOCK.

(Delivered on Thursday Evening, March 5th, 1846.)

"*I will also leave in the midst of thee an afflicted and poor people, and they shall trust in the name of the Lord. The remnant of Israel shall not do iniquity nor speak lies; neither shall a deceitful tongue be found in their mouth; for they shall feed and lie down and none shall make them afraid.*"—ZEPHANIAH iii. 12, 13.

ARE these words spoken of the Jews only, or of Christians also? Yes, of Christians also. The former were designed to be the prefigurations of the latter. "Whatever things were written aforetime were written for our learning, that we through patience and comfort of the Scriptures might have hope." Hence another name is imposed upon the godly in the New Testament: they are called "The Israel of God." There we also read, and this is enough to justify our application this evening, "They that are of faith are blessed with faithful Abraham." "If ye be Christ's then are ye Abraham's seed, and heirs according to the promise." "For we are the circumcision who worship God in the Spirit, who rejoice in Christ Jesus and have no confidence in the flesh."

The words regard their state, their character, and their privilege. "I will also leave in the midst of thee an afflicted and poor people, and they shall trust in the name of the Lord."

I. Where are they to be found? What is their station? You need not wonder at this question. Surely as God is their Father and Friend, and as HE is able to do all things, you will naturally conclude that He will exempt them from everything distressing, and possess them with a sufficiency and confluence of all good things. Such would be the expectation and conclusion of depraved reason, but "the Lord seeth not as man seeth." "My ways are not your ways, neither my thoughts your thoughts, saith the Lord." Therefore He says, "I will leave in the midst of thee an afflicted and poor people."

"An *afflicted* people." "Many are the afflictions of the righteous." They are very deeply sensible of their guilt and depravity and vileness. There is nothing by which they are more afflicted than by their remaining corruptions, their wandering thoughts, their cold affections, their backsliding from God in heart as well as in life. Paul was a sufferer. What a catalogue does he give us in his address to the Corinthians! "Thrice was I beaten with rods, once was I stoned, thrice I suffered shipwreck, a night and a day I have been in the deep." We have not time to read the whole, but this was not his affliction; it was *sin* that induced him to exclaim, "O, wretched man that I am; when I would do good evil is present with me."

But they also have their outward trials. There is not a Christian upon earth but is hated by the world. There is not a Christian but is called to endure some kind of persecution, for "all that will live godly in the present world shall suffer persecution." Yes, Christians are liable to the open and outward calamities of life as well as others. They suffer disappointment and indisposition. Christians also are sometimes too much depressed by these. Many of them have exclaimed in the hour of trial, "I am the man that hath seen affliction by the rod of His wrath. He hath led me and brought me into darkness, and not into light."

They are also a "*poor* people;" this is expressive of their spiritual experience. Therefore our Saviour saith, "Blessed are the poor in spirit, for theirs is the kingdom of heaven." Not the poor in condition, you will observe, but "the poor in spirit." That is, they who know that the fall has deprived them of their righteousness and strength; they who are convinced that in themselves there dwelleth no good thing; they who are made willing (sensible of their poverty) to live on alms, who will readily ascribe to undeserved kindness all they enjoy and hope for. And this may be said regarding all the subjects of divine grace.

But it will apply also to their circumstance. "Hearken, my beloved brethren, hath not God chosen the poor of this world rich in faith, and heirs of the kingdom which He hath promised to them that love Him?" Not that He hath chosen the poor exclusively. In all ages there have been a few taken from the upper ranks, and "*Whosoever* cometh unto Me," saith the Saviour, "I will in no wise cast out." Nor universally has God chosen them; but this is the general complexion of the mass of His followers in all periods. Look at their Saviour:

He was poor. Some of you talk of poverty, but He was poor. "Foxes," said He, "have holes, and the birds of the air have nests, but the Son of Man hath not where to lay His head." He was sustained by the creatures of His power and of His bounty. And where were His followers? "Have any of the rulers," it was scornfully asked, "believed on Him?" But "the common people heard Him gladly." Peter said, "Silver and gold have I none;" and Paul years after this said, "Even to this present time we both hunger and thirst, and have no certain dwelling place." Take any Christian church now, and examine the members; when the congregation withdraw then go and observe the household of faith that surround His table. So it was in the beginning of Christianity, so it is still. As the Apostle says, "God chooses the weak things of the world to confound the mighty." In this Our Saviour more than acquiesced, for He "rejoiced in spirit," and said, "I thank Thee, O Father, Lord of heaven and earth, that Thou hast hid these things from the wise and prudent, and hast revealed them unto babes; even so, Father, for so it seemed good in Thy sight." And when in the latter-day glory there is to be such a revival of the Spirit of the Gospel, how will it be accomplished? "That all shall know Him from the greatest event to the least?" No such thing; but "from the least even unto the greatest." This has always been God's way.

II. Pass we on from their state to observe THEIR CHARACTER; derived from their confidence, excellence, and sincerity.

Their character is derived from their *confidence*. "They shall trust in the name of the Lord." This confidence extends to everything of which they stand in need. They trust in the Lord for eternal life. This is the extent of their confidence. Oh, what an act of trust must that be, which enables me, a sinner, to expect an immensity, an eternity of glory and blessedness from that very Being I offended times and ways without number, and who could so easily and so righteously destroy me! This would have been impossible had they not known there was a Mediator between God and man; that Christ "suffered the Just for the unjust," and that "in Him there is righteousness and strength."

They trust in Him for grace as well as for glory. They know that they are guilty, but that there is pardon through the blood of the cross. They know that they are ignorant, but in Christ there is wisdom; that they themselves are weak, but that in Christ there is strength to make them equal to their day. And their confidence is not presumption; it is founded in knowledge, as confidence always should be, and always will be, unless it is the confidence of fools. "They that know Thy name will put their trust in Thee." "They know whom they have believed." The confidence of the righteous therefore is based on the Word of God, and founded on all the great and precious promises.

This Scriptural and saving confidence is always accompanied by the use of means, and obedience to the revealed will of God. This confidence is founded in holiness. "The remnant of Israel shall not do iniquity." But this is to be taken with qualifications. God forbid we should plead for sin, but we must not falsify the language of Scripture, which assures us that "there is not a just man upon earth;" that "in many things we offend all;" that "if we say we have no sin we deceive ourselves." But sin has not "dominion over them, for they are not under the law but under grace." They do not obey it in the lusts thereof. There is no one sin which they habitually indulge in. Sin of every kind is not only their avoidance, but their aversion. They are "dead indeed unto sin, but alive unto God." Their imperfections are their burden and grief. Their desire is to be delivered from all transgression and to be entirely devoted to the service of God; and the distresses that arise from their sins is a clear proof that God has given them a renewed heart. This is the meaning of the promise, "Blessed are the pure in heart, for they shall see God;" that is, those who love heart purity.

Thirdly, it is derived from their *uprightness*: "nor speak lies; neither shall a deceitful tongue be found in their mouth;" that is, in simplicity and godly sincerity they shall have their conversation in the world. They are like Nathaniel—they are Israelites indeed in whom, though there are imperfections, "there is no guile." They are not like those who profess to know God, but who in works deny Him; they are not like those who have "the form of godliness, but deny the power thereof." They are not like painted sepulchres, "beautiful without, but full of rottenness within." What they appear to be, and what they profess to be, they really are. As an evidence of this they do not consider a faithful preacher their enemy because he tells them the truth. They come to the light that their deeds may be reproved. They try themselves by the divine decision; and, lest after all the examinations of themselves, they should be deceived, they implore divine scrutiny, saying with David, "Search me, O God, and know my heart; try me, and know my thoughts, and see if there be any wicked way in me, and lead me in the way everlasting." There is nothing they more dread than hypocrisy. It is fear of hypocrisy that sometimes keeps them back from a profession of religion, and it is this fear that makes them silent with regard to any communications respecting their own experience, lest they should say more than they feel. Here some of them possess very little light, but their heart is right with God. The Lord has laid hold of their hearts. Their spirit is with Him, and if He obtains the heart, everything else will follow in course, and the way of the Lord will be found to be strength to the upright. The Christian will get clearer views as he goes on, and "the Lord will give grace and glory, no good thing will He withhold from them that walk uprightly."

III. Observe THEIR PRIVILEGE. It is represented historically. The image is common in Scripture, and one that is most pleasing: "They shall feed and lie down and none shall make them afraid."

Consider His charge. Personally considered, they are His sheep. Collectively considered, they are His flock. So we read of "one fold and one Shepherd." Individually considered, these are not only sheep but lambs, and "He feeds His flock like a shepherd, and gathers the lambs in His arms."

The privilege takes in three things.

First, the *pasture*. "They shall feed and lie down." Their food must be spiritual; suited to their characters as new creatures. The things they long after are congenial to their new nature. They must have, therefore, new food. Therefore is it said, "Blessed are they that do hunger and thirst after righteousness." Hence we read of "the bread of life," and "the water of life;" of "the provisions of God's house," and of His promising to "satisfy his poor with bread." Sometimes persons speak of the ordinances as if they were the pastures; but they are not the food, but the meadows in which the food grows, and in which we are fed. Or, to alter the image a little, and to use the language of the Saviour himself, He is the food; for He says, "My flesh is meat indeed, and My blood is drink indeed."

Secondly, observe their *repose:* "They shall feed and *lie down*." This, in connection with the former, is what the Church is inquiring for. "Tell me, O thou whom my soul loveth, where thou feedest, where thou makest thy flock to rest at noon, for why should I be as one that turneth aside by the flocks of thy companions?" In an Eastern country, and on a warm day, and when moving from place to place, how desirable, especially at noon, is it to take repose: and the Lord has provided it for His people! David tells us he was made to lie down in green pastures as well as to feed beside the still waters. I cannot explain this repose to you if you know it not by experience. By believing we enter into rest. "Being justified by faith, we have peace with God through our Lord Jesus." Under the teachings of His Spirit and providence, His people learn "in whatsoever state they are, therewith to be content," and cast all their care upon Him who careth for them. Thus their minds are kept in perfect peace, being stayed upon God, and they feel a degree of that "peace which passeth all understanding."

The third is their *security*: "and none shall make them afraid." Sheep are the most timorous of all creatures; everything alarms them, and this is too much the case with those they represent. How then can it be said, "none shall make them afraid?"

You must make a distinction. The sacred writers often represent things as they ought to be instead of as they are. Thus they teach us much. So Solomon says, "The wicked fleeth when no man pursueth, but the righteous is bold as a lion." That is, he should be bold as a lion; his duty and his principles require it. He ought to be filled with holy courage, though he is not. So here, nothing *should* make man afraid; nothing will, nothing can, hurt him, if God be his protector. For "if God be for us who can be against us?" "Who is he that can harm you, if ye be followers of that which is good?"

Sometimes they are all enabled to realize this. Then their privilege becomes their experience, and they feel a holy confidence in God, in the midst of all their trials—before the face of all their persecutors—while with David they are enabled to say, "The Lord is my light and my salvation, whom shall I fear? The Lord is the strength of my heart, of whom shall I be afraid? Though an host should encamp against me, I will not fear; though wars should rise against me, in this will I be confident."

We here clearly perceive that it is not the will of God that His people should walk mournfully and hang down their heads like bulrushes. He has commanded His servants to comfort them: "rejoice evermore," "rejoice in the Lord always, and again I say rejoice."

We are led to congratulate some of you. Some of you have had your confidence in regard to men abused, but you have been brought to trust in the Lord. What are the things which men so prize, the acquisition of which lead men to congratulate you? They are not such things that regard your substantial, your eternal happiness. But we congratulate those of you who are trusting in the Lord, who are feeding in these pastures, and are lying down in sweet repose, secure and quiet from fear of evil.

And why should any of you, though you have been strangers to all this till now, continue so? Here are persons who, if it were allowable, could rise up and address you, saying, "Come with us and we will do you good; for the Lord hath spoken good concerning Israel." "O, taste and see that the Lord is good; blessed is the man that trusteth in Him!" Why will you not hearken to them? Why not listen to those who have engaged in, and can therefore recommend, His service? who have not only heard of the mercy of God, but have tasted that the Lord is gracious? Listen, not only to the Saints but to the Saviour! "Hearken diligently unto me, and eat ye that which is good, and let your soul delight itself in fatness. Incline your ear and come unto me; hear, and your soul shall live."

XXIX.

THE LORD'S PEOPLE.

(A Thursday Evening Lecture.)

"*And I will bring the third part through the fire, and will refine them as silver is refined, and will try them as gold is tried: they shall call on my name, and I will hear them: I will say, It is my people: and they shall say, The Lord is my God.*"—ZECHARIAH xiii. 9.

THE Scriptures of truth, how precious are they! "More to be desired are they than gold; yea, than much fine gold, sweeter also than honey and the honeycomb." Among other things they shew us a hiding place, a resting place, and a dwelling place; and we need all these. As exposed, we need a hiding place, and we have it. Where? What is it? "Thou art my hiding place," says David, "Thou shalt preserve me from trouble, Thou shalt compass me about with songs of deliverance." As weary, we need a resting place; and we have it. Where? What is it? "Rest in the Lord, and wait patiently for Him." "Return unto thy rest, O my soul." "They have forgotten their resting place," says God by Jeremiah. And we always need accommodation and supplies, and therefore require also a dwelling place; and we have one. Where and what is this? Moses tells us in his sublime song: "Lord, Thou hast been our dwelling place in all generations." For the knowledge of all these things we are indebted to His word, where are exceeding great and precious promises. One of these is to come under our review this evening, and is thus expressed: "I will bring the third part through the fire, and will refine them as silver is refined, and will try them as gold is tried: they shall call on My name and I will hear them: I will say, It is My people; and they shall say, The Lord is My God." Let us here consider four things: The first regards their number; the second regards their condition; the third regards their conduct; and the fourth regards their privilege.

I. Regards THEIR NUMBER. "I will bring the third part through the fire." Not as if only one third were to suffer. No, "whom the Lord loveth He chasteneth, and scourgeth every son whom He receiveth." "As many as I love, I rebuke and chasten." It refers to the nation at large. This is the meaning of "the third part," and this is not to be taken as a definite number of God's people, or as one out of three in a place or number of a nation. We have other representations. One in the parable of the sower. We are told that one part only was fertile. Is there then only one profitable hearer out of three? Elsewhere it is called a remnant or part of the whole.

One day a young man said to Our Saviour, "Are there few that shall be saved?" Without answering *him*, He said to those around, "Strive to enter in at the strait gate;" as much as to say, Whether the saved be many or few, if you would be one, you must strive properly; "for many I say unto you will seek to enter in but shall not be able." Instead of indulging yourself in speculative enquiries concerning the condition of others, be anxious about the state of your own soul.

There are some who reduce the number of the people of God too much; there are others who multiply them too much. While the first of these errs on the left hand, the second errs on the right; for by multiplying them more than the Scriptures justify, two evils will arise. We shall neglect to endeavour to save many of our fellow creatures, supposing them already in a state of safety; and persons will feel more disposed to be easy in their own condition, calculating upon their security, while destruction and misery are in their path. According to the creed of some, there are but few wicked enough to be turned into hell. How then account we for the express declarations of our Lord and His apostles? Our Saviour said, "Strait is the gate, and narrow is the way that leadeth unto life, and few there be that find it;" whereas "wide is the gate, and broad is the way that leadeth to destruction, and many there be that go in thereat." And, says the Saviour, "Fear not, little flock." It is for this reason that John speaks of the unregenerate, as "the whole world which lieth in wickedness." See again, the distinction made in Scripture between the righteous and the wicked. It is the declaration of eternal truth: "Except your righteousness shall exceed the righteousness of the Scribes and Pharisees, ye shall in nowise enter the kingdom of heaven." "Except ye be converted and become as little children, ye shall in nowise enter the kingdom of heaven." "If any man be in Christ he is a new creature." "The grace of God which bringeth salvation teacheth us, that denying ungodliness and worldly lusts, we should live soberly, righteously, and godly in this present evil world." How many are there among those who are hearers of the gospel who receive not the truth; and how many are there among the members of churches, who are professors only, and possess not the grace of God. Yet God always had a people for His name; and I am persuaded that their number is increasing, and "the Lord add unto His people how many soever they be, an hundred fold." And may He hasten the time predicted by Isaiah, when "He shall cause them that come of Jacob to take root; Israel shall blossom and bud, and fill the face of the world with fruit."

II. Note THEIR CONDITION. "And I will bring the third part through the fire, and will refine them as silver is refined, and will try them as gold is tried."

"I will bring the third part through the fire." "Fire," in the language of Scripture, means very sharp and searching afflictions. I need not take up your time to prove this. It is needless also to mention the various kinds of affliction which God's people are called to endure. Formerly they suffered persecution. The Apostle says, "All that will live godly in Christ Jesus shall suffer persecution;" and our Saviour said, "He that taketh not his cross and followeth after me, is not worthy of me." What dreadful scenes of persecution have some witnessed! They were stoned, they were sawn asunder, were tempted, were slain with the sword; they wandered about in sheep-skins; being destitute, afflicted, tormented! We talk of persecution: what persecution have we? What danger have we of losing our lives, or even our liberty or substance by a profession of religion? Some have incurred the loss of friendship, others have been sneered at, slandered and reproached for the sake of religion. But where persecution is not to be found in this way, yet the end can be answered and commonly is, by personal and relative afflictions; and here, every heart well knows its own bitterness. But if they are in the fire, they are not to remain there, they are not to perish in their afflictions. "I will bring them through the fire," says God; and says the Psalmist, "We went through fire and through water, but Thou broughtest us into a wealthy place." "Many are the afflictions of the righteous, but the Lord delivereth him out of them all"—here partially, and hereafter completely. So we read of passing through the waters, and through the floods. Though the people of God may be in floods, they are not to remain there, but to pass through them, and even while they are there, God is along with them, to support and comfort them.

Observe, secondly, they were to derive advantage from them. " I will refine them as silver is refined, and try them as gold is tried." The Apostle addresses the Hebrews, saying, " We have had fathers of our flesh which corrected us, and we gave them reverence: shall we not much rather be in subjection unto the Father of Spirits and live? For they verily for a few days chastened us after their own pleasure, but He for our profit, that we may be partakers of His holiness. Now no chastening for the present seemeth to be joyous, but grievous; nevertheless, *afterward* it yieldeth the peaceable fruit of righteousness unto them which are exercised thereby."

What advantage and what benefit do they derive thereby? Two benefits are here specified. The first is purification. " I will refine them as silver is refined." The furnace takes away the dross from the silver, and renders it less indeed in bulk, but more valuable in quality, and fitter for use. A Christian may be reduced by affliction: but if when he has less of the creature, he has more of the Creator; if when he has less of the world, he has more of the word; and if he gains by his losses more spirituality, he will have no reason to complain. If he becomes more wise, more holy, and more heavenly, he will be better able to serve his generation according to the will of God, and to adorn the doctrine of God his Saviour in all things.

The second is peace: "and will try them as gold is tried." Gold is tried in the fire in order to ascertain its currency and excellency. God knows the religion of His people, for it is all His own production and maintaining and perfecting, but it is necessary that others should know, and it is necessary they should know themselves the reality of their principles, and that they should know the degree of the graces they possess as well as the reality of them. He brings them into circumstances to verify and display them. This display indeed will be made principally at the last day, when God shall have performed the good work He has begun; and therefore Peter says, " That the trial of your faith being much more precious than of gold, which perisheth though it be tried with fire, might be found unto praise and honour and glory at the appearing of Jesus Christ.

III. Note THEIR CONDUCT. " They shall call on My name."

God's people are a praying people. It is not only here implied that they are a praying people, but that they will pray more in their trials, and in consequence of their trials. This is one of the designs of God in sending them affliction: as He says, "I will go and return to my place, till they acknowledge their offence, and seek my face: in their affliction they will seek me early." When this end is answered it is well, and no affliction will be deemed too severe that brings us to a throne of grace. But there are persons who never pour out a prayer but when God's hand is upon them. This is not the case with God's people. They have inward principles and dispositions which actuate them; they have "living waters within them springing up to everlasting life;" but these principles may be aided much by external excitements, and they often are. Therefore the Apostle seems to have prayed more frequently and fervently when he had the "thorn in the flesh," "the messenger of Satan to buffet." "For this thing," said he, "I besought the Lord thrice;" that is, more frequently and fervently.

Then they have "a thorn in the flesh"? Yes, and they have a throne of grace, to which they can repair in all their wants and weakness, and all this is from the supply of the Spirit of Jesus Christ; and they ought to approach this with confidence, knowing that God is able to supply them, and that He will supply them. They want deliverance, but they must seek for it in God's way, and in God's time. Indeed all blessings are to be obtained through Christ; but we read, "for all these things God will be enquired of by the house of Israel, to do it for them." It is no wonder that God should require this, and say, "Call upon me in the day of trouble, and I will deliver thee; and thou shalt glorify me." And it is no wonder that they should exercise this, and say with David, "In the day of my trouble I will call upon the Lord, and He will hear me." They are not to pray in vain: "They shall call upon me, and I will hear." This is enough, Christians. This assurance of God should be enough to induce you to continue instant in prayer. It is desirable to look after answers to prayer, and it is pleasing to observe them; but if you cannot discover them in various instances, and see how your prayers are answered, yet you have enough to rely upon and encourage you. You have the declaration of His own word, that "He never said to the seed of Jacob, seek ye me in vain."

IV. Their privilege. "They shall call on my name, and I will hear them: I will say, It is my people; and they shall say, The Lord is my God."

This is a blessed acknowledgment, and you will observe it is *mutual* too. Everything, indeed, is mutual between God and His people. They love Him because He first loves them. He chooses them, and they choose Him. He calls them His people, and they call Him their God. He says, "This people have I formed for myself;" and they say, "The Lord is my portion, saith my soul." "He takes pleasure in them that fear Him, in them that hope in His mercy;" and they "rejoice in the Lord," and their souls are joyful in their God.

He not only makes them His, but He acknowledges them as His. He says, "It is My people." He is not satisfied with the reality of the thing, but He will proclaim it. They, on the other hand, are not satisfied with the certainty of their interest in Him, they wish also to acknowledge Him, "and they shall say the Lord *is* my God." Well, He says to them, "This is my people,"—in many a devotional prayer, in many a humble hymn of praise, in many a reading of the Scriptures, in many a hearing of His word, and in many a whisper of His Holy Spirit. And what is it that they so long and pray for but this: "Say unto my soul I am thy salvation." "Show me a token for good." On the other hand, He allows them to say, "The Lord is my God." They say this by many a supplication, by many a groan which cannot be uttered, by many a prayer poured into His bosom. God says this practically, "It is my people," that others may know it by deeds as well as words; by interpositions on their behalf in the course of His providence, and by support, and peace, and joy in the course of His grace, and by enabling them to triumph in the valley of the shadow of death. Thus He says in the hearing of others as well as to them, "It is my people." And they say this practically, that those around may know it as well as God Himself. They say "The Lord is my God"—by adhering to His cause, by preferring His will to their own gratification, and by delighting in His service and way; by this they impress others and induce them to say, "This is the seed which the Lord hath blessed," and to take knowledge of them that have been with Jesus.

In conclusion, let me urge you to "take hold of the skirt of him that is a Jew, saying, we will go with you, for we perceive that God is with you." You see who are the blessed people. Congratulations are often addressed to the successful wicked, but "a man's life consisteth not in the abundance of the things which he possesseth." I should rather hail the man whose conscience, awakened from its slumbers, is asking, "What must I do to be saved?" than the man who, convinced of sin, is at the Redeemer's feet crying, "Lord, be merciful to me a sinner." I congratulate such. Though now they may be suffering affliction, they will have occasion to say, "It was good for me to have been afflicted," and soon they will have "quietness and assurance for ever." I have observed persons searching for happiness here, but have clearly seen that they have not found it. Why will you not hearken to those who have made the trial? who from their experience can say, "Wisdom's ways are ways of pleasantness, and all her paths are peace"? They now no longer ask, "Who will show us any good?" for they have found it. May you "acquaint yourselves with Him, and be at peace! thereby good shall come of it." And say with David, "Look Thou upon me, and be merciful unto me, as Thou usest to do unto them that love Thy name."

XXX.

THE KNOWLEDGE AND PRUDENCE OF CHRIST.

(Delivered on Thursday Evening, June 3rd, 1847.)

"*Now when He was in Jerusalem at the Passover, in the feast day, many believed in His name, when they saw the miracles which He did. But Jesus did not commit Himself unto them, because He knew all men, and needed not that any should testify of man; for He knew what was in man.*"—JOHN II. 23-25.

OUR Lord was now at Jerusalem, but Galilee was His principal residence. Though He was born at Bethlehem, He was brought up at Nazareth, and therefore called a Nazarene. Even Pilate inscribed in the title over His cross, "Jesus of Nazareth, the King of the Jews." But Jesus was commonly at Jerusalem at the three grand festivals. First, in obedience to the divine appointment and command, for God had said by Moses to the Jews, "Thrice in the year shall all your males appear before me in Jerusalem." Secondly, to seize opportunities of usefulness, because at these seasons there was always a great multitude, consisting of strangers as well as Jews. Our Lord was now attending the feast of the passover, and we are informed of what took place on the occasion. "Now when He was in Jerusalem at the passover, in the feast day, many believed in His name, when they saw the miracles which He did. But Jesus did not commit Himself unto them, because He knew all men, and needed not that any should testify of man; for He knew what was in man." Let us observe the subject of attention: the many that "believed in His name, when they saw the miracles which He did." The Saviour's conduct towards them: "But Jesus did not commit Himself unto them." Thirdly, the prerogative ascribed to Him: "because He knew all men, and needed not that any should testify of man; for He knew what was in man."

I. THE SUBJECT OF ATTENTION. The "many" that "believed in His name, because they saw the miracles which He did."

What were these miracles? What these miracles were, we are unable to determine; like many others, which, though really performed, were never recorded. Thus our evangelist says, in the close of his gospel, "And many other signs truly did Jesus in the presence of His disciples, which are not written in this book." And again, by a strong hyperbole, he says, "And there are also many other things which Jesus did, the which, if they should be written every one, I suppose that even the world itself could not contain the books that should be written." There are many things of which we may very safely be ignorant, and it is obvious that the Scriptures were not designed to amuse our mind, and gratify curiosity, but "to give light to them that sit in darkness, and the shadow of death, and to guide their feet into the way of peace."

It is probable, however, that one of these miracles was the purification of the temple, spoken of in the preceding words. "And the Jews' passover was at hand, and Jesus went up to Jerusalem, and found in the temple those that sold oxen and sheep and doves, and the changers of money sitting. And when He had made a scourge of small cords, He drove them all out of the temple, and the sheep and the oxen; and poured out the changers' money, and overthrew the tables; and said unto them that sold doves, Take these things hence; make not my Father's house an house of merchandise." Some may be supposed to think that this can hardly be called a miracle, and even the Jews who witnessed it, asked "What sign shewest Thou unto us, seeing that Thou doest these things?" Why, had He not done them? Was not this a sufficient sign? Why, did you suffer Him to do this? Why not resist Him, and drive Him from the suburb of the temple? Men are very tenacious of their property, for nothing are they more ready to strike, and many are more bold and courageous when in company than when alone. Yet here was a man who walked in among these traders alone, without apparent authority, unarmed, with a scourge of small cords; who drove out, not only the sheep and oxen, but the buyers and the sellers, and threw the contents of the tables of the money-changers upon the ground. I can explain this upon no other ground than a supernatural impression and a consciousness of authority.

But what were these believers in His name who saw these miracles? Miracles were not designed for those that believe, but for those who believe not. They are designed and adapted to produce conviction, and they often have produced belief for a time, when, alas, they have produced nothing else. This was the case here. Miracles never really converted a sinner to God, never yet turned a soul from the love of sin to the love of holiness. It was not the miraculous light that changed the heart of Saul of Tarsus, though it smote him to the ground. "No," says he, "God called me by His grace, and revealed His Son in me." From the beginning of the world to the present time, souls have been converted to God in the same way : by the agency of the Holy Spirit. He it is that enlightens us with the light of the living. "He works in us to will and to do of His good pleasure," and enables us to walk in newness of life. Hear the promise of the new covenant : "I will sprinkle clean water upon you, and ye shall be clean; from all your filthiness, and from all your idols will I cleanse you. A new heart also will I give you, and a new spirit will I put within you; and I will take away the stony heart out of your flesh, and I will give you a heart of flesh." "I will pour upon the house of David, and upon the inhabitants of Jerusalem"—not the spirit of signs and wonders, the power of healing and the gift of tongues—but "the spirit of grace and of supplication." "And they shall look upon Him whom they have pierced," that is, they shall believe in a crucified Saviour; "and they shall mourn for Him, as one that mourneth for an only son;" that is, they shall feel a repentance which is unto life, which flows alone from faith in the cross of Christ. Oh, how different is this from that terror which an earthquake or a disease may produce. Real faith is not a mere notion, it is a principle which lures a man from this world, and places him under the influence of another; and this faith unites us to Him in such a way that the natural man perceiveth it not. It must be spiritually discerned, that you and I may experience the influence of that "faith which is of the operation of God's Holy Spirit."

You will observe from the chapter before us, as well as in other places, that many things may produce a faith which does not overcome the world and work by love, by which men do not stand, or walk, or live; and we learn this awful lesson that we may be convinced, and yet not converted ; we may go far, and yet not far enough; we may have our affections excited, and not be renewed in the spirit of our minds; we may have many wishes and resolutions, and yet not come after Jesus and follow Him. And, brethren, many of this class there may be. Many thus believed on Him, and "many" such, says He, "will come to me in that day, saying Lord, Lord, to whom I will declare, I never knew you." Oh, let this produce in you a salutary fear. Remember a Pharaoh who often said, "I have sinned"—a Balaam who admired the people, and wished to die their death—a Saul who had another heart given to him, but not a new one—a Herod who heard John gladly, yet who shut him up in prison, and then beheaded him—and many more who heard the Word with joy, and endured for a time, yet in a season of temptation fell away. Let this lead you solemnly to inquire whether you have any true faith in His name. And Oh that you may be "written among the living in Jerusalem!"

II. Our Saviour's conduct towards them. "But Jesus did not commit Himself unto them."

This is worthy of our attention. "He did not commit Himself unto them." He did not confide in them—He did not believe in their pretensions—He did not reckon them among His followers—He would not be intimate—He would not be familiar with them—"He did not commit Himself unto them." From whence observe two things. First, the prerogative of faith; and secondly, a lesson derivable from the Saviour's history.

First, observe the prerogative of faith. It gains the trust of Christ—He commits Himself to all those who really believe on Him. Yes, faith trusts Christ, and Christ trusts faith. The believer commits himself to Christ, and Christ commits Himself to the believer. What confidence must a man have in Christ before he can commit his eternal all into His hands! Yet such is the confidence of every real Christian. "I know whom I have believed," says he, "and am persuaded that He is able to keep that which I have committed unto Him against that day." Though the salvation of a soul be unspeakably important, and the consequences of a failure here would be remediless, yet says he, "I can trust Him with it, feeling my mind possessed of a perfect peace, being stayed upon Him. And I can also trust Him with every subordinate concern. I can trust Him with my reputation; I can trust Him with my business; I can trust Him with my friends; I can trust Him with my health; I can trust Him with my body; saying, "Though He slay me, yet will I trust in Him."

"My cares, I give you to the wind,
And shake you off like dust;
Well may I trust my all with Him
To whom my soul I trust."

Thus faith trusts Christ, and Christ equally trusts faith ; thus the believer commits himself to Christ, and Christ equally commits Himself to the believer, with all He is, and with all He has. He commits to him His counsels, His cause, and His poor. "The secret of the Lord is with them that fear Him, and He will shew them His covenant." "I can trust," says He, "such a man, for I know the principles and disposition I have wrought in him. I can trust him, and can place him in such a situation, he will not betray me ; I can trust him in any company, for he is not ashamed of Me or of My words. I can trust him even where Satan's seat is, for he will not deny my name ; I can trust him with resources and abilities ; I can trust him with riches and authority ; I know that he will ask, Lord, what wilt Thou have me to do? I know that he will not be high-minded, but fear."

It is because He thus commits Himself unto His people that there is so little minuteness and particularity in the Scriptures. When you have a full confidence in a person, and where there is much love, minuteness need not be enjoined. Upon this principle He does not tell His people how often they are to pray. He knows their disposition, and only says, "Pray, and not faint." He does not tell them how often they are to commune at His table, but only says, "As often as ye eat this bread, and drink this cup, ye do shew forth the Lord's death till He come." In the days of His flesh, with regard to those who really loved and served Him, He became intimate and familiar. He trusted them, yea, He opened His mind as they were able to bear it, and would have told them a great deal more if they could have borne it ; for He had full confidence in them, and said, "Henceforth I call you not servants, but friends, for the servant knoweth not what his Lord doeth ; but I have called you friends, for all things that I have heard of my Father, I have made known unto you."

We may also derive a lesson from the Saviour's example. It regards the Saviour's prudence. It was predicted of Him, "My Servant shall deal prudently." Prudence is wisdom applied to action, and you see how He should be distinguished : "It shall make Him of quick understanding in the fear of the Lord, and He shall not judge after the sight of His eyes, nor reprove after the hearing of His ears." You see this in His answers to questions addressed to Him. You find He does not always answer their inquiries according to their meaning, but according to His own knowledge of their condition. You see it also in caution with regard to characters. Perhaps you think Judas was an exception here. But he was not. "For Jesus knew from the beginning who should betray Him." He was not imposed upon here; and for two reasons He suffered him to be one with the twelve. The first was to show that the whole community is not to be blamed for the sins of one individual; and secondly, that His innocency might be apparent. He thus suffered the spy to live in the camp, and this enemy to live in the household, that it might be apparent that he could bring forward nothing to censure Him, which we may be sure he would if it were in his power. But after all he comes forward, and says, "I have betrayed innocent blood."

This prudence also led Him to decline the offers of some, for He knew them. When the young man said, "Lord, I will follow Thee whithersoever Thou goest," He turned and said, "Foxes have holes, and the birds of the air have nests, but the Son of Man hath not where to lay His head." Thus He discerned and displayed his motives and his principles, that they were selfish and worldly. Thus He teaches us by His own example, that we are not to take everyone into our bosoms; that we are to "distinguish things that differ;" that in our friendships and intimacies we are to be "wise as serpents." It is for this reason He commands us to be "swift to hear, slow to speak;" for oh, it is speech that betrays us into so many difficulties and evils. Of words hastily and carelessly spoken, who can imagine what may be their results? "The tongue is a fire, a world of iniquity."

But here you will observe that while we should learn from the Saviour's example of not committing Himself to everyone, we may carry this too far, and thus imbibe suspicious dispositions, in the exercise of which we may also be mistaken, and discover it afterwards, as David did, who had drawn a very rash conclusion, when he said, "All men are liars;" but he acknowledged that he said this in his "haste."

III. This brings us to observe, thirdly, THE PREROGATIVE ASCRIBED TO OUR SAVIOUR. "For He knew what was in man." It is mentioned as a reason why He did not commit Himself unto them. This kept Him from being mistaken. Observe how far this prerogative is expressed. "He knew what was in man." "He knew what was in" not only those who were near, but those who were afar off; not only those He saw, but those He had never seen with His bodily eyes; not only those who were open and communicative, but also those who were reserved; not only those who were in possession of His grace, but those who pretended to be so; not only those who were His, but those who were not His; and said, "I know the blasphemy of them which say they are Jews and are not, but are of the synagogue of Satan." Princes are obliged to see with the eyes and hear with the ears of others. Judges must call in witnesses to determine things, and sometimes these are perfectly contradictory. Prophets foretold things to come, but not from their own sagacity; these were revealed to them first. The angels know much, but they are learners too; and "now unto the principalities and powers in heavenly places is made known by the Church the manifold wisdom of God." But He needs nothing of this. He knows what is in man. You may know their faces, their names, and their connections, but not their dispositions; you may know what is done by them, but not what lieth in them; you know not what folds there are in their character, which time and circumstances will alone reveal. Yea, men know not what is in themselves. Hazael knew not that there was so much iniquity in his heart: he was sincere when he said, "Is thy servant a dog that he should do this thing?" and yet the dog did it. David said, "Who can understand his errors?" Do you imagine that all the sins you see are all that God sees in you? May you not pray with David, "Cleanse Thou me from secret thoughts"? Not from those that are secret from others, that would be hypocrisy; but from those that are secret to yourself. You therefore should pray, "Search me, O God, and know my heart; try me, and know my thoughts; and see if there be any wicked way in me, and lead me in the way everlasting."

In conclusion, what a view does this give us of the knowledge of Christ! He knoweth all men, He needs no testimony concerning them, He knows all that is in man. Surely this must be the attribute of Deity, and does not Deity proclaim it? Did not God say to Jeremiah, "The heart is deceitful above all things, who can know it? *I the Lord* search the heart, I try the reins of the children of men"? But does not our text express this with regard to Him also? When addressing the seven churches of Asia, He says, "And all the churches shall know that I am He which searcheth the reins and the hearts; and I will give to every one of you according to your works."

Finally, my brethren, let us be all impressed with this, and wherever we are let us say with Hagar, "Thou God seest me." Whatever be our conduct, let us say with Job, "Thou knowest the way that I take." It is an irksome reflection to the wicked and the worldly, but it is a comfortable and satisfactory reflection to the real Christian. He can say, "He knoweth the way that I take." "He knoweth my frame, He remembereth that I am but dust." "He knows all my walking through this great wilderness." "All my desire is before Thee, and my groaning is not hid from Thee."

XXXI.

THE PRIMITIVE CHURCHES.

(Delivered on Thursday Evening, May 16th, 1844.)

"*And so were the churches established in the faith, and increased in number daily.*"—ACTS xvi. 5.

"ALL men," says Paul, "seek their own, not the things which are Jesus Christ's." But the cause of the Redeemer lies nearest to the Christian's heart; "he is sorrowful for the solemn assembly," and grieves when any who profess the name of Christ become a reproach to His cause; he rejoices when in Sion things go well, and His cause flourishes. So "when Barnabas came to Antioch and saw the grace of God, he was glad; and he exhorted them all that with purpose of heart they would cleave unto the Lord." He is affected by it *prospectively:* he rejoices that a King shall reign and prosper; that "He shall have dominion from sea to sea, and from the river to the ends of the earth." He glories in this, because he knows that in Christ all the families of the earth be blessed. He is also affected by it *retrospectively.* In looking back and reading history, persons will be affected according to their peculiar principles and dispositions. "They that are after the flesh do mind the things of the flesh, and they that are after the Spirit the things of the Spirit." Some therefore are more interested by the affairs of life, of commerce and civil freedom; but a Christian is most interested in those times called "Times of refreshing from the presence of the Lord," few of which are recorded in the sacred volume. To such a state of things our text refers; and what crowned the whole was, that the cause went on and prospered. For the inspired penman, having noticed the travels of Paul and Silas, says, "And so were the churches established in the faith, and increased in number daily."

We shall fill up the remainder of the hour in considering some things by way of illustration and improvement.

I. THE FIRST REGARDS THE DISTINCTION. These were the Churches of Syria and Cilicia. The question is, What were these Churches? Now I am not going in this brief and familiar exercise to enter into a controversy concerning church government. I have my own views, others have theirs. "Let every man be fully persuaded in his own mind." But here is a question regarding a matter of fact: What were these churches? All must agree to two things: First, that they were not buildings. They could not have been said to have walked "in the fear of the Lord and the comfort of the Holy Ghost." And all must equally agree that these were not national institutions aided by the civil power. We have seen Christianity spread, not only without them, but in spite of them. Nowhere do we read of the Church of Judea, but of the churches in Judea; of the Church of Galilee, but of the churches in Galilee; of the Church of Samaria, but of the churches in Samaria; of the Church of Galatia, but of the churches in Galatia. Now these were unquestionably certain societies meeting together for the purpose of preaching or hearing the Gospel, according to the promise, "Where two or three are gathered together in my name, there am I in the midst of them"; and it will appear that no edifices were raised and appropriated to the Christian purpose till towards the close of the third century. All the redeemed collectively considered, constitute what the Scripture calls "the Church," comprehending all believers, living in all countries, in all ages, and of all denominations. When the word church is spoken of in the plural number, it means distinct communities, whether large or small. These now go under various names, and, like the individuals composing them, are all imperfect. You must not suppose that any of them have all the truth of the Gospel, and others none. But all those who hold the Head, and profess the truth as it is in Jesus, we are to regard as brethren.

II. THEIR ESTABLISHMENT IN THE FAITH is worthy of our observation. Nothing else is mentioned, though there are many things in which it is desirable to be confirmed in religion, and this shews the importance of faith. It is as the sap which feeds the tree, and the spring that furnishes all the streams. It is by faith we stand, by faith we walk, are justified, and sanctified and saved. It is the life of the Christian. The

Apostle says, "The life I now live in the flesh, I live by the faith of the Son of God, who loved me, and gave Himself for me." How desirable is it that we should pray as the disciples did: "Lord, increase our faith!" and to cry out with the father of the lunatic, "Lord, I believe, help Thou my unbelief." "So were the churches established in the faith." What means this? We apprehend four things implied in it.

First, they were established in the *doctrine* of faith. "It is a good thing that the heart be established with grace"; that is, in the doctrines of grace. It is a sad thing not to be steadfast, immovable, but tossed to and fro with every wind of doctrine. According to some, it matters little what we believe; but if every error be harmless, truth in the same degree is useless. As we think, we feel; as we feel we decree; and as we desire, we act; and by our actions our character is formed and our state determined. "Buy the truth," therefore, "and sell it not."

They were "established in the faith"—that is, in the *joy* of faith. We read expressly of the joy of faith; and joy rises or falls in a Christian with his faith. The Apostle therefore speaks of being "filled with all joy and peace in believing;" and says Peter, "Whom having not seen, ye love; in Whom, though now ye see Him not, yet believing, ye rejoice with joy unspeakable and full of glory." You see how established they were: nothing prevented the exercise of this joy. If they received the Word in much affliction," it was "with joy of the Holy Ghost." Though sensible of their guilt and weakness, they "joyed in God through our Lord Jesus Christ, through whom also they had received the atonement."

"Then were the churches established; that is, in the *obedience* of faith. There is no genuine obedience but what arises from it, and real faith will always produce this. It is therefore worthy of our remark, that those we read of in Scripture as being most remarkable for faith are also most remarkable for obedience. This is no wonder. By faith, Abraham, when he was tried, offered up Isaac; and he that had received the promises offered up his only-begotten son." We read not only of their orthodoxy, but of their sanctity; not only of what faith receives, but of what faith does. Thus faith is said to work by love. James says, "Shew me thy faith by thy works." Thus the thing is seen in the effects, the principle in the practice, and the faith in the conduct.

"Then were the churches established in the faith"; that is, in the *profession* of faith. If to *be* a Christian is all that is required, there never need be a martyr in the Church; but we are not only to be Christians, we are to appear to be such. It is not by our inward experience, which those around us cannot discern, that we make an impression in favour of our religion. We are called not only to "believe with the heart," but also to "confess with the mouth;" we are required not only to hold fast our religion, but "the profession of it without wavering."

III. Then, lastly, we have to consider *their increase.* "They increased in number daily." They increased not only in the graces of the members, but in the number of members. Thus it is said, "So mightily grew the word of God and prevailed;" and again, "The Lord added to the Church daily such as should be saved." This is implied here though it is not expressed.

Whatever were the means used, God was the author of all the success. The principal means He employs for the increase of His church is the preaching of the gospel. This is God's appointed ordinance. He says to every minister of His, "I send thee to open their eyes." Hence the reasoning of the Apostle: "Whoever shall call on the name of the Lord shall be saved. How then shall they call on Him of whom they have not believed? And how shall they believe in Him of whom they have not heard? And how shall they hear without a preacher?" "So then faith cometh by hearing, and hearing by the Word of God"; and you observe when persons come forward for admission to the table of the Lord, how commonly the converts have been the produce of the preached Word.

Yet, Christians, remember again, that the prayers of the Church are a great instrumentality here. There is not a better evidence of God's favour and intending to help us than when a spirit of supplication is poured out. Hence David says, "Thou shalt arise and have mercy upon Zion; for the time to favour her, yea, the set time is come." How did he know this? "For Thy servants take pleasure in her stones, and favour the dust thereof." And oh, when they feel this, when the heart is poured out in prayer, it is a pledge of something good. The graces of the Christian have been seen to flourish, faith has been strong, love to the Saviour, His cause, and His people has been not only sincere but ardent; and hope has been "as an anchor of the soul, both sure and steadfast." The conduct of one believer in the exercise of his graces has been a stimulus to others, and he has said by his conduct, if not in words, "That which we have seen and heard declare we unto you, that ye also may have fellowship with us, and truly our fellowship is with the Father and His Son Jesus Christ."

How much good has often been done by the deportment, temper, and conduct of believers, when these have been exemplary, so that they need not to say anything! How remarkably was this the case with the church we read of in the Acts. It is said, "Of the rest durst no man join himself to them, but the people magnified them. And believers were the more added to the Lord, multitudes both of men and women."

We may therefore observe, that *it becomes us to seek after the increase of our own church.* I do not mean exclusively. No, I do not love to be a party man; yet I have no objection for every man to have a party. It becomes us to seek to bring in fresh recruits to join the army of the living God, in order to supply the places of those soldiers of the cross who from time to time are called to join the ranks above. While we would use precaution not to admit improper persons to fellowship and communion with us, we would not establish a rigid mode of entrance to the table of the Lord. But the way to the church is not designed to be open to all, it becomes us to maintain a holy order, and to adhere as closely as possible to the scriptures of truth. We would hold out the right hand of fellowship to those who give hopeful evidence of genuine discipleship to Christ; and while we exercise kindness and candour to any relation of their experience, we would say, "Come thou with us and we will do thee good; for the Lord hath spoken good concerning Israel." "Come in, thou blessed of the Lord; why standest thou without?"

Again, we should not only be concerned for the increase of our own church, and for the increase of the cause of God in general, *but for our own spirituality*, and that we may "grow in grace and in the knowledge of our Lord and Saviour Jesus Christ." "And this I pray, that your love may abound yet more and more in knowledge and in all judgment; that ye may prove things that are excellent; that ye may be sincere and without offence till the day of Christ, being filled with the fruits of righteousness which are by Jesus Christ unto the glory and praise of God."

XXXII.

DEAD UNTO SIN.

(Delivered on Thursday Evening, July 23rd, 1846.)

"*Likewise reckon ye also yourselves dead indeed unto sin; but alive unto God through Jesus Christ our Lord.*"—ROMANS vi. 11.

THE change made by divine grace is in all the subjects of it real, wonderful, and glorious. Isaiah does not too strongly express it when he says, "Instead of the thorn shall come up the fir tree, and instead of the brier shall come up the myrtle tree: and it shall be to the Lord for a name, for an everlasting sign that shall not be cut off." Nor does the Apostle express it too forcibly when he says, "If any man be in Christ, he is a new creature." His state is new, his relations are new, his views are new, his dispositions are new; he has a new way, and a new end. "Old things are passed away; behold all things are become new." Now this is the estimation the Apostle would have the Romans make of their character and condition. And, says he, Consider yourselves—"reckon ye also yourselves to be dead indeed unto sin, but alive unto God through Jesus Christ our Lord." Christians, therefore, should reckon upon three things: first, that they are dead, "dead indeed unto sin;" secondly, that they are alive, "alive unto God;" thirdly, that they are thus dead, and thus alive, through the mediation of the Saviour. "Likewise reckon ye also yourselves dead indeed unto sin, but alive unto God through Jesus Christ our Lord."

I. The first thing the Apostle would have us reckon upon is, *that we are "dead indeed unto sin."* Now this supposes nothing less than avoiding sin, but it implies much more. A man may be urged to avoid what he yet loves to pursue. There are those who wish that it were lawful for them to live in sensuality, drunkenness, and profanation of the Lord's day and neglect of the public means of grace, and say of the worship of God, "what a weariness is it!" Lot's wife left Sodom, but was not dead to it. Her heart was still there, and this led her to look back, and looking back she became a pillar of salt. If all who profess to leave this sinful world, but who still hanker after it, were to be turned into pillars of salt, we should hardly be able to move about the streets for obstructions; and do you think there would be no awful petrifactions in some of those pews? But now a Christian not only avoids sin, but, as the Apostle says, is dead to it—dead to its very nature, dead to all sin, and not to some particular species of it; there is a natural antipathy to it. They do not relinquish a few vices, to which they may have no inclination in their constitution; no, but they part with their bosom lusts; they cut off right hands, and pluck out right eyes, while they say with Ephraim, "I was ashamed, yea, even confounded because I did bear the reproach of my youth."

My brethren, it will be found the way, and the only effectual way of renouncing all sin, is to be dead to it. Other preventions will frequently fail. But here the believer in Jesus is secure. It is this that distinguishes him from all others. A man is not very likely to fall into what he hates, but what he loves. Religion does not consist in negatives only. The Christian is not only to lay aside "all ungodliness and worldly lusts," but "to live soberly and righteously and godly in this present evil world." He is not only to "put off the old man and his deeds," but to "put on the new man, which after God is created in righteousness and true holiness." He is not only "not to walk after the flesh," but "after the spirit." Therefore the Apostle will have Christians not only "to reckon themselves dead indeed unto sin," but "alive unto God," "for you hath He quickened who were dead in trespasses and sins." "As Christ was raised up by the glory of the Father, even so also should we walk in newness of life." There is nothing that characterises the unsaved man more than his insensibility and indifference to God. Even if we could not discover one immoral action in the whole world, this would be enough to prove the thing that man is "dead in trespasses and sins," that he does not cherish a holy fear of God, does not love to remember Him, to speak of Him, or to hear of Him. Here is a subject dead to his sovereign, a dependant dead in his feelings to his benefactor, a child dead to his father. But man is entirely depraved, and here is an absolute demonstration of it; but real religion commences in the destruction of this insensibility and indifference. The regenerate man is convinced of his conduct and character as a sinner before God, and asks now, "Where is God my Maker, who giveth songs in the night?" and feels after Him, if so be he may find Him.

II. *The Apostle supposes these believers to be alive.* "Alive unto God." They are so in three respects. They are alive to His *favour.* While many are asking, "Who will show us any good?" he prays for the light of His countenance. If therefore he can draw the conclusion that God loves him, he is happy enough, whatever be his outward circumstances. An apprehension of His anger fills him with alarm; the fear of His frown will cut him to the heart. So he "labours that whether present or absent he may be accepted of Him;" not in a way of justification, but in a way of approbation, saying, "Let the words of my mouth, and the meditation of my heart, be acceptable in Thy sight, O Lord."

Secondly, he is alive to God as to His *presence.* His prayer is, "Cast me not away from Thy presence, and take not Thy Holy Spirit from me." Whence is it that he feels the sanctuary such an attraction? Because it is "the place where His honour dwelleth," and because God has said, "In all places where I record my name, I will come unto you; and will bless you." What makes him love retirement? Because he loves to meet with God his Father in secret. And what makes him feel such pleasure in the company of the godly? Because it reminds him of God, who is his all in all. And what makes him long after heaven? Because God will there complete his happiness? Because he shall be freed from toil? Because he shall never, never suffer? No; but because he shall never, never sin; but be "for ever with the Lord."

Thirdly, he is alive to His *honour* and *glory.* He beholds the transgressors and is grieved, "because they keep not His Word." He therefore sympathises with the cause of God in all its changes. If professors fall into sin, he is sorrowful for the solemn assembly. On the other hand, he is glad when he hears that the Gospel spreads, and that believers multiply, and that souls are added daily of such as shall be saved, and that professors "walk worthy of the vocation wherewith they are called," "adorning the doctrine of God their Saviour in all things." He therefore prays, and has done so ever since he prayed at all, "that the Word of the Lord may run and be glorified; that His kingdom may come, and His will be done in earth as it is in heaven." He always considers those the best times when the cause of God flourishes most; therefore he aids it too according to his resources, exertions, and influence. He is brought into the state the Apostle recommends when he says, "Whether therefore ye eat or drink, or whatsoever ye do, do all to the glory of God."

III. The Apostle would have you to be "dead indeed unto sin, but alive unto God *through Jesus Christ our Lord.*" They are to be thus dead, and thus alive, through the mediation of the Saviour—

First, as our *Example.* In His temper, principles, and practice, He pleased not Himself, but always did the things which pleased the Father.

Secondly, as our *Teacher.* Thus He has set before us those arguments and motives which have the greatest tendency to turn us away from sin, and which, blessed be God, are calculated to engage us in His service. What threatenings and what promises too! He has thrown back the veil that hides the future, and shews us a world in flames, and the Judge standing at the door. He is going away, but He will come again and receive His people to Himself, that where He is they may be also.

Then it is also through the *Cross*, for it is all through Him as our dying Friend. "Ye know the grace of our Lord Jesus Christ, how though He was rich yet for our sakes became poor, that we through His poverty might be rich." He died that we might live for ever. Can I then refuse to live according to His pleasure who loved me and gave Himself for me? And shall I, can I, love that which crucified the Lord of life and glory?

"No, my Redeemer, they shall die,
My heart has so decreed;
Nor can I spare the guilty things
Which made the Saviour bleed."

It is there we see the infinite evil of sin. It is there we look into His heart, and behold the dwelling place of pity. There my old man is crucified with Him, "that the body of sin might be destroyed, that henceforth we should not serve sin."

Fourthly, it is through the Saviour's *Meritorious Sufferings.* When He died, He not only atoned for all our sin, but procured for us all the grace that we stand in need of, from the commencement of our course to our journey's end. He obtained the Spirit for us. Watts sings well upon this as upon every other subject—

> "'Tis by the merit of His death
> That hung upon the tree,
> The Spirit is sent down to breathe
> On such dry bones as we."

This accords, too, with what the Apostle says to the Galatians. "Christ hath redeemed us from the curse of the law, being made a curse for us: for it is written, Cursed is everyone that hangeth on a tree: that the blessing of Abraham might come on the Gentiles through Jesus Christ; that we might receive the promise of the Spirit through faith." 'Tis only through Him therefore that we obtain the Spirit. This we have promised us in consequence of His death. The Holy Spirit was not given to particular individuals, but the whole dispensation of it, both in His ordinary and extraordinary operations, was committed to the Mediator, and the right of administration annexed to His office for ever, so that He quickeneth whom He will. It is with Him we have to do in all the concerns of religion. We are to come to Him for faith, hope, and consolation. We are to come to Him, to look to Him, for sanctification, justification, and all the blessings of redemption.

I fear there are some here this evening who are far from exemplifying the character we have been describing. You are indeed dead, but you are dead to God. You are indeed alive, but alive to sin. What a case does this imply! You are alive to folly, to madness, to rebellion, to treason, to sickness, to disease, to all manner of loathsomeness, to wounds and bruises and putrefying sores. These are the representations, not of your preacher, but of God Himself, who can never be mistaken; and what a misery must it ensure! "The wages of sin is death." "The wicked shall be driven away in his wickedness." What a taste does this display! To be dead to the perfections, excellences, and sources of all blessedness! dead to the Fountain of Life! If you are alive to God, God will be alive to you. If you are living to His glory, He will make all things work together for your good, in life, in death, in time, and in eternity. If you walk contrary to Him, He will walk contrary to you; and can your heart endure, or your hands be strong, when He shall come to punish you? O that God may give you repentance unto life! that the rest of your lives may be spent to His praise.

We have not been drawing imaginary characters this evening, but we "testify that we know, and bear witness to that we have seen." We are persuaded there are some present this evening who may reckon themselves "dead indeed unto sin, but alive unto God through Jesus Christ our Lord." It is desirable therefore that you should "maintain a conscience void of offence toward God and toward man;" that your conversation should be such as to correspond with your profession of love to Christ. If you wish to determine what to do at any time, call to mind what you are and what you profess. Reckon yourselves thus in order to keep the world from asking, "What do ye more than others?" Sleep not as do others, walk not in darkness as others, though your light flashing upon them may be offensive. "All who will live godly in this present evil world must suffer persecution." If you oppose them, they will oppose you; if you dissent from them, they will dissent from you. Marvel not, brethren, if the world hate you; it hated the Saviour before it hated you. But rejoice in the Lord as your portion. He is near to justify you. If you are called to make sacrifices, He will more than indemnify you, for "godliness hath the promise of the life that now is, and of that which is to come."

XXXIII.

GOD AND HIS TEMPLES.

(Delivered on Thursday Evening, October 10th, 1844.)

"*For ye are the temple of the living God.*"—2 CORINTHIANS vi. 16.

THE Scripture, my brethren, gives us an awful representation of human nature, and we learn from all observation and all experience that man is far gone from his original righteousness, and as such is alienated from the life of God through the ignorance that is in him, because of the blindness of his heart. God is not in all his thoughts. He endeavours to banish the rememberance of Him from his thoughts, saying unto God, "Depart from us; we desire not the knowledge of Thy ways." "Cause the Holy One of Israel to cease from before us." From such creatures God might righteously withdraw, hold no intercourse, and abandon them for ever. But instead of this, He has devised means that His banished ones should not be expelled from Him. Where sin abounded grace did much more abound; and where sin hath reigned unto death, even there grace reigns through righteousness unto eternal life by Jesus Christ our Lord. "He once suffered the just for the unjust." And now, Christians, ye who sometimes were far off are made nigh by the blood of Christ, and redeemed, and justified, and sanctified, and made the temples of the living God.

Temples of old were named after the deities to whom they belonged. Thus we read of the temple of Bacchus, the temple of Diana, the temple of Mars, and others. But *ye* are the temple of the living God. Let us therefore fill up the remainder of the hour allotted to this exercise by considering two things: first, the character of God; and secondly, the representation of His people.

I. THE CHARACTER OF GOD. "The *living* God." This is

not mentioned without meaning. We should never lightly pass over the words which the Holy Ghost useth, for they are not only words of kindness but of wisdom.

First, He is called "the living God," to distinguish Him from idols. There were of old "lords many and gods many." We read that "men became vain in their imaginations, and their foolish hearts were darkened. Professing themselves to be wise, they became fools and changed the glory of the incorruptible God into an image made like to corruptible man, and to birds, and four-footed beasts and creeping things"; thus they "changed the truth of God into a lie, and worshipped and served the creature more than the Creator, who is blessed for ever." But what succour could any of these afford to those that worshipped them? Many of these were made of dead materials: they were the work of men's hands. They had eyes, but they saw not; ears, but they heard not, neither spake they through their throat. They that made them were like unto them; so is every one that trusteth in them. Now, it seems amazing that man could make a deity and then fall down and adore it, saying, "Thou art my God." Oh, what do we owe to Revelation for showing us the only living and true God who is infinitely worthy of all our regard! who sees every tear, who hears every sigh, and relieves every sorrow!

He is called "the living God" to remind us of the excellency and supremacy of His existence. The kind of life any being in the universe lives must depend upon his nature. A worm as really possesses life as a man, and it is true with regard to a fly as of an angel or an archangel; but what a difference between the one and the other! How does He then possess life whose understanding is infinite, whose power is Almighty, who is everywhere present, who knows all things, who is liable to no dangers, who is without variableness or the shadow of a change, who rules over all, the blessed and only Potentate, who only hath immortality! My soul, who can describe or who can imagine the life of such a Being as this?

He is called "the living God" to remind us of His energy and influence. He has life in Himself, and is able to command it. He is the source of life; hence says David, "with Thee is the Fountain of life." Life in millions of streams issues from Him. He shines in every beam of the sun. He moves in every drop of the ocean. Think of vegetable life, the life of trees and of herbs and of flowers: here He is the living God. Think of animal life. How many creatures, and all creatures visible and invisible in air and earth and sea, all derived their existence from Him! "The eyes of all wait upon Him, and He giveth them their meat in due season." He openeth His hand and satisfieth the wants of every living thing. A life of nature by which we enter the world, a life of grace by which we enter the church, a life of glory by which we enter heaven —all this is only and entirely communicated from Him. He may well therefore be called "the living God."

He is called "the living God" to remind us of the manner in which we are to serve Him; for, my brethren, from His character we may always deduce the nature of that religion which He requires and establishes. Thus, reasoning with the woman of Samaria, He said, "God is a Spirit," and therefore adds, "they that worship Him must worship Him in spirit and in truth." There must be a resemblance between Him and His worship. It is the same with regard to His holiness, and therefore we are to worship God in the beauty of holiness. Therefore says He, "I the Lord your God am holy: be ye holy in all manner of conversation. Because it is written, Be ye holy; for I am holy." It is the same when we consider Him as the God of grace, as He who hears and answers prayer. How are we to approach Him? Are we to approach Him with indifference, insensibility, and dulness? with hosannas languishing on our lips, and our devotion dying? Is there to be no correspondence and suitableness here? We are to be, as the Apostle expresses it, "fervent in spirit, serving the Lord." And he mentions this in his Epistle to the Hebrews in a very interesting connection, saying, "How much more shall the blood of Christ, who through the eternal Spirit offered Himself without spot to God, purge your consciences from dead works to serve the living God."

II. Having glanced at the character of God, let us now look at THE REPRESENTATION OF HIS PEOPLE; for you see they are called "the *temple* of the living God."

This is true of them *collectively* considered. Sometimes thus the term is employed. Paul, in his address to the Ephesians, says, "Ye are built upon the foundation of the apostles and prophets, Jesus Christ Himself being the chief corner stone; in whom all the building fitly framed together groweth into an holy temple in the Lord." And so when the Apostle Paul in his address to the Thessalonians is speaking of the man of sin, he says, "Who opposeth and exalteth himself above all that is called God or that is worshipped; so that he as God sitteth in the temple of God, showing himself that he is God." By "the temple of God" he here means the Church, and so you know it is said of the Messiah in prophecy, "Behold the man whose name is the BRANCH; and He shall grow up out of His place, and He shall build the temple of the Lord, even He shall build the temple of the Lord, and He shall bear the glory."

The people of God in all places, and from the beginning of the world, have formed only *one* Church. As many sheep make only one fold; as many branches make only one tree; as many members make one body; as many stones make only one building, and as in a building some of the stones are nearer the foundation, and others more remote, yet all are resting upon it; and as some occupy more superior positions, and others more inferior ones, yet all are parts of the same edifice, and have a relation to each other; so is it with the Church of Christ. However distinguished Christians have been from each other as to station, or office, or attainment, or even graces, they have all formed only one Church, and this Church is "the temple of the living God."

All other temples are doomed to perish. What now has become of the temples so famous in the heathen world? Where now is the temple built by Solomon, and where the temple built by Zerubbabel, and which continued for so many years? Are they not destroyed? But it is otherwise with the Church of Christ, the temple of the living God. This is made of imperishable materials, and is beyond the reach of men or devils. "Upon this rock," says Christ, "I will build my Church, and the gates of hell shall not prevail against it."

But what is true of the Church of God at large is true of every individual believer. Each believer in our Lord Jesus Christ is a temple of the living God, and so the Apostle Paul means it should be considered here. Every true Christian is called the temple of the living God for three reasons, namely, for consecration, for residence, and for worship: for all these are peculiar to a temple.

First, because of *consecration* he is called so. A temple is sacred to some deity. Some houses are made for animals. If some are made for men these differ much from each other. Mansions are built for nobles; palaces for princes; and temples for gods. Every temple of old was dedicated to some divinity, and particularly appropriated to his service; and now this is the case with regard to every Christian. Therefore says David, "The Lord hath set apart him that is godly for Himself." He hath set Him apart thus for His own purpose and grace, and he is also set apart by his own voluntary surrender of himself to God, for he is made willing in the day of God's power; and he not only comes and prays, saying, "Lord, I am Thine; save me," but he can also say with the Church, "O Lord, other lords beside Thee have had dominion over me; but henceforth will I make mention of Thy name." He is now consecrated to God and made sacred to Him.

Now, to steal from a common house is felony, but to steal from a temple is sacrilege; and with this sacrilege you are chargeable who make a profession of religion, as if you belonged entirely to God and were His temple, yet take your time, and property, and influences, and apply them to any purpose rather than to His praise and glory. "Whether therefore," says Paul, "ye eat or drink, or whatsoever ye do, do all to the glory of God."

Secondly, He is called the temple of the living God because of *residence.* A temple was supposed to be the dwelling place of some divinity. It is the same with the temple of the living God. Each individual believer, therefore, who repairs to Him, is represented as saying, "When shall I come and appear before God?" May you go and follow their example. David therefore says, "Lord I have loved the habitation of Thy house, and the place where Thine honour dwelleth." As a man is known where he dwells, and persons who wish to see him must repair to his house, so the Psalmist expresses his desire to see God's power and His glory, as he had seen Him "in the sanctuary." And again, "They have seen Thy goings, O God, my King, in the sanctuary." Upon the dedication of the temple of Solomon, God came down and took possession of it in a cloud of glory as His own. And He is not less in His people now than He was then, when He gave them such signal proofs of His presence. He is everywhere: His presence fills heaven and earth. But He *dwells* not everywhere. Where then does He dwell? "I will dwell in them and walk in them," says He. "He that dwelleth in love dwelleth in God and God in Him." And says the Apostle John, "Hereby we know that we dwell in God and He in us, because He hath given us of His spirit." Christians have evidences of His presence in them; and there are feelings experienced by them which could only arise from His agency, and agency supposes His presence.

Thirdly, the Christian is called a "temple of the living God" insense of *worship.* A temple was raised for the adoration of the Divinity to which it belonged: God is adored by every Christian; and adored not by bodily exercise which profiteth little. He does not draw nigh to God with his lip while his heart is far from Him; but could you look through the outward man and contemplate the inward man, and could look thus into the the temple of God, there you would see an understanding studying His truth; there you would see a will choosing Him, and a conscience fearing Him; there you would find he was making melody in his heart to the Lord; there you would see his prayer coming up before Him as incense, and the lifting up of his hands as the evening sacrifice.

Now by way of improvement, let us conduct you to the conclusion.

First, by inducing you to admire *the marvellous condescension of God.* David was impressed with this, and therefore exclaimed, "Lord, what is man, that Thou shouldest visit him?" But God does more than this; He not only visits him, but dwells with him. He not only dwells with him as a guest, but dwells with him as a God! and the disposition of the Father was displayed in the Son of His love. When, therefore, Solomon had opened the Temple at Jerusalem for the worship of God, how was he impressed? An ordinary mind would have been most struck with the grandeur of the occasion, and the magnificence of the structure, and the vastness of the multitude; but he was struck with something else, namely, that God should deign to regard him in it, and therefore he exclaimed, "Will God in very deed dwell with men on the earth? Behold, heaven and the heavens of heaven cannot contain Thee; how much less this house which I have built." And can He, you may say, can He really make such creatures as we are His abode? "Depart from me," said Peter, "for I am a sinful man, O Lord." This was not the language of aversion, but of humbleness of mind; impressed with a view of the Saviour's purity and greatness. "Lord," said the centurion, "I am not worthy that thou shouldest come under my roof." And are you worthy of His coming and dwelling in you? But "thus saith the high and lofty One that inhabiteth eternity, whose name is Holy; I dwell in the high and holy place, with him also that is of a contrite and humble spirit, to revive the spirit of the humble, and to revive the heart of the contrite ones."

Secondly, we learn the *duty of a Christian.* For, says the Apostle, "The temple of God is holy, which temple ye are;" and again, "If any man defile the temple of God, him shall God destroy."

It has always been deemed a heinous offence to pollute a temple. Our blessed Lord drove the money-changers and buyers and sellers from the Temple, and said, "Make not My Father's house a house of merchandise."

You may easily see whether your soul is filled with the trifles of earth instead of heavenly realities. Now, would you be shocked to see an idol set up in the middle of the sanctury? But did you never indulge in any vile and lewd imaginations and passions? And are not these sometimes even connected with the service of God? The Apostle, in connection with our text, says, "Be ye not unequally yoked together with unbelievers; for what fellowship hath righteousness with unrighteousness? And what communion hath light with darkness? And what concord hath Christ with Belial? Or what part hath he that believeth with an infidel? And what agreement hath the temple of God with idols? For ye are the temple of the living God; as God hath said, "I will dwell in them and walk in them, and I will be their God and they shall be my people. Wherefore, come out from among them, and be separate, " saith the Lord, "and touch not the unclean thing; and I will receive you and will be a Father unto you, and ye shall be my sons and daughters, saith the Lord Almighty." And this is to extend to the body as well as to the Spirit, for you are to cleanse yourselves from all filthiness of the flesh as well as of the spirit. For, says the Apostle, "Even your bodies are the temples of the Holy Ghost. Wherefore glorify God with your bodies and with your spirits, which are His."

You see, thirdly, *the dignity of Christians.* In their own eyes they are unworthy, and they say with Job, "Behold I am vile." "The world knoweth them not;" and the precious sons of Zion, comparable to fine gold, how are they esteemed as earthen vessels, the work of the hands of the potter! But in the eyes of God what are they? In the eyes of Scripture, what are they? They are the salt of the earth—the light of the world—vessels of honour fitted for our master's use—a holy priesthood—the temples of the Holy Ghost!

Let us judge of them, then, not according to outward condition, but according to their real character, according to their moral and religious worth. Let us seek to resemble a citizen of Zion, of whom it is said, "He walketh uprightly, worketh righteousness, and speaketh the truth in his heart, who backbiteth not with his tongue, nor doeth evil to his neighbour, nor taketh up a reproach against his neighbour, in whose eyes a vile person is condemned; but he knoweth them that fear the Lord." Such are said to be "more excellent than their neighbours."

There is something honourable, therefore, especially in an old Christian, who has been consistent all his days. When I pass such a person, I feel I am passing by a temple of the living God. Ah, it matters not what his outward circumstances may be; he may be poor in this world, but he is rich towards God and an heir of the kingdom which God hath prepared for them that love Him.

Again, this should be *a motive to Christian love.* It may well be considered an act of impiety to neglect a Christian temple. Repair it, if you do not adorn it. How is it here? Is there no door or window that wants attending to? In other words, have you no brethren or sisters naked or destitute? have you this world's goods, and see them in need, and shut up your bowels of compassion from them? If so, how dwelleth the love of God in you? Is a brother or sister overtaken in a fault, and do you not hasten to restore such an one in the spirit of meekness, remembering thyself lest thou also be tempted?

Then finally, as there are some temples of the living God, so there are some temples of the Devil. Indeed, if you are not a temple of the living God, you are a temple of Satan. There is no neutrality here. How dreadful, then, to belong to the Prince of the power of the air, the spirit that now worketh in the children of disobedience. What! to be a habitation ot devils, a dwelling-place of fiends and demons! May Almighty God turn your heart to Himself, and bring you to experience the blessed design of the Gospel in turning you from darkness to light, from the power of Satan unto God, and give you an inheritance among all them that are sanctified by faith which is in Christ Jesus.

XXXIV.

COUNSELS CONCERNING PRAYER.

(Delivered on Thursday Evening, March 7th, 1844.)

"*And herein I give my advice.*"—2 CORINTHIANS viii. 10.

THIS regarded the liberty of the Corinthians in making the collections for the poor saints suffering in Jerusalem, and sending it by messengers who would gladly and safely and faithfully convey it. And if you ask, wherein I am going to give my advice this evening? I answer, the subjects of ministerial admonition are so numerous, that the brevity of this exercise requires selection. My mind this evening leads me to one thing, and to one thing only; namely PRAYER.

The noblest idea we have of real religion is, an intercourse between God and man. There is such an intercourse, and is carried on, on God's side by His word; on our side by prayer. Prayer falls under various characters and distinctions. There is public prayer, family prayer, private prayer, and ejaculatory prayer. It has also various relations and qualities. It is offered only in the name of Jesus, as the only mediator between God and man; "Whatsoever" says the Saviour, "ye ask the Father in my name, He will do it." We also read of our "praying in the Holy Ghost;" because the Spirit teacheth us, and inclines us, and enables us to pray. He is therefore called "the spirit of prayer and supplication." We also are to ask in faith nothing wavering. Our prayers also are to be sincere; "then shall ye find Him, if ye seek Him with the whole heart." "He is nigh unto all that call upon Him, to all that call upon Him in truth." They must also be frequent and importunate; we must therefore resemble Jacob, and wrestle, and say, "I will not let Thee go unless Thou bless me."

But these are not the things on which I am going to enlarge during the remainder of this evening. I am going to deviate a little from my usual textual preaching. The old divines often discussed cases of conscience, and such cases are always to be found in the experience of real believers, who often have their difficulties and doubts.

Asaph was deeply impressed on account of the prosperity of the wicked and the adversity of the righteous; as he says in the seventy-third Psalm, "I was envious at the foolish, when I saw the prosperity of the wicked;" and to such a degree was he impressed, that he was tempted to say, "Verily I have cleansed my heart in vain, and washed my hands in innocency; for all the day long have I been plagued, and chastened every morning." How did he obtain relief? What did he do? He enquired in God's house. "I went," said he, "into the sanctuary of God; then understood I their end." There he saw the clue, and was enabled to unravel the mystery.

Now the case I have to bring forward this evening and concerning which I am going to give my advice is as follows:—*May not a Christian for a time lose much of his earnestness, freedom, and pleasure, in prayer? Though he could not wholly neglect the duty, he may have lost much of the favour and the privilege and freedom; and perform it in a dull and lifeless manner and fall asleep at the throne of grace.*

If there are any here who can rise and say, "I acknowledge I have but imperfectly performed the duty, but I have never to complain in regard to my praying"—to these our subject has no reference. But are there not others who may say, "Well, I cannot hear as I ought, nor pray as I once did. O, that it were with me as in months past, when the candle of the Lord shone round about me, and when by His light I walked through darkness! Then did I love the Sabbath, and I numbered the days that intervened between me and it; then I did not gaze about while I heard the Word, or fall asleep, but either felt as the Jews did, when they cried out and said, What must I do to be saved? or with Jeremiah, who said, Thy words were found, and I did eat them and they were unto me the joy and rejoicing of my heart. Oh, how I sang the praises of God then! how I heard then! But I cannot hear now as I once did. What is to be done?" "Herein I give my advice," and it is comprehended in seven articles.

I. You say, "I cannot pray as I once did:" then carry the case to and lay it before God. If you cannot do anything else, this will be of some avail. The very exercise will be useful. You remember when Hezekiah received the blasphemous letter of Rabshakeh, "He went up unto the house of the Lord, and spread it before the Lord." You remember, when John's disciples took up his body and buried it, they "went and told Jesus." When Martha and Mary sent unto Jesus, they said nothing but, "Lord, he whom Thou lovest is sick;" and it brought Him to Lazarus, though not to raise him up from his sickness, but afterwards to raise him from the grave.

II. Then cause your condition to pass and repass before your mind; go into your closets, walk in your fields, retire somewhere and reflect upon it. Is there nothing to pray about? Nothing to excite you to prayer? What, are you not in the body? and in a world that lieth in wickedness? What, have you not a course of duty to perform? Have you not trials awaiting you? Must you not "pass through the valley of the shadow of death?" Are you yet fully prepared for all your serving, and for all your suffering? What are you relatively? Are you the head of a family? Where is the desire of your eyes? Where are the children of your bosom? Where are your domestics? Have you no friend whose afflictions you are to make your own? with whom you are to weep?

III. "I cannot pray as I did!" Then read a portion of some good book which would serve either to shame you, or enflame you. Above all, take your Bible; take some psalm, as the matter and model of your devotions. Oh! how many are there appropriate to your own case, whatever it may be? Oh, how soon after you took the holy book to read, would you find that it furnishes something answerable to your case! Are you depressed with a sense of guilt? Read the fifty-first psalm, and say "Have mercy upon me, O God, according to Thy loving kindness; according unto the multitude of Thy tender mercies, blot out my transgressions." Are you under affliction? Read such a psalm as the twenty-fifth: "The troubles of my heart are enlarged; O bring Thou me out of my distresses. Turn thee unto me, and have mercy upon me: for I am desolate and afflicted." Or are you depressed in spirit? Read the forty-second psalm; there you hear David express himself: "O my God, my soul is cast down within me; therefore will I remember Thee from the land of Jordan, and of the Hermonites, from the hill Mizar. Why art thou cast down, O my soul? and why art thou disquieted within me? Hope thou in God, for I shall yet praise Him who is the health of my countenance, and my God."

IV. "I cannot pray as I did." Then remember you are heard according as you can pray, and not according as you cannot. How is it now with your own children? Have you a family? One of them can come and ask in proper language; another can only just lisp his desire in broken accents. But the second is heard as well as the first. But here is a third who cannot speak at all, but he can stretch out his little hand; he can cry. Is he to be despised and refused? Why, the big tear in his face—yea, everything pleads for *him*. So our Lord says in His exhortation, "If ye being evil know how to give good gifts unto your children, how much more will your heavenly Father give good gifts to them that ask Him"! They ask according to their ability: He gives "according to his riches in glory by Christ Jesus."

There may be gifts without grace. It is not the arithmetic of your prayers, how many they be; nor the geometry of your prayers, how loud they be; nor the rhetoric of your prayers, how fine they be; nor the music of your prayers, how melodious they be, that is the important thing. But the sincerity thereof, their coming from within, their being the feelings of a broken heart and contrite spirit; the being able to pray with David, "Lord, all my desire is before Thee, and my groanings are not hid from Thee." Or with Job, "Mine eye poureth out prayers unto God." This was his praying; it was also David's. Nor in vain did he address God, and say, "Thou heardest the voice of my weeping." Hezekiah said, "As a crane or a swallow, so did I chatter." Hardly could he use the word "prayer," yet God heard and answered him.

V. You say, "I cannot pray as I did." Then consider your encouragements to pray. Prayer is infinitely important in the Christian life. Not only is it an evidence of it, but the medium thereof; and all such prosperity depends entirely upon it. Let this be considered by you; as Henry says, "Prayer is an outlet and an inlet too—an outlet to grief, and an inlet to grace." It is a duty. Remember, you are to "pray *everywhere*, lifting up holy hands." And as to the continuance, you are to "pray *without ceasing*," to pray and not faint. Is there not enough here to arouse and animate you afresh, especially when you go over the exceeding great and precious promises made to prayer? You hear God saying, "For all these things will I be enquired of by the house of Israel, to do it for them." Is there not enough to excite and encourage you? The God of prayer stands before you as the God of love and the God of all grace and mercy. His hands are filled with all the blessings you need. The throne you approach is a throne of grace, the seat you come to is a mercy-seat, and you have a mediator there to take you by the hand and lead you in and present your services acceptably, offering up your prayer with His own like sweet incense. He gives you His Spirit to help your infirmities. Can you produce no instance of usefulness in prayer? Have you no Ebenezers of your own to raise? Can you not say with David, "It was good for me to draw near to God?"

VI. You say you cannot pray as you once did. Then examine the cause of this. Your state of mind, be assured, is not an instance of Divine sovereignty. There are some persons who carry their views on this subject too far; and because He saves sovereignly, they think He damns sovereignly; but this is a mistake. "He does not afflict willingly, nor grieve the children of men." Is there not a cause? Hear Him state the cause Himself. "Behold, the Lord's hand is not shortened that it cannot save;" "but your iniquities have separated between you and your God, and your sins have hid His face from you, that He will not hear." Hence He addresses the Jews, "Hast thou not procured this unto thyself, in that thou hast forsaken the Lord thy God, when He led thee by the way? And now what hast thou to do in the way of Egypt, to drink the waters of Sihor or what hast thou to do in the way of Assyria, to drink the waters of the river? Thine own wickedness shall correct thee, and thy backslidings shall reprove thee." Again, "O generation, see ye the word of the Lord. Have I been a wilderness unto Israel? a land of darkness? Wherefore say my people, We are lords; we will come no more unto Thee." Yes, there is a reason for this state of mind; and in general a particular cause, and I need not say that we should endeavour to find it out. If you are sincere in your researches, you will soon put your finger on the enemy, perhaps some known duty omitted, some creature improperly regarded; perhaps ingratitude for some deliverance; some ungenerous temper indulged; neglect of the means of grace or indifference to them. In some way or other you may have grieved the Spirit of God who hath sealed you to the day of redemption.

Are the consolations of God small with you? Is there no secret thing by which you may account for this? The gourd withers over your head; is there not a worm at the root?

Thy soul is straitened in the seige; is there no Bichri? no traitor, whose head is to be thrown over the wall, in order that Joab may raise the seige and recall his forces?

Lastly, you say you cannot pray as you once did. Be exhorted to ascertain what it is that hinders thy enjoyment in prayer; whatever this may be, it must be found out. Say with David, "If I regard iniquity in my heart, the Lord will not hear me. What I know not, teach Thou me." Say with Ephraim, "What have I to do any more with idols?" Say with Cowper—

"The dearest idol I have known,
Whate'er that idol be;
Help me to tear it from Thy throne;
And worship only Thee."

And then with him you may add—

"So shall my walk be close with God,
Calm and serene my frame;
So purer light shall mark the road
That leads me to the Lamb."

This is the case of conscience, and "herein I give my advice concerning it." Of what I have spoken this is the sum. It will be well for us to walk so as to please God; but when otherwise, it will be well to be sensible of it, and humbled under it, and say with David, "Thou didst hide Thy face and I was troubled." "Thou hidest thy face"—that was bad; "and I was troubled"—that was well, as it was "a token for good," and implied that a better state of mind was experienced. Jeremiah represents a similar scene, "A voice was heard upon the high places, weeping and supplication of the children of Israel: for they have perverted their way, and have forgotten the Lord their God." "Return ye backsliding children, and I will heal your backslidings." Behold we come unto Thee, for Thou art the Lord our God." Happy children, to respond, "Truly in vain is salvation hoped for from the hills and from the multitude of mountains; truly in the Lord our God is the salvation of Israel." Long as Christians continue here, they will find the Divine life a warfare; "the flesh lusteth against the spirit, and the spirit against the flesh." They are now in the "vale of tears," and will have their complaints while they continue in it; but O, what a state is heaven; there will be no complaints, no fighting there, no fears within. Then that which is perfect will be come, and that which is in part shall be done away. Here you will often have cause to say with David, "My soul cleaveth to the dust; quicken Thou me, according to Thy word." But ever prayer will prevail over every fear and doubt, and a life of prayer end in an eternity of praise. You will soon join the burden of the song with those who are gone before you to dwell in God's house above and are still praising Him.

XXXV.

OUR WEAKNESS AND OUR STRENGTH.

(Delivered on Monday Evening, February 23rd, 1852.)

"*Finally, my brethren, be strong in the Lord, and in the power of His might.*"—EPHESIANS vi. 10.

WHEN the Apostle speaks of strength or might, he means not physical strength, but spiritual; not mental, but moral; not strength for the body, but for the soul; not for the things of time, but for those of eternity.

It is here implied that we want strength, as we have none; and it is here declared that there is strength in another, and that we may and ought to avail ourselves of it.

According to some, religion is a very easy business, and so it is if their views of it be true, that it allows the retaining of every worldly passion; that it requires no privations or sacrifices; that it enjoins no strenuous exertions or self-denial. But this is not the way in which the Scriptures speak of it. *No!* and therefore we read, "*Strive* to enter in at the strait gate; for many, I say unto you, will seek to enter in, but shall not be able." "*Labour* for that meat which endureth unto everlasting life, which the Son of Man will give unto you." "*Work out* your own salvation with fear and trembling, for it is God that worketh in you to will and to do of His good pleasure."

Can a Christian question whether he wants strength, and whether he wants it continually? Why, are you not called to work in the vineyard of the Lord? Are you not enjoined to be always abounding in the work of the Lord? and are you not required to deny yourself, to take up your cross, to follow the Lamb whithersoever he goeth; to deny all ungodliness and worldly lusts, and to live soberly, righteously, and godly in the present world? Are you not required to mortify the deeds of the body, to crucify the flesh with its affections and lusts, to live with your conversation in heaven? At the thought of which you have doubtless often exclaimed:

> "Lord, can a feeble, helpless worm
> Perform a task so hard?
> Thy grace shall all the work perform,
> And give the free reward."

Can you question whether you want strength? Are you not racers, and can you obtain the prize without running? Are you not required to lay aside every weight, and the sin which so easily besets you, and to run with patience the race set before you? Are you not travellers, strangers and pilgrims upon the earth? And have you not a journey before you far more difficult than the ten thousand Greeks under Xenophon, or the Jews under Moses in the wilderness, on their way to the promised land? And do you not find in this journey much up-hill work? Do you not often say with David, "My soul followeth hard after Thee, yet it seems as if I should never overtake Thee"? Are you not warriors? and are you not called upon to "wrestle, not against flesh and blood, but against principalities, against powers, against the rulers of the darkness of this world, against spiritual wickedness in high places"? Did you never reflect upon the power, the number, the malice, the skill, and the success of these enemies? Why, when you look at them, and then look at yourself, it is enough to make a hero turn pale. But when you look at them, and then think of the Captain of your salvation, here is enough to make a coward bold! "They looked unto Him and were lightened, and their faces were not ashamed."

Every Christian finds that without are fightings, and within are fears. We allow we have spoken here figuratively, but then all these figures are founded in fact, and these facts are exemplified in this experience of all real holiness.

But while we are reminded that we want strength, we are equally reminded that we have none of our own, or else we should not be required to seek strength in another, instead of looking for it in ourselves.

Now what is the Apostle's representation of our natural state? "When we were without strength," he says, "Christ died for us." We were without strength, we here see, as we were without righteousness. Men do not easily believe this. They are averse to this fact. They more readily acknowledge their guilt than their weakness. They may confess their sinfulness, but never question whether they can repent and believe and obey, and therefore they resolve to do this at some future period; but, alas! this time seldom ever arrives. Now the reason is, they are not convinced of their real condition by nature. They perceive not their state, and have not made the trial; for if they had made the trial, and made it in earnest, they would have been convinced and brought upon their knees, and induced to beg for what before they thought of buying. They would no longer rely upon their own worthiness before God, but would look to Him through Christ, and place all their dependence for life and salvation upon the atonement of the Redeemer, feeling that their own strength is perfect weakness.

Even the believer does not learn all at once; he is taught it by degrees From the very first, indeed, he is convinced that without Christ there are many things he cannot perform; but after a while he is taught the truth of our Lord's language, "Without Me ye can do nothing;" that he cannot perform the least duties aright if left to himself.

It seems a very easy thing for a man to number his days, for our days are not very numerous: and who is there that cannot number his days without Divine teaching? Yet Moses prays for this, saying, "So teach us to number our days that we may apply our hearts unto wisdom": we cannot learn that common and moral truth to purpose without illumination from above.

It seems to be an easy thing to read this blessed Bible and to understand it; but the king of Israel kneeled and prayed over it to God, saying, "Open Thou mine eyes, that I may behold wondrous things in Thy law." And it is written of our Saviour, that He opened the understandings of His disciples "that they might understand the Scriptures."

It seems an easy thing to pray: and it is an easy thing for some of you to pray. But what says an inspired apostle in regard to praying in the Holy Ghost? "We know not what we should pray for as we ought; but the Spirit itself maketh intercession for us"—by making intercession in us—"with groanings which cannot be uttered."

And as the Christian thus finds he cannot of himself do the least duty acceptably without aid from above, so neither can he keep himself from the greatest sins. He once thought little of this: he thought he was in little danger of falling into gross sins, as intemperance, drunkenness, and various other sins; that with regard to his reputation and profession, he should never fall. That, perhaps, is the reason why some of God's most eminent servants have fallen, not into those esteemed little, but into *great* sins. I have told you before now of one who often prayed, "Lord, keep me from the errors of wise men, and from the sins of good men."

If you look into the Scripture you will see how Noah and David and Peter fell, and fell from their highest excellence; how Moses, the meekest man, spake unadvisedly with his tongue; how Job, the most patient, cursed the day in which he was born; and how Peter, so brave in defending his Master's cause, denied his Lord.

You need not be afraid, Christian, of knowing too much ot your own weakness, or of feeling it too much; for, as the Apostle says to the Corinthians, "When I am weak, then am I strong." But blessed be God, we have strength in another; and hence says the Apostle, "Be strong in the Lord, and in the power of His might." And He in whom our strength is found is Almighty. Omnipotence itself is His. His name alone is Jehovah; and "In the Lord Jehovah is everlasting strength." He can do for us above what we can ask or think; hence the question is asked, "Is anything too hard for the Lord?" However active and strong any man may be, when he has laboured a while he is weary, he must have recourse to food or sleep. In order that he may do something one half of his time, he is obliged to do nothing the other, but be in a kind of insensibility. "But hast thou not known, hast thou not heard that the everlasting God, the Lord, the Creator of the ends of the earth, fainteth not, neither is weary? there is no searching of His understanding." Hast thou not heard of His power? "He giveth power to the faint; and to them that have no might He increaseth strength."

You cannot communicate strength to your fellow-creatures. You may desire it. You may give them medicine, but you cannot give them health. You may give them food, but you cannot nourish them. It is the blessing of God that does this upon the use of those means. You cannot really communicate strength to your fellow-creatures, but God can communicate it. He can make the weak strong. "Will He plead with me," says Job, "with His great power? No, but He will put strength in me." He has done this in the experience of all His people. Look back and read in history what He has done. See how He enabled Abraham, who was no better by nature than you, to offer up his own son Isaac. See how He gave strength to poor Job, who was enabled to say, "Though

He slay me, yet will I trust in Him." See what he has enabled the Martyrs to bear for His sake; and He is "the same yesterday, to-day, and for ever."

Observe, though He strengthens His people, He does not put the stock of strength into their possession, but supplies them as they stand in need. He "renews" it from time to time, and affords them fresh supplies. They come therefore to His throne of grace, that they "may obtain mercy and find grace to help in time of need." And the promise is, "As thy day so shall thy strength be." So God imparts for days of duty, active strength; for days of suffering, suffering strength; for the day of death, dying strength. It does not therefore become you to dread the approach of death now and conclude that you will feel the same when you come actually to die. No!—when you come to the valley of the shadow of death it is enough for you to know that Christ will be with you then, and that His rod and His staff will comfort you. Yes, and I have known many who have wept upon the mountains of Zion, who have sung, *O how loudly*—in the valley of the shadow of death, and have been a wonder to themselves.

"Oh," said Dr. Grosvenor, when dying, "I can now smile, because God smiles upon me."

The great John Goodwin was exceedingly troubled with the fear of death, yet it vanished at last, and he said, "Can this be dying?—Is this what I have dreaded so year after year? Is this death?" He was then blind, and he desired a person to read to him the eighth chapter of Epistle to the Romans, and when the reader came to the passage, "I am persuaded that neither death, nor life, nor angels, nor principalities, nor powers, nor things present, nor things to come, nor height, nor depth, nor any other creature, shall be able to separate us from the love of God, which is in Christ Jesus our Lord"—he said, "Put my finger there; I can die upon that." And, my friends, that chapter still remains, and God is still and ever will be the same faithful God. His mercy is everlasting; therefore put your trust in Him.

Then observe the expression. I was struck with it while coming here. It is not said, "You should be strong in the Lord"; but, "*Be* strong in the Lord." It is not here expressed after the manner of an exhortation; it is a command: "*Be* strong in the Lord, and in the power of His might." So it is intimated that we are not to be senseless and inactive under His influences; but that we should exercise holy activity and diligence.

Now God feeds the fowls of the air; but how does He feed them? He does not send an angel to put food into their mouths, but He gives them wings to fly for it, bills to pick it, crops to hold it, stomachs to digest it, and so on. They feed themselves, but see you not He provides for them and feeds them at the same time? Thus with regard to His people, He is the source of all; He makes them not His work, but His work-*men*, and He works in them to will and to do of His good pleasure. He teaches them, but then they learn. He does not fight the good fight, but enables them to fight. He does not run the race, but enables them to run.

Seek, therefore, my dear brethren, grace and wisdom and strength from the Lord. You have already sought Him, and not in vain. Surely you can say with David, "In the day that I cried, Thou answeredst me, and strengthenedst me with strength in my soul."

"Tho' in ourselves we have no stock,
The Lord is strong to save;
The door flies open when we knock,
And 'tis but ask and have."

The stock, therefore, is not in you.

"Retreat beneath *His* wings,
And in His strength confide;
This more exalts the King of kings
Than all your works beside."

It will help you much to attend upon the means of grace. It is your duty to be found in the use of these means. "Draw nigh to God, and He will draw nigh to you." You will derive profit, refreshment, encouragement, and assistance in a thousand ways by being free and communicative with each other. Thus David said, "Come and hear, all ye that fear God, and I will declare what He hath done for my soul." So it was with Jonathan. He went to David in the wood, it is said, and "strengthened his hands in God." You may thus comfort one another by believing reviews of life, and reviews of the dispensations of Providence and grace; like Asaph, who asked a number of questions—"Will the Lord cast off for ever? Will He be favourable no more? Hath He in anger shut up His tender mercies?" and so on. "But," said he, "This is my infirmity, this is my apprehension, my ignorance, and my unbelief. Well, but what will He do? He cries "This is my infirmity, but I will remember the years of the right hand of the Most High." The right hand is the hand of skill, the hand of power, the hand of donation, by which you give; and therefore the years of the right hand of the Lord are the years in which He has displayed His wisdom, His power, and His goodness. Hence the words of dear Newton:

> "His love in times past, forbids me to think,
> He'll leave me at last in trouble to sink;
> Each sweet Ebenezer I have in review
> Confirms His good pleasure to help me quite thro'."

O, my brethren, trust in Him and be not afraid. "Trust in Him at all times, ye people; pour out your heart before Him; God is a refuge for us. Look to Him in all your duties, submit to Him in all your trials, and expect from Him the fulfilment of the word upon which He has caused you to hope: and remember that "the Lord God is a sun and shield; the Lord will give peace and glory; no good thing will He withhold from them that walk uprightly."

XXXVI.

CHRISTIAN COURAGE.

(Delivered on Thursday Evening, July 10th, 1848.)

"*And in nothing terrified by your adversaries: which is to them an evident token of perdition, but to you of salvation, and that of God.*"—PHILIPPIANS i. 28.

ALL the stars shine, but one star differeth from another star in glory; all the good ground in the parable was productive, but it yielded in some places thirty, and in some sixty, and in some a hundredfold. Now we may apply this to pious individuals. What difference do we perceive here between one Christian and another? Lot, the nephew of Abraham, is called "just Lot," and yet what is he when compared with his godly uncle?

What a difference we perceive between the centurion, who was satisfied with our Lord's word, and Thomas, who said, "Except I see in His hands the print of the nails, and thrust my hand into His side, I will not believe!" which led our Lord to say, "Thomas, because thou hast seen Me thou hast believed; blessed are they who have not seen, and yet have believed." This will also apply to churches and even to primitive churches. There were some good persons in the Church of Corinth; they abounded much in gifts, but they were proud and disrespectful; and with regard to Paul, the more he loved them the less he was loved. He therefore would not be beholden to them. He would not receive anything from them, no, not a penny, and all the while he was with them he laboured, working with his own hands to sustain himself, and said with a noble independence, "We seek not yours, but you." It was far otherwise with the Church of Philippi. What a lovely body of Christians were they! We admire them, if it be only for their behaviour towards Paul himself. Therefore he says, "I rejoiced in the Lord greatly, that now at the last your care of me hath flourished again; wherein ye were also careful, but ye lacked opportunity. Not that I speak in respect of want; for I have learned in whatsoever state I am, therewith to be content. I know both how to be abased, and I know how to abound everywhere and in all things. I am instructed both to be full and to be hungry, both to abound and to suffer need. I can do all things through Christ which strengtheneth me. Notwithstanding ye have well done, that ye did communicate with my affliction. Now ye Philippians, know also that in the beginning of the gospel when I departed from Macedonia, no church communicated with me"—O, what a sad reflection!—"concerning giving and receiving, but ye only. For even in Thessalonica ye sent once and again unto my necessity. Not because I desire a gift: but I desire fruit that may abound to *your* account." He therefore calls them his "brethren," his "dearly beloved," his "joy and crown." And says, "I thank my God upon every remembrance of you, always in every prayer of mine for you all, making request with joy, for your fellowship in the gospel from the first day unto now." Paul was now a prisoner at Rome; he hoped to obtain release, not that he was unwilling to die, for he could say, "I long to depart and be with Christ, which is far better." But to abide in the flesh was more needful for *them*, and therefore he was ready to forego the enjoyment of heaven for a number of years, and to reside in a vale of tears. Such is the benevolence the grace of God inspires, inducing its possessor to imitate Him, who, "though He was rich, yet for our sakes became poor, that we through His poverty might become rich." Therefore says he, "Having this confidence, I know that I shall abide and continue with you all for your furtherance and joy of faith; that your rejoicing may be more abundant in Christ Jesus for me by my coming to see you again. Only let your conversation be as it becometh the gospel of Christ: that whether I come and see you, or else be absent, I may hear of your affairs, that ye stand fast in one spirit, with one mind, striving together for the faith of the gospel; and in nothing terrified by your adversaries."

Thus we reach our text, from which we may consider, their condition supposed, and their duty enjoined. The one showing that they have adversaries, and the other showing that they ought not to be afraid of them.

I. Remark: THEIR CONDITION SUPPOSED. They had adversaries; and had not their Lord and Saviour, to whose image we are predestinated to be conformed, adversaries also, though He could challenge His enemies, saying, "Which of you convinceth Me of sin?" When they took up stones to stone Him, "He enquired, saying, "Many good works have I shown you from the Father, for which of these works do ye stone Me?" They hated Him without a cause. Therefore He said to His disciples, "If they have persecuted Me, they will also persecute you, for the servant is not greater than His Lord." You see, then, they were not taken by surprise, for from the beginning they were told what they were to experience. Therefore our Saviour said, "If any man come to Me, and hate not his father, and mother, and wife, and children, and brethren, and sisters—yea, and his own life also, he cannot be My disciple: and whosoever doth not bear his cross and come after Me cannot be My disciple." He employed two images, the one showing what they had to part with, the other what they had to contend with. "Which of you intending to build a tower, sitteth not down first and counteth the cost whether he hath sufficient to finish it? Lest haply, after he hath laid the foundation and is not able to finish it, all that behold it begin to mock him, saying, This man began to build, and was not able to finish. Or what king going to make war against another king, sitteth not down first and consulteth, whether he be able with ten thousand to meet him that cometh against him with twenty thousand? Or else while the other is yet a great way off, he sendeth an ambassage and desireth conditions of peace. So likewise, whosoever he be of you that forsaketh not all that he hath cannot be My disciple." He therefore said to them again, "Woe to you when all men speak well of you. I send you forth as lambs in the midst of wolves. You shall be hated of all men for My name's sake, but those that persecute you will think he doeth God service. In the world ye shall have tribulation, but in Me ye shall have peace." Therefore said the Saviour to Ananias respecting Paul, when he became converted, "I will show him how great things he must suffer for My sake." Therefore said Paul to the souls he confirmed, "All that will live godly in Christ Jesus must suffer persecution."

Now, I must give you a caution; you must beware, as Peter says, "lest ye being led away with the error of the wicked, fall from your own steadfastness." It is not the cross but the cause that makes the martyr. Your suffering must be for the truth's sake, for righteousness' sake, for Christ's sake, "that the Spirit of glory and of God may rest upon you; that you may rejoice inasmuch as you are partakers of Christ's sufferings, that when His glory shall be revealed ye may be glad with exceeding joy." If we are to suffer let us see to it that it be neither for immoral nor imprudent conduct.

Men are not our only adversaries. What says Peter? "Be sober, be vigilant, because your adversary the devil, as a roaring lion, walketh about, seeking whom he may devour." We know but little of the mode or malignancy of his agency, but the reality cannot be denied, without our denying the plainest declarations of Scripture. You have heard the language of the Apostle this evening, wherein he says, "Ye wrestle not against flesh and blood, but against principalities and powers, against the rulers of the darkness of this world, against spiritual wickedness in high places." Verily Christians have adversaries. How else could they realize the representations given of them in the Gospel? Christians are called "good soldiers of Jesus Christ." They "fight the good fight of faith, and lay hold on eternal life": and under this character provision is made equipment, both defensive and offensive. "Wherefore take unto you the whole armour of God, that ye may be able to withstand in the evil day, and having done to stand. Stand, therefore, having your loins girt about with truth, and having on the breastplate of righteousness, and your feet shod with the preparation of the gospel of peace; above all, taking the shield of faith, wherewith ye shall be able to quench all the fiery darts of the wicked. And take the helmet of salvation, and the sword of the Spirit, which is the Word of God: praying always with all prayer and supplication in the Spirit."

II. Their Duty. They have adversaries, but they are not to be afraid of them. "In nothing terrified by your adversaries."

This is not to be taken in a sense so as to exclude our apprehension of them, so as not to induce us to watch against them; what the Apostle means is, that we are not to be induced to deviate from the truth, or to conceal our principles. We are not to be terrified by their skill, or their malice, or their power, or their number. They have cast down many strong men, yea, they have conquered princes, heroes and philosophers; yea, they have conquered the world, for "the whole world lieth in wickedness." Yet, says the Apostle, "In nothing terrified by your adversaries," and there are good reasons for this. Consider some of them.

First, you should not be terrified by your adversaries, *for they are never unseen by God.* Many of them are indeed unseen by you. It is dangerous to have to do with an unseen adversary, but God knows them all, "the darkness hideth not from Him, but the night shineth as the day." "Hell is naked before Him, and destruction hath no covering." He knows the way that you take; "He knoweth thy walking through this great wilderness;" "He keepeth the feet of His saints, but the wicked shall be silent in darkness."

Secondly, you should not be terrified by your adversaries, *for they can do nothing without God's permission.* They are entirely under His control. Remember this. You see Job: "Hast Thou not made a hedge about him, and about all that he hath?" says Satan, who had searched this hedge all round to see if there were any breach in it, but found it too firm to be penetrated: he examined it to see if it could not be passed over, he found it too high for him; he therefore ascribed all Job's religion to his selfishness, and told God that but for this, his safety and advantage, he would curse Him to His face. "Well, then, try him," says God; "I will allow you to do this, he shall be at your disposal, and in your hand," only observe the Almighty forbids him to touch his life. Thus you see how completely he was under God's control. So Satan was obliged to go and pray to Christ before he could touch Peter. "Satan hath desired to have thee," says the Saviour. The devils could not enter into the herd of swine till they had asked leave. Bunyan has finely pourtrayed this in his account of the hill Difficulty: There was a lion on the right hand and on the left, and Christian was afraid to advance, but he was told that they were chained, and that if he kept in the middle of the path they could not reach him. Remember this, therefore, Christians.

Thirdly, *He who is with you is above them all,* and says, "Fear not, for I am with thee; be not dismayed, for I am thy God." Yes, He is with you. It is beautifully said by Dr. Watts—

> "A thousand savage beasts of prey
> Around the forest roam,
> But Judah's Lion guards the way,
> And brings the strangers home."

It used to be proverbially said of Rome, that it was unbecoming a Roman soldier to fear while Cæsar was alive. I am sure it is unbecoming a Christian soldier to fear, while Jesus his Saviour lives. He hath said, "Because I live, ye shall live also." While Satan may insinuate, "there is no help for him in God," the Christian may exclaim with the apostle, "If God be for us, who can be against us?"

Fourthly, You should never be terrified by your adversaries, *because they can never destroy or injure your main interests.* Though they may take away a little of your spending money, they cannot touch your jewels. The soul is the man, and this is beyond their reach. Therefore said the Saviour, "Fear not them that kill the body, and after that have no more that they can do, but fear Him who can destroy both body and soul in hell." Your treasure is not on earth; then you might well be afraid; but "your treasure is in heaven, where neither moth nor rust doth corrupt, nor thieves break through and steal." The Saviour says, "To him that overcometh, I will give to eat of the tree of life that is in the midst of the paradise of God," and no serpent can ever enter into that garden of the Lord. "My sheep," says the Saviour, "hear My voice, and I know them, and they follow me; and I give unto them eternal life, neither shall any man pluck them out of My hand." We might go on beyond this, and finish with the words of Paul, "I am persuaded that neither life nor death, nor things present, nor things to come, nor angels, nor principalities, nor powers, nor things present, nor things to come, nor height nor depth, nor any other creature shall be able to separate us from the love of God, which is in Christ Jesus our Lord."

Lastly, You should not be terrified by your adversaries, *because you are sure of vanquishing them.* This is not the case in any other conflict. It is, therefore, a proper caution to other warriors, "Let not him that girdeth on his harness boast as he that putteth it off." From some cause or other, the best commanders and the best disciplined troops have sometimes been routed and defeated; but the Christian soldier enters the field under peculiar advantages. If he has not struck a blow, he may strike it with confidence; and if he has fallen through a blow received, he may say "Rejoice not against me, O my enemy; for when I fall, I shall arise again." "Nay, in all these things we are more than conquerors." How? and why? A soldier may barely conquer; had there been a little more resistance, he had fainted and lost the day; but this is not the case with Christians. After they have overcome all their adversaries they could defy thousands and millions more. Moses said to the children of Israel, "The enemies ye see to-day, ye shall see no more for ever," and God said to Israel, by Zephaniah, "The Lord is in the midst of you, ye shall not see evil any more." And as this victory is sure, so it will be equally complete. "Him that overcometh shall inherit all things;" and as it is sure and complete so it is also near. A few more rising and setting suns, and "your sun shall no more go down, nor your moon withdraw itself, for the Lord shall be your everlasting light, and the days of your mourning shall be ended." The helmet will be taken off your heads and a crown of glory put on which fadeth not away.

You, therefore, see from what we have said, that your enemies are always seen by Him who loves you—that they can do nothing without His permission—that He who is with you is above them all—that they cannot destroy or injure your main interest—that you will more than vanquish them, and that this will be speedily. You should therefore examine yourself, and remember, "no cross, no crown." It is a sad evidence against you if you find your religious course no longer a warfare; for a warfare it has ever been found by all the followers of the Lamb. It is an evidence, therefore, in your favour if you find it to be so. How good is the Lord in providing support and consolation under trial! He hath said to His ministers, "Comfort ye, comfort ye my people." His people are also called upon to comfort one another; He would have His people not only safe, but cheerful; He hath said, "Let not your hearts be troubled." You see, though it becomes Christians to take heed, according to the admonition, "Let him that thinketh he standeth take heed lest he fall," yet it also becomes them to exercise holy courage. "The righteous are as bold as a lion," that is, they should be so, their experience requires it. Bunyan with as much truth as genius, has made Mr. Greatheart the conductor of the pilgrims; how much courage it requires to go forth without the camp, bearing His reproach! to follow the Saviour through all opposition! Let, therefore, the weak say with David, "The Lord is my light and my salvation, whom shall I fear? The Lord is the strength of my heart, of whom shall I be afraid? Though an host should encamp against me, my heart shall not fear; though war should rise against me, in this will I be confident."

XXXVII.

A GLORIOUS TRANSLATION.

(Delivered on Thursday Evening, February 27th, 1845.)

"*Who hath delivered us from the power of darkness, and hath translated us into the kingdom of His dear Son.*"—COLOSSIANS i. 13.

DIVINE grace makes a real and marvellous change in all its subjects. Isaiah emphatically expressed this, when he said, "Instead of the thorn shall come up the fig-tree, and instead of the brier the myrtle-tree; and it shall be to the Lord for a name, for an everlasting sign, which shall not be cut off." And this is implied in Paul's question to the Corinthians, "Who maketh thee to differ from another?" so that there is a difference between them and others, such a difference as exists between wheat and tares—between sheep and wolves—between slaves and free men—between the living and the dead. And while they are thus made to differ from others, they also differ from their former selves; and no wonder, "for by nature they were children of wrath, even as others." They are ready to acknowledge this, and say, "We ourselves were sometimes foolish, serving divers lusts and pleasures, hateful, and hating one another. But after this, the loving-kindness of God our Saviour appeared"—for they well know that whatever they are, they are not by birth, but by conversion. They therefore with humble and grateful feelings often look, though not often enough, "to the rock whence they were hewn, and the hole of the pit whence they were digged;" and considering their present privileges, and their future hopes, they can express themselves in the language of the Apostle, "Giving thanks unto the Father, which hath made us meet to be partakers of the inheritance of the saints in light; who hath delivered us from the power of darkness, and hath translated us into the kingdom of His dear Son." Let us consider, first, their natural state; secondly, their new condition; and thirdly, the operation which delivers them from the one and translates them into the other.

I. Let us consider THEIR NATURAL STATE. They were in the possession or under the power of darkness.

"This is a very good and just representation," some may be ready to say," of the state of the heathen without the Gospel, for they are under the rulers of the darkness of this world and spiritual wickedness in high places; they are without God in the world." But, brethren, need you be informed that every unchanged sinner is a little heathen world in himself? He is without the knowledge of our Lord Jesus Christ.

Others say, that there are some who stand in need of conversion, but not all; for there are some who have happily retained their original innocence; and there are others who, though they require an improvement, do not need an entire change. But what saith the Scripture? This assures us that we are all descended from the same original stock, and "Who can bring a clean thing out of an unclean?" that we are not in different states, but only in different degrees of the same state; that we are all going astray, though every one turns to his own way.

But now as to this state and condition—the natural state of God's own people under "the power of darkness." The term is used in Scripture for many things. *Ignorance* is darkness; and under the power of this, they were once "alienated from the life of God through the ignorance that is in them, because of the blindness of their heart." *Sin* is darkness, and they were under the power of this; "sin had dominion over them, and they obeyed it in the lusts thereof." *Misery* is darkness; and under the power of this they found "the way of transgressors was hard"; that "there is no peace to the wicked," but that "destruction and misery are in their path." *Death* is darkness; and under the power of this they felt themselves doomed to die, and subject to bondage through the fear thereof. The *devil* is the prince of darkness, and he had a peculiar influence over them. You remember when our Saviour sent His Apostles to go forth to the Gentiles, He sent them to "open their eyes, and to turn them from darkness to light, and from the power of Satan unto God." There are some persons weak enough to deny his existence; but if there be no such being, our Saviour came into the world to destroy a nonentity, for "He came to destroy the works of the devil."

"The power of darkness" is Satan's tyranny, his agency, his influence. "And we are not ignorant of his devices." "He blinds the minds of them that believe not"; he filled Ananias and Sapphira with deceit; he is "the spirit now working in the children of disobedience"; "the world lieth in wickedness"—or, it lieth in the wicked one; that is, the devil. His government of man was not original, but it is the consequence of rebellion. Having forsaken God, their rightful sovereign, He suffered the enemy to triumph over them. They talk of liberty, but of what a man is overcome, of the same is he brought in bondage. "His servants ye are to whom ye obey, whether of sin unto death, or of obedience unto righteousness." Men express their hatred of slavery, and yet they live in the most dishonourable and rigorous vassalage. They are "taken captive by the devil at his will." Or, to vary the metaphor, though not the meaning, "Ye are," says the Saviour, "of your father the devil, and the lusts of your father ye will do."

II. Let us now turn the medal. Having seen their natural state, let us view THEIR RENEWED CONDITION. "He hath delivered us from the power of darkness, and hath translated us into the kingdom of His dear Son"; where we observe three things: the character of Jesus, His empire, and the privilege of being His subjects.

First, *the character of Jesus*, God's dear Son. Dear to Him, and as Watts says, "Chosen of God, to sinners dear"; but not to all, the greater part of them despise and reject Him; but all awakened and convinced sinners exclaim, "What must I do to be saved?" and to them, Oh how dear is He!

> "And saints adore His name;
> They trust their whole salvation here;
> Nor shall they suffer shame."

"To them that believe He is precious." He takes care to make Himself precious to all of them. He makes Himself infinitely dear, by showing them what He has done, what He has suffered, and what He means to do. This is not all. He is not only dear to saints, but dear to angels. "He was seen of angels" in the days of His flesh.

> "Through all His trials here below,
> They did His steps attend;
> They oft rejoiced, and wondered where
> His course of love would end."

And now that He is in heaven, we are informed that they are adoring Him, and with a loud voice exclaim, "Worthy is the Lamb that was slain, to receive power, and riches, and wisdom, and strength, and honour, and glory, and blessing." But principally He is dear to God. He is His only begotten Son, His Elect, in whom His soul delighteth. We read that "The Father loveth the Son, and hath given all things into His hand." He feels an infinite complacency in His Person, in His work, in His sufferings, and in His Atonement. His offering and sacrifice was a sweet-smelling savour, and through these man was not originally so dear to God as he now becomes when he enters His presence sprinkled with the blood of Christ, and making mention of His righteousness. "We are accepted in the Beloved." So dear is He to the Father, that when we go to Him, and ask anything in His name, He cannot refuse. "Whatsoever," says the Saviour, "ye ask the Father in my name, He will do it."

Then observe, secondly, *His Empire.* For He has a kingdom, "and hath translated us into the kingdom of His dear Son." Once He had not where to lay His head, and widows ministered to Him of their substance; but now He fills the throne of universal empire; now "He is King of kings, and Lord of lords;" now "He changeth the times and the seasons; He removeth kings and setteth up kings," and empires rise and fall at His nod; "He doeth according to His will in the armies of heaven, and amongst the inhabitants of earth;" and "none can stay His hand, or say unto Him, What doest Thou?" Sinners, by an overruling Providence, accomplish His designs. "The wrath of man is made to praise Him." "He is the Governor among the nations."

But He has a kingdom which in the Scripture is called "righteousness and peace, and joy in the Holy Ghost"; a kingdom which "cometh not by observation"; that kingdom of God which is "not in word but in power"; that kingdom of which He spake when before Pilate He made so good a confession, and said, "Now is my kingdom not from hence." It means His *mediatorial* kingdom—that kingdom which was the recompense of His sufferings, the joy that was set before Him, and for which "He endured the cross." "Because He was obedient unto death, even the death of the cross, therefore God also hath highly exalted Him, and hath given Him a name which is above every name, that at the name of Jesus every knee should bow, of things in heaven and things on earth and things under the earth, and that every tongue should confess that Jesus Christ is Lord to the glory of God the Father." Yes, because His soul was to be made an offering for sin He was to see His seed, He was to prolong His days, "and the pleasure of the Lord was to prosper in His hand." He therefore spake of this as a donation, for it is very distinguishable from His original and essential dominion as God. "All power," says He, "is given unto me in heaven and in earth." So in the visions of Daniel. Daniel says, "There was given Him dominion and glory, and a kingdom, that all people, nations, and languages should serve Him: His dominion is an everlasting dominion which shall not pass away, and His kingdom that which shall not be destroyed."

In this kingdom all His followers have an interest, a deep and eternal interest. He therefore said to His disciples previously to His death, "Ye are ye that have continued with Me in My temptations. And I appoint unto you a kingdom as My Father hath appointed unto Me, that ye may eat and drink at My table in My kingdom, and sit on thrones, judging the twelve tribes of Israel."

Observe, thirdly, *the privileges of His subjects.* For you see, it is supposed that it is an inestimable blessedness to be under His empire, to live beneath His reign. "He hath delivered us from the power of darkness, and hath translated us into the kingdom of His dear Son." Oh, what a kingdom is this! a kingdom which can never be destroyed: "the everlasting kingdom of our Lord and Saviour, Jesus Christ"; a kingdom which cannot even be shaken, but must remain. What immunities are attached to this kingdom, and what honours, what privileges, and what benefits are attached to all those who are subjects in this empire! What *security* have they? "Their place of defence shall be the munition of rocks;" "they are kept by the mighty power of God." What *plenty* have they? He furnishes them with a table in the wilderness; and they "are blessed with all spiritual blessings in Christ Jesus." What *peace* have they? "A peace passing all understanding." What *liberty* have they? "The glorious liberty of the sons of God." But if their privileges are so great with regard to their present state, what will be their future enjoyment! The Apostle says, "Eye hath not seen, nor ear heard, neither have entered into the heart of man, the things which God hath prepared for them that love Him." No, "it doth not yet appear what we shall be; but we know that when He shall appear we shall be like Him, for we shall see Him as He is." Well may the Psalmist say, "How great is Thy goodness which Thou hast laid up for them that fear Thee, which Thou hast wrought for them that fear Thee before the sons of men."

III. You have seen their natural state, and viewed their renewed condition. Let us observe next—THE OPERATION WHICH DELIVERS THEM FROM THE ONE AND TRANSLATES THEM INTO THE OTHER.

You will observe first, *this operation is divine.* "*He* hath" done it. "Of Him, and to Him, and through Him are all things, to whom be glory." He gave us "His only begotten Son," and He now gives His Holy Spirit to them that obey Him; and the promise and performance are equally His own where He says, "Then will I sprinkle clean water upon you, and ye shall be clean. From all your filthiness, and from all your idols, will I cleanse you." In this work means are used, but then "the excellency of the power is not of them, but of God." Instrumentality is not incompatible with agency, but supposes it. An instrument can effect nothing without an agent. A sword could not destroy without a hand to wield it. "Who then," asks the Apostle, "who then is Paul? Or who is Apollos? but ministers by whom ye believed?"

This operation as God's own may be so considered two ways: First: as an act of His power. "His people shall be willing in the day of His *power*," and it is an act of His *grace*. This all His subjects will acknowledge; that it is "not of debt, but of grace."

Secondly, *this operation is achieved.* "He *hath*," not that He will. This renovation is not complete indeed now, but it is begun, and the accomplishment is ensured. Therefore, it can be, and ought to be, received as accomplished in a sense already. The meaning is, not that we are now freed from the being of sin, but from the power of it. It is dethroned, and the love of it is destroyed. "Old things are passed away; behold, all things are become new"—new in the degree, but not in the quality. This is the meaning of the Apostle. It is true as yet we do not see the full corn in the ear, but we see the blade: it is true as yet we do not see the day, but we see the dawn. "The path of the just is as the shining light, which shineth more and more unto the perfect day." We therefore read, though we are not acquainted yet with all the privileges of our adoption, "Now are we the sons of God"; and though they are not always assured of their justification, and are sometimes ready to write bitter things against themselves, "There is now no condemnation to them that are in Christ Jesus, who walk not after the flesh, but after the Spirit"; and "he that believeth on the Son of God *hath* eternal life, and shall never come into condemnation, but is passed from death unto life."

Thirdly, *the operation is apprehended.* Paul and his companions do not use the language of doubt or hesitation, or of hope only, but of full conviction and persuasion. "*He hath delivered us* from the power of darkness, and *hath translated us* into the kingdom of His dear Son." It is true all are not able to use language so decisive and conclusive. Were we to affirm this, "we should offend against the generation of God's children." Yet we may say, That all the subjects of divine grace are not satisfied to leave things at an uncertainty; they therefore often pray, "Say unto my soul, I am thy salvation." And this anxiety, by the way, is a token for good. It is possible to come to this blessed conclusion: we have many instances in the Scriptures of truth. Sometimes the Christian can rise into "the full assurance of hope," and can "rejoice with joy unspeakable and full of glory." At other times, there may be many things of which he may not be certain, yet he can say with the man in the gospel, "Whereas I was blind, now I see; I was once senseless, but I now feel the power of divine things;" whereas the Saviour was once an object of indifference, He is now "the fairest among ten thousand, and the altogether lovely."

In conclusion, "Behold how the fine gold is become dim." We are constrained to ask, "Lord, what is man?" We speak not this as to his physical, or mental, or intellectual powers, for there if we look at the discoveries made, and the achievements accomplished, he seems but little lower than the angels. But we speak in relation to his moral power, as a being who appears before God in relation to eternity. Some even here would speak of the dignity of human nature, but where do they find it? Not in the Scriptures of truth, for are we not there assured that "the heart is deceitful above all things and desperately wicked?" And is not our wretched condition implied in all the provisions of the Gospel? For what need have we of a physician if we are not sick? or of a Redeemer if we are not in slavery? Then observe that there is no such thing as neutrality here. "No man can serve two masters." You must be walking after the flesh, or after the Spirit.

Then if God has thus "delivered you from the power of darkness and translated into the kingdom of His dear Son," you will exercise gratitude and thanksgiving, and, constrained by the mercies of God, you will present your bodies "a living sacrifice, holy, acceptable unto God, which is your reasonable service."

XXXVIII.

THREE GRACES.

(Delivered on Thursday Evening, August 14th, 1845.)

"*Remembering without ceasing your work of faith, and labour of love, and patience of hope in our Lord Jesus Christ, in the sight of God and our Father.*"—1 THESSALONIANS i. 3.

WE have some account of the introduction of the gospel into Thessalonica in the Acts of the Apostles, where we read, that "when they had passed through Amphipolis and Apollonia, they came to Thessalonica, where was a synagogue of the Jews: and Paul, as his manner was, went in unto them, and three Sabbath days reasoned with them out of the Scriptures—opening and alleging that Christ must needs have suffered, and risen again from the dead; and that this Jesus whom I preach unto you, is Christ. And some of them believed, and consorted with Paul and Silas; and of the devout Greeks a great multitude, and of the chief women not a few. But the Jews, which believed not, moved with envy, took unto them certain lewd fellows of the baser sort, and gathered a company, and set all the city on an uproar, and assaulted the house of Jason, and sought to bring them out to the people." So they were desired by the brethren to withdraw, and they departed. But though they were so shamefully entreated, the good seed of the kingdom they had sown sprung up and produced, "thirty, sixty, and an hundred fold;" for the Word of God was not bound, but had "free course, and was glorified," and the church formed and established by the Apostle flourished abundantly. When absent in body, therefore, he addressed it by letters. He unites with himself Silvanus and Timothy, though they were far his inferiors, and thus saluted them: "Paul, and Silvanus, and Timotheus, unto the Church of the Thessalonians which is in God the Father and in the Lord Jesus Christ: Grace be unto you, and peace, from God our Father and the Lord Jesus Christ. We give thanks to God always for you all, making mention of you in our prayers;

remembering without ceasing your work of faith, and labour of love, and patience of hope in our Lord Jesus Christ in the sight of God and our Father."

Let us now make a few reflections on this portion of God's Word, considering the Apostle's gratitude on their behalf, the grounds of his remembrance of them, and the character of their graces and their duties.

I. Remark THE APOSTLE'S GRATITUDE ON THEIR BEHALF. "We give thanks to God always for you all, making mention of you in our prayers."

Observe *to whom* his thanksgivings were addressed. "To God," you say, "surely; He is the Fountain of Life; He is the giver of every good and perfect gift." This is very true, but this is not the reason why we notice the object of his gratitude. But, as the Apostle exceedingly extols these Thessalonians, and we have many instances of his approbation, commendation, and even applause; by addressing his thanksgivings to God, he would teach them that he did not absolutely praise them, but would glorify God in them. He would lead them to say, "Not unto us, not unto us, O Lord; but unto Thy name give glory;" he would lead them to acknowledge that "by the grace of God they were what they were."

Then observe the *universality* of this thanksgiving. "We give thanks to God always for you *all*." When ministers look over their congregations, they have often various feelings excited. Some are their comforts, others are their trials; they stand in doubt of some, they are confident with regard to others, that "God who has begun a good work in them will perform it until the day of Christ." While some are advancing, some are standing still, or beginning to look back; but all here were either Paul's "hope, or joy, or crown of rejoicing." The young—the old—the poor—the rich, were all walking so as to please God.

Observe also the *constancy* of it. "We give thanks to God *always* for you all," for their goodness was not "as the morning cloud, or the early dew which soon passes away." They "did run well" and were not hindered. They "began in the spirit," and did not end in the flesh. They were "steadfast, immovable, always abounding in the work of the Lord," so that he had always occasion to abound in praise for them all; not that he could be always actually thinking of them, but then he frequently thought of them, especially in his hallowed moments and devotional exercises.

For, you may observe again, his thanksgiving was always connected with supplication. "We give always thanks for you all, *making mention of you in our prayers.*" There are two connections here worthy of remark. The one is, that prayer should always be accompanied with thanksgiving. So Paul says to the Philippians, "Be careful for nothing, but in everything by prayer and supplication, with thanksgiving"—never omit this in your prayers—"with thanksgiving let your request be made known unto God." "In everything give thanks, knowing that this is the will of God in Christ Jesus concerning you." But if prayer should always be accompanied with thanksgiving, thanksgiving should always be accompanied with prayer. For, brethren, however advanced we may be in the divine life, "we have not yet attained, nor are we already perfect." We can never enter the presence of God without having something to confess, something to deplore, some defect in our actions or experience, without needing something to be added to our graces, or to enliven us in our duties. He has made provision for all we still need, but "for all these things He will be enquired of by us." Therefore we are to "pray without ceasing."

II. Consider THE GROUNDS OF THIS INCESSANT AND GRATEFUL REMEMBRANCE OF THEM. "Remembering without ceasing your work of faith, and labour of love, and patience of hope."

Generally, you observe, the grounds of his thankfulness were for spiritual influences and blessings, not that other blessings are to be overlooked or undervalued. We are not worthy of the least of all God's mercies; and outward benefits and comforts, while we are here, call for our gratitude, but after all we should judge of things according to their real value; for what is the body to the soul? What is time to eternity? What are blessings which appertain only to the present world compared with those which will afford you support, and yield you satisfaction in a dying hour, that will prepare you for all the changes of life, for a passage into "the valley of the shadow of death," and for an appearance at the Judgment Seat of Christ?

The Apostle here mentions, "the work of faith, and labour of love, and patience of hope."

First, he remembers their "*work of faith.*" Much is said in the Scriptures concerning faith. Faith is a fundamental grace. It is represented as a fountain, and you are required "to build up yourselves on your most holy faith." It is a radical grace, that is, it is a root, and this sustains the tree with its branches and its fruit. Some are afraid we should say too much about faith, and seem to think it will lead to licentiousness or to indifference. We will by no means undervalue good works, but no good works are valuable in the sight of God without it. Observe it is not a dormant or dead principle in the mind. James had probably to deal with such a personage as this. He says "Shew me thy faith without thy works," that is, shew me a sun that does not shine; shew me a fire that does not burn, or a fountain that does not flow, "and I will shew thee my faith by my works—I will shew you the spring in the stream; I will shew you my creed in my conduct, and my principles in my conduct;" and this is the best way in which we can shew our faith. For "if the body without the spirit is dead, so faith without works is dead also."

Therefore we read of the "Work of faith." It is, first, a work of *conviction*. It is alarming, humbling. By means of it, "the proud looks of men are brought down, and the Lord alone is exalted." The man no longer goes about to establish his own righteousness, but submits himself to the righteousness of God. He sees that he is not required to build a shelter for himself, but to "fly for refuge to the hope set before him in the Gospel." The first work of faith is to surrender ourselves into His hands, saying, "Lord, I am Thine, save me." "Lord, save, or I perish." It is to keep Him before the eyes of our mind. It is to deal with Him concerning our souls and eternity—in our justification to mention His righteousness only as our acceptance before God. In prayer to use His name, to plead for His sake, "through whom we have boldness and access with confidence," and under a sense of our unworthiness and guilt, to make mention of His name.

Then there is a *purifying* work. So says the apostle, "purifying your hearts by faith," and nothing but the blood of Christ brought into the conscience by faith ever will cleanse the soul from the love of sin, but this can do it. There are thousands now living who by means of it are "dead indeed unto sin, but alive unto God through Jesus Christ our Lord." So it leads to obedience; the subject of it will say, "Lord, what wilt Thou have me to do?" We read of "the obedience of faith;" that obedience which faith demands, and that obedience which faith yields. Those in Scripture mentioned as most remarkable for faith, were also most remarkable for obedience.

Then there is a *conquering* work, for Christians are soldiers;

as such they are called to "fight the good fight of faith," and "this is the victory which overcometh the world, even our faith." It overcomes its smiles and frowns, alarms and menaces; nothing but faith can ever achieve this.

There is also a *loving* work for it to do. "For neither circumcision availeth anything, nor uncircumcision, but faith which worketh by love"—by love to the Saviour, love to His house, and love to His people.

This leads us to consider another ground of His grateful remembrance of them, namely, the "*labour of love.*" As faith is a working grace, love is a very laborious one also. The degree of this love may also be known by a readiness to obey the Saviour's laws. You will by it be made God's willing people, and will not be framing excuses, or pleading for delays, or urging difficulties; no, you will not be satisfied with professions of love in word or tongue, but yours must be "in deed and in truth." You will not say, "Go in peace, be ye warned, and be ye filled;" but the "labour of love" will fill, and warm too. You will not be satisfied with giving a little which you do not want, and which you can never use yourself, in consequence of importunity, but you will be induced to act; you will be induced to "visit the widows and fatherless in their afflictions," as well as to "keep yourselves unspotted from the world."

You may know what the "labour of love" is by its pleasantness. You well know that such labour is not a task, it is no a drudgery. Pharaoh's daughter said to the mother of Moses, "Take this child, and nurse it for me, and I will pay thee thy wages." Here the mother was the nurse. She laboured in this department, but it was the "labour of love" you may be assured; and though she was promised a recompense, she would have done the work without it. How was it with Jacob? He served seven years for Rachel, but it appeared unto him but as seven days, because of the love he bore towards her. This was the "labour of love." Jesus, above all said, "I must work the work of Him that sent me, while it is day." "He went about doing good." "He pleased not Himself," yet He was pleased, and He delighted in it, for it was the "labour of love." Therefore, said He, "My meat is to do the will of Him that sent Me, and to finish His work." So it is with Christians, God pours His love into their hearts, and then the whole of their religion is the "labour of love," so that they feel not "His commandments to be grievous." No, His "yoke is easy, and

His burden light." It is indeed a yoke, but like the yoke of marriage, for which a man blessed God every day for the bondage. It is like a pair of wings to a bird, which gives it buoyancy, and allows it to travel the skies.

Here is another thing: It is the "*patience of hope* in our Lord Jesus Christ, in the sight of God and our Father." As the "work of faith" is the work which faith produces, as the "labour of love" is the labour which love performs, so "the patience of hope" is the patience which hope engenders. Much is said of hope in the Scriptures of truth. If Christians are mariners, this hope is their "anchor, both sure and steadfast." If soldiers, this hope is their "helmet," to guard their heads in the day of battle. If travellers, it is their companion, to soothe and encourage them as they go on.

Patience is required of us for two purposes. First, to enable us to *wait*. Here sometimes much patience is required, for "hope deferred maketh the heart sick, but when the desire cometh it is a tree of life." What an instance have we in Paul, who desired "to depart and be with Christ, which was far better;" yet with all his confidence and desire, he was willing to abide in a poor body in this vale of tears, where he was reproached and persecuted; he was willing to be detained from month to month and year to year. And, Christians, you must not be impatient if you desire heaven and are assured of it, but all the days of your appointed time you should wait, till your change come. So with regard to other things, God does not always immediately answer prayer, or afford deliverance. "He is a God of judgment; blessed are all they that wait for Him." "It is good," says Jeremiah, "that a man both hope and quietly wait for the salvation of God."

But patience is necessary also to *suffer*. It was this that enabled the first Christians to "take joyfully the spoiling of their goods," because they knew they "had in heaven a better and enduring substance." The Apostle Paul could say, "I reckon that the sufferings of this present time are not worthy to be compared with the joy which shall be revealed in us"; and said he, "Our light affliction, which is but for a moment, worketh for us a far more exceeding and eternal weight of glory; while we look not at the things that are seen, but at the things which are not seen, for the things which are seen are temporal, but the things which are not seen are eternal." Who could bear those afflictions, without the hope which the Gospel inspires?

> "A hope so much divine,
> May trials well endure;"

but how are they to be endured without it? You know, and you can say with the Psalmist, "I know, O Lord, that Thy judgments are right, and that Thou in faithfulness hast afflicted me;" you know all is well now, and will be better soon.

> "Yet a season and you know
> Happy entrance shall be given,
> All your sorrows left below,
> And earth exchanged for heaven."

III. There is "the patience of the saints," and there is "the patience of hope," but we must just glance at THE CHARACTER WHICH THE APOSTLE GIVES TO THEIR GRACES. "In our Lord Jesus Christ, in the sight of God and our Father."

The one, you see, is a Christian attribute. These things are in the Lord Jesus Christ, that is as Mediator. He is the Principal and source of them. They are by Him as the procurer. Everything we have is in Him. "For it hath pleased the Father, that in Him should all fulness dwell." All is light around us, but not one ray is transmitted through any other medium; all is mercy, but not a particle flows to us through any other channel.

He is the true Christian who is so in the sight of God and our Father. The question is whether your principles will bear the test. You know "that which is highly esteemed among men, may be an abomination in the sight of God," for "man looketh at the outward appearance, but God looketh at the heart." Will your religion bear the eye of God? This is the thing. It may bear the eye of your fellow-creatures, and of your fellow-members, but how does it appear "in the sight of God and our Father"? You profess to believe—to love, to hope, but will "your work of faith, and labour of love, and patience of hope" abide the scrutiny of God? Oh, let this be your concern, and with David pray, "Search me, O God, and know my heart: try me, and know my thoughts, and see if there be any wicked way in me, and lead me in the way everlasting."

XXXIX.

THE CHURCH IN THESSALONICA.

(Delivered on Thursday Evening, December 21st, 1845.)

"*And ye became followers of us, and of the Lord, having received the word in much affliction, with joy of the Holy Ghost: so that ye were ensamples to all that believe in Macedonia and Achaia. For from you sounded out the word of the Lord, not only in Macedonia and Achaia, but also in every place your faith to God-ward is spread abroad: so that we need not to speak anything.*"—1 THESSALONIANS i. 6-8.

PERHAPS of all the churches the Apostle visited, the Thessalonians were the most endeared to him—as he evinced, first, by his prayers for them. As he says, "We give thanks to God always for you all, making mention of you in our prayers." And secondly, by his praises of them: "Remembering without ceasing your work of faith, and labour of love, and patience of hope in our Lord Jesus Christ."

There are some who think that knowledge of one's self will destroy humility; but if knowledge destroys their humility their humility is of very little worth. The thing is for the man to know his state in the sight of God, and that it is not he, but the grace of God that is in him. But Paul was not afraid to let the Thessalonians know what he thought of them.

We shall make a little alteration in the order of the words, and shall therefore read, "Having received the word in much affliction, with joy of the Holy Ghost, ye became followers of us, and of the Lord.' Here are four relations: first, they were receivers, they received the word in much affliction; secondly, they were followers—"Ye became followers of us and of the Lord"; thirdly, they were ensamples,—"So that ye were ensamples to all that believed in Macedonia and Achaia;" fourthly, they were dispensers, for, says the Apostle, "from you sounded out the word of the Lord, not only in Macedonia and Achaia, but also in every place your faith to God-ward is spread abroad, so that we need not to speak anything." Consider what I say, and the Lord give you understanding in all things.

I. We consider them in the relation of RECEIVERS. They received the Word in much affliction. I need not tell you that *all* to whom the gospel comes do not receive it. Some are spoken of as treading under foot the love of God. They are like those who were bid to the wedding—one of whom had bought five yoke of oxen, and he must needs go and prove them; another had bought a piece of land, and he must go and see it; another had just married a wife, and therefore he could not come. They are running after the things of this world. But as to these Thessalonians, they received the truth in the love of it; they received it not as the word of man, but, as it is in truth, the word of God. They received it, therefore, as an immediate message from God. There is certainly a difference between us and them. We were born in a Christian country, and have long enjoyed our means and our Sabbaths; we were taught to read the Word from childhood, but to them it was a novel thing. To us it is new as regards experience, if indeed we have been divinely illuminated. If a man born blind were to have his eyes opened he would see the same sun which had been shining ever since the world began, but it would be new to him.

There are some who receive the Gospel immediately; like Zaccheus, they make haste and come down and receive the Word gladly. But some receive it gradually; some have to fight their way, and to drop their prejudices by degrees. Another comes into the house of God from no good motive. He is seen, perhaps, standing in the aisle. As the preacher proceeds he feels the subject. He goes home, but being uneasy, he is fretful and peevish. He joins his companions, but he cannot enjoy their society. He feels a dislike to the place where he was made so uneasy. Again he goes, and learns more of his depravity. He now resolves to turn over a new leaf, but he feels he cannot. He goes again, and now he feels that what hinders his salvation is nothing but his own unbelief. There is an ark provided, and he is to betake himself to it. Obedience is required, but this is provided for in that dear One who is righteousness and strength; and constrained by the mercies of God, he presents his "body a living a sacrifice, holy and acceptable to God, which is his reasonable service."

These Thessalonians received the Word of the Lord "in much affliction." They were called to endure great persecution, by which they were exposed to loss of property and to the loss of life itself. None of this is sanctioned in this our happy country by law. But the law cannot remove the malice of the carnal heart, and there are many ways in which the carnally-minded may even now persecute the followers of the meek and lowly Jesus. Besides, how many *private* sufferers are there! "The heart knoweth its own bitterness." How many wounded spirits are there, and how many bleeding hearts! How many whose souls are in heaviness, and their sorrows are known only to themselves! Yes, there are many who receive the Word in much affliction. In comes one bleeding with grief, and says, "Lover and friend hast Thou put far from me, and mine acquaintance into darkness."

These Thessalonians not only received the Word in much affliction, but "with joy in the Holy Ghost." It was not a carnal joy they possessed, but a holy joy. The Apostle Paul's religion made him a sufferer, but it did not deprive him of pleasure, for he says, "I take pleasure in infirmities, in reproaches, in necessities, in persecutions, in distresses, for Christ's sake; for when I am weak then am I strong." When Paul and Silas were in the inner prison, and their feet fast in the stocks, they not only prayed, but they sang praises to God, and at midnight too. Thus you see to have joy in God through our Lord Jesus Christ, and to suffer affliction in the world, are very compatible with each other.

When Peter went down to Samaria to preach Christ unto them there was great joy in that city. So we read of the Hebrews, that they "took joyfully the spoiling of their goods, knowing in themselves that they had in heaven a better and a more enduring substance." These Thessalonians were filled with joy in the Holy Ghost, but we are often filled with despondency; the Thessalonians felt their weakness, but when they were weak then were they strong. And why is it not so with you? Is the Gospel changed? Is not Christ the same? They heard the Word with a holy joy and delight: you, many of you, can go from one Lord's day to another without hearing it at all, and you ask—

"Where is the blessedness I knew,
When first I sought the Lord?
Where is that soul-reviving view
Of Jesus and His word?

"What peaceful hours I once enjoyed!
How sweet their memory still.
But they have left an aching void
The world can never fill."

II. We now hasten to view these Thessalonians in the relation of FOLLOWERS. They became followers of him and of the Lord, or imitators. "Ye became followers of us," that is, of the Apostle Paul and of his fellow-disciples.

Man is an imitative creature. The first efforts of infants are to imitate those around them. Men naturally follow the multitude to do evil. Here the Lord's people are a peculiar people. Thus we see this disposition in the case of the Thessalonians is turned another way. With Moses, they choose "rather to suffer affliction with the people of God than to enjoy the pleasures of sin for a season," their desire and prayer and expectations were heavenward. "Look *Thou* upon me, and be merciful unto me," is their prayer; and the followers of Jesus are those with whom they take sweet counsel.

"Ye became followers of us and of the Lord." Their character and deportment were so manifestly godly, that in imitating the conduct of the Apostle and his associates these Thessalonians might well seem satisfied they were followers of the Lord. The Apostle to the Corinthians says, "I beseech you, be ye followers of me." Did he intend to place himself on an equality with Christ? By no means; but to intimate that he was walking after Christ, and keeping Him constantly in view as his great example. You are to follow no man but as he is a follower of Christ. You are not to pin your faith to the sleeve of your preacher. Good men have their failings. Moses, though so eminently a patient man, spake unadvisedly with his lips. Abraham, the father of the faithful, failed at times in that grace for which he was so distinguished; and Peter denied our Lord. But we have in the Lord Jesus Christ an infallible leader, and we are to follow Him withersoever He goeth.

III. We have seen them as receivers and glanced at them as followers; now let us in the third place view them as ENSAMPLES. "Ye were ensamples to all them that believe in Macedonia and Achaia." These learners now are teachers, and these who were aforetime followers became leaders. What individual is there that is not an ensample to some? You have all some influence. You sometimes, it may be, speak carelessly before children and servants, not thinking that what you say may never be forgotten by them. But, my dear hearers, if you must become copies, take care that you do not become *blotted*. It is an easy thing to become copies of evil things, but the great and grand thing is to become copies to those who maintain a good character. O to be eminently godly, to be eminently holy, to be the children of God without rebuke in the midst of a crooked and perverse generation! O to shine as lights in the world!

It is very probable that some of the churches we read of in the New Testament were in the Lord before these Thessalonians, and that thus the last became first, and the first last. They suffered those who set off after them to pass them upon the road, who were more humble and more spiritually minded than themselves; thus, when they ought to have been teachers, they had need that one teach them again what are the first principles of the oracles of God. You are willing, brethren, to take the lead in other matters, why not in this? May we each study which can adhere most closely to the precepts of the word of truth, while we each esteem others better than ourselves, and love and admire and follow whatever is excellent in them.

IV. We have seen them, as receivers, and as followers, and as ensamples; we have now in the last place to consider them as DISPENSERS. "For from you sounded out the word of the Lord not only in Macedonia and Achaia, but also in every place your faith to God-ward is spread abroad, so that we need not to speak anything! Thus we see they were not receivers, but dispensers; they disseminated the word not only near, but far off. "Your faith to God-ward is spread abroad." It sounded out from them four ways.

First, by their *actions*. Their actions were such as to render the Gospel admired, and—

> "Thus shall *we* best proclaim abroad
> The honours of our Saviour God,
> When His salvation reigns within,
> And grace subdues the power of sin."

Secondly, by their *fearless announcement of it*. By their Christian conversation with individuals, whether in the exchange or in the market, or wherever they went, they would embrace opportunities for usefulness, and when they travelled they would seize occasions for the benefit of those with whom providence might cast them. There are some who go abroad without their religion. They are ashamed of it; but these Thessalonians carried it along with them. There are others who endeavour as much as possible to keep God out of their warehouses and shops, for What business has He there? say their wicked hearts. When Mr. Newton went out into company, he was accustomed to say, "Let us not separate without a word for Christ."

Thirdly, they spread it abroad in their *letters*. A sentiment conveyed in a letter is peculiarly impressive. These, by those beloved, are likely to be read again and again, and pondered over; and especially when the friends are at a distance and have no other means of communication.

And fourthly, they spread it abroad by their *ministers and messengers*. They were anxious that others should enjoy the same blessed privileges with themselves; that to them the Gospel of Christ might be preached, and the way of truth and salvation proclaimed. The same disposition prevails in the heart of the sincere disciple of our Lord. What said David? "Restore unto me the joy of Thy salvation; and uphold me with Thy free spirit; then will I teach transgressors Thy ways, and sinners shall be converted unto Thee." Thus Andrew, as soon as he had found Jesus, findeth his brother Philip and brought him to Jesus. Thus, also, the woman of Samaria, when she became converted, went into the city and said to her neighbours, "Come, see a man that told me all things that ever I did; is not this the Christ?" And does not the Saviour teach us when we pray to say, "Thy kingdom come?" And here you observe, if you remark the order of the words, we are taught to pray, "Thy kingdom come," before we are taught to ask for our daily bread.

Christians are not selfish people, nor ought they to be so; for if ten thousand times ten thousand receive the blessings they themselves enjoy, this rather adds to their blessedness and enjoyment than diminishes it. And such is their love to the Saviour, they are desirous that all others should behold His suitableness to their souls, and through Him be delivered from the power of darkness, and translated into this heavenly kingdom.

Benevolence, my hearers, will plead for the promulgation of the gospel. For what is the body to the soul—what are the trifles of time to the great realities of eternity? And remember that he who converteth a sinner from the error of his way, shall save a soul from death, and shall hide a multitude of sins.

Then the *greatness* of the thing should plead for it. What has the religion of Jesus done for you? How has it relieved you from a burden too heavy for you to bear? How has it supported you under your trials, and given you a hope blooming with immortality and future blessedness? What has it done for you, not only in spiritual but in temporal things, and is it for you to be indifferent about the salvation of others? If you have received the grace of God in truth, you cannot but desire, like these Thessalonians, to sound out the word of the Lord, and you will say:

> "Now will I tell to sinners round
> What a dear Saviour I have found;
> I'll point to His redeeming blood,
> And say, Behold the way to God!"

And not only to sinners in your neighbourhood, but in your own highly favoured land, and throughout the world you will send "the word of the Lord." You will pray that God's way may be known upon earth, His saving health among all nations. Was it not by Christian missionaries that the Gospel was first brought into this highly favoured land? and will you not use all you influence that missionaries may be sent out into other countries, that so the wilderness and solitary places may be glad, and the desert may blossom and bud as the rose?

But are there not many here who as yet know not the way of truth? The Bible is a sealed book to them. Oh, let your prayer be that of the Psalmist, "Open Thou mine eyes, that I may behold wondrous things out of Thy Law." And let the wicked forsake his way, and the unrighteous man his thoughts, and let men turn unto the Lord, and He will have mercy upon them; and to our God, for He will abundantly pardon.

XL.

THE ESTABLISHMENT OF THE HEART.

(Delivered on Thursday Evening, January 8th, 1846.)

"*Be not carried about with divers and strange doctrines; for it is a good thing that the heart be established with grace.*"—HEBREWS xiii. 9.

WE shall confine our attention to the middle clause of this verse—"it is a good thing that the heart be established with grace"—because it contains a subject perfect in itself, independent of the words preceding, and because it will furnish a sufficiency of matter for this brief exercise.

I. GRACE is the favourite word of Inspiration, and a precious term to all true Christians. What does it mean here? It means the Gospel. If you require a proof of this, I could refer you to many passages of Scripture, but let the following suffice: "We then," says the apostle, "as workers together with Him, beseech you also that ye receive not the grace of God in vain." And again, "I have written briefly, exhorting and testifiying, that this is the true grace of God wherein ye stand." And again he speaks of the grace of God which bringeth Salvation, which grace unquestionably means the Gospel.

But if necessary to justify this application of the term, we observe that the Gospel is called the grace of God, *because it flows from grace.* Indeed, this is the case with all our possessions and enjoyments, for we are not worthy of the least of all God's mercies, and if unworthy of the least, how can we be worthy of the greatest? If our bread and water, and raiment, and the air in which we breathe are from free and undeserved favour, surely the Gospel—which is a display of the glorious grace of God, which angels desire to look into, which raises us from the ruins of the fall to a blessed condition, to the estate of angels—surely this can only come to us from free and undeserved favour. And we could no more have produced the Gospel than we have deserved it. Grace gave us this inestimable benefit; grace inspired it; grace wrote it; grace translated it; grace published it; grace preached it; and "unto us is the word of this Salvation sent."

Secondly, the Gospel is called grace, *because it reveals Christ to us.* It makes known the exceeding riches of the grace of God in His kindness towards us through Jesus Christ. It displays all the perfections of Jehovah; it shows us His truth, righteousness, wisdom, and love as as being all harmoniously called into exercise in the salvation of guilty, polluted, helpless creatures. A knowledge of this draws us towards Him, enables us to confide in Him, and to feel attached to Him. He hath told us that He is love; that He "so loved the world that He gave His only begotten Son, that whosoever believeth on Him should not perish but have everlasting life." "He that spared not His own Son, but freely gave Him up for us all, how shall He not with Him also freely give us all things?"

Then, *it produces grace in us.* That is, it renews and sanctifies us, and makes us "meet for the inheritance of the saints in light." God is, indeed, not confined to means, but He has told us that "faith cometh by hearing, and hearing by the word of God;" that we are begotten with the word of truth, that we should be a kind of first-fruits of His creatures; that as new-born babes we are to desire the sincere milk of the word, that we may grow thereby; that when He, the Spirit of truth, is come, He will guide us into all truth; that we are sanctified by His truth; His word is truth.

II. THE HEART physically considered is the great source of vital motion, the vessel by means of which the blood is propelled through the human system. But the heart commonly means the inclinations, and in Scripture it is frequently used for the intellectual part—for man's understanding, for his mind. Hence we read of the blindness of the heart. Hence God says, "I will give them a heart to know me," and hence the apostle says, "With the heart man believeth unto righteousness." When we speak of getting things by heart, we intend not only fixing them in the affections, but lodging them in the memory; and therefore the term, the heart, is used more properly in Divine things for the intelligence of our nature. But the reason, I apprehend to be, is because the knowledge of the Gospel is not speculative, but impressive and influential; it is like the message it conveys, which is not only true but all-important, and which the apostle says is not only a faithful saying, but worthy of all acceptation; and, therefore, can only be known when felt.

III. THE ESTABLISHMENT OF THE HEART requires explanation. This intends not only a clear understanding of the Scriptures, but a heart solidly fixed on Divine truth. We may view it by way of contrast. Thus the apostle in the text opposeth it to divers and strange doctrines, saying, "Be not carried about like a bark on the waves of the sea, or like a feather in the air; be not carried about with divers and strange doctrines; it is a good thing that the heart be established with grace," that is, the doctrines of grace; not in meats and drinks, concerning sacrifices and judging observances.

There are some entirely ignorant of the doctrines of Christianity. There are others who have very indistinct and confused notions of the same—they see men as trees walking, with their roots upwards and their branches upon the ground—they are ever learning and never able to come to the knowledge of the truth. But there are others whose understandings are becoming more and more enlightened, whose principles are more and more fixed and firm, and whose hearts are here said to be established with grace.

IV. "IT IS A GOOD THING that the heart be established with grace," for first, it is *safe.* Hence the apostle recommends "that we henceforth be no more children, tossed to and fro, and carried about with every wind of doctrine, by the sleight of men, and cunning craftiness, whereby they lie in wait to deceive; but speaking the truth in love, may grow up into Him in all things who is the head, even Christ." What trees are the most safe? Why, those that are best rooted and grounded. Therefore the apostle prays for the Ephesians that they might be "rooted and grounded in love." Brethren, we live in a world of error, and though we may not be drawn by any of them fatally, we may be drawn aside so as to sustain much injury; exemplifying the language of Solomon: "The backslider in heart shall be filled with his own ways."

Secondly, "It is a good thing that the heart be established with grace," because it is *honourable.* Without consistency there can be no character, and where there is no character there can be no excellency. Therefore the dying Jacob said of Reuben, "Unstable as water, thou shalt not excel." You have no hold of such an individual; there is no principle upon which you can depend; you can place no confidence in him with regard to anything. It would be like building upon the sand or a quagmire.

Thirdly, "It is a good thing that the heart be established

with grace," for it is *useful*. By this you are furnished for moral stations and relative exertions. This qualifies you to teach your children, to govern your families, to edify the members of the Church. This prepares you to be good neighbours, to comfort the distressed conscience, and to have the tongue of the learned, that you may be able to "speak a word in season to him that is weary." And then you may be able to address those that are without, with the earnestness which real experience will induce a man to use, saying, "That which we have seen and heard declare we unto you, that ye also may have fellowship with us; and truly our fellowship is with the Father, and with His Son Jesus Christ." "Lo, this, we have searched it, so it is; hear it, and know thou it for thy good."

"It is a good thing that the heart be established with grace," because it is *consolatory*. It has connected with it a degree of certainty. To be left in suspense in common cases is painful, but nothing is more distressing than uncertainty, indetermination, and perplexity in cases which are very momentous. This will be the case here.

It may be desirable to specify a few of these to show how much a firm character conduces to our everlasting consolation, as well as good hope through grace.

Take the doctrine of *justification*. How necessary is it that the heart be established here! What else must you do? How can you obtain peace with God now, or hope of future blessedness, but by coming to and believing on Christ alone? We obtain peace by the blood of His cross. There is no robe of righteousness in which you can appear with acceptance before God, but the robe of Christ's righteousness. You cannot be acceptable in His sight in your own filthy garments. See how necessary it is that you should be decided and firm here.

Take the doctrine of *final perseverance*. How well is it that our hearts be established on this point! I have to contend with the powers of darkness, I have to "wrestle not against flesh and blood, but against principalities, against powers, against the rulers of the darkness of this world, against spiritual wickedness in high places." Am I left to my own prowess, and strength, and standing? Then I am sure I cannot succeed; but I have the assurance that I shall in all these things be more than conqueror through Him who loveth me? Oh, how this revives and animates me!

"A Friend and Helper so divine
Does my weak courage raise;
He makes the glorious victory mine,
And His shall be the praise."

Take the doctrine of *Providence*. I mean not only of a general, but of a particular Providence. How desirable is it that we should be established here! Am I left to choose; or am I under the management of my heavenly Father and Friend, of One who is always kind and nigh at hand, and faithful to His promises? Am I in this world the sport of events; or does He care for me? Am I authorised to say, "All the paths of the Lord are mercy and truth unto such as keep His covenant and His testimonies," though some of them seem to be very painful? And may I say, "I know that all things shall work together for good to them that love God, to them who are the called according to His purpose?"

So good is it, therefore, that "the heart be established with grace," because it is safe, because it is honourable, because it is useful, because it is consolatory.

So much for our explanatory notes. Now, as for references on the subject: we observe, first, that whatever we may think of the liberality of mind and freedom of inquiry of which some of our fellow-creatures boast, it is not an enviable state to be always learning and never able to come to the knowledge of the truth; but it is a good thing that the heart be established with grace.

Then, secondly, error is not a harmless thing. In proportion as we allow error to be harmless, we allow truth to be useless. But Divine authority says, "Buy the truth, and sell it not." "For it is a good thing that the heart be established with grace."

Therefore, thirdly, a sound, judicious, and evangelical ministry is a great blessing. We ought, in obedience to our Lord's injunctions, not only to take heed how we hear, but to take heed *what* we hear, for "It is a good thing that the heart be established with grace."

Then, lastly, see the importance of experience. There is nothing that confirms like this. Orthodoxy may be easily severed from mere speculation. What one man puts into your heads, another may easily put out of them. But it is otherwise with regard to what you have derived from divine teaching. And, therefore, hear the conclusion of the Apostle John when he refers to some who threw off the form of godliness, and entered the world: "They went out from us, but they were not of us; for if they had been of us they would no doubt have continued with us, but they went out that they might be made manifest that they were not all of us." "But ye have an unction from the Holy One, and ye know all things. And the anointing which ye have received of Him abideth in you, and ye need not that any man teach you; but as the same anointing teacheth you of all things, and is truth and not a lie, and even as it hath taught you, ye shall abide in Him." Therefore, my beloved brethren, love one another, and walk in love as Christ also hath loved us. And "the rather, brethren, give diligence to make your calling and election sure; for if ye do these things, ye shall never fall; for so an entrance shall be ministered unto you abundantly into the everlasting kingdom of our Lord and Saviour Jesus Christ."

XLI.

CHRISTIAN HUMILITY.

(Delivered on Thursday Evening, November 27th, 1845.)

"*Humble yourselves in the sight of the Lord, and He shall lift you up.*"—JAMES iv. 10.

MUCH of the wisdom of the ancients was delivered in short sentences, easily remembered. Each of the wise men of Greece were distinguished by some adage or maxim. We often read of our Saviour's sayings: "Whoso heareth these sayings of mine"; "If any man have ears to hear, let him hear." Many of these, we may be assured, would be handed down from time to time by traditions. Paul met with one of these: therefore he writes, "Remember the words of the Lord Jesus, how He said, It is more blessed to give than to receive." But many of them were not left to carnal preservation, but are recorded in the Gospels, and not one of them all was more frequently mentioned than this: "He that exalteth himself shall be abased, and he that humbleth himself shall be exalted." We will mention two of the sayings; the first occurred on a *civil* occasion, for our Lord did not deem it beneath Him to teach His disciples good manners and behaviour. So we read that "He put forth a parable to those which were bidden, when He marked how they chose out the chief room, saying unto them, When thou art bidden of any man to a wedding, sit not down in the highest room, lest a more honourable man than thou be bidden of him, and he that bade thee and him come and say unto thee, Give this man place, and thou begin with shame to take the lowest room. But when thou art bidden, go and sit down in the lowest room, that when he that bade thee cometh he may say unto thee, Friend go up higher; then shalt thou have worship of them that sit at meat with thee, for whosoever exalteth himself shall be abased, and he that humbleth himself shall be exalted."

The other was on a *religious* occasion: "He spake this parable unto certain which trusted in themselves that they were righteous and despised others. Two men went up to the temple to pray, the one a Pharisee, the other a publican. The Pharisee stood and prayed thus with himself, God, I thank thee, that I am not as other men are, extortioners, unjust, adulterers, or even as this publican. I fast twice in the week, I give tithes of all I possess. And the publican, standing afar off, would not so much as lift up his eyes unto heaven, but smote upon his breast, saying, God be merciful to me a sinner. I tell you this man went down to his house justified rather than the other; for every one that exalteth himself shall be abased, and he that humbleth himself shall be exalted."

So then we see that the way to be rich in His estimation is to be poor in spirit, and the way to rise is to descend.

We find also that the Apostles of our Lord were led into the same truth. Hence Peter says, "Ye younger, submit yourselves unto the elder. Yea, all of you be subject one to another, and be clothed with humility; for God resisteth the proud, but giveth grace unto the humble." "Humble yourselves, therefore, under the mighty hand of God, that He may exalt you in due time." So James in our text says, "Humble yourselves in the sight of the Lord, and He shall lift you up."

So far what we have considered has been to give the words a character of importance; we must now hasten to their intention, and let us first examine the humiliation here enjoined; secondly, the exaltation here promised.

I. THE HUMILIATION HERE ENJOINED. "Humble yourselves in the sight of the Lord."

We should humble ourselves "in the sight of the Lord," even as *creatures*, for as such we are nothing, "less than nothing and vanity." Yet we are the work of His hands, "and fearfully and wonderfully made." But we should humble ourselves especially as *sinners* before Him. We have not only neglected, but have opposed Him, and declared ourselves His enemies by wicked works.

This humiliation before Him will include particularly three things, though not exclusively. First, you must humble your reason with regard to His revelation, receiving His word with meekness, and, as the Apostle says, "Casting down imaginations, and every high thing that exalteth itself against the knowledge of God, and bringing into captivity every thought to the obedience of Christ"; for there is much in the Scriptures beyond our comprehension, and we are not ever prone to ask, "How can these things be?" But we are to become fools that we may be wise; we are to receive the kingdom of God as a little child receives a declaration from its father; that the sunshine of God's word may be added to the glimmering of your lamp. Thus shall your hearts be illuminated thereby. If you can believe nothing more of what God says than you can comprehend, you treat Him as a suspected witness in court, whose testimony is no further regarded than it is clearly supported; you disgrace His wisdom, as if He knew no more than you know; and also His veracity, as if He were not to be depended on.

Secondly, you must "humble yourselves" with regard to the method of salvation. This is what the Jews were destitute of. Therefore says the Apostle, "Being ignorant of God's righteousness, and going about to establish their own righteousness, they have not submitted themselves to the righteousness of God." For, my brethren, His way of salvation is not only holy, and so opposed to our depraved nature, but it is gracious, and it is free; it secures the undivided praise to God, and leaves us nothing wherein we may glory before Him. Accordingly we read, "He that glorieth, let him glory in the Lord." You remember the case of Naaman, who wished for a cure: Elisha sent a messenger to him, and said, "Go, and wash in Jordan seven times, and thy flesh shall come again to thee, and thou shalt be clean. But Naaman was wroth, and went away, and said, Behold, I thought he will surely come out to me, and stand, and call on the name of the Lord his God, and strike his hand over the place, and recover the leper. Are not Abana and Pharpar, rivers of Damascus, better than all the waters of Israel? May I not wash in them and be clean? So he turned and went away in a rage." And he would have been, through his pride, deprived of a cure, had not his servants come near and said, "My father, if the prophet had bid thee do some great thing, wouldst thou not have done it? how much rather, then, when he saith unto thee, Wash, and be clean?" Do you remember nothing answerable to this, in your former experience, Christians? What was Paul's experience in reference to this? "What things," says he, "were gain to me, those I counted loss for Christ, yea, doubtless, and I count all things but loss for the excellency of the knowledge of Christ Jesus my Lord." You will observe that this submission here is necessary, because there is no other Saviour, because no man cometh to the Father but by Him. But men are made willing in the day of His power, and their minds are enlightened so that they see enough in the scheme of salvation to approve of it, to acquiesce in it, and to glory in it.

Again, you must humble your will to His government, so as to resign yourselves to His providence as to your condition and your circumstances in life; that He may choose your inheritance for you; that you may be at His disposal and not your own. Then will you say, "Here I am, do with me as seemeth Thee good," and committing yourself to His dispensations you will "learn in whatsoever state you are therewith to be content," and to say with the Apostle, "I know both how to be abased, and I know how to abound: everywhere and in all things I am instructed both to be full and to be hungry, both to abound and to suffer need." This was the case with David. His connection in life was not of his own choosing; he arose from obscurity to wealth, splendour, and eminence, and the courtiers of Saul condemned him as an ambitious youth struggling into notice; but he could appeal to God, and say, "Lord, my heart is not haughty, nor mine eyes lofty; neither do I exercise myself in great matters, or in things too high for me. Surely I have behaved and quieted myself, as a child that is weaned of his mother: my soul is even as a weaned child." He would leave it for the Lord to decide whether he should serve Him in public, or only in private life. This resignation will apply especially to affliction; this is what the Apostle means when he says, "Shall we not much rather be in subjection unto the Father of Spirits and live?" so as to endure the rod, and submit without repining; and in regard to death to be able to say, The when, the how, the where—all this, my Sovereign Disposer, I leave to Thee. Thus in life and in death we are to be subject to His pleasure.

But you see the requisition demands not only that we should humble ourselves, but that we should humble ourselves "in the sight of the Lord." The question is, whether this refers to the motive of the thing, or to the manner, or to both?

If it refers to the *motive*, then the meaning is, "Humble yourselves in the sight of the Lord," because you are always in His sight. Thus God said to Abraham, "Walk before Me, and be Thou perfect." Thus David says, "All my ways are before Thee." Thus Cornelius the centurion said to Peter, "We are all here present before God, to hear all things that are commanded thee of God." This abasement "in the sight of the Lord," may alienate some from you, and may lead some of your fellow-creatures, and even some of your friends and relations, to suppose that you are distracted, or falling into despair, but He who is high hath respect unto the lowly, though the proud He knoweth afar off." He hath said, "To that man will I look, even to him that is poor and of a contrite spirit, and that trembleth at My word." "The sacrifices of God are a broken heart; a broken and a contrite spirit, O God, Thou wilt not despise."

If it refers to the *manner*, then the meaning is, that we must humble ourselves sincerely, so that it will bear the view of God, for "God seeth not as man seeth, for while man looketh at the outward appearance, God looketh at the heart." That which is highly esteemed among men is often an abomination in the sight of God.

> "God is a Spirit just and wise,
> He sees our inmost mind;
> In vain to heaven we lift our eyes,
> And leave our *souls* behind."

The great question, therefore, is, not what my fellow-men or fellow-members think of me, but what does God think of me? How do I appear in His sight? It should be "a very small thing to be judged of man's judgment" at any time. He that judgeth us is the Lord, and O, how little of our humiliation will bear the examination of His eye!

II. Now let us hasten to consider:—

THE EXALTATION HERE PROMISED. "And He shall lift you up."

There are three ways in which this elevation may be exemplified, as temporal, spiritual, and eternal. The first is conditional, the second is partial, and the third is complete. In a general way God loves to keep His people low; He knows that a low condition is best for them, yet sometimes He raises them up to office and elevates them in their temporal affairs, and this would be the case with you all, if you could bear it; but God sees that you could not bear it, or you might be as sure of it as of your own existence, for "no good thing will He withhold from them that walk uprightly." "They that seek the Lord shall not want any good thing." Then who is to be the judge? We are not qualified to be the judge, owing to our ignorance, our carnality, and our impatience. No, "we know not what a day may bring forth;" we know not what is best for us. No, says Solomon, "For who knoweth what is good for a man in this life, all the days of his vain life which he spendeth as a shadow?" But,—

> "Since all the downward tracks of time
> God's watchful eye surveys,
> O, who so wise to choose our lot,
> And regulate our ways,"

as a Being who is infallible, who sees the end from the beginning, who can distinguish appearances from reality, who knows not only what is good for us in time, but in eternity?

But then there is a condition of *spiritual* elevation. For your outward condition, Christians, may sometimes be very low, and yet you may be exalted as to your spiritual state. Your soul may prosper and be in health: you may be elevated above those doubts and fears that sometimes distress you; you may realize what David says, "Blessed are the people that know the joyful sound; they shall walk, O Lord, in the light of Thy countenance. In Thy name shall they rejoice all the day, and in Thy righteousness shall they be exalted." You are not to judge of your spiritual condition by your outward circumstances. Our Saviour says to the Church of Smyrna, "I know thy works, and tribulation, and poverty (but thou art rich)." O Christians, it is in the night's darkness that you see the stars. You may not be aware of it, perhaps, some of you, but if you were in a very low pit, and looked up, you might see the stars, even at noonday. God may spread a night over His people, or place them in such a low station as this, and yet they may be blessed with heavenly discoveries, manifestations and consolations, to which they were strangers at other times. Oh, how does He exalt you in your spiritual condition! The world is not worthy of such; you are more excellent than your neighbours; you are "the sons and daughters of the Lord Almighty;" you are "heirs of God, and joint heirs with Christ." Oh, how does God elevate you, verifying the words of David, "He raiseth up the poor out of the dust, and lifteth up the needy out of the dunghill, that He may set him with princes, even with the princes of His people."

But principally this elevation is *future*, it is eternal. What a state does the Saviour find you in originally! "He remembered us in our low estate." How low was it? Dr. Watts has told us:

> "At hell's dark door we lay,
> But we arise by grace divine,
> To see a heavenly day."

Oh, what a day will that be? for "Eye hath not seen, nor ear heard, neither have entered into the heart of man the things which God hath prepared for them that love Him." You will "not be ashamed before Him at His coming," for He will confess you before His Father and before His angels. He will say of those duties over which you have wept and blushed, "Well done, good and faithful servant; thou hast been faithful over a few things, I will make thee ruler over many things; enter thou into the joy of thy Lord."

So much for the existence of this promise. What is its *certainty?* For the richer the privilege the more anxious are we to ascertain and secure it. Well, and is it not here said, "Humble yourselves in the sight of the Lord, and He shall lift you up?" Oh, you say, but then we have it only in words, and are we to hang our eternal happiness upon mere words? But you must consider whose word it is. It is the saying of a faithful God, and—

"His every word of grace is strong
As that which built the skies;
The voice that rolls the stars along,
Spake all the promises."

He it is who here speaks; and He has not only promised, but "He has sworn, and because He could swear by no greater He swore by Himself." And that is not all. "He brought again from the dead our Lord Jesus, that great Shepherd of the sheep, through the blood of the everlasting covenant." "He spared not His own Son, but freely gave Him up for us all, how shall He not with Him also freely give us all things?" Did He die in order that His people might possess all this blessedness and glory and immortality, and died He in vain? No, "He shall see His seed, He shall prolong His days, and the pleasure of the Lord shall prosper in His hands."

XLII.

SPIRITUAL LIFE.

(Delivered on Thursday Evening, July 17th, 1845.)

"*He that hath the Son hath life.*"—1 JOHN V. 12.

HERE we see a character referred to, a possession expressed, and a life ennobled.

I. Here is A CHARACTER REFERRED TO. You well know who is to be understood by this term Son of God.

There is a sense in which the term applies to every human being because they are the creatures of God. He made them and not they themselves. He formed their bodies and formed their souls within them.

It is applied to Christians in distinction from mankind generally in a way of adoption and regeneration. Adam is called the son of God in a most particular sense, as he was produced not according to the course of ordinary generation, but by the mere agency of God.

Angels are in a higher sense the sons of God. Thus it is said, when the world was produced, "the morning stars sang together, and all the sons of God shouted for joy."

But you will observe that no one of them is called, as Christ is called, His own Son—the Son of His love—the only-begotten of the Father, in whom His soul delighteth, and in whom He is well pleased (with us for His sake). He "being the brightness of His glory, and the express image of His person, and upholding all things by the word of His power, when He had by Himself purged our sins, sat down on the right hand of the Majesty on high; being made so much better than the angels, as He hath by inheritance obtained a more excellent name than they. For unto which of the angels said He at any time, Thou art my Son; this day have I begotten thee? And again, "I will be to Him a Father, and He shall be to me a Son. And again, when He bringeth in the first-begotten into the world, He saith, And let all the angels of God worship Him." Here we find a glory and dignity ascribed to the Saviour, surpassing all created dignity: and the glory is enhanced when it is said, "He made Himself of no reputation, and took upon Himself the form of a servant and was made in the likeness of men; and being found in passion as a man, He humbled Himself, and became obedient unto death, even the death of the cross." This also tends to exalt our hope and to justify our confidence in Him.

II. But you will observe, there must be a possession of Him in order to our deriving salvation from Him, and the person of whom our text speaks has THIS POSSESSION OF HIM. This refers to the exercise of faith and requires a few moments' reflection.

God spared not His own Son, but delivered Him up for us all—in His incarnation, suffering, and death—that whosoever believeth in Him should not perish, but have everlasting life. The Gospel not only describes Him, but presents Him to us; and believers accept Him and receive Him: and this serves to show the nature of genuine saving faith, that it is not a barren inactive principle, not a mere opinion, or a mere assent of the truth and doctrine concerning Him in His person, and work, and grace, and sufferings, and glory. This is indeed necessary; it is fundamental to everything else; but if it goes no further it is nothing; it is dead, being alone. There must be a reception of Him arising from a conviction of our absolute need of Him, and of His all-sufficiency and suitableness to save us; and this reception of Him must have two characteristics:

First, it must be *cordial.* Therefore the Apostle says "With the heart man believeth unto righteousness." For this submission is not compulsory. *No;* He worketh in us to will and to do of His good pleasure. We are made willing in the day of His power. We therefore cheerfully and thankfully acquiesce in the dispensation. Instead of being ashamed of our profession of Him, we glory in it, and resolve with the Apostle to glory in nothing else.

Secondly, it must be *universal.* We must receive Him in all the offices and characters in which He is revealed, and we are told He is exalted to be a Prince and a Saviour, to give repentance unto Israel and the remission of sins. He comes to the soul, as He came in the days of His flesh, by water and by blood. Hence there is a vital union between Him and them. He is the Head, they are the members. He is the Vine, they are the branches. Without this union with Him there can be no communion. The influences derived from the head actuate only the members of his own body; and the sap flows from the vine only into its own branches, not into those which are external, however near they may be placed, or united by external ligatures. But by reason of this we are one with Him, and called to the fellowship of Jesus Christ our Lord.

III. We are now led to observe, here is A LIFE ENNOBLED. "He that hath the Son hath *life.*"

There is nothing to which men are so much attached as life. The reason is, it is the foundation of every enjoyment. Solomon therefore says, "A living dog is better than a dead lion;" and Satan spake the truth when he said, "Skin for skin, all that a man hath will he give for his life." How we value the food that sustains it! How anxious are we for its preservation! How soon we take the alarm when any danger attends it! How thankful when you escape from any perilous accident or disease! You see this in Hezekiah; upon his recovery, he says, "The living, he shall praise Thee, as I do this day, the father to the children shall make known Thy truth."

But, now, what is this life which engrosses so much of your concern? Jacob gave a true representation of it when before Pharaoh, he was asked concerning his life, and he answered, "Few and evil have the days of the years of my life been." Brevity and misery not only characterised his life, but attach to human life generally. Therefore we read, "Man that is born of a woman is of a few days and full of trouble. His life is as a vapour, which appeareth for a little time, and then vanisheth away;" it is as a tale that is told, as a dream when one awaketh, a series of cares and fears, of mortifications and of distresses.

But there is a life which is worthy of the name, a life which regards the soul and eternity, the life of God; and "He who hath the Son hath life"—the life of *righteousness*, the life of glory; a life which consists in a deliverance from the penalty of the law we have transgressed; and the curse enters with transgression, and therefore says the Apostle, "Cursed is every one that continueth not in all things written in the book of the law to do them." There is no possibility of escaping from this sentence, which renders us dead in the eyes of the law, but by Him who is "the end of the law for righteousness to every one that believeth." He bore our sins in His own body on the tree, and He bore away the penalty and set us free. "And by Him all that believe are justified from all things, from which they could not be justified by the law of Moses." This accords with His own declaration, for said He to the Jews, "He that heareth my word, and believeth on Him that sent me, hath everlasting life, and shall not come into condemnation; but is passed from death unto life." And the apprehension of this by faith produces peace of conscience, peace within arising from peace above; and affords the believer in Jesus boldness and access with confidence by the faith of Him.

"He that hath the Son hath life"—the life of *renovation;* and the consequences of this renovation take place in all believers, of whom it may be said, as the Apostle said of the Ephesians, "You hath He quickened who were dead in trespasses and sins."

Now there is a difference between a picture and a living man. There is a likeness in a picture, sometimes very striking. It seems to survey all in the room. We read of the breathing canvas. But it has no breath. Feel it, it is cold. It moves not, but remains the same. It is the same with mere professors of religion, who have a name to live but are dead, who have the form of godliness but deny the power thereof. But now as to real Christians, they are dead indeed unto sin but alive unto God through Jesus Christ our Lord. They are living characters. They have spiritual *senses* to exercise. They look at those things which are unseen and eternal; they hear the voice of the Son of God, and live; they feel the powers of the world to come; they taste that the Lord is gracious. They have spiritual *appetites* to be supplied: they hunger and thirst after righteousness, and they feast upon Christ the living bread which came down from heaven. They have spiritual *actions* to perform. They have to walk, they have to fight, they have to run the race set before them.

"He that hath the Son hath life," a life of *faith.* This is obvious from the Apostle's expression, "I am crucified with Christ; nevertheless, I live; yet not I, but Christ liveth in me; and the life I now live in the flesh, I live by the faith of the Son of God, who loved me, and gave Himself for me."

"He that hath the Son hath life"—a life of *glory.* Speaking of this life under the image of water, our Saviour says to the woman of Samaria: "The water that I shall give him shall be in him a well of water springing up unto everlasting life."

This shows us its tendency, and also the constancy and permanency of its effects. It is in the man as a heavenly and immortal principle. Death, which is the destroyer of everything else, makes this even flourish more and more.

And not only have we from this blessed Saviour, life, but life *more abundantly*. We obtain a greater degree of life than even Adam had in Paradise, or even the angels in glory; for the saints are represented in the Revelation as nearer the throne than they; and,

> "Never did angels taste above
> Redeeming grace, and dying love."

Oh, that is "life," indeed. There will be no languor there, no cold affections, no wandering thoughts, no imperfections in duty. The days of their mourning shall be ended, and all tears shall be wiped from the eyes.

The body is to be made partaker of this life. The body which was sown in dishonour, will be raised in glory; and sown in weakness, shall be raised in power; this vile body shall be fashioned like unto the glorious body of Christ. "And as we have borne the image of the earthy, we shall also bear the image of the heavenly.

But we attempt not a description of His glory. "Eye hath not seen nor ear heard, neither have entered into the heart of man the things which God hath prepared for them that love Him." And instead of indulging in curious enquiries after many things, it would be far better for you to use and improve what is plainly revealed. Your treasure, Christian, is in heaven, let your heart be there also; your country is in heaven, let your conversation be there too. Get as much of this future life as you possibly can here. Be always looking for that blessed hope and the glorious appearing of our Lord and Saviour Jesus Christ.

But remember, while you are in expectation of this, how you obtain it; that is only in communion with Him who is our life. He said therefore, "He that believeth on Me hath everlasting life"—not only a life of righteousness, and a life of renovation, but also a life of glory. "He that hath the Son hath life."

And need you wonder that he has it already, since it is paid for, and by a price of infinite value; and insured by promise and by oath—and by the oath of God? Yes, Christians have already earnests and first-fruits and foretastes of this blessed life. Grace and glory may be considered as not different states, but only different degrees of the same state. Grace is glory in the bud, and glory is grace in the full-blown flower; grace is glory in the dawn, and glory is grace in the day; grace is glory in the child, and glory is grace in the fulness of the stature of a man in Christ.

In conclusion, we observe, first, that the opposite of the proposition in our text is true. As he who hath the Son hath life, so he who hath not the Son hath not life. The apostle does not leave us to draw the conclusion; he immediately asserts, "And he who hath not the Son hath not life." Oh, what a lamentable state are such in—strangers to a believer's deliverance from the sentence of the law, they have to meet its direful charges in their own person. How will they be able to do so? Strangers to that grace which enables believers to have their conversation in heaven while they remain in this present world, they are dead to the things of God, and feel what a weariness it is to serve the Lord, for their hearts are not right in His sight. They are destitute of that hope which believers rejoice in, or if they indulge a hope respecting future blessedness, it is a hope which will make them ashamed in the end. Thus he who hath not the Son hath not life, whatever be his outward character or circumstances.

What, then, should be your concern? for be it observed, and it is with pleasure we mention this—though your state is dangerous, it is not desperate. You cannot save yourselves, but there is an all-sufficient and suitable Saviour. Seek ye the Lord, therefore, while He may be found; call ye upon Him while He is near. Let the wicked forsake his way, and the unrighteous man his thoughts, and let him return unto the Lord, and He will have mercy upon him; and to our God, for He will abundantly pardon.

Then how valuable is this Saviour! You need not wonder that He is called God's unspeakable gift. You need not wonder that He is called the consolation of Israel, the Saviour thereof in time of trouble. For all that we can hope for is to be found only in Him, and is derived from Him who is made unto us "wisdom and righteousness, sanctification and redemption." You need not wonder that Christ is everything to the true Christian, seeing He is everything in Himself. He is a Sun and Shield, a Rock and Refuge, everything a believer needs. Therefore says the Apostle, "To them that believe He is precious," but not half precious enough.

"Jesus is worthy to receive
Honour and power divine;
And blessings more than we can give
Be, Lord, for ever Thine."

Then, how anxiously should you enquire whether you *have* the Son! Your happiness must depend upon the answer to this enquiry. We don't wonder that you should rejoice in Him with joy unspeakable and full of glory. Then the question returns, *have* you the Son? You have often heard of Him and read of Him, but have you received Him? You have Him in your country, you have Him in your churches, you have Him in your houses, you have Him in your Bibles, but have you Him in your hearts? This is the grand enquiry. O God, put these words into the minds, and write them in the hearts of these hearers; and henceforth may they remember that "he who hath the Son hath life, and that he who hath not the Son hath not life, but the wrath of God abideth on him"; and command Thy blessing upon the word spoken, for Christ's sake. Amen.

SERMONS

PREACHED ON

SPECIAL OCCASIONS.

I.

DAYS TO BE REMEMBERED.

(Preached on Sunday Morning, December 29th, 1850.)

"*This day shall be unto you for a memorial.*"—EXODUS xii. 14.

MARCUS Aurelius was a Roman Emperor, and was one of the best of that bad body. He was a man of reflection, and speaking of the division of time he said, "We should give the future to Providence, the present to duty, and the past to oblivion." Now, we readily admit the first and the second of these divisions. Yes, we would resign the future to Providence, "casting all our care upon Him who careth for us," ever saying, "If the Lord will, we shall live, and do this or that." And we would give the present to duty, doing the work of the day in the day, and never growing weary in well doing. But we cannot consent to give the past to oblivion. No; Solomon says, "God requireth that which is past." "No," says Moses to the Israelites, "Remember the days of old, consider the years of many generations: ask thy father and he will shew thee; thy elders, and they will tell thee." And so says Moses in the words before us, "This day shall be unto you for a memorial."

It refers to the passover. The passover may be considered two ways. First, *symbolically:* and it would be easy to trace the resemblance between the figure and the reality; and therefore says the Apostle to the Corinthians, "Christ our Passover is sacrificed for us . . . Therefore let us keep the feast, not with old leaven, neither with the leaven of malice and wickedness, but with the unleavened bread of sincerity and truth."

Secondly, it may be viewed *commemoratively.* "Ye shall observe the feast of unleavened bread, for in this self same day have I brought your armies out of the land of Egypt; therefore shall ye observe this day in your generation by an ordinance for ever." "And it shall come to pass, when ye be come to the land which the Lord will give you, according as He hath promised, that ye shall keep this service. And it shall come to pass when your children shall say unto you, What mean ye by this service? that ye shall say, It is the sacrifice of the Lord's passover, who passed over the houses of the children of Israel in Egypt, when He smote the Egyptians and delivered our houses."

Let us now leave the original reference of these words, and apply them to some other subjects, and as Tuesday will end the old, and as Wednesday will begin the new year, surely these reflections will not be deemed premature, but appropriate, and, we hope, useful.

Now there are nine days which ought to be for a memorial.

I. Take the Sabbath Day. This day should be unto you for a memorial.

> "Day of all the week the best,
> Emblem of eternal rest."

Yes, says the Apostle to the Hebrews, "There remaineth a rest for the people of God;" the margin says, a sabbathizing, or keeping Sabbath. And Christians call the Sabbath "a delight, holy of the Lord, honourable." They can say with our hymn—

> "Thine earthly Sabbaths, Lord, we love,
> But there's a nobler rest above."

Here the Sabbath is soon ended, and we return again to the cares and perplexities of the world, but *this* Sabbath will be perpetual. Here you serve God with numberless imperfections; and though you are not weary of this service, you are weary *in* it, but there your powers will be equal to your work, and your dispositions equal to your powers. There will be no feeling of hunger, or need of repose.

It is also a memorial, not only of heaven, but also of the Saviour's resurrection from the dead. Then, as the Apostle says, "He ceased from His work and entered into His rest.' The Saviour in this intercessory prayer therefore said, "I have finished the work what Thou gavest me to do;" and when He was expiring, He said, "It is finished;" and "He triumphed over principalities and powers, making a show of them openly, and nailing them to His cross." And then He ascended to

His "Father and to our Father, to His God and our God, and is set down on the right hand of the Majesty in the heavens."

The primitive Christians were accustomed to meet one another on the morning of the Sabbath, and to say, "He is risen," as if they would say everything by saying one thing. And, indeed, what is not implied in this one thing? Well, we do often the same; yea, we say—

> "To-day He rose and left the dead,
> And Satan's empire fell;
> To-day the saints His triumphs spread,
> And all His wonders tell."

This therefore is called The Lord's Day. "This is the day which the Lord hath made; we will be glad, and rejoice in it." He made it also for the salvation of sinners, and on a Lords' Day morning you would do well to reflect on the glorious achievements of this day. How many millions on this day have been "turned from darkness to light, and from the power of Satan unto God!" How many saints have been made joyful in this house of prayer! The Lords' Day, therefore, may be peculiarly called the day of salvation.

II. Take the Day of Holy Communion. This day should be unto you for a memorial. Our Lord designed and appointed it to be so, and when He established the Institution, He said, "Do this in remembrance of Me." Here He has employed our very senses to aid our faith, and by things seen and temporal to help us to hold communion with things unseen and eternal. Here we have emblems as well as memorials. Here before our eyes Jesus Christ is evidently set forth crucified among us, by the bread and the wine which represent Him as the food of the soul; by the breaking of the one, and the pouring out of the other, are set forth the medium by which we receive His blessings; our eating the one and drinking the other is a representation of our realizing Him as our Saviour by faith; and the participation of these elements by all holds forth the communion of saints, and shews that we are all one in Christ Jesus.

Now this was not to be a temporary observance as was the passover, but was to be a perpetual ordinance. "As often as ye eat this bread, and drink this cup, ye do shew forth the Lord's death till He come."

To many, alas, the table of the Lord is contemptible. There

are many who partake of it ignorantly; many who pervert it; many who make it a passport to heaven, and place it in the room of that Saviour it is designed to display. But surely you look beyond the sign to the thing signified; surely He is known of you in the breaking of bread; surely your fellowship here is with the Father and His Son Jesus Christ; surely you remember His love more than wine; and surely as you look back you can say, "I sat down under His shadow with great delight, and His food was sweet to my taste.'

III. TAKE YOUR BIRTHDAY. This day should be unto you for a memorial. Though of course you cannot know this day of yourselves, it has been so registered by your parents, and so connected by circumstances that it is easily found out. And oh, what a period is that to review, when you began an existence which is to continue for ever, an existence in which you shall see "the heavens pass away with a great noise, and the elements melt with fervent heat, the earth also and the works that are therein burnt up;" in which you will survive the universe, and live for ever in raptures or in woe! Surely you cannot think of your creation without being reminded of the Creator. He made you and not you yourselves. He formed your body, and He framed your spirit within you. "He has taught you more than the beasts of the earth, and shewed you more than the fowls of the air, for there is a spirit in man, and the inspiration of the Almighty giveth him understanding." You should therefore say with David, "O Lord, I will praise Thee, for I am fearfully and wonderfully made: marvellous are Thy works, and that my soul knoweth right well. My substance was not hid from Thee, when I was made in secret, and formed in the lowest parts of the earth. Thine eyes did see my substance, yet being unperfect; in Thy book all my members were written, which in continuance were fashioned, when as yet there were none of them." The young are called to "remember God their Creator in the days of their youth." Are others to forget Him? Surely your birthday properly considered is a very solemn period, and you should not be satisfied with compliments and flatteries on the occasion, nor even with the allowed endearments of relative and friendly congratulations. Can you think of the day on which you were born, and not ask yourselves for what purpose you were born, for what end you came into existence, and how you have answered that end? For whether you have lived fifteen years or fifty surely conscience will ask you on that day, "How old art thou?" For, my brethren, you should remember that none of these years can be recalled, no part of your life can be seen over again. There can be no second edition of the period of human life, for as the dust returns to the dust as it was, the spirit goes to God who gave it, and after death the judgment; and then the Divine fiat runs, "He that is unjust, let him be unjust still; and he that is filthy, let him be filthy still; and he that is righteous, let him be righteous still; and he that is holy, let him be holy still."

Can you think of your birthday and not thank God that you were not born in a heathen country, or in a Mahommedan or a Popish country, but that you were born in a Christian and a Protestant land, where your understanding meets with every advantage; a land of vision—a land of bibles—a land of privileges, where the lines are fallen to you in pleasant places, and you have a goodly heritage; where you are fed with the finest of the wheat, and where with oil got of the Rock you are satisfied; where your advantages far surpass those of God's people of old? "Many prophets and righteous men have desired to see those things which ye see, and have not seen them; and to hear those things which ye hear, and have not heard them. But blessed are your eyes, for they see; and your ears, for they hear."

Can you think of your birth and not thank God that you were not born in an earlier age of the world? For I hope you are not silly enough to enquire, Why were the former days better than these? for you would not enquire wisely concerning this matter. You live in a day when all kinds of improvement abound. Oh, what has God wrought in our own day! What comparison may be made between the present and the past! I had rather live in the present day than in any period of the world since the Creation.

Can you think of the day on which you were born and not bless God that you were born, not of infidel or ungodly parents, but of those who dedicated you to Himself, and who trained you up in the nurture and admonition of the Lord, and from whom you have derived a thousand advantages? Can you help thinking of Him? You might have been born with a deformed body, or an unhealthy constitution, or you might have been made to posess mouths of vanity, and had wearisome nights appointed you! Then you would never have tasted pleasant meat; then from a series of trials and punishments you might have been inclined, like Job, to curse the very day of your birth! And oh, what ought to be your praise if to your natural birth you can add a spiritual; if you are born again; if you can say with the Apostle, "God who separates me from my mother's womb, hath called me by His grace, and revealed His Son in me?"

IV. Take THE DAY OF CONVERSION. This day should be unto you for a memorial. Hear what God said to the Jews: "Thou shalt remember the day that thou camest out of Egypt, all the days of thy life;" as if He should say, "this should never be forgotten." O Christian, you can say, "I was once far off but am now made nigh by the blood of Christ; I was once in darkness, but am now light in the Lord; I was once a stranger and a foreigner, but am now a fellow-citizen with the saints and of the household of God." Some can remember the peculiar circumstance of this happy day. Some can remember the very place where they had their first interview with the Saviour, and said, "Lord, I am Thine; save me." Some can remember the instruments He employed for this purpose, and can say, "O that dear minister, who turned my feet unto the way of peace! O that sermon, that roused my careless soul! O that book, that alarmed me; that friend that allured me; that trial that broke up my creature comforts, and said, Arise and depart, for this is not your rest." In some this work is more slow, in others more rapid. Some are saved by fear, and are saved so as by fire; others are drawn by love, and with the bands of a man. But where no such particularity or minuteness exists, yet the individual can say, "Whereas I was blind, now I see." I know that once I was dead in trespasses and sins, but am now alive unto God; and with our admired poet—

"'Tis done; the great transaction's done,
I am my Lord's, and He is mine;
He drew me, and I followed on,
Glad to confess the voice divine.

High heaven that heard the solemn vow
That vow renewed shall daily hear,
Till in life's latest hour I bow,
And bless in death a bond so dear."

V. Take THE DAY OF BEREAVEMENTS. This day should be unto you for a memorial. And who has not had such a day? Who has not said, "Lover and friend Thou hath put far from me, and mine acquaintance into darkness?" Then Rachel weeps for her children, and refuses to be comforted, because they are not. Then David says, "I am distressed for thee, my brother Jonathan." Then Ezekiel hears the sentence, "Son of man behold I take away the desire of thine eyes with a stroke." Then a father thinks of his son, who seemed destined to be his companion, honour, and comfort, and inscribes upon his early tomb, "Childhood and youth are vanity."

> "Friend after friend depart,
> Who has not lost a friend?
> There is no union here of hearts
> That does not find an end."

> "If this frail world were all our rest,
> Living or dying none were blest."

As to some, they have been so peeled and bereaved, that they seem like a beacon on a mountain, or an ensign on a hill. They gaze around, and ask, "What do I here?" "What have I here?"

> "There my best friends my kindred dwell,
> There God my Saviour reigns."

Can you ever forget those with whom you walked and took sweet counsel? You still are united to them, for

> "The saints below and all the dead
> But one communion make,
> All join in Christ their living head,
> And of His grace partake.

Can you ever forget that dreary hour in which you saw life quivering upon the lip, and the glazing eye closing in darkness? Can you forget the hour when nature opened the floodgate of grief, and the world became a wilderness, and all its scenes, however pleasing and interesting before, unmeaning and dull? Can you ever forget the field of Machpelah? "There they buried Abraham, and Sarah his wife. There they buried Isaac, and Rebekah his wife, and there I buried Leah." Has this passed away without any real and lasting benefit? Was it attended with a heart torn, without being changed or made better? Have you realised the words of Solomon, "It is better to go to the house of mourning than to the house of feasting?" Oh, it is a sad thing to lose an affliction, and above all to lose a bereavement.

Take care that you not only weep, but that you sow in tears, and then you will have something to reap in joy; and then "light afflictions, which are but for a moment, shall work out for you a far more exceeding and eternal weight of glory.

VI. Take THE DAY OF YOUR MARRIAGE. This day *should* be unto you for a memorial. There are no marriages in heaven, and in the resurrection they neither marry nor are given in marriage. But now, in the designs of God in nature, providence, and grace, marriage is expedient, marriage is necessary, marriage is honourable. For then you enter into a state which is to exceed and surpass even natural relationship. "For this cause shall a man leave his father and mother, and shall cleave unto his wife, and they two shall be one flesh." Then you are no longer your own, and

> "Though you leave a father's wing,
> Nor longer ask his care,
> It is but seldom husbands bring
> A lighter yoke to wear."

It is a connection, remember, for life; and when the parting hour arrives, "'Tis the survivor dies." When properly contracted, marriage is a source of the greatest domestic peace, and has far more contributed to the public weal than any other institution. Yet how carelessly, how thoughtlessly, how prayerlessly, do many enter into this state! And if any of you, regardless of God's warning advice not to marry but in the Lord, have been led astray by folly and affection, no wonder if you now have inward feelings and outward circumstances which remind you of God's menace to the Jews, "If ye walk contrary to me, I will walk contrary to you." And O, hasten by prayer to Him who is ready to forgive, and who can make all things work together for good, and beseech Him to turn the curse into a blessing. But if you have been directed aright, if you have chosen wisely; if you have given yourselves to the Lord, and then to each other by His will; if you have been walking together as fellow-heirs of the grace of life, and your prayers have not been hindered, acknowledge gratefully with Solomon, that "He that findeth a wife findeth a good thing, and shall obtain favour of the Lord."

And when you look back to the day of espousal, and to the gladness of your heart, it may be well to enquire how the confidence and generous affections of that day have worn with the lapse of years. Has there been no diminutions, no variations of the love which united your hearts then as well as your hands? Have you soothed each other's sorrows? Have you borne each other's burdens? Have you been deaf and blind to each other's infirmities? Well, if so, a wise retrospection here may aid you in regard to the future. See that ye abound therein more and more.

VII. Take THE DAY OF PROVIDENTIAL INTERPOSITION. "This day shall be to you a memorial." We have many of these interpositions recorded in Scripture. Doubtless Joseph remembered the day that delivered him from prison, and that rescued his feet from the rude iron and fetters. Doubtless Daniel remembered the day when he was saved from the lions' den. Doubtless the Israelites often looked back to the day when they were brought out of Egypt. It is true that these and many other instances recorded in Scripture were miraculous; and you, unless you are enthusiasts, will not look for miracles now, but you may look to Him who performed these, and who is "the same yesterday, to-day, and for ever;" who has said, "I will never leave you nor forsake you." "As thy day so shall thy strength be." "I will bless thy bread and thy water." And sooner all nature shall change than one of His promises fail. Perhaps you have been in straits, and, looking at your little ones, have said, "What shall we eat, and what shall we drink, and wherein that shall we be clothed?" And though you have not been fed by ravens, yet from the most unlikely sources you have received help and relief. Perhaps you have had dark days, very dark, but at eventide it has been light. Perhaps death hovered over you; perhaps you have been brought down to the borders of the grave and looked into eternity, but you shrunk back, and said, "O spare me a little, that I may recover strength before I go hence and be no more seen;" and He said, "Return ye children of men," and re-coloured your check, and renewed your strength, and raised you up to walk before the Lord in the land of the living, and

"Why should the miracles He hath wrought
Be lost in silence and forgot?"

VIII. Take THE LAST DAY OF THE YEAR. This day shoul be unto you for a memorial; and surely this day is near enough to awaken and justify reflection, for this is the last Sabbath in the year. Surely such a day as this ought to be improved. "O that you were wise; that you understood this; That you would consider your latter end." To some of you it has been a very expensive year. You remember the wormwood and the gall, your soul hath them still in remembrance, and is humbled within you; but extending your thoughts beyond your own circle, who can help on such a day reflecting on what a number have gone down to the grave, and how many have been carried off in their sins? Who can help exclaiming, "When a few years are come, then I shall go the way whence I shall not return?" Who but must say with the butler, "I do remember my faults this day?" Who can but say with regard to his trials, "He hath not dealt with me after my sins, nor rewarded me according to my iniquities?" Who, reflecting upon his deserts, but must say, "It is of the Lord's mercies that we are not consumed, because His compassions fail not?" Who, on reflecting upon His mercies, but will say, "What shall I render to the Lord for all His benefits towards me?"

> "Dangers stand thick through all the ground,
> To push us to the tomb;
> And fierce diseases wait around
> To hurry mortals home."

You have not been hurried home; you are still in the land of the living, and the place of hope. You are not only alive, but your limbs have been preserved; your reason has been continued, and the use of your senses, and your relative comforts, and the Gospel throughout the long year.

> "The Gospel throughout the long year,
> From Sabbath to Sabbath He gave;
> How oft has He met with us here,
> And shewn Himself mighty to save!"

Can you on such a day refuse praying, "Lord make me to know mine end, and the measure of my days what it is, that I may know how frail I am?"

IX. Once more, and only once, take THE FIRST DAY OF THE YEAR. This day should be to you for a memorial. But here you charge me with a blunder. Here you may ask, "What have we to memorialize on a New Year's Day? it is only just the beginning of the year?" Well, if there be nothing on such a day, it is to be memorialized; there is much, however, that will be impressive and improvable. People at such a time look into their circumstances and endeavour to balance their secular affairs; and does it not become you to enquire how matters stand between God and your souls, and what readiness you are in for your eternal state? The New Year's Day is a day of joy and congratulation. We do not oppose this, but only call upon you when you rejoice, to rejoice with trembling. This we should do with regard to everything we possess and enjoy here. Another year will soon open upon you, and you will not know what a day of it will bring forth, but a Christian can say:—

> "It can bring nothing with it
> But He will bear us through."

Trials may abide you, and of every kind while you are here; but they are Divinely appointed. You know who hath said, "I will be with thee in trouble: call upon me in the day of trouble, and I will deliver thee." You know there might be numberless duties which you will be required to perform, and your strength is small. But His grace is sufficient for you, and His strength is made perfect in weakness. You know that Moses set up the tabernacle on the first day of the year, not that it was a better day for the purpose, but it would render it more memorable and striking. Have none of you to set up family worship? Can you be a Christian, and live without God in your families? Have none of you to abandon intemperance? Have none of you to begin rising earlier and to improve your time? Are there not many things which you should bring under review? I pity those who will go into the next year without God. Oh, how anxious should you be to have God for your God, and your guard, your patron, and your comfort!

I cannot say to any of you as Jeremiah said to Hananiah, "This year thou shalt die;" but I can say to any one of you, this year you *may* die; and therefore be concerned to give up yourselves to Him, so that you may say, "If I live, it will be to serve Him; and if I die, it will be to enjoy Him."

To conclude, of what importance is this remonstrance! Endeavour to strengthen it, avail yourselves of eternal aids and excitements. Samuel took a stone and set it up between Mizpah and Shem, and called it Ebenezer. Moses had two sons, and gave them names, one of which would always remind him of his trials and the other of his mercies.

Diaries were very common formerly, and they have been much abused; but they may serve to aid us in reviewing past experience, and the dealings of God in His providence.

Then remember, if we forget these things, they are not forgotten elsewhere. We are a spectacle to angels as well as to men, and "all things are naked and open to the eyes of Him with whom we have to do." He sees and hears all, and records it in the book of His remembrance. For what purpose? Solomon tells us. "God will bring every work into judgment whether it be good or whether it be evil."

Then observe, the true way of remembering the past is to improve the present and the future. "If ye know these things, happy are ye if ye do them." There are some that look back, but it is all in vain. There are but few persons who have no spasms and fits of reflection and seriousness, but they are like the morning cloud and early dew. Some are saints on the Sabbath and devils all the week. There are some who are devotional in the House of God, but they leave it there to be brushed out with the dust on the Monday morning. This is not religion. Religion is a whole and complete garment that is to be worn always.

You must remember Jesus Christ. Raise as many memorials as you can, but set them all up around the Cross; I say, set them all up around the Cross. What is there in your history and character, when you examine them, which do not display your sins and deficiences? And, Oh Christian, what would you do without His atoning blood and righteousness, and without His Spirit? What will you do on Tuesday when you enter your closets, and ask:—

> "What have I done for Him who died
> To save my wretched soul?
> How are my follies multiplied
> Fast as my minutes roll!"

What will you do next Wednesday when you enter your closets, and say,

> "Lord with this guilty heart of mine
> To Thy dear Cross I flee;
> And to Thy hands my soul resign,
> To be redeemed by Thee"?

Oh Christians, in prosperity or adversity, in life or in death, say as Flavel did at the end of all his numerous sermons, "Blessed be God for Jesus Christ." Amen.

II.

FORWARD!

(Preached on Sunday Morning, January 4th, 1853.)

We are going to surround the table of the Lord, and to eat the bread and drink the cup in remembrance of Him who died for us and rose again ; and, as you well know, in these religious services I endeavour to introduce a suitableness of reflection and improvement. There are few subjects that have not a real if not an immediate reference to the dear death we are going to commemorate. But I feel the importance of the season, and I must yield to it. We have passed from one year to another, and the transition has been so recent as to allow of an appropriate address, in addition to the many excellent things you heard from our brother* on Thursday evening from the blessing of Ashur, "As thy day so shall thy strength be." Let me now read the text I have selected for our present meditation, which you will find in Exodus xiv. 15.—"*Speak unto the children of Israel that they go forward*," which command we are going to consider three ways, upon which I shall enter as soon as you have done shuffling your Bibles in looking for the text. Is it not strange that you cannot believe I read it aright, without searching to see? In that you often lose an introductory observation, that may serve as a clue to the whole discourse. Well, then, "Speak unto the children of Israel, that they go forward." As we said, we shall consider these words three ways. First, in reference to the command given to the Israelites ; Secondly, in reference to the advancement of Christians in the Divine life ; Thirdly, in reference to the progress of time. What may not appear clear in the division, for the sake of brevity, I hope will be made plain in the development.

I. We consider these words in reference to THE COMMAND GIVEN TO THE ISRAELITES.

---

* Rev. Mr. Parks, Bridgewater.

With the history of the case you are familiar. By a succession of dreadful judgments, Pharoah was at last brought to be willing to let the children of Israel go; but no sooner had they departed, than he resolved, if possible, to bring them back, and immediately pursued after them with all his horses and chariots, his horsemen, and his army, and they were sore afraid: and the children of Israel cried unto the Lord. "And they said unto Moses, because there were no graves in Egypt, hast thou taken us away to die in the wilderness? Wherefore hast thou dealt thus with us, to carry us forth out of Egypt? saying, let us alone that we may serve the Egyptians; for it had been better for us to serve the Egyptians than that we should die in the wildernesss." So early began the murmurings and rebellions of the people. "And Moses said unto the people, Fear ye not; stand still, and see the salvation of the Lord, which He will show you to-day; for the Egyptians whom ye have seen to-day, ye shall see them again no more for ever."

This indicates strong confidence in Moses, and the confidence was not presumption, but a confidence connected with prayer. It does not appear that Moses said anything in prayer on this occasion audibly. He seems to have withdrawn from public view, and was prostrate upon the ground, intent in prayer, with groanings which could not be uttered. "And the Lord said unto Moses, wherefore criest than unto Me? Speak unto the children of Israel, that they go forward." Thus teaching us that as duty is not to call us from prayer, prayer is not to keep us from being forward in the use of those means which God has ordained.

Let us reflect upon the situation of these people; for if the army of Pharoah was behind them, the sea was immediately before them, and if they were to proceed it seemed to be advancing into the sea itself. But, my brethren, it became them, and it becomes us, to obey whenever and whatever God enjoins us, and that for four reasons:—

First, Because He has a right to command. He is the Sovereign, we are the subjects; He is the Master, we are the servants; He is the Father, we are the children. "And if I be a Father, where is mine honour? and if I be a Master, where is my fear? saith the Lord of Hosts."

Secondly, Because none of His commands are arbitrary. We may not be able to perceive the reasons upon which they are founded, but there are reasons; and these reasons are now satisfactory to Him, and they will be more than satisfactory to us when they come to be disclosed, and in God's light we shall see light. Our Lord, therefore, traces up the dispensation which drew from Him not only submission but adoration and praise, not to the will of God, but to His wisdom. "I thank Thee, O Father, Lord of heaven and earth, because Thou hast hid these things from the wise and prudent and hast revealed them unto babes; even so, Father, for so it seemeth good in Thy sight."

Thirdly, Because all His commands are beneficial, and regard our welfare as well as His own glory. "In keeping His commandments there is great reward."

And Lastly, Because they are all practicable. They all imply a power to obey; a power, if not possessed, yet attainable; if not in ourselves, yet in another, who is at all times accessible. While we are not sufficient of ourselves, even to think anything of ourselves, our sufficiency is of God. And while without Him we can do nothing, by His strengthening of us we can do all things. You will observe, therefore, that His commands are so many intimations and assurances of success.

A British General some years ago having reconnoitred a strong force was about to attack a certain fort, when his men said, "It cannot be taken;" but, said he, "It *can* be taken, for I have the command in my pocket." Now men may require what is really impossible, but "with God all things are possible." "Stretch out thine hand," said the Saviour to the poor creature who had his hand withered. Did he reply, "Lord I cannot strerch it forth; it is withered?" No, he stretched it forth, and an energy accompanied the Saviour's word, and his hand was restored whole as the other. "Prophecy to these dry bones," said God to Ezekiel, and he replied, "Lord it is perfectly useless; they can neither hear nor feel!" No; but he prophesied, and they sprang up an exceeding great army. "Go forward" said He unto Moses. Did he reply, "What, and be drowned in the sea?" They went forward, the sea opened before them, and they passed through it as on dry land.

Now all this is very instructive and edifying. It should teach us to do all things in religion without murmuring and disputing. It teaches us to be followers of God as dear children; that there is nothing that more becomes us than a childlike disposition, a very implicit confidence in God, and an unhesitating obedience to His orders and commands. It is this alone that can show you to be the children of our father

Abraham. God sa... o Abraham, when he was seventy-five years of age, "Get thee out of thy country and from thy kindred;" a command not very easy to comply with. The heart at seventy-five begins to cleave to places and objects to which it has been long accustomed. A native country is dear; a father's house is dearer still. Then he knew not whither he was to go. Did he say, "Lord, before I leave where I am, inform me where I am to be?" No, he immediately obeyed, and "went forth, not knowing whither he went." So, too, when God said to him, "Take now thy son, thine only son Isaac, whom thou lovest, and get thee unto the land of Moriah; and offer him there for a burnt offering upon one of the mountains which I will tell thee of." What did he? He arose early in the morning and prepared to obey this strange, this mysterious, this inexplicable command: and obtained from God this testimony, "Now I know that thou fearest God, seeing thou hast not withheld thy son, thine only son, from me."

And, my brethren, this will apply to the declarations of Scripture as well as to commands. If God is pleased to reveal such and such things, we are to believe them upon His own authority. It is an homage due to His wisdom and to His faithfulness; for, "He is too wise to err, too good to be unkind." Whereas, if we say, "How can these things be?" instead of receiving them as a little child the declarations of its father, without suspicion, and place our faith only upon our knowledge, how is it possible that we can honour God? If a person were to tell you that there is such a place as Paris, and you were to say "I will believe it, sir, as soon as I have seen it," would he not deem this an insult?

Yea, further, this will also apply to the dispensations of Providence, as well as to duties and declarations. When any of these dispensations seem to be against us and at variance with our welfare, we are to remember that all the ways of the Lord are mercy and truth to those that fear Him, and therefore we should say with Eli, "Let Him do as seemeth Him good."

II. Let us pass from the Jews to Christians. This is the second application of our subject, in which we are to view this command in reference to THE ADVANCEMENT OF CHRISTIANS IN THE DIVINE LIFE. For, my brethren, as the Israelites were to advance on their way from Egypt to Canaan, so Christians are wayfaring men, seeking a better country, and it becomes them to be always advancing in the way everlasting. "Speak to the children of Israel that they go forward."

It is an awful thing when Christians are inclined to look back; yet this is no uncommon case. David went back. We read of the first ways of David as being his best ways, and they were so. The King of Jerusalem never equalled the shepherd in Bethlehem in character. The Ephesians went back, and so they are called to do their first work, and to walk in their first ways, and to repent or to lose the privileges with which they were indulged. The Church in the day of Osea had gone back, and therefore she was brought to say by a series of afflictions, "I will go and return to my first husband, for then was it better with me than now." Christian went back in order to find and fetch his roll which he dropped when he slept in the arbour. And how many more living have gone miles back, and are ready to say,

> "Where is the blessedness I knew
> When first I saw the Lord?
> Where is the soul-reviving views
> Of Jesus and His word?
>
> What peaceful hours I then enjoyed,
> How sweet their memory still,
> But they have left an aching void
> The world can never fill."

'Tis sad when Christians are but even where they were, standing still as it were, instead of progressing in godliness. An old writer says, "A Christian should never pitch his tent twice in the same place, but with every fresh rising sun there should be fresh advancement."

There are some who deny a growth in grace, and no wonder *they* should deny it, because they deny a work of grace in *reality* in the man. All their religion is in moral relations, and in outward things. But our Saviour says of the water He gives us, that it shall be in us "a well of water *springing up into everlasting life.*" And the Apostle says to the Philippians, "Being confident of this very thing, that He who hath begun a good in you will perform it unto the day of Jesus Christ," where he shows us that this work is not only interior, but also progressive. And what do persons mean when they deny or endeavour to ridicule the possibility of growth in grace? What! Is it not possible to obtain clearer views of Divine truths? Is it not possible to be more patient under our trials of afflictions, and to have a greater concern for the salvation of those around you? "Speak unto the Children of Israel that they go forward."

In order to see the possibility, the propriety, the importance, the expediency, and the necessity of this advancing in the Divine life, turn to the commands of the Scriptures, such as the following :—" Grow in grace, and in the knowledge of our Lord and Saviour Jesus Christ." "Add to your faith, knowledge, temperance, patience, brotherly kindness, charity," and "let these things be in you and abound."

We may learn this also from the images God has employed in His word to excite you onward. "The path of the just is as the shining light which shineth more and more unto the perfect day." "There is first the blade, then the ear, after that the full corn in the ear." In the household of faith you have babes, and young men, and fathers in Christ. Does not this imply, and even express, progression?

Turn you then to the examples which are held forth in the word of truth. Look at the Thessalonians : says the Apostle, "Your faith groweth exceedingly, and the charity of every one of you towards each other aboundeth." Look at Moses : he knew more of God than any human being in the world then, and yet he prays, saying, "O Lord, I beseech Thee show me Thy glory." Who ever had made such advancement in the Divine life as the Apostle of the Gentiles? and yet says he, "I have not yet attained, I am not already perfect; but this one thing I do, forgetting the things which are behind, and reaching forth unto those things which are before, I press towards the mark for the prize of the high calling of God in Christ Jesus." And he adds, "Let as many as be perfect be thus minded."

Then turn you to the promises with which the Scripture abounds : "I will be as the dew unto Israel; he shall grow as the lily, and cast forth his roots as Lebanon. His branches shall spread, and his beauty shall be as the olive tree, and his smell as Lebanon. They that do dwell under his shadow shall return ; they shall revive as the corn, and grow as the vine; the scent thereof shall be as the wine of Lebanon." "They that have clean hands," says Solomon, "shall wax stronger and stronger."

Then turn to the advantages of progression in religion ; for, as you advance you will improve ; as you advance, you will rise ; and as you advance, you will be changing "from glory to glory, as by the Spirit of the Lord." Every step you go adds to your dignity ; every step adds to your usefulness, and enables you the more to adorn the doctrine of God our Saviour in all things, to recommend His service to all around you. Every step you take will add to your comfort, and will contribute to the evidences of your state and character before God. See for example the words of our Saviour: "Herein is my Father glorified, that ye bear much fruit; so shall ye be my disciples," as much as to say, this will exemplify you as such.

No wonder, therefore, that Moses should say to the children of Israel "go forward." Let nothing hinder you in your course. Let not sleep or sloth hinder you; let not a fear of loneliness hinder you; let not a fear of the difficulties of the way hinder you. You shall "tread upon the lion and adder, the young lion and the dragon shalt thou trample under feet." Let not the powers of darkness hinder you. If Apollon straddles across the whole road, and tells Christian he shall either die or go back, "resist the Devil, and he will flee from you." "As thy day so shall thy strength be."

"Hell and thy sins resist thy course,
But hell and sin are vanquish'd foes;
My Jesus nail'd them to the cross,
And sung the triumph when He rose."

"Go forward," then, Christians, fighting the good fight of faith in the strength of the Lord.

"Onward, Christians! onward go,
Join the war and face the foe;
Faint not, much doth yet remain
Of the trying fierce campaign.

Shrink not, soldiers! will you yield?
Will you quit the painful field?
Will you flee when dangers low'r?
Know you not your Captain's power?

Let your drooping hearts be glad,
March in heavenly armour clad;
Fight! nor think the battle long,
Vict'ry soon shall tune your song.

Let not sorrow dim your eye,
Soon shall every tear be dry;
Let not gloom your course impede,
Great your strength, if great your need.

Onward, then, to battle move,
More than conquerors you shall prove,
Though opposed by many a foe,
CHRISTIAN SOLDIERS! ONWARD GO!"

III. Let us consider the command in reference to THE PROGRESS OF TIME.

You will immediately see that the design of this address cannot mean you should go forward with time itself, for this is unavoidable. Time is always advancing; the hour is going forward; the day, the week, the year is going forward, and does it leave you behind? No; you advance with as much rapidity as the vessel which bears you along. Time has been moving on since we have been assembled together. And have you not been going on? Are not you every day and every hour nearer—Where?—What?—*Conscience*, answer!

You are not therefore to consider us here as exhorting you to go forward with time, but we would point out the way you ought to advance. Hear, therefore, the following admonitions:—

First, go forward *with humbleness of mind*, not strutting into the new year as if you had been acting wisely, worthily, and religiously only, during the year that is past, but being clothed with humility, and walking humbly with your God. If you are sensible of your unworthiness; if you reflect, not only upon your sins since you have known God, or rather have been known of Him; if you reflect, not only upon the sins of the week, but upon the sins of the Sabbath, and of those sins connected with your most holy things; can you help exclaiming with Job, "Behold I am vile! how shall I answer Thee?" or with Jeremiah, "It is of the Lord's mercies we are not consumed, and because His compassions fail not."

Secondly, "Go forward" *in remembrance of His mercies.* Have they not been new every morning? Has not the Lord been loading you with His benefits? How many of your fellow-creatures have gone down to the grave and seen corruption! Who is it that has held your souls in life? Who has preserved you in your going out and in your coming in? Who has filled the tabernacles of your house with the voice of peace and comfort?

> "His gospel throughout the long year
> From Sabbath to Sabbath we hear:
> How oft has He met with us here,
> And shown Himself mighty to save."

What enjoyment have we had in His house and ordinances! Whose Spirit has helped our infirmities? Whose joy has been our strength? Whose arm has been our support?

Then "Go forward" *under a sense of present mercies*, in opposition to complaining and murmurings. Admitting that the new year has found you still in the wilderness, yet like the Israelites of old, have you not found grace in the wilderness?

and cannot you distinguish between your wants and your supplies? Need you be told that you are not alone there? that you have the fiery cloudy pillar to guide you there? that you have water from the rock to follow and to refresh you there? that you have manna from the clouds to sustain you there? that you have Moses and Aaron and Miriam—that you have the mercy-seat, and God holding communion with you from off that seat, and always ready to hear and answer your prayer!

Then "Go forward" always *with a firm confidence as to what may befall you in the future.* Reflection is enough to encourage you here. Surely we may all say—

"His love in times past
  Forbids me to think,
He'll leave me at last
  In trouble to sink;
Each sweet Ebenezer
  I have in review,
Confirms His good pleasure
  To help me quite through."

How much more when He promises to meet all your circumstances, and provide for all the contingencies of futurity! 'Tis true, you know not what a day may bring forth, but you know who has said, "I will never leave thee, nor forsake thee." You will have continually your wants, but He will supply them all from His riches in glory by Christ Jesus. You will have fresh duties to perform, but His strength shall be made perfect in your weakness. "Trials may and will befall," but if the road be rough, and your feet be tender, your shoes shall be iron and brass, and as your day so shall your strength be. You may look for continual conflict with enemies, but, "Fear not, thou worm Jacob, and ye men of Israel, I will help thee, saith the Lord, and thy Redeemer the Holy One of Israel. Behold thou shalt thrash the mountains, and beat them small, and shall make the hills as chaff." Yea, in all these things ye shall be "more than conquerors through Him that loveth you."

Again, "Go forward" with *earnest and constant prayer.* "If any man lack wisdom, let him ask of God, who giveth to all men liberally and upbraideth not, and it shall be given him." If you do not use this armour you are open to every kind of danger, whereas if you abound in this, your soul shall "prosper and be in health," for He hath said, "Their hearts shall live that seek God." Perhaps some years ago you were ready to resolve and to vow, and to enter into a covenant with God, unconscious of your own frailty; but now, I hope, you are more disposed to say with David, "I will go in the strength of the Lord God," as well as make mention of His righteousness, of His only. You have trusted in your own hearts, and have been ashamed. You have seen the vanity of your own purposes, and how your iniquities like the wind have carried you away, and I hope you are now prepared to be "strong in the Lord and in the power of His might," and to hear as an admonition, "Be strong in the grace that is in Christ Jesus;" "Come boldly to the throne of grace, that you may obtain mercy, and find grace to help in time of need."

Once more, "Go forward" *with frequent thoughts of your journey's end:* for it will have an end, and you are brought one year nearer to it. Have you not heard a voice lately, saying, "It is high time to awake out of sleep, for now is our salvation nearer than when we believed. The night is far spent, the day is at hand: let us therefore cast off the works of darkness, and let us put on the armour of light. Let us walk honourably as in the day; not in rioting and drunkenness, not in clambering and wantonness, not in strife and envying; but put ye on the Lord Jesus Christ, and make not provision for the flesh, to fulfil the lusts thereof."

Jeremiah said to Hananiah, "This year thou shalt die," and so it was. I am not authorised to say so to any individual here this morning, "this year thou shalt die;" but I am authorised to say to every individual here this morning, "this year you *may* die," and O, sinner, is this the case with you? And may you die this year? May the bridge be drawn? May the door be shut? And may you be forced to exclaim, "The harvest is past, the summer is ended and I am not saved? O sinner, may you die this year? Are you prepared to meet the King of Terrors? Are you prepared to pass through the valley of the Shadow of Death? Are you prepared to enter a world in which as you have no hope, so after which you can have no desire? Are you prepared to appear before the judgment-seat of Christ, to give an account of the deeds done in the body whether they be good or evil?

O, Christian, may you die this year? What! may you go home this year? What! may you leave all the winds and the waves this year, and enter into your desired haven? What! may you this year get rid of the burden of the flesh and the body of this death? What! may you this year be freed from all your afflictions and from all your infirmities, and have no more darkness in your mind, no more rebellion in your will, no more sensuality in your affections? What! may you this year get rid of a wicked world without and a wicked heart within? What! may you this year behold Him, whom, having not seen, you love? "In whom though now we see Him not, yet believing, we rejoice with joy unspeakable and full of glory." Ah, Christian! die when you may, you will be introduced to Him whom your soul loves; you will see Him as He is; you will be for ever with Him—with Him who "loved you and gave Himself for you," "an offering and a sacrifice of a sweet smelling savour;" who is now your advocate with the Father, having been the propitiation for your sins.

And now you are going, Christian, to celebrate the supper of your dying Lord, and eat and drink in remembrance of Him. And what subject is there that does not lead us to Him? Did I not tell you it would be always attractive, always desirable, always necessary, always consoling? I trust you feel the Redeemer to be more precious to your soul than ever, and that He is increasingly dear as you advance towards your journey's end. Feel you not, Christian, that whatever be your external circumstances, He is all your salvation and all your desire. Let us therefore go to His table singing or sighing—

> Perpetual blessings from above
> Encompass one around,
> And yet how few returns of love
> Hath my Redeemer found?
>
> Lord, with this guilty heart of mine
> To Thy dear cross I flee;
> And to Thy grace my soul resign,
> To be renewed by Thee.
>
> What have I done for Him who died
> To save my wretched soul?
> How have my follies multiplied,
> Fast as my minutes roll!

"God be merciful to me a sinner." Amen.

III.

THE HARVEST FEAST.

(Preached on Sunday Morning, October 10th, 1847.)

"*When ye have gathered in the fruits of the land, ye shall keep a feast unto the Lord.*"—LEVITICUS xxiii. 39.

WE are going to consider these words; not only, or principally, in reference to those to whom it was originally addressed. It regards one of the annual festivals of the Jews. Of these festivals there were three. (I hope you will soon have done turning over your Bibles, for you may depend upon it it is true, and I have read it correctly),—(referring to the words of the text). There were three of these annual festivals. They were divinely enjoined. "Three times in the year shall all your men-children appear before the Lord God, the God of Israel. For I will cast out the nations before thee, and enlarge thy borders; neither shall any man desire thy land, when thou shalt go up to appear before the Lord thy God thrice in the year." These festivals were designed to accomplish five purposes. First, to point to a grand reality. So they were shadows of good things to come, of which the body was Christ. Sccondly, to afford an opportunity for the people to hear the Law of God, and to keep up an acquaintance with the ordinances of the Lord. Thirdly, to allow an interval for intercourse with their relations and friends, and thus to cherish relative and social affection. Fourthly, to furnish them a suitable reason for relaxation and recreation; for He that is the Saviour of the soul is not the destroyer of the body. And, lastly, to perpetuate the memory and the lively recollection of God's mighty works.

"When ye have gathered in the fruit of the land, ye shall keep a feast unto the Lord." This command was binding upon His people the Jews so long as the dispensation under which they lived continued; but when the "fullness of time was come" it was abolished,—abolished ceremonially, but not abolished morally; the spirit of it remains, and calls upon us as much as upon the Jews; and it never called louder than at the present time. Some months ago a fast was appointed, and we were called upon to humble ourselves before God on account of our manifold sins, and to implore Him to remove the judgments of His heavy hand, which was then abroad in the earth, and pressed sore upon ourselves. This day was solemnly observed; the nation was impressed; our prayers were in the spirit of grace and supplication; addresses were delivered from the pulpits, suitable, instructive, aud profitable, and we are fully persuaded the Lord regarded it for good. Is this belief enthusiasm? Is there not a God that judgeth the earth? Is not He the Governor among the nations? Cannot God really and obviously bless a nation? And if He does this, must He not do it in time, for there are no nations found in eternity, but only individuals? Is not God the hearer of prayer? Has He not encouraged us to hope in His Word? Does not the Saviour teach us to ask from day to day our "daily bread," and say to you, "Prove Me now herewith, if I will not open you the windows of heaven, and pour you out a blessing that there shall not be room enough to receive it. And I will rebuke the devourer for your sakes, and he shall not destroy the fruit of your ground; neither shall your vine cast her fruit before the time in the field, saith the Lord of Hosts. And all nations shall call you blessed, for ye shall be a delightsome land, saith the Lord of Hosts." I hope we have all blessed Him already privately, in our closets, and in our social meetings; but, my brethren, public blessings demand public acknowledgment. Some of our brethren have indeed already had public Services in their churches, and we should not have tarried in this well-doing but for a full expectation that as a day was appointed for thanksgiving, and as the issue of a mere form of prayer was not considered necessary for the one, so the mere stated prayer would not be considered enough for the other. Many will be disappointed, but it will be well for them to remember, though they should have been glad to "enter His gates with praise" with their country along with them, their duty never depends upon the example of a number or the sanction of a multitude. What is the duty you ask? "When ye have gathered in the fruits of the land, ye shall keep a feast unto the Lord." Observe the boon; observe the season; observe the service; observe the aim. "Consider what we say, and the Lord give you understanding in all things."

I. Observe THE BOON: "The fruit of the land." This comprehends and regards all the land; the increase of the field and of the garden, the peaches, grapes, figs, olives, pomegranates, and many other inferior productions. Those with regard to us may be arranged in three classes: Those that regard the animal, those that regard our indulgences, and those that regard our support.

The fruits of the land with us include the brute creation. They have their suffering as well as we. They are as capable, in their measure, of relief and satisfaction as ourselves. And "doth God care for oxen?" Yes! He hears "the young ravens when they cry." Yes, all wait upon God, and He giveth them their meat in due season; "He openeth His hand, and satisfieth the desire of every living thing." Solomon observes that "a righteous man regardeth the life of his beast; but the tender mercies of the wicked are cruel." We see this contrast in Eleazer and Baalam: the one would not feast until he had foddered his cattle, the other spurred his ass till he spake as with a man's voice, and forbade the madness of the prophet. And God as well as man will always rejoice to see provision made even for the brute creatures. Many of these are in man's employ as beasts of burden, by which he conveys and carries things from place to place. And he derives a thousand comforts from them, and should therefore feel an interest in their welfare on his own behalf. You see the Scriptures regard these always. Thus we read in the twelfth chapter of Deuteronomy, "I will give you the rain of your land in his due season, the first rain and the latter rain, that thou mayest gather in thy corn, and thy wine, and thine oil; and I will send grass in thy fields for thy cattle, that thou mayest eat and be full." Here Solomon has the same remark, "Be thou diligent to know the state of thy flocks, and look well to thy herds, for riches are not for ever; and doth the crown endure to every generation? The hay appeareth, and the tender grass showeth itself, and herbs of the mountain are gathered. The lambs are for thy clothing, and the goats are the price of the field: and thou shalt have goat's milk enough for thy food, for the food of thy household, and for the maintenance of thy maidens."

Then in the "fruit of the land" we include those that are for our indulgence. It is obvious God designed not only our support, but our gratification and enjoyment. How wonderful is this! Look now over the earth, and survey its productions and profusion. Who would ever suppose that a region thus furnished was ever intended for the residence of sinners, rebellious, unworthy and helpless? It is obviously for our indulgence. What are the daisies for? What are the gillcups for? What is the hawthorn on the hedges for? What are the wild flowers on the banks for, but to aid the loveliness of Nature, and the advantages and pleasures to be derived from variety? What charms there are in Nature for the eye! What sermons in a simple flower! Take now the apple tree; how lovely is it in its blossoms! such a mixture of red and white! it could have been without blossom, but it is the beautiful blossom to please the eye, before the fruit meets the taste. There are other instances in which we behold the extent of the loving-kindness of God; by which we see not only that in Him we live, and move, but have all things richly to enjoy.

In the "fruits of the land" we are above all to include that which regards our support and sustenance: barley and wheat. The latter deserves peculiar notice. It is called "the staff of life," upon which we lean more than anything else, the failure of which occasions a famine of bread. Vegetables also may come under this division. They are very nutritive, and one requires peculiar notice. The potato entered this country a few years ago from abroad. For a considerable time it was a rare article, and was seen only at the tables of princes; but after a time it became exceedingly multiplied. It has now become almost a necessary of life, especially with the peasantry, and more especially with the peasantry of our neighbouring island, Ireland. Their very existence seems to depend on it.

II. Let us pass from the boon to THE SEASON. "When ye have gathered in the fruit of the land." What a difference between this season and the season of spring! Then we hear a voice saying: "Rise up, my love, my fair one, and come away. For lo, the winter is past; the rain is over and gone; the flowers appear on the earth; the time of the singing of birds is come, and the voice of the turtle is heard in our land." We obey; we go forth and we see nature renewed. The lovely valleys "stand thick with corn," and the "little hills rejoice on every side;" and we observe "first the blade, then the ear, and after that the full corn in the ear." We walk through the field, and see it has a "wave offering to the Lord," and exclaim with David, "Thou hast prepared of Thy goodness for the poor." Then cometh harvest; the mower is seen filling his hand with corn, and binding his sheaves to his bosom; and as we pass by we say, "The blessing of the Lord be upon you, we bless you in the name of the Lord."

If we go forward, what changes do we see! the treasures we saw so recently in the fields are reduced to stubble. The trees drop their foliage, and everything seems hastening to a kind of sameness. This season is more sober and sombre; but though it has not the attractions of spring, it is not without its use. Now the painter who sketches your landscapes goes forward. Now the moralizer goes forth musing as he walks on the romantic hills. He feels himself changed with the period; he remarks the lapse of time; the sun is shortening his visits, and he says, sighing as he sees it, "All the glory of man is as the flowers of the field." And as the season of winter is seen approaching, he exclaims—

> "All, all on earth is shadow,
> All beyond is substance;
> The reverse is folly's creed;
> How solid all when change
> Shall be no more!——"

Thus, says the man, "my comforts are removed; my connections are gone. Lover and friend hast Thou put far from me, and mine acquaintance into darkness. What have I here? What do I here? Henceforth my home is in the skies."

> "There my best friends and kindred dwell,
> There God my Saviour reigns."

Now the husbandman goes forth, and he is now free from those cares that corrode him, and from those fears that alarm him. There are no mildews, no insects, no droughts, no excessive rains now! His wishes are accomplished, his hopes fulfilled, his labours crowned with success! He has sown in tears, but reaped in joy. Now all his corn is secure; all is in the stack or the garner, and there is seed for the sower, and bread for the eater. Let us pass to the service.

III. "When ye have gathered in the fruits of the earth ye shall make a FEAST unto the Lord." This feast, being among the festival seasons, was to express gladness and gratitude, rejoicing and thanksgiving. "A feast," says Solomon, "is made for laughter." And if you were to see many "feasts," you would soon see it was not made in vain. Then we see joy becomes a feast, and then we remark this was always connected with Divine appointment. I shall only refer you to one passage in the book of Deuteronomy: "Thou shalt observe the feasts of tabernacles seven days after that thou hast in thy corn and thy wine, and thou shalt rejoice in thy feasts, thou, and thy son, and thy daughter, and thy man-servant, and thy maid-servant, and the Levite, the stranger, and the fatherless, and the widow, that are within thy gates." Oh! how good is God to us, not only to allow us to rejoice, but to require us to do it, and to make it our duty, for He would have His servants feasted while they attend upon Him in the discharge of their duty! He does not therefore drive you from Himself, as some people imagine, but He feels a pleasure in you, and not only requires you to come before Him, but to come before Him with singing. You must not be afraid to rejoice in His presence. "In His presence there is fulness of joy." Yea, they are commanded to joy before Him as men in harvest. Here to enjoy is to obey, to feast on the abundance of nature and providence. He does indeed forbid the pleasures of sin, and why? Because it strains the mind and stings the conscience; it degrades and defiles the man; because it enslaves, and finally destroys him. He forbids no other pleasure. Where does he ever enjoin self-tormenting? Are we not assured He takes pleasure in the prosperity of His servants? Does He not say, "Behold, my servants shall eat, but ye shall be hungry? Behold, My servants shall rejoice, but ye shall be ashamed? Behold, my servants shall rejoice and shout for joy, but ye shall wail, and sorrow, and affliction of spirit shall be upon you?" We love sanctity: we equally dislike sanctimoniousness. We love serious reflection, but not sorrowful spirits, or loud noises. It is the creeping of the waggon as it comes along the road with the last part of the harvest in from the fields, with the rustics' shouts bringing their sheaves, and shouting as the villagers are passing by. We would not despise this song: we see how much the harvest-home falls in with the Divine appointment; and yet how much has this been given up through covetousness, under the pretence of some irregularity, or of some little excess, by some of those who while they sit and carouse at the table talk scandal by the hour. Thus everything that administers to the comfort and pleasure, especially of the poor, is abolished. But by whom? Does God require this? Is it God that forbids to marry and to abstain from meats? No; for every creature of God is good, *if* it be received with thanksgiving; and sanctified by the word of God and prayer. No! No! It is the religion of Hell that says "touch not, taste not, handle not (which all are to perish with the using). After the commandments and doctrines of men, such things have indeed a show of wisdom in will-worship, and humility, and neglecting of the body, not in any honour to the satisfying of the flesh."

But, my dear brethren, whilst man is remembered, let not God be forgotten. This feast is finally to express joy and gladness with thanksgiving—"thanksgiving." This, remember, is added to the former. How little of this, alas! is to be found even among the professors of godliness. "They that dwell in His house shall still *praise* Him;" where else shall we find it? Archbishop Leighton says, "How lamentable is it that the earth should be so full of the goodness of God, and so empty of His praise." And David groans three times in one Psalm, "Oh, that men would praise the Lord for His goodness, and for His wonderful works to the children of men!" Doctor South says, "An ungrateful man is like the sea, constantly receiving the showers of heaven and turning them to his own account. Yea! he is like the grave, which is saying, 'Give, give;' always receiving, and never restoring." The Lacedemonians punished ingratitude with the greatest severity. There is no one thing so lamentable as ingratitude, when it is manifested to your own dear selves. What is your ingratitude to your fellow-creatures compared with your ingratitude to God? What is all the kindness of your fellow-creatures compared with your infinite Benefactor? An old writer has said, "Ingratitude is the only one thing that never had an advocate." But while there is no one who will plead for it, how many are there who practise it!

How much is there to call forth your gratitude and praise at the season upon which I now address you! And in order to induce you to be thankful, shall I lead you back a few months, when destitution, disease, and desolation were seen from one end of our land to the other? Or shall I lead you forward to the prospect before us? Was there any one of you that was not shocked at the reports from many parts in Scotland, and almost all of Ireland? Shall I refer you to the starving multitude—to children pouring out their lives in their mother's bosom—to the torture of parents—to the diseases of the dying—to the dead and the unburied—to the dog-mangled carcasses? Or shall I refer you to the abundant harvest with which God has blessed us: so abundant as not to be denied even by the farmers themselves? Or shall I refer you to the excellency of the produce: so excellent that even the farmer for once owns it! Or shall I lead you to observe that the same abundance, the same excellency, have been found abroad? We should be thankful and grateful even for this; for one nation can never be independent of another. Or shall I refer you to the favourable weather? How few days have there been in which the work of the husbandman could not be pursued! How few have been the days in which the labour connected with the "fruit of the land" could not be carried on! Let us therefore exclaim with David, "The Lord hath done great things for us, whereof we are glad;" only adding one thing, "The Lord hath done great things for us, whereof we are *grateful.*" Oh! that you could all say so!

III. Let us pass on to consider THE AIM. "Ye shall keep a feast unto the Lord."

You will remember, perhaps, the language of Hosea:—"Israel is an empty vine, he bringeth forth fruit unto himself." Persons may be fruitful in profession, and yet very barren in practice. Remember the question God Himself addressed to the Jews in the Babylonian captivity: "When ye fasted and mourned in the fifth and seventh month, even those seventy years, did ye at all fast unto me—even to me? And when ye did eat, and when ye did drink, did not ye eat for yourselves, and drink for yourselves?" Oh, my dear hearers, how does this question shake the self-righteousness which had occupied so great a part in ourselves? How does it admonish us in our religious services! How little have we ever done, and how much of that little have we done to ourselves, instead of attending to the grand direction, "Whether ye eat or drink, or whatever ye do, do all to the glory of God." We cannot consider this service a feast unto the Lord, unless we ascribe the bounty to His agency, and improve it to His glory and praise.

We cannot observe this feast unto the Lord unless we ascribe it all to His agency. How senseless are mankind naturally! As Isaiah says, "They regard not the work of the Lord, neither consider the operation of His hands." Thus with regard to the course of nature, everything seems convenient—seed time and harvest, summer and winter, night and day, heat and cold; so they rely on the established order of things, and think God has nothing to do with them. But in time He distorts and controls the whole, in order that He may break this usual course in nature, and in providence, and come forth, as He has done to our experience before, and do "His strange work." Let us remember that everything is of God's appointment, and that while He is seeming to do nothing in our world, He is doing all; and "that every good gift and every perfect gift is from above, and cometh down from the Father of lights, with whom is no variableness neither shadow of turning." However poor the means employed may be; however real the operation of second causes may appear; may we remember God is the original mover of the whole! "I will hear the heavens," says God, "and they shall hear the earth; and the earth shall hear the corn and the wine and the oil; and they shall hear Jezreel." To Him, therefore, everything must be ascribed, and to Him be all the praise.

Surely it is important to reflect upon such things as these. There is such perfection and harmony, such displays of infinite variety, and all the result of some few simple elements; and we should remember that all His works display the same wisdom. "In wisdom hast Thou made them all." His wisdom is as much displayed in the salvation of a soul as in the creation of a world. "Whoso," says David, "is wise and will observe these things, even they shall understand the loving kindness of the Lord."

But as we are required to ascribe the bounty to His agency, so we are equally required to improve all to His praise. We are capable of doing this, and we *only*. All animals are His creatures, but we are His subjects. They are not endowed with reason. He teaches us more than the beast of the field, and maketh us wiser than the fowl of the air, for there is a spirit in man, and the inspiration of the Almighty giveth him understanding." The brutes that perish, they eat their food and know nothing of the source from which it comes. But we do! We know our resources, we know our obligations, and we know it is of "His mercy that we are not consumed." We know that the earth is full of His riches. We know that His paths drop fatness. We know that He crowns the year with His goodness. And shall we pass these benefits by perpetually? Shall we, like Israel, take of the holy things, and prepare them for Baal? Rather let His goodness fill up our thoughts and employ our tongues, that we may exclaim with David, "They shall abundantly utter the memory of Thy great goodness, and shall sing of Thy righteousness." Let us not be satisfied with giving Him lip service. "Let us show forth His praise, not only with our lips, but in our lives, by giving up ourselves to His service, and walking before Him in holiness and righteousness all our days." Oh! let us not incur the reproach of the Lord, "The ox knoweth its owner, and the ass its master's crib, but Israel doth not know, my people do not consider!" Oh, let us not expose ourselves to the charge of Jeremiah, "Neither say they in their heart, let us now fear the Lord our God, that giveth rain, both the former and the latter in His season; He reserveth unto us the appointed weeks of the harvest." My brethren, "thanksgiving," as Mr. Henry observes, "is good, but thanks-*living* is better;" and therefore we beseech you, "by the mercies of God, to present your bodies a living sacrifice, holy, acceptable to God, which is your reasonable service."

Thus far I have spoken of earthly things: I have now to speak of heavenly. I have been addressing you as Britons: I now address you as heirs of immortality. I have been addressing you as creatures: I must now fulfil my commission, and address you as sinners. I have been speaking to you of the abundance of Providence: I now invite you "to the exceeding riches of His grace, His long-suffering and goodness, which are by Jesus Christ." I have been speaking of a corporeal feast: I now tell you of a "feast of fat things, a feast of wines on the lees; of fat things full of marrow, of wines on the lees well refined," and would say "Come, for all things are now ready." "Man liveth not by bread alone;" he has a soul within him; he has an eternity before him. He would be worse than a brute if he were not concerned for blessings superior to those which belong to the inferior part of his nature and to the shortest period of his being; for he will have lived but two or three moments, when behold, "the heavens shall pass away with a great noise and the elements shall melt with fervent heat, the earth also, and the works that are therein shall be burned up." And is it so? "Seeing, then, that all these things shall be dissolved, what manner of persons ought ye to be, in all holy conversation and godliness!"

I shall be sorry if any one of you should go away this morning unimpressed with the goodness of God. I hope not a few will go away affected—properly affected—with the goodness of God in nature and providence, blessing Him for our creation, preservation, and all the blessings of this life, but above all for the redemption of the world by our Lord Jesus Christ, for the means of grace, and for the hope of glory. How many are there who will be thankful for this? This is the test by which you ought to judge of yourselves. The natural man will be thankful for temporal blessings; but the spiritual man will be thankful for spiritual blessings. I hope, therefore, that every man here who has duly fed on the kindness of nature and Providence will be thankful: but above all, say, as he retires, "Thanks be unto God for His unspeakable gift." "Blessed be the God and Father of our Lord Jesus Christ, who hath blessed us with all spiritual blessings in heavenly places in Christ Jesus."

How I pity those who have their portion in this life, and are unconcerned for a better! How can I conclude without addressing you in the language of the prophet, "Wherefore do ye spend money for that which is not bread, and your labour for that which satisfieth not? hearken diligently unto me, and eat ye that which is good and let your soul delight itself in fatness. Incline your ear, and come unto me; hear, and your souls shall live; and I will make an everlasting covenant with you, even the sure mercies of David." "Seek, therefore, those things that are above, where Christ sitteth at the right hand of God."

Can you die, my dear hearers, can you die happy without this? Alas! you will not be able. You will die certainly: you may soon. Suppose, now, before we conclude this service you should be called by the messenger of death, and carried home, and laid on the bed of languishing; notice the whispering of friends and relations, "There is no hope!" Everything within you is saying, "One thing thou lackest." Everything else is done, "but one thing thou lackest." The Judge is at the door; you are dying; where are you now? What is your condition? What your feelings? What will you do now without a connection with the Saviour? Are you able to rejoice in His righteousness and strength? But before this period arrives, what may you not suffer? What will you do then without this better blessing? How uncertain, need I remind you, is this life! "Man that is born of a woman is of few days and full of trouble." He is like the sparks that fly upwards, and shine for a moment and then expire! Need I tell you how soon the lamp will expire, and no Sun of righteousness shine upon you with healing in His wings? Can you say with Mrs. Rowe, on the death of her husband,—

"Thou dost but take the lamp away
To bless me with unclouded day."

But what will you do in such a condition as this? There are

many persons here who can testify they have obtained a better blessing, and in their own experience, and with propriety, they can say, "Oh, taste and see that the Lord is good: blessed is the man that trusteth in Him." But I must conclude; for neither my strength or your patience will allow me to enlarge. "O! labour not for the meat that perisheth, but for that which endureth unto everlasting life, which the Son of man shall give unto you, for Him hath God the Father sealed." Oh, come to Him and say, "Lord, evermore give us this bread. Lord, give me this water, that I thirst not, neither come hither to draw." This is the day of salvation, may you each know the things that belong unto your everlasting peace, before they are hid from your eyes. This is your summer—your harvest; let it not be any of your lots to exclaim "The harvest is past; the summer is ended; and we are not saved!"

IV.

THOUGHTS FOR THE NEW YEAR.

(Preached on Thursday Evening, January 1st, 1846.)

"*And Elisha died, and they buried him. And the bands of the Moabites invaded the land at the coming in of the year.*"—1 KINGS xiii. 20.

HERE are three things to observe and improve. First, death: "And Elisha died." And what man is there that liveth and shall not see death? The good die, the great die, the useful die. Even Elisha, that man of God, who performed such miracles, wonders, and signs, was not suffered to continue by reason of death. I daresay they made great lamentation over him; for if God's servants are not prized while they live, they are lamented when they die. "How blessings brighten when they take their flight!"

Secondly, an invasion: "And the bands of the Moabites invaded the land." They were not only neighbours to the Jews, but enemies, and always ready to seize an opportunity for mischief. Their aim now was to rob, to spoil, to desolate and enslave. We find this mentioned apparently, and I believe really, as the result of the death of the prophet. While Elisha was alive, by his presence, prayer, and power with God, he was "the chariots of Israel and the horsemen thereof." In our breaches, God's people stand in the gap, and hold back invading judgments. But their removal opens a free passage for these. When God calls home His ambassadors, it is a fearful intimation that He is going to proclaim war. Therefore Isaiah complains, "The righteous perisheth, and no man layeth it to heart; and merciful men are taken away, none considering that the righteous is taken away from the evil to come." And David says, "Help, Lord; for the godly man ceaseth; for the faithful fail from among the children of men." And therefore "thus saith the Lord, As the new wine is found in the cluster, and one saith, Destroy it not; for a blessing is in it: so will I do for my servants' sakes, that I may not destroy them all."

Thirdly, a season: "And Elisha died, and they buried him. And the bands of the Moabites invaded the land at the coming in of the year." So the year came in cloudy and dark, and furnished very little congenial with that cheerfulness which the season commonly inspires. Whether this is the case with us appears in the sequel of the discourse, but I address you at the same season, and hasten to improve the coming in of the year. And this may be done five ways: It may be done, first, in a way of reflection; secondly, in a way of humiliation; thirdly, in a way of thanksgiving; fourthly, in a way of resolution; and, fifthly, in a way of prayer.

I. It requires REFLECTION. You say, What is the subject of our reflection? I reply, a thousand things are deserving it; but I must confine your attention this evening to one. It is the importance of such a measure of time as you have just passed through. It is hardly necessary to remark that there is nothing concerning which men are so thoughtless as their time. They carelessly squander it away, and it seems to be the chief labour of many to get rid of it. When I survey some of you, judging by your lives, no one would ever imagine that you attach the least value to a day, or a week, or a year. Yet what tongue can express how important such a period as you have just passed through is?

It is important, first, from the *brevity* of your time. If you had to reckon upon hundreds of years, as many before the flood had, why you need not be so much affected with the lapse of one year. But what is the truth with regard to you? "The days of our years are threescore years and ten, and if by reason of strength they be fourscore years, yet is their strength labour and sorrow; for it is soon cut off, and we fly away." "For what is your life? It is even a vapour, that appeareth for a little time, and then vanisheth away." It is as a flood—as a watch in the night, as a tale that is told. God has made our days as a handsbreadth, and our age is as nothing before Him. "Surely man at his best estate is altogether vanity." And of this short period, how little is appropriated to the grand purpose of our being! How much of our time is consumed by sleep! How much in frivolous discourse! How much in necessary refreshment, and the recreations of life!

Important, secondly, from the *uncertainty* of your time.

The longest duration upon earth is very short; but how few reach this boundary! You cannot call a week or an hour your own; and when you consider the accidents and diseases to which you are exposed, and the frailty of your frame; when you consider that your breath is in your nostrils, that you are crushed before the moth, that your life is in jeopardy every hour, you can easily see that there is but a step between you and death. And when you perceive the death of the young, the death of the strong, and of those who are suddenly hurried into an eternal world, you are also told plainly enough, that the Son of Man cometh in an hour when ye think not, and when you are not aware.

Important, thirdly, from the *irrecoverableness* of your time. When once gone, it is gone for ever. Where now is the past year? Where are the days of the past week? And where the past hours of the days? Where are the past moments of this hour? Why, gone to join the years before the Flood. You cannot live one of those hours or moments over again. If you lose your friends, or your riches, or your health, it is possible you may recover these; but if you lose a day or an hour, it is lost for ever, and will through eternal ages wear the very character you have impressed upon it.

Important, lastly, from the *influence* of your time. Now you will observe, and it is this that renders it so momentous, that your time has an intimate connection with eternity; and the present life issues in a never-ending eternity, so that the lapse of a year not only brings you nearer to the grave, but nearer to heaven or to hell; nearer to the lake that burneth with fire and brimstone, or to the river of the water of life; for when the dust returns to the earth as it was, the spirit goes to God who gave it, and after death there is the judgment.

How much happiness or misery then can one year in the review furnish in another world, for life now is seed-time, hereafter is the harvest, and "be not deceived; God is not mocked; for whatsoever a man soweth, that shall he also reap. For he that soweth to his flesh shall of the flesh reap corruption; but he that soweth to the Spirit shall of the Spirit reap life everlasting."

We must not enlarge here, as we have much before us; but if a single year, such as we have just passed through be important in all cases, it must be peculiarly so in some cases. We will, therefore, mention two of these. The first regards the aged. My old friend, if you had only seven sovereigns in your purse, after you had drawn forth the fifth and sixth, you would use the remainder with much care and caution; and how is it then with you? Grey hairs are here and there upon some of you, and I fear you perceive it not; and your infirmities, and limbs, and senses tell you that you are going the way of all the earth, but you do not lay it to heart. When you awoke this morning, you might have been aroused with an awful reflection, and said, "*What!*" is another of my years gone? and am I still destitute of pardoning mercy, and sanctifying grace? And what right have I, what reasonable right have I, to conclude that I shall see the end of another? Lord, so teach me to number my days that I may apply my heart unto wisdom. Oh, that I were wise, that I understood this, that I considered my latter end!"

The other regards youth. The young imagine they may lavish their time away. Though they would think it improper for the aged to do so, they think it is of little consequence for them to waste a year, since so many are before them. But remember, first, not one of you, my dear young friends, is sure you have another year to live. It is proverbially said—The old must die, the young may. Whom are we continually following to the grave? Are there not some present mourning over the death of some younger than themselves? And, secondly, if there were many years before you, you would be mistaken in your conclusion. As to an old man, the most of what he had to do is done; his connections in life are all formed, and his course is ended, but yours is commencing; yours are to be formed; how much depends upon every step you now take! There is the honour or disgrace that will attend your course; and how much arises from what you are, and what you do through a single year of your life! For what is the present season with regard to you? It is the morning of life, and an hour in the morning is worth two afterwards. It is the spring of life, and if in the spring there be no manuring, and ploughing, and sowing, there will be no reaping in the autumn, and no provision for winter.

II. In a way of HUMILIATION. And I hope you will never never consider humility injurious. It is not only safe but every way profitable, for "God resisteth the proud, but giveth grace unto the humble." And surely there must be enough in the review of one year to hide pride from man, and to induce him to bring to God the sacrifices of a broken and contrite spirit, which blessed be His name, He will not despise.

Now, to aid you in this, let me call upon you to consider

four things. First, the sins you have committed during the past year. Alas! perhaps you have forgotten them, especially those that consisted in thought, affection, and imagination. But God has them all in remembrance before Him; they are all written in His book. Many of these sins are not so vicious and gross as others, but all are more or less aggravated, by reason of your privileges and advantages, for where much is given much is required. If, therefore, God should say your sins are more in number than the hairs of your head, He would not exceed the truth, especially if He place in the number of all your outward and inward sins your *omissions*, for God takes these into account. A servant despises his master as much in neglecting duty as in doing what he has forbidden. How has it been with you during the past year? Have you always loved God supremely, and been alive to the divine glory, and kept your hearts with all diligence? When Dr. Robt. Harris was dying, a person said to him, "Oh, sir, you may now take comfort from your labours; you have done so much for God in your day and generation." He answered, "I am an unprofitable servant; I have done comparatively little for God and others, and the loss of time sits heavy upon my conscience." Archbishop Usher, that great scholar as well as divine, often prayed, "O Lord, pardon my sins and negligences." And when a clock struck, how often did he remark with solemn feelings, "There is another hour gone for ever."

Then, secondly, consider how much good you might have done during the past year. How much might you have done had you gone in search of opportunities, and had you improved the seasons when presented to you! But have you not often declined in both cases?

A word spoken in season how good is it! like apples of gold in pictures of silver. How much might you have done by a word of comfort to the mourner—to inform the ignorant—to strengthen the feeble-minded—by inviting persons to the house of God, and saying with David, "O taste and see that the Lord is good: blessed is the man that trusteth in Him."

How much good might you have done by your actions; for nothing is so forcible in addressing men as the silent eloquence of an amiable, consistent, and holy life. Have you adorned the doctrine of God your Saviour in all things, by a proper example of submission under trials, of contentment under privations, and forgiveness of provocations and injuries received? Have you been exemplary in your relations as husbands and wives, parents and children, masters and servants?

How much might you have done by your substance, according as God has prospered you. As you have had opportunity, have you done good "unto all men, especially unto them who are of the household of faith?" Have you fed the hungry, and clothed the naked, and visited the sick, and complied with the admonitions of Solomon, "Withhold not good from them to whom it is due, when it is in the power of thine hand to do it. Say not unto thy neighbour, 'Go, and come again, and to-morrow I will give;' when thou hast it by thee."

Consider, thirdly, how during the past year you have been favoured with religious privileges and the means of grace. Have you improved these? Under the law there was a lamb sacrificed every morning and every evening throughout the year, but on the Sabbath there were to be two lambs every morning and two every evening. This clearly enough teaches us that while we stand in need of daily forgiveness, we need especially forgiveness for our Sabbath sins, for guilt results more from our privileges than from our privations; and sins connected with our holy things are more heinous than in common things. O sinner, for I scorn to give flattering titles to any, O sinner, you are seventy years old; are you aware of what I am going to tell you? Are you aware that three thousand Sabbaths have passed over your ungodly head, and your ungodly heart; that three thousand Sabbaths are standing at the Bar of God to bear witness against you, unless you turn and repent, and believe? And oh, professor of religion, let me remind you, that you have passed through another year; that you have had fifty-two more of those days which may well be called "days of heaven upon earth." How many sermons during this period have you heard! You have been alarmed under some and melted under others. But you may now be ready to exclaim, "My goodness has been as a morning cloud, and as the early dew it goeth away." I have had opportunities of hearing the Word which I should have improved; I have read many excellent books; I have surrounded some dying beds; I have had many instructive providences, yet how dull of hearing have I been! and how slow of heart to believe! The sun of my profession, like Joshua's sun, has gone many degrees back. Oh, that it were with me as in months past!

> Where is the blessedness I knew,
> When first I saw the Lord?
> Where is the soul-refreshing view
> Of Jesus and His Word?

What peaceful hours I then enjoyed,
How sweet their mem'ry still;
But now I find an aching void
The world can never fill."

Then, lastly, consider the corrections you have been exercised with, and the little benefit you have derived from them. You will remember that God doth not afflict willingly, nor grieve the children of men without design. He intends by it to embitter sin, to wean His people from the world, to endear His Blessed Book to your minds. Oh, that sympathy of that Great High Priest, who is still touched with a feeling of your infirmity! We ought to pray for a blessing upon our daily rod, as upon our daily bread. It is sad when your food does you no good; but when your medicine fails, and the physician is employed in vain, the case looks awful. Oh, it is a great thing not to lose the benefit of an affliction or trial. Perhaps this has been a very expensive year to some of you; perhaps providence has laid bare your worldly schemes; and yet you have not been induced to serve the Lord better. Perhaps in your passage through life you have said "all men are liars," but have not said with Micah, "Therefore I will look unto the Lord; I will wait for the God of my salvation; my God will hear me." Perhaps God has broken up your domestic comfort. You sit down at your table, but David's place is empty. He has, perhaps, removed the guide of your youth, or taken away the desire of your eyes; yet, perhaps, if compelled to speak the truth, you would after all say, "Here I am still a poor senseless creature, and no better for the chastisement. I have been wooed and awed, blessed and chastised, yet remain a rebel still."

III. Let us pass on to observe that the coming in of the year requires THANKSGIVING. Here let me enter a little into details, and view gratitude as having claims upon you under five characters.

And first, you ought to be grateful as *creatures*. Here you should look back and call your own history to remembrance. Some during the past year have had their sanguine wishes accomplished—some have recovered from a bed of sickness—some have been brought back from the very verge of the grave—some during the past year have been blessed by Providence in the labour of their hands, so as to add to their income—some have been exempted from evils which have fallen upon those around them; and as to the afflictions you have experienced, have you had no alleviation? and might not your trials have been much more severe than they have been? If one resource has failed, have not others opened? If you have had hours of sickness, have you not had days of ease? Is there any who can stand forth this evening, and say, "I have not been under any obligations to God during the past year?" Under no obligations! Who has fed you from His table, and clothed you from His wardrobe? Who has drawn the curtain of darkness around your bed, and commanded all nature to be quiet while you have slumbered and slept? Surely it becomes you to say, "His mercies have been new every morning, and repeated every evening. Bless the Lord, O my soul, and all that is within me, bless His holy name."

Secondly, you ought to be thankful as *partakers of Divine Grace.* Having been blessed with all spiritual blessings in Christ, surely you will say this evening—

"Here I raise my Ebenezer,
Hither by thy help I'm come;
And I hope, by Thy good pleasure,
Safely to arrive at home.

Oh, to grace how great a debtor
Daily I'm constrained to be!
Let that grace, Lord, like a fetter,
Bind my wand'ring heart to Thee.

Oh, how oft during the past year have you seen this power and this glory in the sanctuary! By waiting upon God your strength has been renewed like the eagle's. With Jonah you may have sometimes said, "I am cast out of Thy sight," but you have added, "Yet will I look again toward Thy holy temple." You have sometimes said, "I shall one day perish by the hand of my spiritual enemy;" but at other times you have said, "Our heart is not turned back, neither have our steps declined from Thy way; though Thou hast sore broken us in the place of dragons, and covered us with the shadow of death." "If I have not been alive in duty, I have not been allowed to restrain prayer before God. During many a dark hour, I have waited for Him more than they that watch for the morning; I say, more than they that watch for the morning. Though the thorn in the flesh has not been removed, I have been enabled to resign myself to the divine will. My adversaries have struck sore at me, but have not prevailed against me; I have had enemies but God has been my friend and keeper.

I am not in the land flourishing with milk and honey; but I have been fed with manna, and with water out of the rock; I have been sustained, I have had grapes from Eschol, which tell me where they grow, and whither I am going."

Then, thirdly, you ought to be thankful, as *Britons;* and if you have English hearts in you, which I hope you have, you will say with Cowper, "England, with all thy faults I love thee still." We have had our national trials and embarrassments; but you must be devoid of every feeling of ingenuousness, if you can contrast the condition of your country with that of others without gratitude. God has not as a nation dealt with us after our sins—nor rewarded us according to our iniquities. The heavens over our head might have been brass, and the earth under our feet might have been iron, instead of which the earth has yielded her increase, and God, even our own God, has blessed us.

A strange disease affected one article of our food, and which belongs more particularly to the poor, yet we have reason to believe that the cry has been greater than the calamity.

We have had some improvement in our laws, and some liberal measures have been advanced, and we have reason to believe that the corn laws will be abolished, and freedom of trade will be the result.

Surely we must own that the Lord has crowned the year with His goodness, and that His paths drop fatness.

Fourthly, you ought to be thankful *as the lovers of Zion.* I hope there are some here before God who love the Redeemer's cause even better than they love their lives, and can say with Isaiah:—"For Zion's sake will I not hold my peace, and for Jerusalem's sake I will not, until the righteousness thereof go forth with brightness, and the salvation thereof as a lamp that burneth." I hope there are here those who, if they could be assured that the cause of God prospered, would find enough in this to comfort them amidst all their personal and relative trials; who say, "Well, it is of little importance whether I live or die, if His name be made known; it is of little importance if my schemes fail, if His flourish, and if, as a King, Christ reigns in righteousness." Popery has been very active during the past year; but corresponding zeal has been awakened amongst Protestants. Some additions have been made to Babylon. but more, I trust, have been drawn from it. It has received several checks, and its advocates are compelled to employ lies in hypocrisy, to retain the loaves and fishes along with their errors.

It is difficult to accomplish good in such a world as this, but think of the Evangelical alliance, by which ministers of all denominations agree to maintain unity and harmony without compromise. I view this as a wonderful instance of the goodness of God, being fully persuaded it is pregnant with blessings; that it must tend to reduce all exclusive principles, diffuse liberality, bring Christians nearer together, and show to the world that though in some things we differ, we agree in the main; and though not all of the same size and age, yet we wear the same garments, and are all children of the same family. I do not envy that man who cannot say, "Grace be with all them that love our Lord Jesus Christ in sincerity."

Once more, you should be thankful as *members of your own Christian Church*, to which you have given yourselves. I would not have you be exclusive here. It may hardly be delicate in your preacher to refer to himself; but your Pastor's life has been preserved through another year, and his capacity for action continues, and I trust his acceptance and usefulness; though after fifty-five years of labour the novelty must have worn off, yet there is the same good attendance that followed his youthful days.

As a Church you have shown growth of a public spirit, and your last works have been more than your first. You still hold the unity of the Spirit in the bond of peace, and there have been no breakings in, or breakings out among us, and many have been added to the Church of such I trust as shall be saved. These are the reasons why we call upon you at the coming in of the year to exercise thanksgiving.

IV. The coming in of the year ought to be improved by RESOLUTION—by a determination to correct whatever is wrong, and a determination to cherish whatever is right in your character and conduct. It will be well to take advantage of everything that may aid the impression, for we need every kind of auxiliary and influence. God hath Himself set the example. The tabernacle was a work of great expense and labour, but when everything was ready, God would not suffer it to be set up till New Year's day. "Therefore the Lord spoke unto Moses, saying, On the first day of the first month shalt thou set up the tabernacle of the tent of the congregation." Now examine yourselves, and see if there is anything to begin the year with in a way of improvement. Have you kept company with evil companions? Begin by abandoning them, and say with David, "Depart from me ye evil-doers." Have you neglected the Scriptures? Begin this year by attentively reading them. "Bind them upon thine heart, and tie them about thy neck. When thou goest, it shall lead thee; when thou sleepest, it shall keep thee; and when thou awakest, it shall talk with thee." Have you neglected prayer? Begin this year by entering your closet, by praying to your Father in secret, and your Father who seeth in secret shall reward you openly. Have you neglected family worship? Begin by erecting an altar to God, saying with Joshua, "As for me and my house, we will serve the Lord." Have you disregarded the dear Saviour? Oh, begin the year by looking to Him, by fleeing to Him, by confiding in Him, by giving up yourselves into His hand, and by dedicating yourselves to His service, and by exercising beneficence according to your means, every one laying by in store as God has prospered him, and be ready to distribute, willing to communicate; so shall the blessing of the Lord rest upon you.

V. It requires PRAYER, and the former will be perfectly vain without this. Therefore the Church says, "O Lord, other lords have had dominion over us; but by Thee only will we make mention of Thy Name." Hence David says, "Through God we shall do valiantly, He it is that treadeth down our enemies." Can you trust any longer to your own heart? Have you not proved its deceitfulness? Have you not seen the instability of your convictions? Can you not say,

"Prone to wander, Lord, I feel it,
Prone to leave the God I love"?

Surely, Christians, you will be excited and encouraged to address the throne of grace, that you may obtain grace in time of need. For consider how vain are the vows you have often made in former years. You have laid down rules which you have soon violated, because you have not been strong in the grace of God. His grace only is sufficient for us. Oh, seek therefore for pardon, for holiness, and sanctification. Before you retire this evening, say,

"Lord, with this guilty heart of mine
To thy dear cross I flee,
And to Thy hands my soul resign,
To be renewed by Thee."

Seek wisdom to know, and power to do, and patience to suffer all the will of God. Seek grace that you may be prepared for all that lies before you in the futurities of the year. It is a dark unknown. "Boast not thyself of to-morrow; for thou knowest not what a day may bring forth." At present you may have comforts, but how soon may God give you the bread of affliction! You have health now, but before the end of the year you may be made to possess mouths of vanity, and wearisome days may be appointed to you. Perhaps though now you are surrounded by endeared connections, before the end of the year you may have cause to say, "Lover and friend hast Thou put far from me, and mine acquaintance into darkness." Perhaps this may be the last New Year's Day with regard to some of you. If I had now the gift of prophecy, I might see the mutes and hearse before your door, ready to convey you to the tomb; and before this season returns you will be sleeping in the dust. Perhaps before this season returns, another may be occupying this pulpit; and others may be in this or that pew.

If at the coming in of the year you have found no Redeemer, O sinner, delay not now to seek Him; and if the year is opening upon you, Christian, with dark clouds of the sky, still

> "Ye feeble saints, fresh courage take;
> The clouds ye so much dread,
> Are big with mercy and will break
> In mercy on your head."

Your God has provided for every case in which you may be. If the road be rough, He has promised that "your shoes shall be iron and brass, and as your day so your strength shall be." What, Christian, if this should prove the year of release? O ye nations of the sky, ye cannot continue much longer here. A very few more rising and setting suns, and you shall see Him who has found a way to your hearts, and who has promised that you shall dwell with Him above. Yes, and there will He wipe away all tears from your eyes, and you will be *like* Him, too, as well as see Him as he is. You shall be caught up together with the redeemed in the clouds, and shall dwell for ever with the Lord. Wherefore comfort one another with these words. "Having, therefore, these promises, dearly beloved, let us cleanse ourselves from all filthiness of the flesh and spirit, perfecting holiness in the fear of the Lord."

There are those of our brethren and sisters who are gone

before and are beyond the reach of suffering and temptation and sin.

> "Once they were mourning here below,
> And wet their couch with tears;
> They labor'd hard, as we do now,
> With sins and doubts and fears."

They, too, were exercised with an evil heart within, and a wicked world without, and a body of sin and death; but they have overcome by the blood of the Lamb and by the word of His testimony. They once mourned, but the days of their mourning are ended. While we sigh they sing. They once fought their way to the Kingdom, but they now wear their crowns and carry their palms of victory. But their joys and their songs cannot be complete till we are called up to join them. See how they beckon us to come and call us away from these low and grovelling scenes of earth and time. And we hope ere long to join this blissful throng, and with angels and the multitude of the redeemed from amongst men will we sing—

> More sweet, more loud,
> And Christ shall be our song.

> "See the kind angels at the gates
> Inviting us to come;
> There Jesus, the Forerunner waits,
> To welcome travellers home."

Thus have we observed the coming in of the year requires Reflection, Humiliation, Thanksgiving, Resolution, and Prayer. May you meditate upon these things.

And what more remains, but for me to give you the congratulations of the season, and wish you all a happy new year? But then I have no notion of happiness separate from holiness. Good Mr. Henry says, "A year cannot be a happy one without the the peace of God." It can be a happy one with it. I have passed through many such, and now I am looking for a more happy day.

May the God of all grace bless this people! May He bless our Sovereign, our rulers, our magistrates! May He abundantly bless our dear missionaries, and be a little sanctuary to them! May He bless all the ministers of Christ of every name, and make them blessings to the Church and the world! The Lord bless our families, our wives, and our children! "Let

Thy work appear unto Thy servants, and Thy glory unto their children; and let the beauty of the Lord our God be upon us; and establish Thou the work of our hands upon us; yea, the work of our hands establish Thou it." "The Lord bless you, and keep you; the Lord make His face to shine upon you and be gracious unto you. The Lord lift up His countenance upon you, and give you peace." "And may the grace of the Lord Jesus Christ be with you all." Amen.

V.

MEMORABLE DAYS.

(Preached on Sunday Morning, January 2nd, 1848.)

"*These days should be remembered.*"—ESTHER ix. 28.

HERE is a part of Scripture in which the name of God is not mentioned. But how is His agency, and how is His glory displayed! and at each execution and development we are constrained to exclaim, "The thing proceedeth from the Lord, who is wonderful in counsel, and mighty in working."

Were we to cast a general glance over the contents of the whole Book, we should here observe facts which took place in the history and experience of individuals varied and striking. There are some whose course of life passes on evenly and smoothly, but others are a wonder unto many. Take David, for instance, who was called from the sheepfolds: "from following the ewes great with young, He brought him to feed Jacob His people, and Israel His inheritance." Here again, we see a little ark floating along the water, in which we see a babe weeping. That babe becomes the wonder of ages, the scourge of Pharaoh, the destroyer of the Egyptians, the king in Jeshurun, and the prophet who saw God face to face. Here is a poor young female, who was early left an orphan, brought up by her uncle Mordecai, becoming the wife of Ahasuerus, and the queen of a hundred and twenty-seven provinces. "This is the Lord's doings, and is marvellous in our eyes."

We further observe, that "the Lord knoweth how to deliver the godly out of temptation," while He reserves the wicked for punishment. Thus we see Noah preserved while the ungodly perished. So, in the overthrow of Sodom and Gomorrah, Lot was remembered, whose "righteous soul was vexed with the filthy conversation of the wicked." So again, the Lord placed a fiery cloudy pillar between the Israelites and the Egyptians, having a dark side to the one, and a light side to the other.

And here we see the Jews delivered from sore destruction, while their bitter adversaries were disappointed in their wicked devices, and Haman was hanged on a gallows fifty cubits high.

Thirdly, we see here that our extremity is God's opportunity. He loves to display His glory on the dark ground of human despair. He waits to be gracious. Then we should learn to trust Him in all future difficulties. Thus the altar was raised, and the wood laid upon it, and the victim bound, and the hand had seized the knife, before the voice was heard—"Abraham, forbear; the Lord hath provided Himself a ram for a burnt-offering." So here everything seemed on the very brink of ruin. The decree was passed; the decree was sealed; the decree was sent forth, and the execution seemed to be inevitable, when the triumph of divine providence appeared. "When the Lord turned again their captivity, they were like men that dreamed. Then was their mouth filled with laughter, and their tongue with singing. Then said they among the heathen, the Lord hath done great things for them. The Lord hath done great things for us, whereof we are glad."

What now should we have thought of them, if they had not endeavoured to perpetuate the memory of such deliverances? But they did. They made these days "days of gladness and of feasting, and of sending portions one to another, and gifts to the poor; wherefore they called these days Purim, after the name of Pur. Therefore the Jews ordained, and took upon them, and upon their seed, and upon all such as joined themselves unto them, so as it should not fail, that they should keep these days, according to their writing, and according to their appointed time every year. And that these days should be remembered and kept throughout every generation, every family, every province, and every city, and that these days of Purim should not fail from among the Jews, nor the memorial of them perish from their seed."

My brethren, we wish to bring this home to you. Marcus Aurelius was one of the Roman emperors, and one of the best of all this bad body of monarchs. He is reported to have said that we ought to give the future to providence, the present to duty, and the past to oblivion. Now I hope you will remember and admire the two former of these admonitions, but not the third. We should give the future to providence, "casting all our care upon God who careth for us." "Commit thy way unto the Lord; trust also in Him, and He shall bring it to pass"; and say, "The Lord shall choose my inheritance for me." You should give the present to duty, by letting the work of the day be performed in its day, and never grow "weary in well doing." "Whatsoever thy hand findeth to do, do it with thy might." But never give the past to oblivion. "God requireth that which is past," and requireth it in a way of responsibility, and in a way of improvement. Therefore in the Scriptures we are called to recollection. Thus Moses blessed his people just before his death: "Remember the days of old, consider the years of many generations. Ask thy father and he will shew thee, thy elders and they will shew thee." And thus I address you this morning. "These days should be remembered." What days? Days of unregeneracy—days of conversion—days of persecution—days of bereavement—days of providential interposition—and days of particular speciality. "Consider what I say, and the Lord give you understanding in all things."

I. Days of unregeneracy. "These should be remembered." And where is the person who has not these to review? for there are but very few who like Jeremiah are sanctified from their youth; there are but few that can say with Watts,

"And from my mother's painful hour,
I was entirely Thine."

No, says Paul, "We were by nature children of wrath even as others." "We ourselves were sometimes foolish, disobedient, serving divers lusts and pleasures, living in malice and envy, hateful, and hating one another;" but "after this the loving-kindness of God our Saviour appeared." Those days should be remembered. You should comply with the admonition in Isaiah: "Look to the rock from whence ye are hewed, and the hole of the pit from whence ye are digged." And says the Apostle to the Ephesians, "Remember that ye being in time past Gentiles in the flesh, who are called uncircumcision by that which is called the circumcision in the flesh made by hands, that at that time ye were without Christ, being aliens from the commonwealth of Israel, and strangers from the covenants of promise, having no hope, and without God in the world." "Oh," says one, "I ought to remember those days, for, alas! they were many with me. Had I passed only one of them in a state of alienation from God, it would have been too much: but, alas! year after year passed away, and through the progress of childhood, and youth, and manhood, I have consumed twenty, thirty, forty years in going astray from God."

"Oh," says another, "I ought to remember those days, for I went great lengths in sin. I was a blasphemer, a profane swearer, a persecutor of all them that were good, waxing worse and worse, corrupt, and corrupting all around me." And says another, "I ought to remember those days, for if I were not grossly immoral like some, I was a heinous transgressor by reason of the advantages I possessed. Oh, how I laboured to stifle conviction! I had two pious parents, and the advantages of their instructions and example. From a child I knew the Holy Scriptures, which were able to make me wise unto salvation. I heard sermons the most clear, and convincing, and alluring, but I went on disregarding counsel after counsel, and admonition after admonition, and He could have cut me down as a cumberer of the ground; yet He bore with me. Oh, had I died in the state I was then in! But He preserved me by His love, He called me by His grace, and led me to Himself with a broken heart and a contrite spirit, and now with a soul full of gratitude, I call to remembrance such times as those."

II. Days of conversion. "These should be remembered." The former were days of nature, these are days of grace. "I," may the Christian say, "I was once far off, but He made me nigh; I was asleep, but He awoke me; I was in darkness, but He called me out of darkness into His marvellous light."

"'Twas grace that taught my heart to fear,
And grace that fear relieved;
How precious did that grace appear,
The hour I first believed."

There are some among Christians who can remember particular circumstances; some can call to mind, perhaps, the very place where God first met with them, and how they were brought into that place on purpose for this blessed design. Others can remember the dear minister whose preaching turned their feet into the way of peace, the sermon which first aroused their attention, the friend that reproved them, the book they read, or the tract that was given them, and by which they were impressed. There was "diversity," in the operation, but "the same Spirit." In some the work was slow; others, like Zaccheus, "made haste, came down, and received Him joyfully." In some the man was, to use the words of Jude, "like one pulled out of the fire," his clothes burning, with his hands, face and feet burnt; while others were drawn with the cords of a man, and by the bonds of love. But where there is no such particularity, the man can say, "One thing I know: whereas I was blind, now I see; I was once dead, I now feel the things of religion; He who 'was despised and rejected' is now to me 'the chiefest among ten thousand, and the altogether lovely.' 'Tis done." What is done? "Why He has done a work for me, the best He ever performed. His making me a new creature is far better than His creating me at first. 'Tis done." What is done? "He has delivered me from the spirit of the world, and has made me a partaker of His own likeness. He has constituted me an heir of the glory which is to be revealed."

"'Tis done, the great transaction's done,
I am my Lord's, and He is mine;
He drew me and I followed on,
Charmed to confess the voice divine.

"O happy day that fixed my choice
On Thee, my Saviour and my God;
Well may my grateful heart rejoice,
And tell its raptures all abroad."

And can you ever forget this? Will you not always acknowledge that He hath delivered your soul from death, in order that you "may walk before the Lord in the land of the living, and shew forth all His praise?"

"High heavens have heard that blessed vow;
That vow renewed, shall daily hear;
Till in life's latest hour I bow,
And bless in death a bond so dear.

III. Days of persecution. These should be remembered. How pleasing is it to look down upon a congregation like this, and see them exemplifying by happy experience the words of Isaiah, "Though the Lord give you the bread of adversity and the water of affliction, yet shall not thy teachers be removed into a corner any more, but thine eyes shall see thy teachers; and thine ears shall hear a word behind thee saying, This is the way: walk ye in it, when ye turn to the right hand, and when ye turn to the left." How pleasing to see you sitting under your vines and fig-trees, none daring to make you afraid; and to hear you also calling your neighbours to come and partake with you in your privileges, and to co-operate with you in your exertions. But was this always the case? What says Paul to the Hebrews? "But call to remembrance the former days in which after ye were illuminated ye endured a great fight of afflictions, partly whilst ye were made a gazing-stock, both by reproaches and afflictions, and partly whilst ye were companions of them who were thus used. For ye had compassion of me in my bonds, and took joyfully the spoiling of your goods." Read the Book of Martyrs; read Neil's History of the Puritans, and Palmer's Memorials of the Nonconformists. Read their exiles from their own country, and their exclusion from their own people; the insults they endured, their fines, and their imprisonments; and then compare their condition with your own. Our worship is legally established, and the law says, "He that toucheth you toucheth the apple of my eye." And you must adore and bless that God who has all events at His disposal, and all hearts under His control. You should be thankful for those who have resisted unto blood, and by whose means these privileges have been obtained; for those who bore "the burden and heat of the day" for you, which you would not have courage or confidence to do. They have laboured, and you have entered into their labours. They were men of God indeed; they preached in season, and out of season; when they could not preach publicly, they preached more privately; when they could not preach by day, they preached by night; when they could not proclaim the word of truth in their own congregations, they did so in woods, and caves and dens of the earth. And shall we ever forget these men of God? No, we will visit from time to time your tombs, and if your names are erased, we will inscribe them, and underneath we will write, "Of whom the world was not worthy."

IV. Days of bereavement. These should be remembered. And who has not such days to remember? There is Rachel weeping for her children, and refusing to be comforted, because they are not. There is he who hears the announcement, "Son of man, behold I take away the desire of thine eyes with a stroke." There we see the widow coming up out of the wilderness, no longer leaning upon her beloved: she must finish her journey alone. There we see the father weeping for his hopeful son, who seemed not only destined to be his heir, but his companion, and sighing, "Thou destroyest the hope of man." And who has not been striped and peeled?

> "Friend after friend departs:
> Who has not lost a friend?
> There is no union here in hearts
> That does not find an end."

'Tis affecting to review scenes like these. 'Tis painful to

hear the last farewell, and to know that we shall see their face, and hear their voice no more. But we are united still, for—

> "The saints on earth and all the dead,
> But one communion make:
> All join in Christ their living Head,
> And of His grace partake."

Shall the friends who have gone before us draw us upward to the skies, and induce us to say, "What do I here? What have I here?"

> "There my best friends, my kindred dwell,
> There God my Saviour reigns."

V. Days of providential interposition. These should be remembered. Our text refers to one of these, and a very remarkable one, which you will perceive on reading the Book. But many more are recorded in the Scriptures. Some of these, indeed, are miraculous. We are not to look for miracles now; but we may look for the God who wrought these miracles. We may look for Him who is still "the same yesterday, to-day, and for ever," and who would perform them did His word render it necessary, for,

> "Sooner all nature shall change,
> Than one of His promises fail."

How many of His dispensations are there, in which, if there is nothing miraculous, there is a great deal that is merciful? You have had your straits, and deep distresses, and manna has not dropped from the clouds; yet God has raised up friends who have brought you very unexpected relief. You have had your days of darkness, but at eventide it has been light. You have had your fears, but He has turned the shadow of death into the morning, and you have been enabled to say,

> "The Lord can change the darkest skies,
> Can give us day for night;
> Make sacred floods of sorrow rise
> To rivers of delight."

And well may we ask:

> "Why should the wonders He has wrought,
> Be lost in silence and forgot?"

Well may we say with David, "Bless the Lord, O my soul, and forget not all His benefits." "O praise the Lord, bless

His name, and declare His doings among the people"; or at least you should say with him, "Come and hear, all ye that fear God, and I will declare what He hath done for my soul."

VI. Days of particular specification. These should be remembered. We will mention three of these. Birthdays, Nuptial days, and New Years' days.

First, *Birthdays*. These days should be remembered. Then you come into contact with God as His creatures, for He has made you, He formed your bodies, and framed your spirits within you, and you are called upon to "Remember your Creator in the days of your youth." And you ought to look back upon that period, and say with the Psalmist, "O Lord, I will praise Thee, for I am fearfully and wonderfully made. Marvellous are Thy works, and that my soul knoweth right well. My substance was not hid from Thee when I was made in secret, and curiously wrought in the lowest parts of the earth. Thine eyes did see my substance yet being imperfect, and in Thy book all my members were written, which in continuance were fashioned, when as yet there was none of them." And as you think of the country in which you were born, you should daily bless God that you were not brought forth in a heathen, or Mahommedan, or a Jewish, or a Popish country, but you have had your existence where "the lines have fallen unto you in pleasant places;" where your understandings have had every advantage; where you have civil and religious freedom, and where spiritually too, you are fed with the finest of the wheat, and where with oil out of the rock you have been satisfied. How thankful should you be that you are not in the condition of poor Job, whose suffering and anguish of spirit constrained him to say, "Let the day perish wherein I was born. Let that day be darkness; and as for that night, let it not come into the number of the months."

I suppose there is no harm in a man stealing from himself; let me therefore read a few lines derived from "Jay's Morning Exercises:" "How dreadful must it be to say with Voltaire, 'who can without horror consider the whole world as the empire of destruction? It abounds with wonders: it also abounds with victims. It is a vast field of carnage and contagion. In man there is more wretchedness than in all the other animals put together. He loves life, and he knows that he must die. If he enjoys a transient good he suffers various evils, and is at last devoured by worms. This knowledge is his fatal prerogative: other animals have it not. 'He spends the transient moments of his existence in diffusing the miseries which he suffers; in cutting the throats of his fellow creatures for pay; in cheating and being cheated; in robbing and being robbed; in serving that he might command; and in repenting of all he does. The bulk of mankind are nothing more than a crowd of wretches equally criminal and unfortunate; and the globe contains rather carcases than men.' I tremble at the review of this dreadful picture to find that it contains a complaint against Providence itself: '*and I wish I had never been born.*'" Now let us hear the language of the excellent Hallyburton: "I shall shortly get a very different sight of God from what I have ever had, and shall be made meet to praise Him for ever and ever. Oh, the thoughts of an incarnate Deity are sweet and ravishing. Oh, how I wonder at myself, that I do not love Him more, and that I do not admire Him more. What a wonder that I enjoy such composure under all my bodily pains, and in the view of death itself! What a mercy that, having the use of my reason, I can declare His goodness to my evil! I long for His salvation; I bless His name; I have found Him, and die rejoicing in Him. Oh, blessed be God that *I was born!* Oh, that I was where He is! I have a father and mother, and ten brothers and sisters in heaven, and I shall be the eleventh. Oh, there is a telling of this Providence, and I shall be telling it for ever! If there be such a glory in His conduct towards me now, what will it be to see the Lamb in the midst of the throne? Blessed be God that *ever I was born!*"

Well, now, what a mercy is it, if you can connect your new birth with your first, and can say with Paul, "God who has separated me from my mother's womb, hath called me by His grace, and revealed His Son in me." If this be not your case, my dear hearers, at the beginning of this year, let me beseech you to pray that it may be so.

Secondly, *Nuptial Days.* These should be remembered. They are some of the most important and most interesting in the whole course of your lives. Then it is that you leave individuality, and enter upon social life, and you find yourself in a state of relationship that surpasses all natural ties. "For this cause shall a man leave his father and his mother, and shall cleave unto his wife, and they twain shall be one flesh." And Oh, what reason have you to be thankful, if you have a helpmeet; if now you are walking together as fellow heirs of the grace of life, and are helpful to each other in the way everlasting. If, indeed, you have disregarded the divine command to "marry only in the Lord," why you may expect that, having walked contrary to Him, He will walk contrary to you, and cause your own backslidings to reprove you. And if you, O wife, instead of finding the days of your espousals the gladness of your heart, have been deceived without any blame on your side, still may you look up to the Lord, and say, "Save with thy right hand, and hear me!" If you cannot take sweet counsel together, and walk to the house of God in company, seek Him alone; He can sanctify, and overrule this deepest of all afflictions. I have known more than one who has been chosen on this furnace of affliction, and where a bad husband has done what many ministers have laboured in vain to accomplish.

Thirdly, *New Years' Days.* These should be remembered. We have entered upon a new period of existence, and you should remember you never had such a New Year's Day before, because it has left you one year nearer the Bar of Christ, where you will have to give an account of the deeds done in the body, whether they have been good or whether they have been evil. We wish you to remember that, though you have been brought through another year, many have been carried down to the regions of death. They have now seen corruption, while you are living to praise God.

We would have you praise as well as rejoice at such a time, and surely you will indulge one reflection before we proceed further, and say with Job "when a few years are gone, I shall go the way whence I shall not return." Would it be useful for you to ask "May I not this year die? Have I guarantees to pass safely through? Is not life uncertain?" Oh, how many dangers are there that lie in wait to make us afraid! Surely you would not think of entering upon a new year without praying that you may be prepared for all that awaits you, and without asking God to be your companion and guide. What would you think of passing through another year without seeking God to be your Guide and Guard and Comfort? without seeking His pardon and sanctifying grace, and the supply of the Spirit of Jesus Christ for all your duties and trials, that though you know not what a day may bring forth, you may still rejoice; knowing that

"It can bring nothing with it,
But He will bear you through."

He will never leave nor forsake you ; that if you live it may be to serve Him, and if you die, it may be to enjoy Him for ever. I wish you all, therefore, a Happy New Year ; but then it must be a holy one in order to be a happy one. May great grace descend upon you all ! "The Lord bless you and keep you. The Lord make His face to shine upon you, and be gracious unto you. The Lord lift up His countenance upon you, and give you peace."

VI.

FORGETFULNESS OF GOD.

A Fast-day Sermon.

(Preached on the 28th of September, 1849.)

"*And the pride of Israel testifieth to his face: and they do not return to the Lord their God, nor seek Him for all this.*"—Hosea vii. 10.

The history of the Jews is very peculiar; it abounds with wonders, miracles, and signs; and in perusing it, nothing strikes us more than the frequency and severity of God's reproaches concerning them, some of which may be considered as expressed by the eloquent Isaiah: "Hear, O heavens, and give ear, O earth: for the Lord hath spoken. I have nourished and brought up children, and they have rebelled against me. The ox knoweth his owner, and the ass his master's crib, but Israel doth not know, my people doth not consider. Ah! sinful nation, a people laden with iniquity, a seed of evil-doers, children that are corrupters. They have forsaken the Lord; they have provoked the Holy One of Israel unto anger; they have gone away backward." Hence some may be tempted to suppose that their case was peculiar, but are we better than they? By no means. They were fair specimens of our common nature; and we may say in the words of Dr. Watts,—

> "There in a glass our hearts we see,
> How fickle and how false are we!"

And we wonder not that Adam in his private thoughts should say, "I should never have been able to believe in the truth of the history of the Jews had I not known my own heart, and known that it is deceitful above all things and desperately wicked." The general resemblance between them and us, especially as to the means of improvement, and the non-improvement of these means, is the ground of our discourse this morning, in which we join our brethren in the Establishment in calling upon you to humble yourselves under the mighty hand of God, and to return to Him that smiteth you. God forbid we should incur the reproach of the Jews, "they do not return to the Lord their God, nor seek Him for all this." Let us consider three things: First, the Duty; secondly, the Neglect of the Duty; and thirdly, the Aggravation of the Neglect.

I. THE DUTY. It is to seek Him. In Scripture this stands for the whole of religion. Hence we read of the generation of those who seek Him. Religion is thus expressed, for two reasons. First, *because with Him we have principally to do.* He is the greatest, He is the best of beings, and we are most importantly related to Him. He is our Proprietor, our Benefactor, our Governor, and our Judge; and, my brethren, *before we can have anything to do with Him, we must find Him.* God is indeed not far from every one of us, for "In Him we live, and move, and have our being"; "He is about our path, and about our bed, and spieth out all our ways."

> "O may these thoughts possess my breast,
> Where'er I roam, where'er I rest;
> Nor let my weaker passions dare
> Consent to sin, for God is there."

But morally and spiritually considered, we are away from God, and God is away from us, we having left Him criminally, and He having left us penally. So then we are said to be far off, and even to live without God in the world. Our first concern, therefore, is to find God, and if it be asked, "Where shall we find Him?" we answer, in heaven. Therefore our Saviour taught us to address Him, saying, "Our Father, which art in heaven." But you must find Him before you get there, if ever you do get there. You cannot get to heaven without finding Him. He is to be found in the Son of His love. Without Him, He is a consuming fire; in Him, He is reconciling the world unto Himself, not imputing their trespasses unto them." He is to be found in His house. He has promised to be there. "In all places where I record my name I will come unto thee and bless thee"; and His people in all ages have seen the goings of their God and King in His sanctuary, and have found Him in His palaces for a refuge. He is to be found at His table, at the family altar, and in the closet.

> "Where'er we seek Him He is found,
> And every spot is holy ground."

Let us penetrate farther into this subject, and observe four purposes for which we are to seek God which enter deeply into true religion. First, we are to seek to *know* Him. "This is life eternal," says the Saviour, "to know Thee, the only true God, and Jesus Christ whom Thou hast sent." Paul says "Some have not the knowledge of God: I speak this to your shame." It could not be to their shame unless it was their sin; and it could not be their sin unless it was avoidable; but it is avoidable. And we read, "If any man lack knowledge, let him ask of God, who giveth to all men liberally and upbraideth not, and it shall be given him." "I will give them," says He, "a heart to know me;" and again, "Let not the wise man glory in his wisdom, nor the strong man glory in his strength, neither the rich man glory in his riches, but let him that glorieth glory in this, that he understandeth and knoweth Me; for I am the Lord which exercise loving-kindness, judgment, and righteousness in the earth, for in these things I delight, saith the Lord."

Secondly, are we to seek to *enjoy* Him. In order to do this we must be reconciled to God. Till His anger be turned away, we cannot enjoy His comfort. Till we are justified by faith, we cannot have peace with God; we cannot rejoice in Christ Jesus till we have believed in Him; but then "we have boldness and access with confidence by the faith of Him;" then we can draw near to God as our exceeding joy; then our souls can be satisfied, as with marrow and fatness, and our mouths can praise Him with joyful lips. Then His favour is life, and His loving-kindness is better than life; and therefore while the many say, "Who will shew us any good?" the desire of the Christian is, "Lord, lift Thou up the light of Thy countenance upon us."

Thirdly, we are to seek to find Him, not only as our portion to enjoy, but as our Master to *obey*. They are servants to receive and execute His orders, and inquire, "Lord, what wilt Thou have me to do?" His service is perfect freedom; His work is honourable and glorious; His yoke is easy, and His burden is light; and in keeping His commandments there is great reward.

We should also seek to *resemble* Him. It is the essence of religion to resemble God. We have lately endeavoured to show this in addressing you from those words, "That ye should shew forth the praises of Him who hath called you out of darkness into His marvellous light," when we remarked that it was shewing forth the *virtues* of Him, and that the best way we can show them forth is by exemplifying them; by being holy as He is holy, in your measure and degree. And, my brethren, as we advance in this, and are renewed in the image of Him that created you in righteousness and true holiness we are changed from glory to glory as by the Spirit of the Lord.

II. We have to observe THE NEGLECT OF THIS DUTY. "They do not return unto the Lord, nor seek Him for all this." How far does this omission extend? Are there no exceptions? Yes; blessed be God, there are; and it is well for us there are; for "Except the Lord of Hosts had left unto us a very small remnant, we should have been as Sodom, and we should have been like unto Gomorrah." We should have had no chariots of Israel, or horsemen at all; we should have had no persons to stand in the breach; we should have had no repairers of the breaches, no restorers of paths to dwell in. But still the language of Scripture is very useful on this subject. Isaiah said in his day, "There is none that calleth upon God, there is none that stirreth up himself to take hold on God." And Paul says, "There is none righteous; no, not one; there is no fear of God before their eyes." And John says, "The whole world lieth in the wicked one." This language, if it does not imply universality, unquestionably expresses generality. Let us see, therefore, how far this testimony is true and is confirmed by experience and observation. For this purpose we will glance at five classes of persons; and Oh, how many are there to be found amongst us!

In the first class we place *infidels*, who, if they do not deny the being of a God, deny His moral Providence and look upon the Revelation He has given us as nothing better than a cunningly devised fable. Infidels are not so numerous now as they were some years ago, soon after the French Revolution. Perhaps through shame, they have been driven into silence or concealment. It is worthy of remark that no infidel ever attempted to confute any of our best writers, such as Grotius, or Paley, or Doddridge, or Watson. But there are enough to be found even now in the midst of us. And there is some difference between the present and the former times. Formerly infidels were found among the learned, now they are found among the illiterate. Formerly they were found among the philosophers, now they are found among shopmen, and even apprentices will attempt to pity the folly of such men as Newton, and Blair, and Locke, who could be carried away by such delusions, forsooth!

In the second class we place the *profligate.* These hide not their sin, as Sodom and Gomorrah, but publish it ; such are swearers, liars, drunkards, fornicators, adulterers, and so on. All these are labelled upon their character. You see inscribed upon them in large letters, "I am on the devil's side : I am bound for hell." These do not "return unto the Lord, nor seek Him for all this."

In the third class we place the *careless.* Though they are not outwardly vicious, yet they are indifferent to everything of a religious nature. Gallio-like, they care for none of these things. These have cast off fear ; they have restrained prayer before God. They rarely read the Scriptures, or hear the Word, or attend the House of God, unless from regard to their reputation and connections. They observe not the Sabbath to keep it holy. Heaven is hid from their view. Earth contains all their desire. To get money, to adorn the body, to nurse it in sickness and pamper it in health, and to answer the question, "What, oh ! what shall I drink ? and wherewithal shall I be clothed ?" This engrosses the whole of their attention. Did you never hear them utter the sentence, "I no more think of heaven than I do of my dying day" ? I have. So one day when I reproved a servant for evil conduct, and asked how she expected to give an account thereof at the day of judgment, she sneeringly said, "That is the last of all my concerns," and what she dared to utter there are thousands who dare to think. These do not seek the Lord.

In the fourth class we place the *moralist.* God requires "truth in the inward parts ; and in the hidden part Thou shalt make me to know wisdom." "God is a Spirit, and they who worship Him must worship Him in spirit and in truth," or they do not in His estimation worship Him at all. We read of some in the days of Isaiah, of whom it is said, "Yet they seek Me daily, and delight to know My ways, as a nation that did righteousness, and forsook not the ordinance of their God." But how was it really ? They drew near to Him with their mouths, and honoured Him with their lips, while their heart was far from Him. They sang, but not with grace in their hearts, making melody as unto the Lord. They heard His Word, but were not doers of the same. They had a name to live, but were dead : they had a form of godliness, but denied the power thereof. What numbers are even members of Christian churches who yet are not partakers of Christian principles ! These do not seek the Lord their God.

In the last class we place *backsliders and apostates.* For

there are comparatively few who have not what are called fits and starts in religion. There are but few who have not recourse to religious exercises at certain times. How numerous are they who are religiously impressed, and who, though they may not be insincere at the time, yet their goodness is as the morning cloud and early dew, which soon passes away. They appear at least to begin in the spirit, but end in the flesh; they seem well for a time, but Satan hinders them. Their religion depends upon external excitements, and not upon internal principles, and therefore falls with these excitements. Their religion is like a tree without roots, which withers and dies; or like a land-flood, which soon dries up, having no fountain to support it. Ephraim, says God, is "like a cake not turned," neither bread nor dough. Our Lord says of the Church of Laodicea, "neither cold nor hot." Alas, what numbers are there who go far, but not far enough, who are not made partakers of the Divine nature and not renewed in the spirit of their minds! There are but few who think themselves sufficiently wicked to perish, but God hath said "The wicked shall be turned into hell, with all the nations that forget God."

We hasten to consider:

IV. THE AGGRAVATIONS OF ALL THIS NEGLECT. "But they do not return unto the Lord their God, nor seek Him for all this. All what? Here a wide field opens to our view, for how vast, how numerous the means God is providing, and which He perpetually employs, for the prevention of sin, and as the instrument of holiness to induce men to seek the Lord their God. What are they?

We may mention a *profusion of benefits* to draw you to God by the cords of love, and to allure you to Himself. There are benefits flowing to us in nature and Providence and grace—social advantages, commercial advantages, civil advantages, intellectual advantages; mercies new every morning, and repeated every evening; blessings which fly on the wings of every hour. All God's works praise Him, and call upon us to do the same, never leaving Him without witness, in that He is continually doing us good, in sending us rain and fruitful seasons, and filling our hearts with food and gladness. The earth is filled with His riches. The year is crowned with His goodness. But notwithstanding they are thus favoured, yet "they do not return unto the Lord their God, nor seek Him for all this."

We ought to mention *the Scriptures in their own hands, in their own tongue.* "What advantage," saith the apostle, "hath the Jews, or what profit is there of circumcision? Much every way; chiefly because that unto them were committed the oracles of God." We are indulged, and indulged in a much higher degree, in this respect, because that to us is the word of this salvation sent, but sent in its complete form; for we have in addition to Moses and the prophets, the evangelists and the apostles. We have this blessed book, containing the glad tidings of salvation. We have this blessed book filled up with doctrines, and precepts, and promises, and invitations, and principles, addressed to every passion of the human bosom! What an advantage is this! What benefit is to be derived from hence! Yet, notwithstanding these, "they return not unto the Lord their God, nor seek Him for all this."

We might mention *His sending His ministers that we may not only read the word of God, but hear the word of life.* They have the advantage of a living address from man to man! Among the number whom God raises up, who employ their natural talents, and their graces, gifts, and peculiar manner to prevail, some, like David, can play well on an instrument; some are as Boanerges, sons of thunder; and others as Barnabas, sons of consolation, who speak a word in season to him that is weary. Thus God is continually addressing them. Thus He ariseth up early and sendeth them, but in vain; for "they do not return unto the Lord their God, nor seek Him for all this."

Then we might mention *the power of conscience.* Some men find the way of transgressors to be hard. Some find it very difficult to go on in sin. Conscience has withstood, like the angel with a drawn sword threatening them. Conscience has said to this man, "Dare you to adventure? There is destruction in that course, and in the step you are about to take, you will plunge yourself into destruction. Oh, pause and forbear." Yet he goes forward still, but oh! what are his reflections afterwards? These also, after awhile, are disregarded. Yes; they endeavour to get rid of them; they shut their eyes against the sight; they close their ears against the sound; they restrain conscience by a curb; they stupefy it with an opiate; they kill it with a stab. Notwithstanding "they return not unto the Lord their God, nor seek Him for all this." This is sad.

We might mention *the various respects, advantages, and encouragements to be derived from their various connections.* A godly father says, "My son, if thou be wise, my heart shall rejoice, even mine." A pious mother says, "What, my son? and what the son of my womb? and what the son of my vows?" A sister mourns over her brother, and says, "Alas! my brother." And friends come and warn them, and "faithful are the words of a friend." Even children come, and teach their own parents, from whom they should have learned. Even the various kinds of birds and brutes around will teach them. Yet "they turn not unto the Lord their God, nor seek Him for all this."

We may mention also *afflictive dispensations.* Sometimes man's schemes are broken off, and sometimes their worldly substance is removed, to induce them to seek in heaven "a better and an enduring substance." Sometimes death comes into their family, and bears off a member of it—

"The dear delights they once enjoyed,
And fondly called their own;"

and they have cause to say, "Lover and friend hast Thou put far from me, and mine acquaintance into darkness." Their life has been threatened by an accident, and the man found there was but a step between him and death; then sickness seized him, and drew him down to the very gates of the grave, through the bars of which he gazed into an awful eternity, and said, "O spare me, that I may recover strength before I go hence and be no more." And, would you believe it? yet do they not "return unto the Lord, nor seek Him for all this."

We may mention *judgments,* that are public calamities! God Himself calls these judgments, Who by His servant says, "When Thy judgments are abroad in the earth, the inhabitants thereof shall learn righteousness." This is the design of them, for God does not "afflict willingly nor grieve the children of men."

You see this exemplified in the Jews. The Jews were visited with very sore judgments.

The first we name was wild beasts. From these we have been exempt. We have had no wild beasts of prey surrounding our dwellings, no prowling bears, or roaring lions, or ravening wolves; no myriads of locusts darkening the air and eating up every green herb.

The second we name was war. To this we have not been entire strangers. It is very true that while war has not raged in the midst of us, nor have foreign foes invaded our land; yet if we look back we behold that half our time has been consumed in war! What thousands of our fellow-creatures have perished abroad! leaving *what?* Numbers of widows and orphans to lament their loss; while, as a consequence of war, taxes—*taxes*, like the plague of frogs upon Pharaoh and his servants—have come up into our habitations, and into our warehouses, and into our ovens, and into our kneading troughs, into our pockets, and into our very mouths.

The third was famine. Now for a great length of time, we have not had a famine of bread, blessed be God. Though disease has for the last five years nearly wasted a vegetable upon which very many principally depended for their subsistence, yet we have to bless the name of the Lord that it has not been the case the present year.

The fourth judgment sent among them was the pestilence. And here we have suffered severely. We have had our pestilence. A pestilence that walketh in darkness; a pestilence, the secret of which God holds in His own eternal mind; a pestilence that has left investigators at a loss for its origin, physicians perplexed as to its nature and the means of its removal. But you know something concerning it. You know its mortal issue. You know its torturing pang, you know its speedy execution, you know its ravages are not confined; and though it will be acknowledged that it more commonly arises in scenes of filth and intemperance, yet it occasionally siezes others; the high as well as the low, the rich as well as the poor, and the temperate as well as the intemperate. You know that it has visited us a second time, and more severely than before. You know the fears that many have entertained; you have heard the cries of those who have been ready to break forth and exclaim, "Who shall live when God doeth this?" For this cause we are assembled together this morning. We expected a day would have been appointed by Government for the observance of the whole realm, but we have since been better satisfied by a day only being recommended to be appropriated as a day of humiliation and prayer; because by this the more voluntary disposition has been displayed, and persons have in different places successively come forward to improve the event. Some have lamented that a day sooner has not been observed; but even this has been over-ruled, and we have derived from the delay an opportunity to "sing of mercy" as well as of judgment: not only in the limitation and abatement of the pestilence, but as it respects the ingathering of the harvest. And, Oh, how ungrateful, how sinful should we be, if we were not to observe here that God hath in judgment remembered mercy. What a plentiful harvest have we had, and of what an excellent quality has been the grain, and with what favourable weather have we been favoured for securing the produce! God forbid that the charge brought against the Jews of old should apply to us: "This people hath a revolting and a rebellious heart; neither say they in their heart, Let us now fear the Lord our God who giveth rain, both the former and the latter in his season; He reserveth unto us the appointed weeks of the harvest." We are the more readily disposed to mention this, because we are persuaded that repentance (and this we wish you to observe)—that repentance is never produced by pure unmixed terror. Terror may drive, but goodness alone leadeth to repentance. It becomes us not to yield entirely to the side of despondency and gloom. Our case is not desperate. "There is hope in Israel concerning this thing." "God," as we are allowed to argue, "God will not cast away His people whom He foreknew, because it pleased Him to make them His people."

I never felt less despondency in regard to my country in my whole life. I consider its rebukes as tokens for good. You do not prune a tree when you are about to cut it down; nor do you spare the rod when you wish to correct the child; and your correcting him is a token of your regard. Since I began my ministry sixty-four years ago, Oh, what hath God wrought in this land! We have a thousand improvements in our laws and institutions and government. God has a cause in our country to which He is infinitely attached, and He is engaged to carry it on. The number of those who believe to the saving of the soul, and who have power with God and prevail, is, we are fully persuaded, increasing. And if formerly for ten righteous men God would have saved the cities of the plain, what think you of the thousands of the Israel of God who, whether they eat or drink, or whatever they do, do all to His glory? Can we for a moment suppose that when God is about to bring our country into a state worth living in, He is going immediately to destroy it? It cannot be.

The reflection derived from our discourse turns upon the goodness of God and the depravity of man, alike calling into notice a display of the grace and forbearance of God on the one side, and a display of depravity and guilt on the other.

The first reflection derived from our discourse turns on the goodness and grace of God. Think, now, how many sins have been committed in one day, how many in a month, how many more in a year! How many by one individual, how many by a family, how many more by a town, how many more by a nation! And God sees all these: He knows them all, and could as easily as righteously punish the transgressors. But He is slow to anger, and is anxious for their welfare and salvation. He hath declared by the prophet, "as I live, saith the Lord God, I have no pleasure in the death of the wicked;" and again He says, "Wherefore turn, and live ye." Yet, behold the depravity of man in answer to this, "God speaks once, yea, twice; yet man perceiveth it not." And saith the inspired word, "Because sentence against an evil work is not executed speedily, therefore the heart of the sons of men is fully set in them to do evil." Thus is man continually neglecting or affronting his great Creator. Thus we see his depravity and guilt displaying itself, and instead of falling in with the method of God's goodness, saying, "Depart from us, we desire not the knowledge of Thy ways." Is not man a fallen creature? Do you imagine that God made Him such? I could as soon imagine that He made a demon, as that He made man in his present state. No, "the heart is deceitful above all things, and desperately wicked." How, then, has this goodness and this depravity displayed itself in our country? You shall hear God's own declaration, "My well-beloved hath a vineyard in a very fruitful hill; and he fenced it, and gathered out the stones thereof, and planted it with the choicest vine, and built a tower in the midst of it, and also made a wine press therein, and he looked that it should bring forth grapes, and it brought forth wild grapes." "And now, O inhabitants of Jerusalem, and men of Judah, judge, I pray you, betwixt me and my vineyard. What could have been done more to my vineyard that I have not done in it? Wherefore when I looked that it should bring forth grapes, brought it forth wild grapes?" "He that being often reproved hardeneth his neck shall suddenly be destroyed, and that without remedy."

But I must leave the nation, and come to yourselves. There is always a great danger in public assemblies that individuals will escape, thinking of others instead of themselves. And woe to that preacher who suffers them to depart without saying to each of them, "*Thou* art the man!" and without "commending himself to every man's conscience as in the sight of God."

I much fear this day will be only a day of mere pretence or of formality with many. But it need not be so with any of you. If you will humble yourselves before God and seek His face, He will not pass you by; no, He will not. "He looketh upon man, and if *any* say, I have sinned, and perverted that which was right, and it profiteth me not, He will deliver his soul from going into the pit, and his life shall see the light." He says, "To that man will I look, even to him that is poor and of a contrite spirit, and who trembleth at My word."

We first wish to individualize you *in your gratitude.* Don't leave the giving of thanks to the public. Say, "Bless the Lord, O *my soul,* and all that is within me bless His holy name." Ah! in how many congregations this morning will there be found those who are in mourning! If you could look into some of them, you might see Rachel weeping for her children and refusing to be comforted, because they are not. We should see children mourning over the loss of their parents, husbands their wives, and the wife the guide of her youth; while, perhaps, there is scarcely a family here this morning or an individual who has lost a friend by the prevailing epidemic.

We wish to individualize you also *as to your penitence and conviction.* Don't say, "We are all sinners, and the Lord knows we are all bad enough." But ask, "What have *I* done, I as a master or a servant, whether rich or poor? How have *I* added to the national transgression? And let me cry, 'God be merciful to me, a sinner!'"

We wish to individualize you also *as to your danger.* Don't think simply of the destiny of your country, but remember that "Except ye repent, ye shall all likewise perish;" that though you may escape the cholera, God can lay hold of you in ten thousand other ways. Your breath is in your nostrils; you are "crushed before the moth"; a grape-stone or a fly may be fatal to your life. The falling of a tile from a building, or the rupture of a small blood-vessel may hurry you into eternity.

We wish to individualize *your hopes also.* We would not have you forget that blessed promise, "At what instant I shall speak concerning a nation, and concerning a kingdom, to pluck up, and to pull down, and to destroy it, if that nation against whom I have pronounced turn from their evil, I will repent of the evil that I thought to do unto them." And again He hath said, "He who confesseth and forsaketh his sins shall have mercy." Oh, give up yourselves to Him, according to His gracious admonition. "Let the wicked forsake his way, and the unrighteous man his thoughts"—whatever be his thoughts—"and let him turn unto the Lord, and He will have mercy upon him; and to our God, for He will abundantly pardon." Then, if the plague should spread or continue, He can make a way for your escape; He can cover you with His feathers, and under His wings shalt thou trust. He has chambers of safety in which He can hide His people. Hear Him say, "Come, My people, enter thou into thy chambers, and shut thy doors about thee: hide thyself as it were for a little moment, until the indignation be overpast." Or, if you should fall by the plague or pestilence, you may rest assured that it shall be well with them that fear God; that death will be to you everlasting gain; that it will only remove you from a world of sin and sorrow into Immanuel's land, where nothing will be seen but joy and gladness, nothing heard but thanksgiving and the voice of melody: for "when that which is perfect is come, then that which is in part will be done away.'

"Just as a hen protects her brood
From birds of prey that seek their blood,
Under her feathers, so the Lord
Makes His own arm His people's guard.

"If burning beams of noon conspire
To dart a pestilential fire,
God is their life, His wings are spread
To shield them with a healthful shade.

"If vapours, with malignant breath,
Rise thick and scatter midnight death,
Israel is safe, the poison'd air
Grows pure, if Israel's God be there!

"What if the fire, or plague, or sword,
Receive commission from the Lord
To strike His saints among the rest?
Their very pains and deaths are blest.

The sword, the pestilence, or fire,
Shall but fulfil their best desire;
From sins and sorrows set them free,
And bring Thy children, Lord, to Thee."

VII.

THE SPIRIT OF CHRIST.

(Preached on Whit Sunday, May 26th, 1844.)

"*Now, if any man have not the Spirit of Christ, he is none of His.*"—ROMANS viii. 9.

"THE words of the wise," says Solomon, "are as goads and as nails;" "as goads," to stimulate, and "as nails" to fasten. "If thou take forth the precious from the vile, thou shalt be as my mouth." This was the promise of God to Jeremiah. "Study to shew thyself approved unto God, a workman that needeth not to be ashamed, rightly dividing the Word of Truth." This was the injunction of Paul to Timothy. Both these are opposed to the mode of preaching which generalizes, and individualizes, unaccompanied by a *Scriptural portrayal of character.*

There are many now who are ready to say, "The temple of the Lord, the temple of the Lord, the temple of the Lord are we." Well, are these Christians? We are to describe their principles and dispositions; and to place before them the evidences of divine grace. If they are such who love sin, and "walk according to the course of this world," it matters not who they are, or what they possess, we must endeavour to tear away from their eyes the bandage which keeps the Saviour from their sight, and to exhibit Christ as the only basis on which they can rest; whilst we show them the fallacy of that foundation on which they are building. The alarm may give them some disturbance at first, and spoil their sleep; but it does not follow that the alarm we give is unreasonable. The attempt, however painful, is necessary. Fidelity to our office, love to souls, and common humanity requires it.

You know I am accustomed to observe times and seasons without being superstitious. I know but of one day divinely appointed, and whose authority is therefore binding on the conscience; but for the sake of variety and excitement, and because something is generally expected on these occasions, I notice them.

In view of the services of this day several texts occurred to my mind, some of which relate more to the event; one of which I hope to take in the evening.* How many are there who will this day make some reference to the descent of the Holy Spirit! Merely to confine ourselves to the event might, however, do little to bring home conviction of the Spirit's work, commending it to every man's conscience in the sight of God: therefore before I withdrew from the study, "I sware unto the Lord, and vowed unto the mighty God of Jacob," that I would not keep the sword of the Spirit this morning hung up in its scabbard, nor brandish its shining blade into the air, but drive it to the heart, even to the hilt.

From the words before us let us consider, first, the subject of your attention: "The Spirit of Christ;" secondly, The way in which it is possible for us to possess the Spirit of Christ now; thirdly, The threatening found in the absence of the Spirit; and, lastly, An assurance implied,—the reverse of the decision of our text is equally true: "If any man have the Spirit of Christ, he *is* His."

Consider, first, THE SUBJECT OF YOUR ATTENTION: The Spirit of Christ, so called not only here, but, as you may have observed, in several other places. For instance, when Peter was speaking of the prophets, he says, "Searching what, or what manner of time the Spirit of Christ which was in them did signify, when it testified beforehand the sufferings of Christ and the glory that should follow." Paul, in speaking to the Philippians, says, "For I know that this shall turn to my salvation through your prayer, and the supply of the Spirit of Jesus Christ." To the Galatians he says, "Because ye are sons, God hath sent forth the Spirit of His Son, crying, Abba, Father."

It is called "The Spirit of Christ," because as *man*, He possessed it in all its gifts and in all its graces, qualifying Him for His office and work. Thus He speaks in Isaiah, "The Spirit of the Lord God is upon me, because the Lord hath anointed me to preach good tidings unto the meek." Isaiah says, "The Spirit of the Lord shall rest upon Him, the spirit

---

* Unfortunately the notes of this sermon have not been preserved.

of wisdom and understanding, the spirit of counsel and might, the spirit of knowledge and of the fear of the Lord." Thus His people possess this Spirit, but not like Him; "He was anointed with the oil of gladness *above* His fellows." Thus we read of Jesus being "*full* of joy and of the Holy Ghost"; of His being "*full* of grace and truth." We read indeed of Barnabas being "full of the Holy Ghost and of faith." But this is spoken of comparatively; for there were other things of an adverse nature in him, but there was no imperfection in the Holy Son of God.

It is called "the Spirit of Christ," because as Mediator He obtained it for us. Thus you often sing—

"'Tis by the merits of His death
Who groaned upon the tree,
The Spirit is sent down to breathe
On such dry bones as we."

This is not only poetry, but truth; and Dr. Watts has versified the language of the Apostle to the Galatians, when he says, "He hath redeemed us from the curse of the law, being made a curse for us . . . that we might receive the promise of the Spirit through faith."

It is called "the Spirit of Christ," because as the treasurer of His Church it resides in Him for communication to His followers. Now you may by your influence and intercession prevail upon a benefactor to bestow relief upon the distressed, but he may not impart it by you or by another, but he may do it himself. God does nothing immediately with us, but transacts all His concerns with us through the medium of Christ. Therefore we read, "It hath pleased the Father that in Him should all fulness dwell"; that "from His fulness have we all received, and grace for grace"; that "He hath given us eternal life, and this life is in His Son." Therefore, as when Pharaoh saw the famishing multitude, and heard them cry for bread, he said, "Go to Joseph," so God tells us by the Gospel, "Go to Jesus"; and all that have heard and received of the Father, come unto Him.

Nothing is more obvious in the Scriptures than that the whole dispensation of the Spirit is lodged in the hands of the Saviour; and that the blessings of that dispensation it is His office and His honour to bestow. This is the "joy set before Him," for which He "endured the cross, despising the shame." Therefore said He to His disciples when He was about to leave them, "If I go not away the Comforter will not come unto you." Peter said on the day of Pentecost, "Him being at the right hand of God exalted, and having received of the Father the promise of the Holy Ghost, He hath shed forth this which ye now see and hear." And Paul declares that "God hath highly exalted Him, and given Him a name which is above every name"; therefore, "through His name whosoever believeth in Him shall receive remission of sins." This is the import of the blessing here spoken of.

II. Consider, secondly, THE WAY IN WHICH IT IS POSSIBLE FOR US TO POSSESS THE SPIRIT OF CHRIST NOW. Now there are some who consider the ministration as having ceased. Yet persons are said to be "born of the Spirit"; to, "live in the Spirit"; to "walk in the Spirit"; and to "pray in the Spirit." But all this, we are told, is mere enthusiasm.

We readily allow a distinction is here necessary; we have not now the "Spirit of Christ" in its miraculous operations. We frequently read this in the Scriptures. But by some its influences are ignorantly or intentionally misunderstood. We plead not now for the discernment of spirits—for speaking with tongues, or for the healing of disease with a word. These were known in the Apostles' days, and were confined to them; but these were the things that sometimes, but not always accompanied salvation in those days. Judas performed miracles as well as the other apostles, but he "hanged himself," and "went to his own place"; Balaam prophesied, as well as Isaiah, and was slain, fighting against "the Israel of God." Our Saviour tells us that many will come to Him in that day, saying, "Lord, Lord, have we not prophesied in Thy name, and in Thy name have cast out devils, and in Thy name done many wonderful works?" "Then will I profess unto them I never knew you; depart from me ye that work iniquity." We only plead therefore now for what are called the ordinary operations of "the Spirit," because they belong to the Church of God under every economy and in every period. These are rendered absolutely necessary by the corruption and weakness of our fallen nature.

Therefore they who have now the Spirit have it under a fourfold character: As an *enlightener*, to lead them into all truth and to make them wise unto salvation; as a *sanctifier*, to "renew them in the spirit of their minds," and to make them partakers of His holiness; as a *comforter*, to sustain them amidst all their internal conflicts and outward trials; and as a *witness* and *seal*, to "seal them unto the day of redemption," and to "witness with their spirit that they are the children of God."

III. Now let us advance to an awful part of our subject, namely, THE THREATENING FOUND IN THE ABSENCE OF THE SPIRIT: "Now if any man have not the Spirit of Christ, he is none of His." How shall we manage this part of our subject? Let us take three views of it.

Let the first regard its *certainty*. Is it necessary for me to enlarge here? Do you believe that the Scriptures are the Word of God? If so, then here are the "true sayings of God," and which are too plain to require philosophy to decide, for "the unrighteous shall not inherit the kingdom of heaven." "They that are Christ's have crucified the flesh with its affections and lusts." Why should I multiply words? One declaration of God renders a thing as certain as a thousand. What says our text? "For if any man have not the Spirit of Christ he is none of His."

So you have no reason to suppose you are His, unless you have His Spirit. There can be no bond of union between Him and you; no suitableness; no conformity, for "How can two walk together unless they be agreed?" "What communion hath light with darkness? What fellowship hath righteousness with unrighteousness? and what concord hath Christ with Belial? or what part hath he that believeth with an infidel?" "He that is joined to the Lord," says the Apostle, "is one spirit."

The church of God is not like the image of Nebuchadnezzar, whose head was of gold, and the inferior members of baser metal. No, but there is a sameness here between the Head and the members. No, "as is the heavenly, such are they also that are heavenly, and as we have borne the image of the earthy, we shall also bear the image of the heavenly."

Let us take take another view of this exclusion, and let it concern the *dreadfulness* of it. "He is none of His," for he has no part in Him; he does not belong to Him; he has nothing to look for from Him, either in this world or in another. Christ has a school, but "he is none of His" disciples; not a pupil in the lowest class. "He is none of His." Christ has a flock, but "he is none of His"; not a sheep, not a lamb. "He is *none* of His." Christ has a mystical body, but "he is none of His," not "an eye," not "an ear," not a "foot," not a hair of the head. Christ has a family, but "he is none of His," not a child, not a servant, not a dog under the table to eat the crumbs that fall. Christ has a garden; as you have been singing,

> "We are a garden walled around,
> Chosen and made peculiar ground;"

but "he is none of His," not a tree, not a plant, not a shrub growing there.

This may seem indeed a light thing to some of you according to your present views and feelings; for you may now resemble the swine, that knows not the value of the jewel, and therefore tramples it under foot. But what will be the discoveries of an awakened conscience, when brought to exclaim, "What must I do to be saved?" What will you think of it in a dying hour? What will you think of it in the judgment of the great day? Hear how the Apostle speaks: "Yea, doubtless, and I count all things but loss," and "do count them but dung," so "that I may win Christ, and be found in Him." If He were an indifferent person, the exclusion would not be so dreadful; but the fact is, every thing you need is only to be found in Christ. No one in the universe can supply His place. How dreadful, then, to be "none of His"! Fancy not you have no need of Him; without Him you have no surety, no righteousness and strength. These are only to be found in Him. Without Christ you can have no access to God, "for no man cometh unto the Father but by Him. Without Him you cannot be saved; for "there is salvation in no other," yea, "there is no other name under heaven given among men whereby we may be saved."

And to finish the awfulness of this exclusion, what must be the alternative? Whose are you? There is no neutrality here! Jesus hath said, "He that is not for me is against me; and he that gathereth not with me, scattereth abroad." Whose are you? You belong to the prince of the power of the air, the spirit that now worketh in the children of disobedience. Our Saviour also says, "Ye are of your father the devil, and the lusts of your father ye will do."

The third view of this exclusion regards its *universality*. The Apostle makes no scruple to say, "If any man have not the Spirit of Christ, he is none of His." Some would think these things true with regard to the Jews and heathens, and so they are with regard to persons born in a Christian land; to such who may have been baptized in their infancy, wherein they are said to be "made the children of God, and inheritors of the kingdom of heaven." And can you suppose a little water thrown on the face by a parson or a fiddling priest can make you "new creatures"? or form your hearts anew? or can mere education change your natures? Take a babe and teach him the actions of a man, he would bear still the marks of a child. Take a blind man and you will find that the sunshine and the shade are both alike to him. Are we not "born in sin," as well as Jews and heathens? Are we not by nature the "children of wrath even as others"? Does God only work upon heathens? Does He not work the same changes morally and spiritually as formerly? "We speak that we do know, and testify that we have seen." We have seen, blessed be God! instances of men who have become the very reverse of what they were before. Not only as to their actions, but as to their dispositions. And who has accomplished this change in them? Did Paul or Apollos create them anew in Christ Jesus? "Who is Paul, and who is Apollos, but ministers by whom ye believed. I have planted, Apollos watered; but God gave the increase. So that neither is he that planteth anything, neither he that watereth; but God that giveth the increase."

Thus we see this exclusion bears down upon ourselves. So we see the truth of that which we have been reading. "That which is born of the flesh is flesh, and that which is born of the Spirit is Spirit. They that are after the flesh do mind the things of the flesh; they that are after the Spirit the things of the Spirit."

Let us then view this assertion with regard to ourselves. According to the Apostle, there is nothing in the world to insure your being a Christian, but your having the Spirit. "If any man have not the Spirit of Christ, he is none of His."

How can it be otherwise? Here is a man who has mental endowments; he can penetrate into the secrets of nature, and be familiar with the stars, and he is able to speak various languages. We do not decry talent, we admire it, but talent is not grace. Whatever be your intelligence, if you have not the Spirit of Christ you are "none of His."

Here is a man of a lovely natural temper, who has much of the milk of human kindness flowing through his veins; this is a source of pleasure to himself and a satisfaction to those around him: but complacency of disposition is not grace. Whatever, therefore, be your natural temper, if you "have not the Spirit of Christ" you are "none of His."

Here is another distinguished by morality; he is sober in his habits, just in his dealings, and diligent in his business. Do we disparage this? These things, as the Apostle says, "are good and profitable unto men." They adorn the character of a man and secure esteem; but they may spring from other causes, and cannot be grace. Without morality we cannot be Christians, mind this; but there may be morality without grace, mind this too. And whatever be your morals, if you "have not the Spirit of Christ" you are "none of His."

Here is another who can only bear to hear the pure gospel; who discerns the least deviation from orthodoxy; who makes a man "an offender for a word," and is a zealous contender for the truth. "Devils also believe and tremble." It matters not what you know, unless while you know these things you do them. It matters not what you believe, unless your faith is of the operation of the Spirit. It is well to be informed, but whatever you may have been taught, it will not avail you much, unless you have been taught to deny ungodliness and worldly lusts, and to live soberly, righteously and godly in this present evil world. "Now if any man have not the Spirit of Christ, he is none of His."

We mention these things the more plainly, because there are many persons now who are ready to exclude from the Church of God all those who differ from them. *They*, forsooth, understand the counsels of the Almighty; they think themselves to be His, while they think none beside, or very few beside, are so. But suppose *they* should be excluded; and this will, this must be the case with all, whatever be their pretensions or boastings, if they have not the Spirit of Christ! It may be well to compare *His* Spirit and their spirits together, while you remember the words of our text. "If any man have not the Spirit of Christ, he is none of His."

IV. But, lastly, here is AN ASSURANCE IMPLIED; the reverse of the decision of our text is equally true and scriptural, and we dare not pass it by. We therefore say, "If any man *have* the Spirit of Christ, he is His." The grand thing for you is to ascertain the possession of the principle, and then to surrender up your souls to the enjoyment of all the privileges connected with the blessing. The question, therefore, is whether you "have the Spirit of Christ." All depends upon this. Hence the absolute necessity of self-examination. Behold the criterion whereby you may judge of yourself.

We also see the folly of leaving things that are of infinite importance at an uncertainty. Should you be under a mistake, is it not desirable to discover it in time to alter? Do you ask how you are to know whether you have the Spirit? Not by a direct assurance from Heaven; not by any sudden impulse of mind. No; but by the effects produced. This is the way the sacred writers lead us to determine. If the Spirit of Christ be in you, you may be sure it will be active there; that it will banish the love of sin; that it will inspire a desire to please and glorify God. Examine the history of the Son of God; observe His language; see Him going about doing good; see Him, "meek and holy in heart;" hear Him say, "My meat is to do the will of my Father, and to finish His work." Oh, if you have *His* Spirit, could you live, as some of you are living, without prayer? Remember, the Spirit of God is called "the Spirit of Grace and of Supplication." It is His office to take up the things of Christ, and to reveal them unto you.

Well, if you *are* His, we have reason to hail you. You need no more to fill you with joy unspeakable and full of glory, than a pleasing sense of this. You need fear no "condemnation," as you have heard, for "There is therefore now no condemnation to them who are in Christ Jesus, who walk not after the flesh, but after the Spirit." That is, though Satan may accuse and condemn you; though the world may accuse and condemn, God hath justified you. "Who is he that condemneth? It is Christ that died, yea, rather that is risen again, who is even at the right hand of God, who also maketh intercession for us."

Then you need fear no separation. For, as we read in the chapter before us, "I am persuaded that neither death, nor life, nor angels, nor principalities, nor powers, nor things present, nor things to come, nor height, nor depth, nor any other creature, shall be able to separate us from the love of God, which is in Christ Jesus our Lord.

Then you need fear no exigency. For your "God shall supply all your need according to His riches in glory by Christ Jesus." "There is no want to them that fear Him." "He," says the Apostle, "that provideth not for his own is worse than an infidel." Does not God, think you, provide for His own? Does not the Saviour provide for His own?—those for whom He suffered, bled, and died? Yes. All the promises are theirs. All the treasures of grace and glory are theirs. Nature and Providence, too, are theirs. All things are theirs; whether Paul, or Apollos, or Cephas, or the world, or life, or death, or things present, or things to come; "All are yours, Christians, for ye are Christ's, and Christ is God's."

There is one remark with which we conclude. There may be in this large assembly some who have *not* the Spirit, *and they know it.* Your case is truly awful, but we would not drive you to despair. There is hope in Israel concerning this. There is hope regarding your salvation. The Apostle's language in our text is, "Now if any man hath not the Spirit of Christ, he *is* none of His." But he does not say, "He *shall* be none of His; that there exists an impossibility of his ever being one of Christ's." Oh, no. What were those *once*, now in a state of union and communion with Him? Hear them saying, "Not unto us, not unto us, O Lord: but to Thy name be all the glory." "O taste and see that the Lord is good," for yourselves, "blessed are all they that put their trust in Him." "That which we have seen and heard declare we unto you, and truly our fellowship is with the Father and with His Son Jesus Christ." Behold Him, therefore, exalted at the right hand of God, waiting to be gracious; go and plead with Him; hearken to His language. "If ye, being evil, know how to give good gifts unto your children, how much more shall your heavenly Father give the Holy Spirit to them that ask Him?" When Mr. Newton was first awakened, he says he was impressed with these words, and they afforded him encouragement. "I said to myself, 'If the Bible be true, why then this promise must be true, and if this promise be true, then if I ask I shall receive.' I *did* ask," he tells us, "and I received; I did seek, and I found; I did knock, and the door of mercy opened. Now I stand before Him, as a monument of His goodness, to excite and induce others to believe on Him to life everlasting." Amen.

VIII.

EASTER HOPES.

(Preached on Easter Sunday, April 23rd, 1840.)

"*Knowing that He which raised up the Lord Jesus shall raise up us also by Jesus, and shall present us with you.*"—2 CORINTHIANS iv. 14.

FOR many years I have been in the habit at the return of this season, as you well remember, of considering the resurrection of Christ in the morning, and that of His people in the evening; but as now I have only to address you once, I combine them both in our present exercise, according to the language of our apostle in the text, "Knowing that He who raised up the Lord Jesus shall raise up us also by Jesus, and shall present us with you." Now here are four things which we shall endeavour to explain and improve. The first regards a fact; "God raised up the Lord Jesus." The second regards the inference derivable from it; "He shall raise up us also by Jesus." The third regards a privilege: fellowship; "and shall present us with you." The fourth regards a knowledge of this: "we know it," say Paul and Barnabas, the speakers in our text. "Knowing that He which raised up the Lord Jesus shall raise up us also by Jesus, and shall present us with you."

I. The first regards A FACT. "God raised up the Lord Jesus." We call it a fact because it has been acknowledged as such for nearly two thousand years, and because it has been so acknowledged by men the most capable of understanding the force and value of evidence; because it is a subject that demands all our attention and all our belief; and because we can bring forward in defence of it, probabilities, proofs, and even demonstrations which no man can reasonably gainsay or resist.

Jesus died. Here we begin. This was never denied: It could not be denied. He was publicly executed on a hill, at the time of a festival, and before a vast number of spectators. His death was ascertained even while He was yet upon the cross. When the executioner had broken the legs of the malefactors that were crucified with Him, they brake not His legs because they found He was dead already. "Then Joseph of Arimathea took down the body of Jesus. And Nicodemus brought a mixture of myrrh and aloes," and anointed the body, and then He was conveyed to the grave, which was a new tomb wherein never man was laid. To prevent all deception His adversaries set a watch, and sealed the stone of His sepulchre with the Governor's seal. But yet the third day the body was gone. What became of it? The guard was answerable for it, it was committed to their keeping, and that those poor timid suffering disciples came and drove away these veterans of the world and took the corpse was too absurd for them to report; therefore they were taught to say, "that His disciples came by night, while we slept, and stole him away." But here was a reflection upon the Roman soldiers, who were said to sleep while on watch. Then, secondly, how came they all to be asleep, no individual among them being awake? Then, thirdly, this instance is the first time in all the annals of history of a party coming into court for the purpose of swearing to a thing which took place while they were asleep. But infidelity stops at nothing. There is nothing too inconsistent —too improbable—too impossible—with men when they oppose the truth of God.

We may remark also, the disciples were not men of hasty credence; they were full of despondency; nothing but the most strong and convincing proofs would have satisfied them; but the weakness of their faith is the strengthening of ours.

They were favoured to be the witnesses of His resurrection; and what were these witnesses? What was the number of them? It is said "In the mouth of two or three witnesses shall every word be established." Our Lord appeared to several individuals alone. He appeared unto two of His disciples as they were going to Emmaus. Twice He appeared to His disciples when assembled at Jerusalem. Again He appeared to seventy of them at the Sea of Galilee; and afterwards He appeared to above five hundred at once. What were their qualities as witnesses? They were eye-witnesses and ear-witnesses; they were manual witnesses. And what time had they to observe whether this were a reality? Why, "To them He showed Himself alive by many infallible proofs, being seen of them forty days, and speaking of the things pertaining to the kingdom of God." Thus they could not be imposed upon themselves.

Let us ask, what could have induced them to want to impose upon others? What prospect had they of success? What were they to gain? What honour, or wealth, or safety by their lies? But, my brethren, as we have proofs as well as probabilities to adduce, we have also demonstrations. These men came forward and vowed that He whom they had crucified had risen; that He was actually now alive. "You know we have no learning; we can only speak our own tongue," might they say, "but we will call upon Him, and we will immediately speak off eloquently thirteen languages which we never knew, and persons from various countries shall hear in their own tongue the wonderful works of God. We are mere men, we are acting in His name and in His strength; and if you question this, bring forward your blind and we will give them sight, your deaf and we will cause them to hear, your dead and we will raise them to life by a word."

> "Hence and for ever from my heart,
> I bid my doubts and fears depart;
> And to His hand my soul resign,
> That bears credentials so divine."

So far, my brethren, we have considered His resurrection as certain, but we may also view it as magnificent. The air was clear and cold; the pale moon was shining on the helmets and shields of the soldiers, when the earthquake shook the ground; and then an angel of the Lord descended from heaven, and rolled away the stone from the door of the sepulchre and sat upon it. Why do not these guards drive him away? Why do they suffer this to take place? But these guards trembled, and became as dead men, and fell to the ground, while he sat upon the stone with folded arms defying all their power: well, but they had viewed many terrible things; they had made the earth to tremble with their exploits; and now they tremble and shake! But this is not all. Here was magnificence of mercy as well as might. Here were women: where were the Apostles? Here were women, the last at the cross, and the first at the sepulchre; they came very early while it was yet dark; they were not terrified at those Roman guards; but though they were not afraid of these, they obviously were afraid of the shining figure on the stone. Yet this fear was perfectly groundless. "And the angel answered and said unto them. Fear not; I know that ye seek Jesus which was crucified. He is not here, but is risen, as He said. Come, see the place where the Lord lay; and go quickly and tell his disciples that He is risen from the dead; and behold He goeth before you into Galilee, there shall ye see Him; lo, I have told you. And they departed quickly from the sepulchre with fear and great joy, and did run to bring His disciples word." What tenderness was here displayed towards these females! and what relief and consolation was afforded to His disciples!

So far have we considered His resurrection as certain and as glorious, but we must not forget that it was all important too, for, "If Christ be not risen, then is our preaching vain, and your faith is also vain; and ye are yet in your sins." The apostle, therefore, makes this a higher ground of triumph than the death of Christ. "Who is he that condemneth? It is Christ that died, yea, rather that is risen again." "He was delivered for our offences, and raised again for our justification." The apostle speaks of the power of His resurrection as well as the fellowship of His sufferings. There is power to establish our faith; power to evince and prove His messiahship, the acceptance of His sacrifice, and the safety and welfare of His people.

II. Having considered the fact we pass on to observe THE INFERENCE DERIVABLE FROM IT. "He that raised up the Lord Jesus will raise up us also by Jesus."

You will observe the resurrection the Apostle here speaks of is the resurrection of believers. All, indeed, will rise; the resurrection will be an universal event, but not an universal blessing. It would be well for the wicked if their bodies were allowed to remain where death had consigned them. What benefit will it be to them to be taken from worms and consigned to the flames? Because they could derive no advantage from the resurrection, it is seldom mentioned with regard to them; but with regard to Christians it is of unspeakable value. It will not be a mere revival of the body, but a restoration of it with infinite improvements. What a difference was there between the tabernacle in the wilderness and the temple at Jerusalem? But there will be a much greater here. Such are the infirmities of the body now, that it would seem unworthy to be re-entered; but you must not compare the state of the future bodies of Christians with their present. "No," says the Apostle, "there are celestial bodies, and bodies terrestrial, but the glory of the celestial is one, and the glory of the terrestrial is another." The body of the believer in the resurrection is not to be found like Adam's in Paradise. "The first man is of the earth earthy, the second man is the Lord from heaven. As is the earthy, such also are they that are earthy, and as is the heavenly such are they also that are heavenly; and as we have borne the image of the earthy, we shall also bear the image of the heavenly." What an idea is this! your bodies are to be "fashioned like unto His glorious body," that body in which He appeared to Saul of Tarsus, which "shone above the brightness of the sun"; that body in which He will judge the world in righteousness, and through which we shall hold communion with the Deity for ever and ever.

You will remark, therefore, though the sacred writers admit of an intermediate state, yet when they speak of the consummation of the Christian's hope and happiness, they carry us forward at once to the resurrection of the dead. "They shall be recompensed at the resurrection of the just," says the Saviour; and says the Apostle, "He is able to keep that which I have committed to Him against that day"; and again, "The crown of glory which the righteous Judge shall give unto me at that day."

Let us observe here two things. The Apostle remarks the connection there is between the resurrection of Christ and the resurrection of Christians, and also the agency by which it is to be accomplished.

Observe, first, the connection there is between the resurrection of Christ and that of His people. The Apostle clearly infers this one from the other. Let us examine it. The first thing in it observable is, we see in His resurrection the possible resurrection of His people. With God all things are possible. "Why should it be thought a thing incredible that God should raise the dead?" There were several individuals raised from the dead, and each prove that our resurrection is possible, but it does not infer that others will rise also. The resurrection of Christ possesses a peculiar character. He is called, "The first-begotten from the dead;" "the firstborn among many brethren," and possesses a peculiar influence, producing and ensuring ours. The redemption of His people extends to the whole man, the body as well as the soul, and He will claim His ransomed; and is assured also from the relation there is between them. There is an union, a vital union, between Christ and Christians, so that what pertains to one pertains to the other. When He died, they died; and when He arose they also arose; and because He lives they shall live also. He is the Master, where are the servants? "Why," says the Saviour, "where I am there also shall my servant be." He is the Head, where are the members? The body would be defective if it had the head without the members, but these are inseparably united. "But now is Christ risen from the dead and become the first-fruits of them that slept." "For since by man came death, by man came also the resurrection from the dead." "And as in Adam all die, so in Christ shall all be made alive; but everyone in his own order: Christ the first-fruits, and afterwards they that are Christ's at His coming." You see, therefore, that He has gone before us; that He has entered into the presence of God, there to appear for us; and He appears there as our forerunner. This shews a connection with us. When He appeared He announced our arrival and prepared for it; "I go," said He, "to prepare a place for you." He has entered the heavenly country and has prepared a safe landing-place for you. He is now ready to receive you and to welcome you there, that where He is you may be also. Whenever you die, therefore, there is a place ready for you. You have not only the promise of heaven, though this is much, but you have taken possession of it representatively, in the person of your Lord and Saviour. "For," as the Apostle says, "ye are quickened together with Christ, and raised up and made to sit together in heavenly places in Christ."

Having noticed the connection between the resurrection of Christ and that of Christians, and how the one is inferred from the other; mark also the Agency by which it is accomplished. "*He* shall raise us up also by Jesus." I say Agency here rather than instrumentality. We are not to consider Him as a mere instrument. We often speak of God in Christ, and perhaps we too much limit the expression. We do not consider how far His mediation extends. We are expressly told that "The Father loved the Son, and hath given all things into His hand"; that "The Father judgeth no man, but hath committed all judgment unto the Son." We are expressly assured that by Him God made the world; no wonder, then, He is said to redeem and save; no wonder that the name of Jesus should be given Him because He should save His people from their sins, as well as deliver them from the wrath to come; and no wonder, therefore, He is to recover them from the dishonour of the grave. We are told that all that "are in their graves shall hear His voice," and He is Lord both of the dead and of the living. "I am," said He, "the resurrection and the life," and several times in one chapter, addressing the Jews, He says, "I will raise him up at the last day."

But what a work will this be! Only consider the immensity of the number to be raised, and that each body will be a thousand times more beautiful than before. What said the Saviour to John in Patmos? "I am Alpha and Omega, the beginning and the ending, saith the Lord; which is, and which was, and which is to come, the Almighty." This is enough, He is the Almighty; and therefore, as the Apostle says, "We look for the Saviour, the Lord Jesus Christ, who shall change our vile body, that it may be fashioned like unto His glorious body, according to the power whereby He is able to subdue all things unto Himself."

III. Let us observe THE PRIVILEGED FELLOWSHIP. "And shall present us with you."

There are several presentations mentioned in the Word of God, and it may not be improper to notice them.

You will find then a *personal* presentation made by believers themselves, and of which the Apostle speaks when he says, "I beseech you, brethren, by the mercies of God, that ye present your bodies," meaning by a figure of speech which takes a part for the whole, "your entire selves,"—"We beseech you, brethren, that ye present your bodies a living sacrifice, holy, acceptable unto God, which is your reasonable service." In the experience of every believer, there was a time when he first began to seek the Lord, a time when he said, "I am Thine; save me." Perhaps some of you can remember the very period. Oh, what a time of love was it to your souls! Perhaps you can call to mind the very place. Perhaps it was in such a room, or perhaps at eventide when meditating in the field, or, which is most commonly the case, under the Word. Then you said, "Lord, what wilt Thou have me to do? I now yield myself to Thee: my body is Thine, my soul is Thine." How finely does Doddridge speak of this transaction—

"O happy day, that fixed my choice
  On Thee, my Saviour and my God!
Well may this glowing heart rejoice,
  And tell its raptures all abroad.

"'Tis done, the great transaction's done;
  I am my Lord's, and He is mine;
He drew me and I followed on,
  Charmed to confess the voice divine.

"High heaven, that heard the solemn vow,
That vow renewed shall daily hear,
Till in life's latest hour I bow
And bless in death a bond so dear."

There is also a *ministerial* presentation. Our Apostle says, "I am jealous over you, that I may present you as a chaste virgin to Christ."

Then there is also a *divine* presentation; that is, not a presentation to God, but a presentation by God. Of this Jude speaks, when he says, "Now unto Him that is able to keep you from falling, and to present you faultless before the presence of His glory with exceeding joy." And of this also Paul speaks in addressing the Colossians: "You who were sometimes alienated and enemies in your minds by wicked works, yet now hath He reconciled in the body of His flesh through death, to present you holy, and unblamable, and unreprovable in His sight."

Then, lastly, there is an *united* presentation, for, says the Apostle, "He shall present *us* with *you*. He shall present us with you, Corinthians, among whom we have laboured." Now this extends equally to other ministers and their converts, and by a parity of reasoning to other connections in this world. Observe, the Apostle does not say, "you shall be presented with us," but "we shall be presented with you," as if they were chief. Therefore, he says in another place, "we are your servants, for Jesus' sake"; "we do not wish to take the lead, we are satisfied to follow in your train, and to be presented together with you." Oh, what a noble disposition does divine grace produce! The spirit that is in us naturally lusteth to envy; but divine grace dethrones envy, if it does not destroy it. It produces something of the temper of angels who rejoice over sinners that repent, and when they know that they shall be raised to a condition above their own.

Three things seem to be inferred when the Apostle says, "and shall present us with you." The first is *unity*. The difference of office and station here will occasion no difference in our condition in future life. The poor will be presented with the rich; the servants with the master; the subjects as well as the sovereign. The Apostles were men of extraordinary endowments and extraordinary achievements, yet Paul always calls common Christians "brethren," and even implores their prayers on his behalf. Yes, and this unity begins even now. They worship in the same sanctuary; they surround the same board; they are partakers of the same common salvation; and there is now neither "Greek nor Jew, barbarian, Scythian, bond nor free, for all are one in Christ Jesus."

Secondly, *sociality.* Every representation given of it in Scripture expresses or implies this. We know man was formed for this, and he derives much of his pleasure now from social intercourse. Thus Paul speaks of "the comfort of love;" and remember that then all the comforts of society will be enjoyed without any of its bitters.

Then, thirdly, surely the passage befriends the *recognition* of each other in another state. This is a pleasing idea, and which the Apostle seems so fully to establish when he says to the Thessalonians, "For what is our hope, or joy, or crown of rejoicing? Are not even ye in the presence of our Lord Jesus Christ, at His coming? For ye are our glory and joy." And our Lord says, "Make to yourselves friends of the mammon of unrighteousness, that when ye fail—and when by your liberality you have befriended persons here, in that world of light and love, when you fail—they will receive you into everlasting habitation." Yes, Martha and Mary will know Lazarus again; the child will know its mother again; and the husband the desire of his eyes that was taken from him with a stroke. Yes, if Paul and the Corinthians were presented together, surely they would know each other.

But where will some of you be presented? And how will you be presented hereafter? Not with those you now dislike; not with those whose names you now cast out as evil. No, you have turned from them; as David says, "As for such as turn aside unto their crooked ways, the Lord shall lead them forth with the workers of iniquity." We know too well with whom you will be presented, living and dying, as you are. "Depart from me," will the Saviour say, "ye workers of iniquity, into everlasting fire, prepared for the devil and his angels."

IV. THE KNOWLEDGE OF ALL THIS. "*Knowing* that He, which raised up the Lord Jesus, shall raise us up also by Jesus, and present us together with you."

Paul and Barnabas knew this three ways. First, as an article of faith. The Apostle receives the doctrine of the resurrection from the dead as one of the first principles of our religion. We know that "faith is the substance of things hoped for, the evidence of things not seen!" "By faith we understand the worlds were made," and if you go forward you will have an understanding of the dissolution of the present system, and will behold "new heavens and a new earth wherein dwelleth righteousness." All we know of divine things is not from reason but faith; not from nature but Scripture. Therefore those who are destitute of Scripture, we consider as rolling in darkness and having no light. The doctrine of the resurrection is a doctrine of pure revelation of which heathens never entertained a conception. At death they bore their friends to the grave, and there left them in the dust, and said "Farewell! Farewell for ever!" But it is not so with Christians when they inter their friends; they sorrow not as those who have no hope. "For if we believe that Jesus died and rose again, even so, them also which sleep in Jesus will God bring with Him."

Then, secondly, they know it *as an assured privilege.* Balaam said, "I shall see Him, but not nigh." And our Lord tells us there are many who shall see Abraham, Isaac, and Jacob, in the Kingdom of God, while they themselves are thrust out." There are many—you all know this—there are many who feel satisfied that there will be a glorious resurrection, who will not partake of it. But this knowledge is possible. Job said, "I know that my Redeemer liveth, and that He shall stand at the latter day upon the earth: and though after my skin worms destroy this body, yet in my flesh shall I see God! whom I shall see for myself, and mine eyes shall behold, and not another." Oh, how desirable is this! It is strange that any of us should rest satisfied without attaining it. Men do not easily rest satisfied with regard to their title to an estate; yea, they often give much to ensure it. Why do not we give all diligence to make our calling and election sure? Why do we not prove our own selves?

Then, thirdly, they know it *as a practical principle,* and not merely as a speculative. It is a vital truth that worketh in them. We see the effects of this in the speakers here, under the two facts spoken of as resulting from this knowledge. The first regards their profession, which we have in the verse preceding our text. "We have the same spirit of faith, according as it is written. I believed, and therefore have I spoken. We also believe, and therefore speak." Yea, how can we believe the truth and importance of a thing without wishing to make it known? Surely the belief of the heart will produce the confession of the mouth, and if the Spirit of God dwell in you, He will open your mouth, and your lips will show forth His praise; you will hold fast the profession of your faith without wavering, knowing that He is faithful who hath promised, who also will do it. And the second effect you see resulting from their knowledge is in their suffering, for as it led them to act, so it led them to suffer and endure. Hence the words that follow our text, "For which cause we faint not; but though our outward man perish, our inward man is renewed day by day. For our light affliction, which is but for a moment, worketh for us a far more exceeding and eternal weight of glory;" as much as to say, "Having such a destination, we can bear our losses and afflictions." "A hope so much divine, may trials well endure." Oh, how this smooths the rugged path of life! Oh, how it lines with down the yoke of suffering imposed on the believer's neck! Oh, how it gilds with glory the valley of the shadow of death. The Christian, like a bird, can sing in his cage, though the wires of his prison confine him. He can also sing in the night. Hear the language of Asaph; I was struck with it in my reading this morning; he marvelled at the prosperity of the wicked, and the adversity of the righteous, and his wonder increased by every fresh investigation, "Until," says he, "I went into the sanctuary of the Lord, then understood I their end." And he says, "What have I been doing? I have been reasoning as if I were at home, whereas I am only a stranger here; I have been reasoning as though my portions were in this world, whereas my treasure is in heaven; as if my happiness depended upon creatures, while God over all, blessed for evermore, is mine; is all my salvation and desire. I have been acting the brute instead of the man. "So foolish was I, and ignorant, I was as a beast before Thee. Nevertheless, I am continually with Thee; Thou shalt guide me with Thy counsel, and afterwards receive me to glory." "Whom have I in heaven but Thee, and there is none upon earth I desire beside thee. My flesh and my heart faileth; but God is the strength of my heart, and my portion for ever."

May this be our experience, for the Redeemer's sake. Amen.

IX.

THE CITY OF THE SAINTS.

A Sermon preached on behalf of the Evangelical Alliance on Sunday Morning, September 6th, 1846.

"*Now, therefore, ye are no more strangers and foreigners, but fellow citizens with the saints, and of the household of God.*"—EPHESIANS ii. 19.

PAUL takes it for granted that there is such a corporation as this, and such a family as the "household of faith." God has a people, and if they are not the most numerous party now, they will be so in due time, when "a nation shall be born in a day"; when "He shall sprinkle many nations," and when "all nations shall call Him blessed." They are more numerous now than many imagine, for He has always had His hidden ones—hidden by the obscurity of their station, hidden by the timidity of their disposition, and hidden by the imperfections of their character. Elias supposed that he was the only true worshipper in all Israel, while God "reserved seven thousand who had not bowed the knee to Baal." The number also is perpetually increasing, "and the Lord add to His people, how many soever they be, a hundredfold!" If they fill not the high places of the earth, they are "more excellent than their neighbours," and are distinguished from the rest of the world. Our Saviour therefore said to Saul of Tarsus, "I send thee to open their eyes and to turn them from darkness to light, and from the power of Satan unto God, that they may receive forgiveness of sins, and inheritance among them which are sanctified by faith that is in me." So the first Christians said to those around them, "That which we have seen and heard, declare we unto you, that ye also might have fellowship with us." It might have been said in reply, "Is this such a privilege, then, to have fellowship with you? Are you not poor, and despised, and persecuted, and deemed the offscouring of all things? Is it such an invaluable privilege to have fellowship with *you?*" "You judge," say they, "by a wrong standard, for truly our fellowship is with the Father, and with His Son Jesus Christ." So says Paul here, "Now, therefore, ye are no more strangers and foreigners, but fellow-citizens with the saints, and of the household of God."

A preacher, in the discussion of a text, must feel very differently according to the subjects of his addresses, according as they call for reflection or praise. For instance, if his text appeals in a way of reproach and condemnation, it is pleasing for him to know that those to whom he speaks are not those of whom he is speaking; and, therefore, the apostle to the Hebrews, when speaking of apostate professors, says: "But beloved, we are persuaded better things of you, and things that accompany salvation, though we thus speak." On the other hand, when the text appeals in a way of privilege and promise, it is pleasing to know that the individuals he is speaking *to* are the very persons he is speaking *of*, and that these blessed persons are not only to be found in the world, or in the neighbourhood, but in the very congregation before him. Now this was Paul's happiness, as you have heard in the words I have read, for addressing these Ephesians to whom he wrote, he said, "Now therefore *ye* are no more strangers and foreigners, but fellow-citizens with the saints, and of the household of God." And this is my happiness, for there are persons here, who are waiting to surround the table of their dying Lord, and who are the very characters we are about to endeavour to describe. Not that all here are so, would to God they were! and that I had returned after an absence to a congregation all of which were persons who worship "God in the Spirit, who rejoice in Christ Jesus, and have no confidence in the flesh."

The division of our subject is very simple and easy to be remembered. It consists of two truths: First, you are told what the Ephesians once were; secondly, what they now are.

We are told WHAT THEY ONCE WERE: "*strangers and foreigners;*" for in saying that they were *not* so now, Paul fully admits that they were such before.

But who are these characters? According to some those who were converted to Christianity from heathenism, and such the Ephesians had been. They had served "divers lusts and pleasures," and "at that time were without Christ, being aliens from the commonwealth of Israel, and strangers from the covenants of promise, having no hope, and without God in the world." But how was it with regard to the Jews? Addressing them he says, "Among whom also we all had our conversation in times past in the lusts of our flesh, fulfilling the desires of the flesh and of the mind, and were by nature the children of wrath even as others." Thus both Jews and Gentiles are all guilty before God. All need the same redemption, the same justification, the same renovation. We who live in a land of vision and in a Christian country need the same change. Did not our Saviour say, "Except a man be born again he cannot see the kingdom of God"? Did not Paul say, "If any man be in Christ he is a new creature?"

There is indeed a sense in which Christians are all "strangers and foreigners"; thus the patriarchs are spoken of as "not having received the promises, but having seen them afar off, they confessed that they were strangers and foreigners upon earth." So Peter says "I beseech you, brethren, as strangers and pilgrims, abstain from fleshly lusts which war against the soul," and it would be well if in this sense you were more as "strangers and foreigners," remembering that you are born from above, and bound for glory, and ever hearing a voice crying, "Arise and depart, for this is not your rest." It will be for you to declare more plainly that you "seek a country, even a heavenly one," and to judge of yourselves not by what you are in the way, but of what you will be at home. "There I am to dwell for ever, there lies my inheritance."

> "There my best friends, my kindred dwell;
> There God my Saviour reigns."

But brethren, you are "now no longer strangers and foreigners" as to the things of God; as to your illumination by the Holy Spirit; as to the preciousness of a Saviour, and your glorying in Him; as to a "hope full of immortality"; as to Immanuel's land; and as to your connection and communion with the people of God. You were once strangers; you attended perhaps the very same place that God's people attended, but you had no vital union with Christ. If you had the form of godliness, you knew nothing of its power. You *were* "strangers," but now you are no more such; "*Now* ye are fellow-citizens with the saints, and of the household of God."

Hence we make two remarks by way of concluding this first division of our subject.

First, there is no difference between the people of God and the people of the world naturally. They will own this themselves. Paul, who was a moral man before his conversion, owned it, and said, "We ourselves also were sometimes disobedient, serving divers lusts and pleasures, living in malice and envy, hateful and hating one another."

But secondly, God never leaves His people as He finds them, or what He finds them. He finds them afar off, but He brings them nigh: He finds them with the men of the world, who have their portion in this life, "but now they desire a better conntry."

This brings us to consider—

II. WHAT THEY NOW ARE: "But fellow-citizens with the saints, and of the household of God."

Here are two representations of them in their present state, and both of them, you see, are metaphorical. Now in the treatment of a metaphor, there are two extremes to be avoided. "When," says an old writer, "a metaphor offers to go with us a mile, we must not compel it to go with us two." We must take its plain aim and design, but we must not overlook "the words which the Holy Ghost teacheth," for they are words of wisdom as well as truth. Let us therefore enter a little into these two representations. One is taken from a city, the other from a household.

The first is taken from a city: "Ye are fellow-citizens with the saints." Therefore ye are not strolling gipsies, living under hedges. Ye are not a set of vagrants; not a banditti, but under a regular government. Ye are a body politic. Every believer is among those who are "written as the living in Jerusalem," and he is entitled to all the rights and immunities of the state and place. Therefore our Saviour said to His disciples, when they returned rejoicing at their miraculous attainments and achievements, "But rather rejoice because your names are written in heaven."

"Ye are fellow-citizens with the saints." Yes, ye are citizens of no mean city, but the most remarkable city ever known. As to the nature of this city, it is not of this world, and its inhabitants are not of this world. "Glorious things are spoken of thee, thou city of God." It is the most renowned city in the world; "it is the city of the living God, the heavenly Jerusalem." Its "Builder and Maker is God."

Let us observe its extent. Properly speaking, this city consists of two parts, the Upper and the Lower town. By far the larger part of this city is above. Oh, what multitudes of citizens are there! There are patriarchs, and prophets, and apostles; there is the "glorious army of martyrs"; there are many of your own beloved connections. Many are continually entering the city. Some have entered since we have been assembled together, and some are entering now; at this very moment some have entered upon the enjoyment of life eternal. But you will observe, that all those who are in the Upper town have been added from the lower part, which is this earth, and comprehend all those "who love our Lord Jesus in sincerity"; for all those who are residing in this lower town are equally citizens with those above; and this upper and lower town are connected by means of a trying round of steps. This is death: *this* is the way, the only way, from one to the other.

The Governor of this city is the most Glorious Person in the universe. "He is fairer than the children of men." "He is the only King in Zion." "He is the Head over all things to His Church." He has the bestowal of all blessings, and the control of all events; nothing can take place without His knowledge. There are great diversities and degrees among His servants, but He provides for their accommodation, for their protection and instruction. He has promised to be with them even unto death. You remember that at the close of Ezekiel it is said, "The name of the city shall be, The Lord is there."

The laws of the city are "holy, just, and good," founded in a regard for the welfare of the citizens, as well as for the honour of the Governor. And the privileges thereof are inconceivable and unspeakable. For instance, what can equal their safety? "Their place of defence shall be the munition of rocks." None of their adversaries violate or infringe upon the privileges of the Citizens, who are, we are assured by unerring truth, "kept by the mighty power of God." How safe as well as happy are they! How well did Balaam exclaim, "Surely there is no enchantment against Jacob; neither is there any divination against Israel." "No weapon that is formed against thee shall prosper, and every tongue that riseth up in judgment against thee, thou shalt condemn." They may, therefore, well rejoice in their security; they may well sing with the Church in the days of Isaiah, "We have a strong city, salvation doth God appoint for walls and bulwarks."

Think, brethren, of the plenitude of the place. The inhabitants thereof are not only fed, but feasted: "In this mountain," says Isaiah, "shall the Lord of Hosts make unto His people a feast of fat things; a feast of wines on the lees, of fat things full of marrow, of wines on the lees well refined." The Lord spreads a table for His people in the presence of all their enemies.

Think of the freedom of this city; the citizens have liberty to "sit under their own vine, and under their own fig-tree, none daring to make them afraid." They have a freedom that others know nothing of—a freedom from condemnation; a freedom from the tyrannical powers of darkness, for they are no longer "led captive by the devil at his will;" a freedom from the dominion of sin, for "sin shall not have dominion over you;" freedom from the lashes of a guilty conscience, and from our anxiety respecting all future events, being enabled to "cast all their care upon God, who careth for them." They feel "a peace that passeth all understanding." Thus are they free to walk into God's house, and sit down at His table, to lean upon His arm, and to rest upon His bosom. "Oh, how great is Thy goodness which Thou hast laid up for them that fear Thee, which Thou hast wrought for them that trust in Thee before the sons of men!" Such is the freedom of this city.

There are three ways by which the citizens are made free: by gift, by purchase, and by birth; and all these will apply in different respects to the citizens of Zion. Sometimes by *gift*. This may be for some distinguished services: now our services are never meritorious, but Jesus has made them rewardable. Concerning those performances over which we blush, and ought to be ashamed, He will say, "Well done, good and faithful servant; thou hast been faithful over a few things, I will make thee ruler over many things, enter thou into the joy of thy Lord." Then it is sometimes obtained by *purchase*. Thus the chief captain answered Paul: "With a great sum obtained I this freedom." So may every Christian say, for he has obtained it by a price of infinite value, even by the precious blood of Christ. Then this freedom is sometimes obtained by *birth*. Paul said, "But I was free-born." Thus may every believer in Christ say: "And of Zion it shall be said, This and that man was born in her, and the Highest Himself shall establish her. The Lord shall count, when He writeth up the people, that this man was born there." Thus the freedom of the city is obtained.

But here another source of reflection opens; and I may address you in the words of the sacred writer, "These things, brethren, I have transferred to you in a figure." But here is a difficulty, for all the images by which divine realities are held forth, are very inadequate to the purpose. The sacred writers who employed them were fully aware of this, and in order to supply this deficiency, they did three things: First, they stripped these images of every imperfection. Then they added to them attributes which are not naturally inherent in them. Thus, as Watts says—

> "Nature, to make His glories known,
> Must mingle colours not her own."

So that art must blend with nature. Then, thirdly, they multiplied, adding one figure after another, that we might gain a knowledge of the idea they would present to us. Here you see some change in the imagery. There, you see the Governor of the city now becomes the Master of the household; and the "fellow-citizens of the saints" are drawn into closer contact and more intimate alliance, being fellow-domestics. If, therefore, this figure seems less expansive than the former, be it remembered, it is more attractive, and comes more home to our feelings; it is more attractive. "A household" gives us an idea of a home of which every believer can say—

> "There is my rest, my portion fair,
> My treasure and my heart are there,
> And my abiding home.
>
> "For me my elder brethren stay,
> And angels beckon me away,
> And Jesus bids me come."

Yes, they are not "strangers and foreigners, but fellow-citizens with the saints, and of the household of God."

This "household" takes in two classes of persons, servants and children. It takes in servants. If the Queen of Sheba, when she saw Solomon's domestics, said, "Happy are thy men; happy are these thy servants, that stand continually before thee, and that hear thy wisdom;" how much more may we say, "Blessed are they that dwell in Thy house; they will be still praising Thee. They shall be abundantly satisfied with the fatness of Thy house; and Thou shalt make them drink of the river of Thy pleasures." It also takes in children. So we read of "the sons and daughters of the Lord Almighty." "Behold what manner of love the Father hath bestowed on us, that we should be called the children of God!" "Beloved, now are we the sons of God."

But what now is the evidence of this affinity and alliance? How may you know that you are "of the household of God?" Do you remember the address of our Saviour when told that some of His relations wanted Him? He said, "Behold my mother and my brethren, for he who doeth the will of my Father which is in heaven, the same is my brother, and sister, and mother"; that is they are equally related to Him, they are equally beloved by Him.

But we must draw to a conclusion.

Let this view of the Church of God, "fill us with joy and peace in believing." For think you not that He who is the Father of mercies will provide for His children?

Those who belong to this family should learn to love as brethren; and act so as to induce those who see them to exclaim "Behold how good and how pleasant a thing it is for brethren to dwell together in unity." "By this," said the Saviour, "shall all men know that ye are my disciples, if ye have love one to another." Now this has been the design of the "Evangelical Alliance." Its great and blessed design has been realized already in a great degree, and must accomplish great good. The members of many religious communities have met together, and while agreeing to hold the Head, their own particular opinions have disappeared. They consider all as their brethren, and as "one in Christ Jesus," who agree in the truths which form the essentials of the Gospel. I have, during my absence, had an opportunity of attending one of its meetings; but, unless you had been there, it is impossible to convey an adequate idea of the impressions produced by the largeness of the assembly, by the quality of the speeches, and by the spirit of devotion which was displayed; of the pleasures produced, and the tears drawn forth by the speakers, who seemed to be all but inspired. You may deem it extravagant, but I thought then, and think the same now, that it would be worth Christians' coming down from heaven to see what was then seen, and to hear what was then heard. This subject shows us that religion is a social thing, as well as personal. Let there be no selfishness prevailing in us, but, like "the household of faith," may we look no more "on his own things, but every one also on the things of others."

This subject also preaches humility. You were once "not a people, but are now the people of God." It also preaches thankfulness, for, you are "now no longer strangers and foreigners, but fellow-citizens of the saints, and of the household of God." The subject also preaches joy. "Let the children of Zion be joyful in their King." We hail you as the blessed of the Lord, who have reason to "rejoice with joy unspeakable and full of glory."

But what shall we say to others? May there not be many here, who know nothing of all this? Alas, you are "strangers and foreigners." This is your unhappiness, but it is also your fault and your guilt. "Some have not the knowledge of God; I speak this to your shame." It would not be their shame, unless it were their sin; and it would not be their sin, unless they could have escaped from it. The blessings of the Gospel were placed within their view and within their reach, and yet the Saviour complains of them, "Ye will not come unto me that ye might have life." The gates of this city are now open! the doors of this house are now unclosed; and a thousand voices are heard to exclaim, "Come in, come in; and He will receive you graciously and love you freely." "Behold, now is the accepted time; behold, now is the day of salvation." That door will soon be shut, and the Saviour will exclaim, "The harvest is past, the summer is ended, and ye are not saved."

X.

THE WORD OF CHRIST.

(A Sermon preached on behalf of the British and Foreign Bible Society, on Sunday Morning, March 9th, 1845.)

"*Let the word of Christ dwell in you richly in all wisdom.*"—COLOSSIANS iii. 16.

A PREACHER of the gospel has various duties to perform, and in the performance of them he is not to be governed by his own feelings, or the opinions of his hearers, but, commending himself to every man's conscience, in the sight of God, he is to declare the whole counsel of God; to keep back nothing that is profitable for doctrine, for reproof, for correction, for instruction in righteousness, that the man of God may be perfect, thoroughly furnished unto all good works. Sometimes he is to alarm, sometimes he is to encourage, sometimes he is to inform, and sometimes to admonish. With regard to many, especially those who are favoured with the means of grace, they require to have their pure minds stirred up by way of remembrance. They know the truth, but their experience and practice do not keep pace with their knowledge. Our Saviour therefore says, "The children of this world are in their generation wiser than the children of light." It is seldom necessary to have a monitor in the exchange, or in the market, or in the warehouse, or in the shop, but in divine things *there* "precept must be upon precept, precept upon precept; here a little and there a little." And the minister must often say to his people, as the Apostle does to the Hebrews, "I beseech you, brethren, suffer the word of exhortation"; and what does he say to you this morning? "Let the word of Christ dwell in you richly, in all wisdom. If such an exhortation were necessary for these Colossians, in whom the Gospel had not ceased to bring forth fruit from the day they heard it, and knew the grace of God in truth, can it be needless for us?

Let us then consider, first, the subject of attention; secondly, the manner in which we are to regard it; thirdly, the motives which should excite us; and fourthly, the bearing of the whole upon an institution concerning which we shall have to give notice at the close of the exercise.

I. THE SUBJECT OF ATTENTION. "The word of Christ." I need hardly say this means the Scripture. In Paul's commendation of Moses, he says, he chose rather to suffer affliction with the people of God than enjoy the pleasures of sin for a season, esteemed the reproach of Christ as greater riches than the treasures in Egypt. Why did he call this "the reproach of Christ?" Because he endured it in His cause, and for His sake, and for the sake of His people who where His mystical body. It was therefore called the reproach of Christ, because of its relation to him. So the Scripture is called the Word of Christ because of its relation to Him; and this relation is twofold.

First, It has a relation to Him as the *Author.* "Holy men of old wrote as they were moved by the Holy Ghost." And whose influence was it that inspired them? Hear Peter: "Of which salvation the prophets have enquired and searched diligently; who prophesied of the grace that should come unto you, searching what or what manner of time the *Spirit of Christ* which was in them did signify, when it testified beforehand the sufferings of Christ and the glory that should follow." All revealed knowledge is from Him. As the apostle says, "He is the author and the finisher of faith;" the word "our" in this passage you will find to be in italics. "The faith once delivered to the Saints." He began it in Paradise and ended it in the Isle of Patmos, and then said, "I testify unto every man that heareth the word of the prophecy of this book, if any man shall add unto these things, God shall add unto him the plagues that are written in this book, and if any man shall take away from the words of the book of this prophecy, God shall take away his part out of the book of life, and out of the holy city, and from the things which are written in this book."

Secondly, It has a relation to Him as the *substance*: for it is not only a revelation from Him but a revelation of Him. In some places it points to His divinity, in some to His humanity; in some places to His birth, in some to His death; in some places pointing to His suffering, and in others to His glory. Wherever on this holy ground you hearken you immediately hear a voice saying, "Behold the Lamb of God which taketh

O O

away the sin of the world." Wherever you look you see a star going before you that stands over where the young child was. Wherever you open these sacred pages, His name is as ointment poured forth. Whenever, as Ministers of the Gospel we preach the Word, we hold forth this all-sufficient Saviour in whom we have redemption through His blood, even the forgiveness of sins, in whom we are blessed with all spiritual blessings in heavenly places; we hold Him forth as descending from the throne to the cross, and as ascending from the cross to the throne. This is the grand theme of revelation. There is something in it infinitely delightful, wonderful, and sublime. While, as to us, it is "all our salvation and all our desire."

Let us divide the word of Christ into five parts, and we shall see how He is all and in all therein.

Take the *historical* part. Here you see Him in Isaac, as a type of Him who was slain for us; in Joseph, as the Saviour of His father's house; in Moses, as the law-giver; in Aaron, as the high-priest; in Joshua, as the conqueror; in Solomon, as the prince of peace; in Zerubbabel as the restorer of the Temple.

Take the *ceremonial* part. The sacrifices under the law were shadows of good things to come, of which the body was Christ. We read of the rock furnishing the Israelites with refreshing streams in their travels through the wilderness, and, says the Apostle, "that Rock was Christ." We read of the manna which came down from Heaven, and this prefigured the living Bread, of which if a man eat he shall live for ever. And every victim bleeding upon the altar proclaimed Him as taking away sin by the sacrifice of Himself. He was the true tabernacle—the tabernacle which the Lord pitched and not man. He was the real Temple, in whom dwelt all the fulness of the Godhead bodily.

Take the *prophetical* part. To Him gave all the prophets witness; and said the Angel to John, "The testimony of Jesus is the Spirit of prophecy."

Take the *promissory* part. Is this Book of God filled with exceeding great and precious promises? "All the promises of God in Him are Yea, and in Him, Amen, to the glory of God, by us."

Finally, take the *evangelical* part. We see Him in Moses and the prophets. And if Moses wrote of Him, how much more did Paul; and if He be found in the book of Leviticus, how much more in the four Gospels, and in the writings of the New Testament! Therefore the New Testament excelleth in glory. Here, the veil is taken off, and we, with open faces, behold His glory, "the glory as of the only Begotten of the Father, full of grace and truth."

II. We pass from the subject of attention to consider, secondly, THE MANNER IN WHICH WE ARE TO REGARD IT. "Let the word of Christ dwell in you richly, in all wisdom."

According to the Apostle this includes four things.

First, that it should be *in* us, "Let the word of Christ dwell *in* you." It is a great mercy to have the Word of God in the world; to have it in our own country; in our churches and in our houses. But we must have it in ourselves; all our religion lies in this Word of Christ dwelling *in* us The grand business of our lives is to get it out of the Book into the man, and this may be accomplished. It may be in us—in us as a well of water springing up unto everlasting life; in us, like leaven, which a woman took and hid in three measures of meal till the whole was leavened; in us, as the soul is in the body, enlivening every limb, and influencing every motive.

But, secondly, the Apostle tells us that this word of Christ must *dwell* in us; that is, it must have an abiding and permanent place in our hearts and affections; unlike a traveller at an inn, who turneth aside to tarry for a night; or the temporary residence of a visitor. It must not be a traveller or a mere guest, but an inhabitant; one taking up his abode there; and it must not be its resting-place only, but its dwelling-place. It must be its house; not its summer-house only, or its winter-house; but its *only* house. It must dwell in you. "If," says the Saviour, "If ye abide in Me, and My words abide in you, ye shall ask what ye will, and it shall be done unto you." "And," says John, "the anointing which ye have received of Him, abideth in you, and ye need not that any man teach you; but as the same anointing teacheth you all things, and is truth, and is no lie, and even as it hath taught you, ye shall abide in Him."

Then, thirdly, the Apostle would have the word of Christ dwell in us *richly*, that is, abundantly or plenteously, as some read it. Let it occupy the largest room in the house, and not a small upper story or attic. The word of Christ should be found in all the powers of the soul; it should be found in the understanding, in the will, in the conscience, and in the affections. It cannot dwell in you richly unless it dwell in you in all its parts. "Every word of God is pure," and "all scripture is given by inspiration of God, and is profitable for doctrine, for reproof, for correction, for instruction in righteousness, that the man of God may be perfect, thoroughly furnished unto every good work." "Whatsoever things were written aforetime were written for our learning, that we through patience and comfort of the scriptures might have hope." There are some who confine their views to one particular doctrine, or to a few familiar phrases, or to some creed or system drawn up by fallible men, but the Apostle prays for these Colossians that they may be "filled with the knowledge of His will in all wisdom and spiritual understanding; that they might walk worthy of the Lord unto all pleasing, being faithful in every good work and increasing in the knowledge of God." And hear how Paul reproves the Hebrews for the slender knowledge they had: "When for a time," says he, "ye ought to be teachers, ye have need that one teach you again which be the first principles of the oracles of God; and are become such as have need of milk and not of strong meat, for every one that useth milk is unskilful in the word of righteousness; for he is a babe. But strong meat belongeth to them that are of full age, even those who by reason of use have their senses exercised to discern both good and evil." And hear therefore what he adds in the commencement of the next chapter. "Therefore leaving the principles of the doctrine of Christ, let us go on unto perfection"—perfection of knowledge—"not laying again the foundation of repentance from dead works, and of faith towards God, of the doctrine of baptisms, and of laying on of hands, and of resurrection from the dead, and of eternal judgment."

Then, fourthly, the Apostle would have the "word of Christ dwell in us richly in all *wisdom*." A man may have a large fortune and yet not know how to employ it; he may have much learning, and yet play the fool. Some have a considerable stock of scriptural knowledge, and yet not know how to use it. But Oh, to know how to use this book well, which we cannot do unless we properly apply its various parts to their respective states. Some condemn themselves while reading or hearing those portions which ought to comfort them; and some comfort themselves by parts which ought to condemn them. We ought to learn how to harmonize doctrine and practice, commands and promises, duty and privilege, justification and sanctification.

It cannot dwell in us richly unless we can distinguish things that differ, and regulate the degree of our attention from the importance of the subject, and, unless we are principally concerned by perusing it, to learn the way of salvation, for this is its grand purpose. The things recorded in the scriptures are written "that ye might believe that Jesus is the Christ the Son of God; and that believing ye might have life through His name."

It cannot dwell in us richly in all wisdom, unless we make it the man of our counsel; unless we make it a lamp to our feet and a light unto our path, and regulate our conduct by it in all the relations and circumstances of life.

So much for the second part, namely, the manner in which we are to regard this subject.

III. Let us now consider THE MOTIVES WHICH SHOULD EXCITE US TO REGARD IT. These are various; we will make a selection of four, and

First, because it is the *command of God.* We are commanded by God to "take the sword of the Spirit, which is the Word of God." The Saviour said "Search the scriptures; they are they which testify of me." Now see how far this authority extends. Moses addresses the whole body of the Jewish people thus, "These words which I command thee this day shall be in thine heart, and thou shalt teach them diligently unto thy children, and shalt talk of them when thou sittest in thine house, and when thou walkest by the way, and when thou liest down, and when thou risest up. And thou shalt bind them for a sign upon thine hand, and they shall be as frontlets between thine eyes. And thou shalt write them upon the parts of thine house and on thy gates." Hear how the Lord addresses Joshua, the leader and commander of Israel, as he was entering the promised land, "This book of the law shall not depart out of thy mouth; but thou shalt meditate therein day and night, that thou mayest observe to do according to all that is written therein; for then thou shalt make thy way prosperous, and then thou shalt have good success." Let us hear what the king was to do, when he was to sit upon the throne of Israel. "And it shall be," says God, "when he sitteth upon the throne of his kingdom, that he shall write him a copy of this law in a book, and it shall be with him, and he shall read therein all the days of his life, that he may learn to fear the Lord his God, to keep all the words of this law, and these statutes to do them; that his heart be lifted up above his brethren; and that he turn not aside from His commandment to the right hand or to the left; to the end that he may prolong his days in his kingdom, he and his children, in the midst of Israel." Here, now, is an authority from which there is no appeal. We see station would not exempt him from the obligation. God commands, and commands it not from a principle of sovereignty, but from a regard to our own welfare; not because He would rule, but because He loves us, and is concerned in our spiritual and everlasting welfare.

Secondly, *because it is the word of Christ.* With what eagerness do you peruse a book written by, or that might treat of, an eminent and distinguished individual! Here we have a volume which contains the life and sayings of the most wonderful and most lovely Being in the universe. If you are the subject of true religion, you will love Christ supremely, and will esteem the words of His mouth more than your necessary food; and if the word of Christ dwell in you richly in all wisdom, you will love everything that belongs to Christ. You will love the Sabbath because it is the Lord's day; you will love the sanctuary, because it is the place where His honour dwelleth; you will love His people, because they are His followers; you will love His ministers, because they are the servants of the Most High God, who show unto men the way of salvation; and you will love the Scripture because it is the word of Christ; the word of Him who loves you and gave Himself for you, who ever liveth to make intercession for us, and who is making all things to work together for our good. Justin says: "I have lost all relish for the sciences, because I could not find in them anything of Jesus." But here we find it—

> "Here my Redeemer's face I see,
> And read His love, who died for me."

Here is the field of which our Saviour speaks, and happy is he who goeth and "selleth all that he hath and buyeth that field." Oh, that with the apostle you may say: "I am determined to know nothing among men, save Jesus Christ and Him crucified." "Which things," says Peter, "the angels desire to look into."

Thirdly, *the estimation by which it is held by good men.* The godly are always distinguished by their love for the Scriptures of truth. Inspiration describes them as such: "Blessed is the man that walketh not in the counsel of the ungodly, nor standeth in the way of sinners, nor sitteth in the seat of the scornful. But his delight is in the law of the Lord, and in His law doth he meditate day and night." Hear Job: "I have esteemed the words of Thy mouth more than my necessary food." Hear the weeping prophet: "I found Thy word, and I did eat it: and Thy word was unto me the joy and the rejoicing of my heart." And, oh, how does David express himself! "More to be desired are they than gold, yea, than much fine gold; sweeter also than honey and the honeycomb. Oh, how love I Thy law; it is my meditation all the day." What said Mrs. Savage? "I prefer one page of the Sacred Scriptures to all other writings beside." Said Judge Hall, "If I leave my house before I have perused some portion of God's word, nothing ever goes well with me all the day." And we have read of a husbandman who gave a whole load of hay for one leaf of the Epistles. Oh, let us go forth by the footsteps of the flock; let us be followers of those who through faith and patience are now inheriting the promises.

The fourth shall be taken from *the advantages derived therefrom*, compared with the works of men. "By the word of Thy lips I have kept me from the paths of the destroyer. The entrance of Thy word giveth life; it giveth understanding to the simple."

You shall be preserved from being carried about by every wind of doctrine; you shall have your heart established with grace; and he that believeth hath the witness in himself. What do you think of pleasure? What says Young? "Retire and read thy Bible, and be gay." This is what David did. "I will delight myself in Thy statutes; I will not forget Thy law. Thy testimonies are my delight and my counsellors; I have made Thy statutes my song in the house of my pilgrimage." And again, "I will delight myself in Thy commandments which I have loved." Or do you value your mercies? You are passing through a vale of tears, and man is born to trouble as the sparks fly upward. And you, awakened and convinced sinner, how did you obtain relief from a burden too heavy for you to bear? What was it that freed you from tormenting fear? You were enabled to flee for refuge, to lay hold upon the hope set before you in the Gospel. And what placed it within your reach, but this blessed book? Oh, may it dwell in you richly in all wisdom!

Mr. Jay's observations under the fourth head of this discourse have, unfortunately, not been preserved.

XI.

CHRIST'S MISSION.

(Preached on the 25th of December, 1848.)

"*This is a faithful saying, and worthy of all acceptation, that Christ Jesus came into the world to save sinners.*"—1 TIMOTHY i. 15.

MUCH of the wisdom of the ancients was wrapt up in a single sentence which could easily be remembered and easily repeated. Each of the wise men of Greece was distinguished by some remarkable expression. That which pierces must be pointed. It is difficult to remember a loose statement. Long paragraphs and consecutives generally fail in regard to the mass of hearers and readers. God, therefore, has not delivered the scriptures to us in the form of a system. What would the poor and common people do with a huge volume or body of divinity like those of the schools? The Gospel was a very plain and familiar thing before philosophy was brought in to aid the Christian learner, and while the people were satisfied with the words which the Holy Ghost used without anything human, and before those vain janglings arose in the Church which have gendered so much bad temper, and wasted so much precious time.

Much of the teaching of our Saviour consisted in particular sayings. Hence we read, "He that hath these sayings of mine:" "He that keepeth these sayings of mine shall never see death." You may have observed that in some such way as this the common people frequently express themselves; "as the saying is," &c. This was the case with the first Christians, and they diffused the principles of the Gospel in a kind of proverbial phraseology. I could easily refer to various instances. Thus they said one to another, "It is a faithful saying, brother, for if we be dead with Him, we should also live with Him." "If we suffer, we shall also reign with Him; if we deny Him, He will also deny us." "If we believe not, yet He abideth faithful; He cannot deny Himself." "For bodily exercise," as the saying is, "profiteth little, but godliness is profitable unto all things, having promise of the life that now is and of that which is to come." "This is a faithful saying, and worthy of all acceptation." No wonder therefore that the words of our text should have become in time one of the common sayings, that in their walks, at their work, and at their meals, at their meetings, and at their partings, through life and in death, they were heard saying, "It is indeed a faithful saying, and worthy of all acceptation, that Jesus Christ came into the world to save sinners."

Perhaps there are no words so commonly employed at this season as the words I have now read; but you see I have not declined them on this account. Yea, I have rather *chosen* them on this account. There is nothing I dislike so much as the affectation of novelties. Human sciences are continually receiving fresh accessions of discovery; but Christianity is a Divine testimony, to which nothing is to be added. It was complete long ago, and Jesus was the finisher as well as the author of your faith.

Let us consider three things. First, the subject of this saying; secondly, the truth of this saying; and thirdly, the excellency of it.

I. Let us notice THE SUBJECT OF THIS SAYING.

This includes two things—His advent, and His design. "Christ Jesus came into the world to save sinners."

First, *His Advent*, "He came into the world." Sometimes He is spoken of as being sent into the world, but here He is said to *come*, for though in the economy of salvation He was sent and was given of the Father, this did not invalidate His independency and voluntariness. Therefore we read, "He loved us, and gave Himself for us." And here, "He *came* into the world to save sinners." Therefore we read, "He who was rich for our sakes became poor." But how did He become so? How was this accomplished? By accident or by compulsion? No: "He made Himself of no reputation; He took upon Him the form of a servant, He humbled Himself, and became in fashion a man, and became obedient to death, even the death of the cross."

"He came into the world." He had come into the world long before, and He frequently appeared in human form; for He rejoiced in the habitable parts of His earth, and His delights were with the sons of men. At last, He came in the flesh. "The Word was made flesh, and dwelt among us, and we beheld His glory, the glory of the only begotten of the Father, full of grace and truth," walking up and down this earth in all the sinless attributes and infirmities of human nature.

"He came into the world." Others had come into the world before Him, but they had no existence before; but "*His* goings forth were from of old, from everlasting! They came according to the course of nature, but here we behold a new thing in the earth, for "Unto us a child is born, unto us a Son is given, and the government shall be upon His shoulders;" and "His name shall be called Immanuel, God with us." They were shapen in iniquity and in sin did their mothers conceive them; but He was the Holy One and the Just. He did no sin, neither was guile found in his mouth. At their birth, even in their highest ranks, all things went on as they were; but when He, the desire of all nations, came into the world, God shakes the heaven and the earth, and the sea and the dry land, and all nations; and a new star guides the Eastern sages to the places where He was; the angel of the Lord appeared to the shepherds and said, "Behold, we bring you glad tidings of great joy which shall be to all people. And a multitude of the heavenly host appeared, praising God, and saying, Glory to God in the highest and on earth peace and good will towards men."

Secondly, we have *His design.* "He came into the world to save sinners." Another Being had come into the world. He entered it very early. He walked about in Paradise in search of his victims there, and he found them, alas! for he came to traduce, and to corrupt, and to destroy, for he was a murderer from the beginning, and abode not in the truth. "But," says Jesus, "The Son of Man came to seek and to save that which was lost." "I am come that they might have life, and that they might have it more abundantly." "For this purpose the Son of Man came into the world, that He might destroy the works of the devil."

"Thy hands, dear Jesus, were not arm'd
With a revengeful rod;
No hard commission, to perform
The vengeance of a God."

He might have come to smite the world with a curse, but "He came not to condemn the world, but that the world through Him might be saved."

The question is, how this was to be accomplished by the Saviour? We answer immediately, not only or principally by His doctrine and His example. We readily allow He was a teacher. "For this end," says He, "was I born; and for this purpose came I into the world, that I might bear witness unto the truth." And He was an example. "He that saith He abideth in Him ought himself also to walk even as He walked."

But, my brethren, this does not reach the main thing. The Son of Man came to give His life a ransom for many, and to bear our sins in His own Body on the tree; to bring in everlasting righteousness, and to be a propitiation for their sins. And, therefore, in Him we have redemption through His blood, even the forgiveness of sins; and therefore through Him we have received the atonement. Hence, He said, when He expired upon the cross, "It is finished!" And it was then finished. But *what* was then finished? The purchase of this Salvation only. How then is it applied? We are reconciled unto God by the death of His Son; but, as the Apostle says, "We are saved by His life." What He procured for us on the cross is communicated to us on the throne. He is now at the right hand of God "to give repentance to Israel," as well as the forgiveness of sins. We are now saved "by the washing of regeneration and the renewing of the Holy Ghost." And "if *any* man"—for there is no exception—"if any man be in Christ Jesus, he is a new creature. Old things are passed away: behold all things are become new," that is, in measure and degree. His understanding, therefore, which was once darkness, is now light in the Lord; his conscience, which was before defiled, is now purged from dead works to serve the living God; his will now bows to the authority of God in His commands and in His prohibitions; his affections are now set upon things which are above; and his conversation is in heaven. The grace of God, which bringeth salvation, teaches him that, denying ungodliness and worldly lusts, he should live soberly, righteously, and godly, in this present evil world.

The work, indeed, is not complete. While here, the believer sees but in part; he is sanctified but in part; he enjoys but in part; he groans under a burden of natural and moral infirmities. And is this all the Saviour came down from heaven to accomplish for him? Oh, no! In due time He will perfect that which concerneth him. Oh, no! At death He receives his soul to heaven; He joins it with the spirits of the just made perfect. At the Resurrection He changes his vile body that it may be fashioned like unto His own glorious body; and at the Judgment of the last day, He says, "Come, ye blessed of My Father, inherit the kingdom prepared for you from the foundation of the world."

This, my brethren, was the design of His coming into the world: it was to save sinners; and it should remind us of five things.

It should remind us, first, of *the value of Salvation.* You can read and hear of it without emotion; you can neglect so great Salvation; you can sacrifice it, though it is so great, for worldly interests, for momentary gratification, or for the love of honour. Were we to judge of it by your conduct, we should consider it a thing of nought. It is well He did not estimate Salvation as you do! It is well He deemed it worthy of His incarnation, and to procure which He despised the shame, and endured so much suffering and privation. And was it a trifle, do you imagine, that induced Him to descend from the throne to the cross, and again to ascend from the cross to the throne? It was to save thy soul.

Secondly, It should remind you of *the difficulty of salvation.* You have low views of the evil of sin, of the excellency of holiness and of righteousness, and are therefore little struck with the difficulties that stood in the way of our salvation. But God does nothing in vain. The vastness of the preparation serves to show us the magnitude of His design, and the expansiveness of the remedy proves the desperateness of the disease. What! in order to save you must He be born of a woman, must He be laid in a manger, must He be for thirty-three years a man of sorrows and acquainted with grief? Must He agonize in the garden and on the cross, and enter the lower parts of the earth? Why could not an inferior personage accomplish this, as well as God's only begotten Son? and why not He in some other way? Why could He not deliver you from the bondage of corruption, as He did deliver the Jews from Egyptian bondage; that is, by a high hand and by an outstretched arm? When He made the world He spake and it was done; he commanded, and it stood fast. He made it at the expense of His breath; he redeemed it at the expense of His precious blood!

Thirdly, It should remind you of *the success of the undertaking.* He came into the world to save sinners, and He will "not fail nor be discouraged before He have set judgment in the earth, and the isles shall wait for His law." He will not expose Himself to the reproach "This man began to build and was not able to finish." *No;* He will not leave the work unaccomplished. *No;* He is mighty to save; able to save to the uttermost all who come unto God by Him. Every believer therefore may say with Paul, "I know whom I have believed, and that He is able to keep that which I have committed unto Him against that day." I know His blood was not shed in vain. Is not His righteousness all-sufficient to justify even the ungodly? Is not His Spirit able to take you from the ruins of the fall, and to make you an eternal excellency, the joy of all generations? What did He in the days of His flesh? What wonders He performed on the bodies of man; and if in the natural world, much more in the spiritual world, He opens the eyes of the blind, He makes the deaf to hear, and the dumb to speak, and the dead to live.

Fourthly, It should *encourage your hope.* If He came into the world to save sinners, you may be assured when you go to Him for that very purpose He will not refuse you; if you go and say, Lord I am willing that this heart should be renewed, O save me and work in me to will and to do of Thy good pleasure, and may the Redeemer see of the travail of His soul and be satisfied.

Lastly. It should *excite your emulation.* You should be concerned to resemble Him who came into the world to save sinners. And be you anxious to save. "*We cannot* save." I know you cannot save meritoriously, or efficiently, but you may save instrumentally. Therefore James says, "Brethren, if any of you do err from the truth, and one convert him, let him know that he which converteth the sinner from the error of his way shall save a soul from death and shall hide a multitude of sins." *Fathers*, have you no children to save? Masters, have you no servants to save? Neighbours, have you no neighbours to save? Friends, have you no friends to save?

What should influence you in a cause like this, so much as the example of Him who came into the world for this very purpose—to seek and to save that which was lost? O, what a work for you to be honoured with, and for you to be engaged in. Whose birthday do you suppose is kept in the courts of heaven? A Wellington's or a Whitfield's? A Nero's or a Howard's? "Verily I say unto you, There is joy in the presence of the Angels of God over one sinner that repenteth.

"Then Satan hath a captive lost, and Christ a subject born."

II. We proceed to consider THE TRUTH OF THIS SAYING.

Half the sayings we hear are wholly or partially falsehood; so I consider. Is it true then that Jesus Christ came into the world to save sinners? It is true "It is a faithful saying?" And here we shall have to do with two classes of persons; to bring forward the subject to encourage the believer, and to oppose the disbelief of the infidel.

We first seek to encourage the believer. We call not upon you to follow cunningly devised fables. No doctrine has a higher authority than the testimony of God. "If we receive the testimony of man the testimony of God is greater." O, you say, we admit this. We acknowledge that this is stated in the Scriptures. But are the Scriptures true? You are ready to say with the tempter of old, "We know you say it as a creature and professor of religion; but hath God said it? We know it is said in your book; but is that book true?" Now in answer to this I observe you cannot deny but that this may possibly be true. Yes, you often feel, much oftener than you allow, that it may *probably* be true, hence your anxiousness of mind, hence your endeavour to make proselytes that you may support your poor tottering faith. But we come forward and say, *Is this true?* And where then is certainty? Where are we? Why, in company with the best of men who have washed their robes and made them white in the blood of the Lamb; in company with the greatest of men, well qualified to judge, who have employed all their capacity to judge. We can appeal to prophecies, many of which have been accomplished, and others are evidently fulfilling. We can appeal to miracles performed before *enemies themselves.* We can refer to the progress of Christianity by means inadequate to its promulgation if alone without a Divine agency. We can appeal to the suitability and harmony of the doctrines of revelation; we might point you to the benevolence, the morality, and exalted character Christianity has produced in those who have embraced it and adhered to the precepts of the Scriptures, whether we consider it individually or socially.

"Hence and for ever from my heart
I bid my fears and doubts depart;
And to His hands my soul resign,
Which bear credentials so Divine."

But we must oppose it also to the unbelief of the sceptic. There are objections much greater than those bandied about in coffee-houses, or those published by the workers of iniquity.

These do not get near enough to view it: but look at the man smarting under a sense of his guilt, who sees the wrath of God coming upon him, who asks in anxiety and earnestness, "What must I do to be saved?" who feels the need of the salvation there is in Christ, and who is assured there is salvation in no other. But all this for the time produces a kind of incredulity, such as it is said of the disciples. "They believed not for joy." O, says he, my unworthiness, and the number and the nature of my sins! There *is* salvation, but is there salvation for me? Now my brethren, before he ventures here, he requires evidence, full evidence, clear evidence, to venture *his eternal* all! and such evidence as he requires we can furnish. Our Saviour hath declared, "My Father worketh hitherto, and I work. The works that I do in My Father's name, they bear witness of Me. Believe Me that I am in the Father, and the Father in Me, or else believe Me for the very works' sake." Hence we come forward with invitations and promises of His Word, and say, these are not to deceive your hopes or entrap your confidence. If these things were not so, we should have told you. He is too good, as well as too great, to deceive you. Suppose after a prince had proclaimed pardon to all those who should submit themselves, a rebel should come and bow at his feet, and he should have him hanged! What a disgrace this would be, though he might have *deserved* his doom. My brethren, there is nothing by which you can honour God so much as by your confidence. What would you think of a man, if a dove were to fly into his bosom for protection from a hawk, he were to take advantage of the circumstance by depriving it of its life? What a disgrace to humanity. Why, the Saviour desires sinners to come unto Him, and O, how many have found life and liberty, and every kind of blessing, by applying to Him. They therefore can bear witness that it is a true saying. How many can say, We repaired to Him, and He received us graciously; we applied to Him, and He freed us from our burden, He supplied all our need; He sympathized with us under a sense of all our troubles; we have never called upon Him in vain. O, that you would make the trial yourselves, and you would soon enjoy the same blessing. "We have the witness in ourselves, and those things which we have seen and heard declare we unto you, that ye also may have fellowship with us; and truly our fellowship is with the Father, and with His Son Jesus Christ."

Well, we have seen the subject of this saying, and considered the truth of it.

III. Let us observe THE EXCELLENCY OF IT. For, my

brethren everything important *must* be true, but everything true is *not* important. This saying *is* important; it is most excellent. As it is a *faithful* saying so it is *worthy of all acceptation*. O how it harmonizes the Divine perfections and displays them! O how it brings glory to God in the highest! O how it publishes peace on earth and goodwill towards men! O how it shows to us the things freely given to us of God! It comes and resolves what reason has failed to resolve, and concerning which all philosophy is dumb, and furnishes in answer to the question, "How shall I come before the Lord, and bow my knees before the high God?" and cries, "Behold the Lamb of God which taketh away the sin of the world." O my brethren, it is just such a truth as you and I want. It tells us that which we wanted to know, that there is a mighty, a willing, an all-sufficient Saviour, "whose heart is made of tenderness, whose bowels melt with love." Yes, here we have it. There are many things which are possible in the acquisition and yet useless in the possession. There are many studies for mere amusement: they do not make the man *truly wise*, or "*wise unto salvation*." Yes, Solomon says, "In much wisdom there is much grief; and he that increaseth knowledge increaseth sorrow." But here we find knowledge and happiness combined. "Blessed are the people who know the joyful sound. In Thy name shall they rejoice all the day and in Thy favour shall they be exalted." What is practical knowledge compared to the knowledge of our Lord Jesus Christ? Why, *society will soon be broken up!* and we shall want no Statesman, or Counsellor or Magistrate in our land. What is the knowledge of the world, the knowledge of the arts and sciences, and of various languages? for, "whether there be tongues they shall cease; whether there be knowledge it shall vanish away." And it is an affecting thought, that so much of that knowledge which often costs so much to acquire, and often at the expense of one's health, will soon be of no avail. "For what is your life? it is even a vapour which appeareth but for a little time, and then vanisheth away."

O my dear hearers, What is the body to the soul? What is time to eternity? But the Gospel comes and fixes its residence in the soul of man and blesses him there with all spiritual blessings in heavenly places; and exerts its influence through an immensity of ages! therefore it is worthy of all acceptation.

Then, as it is worthy of all *manner* of acceptation, so it is worthy to be received *with the firmest conviction*, with the deepest reverence, with the highest admiration, with the devoutest affection, with the warmest gratitude, and with the utmost exaltation and rapture!

It is worthy of all acceptation, that is, it is worthy of the acceptation of all, and so it was formerly rendered, whether Jew or Greek, Barbarian, Scythian, bond or free, it is worthy the acceptation of all.

> "'Tis not confined to sex or age,
> The lofty or the low."

It is worthy of all men to be received. Kings are out of my address this morning, or I would say, O see how your throne shakes. I see none more exposed than yourselves. Remember you are only men. You see all is vanity and vexation of spirit. "Be wise now, therefore, O ye kings; be instructed ye judges of the earth. Kiss the Son lest He be angry, and ye perish from the way when His wrath is kindled but a little; blessed are all they that put their trust in Him." But the kings are not within my reach: there are many we may address this morning, and O let me beseech you to hear, to read, to accept, and to realise this faithful saying and worthy of all acceptation as *true.* It recommends itself to your understanding, to your judgment, and to your will. It claims your acceptance if you are wise. It demands your acceptance if you would be happy.

Receive it, ye *vilest of the vile;* you have gone far; but in His bosom and in His heart there is yet room for such as you!

Receive it, ye *moral and self-righteous*; you need a better righteousness than your own, and without it you cannot appear with acceptance before God.

Receive it, ye *learned;* it will scatter all your remaining ignorance and make you the children of the light and of the day.

Receive it, ye *poor;* it will sanctify all your poverty and bless your labour and your toil.

Receive it, ye *rich;* it will sanctify all your riches and preserve you from making gold your trust and fine gold your confidence, and you will become rich in faith and heirs of the kingdom.

Receive it, ye *old;* it is time, high time, to awake out of sleep but, blessed be God, it is not too late even for you, and then at eventime it shall be light.

Receive it, ye *young;* it will save you from many a snare; it will turn your feet into the path of peace, it will prepare you for life or for an early grave. O how often have you been reminded that youth is no preservative from an early grave;

and how often have you been told that true religion will prepare you for all your trials if your lives are spared; and when time shall snow upon your heads, your grey hairs will be a crown of glory, and God looking back upon your former services will kindly say: "I remember thee, the kindness of thy youth, when thou wentest after me in the wilderness."

And *O ye dear children*, receive it and He will take you up in His arms and say, "Suffer little children to come unto me, for of such is the kingdom of heaven." "I love them that love me, and those that seek me early shall find me."

Thus it is "worthy of all acceptation," or worthy the acceptation of all. Then *how privileged are you* who live in this land of light and liberty, where this truth is perpetually presented to your eyes and your ears in the preaching of the Gospel.

> "How blessed are your eyes
>   That see this heavenly light,
> Which kings and prophets waited for
>   And died without the sight;
> How blessed are your ears,
>   That hear this Gospel sound;
> Which kings and prophets waited for
>   And sought but never found."

"How blessed are your eyes for they see, and your ears for they hear!" *or else* how inexcusable will it be if *you* perish! Is there not a Saviour provided? are you not informed of everything concerning Him? In vain you talk of your *weakness* while He says, "My grace is sufficient for you." And why should you question whether He is *willing* to save you while He cries "Come unto me all ye that are weary and heavy laden and I will give you rest." The question is not whether you can save yourselves; we know this is impossible; but will you come to Him, who is waiting to receive you and exalted to have mercy upon you. From whence will your destruction arise if you perish? Be not deceived, you will be *suicides*. You will be charged with the murder of yourselves! Ye will not, says the Saviour, come unto me that ye might have life. How often would I have gathered your children together, as a hen gathereth her brood under her wings; but ye would not.

Have you, my dear hearers, accepted this faithful saying so *worthy* of *all* acceptation? Is it lodged in the recesses of your souls? Is it pervading every thought and power of your minds? Is it operating upon your lives? Have you welcomed the

Saviour this morning, and said with the Church of old "Lo, this is our God, we have waited for Him and He will save us. This is the Lord, we have waited for Him; He will be glad and rejoice in His salvation." Then, rejoice in the Lord always, and again I say rejoice.

Men, brethren and fathers. We have been looking backward: we may now look forward. "Once in the end of the world hath He appeared to put away sin by the sacrifice of Himself: and as it is appointed unto men once to die but after this the judgment, so Christ was once offered to bear the sins of many; and unto them that look for Him shall he appear the second time without sin unto salvation." *Lord prepare us for that interview!*—Amen.

XII.

THE PURPOSE OF THE INCARNATION AND DEATH OF CHRIST.

(Preached on Good Friday, March 21st, 1845.)

"*Forasmuch, then, as the children are partakers of flesh and blood, He also Himself likewise took part of the same; that through death He might destroy him that had the power of death, that is, the devil; and deliver them who through fear of death were all their lifetime subject to bondage.*"—HEBREWS ii. 14, 15.

WE acknowledge but one day of divine appointment, and which is binding upon the conscience. This is the Lord's day. All other sacred days are human ordinances; and as they are not of divine appointment, we are reminded of the language of the Apostle, "Let every man be fully persuaded in his own mind. One man esteemeth one day above another; another esteemeth every day alike. He that regardeth the day, regardeth it unto the Lord; and he that regardeth not the day, to the Lord he doth not regard it."

But in the words of our text, I have read three things worthy your attention, not only on Good Friday, but on every day throughout the year. The reality of Christ's incarnation; the victory of His death; and the redemption of His people.

I. THE REALITY OF HIS INCARNATION. "Forasmuch as the children are partakers of flesh and blood, He Himself also took part of the same."

Humanity, you see, is here expressed by "flesh and blood." To His humanity John frequently refers in his Gospel. "He grew in wisdom and in stature." "He hungered" and "was athirst." "He groaned," and felt our aversion to pain, and prayed, "Father, if it be possible, let this cup pass from me." But we observe He was made only "in the *likeness* of sinful flesh;" though He was made in all points like unto us, it is added, "yet without sin." "He was manifest to take away our sins, but in Him was no sin." He is therefore called "the Holy One, and the Just." As Cowper says—

> "He who doth for sin atone,
> Must have no failings of his own."

"He took part of the same" *supernaturally*. In this He is very distinguishable from every other partaker. "He was made flesh and dwelt among us." "He was made of a woman;" a body was prepared for Him. The Angel said, "A virgin shall conceive, and bear a son; and they shall call His name Immanuel, which being interpreted is, God with us." There were no attendants waiting to welcome Him when He came, no palace for His reception. He was born in a stable, and laid in a manger. He had no title to any earthly distinction. "He was despised and rejected of men." "The foxes have holes, and the birds of the air have nests, but the Son of Man hath not where to lay His head."

He also partook of this *voluntarily*. The very language implies this. "He also Himself *took* part of the same." In the economy of salvation it is said, "God *sent* His Son," and He is spoken of as being given; but this is not incompatible with His choice. He therefore is said to have "come to seek and to save that which was lost." "He loved us, and gave Himself for us." We are therefore told that "He who was rich, for our sakes *became* poor, that we, through His poverty, might become rich;" that "He who was in the form of God, and thought it no robbery to be equal with God, *made Himself* of no reputation," and "*became* obedient unto death, even the death of the Cross." Nor was He at all beguiled into an undertaking of which He afterwards repented. All He was to do and suffer was spread out before Him; He viewed it all, and acquiesced in it, not with reluctance, for He said, "Lo, I come to do Thy will, O God." "Thy law is within my heart." And as the hour of suffering approached He said, "I have a baptism to be baptized with, and how am I straitened till it be accomplished!"

But we observe the ground of this partaking of flesh and blood. It was necessary that He who came to save sinners should have the same nature as they. "Therefore," says the Apostle, "Forasmuch then as the children are partakers of flesh and blood, He also Himself took part of the same." "For, verily, He took not on Him the nature of angels; but He took on Him the seed of Abraham. Therefore, in all things it behoved Him to be made like unto His brethren, that He might be a merciful and faithful High Priest, in things pertaining to God, to make reconciliation for the sins of the people."

This is the great mystery of godliness, and there is very little godliness where it is denied or concealed. And it is not only a great mystery, but a mystery without controversy. The importance of it may be inferred from the expression of Paul to the Hebrews, wherein he says, "Having therefore boldness to enter into the holy of holies, by the blood of Jesus, by a new and living way which He hath consecrated for us, through the vail, that is to say, His flesh"—namely, through His humanity and incarnation. Without this, even as a Teacher, His terror would have made us afraid, and we should have felt as the Jews did when they heard the thunder, and said to Moses, "Speak thou to us; but let not God speak to us, lest we die." This aids us in our apprehensions of Him, and in our approaches to Him. His greatness would otherwise overpower us. How can you draw near to Him who is infinite? But His humanity is a temple in which we can worship Him, for "in Him dwelleth all the fulness of the Godhead bodily." Here is something we can reach; something we can fix upon; something that can soften down the effulgence of the divine throne. Here is a medium between God and us.

By assuming our nature, He also became our example: a perfect example, which He could not have been without this. Without this He could not have gone before us in the performance of those duties which imply reverence, subjection, obedience, and suffering; whereas now He goes before us in all this, and as He is, so are we in this world. Unless He had been made a partaker of our nature, He could not have sympathized with us under our woes and sorrows, whereas now "He is touched with the feeling of our infirmities." Above all, without this He could not have "borne our griefs and carried our sorrows." We were under the curse, and therefore to redeem us from the curse of the law, He was made a curse for us. We were exposed to death, and therefore as our Substitute, "He once suffered for our sins, the Just for the unjust, that He might bring us unto God." As Divine, He could not suffer and die; but as human, He could. Therefore it is said, He purchased the Church with His own blood.

II. We are told of THE VICTORY OF HIS CROSS. "That through death He might destroy him that had the power of death, that is, the devil."

Here we see that the Saviour assumed our nature to suffer on our behalf, and to die. When they went to crucify Him, He went forward to meet them. His death, therefore, was not an accidental one, but it was designed. It was not subordinate, but supreme. Let us just glance at the victory.

We see here *the greatness of the foe.* A conqueror is to be judged of by the enemy he subdues. Because David conquered Goliath, and Saul only common men, the women sung, "Saul hath slain his thousands, but David his ten thousands." It is no easy thing to conquer such a foe as is here referred to, who had reigned from the beginning, and whose reign was as extensive as mortality itself. "He destroyed." Whom did He destroy?" "Him that had the power of death, that is the devil." Some tell us there is no such being! but how then is the Saviour described as having destroyed him? If you consider death temporally, he introduces it, for death is the effect of transgression, and of his temptation. Death is not, as some call it, a debt of nature, but a debt to the justice of God, and it was introduced through the instrumentality of this wicked one. He delights to see death in excesses, in war, in the effect of disease, and urges men in their career of drunkenness and bloodshed, in idleness, in lying much in bed, in everything that can keep people from living out half their days. Then if you consider death spiritually, he introduced this. Men are "dead in trespasses and sins." He feeds this death by every kind of depravity; and if we consider death eternal, he introduced this. He now reigns in the infernal regions, and he now exercises, upon the wicked here, the most oppressive, galling tyranny. God does not immediately punish sinners; but His wrath is in reserve for them, and let them remember that he who now tempts them will hereafter torment them. You serve him now, and he will be found a dreadful master, for "the wages of sin is death."

Then consider *the means of the Saviour's vanquishing this foe.* Is anything more unlikely than this? In itself it seemed his hour and the power of darkness; as, therefore, it drew on, he tempted Judas to betray Him, false witnesses to accuse Him, the high priest to arraign Him, and the multitude to call for His crucifixion, and Pilate to condemn Him. And after that He had been nailed to the tree, and buried in the tomb, "Now," says he, "I shall hear of Him no more; His cause is now ruined, and will perish." But, brethren, his triumph was short. 'Tis true, Satan, He has fallen, but in falling He has conquered! 'Tis true He died, but in dying He vanquished death! Yes, it was "through death He destroyed him that had the power of death, that is, the devil." How extraordinary! He destroyed him, not physically, but as to his influence; not by annihilation of him, but by the subjection of him. MacKnight renders it, "He dethroned, He deposed, He degraded him who had the power of death, that is, the devil." As the Apostle says, "He spoiled principalities and powers, making a show of them openly, and triumphing over them in it." "And now," said He Himself, as His hour approached, "now is the prince of this world cast out; and now when I am lifted up, the world shall change masters, for I will draw all men unto Me."

And all this was effected by taking away sin, for Satan's power is founded in sin. With regard to the people of God, the guilt of sin, and the dominion of it also, are done away by the sacrifice of Himself; and though the remains of sin are not immediately done away, they will be eventually and surely. The process begins in the soul and ends in the body. The soul is freed at death; the body is freed at the resurrection from all remains of sin. The Apostle says, "The body is dead because of sin, but the spirit is life because of righteousness;" "and if the spirit of Him who raised up Jesus dwell in you, He that raised up Christ from the dead, shall also quicken your mortal bodies, by His Spirit that dwelleth in you?" Then, "having borne the image of the earthy, you shall bear the image of the heavenly."

III. We come to consider THE REDEMPTION OF HIS PEOPLE. "And deliver them who through fear of death were all their lifetime subject to bondage."

It is worthy of observation that the period called by Isaiah "the acceptable year of the Lord," is called also "the day of vengeance of our God," and for a very good reason, for the overthrow of their enemy is the release of His people. The destruction of the tyrant is the rescue of his wretched vassals. Now, here a question arises of great importance, and relating to the experience of Christians. What does the Apostle intend by this deliverance? I venture to affirm that this deliverance from him who hath the power of death is a deliverance from his vassalage, from his wicked designs, and from his cruel power to injure them; the very thing the Apostle expresses when addressing the Colossians: "Who hath delivered us from the power of darkness, and hath translated us into the kingdom of His dear Son." This is it, and not only and "*principally the fear of death.*"

In proof of this we advance three reasons.

First, it would be a very inferior design. The "fear of death" is troublesome and trying, but it can only affect you for awhile as Christians. It does not affect your safety for ever; or at all. The deliverance therefore would be exceedingly limited and temporary, if this only were the design of the Saviour in His Incarnation.

Then, secondly, this end is not universally or generally fulfilled. When we come to look into the state of things, how few Christians comparatively are free from the existence of this fear! Which of them all is free from the liableness of it? And who is not subject to it all through life?

Therefore, thirdly, such exemption might alarm and affect many, who would be ready to say, "I cannot be the subject of this deliverance, because I often feel this fear of the king of terrors." He came to "deliver those who through fear of death are all their lifetime subject to bondage" is added, not to specify the evil from which they are delivered so much as to characterize the subjects of those who are interested in this deliverance, and who will soon have Satan buried under their feet. In some the fear of death is perfectly natural, or else the words, "in the day thou eateth thereof, thou shalt surely die" was not threatening. Our Saviour is spoken of in prophecy as being heard in that He feared. It is natural to feel an aversion to pain. If you saw the poisonous fang extracted from a serpent, and were persuaded that it was so, yet you might find it difficult to take it into your bosom, or even into your hand. Yes, there is a fear of death which arises from grace itself. Christians had not this once, and others have not it now. There are those who are seeking to drive it from them as long as possible, through ignorance, unbelief, business, amusements, and the bowl of intoxication; though these cannot remove the stroke, the reflection may be drowned for a time. And some have in a sense kept off the dread till the day of their death, so that they have no bonds in their death, and their strength is firm. But this is not the case with real Christians, they wish to consider the consequences of death, and see whether they have a title to heaven and a meetness for it.

There are many things from time to time which keep the believer in bondage and which render him subject to this fear of death. We do not applaud or recommend this subjection, and there is a provision made for the believer's deliverance. This is a great privilege which you should seek after, and if the *evil* of death be removed, well may the *fear* of it cease.

For what, Christian, is death to you? Can it harm you? Impossible. Cannot it in every way benefit you? Is not the curse turned into a blessing, and the enemy into a friend? Will not death be "gain" to you? Live, therefore, nearer to God and your evidences will be more clear and bright. "Set your affections on things above, not on things on the earth." Maintain a single and entire reliance on Him who died for you and rose again. Beware of a legal bias. Beware of looking after something in yourselves, instead of saying, "In the Lord have I righteousness and strength." Think more of Him who "hath abolished death, and brought life and immortality to light through the Gospel." Think more of Him who is "the resurrection and the life," who hath opened the kingdom of heaven to all believers, and who hath said, "If any man keep my sayings, he shall never see death." What! is he not mortal then? Yes, but then to him, dying is going home; it is to fall asleep; it is "to depart and to be with Christ which is far better." Death is so changed with regard to him, that it shall no longer go by that name.

Two things result from this subject. The one is, how should you remember the love of Jesus! We call friends benefactors. Ah, what a benefactor is He! What self-denial, what sacrifice, what sufferings did He experience for you! He took upon Him flesh and blood, "that through death He might destroy him that had the power of death." Say, therefore, with the Apostle, "the love of Christ constraineth us, because we thus judge that if one died for all, then were all dead, and that He died, that those who live should not henceforth live unto themselves but unto Him that died for them and rose again." And may you present your bodies as living sacrifices, holy, acceptable unto God, which is your reasonable service, saying, "What wilt Thou have me to do?"

The second is, we should estimate very highly the death of Christ. It was "to the Jews a stumbling block and to the Greeks foolishness." But can it be so to you, Christian? It ought to be everything to you; it *will* be everything to you if you are like-minded with Paul, who as a minister said, "I am determined to know nothing among you but Jesus Christ and Him crucified;" and who as a Christian said, "God forbid that I should glory save in the cross of our Lord Jesus Christ."

XIII.

THE UNCERTAINTY OF LIFE.

(Preached on Sunday Morning, December 30th, 1849.)

"*For that ye ought to say, If the Lord will, we shall live, and do this, or that.*"—JAMES iv. 15.

THE Bible, my brethren, gives us the wisest and sublimest view of every subject on which it treats; and of what subject important and interesting to our welfare does it not treat? Its aim, indeed, is not to amuse our minds by gratifying a vain curiosity and to furnish matter for criticism and vain disputation. Its grand message is the faithful saying worthy of all acceptation, "That Jesus Christ came into the world to save sinners;" that "He was delivered for our offences, and raised again for our justification;" and that "He ever liveth to make intercession for us." But it is also a proper directory of life. It is "a lamp unto our feet, and a light unto our faith." It shews what God requires of us in all the relations, conditions, and circumstances in which we are placed. We kneel before living oracles, and hear a voice, saying, "Whatsoever ye do in word or deed, do all in the name of the Lord Jesus." "So speak and do as those who will be judged by the perfect law of liberty;" and "let the words of my mouth, and the meditation of my heart, be acceptable in Thy sight, O Lord, my strength and my Redeemer." I love those general aphorisms and maxims with which the Bible so much abounds, which are of uuniversal application; which convince and strike as soon as proposed; which require no depth of understanding to comprehend, or strength of memory to retain.

One of these we have chosen for our improvement this morning: "Ye ought to say, If the Lord will, we shall live, and do this, or that." Now there is a difference between what we say and what we ought to say, an instance of which we have in the preceding verses, especially if we put their conduct into language. "Go to now, ye that say, To-day or to-morrow we will go into such a city, and continue there a year, and buy and sell, and get gain; whereas ye know not what shall be on the morrow. For what is your life? It is even a vapour that appeareth for a little while, and then vanisheth away." Here is language founded in entire regardlessness of Providence. You see how far it extends. They speak as if all were within the compass of their control, both as to the duration of life, and as to the success of their endeavours. First, as to the duration of life: "We will go into such a city, and continue there a year. We will arrange our affairs without difficulty; we will march off without accident, we will travel without injury, and will reach the place of our destination in safety; and all through the year we will have health of body, and a sound mind, and be able to pursue our plans." Secondly, As to the success of their endeavours: "We will buy and sell, and get gain. We will have no unfavourable season, no failure of crops, no unfaithful servants; we will have no treacherous friends; we will have no unprincipled customers; we will have no bad debts, no dear buyings or cheap sellings." Here you see the Apostle speaks of what they do say, but says he, "all such boasting is vain, and all such rejoicing is evil," for the events upon which life depends are uncertain. "Ye know not what shall be on the morrow. For what is your life? It is even a vapour that appeareth for a little time, and then vanisheth away." Then he tells us what we ought to say, "for that ye ought to say, If the Lord will, we shall live, and do this, or that." Let us consider *how* we ought to say this; and what the sentiment expresses or implies. These reflections will be appropriate, so near are we to the end of the old and the beginning of the new year. Consider what I say, and the Lord give you understanding in all things.

It may be necessary to consider HOW WE OUGHT TO SAY THIS. "If the Lord will, we shall live, and do this or that."

Now, are we always to use these very words, and confine ourselves in all our communication to this phraseology?

In answer to this, we may observe, first, that it is wise and well in us to accustom ourselves to holy and scriptural modes of speech. God demands the fruit of the lips. "Let no corrupt communication proceed out of your mouth, but that which is good to the use of edifying, that it may minister grace to the hearers." "Let your speech be always seasoned with salt." James is very express on this subject; he tells us, "If a man offend not in word, the same is a perfect man, and able also to bridle the whole body." And he says—O that you would reflect upon it—"If any man among you seem to be religious and bridleth not his tongue, but deceiveth his own heart, this man's religion is vain." The Saviour has said enough to make us shake from head to foot: "For every idle word that men shall speak, they shall give account thereof in the day of judgment; for by thy words thou shalt be justified and by thy words thou shalt be condemned." You would do well to observe how the servants of God recorded in the Scriptures were accustomed to express themselves. Moses said, "If Thy presence go not with us, carry us not up hence." Jacob: "And Jacob vowed a vow, saying, If God will be with me and keep me in this way that I go, and will give me bread to eat and raiment to put on, so that I come again to my father's house in peace, then shall the Lord be my God." Paul: "I will come to you shortly, if the Lord will."

We wish you to observe, secondly, that words are but air and not infallible proofs of sincerity. Mark what the sacred writers say. John: "Let us not love in word and tongue, but in deed and in truth." So James here says, "If a brother or sister be naked and destitute of daily food, and one of you *say* unto them, Depart in peace; *be ye* warmed, and *be ye* filled; notwithstanding ye give them not the things which be needful for the body, what doth it profit?" So says he again, "What doth it profit, my brethren, though a man say he hath faith, and have not works? can faith save him?"—that is, Can such faith save him? So it is here with regard to these words. There are some that use them thoughtlessly, and some from custom. My predecessor once gave notice from this desk, "There will be no service here on Wednesday, '*God willing.*'" So there are some who use these words sanctimoniously; they would appear more sanctified than others; they have religion at their tongues' end. And there are some good people who use the phrase "If the Lord will," in all their letters, and in all their advertisements, so as to make it almost nauseated by some, while it is turned into ridicule by others, so that their good is evil spoken of. Baxter, in his life of that most excellent character Judge Hale, says, "I feared for some time that he was wanting in evangelical experience. He spoke so little of his own religious views and feelings, pains and pleasures, conflicts and trials; but I was mistaken, and I soon found the reason was his having heard so much of the experience of persons who gave evidence of not being born from above and bound for glory." He heard so much of religious cant as to be driven into comparative silence. And I have known instances of the same kind with regard to others whose tempers and lives falsify all their language. Paul speaks of "vain talkers and deceivers." A friend of mine had been so injured by one of these talkative professors, who in all his devotions so upturned his eyes towards Heaven that you could only see the whites of them, "so that ever since," said he, "I have been afraid of these white-eyed professors." My dear brethren, in all cases the reality should surpass the appearance. It is worthy of observation, that when angels appeared, they always appeared less than they really were. They appeared in the form of men; but when Satan appeared, he would be greater than he really was; he transformed himself into an angel of light. It is worthy of observation, that in such language as this, "If the Lord will, we shall live, and do this or that," the heart should always keep the tongue under. It is better being under the impression of a principle, than always using the very words. If we are influenced by this principle, we may, without sinning, frequently omit the expression itself. Accordingly we observe that good men do not always utter them in the same way. It is enough if you find yourself in that state of faith and feeling which the language expresses and implies.

II. This leads us to consider, secondly, WHAT THE SENTIMENT REALLY CONTAINS when we say, "If the Lord will, we shall live, and do this or that." It contains, we apprehend, three things, and may be described three ways: dependence upon God, enquiry of God, and submission to God. Let us observe and review each of these.

First, the sentiment includes *dependence upon God,* and if you ask in what this dependence is to be shown, we answer in everything. We are not to promise ourselves anything without God's permission. We are not lords of our own lives, or our own actions, but depend upon Him whose sovereign providence extends over—what? over our lives, and over events.

"If the Lord will, we shall *live,*" and not otherwise. It does not depend upon enemies to shorten, or friends to lengthen the cords of life. "If the Lord will we shall live"; and this will be enough to spare us in the midst of the pestilence and the destruction that wasteth at noon-day.

"Dangers stand thick through all the ground,
 To push us to the tomb;
And fierce diseases wait around,
 To hurry mortals home."

But they cannot hurry us faster than the pleasure of God; and on the other hand, "If the Lord will that we should not live, it is in vain that youth be on our side, or strength be on our side, or usefulness be on our side, or a thousand connections. "He turneth man to destruction, and saith"—so easy is it to Him, "and saith" only—"Return, ye children of men;" and then "his breath goeth forth, he returneth to his earth, in that very day his thoughts perish." And wilt thou then, O vain man, lay out schemes for years, when thou art not sure of a week or of a day? If any of you could look into futurity, perhaps in the course of the approaching year you might see the grave opening before you, in which would be interred the fondest wishes of your heart.

That which condemns vain presumption serves also to show the vanity of man as to our fears and cares as to the future. I knew a man whose support depended upon an income, which was to leave him on such a day, and on the morning of that day he expired, and found the groundlessness of all his anxieties and apprehensions.

But we find it extending to events as well as our lives. Therefore, adds the Apostle, not only should we say, "If the Lord will, we shall live;" but, "we will *do* this and that." The success of all our endeavours depends upon His providence, and if what Dr. South says be true, "No man ever grew rich without asking his wife's leave," how much more true is it with regard to God! We may form our plans, but as Solomon says, "A man's heart deviseth his way, but the Lord directs his steps." You may think you have acted wisely, and, perhaps, you may have done so, but you cannot add efficiency; and you may avail yourself of means by which you may promise yourself success, but unlooked-for opposition, either by skill or force, may counteract all your endeavours. "The hand of the diligent maketh rich;" but God can paralyze that hand, so that it may forget its cunning. The deceiver as well as the deceived are as the smith that bloweth the coals in the fire. Frost is His; hail is His; drought is His; mildew is His. "The race is not to the swift, nor the battle to the strong, neither yet bread to the wise, nor yet riches to men of understanding, nor favour to men of skill, but time and chance happeneth to all."

Now, have you a project before you? You should do just as Abraham's servant did, when going in search of a wife for his master's son. "O, Lord God," said he, "send me good speed this day." You should make use of means. You should exercise prudence. You should imitate Jacob when he went to meet his brother Esau, who determined to destroy him. He did all that prudence could do, and when he had done all committed himself to God, saying, "Send now, O Lord, I beseech Thee, prosperity; deliver me, I pray Thee, from the hand of my brother, from Esau, for I fear him, lest he will come and smite me and the mother with the children; and Thou saidst I will surely do thee good, and make thy seed as the sand of the sea, which cannot be numbered for multitude." Or, if you prosper in the earth, you are to remember the language of Moses to the Jews, "Thou shalt remember the Lord thy God, for it is He that giveth thee power to get wealth." You are not to "sacrifice to your own net or burn incense to your own drag," as if by these your portion was made plenteous. Whatever be the degree of your prosperity and success, you will lose its sweetest relish if you do not remember it is "the blessing of the Lord that maketh rich, and He addeth no sorrow therewith."

So much for the first article, Dependence upon God.

The second thing is *enquiry of Him*, that is, enquiry whether it accords with His pleasure and our venturing upon nothing without asking counsel of Him: for whatever object you have in view, you are essentially wrong unless you preface it with, "If the Lord will, I shall live, and do this, or that." Oh, how many things would be dropped, if persons thought of appealing to God to know if He approved of them. For could you say, "If the Lord will, I shall go to the playhouse to-morrow, and retain my spirituality as much as ever." "If the Lord will, I shall attempt to deceive the dealer in such a transaction." "If the Lord will, I shall call at the house of such a friend, and calumniate and backbite my neighbour."

How does the matter stand with regard to your own feeling? Are you conscious you could not enter upon any course, if inconsistent with His will? Can you say, "Lord, is it Thy pleasure I should form such a connection? Is it Thy pleasure I should go to such a place? Is it Thy pleasure I should take such an office upon me;" and so of everything else. Is this your concern? Is this your sincere saying, or a mere vain pretence? There are some who, after they have come to a determination about a thing, say "Lord, I shall be much disappointed if Thou dost not answer me according to my wishes and desires." Others are afraid of the result, and would be afraid of the answer if they thought it would be an adverse one.

Then there are others who enquire, but make no distinction between God's permission and God's approbation; for God permits many things He does not approve of, and yet some judge of one by the other. Balaam asked God whether, if the messengers came for him, and prayed him to go, he might do so, wishing and hoping that God would say "Yes." And God, knowing his wish and inclination said, "Yes; go. You are disposed for it; if they come, go; go, and take the consequences." See what God said to Ezekiel: "Son of man, those men have set up their idols in their hearts, and put the stumbling-block of their iniquity before their face. Should I be enquired of at all by them? Therefore speak unto them, and say, 'Thus saith the Lord God, every man of the house of Israel that setteth up his idols in his heart, and putteth the stumbling-block of his iniquity before his face, and cometh to the prophet, I, the Lord, will answer him that cometh, according to the multitude of his idols.'"

If you ever engage in any concern or enterprise without enquiring His pleasure concerning it, one of these two things will be sure to follow, He will either plague you with disappointment, or He will curse you with success.

First, He will plague you with disappointment. He can turn every comfort into sorrow, every blessing into a curse, every friend into a foe; and every succeeding course shall set you more distant from prosperity. For says He, "If ye walk contrary to me, I will also walk contrary to you, and will punish you yet more for your sins."

Or otherwise, if He does not plague you with disappointment, He will curse you with success. The Israelites would have a king and be like the other countries; "You shall have one," said God, "and He gave them a king in His wrath." "We will have flesh," said they, "as well as this manna." "You shall have it," says God; but He sent leanness into their soul, so that while the flesh was between their teeth, the wrath of God came upon them. How wisely does Dr. Young express himself when he says:—

"God's choice is safer than our own;
Of ages past enquire,
What's the most formidable thing?
To have our own desire!"

So much for the second article,—Enquiry of Him.

Thirdly, it includes, *submission to Him.* It is a resigning ourselves to His will, and leaving our plans and schemes with Him, to crown or to frown upon, to prosper or to disappoint. We may desire success, and we may make known our wishes to God, but we must say, "Lord, my desire is not absolute; my desire is conditional. If it be for Thy glory and for my good, I pray Thee to succeed and bless. I have put myself under Thy guidance, and therefore it does not become me to choose, but to acquiesce in Thy will." Thus it was with David, when exiled from his palace. He went up on the hill, on the side of which the Lord agonized, and he said unto Zadok, "Carry back the ark of God into the city; if I shall find favour in the eyes of the Lord, He will bring me again, and show me both it and His habitation. But if He thus say, I have no delight in thee; behold, here I am, let Him do with me as seemeth good unto Him." And on another occasion he said, "Lord, my heart is not haughty, nor my eyes lofty, neither do I exercise myself in great matters, or in things too high for me. Surely I have behaved and quieted myself as a child that is weaned of his mother; my soul is even as a weaned child, and I leave myself entirely at Thy disposal."

Now there are three things which enter materially into this acquiescence, and leaving God to determine.

First, He has a *right* to determine, and we have no claim upon Him; "We are less than the least of all His mercies." "It is of the Lord's mercies we are not consumed, because His compassions fail not." He has a right to do what He will with His own; surely He may frown upon my plans and my schemes, and remain righteous still, wise still, gracious still.

And secondly, He has the *ability* to determine. His understanding is infinite—He is a God of Judgment. We know not what is best for us; but He knows, for He sees the end from the beginning, He can distinguish between appearance and reality; He *cannot* err.

And thirdly, because He is *willing* and *engaged* to determine: if you cast all your care upon Him you may be sure He careth for you; and is not the care of God sufficient in your affairs without the addition of your poor paltry anxiety? "For which of you by taking thought can add one cubit unto his stature?" Therefore says David, "Commit thy way unto the Lord; trust also in Him, and He shall bring it to pass," that is, if it be for your welfare. Again says Solomon, "Commit thy works unto the Lord, and the thought of thy heart shall be established," that is, you shall be free from that ferment, that ruffle of mind, which arises from anxiety and uncertainty.

There is nothing therefore which you should not bring before

God in prayer and leave with Him; as saith the Apostle, "Be careful for nothing, but in every thing by prayer and supplication with thanksgiving let your requests be made known unto God; and the peace of God, which passeth all understanding, shall keep your heart and mind through Jesus Christ." The only way in which you can have your mind kept in perfect peace is to have your mind stayed on God, and oh, what a relief, what a satisfaction is it to be enabled to leave all with Him.

I was thinking this morning in my retirement with regard to all the events and affairs of this life; I was thinking of four proposals, and suppose they were made to you which of these would you choose? First, would you like for all these things to be unarranged? Would you wish them all left to chance? After the vessel is unmoored would you like it to go on without a rudder, or pilot, or mast? Should you like this? If not, secondly, would you like any of your fellow-creatures to manage for you? One of your enemies? Certainly not! One of your friends? What friend do you know who is wise enough, patient enough, kind enough, and powerful enough, to manage all? Oh, you hear a voice, saying, "Cease from man whose breath is in his nostrils, for wherein is he to be accounted of?" Then, thirdly, should you like to have the management yourself? Many of you think more highly of yourselves than you ought to think, but are there any of you so proud as to desire to have the management of everything in your own hands? Do you believe you are wise, and patient, and powerful enough to regulate all yourself? Would you not look back directly upon life, and say, "How often have I desired a thing, which after a while I saw would be for my mischief and misery! How often have I wished to escape those things which proved to be my chief mercies?" And have you not all through life been learning this lesson, that "the way of man is not in himself; it is not in man that walketh to direct his steps"? Well then, if you would not like these things to be left to chance, if you would not like for a fellow-creature to have the management of them, if you would not like to have the regulation of them yourself; then, fourthly, how should you like to have them left with God, with a Being possessed of infinite perfection? Would you not like for Him to take the reins and govern the whole, saying, "Lord, here I am, do with me as seemeth Thee good"?

Now of that which we have spoken, this is the sum:

"Trust in the Lord with thy whole heart, and lean not to thine own understanding. In all thy ways acknowledge Him, and He shall direct thy paths." Oh, we have all need of this admonition. We are all prone to leave God out of our concerns. As to the wicked, God is not in all their thoughts; they wish not to think of Him. "He is not far from every one of them, for in Him they live and move and have their being;" but, they never see Him, never hear Him, never speak of Him, unless, indeed, when they take His name in vain. Now from these some are made to differ by the agency of divine grace, and yet they are only sanctified in part; as yet there are awful remains of this old Atheism; and there is a great difference between having a principle and making use of it, and between using it partially and occasionally, and using it constantly and universally. Some on the occurrence of anything peculiar or extraordinary are heard to say, "This is very providential." Why, *everything* is providential, and we ought to recognise this in little things, for what grand results originate from little things! "What a great matter does a little fire kindle." Jacob called Joseph and said, "Go and enquire after thy bre hren's welfare." Ah, little did he think he was sending his beloved son by a way which he should never return; that he should not see him for one-and-twenty years; that he should be intentionally murdered, but miraculously saved, and should become the saviour of the surrounding nation. Why you may go out in the morning, and before you return you may meet with something that may give a complexion to the whole of your future life. I say this is enough to make one cautious, prayerful and serious. It *should* produce these effects, and you should be in the fear of the Lord all the day long, and every day, and combine everything with His providence, agency and fear. Your religion is to consist in walking with God, in communing with Him not only in His ordinances but in His dispensations; in communing with Him not only in His word, but in His worship; and not only in His worship, but in His ways, till you are prepared for that blessed state where God will be all in all.

Men, brethren, and fathers, the sands of another period of your time are nearly run out. To-morrow you will see the end of the present year. It has been a remarkable year with regard to national concerns. It has been a very important year with regard to some of you, as it hath deprived you of

"The dear delights you once enjoyed,
And fondly called your own."

Your circle has been diminished. You enter the room, and you take up the Bible, and open the leaf which the hand of the dear deceased had folded down. You sit down at the family table, and David's place is empty. You think of the house of God, but you can no longer take sweet counsel and go to the house of God in company.

> "All, all on earth is shadow; all beyond is substance;
> How solid all where change shall be no more."

The year which is so soon to close, is the most important year you have ever past, because it brings you nearer to your dying hour—nearer to the house appointed for all living—nearer to the judgment day; and surely you would not let this morning pass away without the serious reflection, "When a few years are come, then I shall go the way whence I shall not return"; without the acknowledgment, "I know Thou wilt bring me to death and to the house appointed for all living"; without the prayer, the earnest prayer, "So teach us to number our days that we may apply our hearts unto wisdom."

On Tuesday you will find yourselves launched into another year, not knowing either what a day or an hour of that year may bring forth. But be assured that it will yield perpetual temptation; that bonds and afflictions will await you; that in whatever condition you may be found, that with all your indulgences—and how many of these have you!—still you are in a wilderness. But you are passing through it; you will soon reach your Father's house, and rejoin those who have gone before you, who are waiting to receive you into everlasting habitations.

There are but very few who at the beginning of the year have not some schemes to accomplish, some connections to form, some removals to take. Well, whatever of the kind you have before you, oh, take our text into the new year, and say, "If the Lord will, we shall live and do this or that."

When Moses had finished the tabernacle, he chose to rear it on the first day of the month, that is New Year's day; not that it was a better day than any other, but it was attended with more impression and influence. I hope there are persons here who seek after moral changes. Few I believe ever begin the year without resolving to avoid what they have condemned in themselves through the past year. We hope some of you will no longer suspend the concerns of the soul to a future period, but that you will immediately "seek the Lord while He may be found, and call upon Him while He is near." We hope there are some of you, dear young friends, who will begin from this coming year to "Remember your Creator in the days of your youth"; and then from that day, says God, "I will bless you." I hope that some who have not yet had an altar for God in their families will say with Joshua, "As for me and my house, we will serve the Lord." I hope some of you will rise earlier, and not degrade and injure yourselves by lying long in bed, but be more concerned to redeem your time. We hope some of you will be more disposed to be generous and assist all who need, especially those who are of the household of faith. We hope these may be your resolves; but make them in the strength of the Lord and the power of His grace, and say with the Apostle, "And this will we do, if God permit." And remember that His permission in such a case includes agency and influence; and "that of Him, and to Him, and through Him are all things, to whom be glory for ever. Amen."

XIV.

ADVENT FACTS AND ADMONITIONS.

(Preached on Sunday Morning, December 29th, 1844.)

"*And we know that the Son of God is come, and hath given us an understanding, that we may know Him that is true, and we are in Him that is true, even in the Son, Jesus Christ. This is the true God, and eternal life. Little children, keep yourselves from idols. Amen.*"—1 JOHN v. 20, 21.

IT was a true saying of the wise man, that "Pride goeth before destruction; and a haughty spirit before a fall." Therefore "let us not be high-minded but fear." "Let him that thinketh he standeth take heed lest he fall." Yet, my brethren, consistent with the self-diffidence and jealousy of oneself which the professors of religion should cherish is our seeking "a full assurance of hope," and a firmness of our principles, for the religion of the Gospel always inspires satisfaction of mind. The believer in Jesus is not the dupe of delusion; he is not driven about with every wind of doctrine; he does not flounder about in the mud and mire where there is no standing; his feet are founded upon a rock; his goings are established, and a new song is put into his mouth, even praise to our God. Yes, "He that will do His will, shall know of the doctrine whether it be of God." "He that believeth hath the witness in himself." Much of this evidence will not be convincing to others, but it will afford great consolation to his own mind, and he will rejoice in feeling that "it is a good thing for the heart to be established with grace." Hence the language of the first Christians in the words of our text: "And we know that the Son of God is come, and hath given us an understanding, that we may know Him that is true, and we are in Him that is true, even in His Son, Jesus Christ. This is the true God, and eternal life." If it be said that a considerable difference exists between us and these Christians to whom John wrote, we allow that there does; but this principally regards their supernatural endowments, not the ground of their confidence. They could not infer that they were in a state of salvation because they could speak with tongues, or raise the dead, or discern spirits, or foretell things to come. Our Saviour tells us that the possession of these was no evidence of divine grace, and that many who professed and exercised them will be despised by the Saviour in the last day. "On that day many will come to me, saying, 'Lord, Lord, open to us.' But I will profess unto them, I never knew you. Depart from Me, ye that work iniquity." If it be said, they were aided in their confidence by the miracles which they saw, we, brethren, have the same advantage. They were eye-witnesses, and ear-witnesses, but these things are recorded for our advantage, "that we, through patience and comfort of the Scriptures, might have hope." Let us, then, look at the contents of our text. Here we find four things:—A known fact, an interesting experience, an exalted character, and a very needful admonition.

I. We have A KNOWN FACT. "We know that the Son of God is come."

Upon this we shall not much enlarge; not because it possesses little importance, for it is all-important. His coming was prophesied ages before, and announced by a succesion of prophecies, becoming more and more evident, for the revelation of Him was "as the shining light, shining more and more unto the perfect day." To His Advent the godly looked forward in every age, regarding Him as "The Hope of Israel; the Saviour thereof in time of trouble." In all their external difficulties, or internal depression, the prophets led them to Him as the "Consolation of Israel." Zechariah said, "Sing and rejoice, O daughter of Zion: for lo, I come, and I will dwell in the midst of thee, saith the Lord." And says Isaiah, "Unto us a Child is born, unto us a Son is given, and the government shall be His shoulder; and His name shall be called Wonderful, Counsellor, the Mighty God, the everlasting Father, the Prince of Peace." But we enlarge less on this, because we have so largely noticed it on Sabbath evening, from the words of Micah, "And thou, Bethlehem Ephratah, though thou be little among the thousands of Judea, yet out of thee shall He come forth unto me, that shall be ruler in Israel; whose goings forth have been from of old, from everlasting;" and on Wednesday morning, from the language of David, "Blessed is he that cometh in the name of the Lord." We have considered the place, the time, and the manner of His Advent. We have called upon you to hear the language of the angels to the shepherds, "Fear not, for, behold, we bring you glad tidings of great joy, which shall be unto all people;" and to listen to the song of the heavenly host, "Glory to God in the highest, on earth peace and goodwill towards men." We have gone with you to Bethlehem, and have seen the Babe, wrapt in swaddling-clothes, lying in a manger; we have called you out to gaze on the star in the East, and have entered with the wise men who came to worship Him, and have seen them presenting Him "gifts—gold, frankincense, and myrrh." We have seen Simeon embracing Him, when he longed to be gone. We have heard Anna, the prophetess, speak of Him to all those who looked for redemption in Israel; and we would now only lead you back to the language of Moses on another occasion, "Ask, now, of the days that are past, which were before thee, since the day that God created man upon the earth; and ask from the one side of heaven unto the other, whether there hath been any such thing as this great thing, or hath been heard like it?"

II. We notice AN INTERESTING EXPERIENCE. This consists of two parts, distinct, indeed, but yet inseparably connected:—A knowledge of Him, and a union with Him.

First, a knowledge of Him. "He hath given us an understanding, that we may know Him that is true." This does not mean a new natural vision, but a spiritual discernment, so that we possess a view of Christ we never had before, and which issues in devoted attachment to Him, in dependence upon Him, and in obedience to His precepts, and desires after Him, and in concern to make Him known to others; for—

> "His worth, if all the nations knew,
> Sure all the earth would love Him too."

Knowledge is valuable according to its object. The knowledge of some things is vexatious, the knowledge of others is useless, but the knowledge of others is most desirable and excellent. It is even necessary, yea, absolutely necessary, "and this is life eternal, that they may know Thee the only true God, and Jesus Christ, whom Thou hast sent." Hear, therefore, the language of the Apostle with regard to this: "Yea, doubtless, and I count all things but loss for the excellency of the knowledge of Christ Jesus, my Lord."

But, brethren, as He is the Object, so He is the Author of

this knowledge. It is worthy of your remark, that *He* "hath given us an understanding, that we may know Him that is true." He has done it, who is "the Sun of Righteousness." It is by His light alone that we see light; and as the natural sun is only to be seen by his own shining, so is "the Sun of Righteousness," and is only discovered as He makes Himself known. Hence said the Saviour to His disciples, "I will manifest Myself unto them." Hence, says the Apostle John, "We have an unction from the Holy One"—from the communication of His blessed Spirit, who takes of the things of Christ, and reveals them unto the believer. For "the natural man knoweth not the things of the Spirit of God, neither can he know them, because they are spiritually discerned."

Secondly, consider our union with Him: "and we are *in* Him Him that is true." Not only have we an understanding to know Him, but we are also in Him. The language is expressive, and it is peculiar to Scripture; it implies no ordinary union, but a federal and vital union subsisting between Christ and Christians. They are in Him, as the constituents are in their representatives; as debtors are in their sureties. There subists not only a real union, but a very intimate one; every kind of connection is made use of to express it; as branches in the vine, through which they bear much fruit; as Noah, in the ark, and so safe from the deluge; as the man-slayer in the city of refuge, and so safe from the avenger of blood. Of what importance it is for us to be in Him, we may infer from the words of the Apostle, when he says, "That I may win Christ, and be found in Him;" and from his declaration, "There is now no condemnation to them that are in Christ Jesus."

Then, as it is of so much importance, you need not wonder that he should describe those who are the subjects of it, and say, "If any man be in Christ Jesus, he is a new creature. Old things are passed away; behold, all things are become new." For it is not to be supposed, without absurdity, that a living Saviour has dead members. But the disciples of Jesus have the same mind in them as was in Christ Jesus. This connection is indispensable, and there is no difference between Jew or Greek, but they are all one in Christ Jesus. Let us, therefore, notice:

III. An exalted character here mentioned. It regards Him whose advent we have been commemorating, "Whom having not seen we love, in whom though now we see Him not, yet believing, we rejoice with joy unspeakable and full of glory." It is a character which is threefold; it is *reality*, *divine* and *mediatorial*.

First, it is reality in Him that is true. How is this? Was this name given Him in reference to numbers of impostors, concerning whom he said, "Many will come in my name and will deceive many, and when they shall say, Lo, here is Christ, or lo, there, believe them not"? Or is He called so in reference to those who denied the truth, the reality of His incarnation—who would make His appearance only visionary? For while some have denied His divinity others have denied His humanity. He was not only divine, but He was truly man. He was a real personage. Thus the Apostles saw and heard and handled the word of life. "This is He that is true, and we are in Him that was true." Or was He called so in reference to the types and shadows that prefigured Him? "He was the bread of life;" He was the true rock whose streams flowed through the wilderness; the true altar; "the true tabernacle which the Lord pitched, and not man"; the true temple in which dwelt "all the fulness of the Godhead bodily." Or was He called so to distinguish Him from error? Everything seemed as nonentity compared to Him. He said, "If the Son make you free, ye shall be free indeed," as if every other freedom was pretence. "My flesh is meat indeed, and my blood is drink indeed," as if all other food was nothing. So those possessing Him are spoken of as having the "true riches," as if all other riches were lies. So with regard to this character given Him in our text. He is called "true." He is elsewhere called "the Faithful Witness." He can be depended upon in all His declarations, in all His threatenings, and in all His promises; whatever He said may be relied upon with absolute confidence. If He said, "Come unto me all ye that labour and are heavy laden, and I will give you rest," it is true, and you will find it even as He said. If He declared, "The water that I shall give him, shall be in him a well of water springing up into everlasting life," this is *true* of Him, and you will find it even as He hath said, for "the Scripture cannot be broken."

His affection as well as His wisdom prevents His being unfaithful. It is remarkable, therefore, that when He said to His sorrowing disciples, "Let not your hearts be troubled, ye believe in God, believe also in me. In my Father's house are many mansions"—He added, "If it were not so I would have told you." You may be sure I cannot impose upon you; I would not trifle with your love and confidence. "If it were not so I would have told you; I go to prepare a place for you."

Secondly, He is also *divine*. "He is the true God." He is so in distinction from all false divinities. "By Him were all things created, and without Him was not anything made that was made." Not only were "all things made by Him, but for Him and by Him all things consist." If He upholds all things by the might of His power, and if we are to honour the Son even as we honour the father; if Apostles prayed to Him, "Lord, increase our faith"; if Stephen when dying, "being full of the Holy Ghost," and not likely to be in error, invoked Him, saying, "Lord Jesus, receive my Spirit," and cried with a loud voice, "Lord, lay not this sin to their charge"; if "when God bringeth in His first begotten Son into the world, He saith, And let all the angels of God worship Him"; if this be true, then has He an infinite might in His arm, an infinite perfection in His righteousness, an infinite value in His blood, an infinite love and tenderness in His heart, and this is true.

Thirdly, He is also *mediatorial*, and "eternal life." How full is the language! Scripture tells us that "God hath blessed us with all spiritual blessings in Christ"; that also "it hath pleased the Father that in Him should all fulness dwell"; that He makes us wise, and righteous, and holy; that "He is made of God unto us wisdom, righteousness, sanctification, and redemption"; not that He strengthens you, but is our strength absolutely. "He is all our salvation and all our desire." And He is our "eternal life." We take it for granted that you believe that there is such a state of blessedness. It is not necessary to prove this, but it may be necessary to remark that this does not mean merely a perpetual existence, or a state of mere immortality, but an immortality having the highest degree of happiness connected with it, for, "Eye hath not seen, nor ear heard, neither have entered into the heart of man the things which God hath prepared for them that love Him." And we are to view this as connected with Him, for Who is the Author of it? "I am come that they may have life, and that they may have it more abundantly." Who is the Keeper of it? "This is the record which God hath given to us, eternal life, and this life is in His Son." Who is the Giver of it? "My sheep hear my voice, and I give unto them eternal life, and they shall never perish, neither shall any pluck them out of my hand." What is the Substance of it? "And so shall we ever be with the Lord." No wonder then it is called "eternal life." "This is the true God and eternal life."

IV. Here is, lastly, a VERY NECESSARY CAUTION AND ADMONI-

TION. "Little children keep yourselves from idols." Nothing seems so absurd as idolatry. One would be ready to suppose that no rational being would fall down before animals and reptiles, saying, "Ye are our gods." One would think it impossible to make an idol and then fall down and worship it. Yet you know how early idolatry commenced, and how widely idolatry spread. The Jews, to whom were committed the oracles of God, always had a propensity to this, and it required a captivity of seventy years to free them from a tendency and attachment to it.

But there is another kind of idolatry; there is an idolatry which is mental and spiritual. For what is idolatry? It is a transfer of something to a creature which belongs to "God over all, blessed for ever"—the transfer of love, or fear, or dependence, or obedience. Some prefer the honour which cometh from men, to the honour which cometh from God; some are lovers of pleasure more than lovers of God; some rest upon their orthodoxy, some upon their baptism, some upon the Lord's Supper. How do such idolize themselves? We may see, therefore, the propriety of the admonition, "Little children keep yourselves from idols."

Let us examine ourselves by the conduct of Our Lord Jesus Christ, and I presume there is not an individual present but would say with John, "We know that the Son of God is come." But do you know Him, and are you in Him? Do you believe in Him that is true? Do you worship Him that is divine? and are you looking to Him for eternal life who is "the only Mediator between God and man?" Perhaps some present are yet strangers to Him. This is an awful thing; while you remain in this state, to what dangers are you exposed! for He tells you in His word, because they are "a people of no understanding, therefore He that made them will not have mercy on them, and He that formed them will show them no favour." It is an awful thing to be out of Christ, because in this state you are exposed to the wrath of Him who is a consuming fire. "But it is a faithful saying and worthy of all acceptation, that Christ Jesus came into the world to save sinners." He invites us to come to Him, and says, "Him that cometh unto me I will in no wise cast out." If you will repair to Him, you will find a more blessed reception than ever a dear child received from the most affectionate parent. He will receive you to Himself now in a way of grace, and at death in a way of glory, that where He is, there you may be also. But remember, if you have no interest in Him, that He will be a destroyer instead of a saviour. He is coming again to deal with you. "Behold He cometh with clouds, and every eye shall see Him, and they also which pierced Him, and all kindreds of the earth shall wail because of Him." "Once in the end of the world hath He appeared to put away sin by the sacrifice of Himself, and unto those that look for Him"—God grant that this may be the case with you all!—"will He appear the second time without sin unto salvation." Endeavour to gain that state of mind which rises above doubts and fears and distressing apprehensions; endeavour to come to a certainty with regard to your state, till you can say with Job, "I know that my Redeemer liveth;" and with Paul, "I know whom I have believed." Be not only importunate with regard to the things which will prepare you for death, but for that state of mind which will aid you in all your dealings with others, by which you may recommend the Saviour, and be able to say, "That which we have seen and heard declare we unto you, that ye also may have fellowship with us, and truly our fellowship is with the Father, and with His Son Jesus Christ."

Then, again, remember: If you confess Him before men, He will confess you before His Father and His holy angels; if you deny Him, He also will deny you; if you are ashamed of Him, He will also be ashamed of you. Therefore be openly and unquestionably His. Do not use ambiguous terms, like those who wish to introduce error; not like Isaiah's wizards, who "peep and mutter." Do not be afraid to let it be known to whom you belong, and what you believe. *Abandon Him at once*, or hold fast the profession of your faith without wavering, knowing that He is faithful who hath promised. Then whatever lovers others may follow, and however they may divide their affections, show to all around that you love Him, that His love is shed abroad in your heart, "who died for you and rose again;" not only that you love Him, but that you love Him *supremely*, that you have no idols who rival Him. Remember, that you do not love Him unless you love Him *above all;* that He hath said, "He that loveth father or mother more than me, and he that loveth son or daughter more than me, is not worthy of me." He demands your heart, and oh, how infinitely He deserves it! Let Him have it undividedly.

XV.

OUR HIGH PRIEST.*

(Preached on Sunday Morning, June 5th, 1845.)

"*For we have not an high priest who cannot be touched with the feeling of our infirmities; but was in all points tempted like as we are, yet without sin.*"—HEBREWS iv. 15.

CHRIST is called in the Scriptures "the friend of sinners," and "the consolation of Israel." He is our refuge from the wrath to come. He is the foundation on which we may build for eternity; "and He is the fountain opened for sin and uncleanness." Faith finds in Him "a balm for every wound, and a cordial for every fear." Peter addresses the Christians scattered abroad, and says, "Whom having not seen, ye love; in whom though now ye see Him not, yet believing, ye rejoice with joy unspeakable and full of glory." Christians on your way to the table of the Lord, we hope that you are come here this morning counting "all things but loss for the excellency of the knowledge of Christ Jesus Our Lord"; and if you are, hear what the Apostle says: "For we have not an high priest who cannot be touched with the feeling of our infirmities."

We may premise two things before we come to the illustration of the passage.

First, our text furnishes an answer to the words immediately preceding it. "Seeing then that we have a great high priest that is passed into the heavens, Jesus the Son of God, let us hold fast our profession." But we may be ready to suppose, as He is no more in the world, and has passed into heaven, that His concern for us and His communion with us have ceased. As when a friend is gone far away, we think of the proverb, "Out of sight, out of mind"; and when persons rise

* This sermon was accidentally omitted from the volume of Morning Sermons, and it is therefore inserted here.

in their condition they often get very bad memories; they forget those in humbler spheres, from whom they have derived many favours and benefits, and hardly know them when they meet. Thus it was, you know, with the chief butler after his promises to Joseph. "Yet did not the chief butler remember Joseph, but forgat him." But, brethren, it is otherwise here, for whether we wake or sleep we live together with Him. The ligature between Him and us is unbroken, and will ever remain so. He remembers us now He is come into His kingdom, and now that He has obtained "a name which is above every name."

Secondly, two negatives make a strong affirmation. Therefore when the Apostle says, "We have not an high priest who cannot be touched with the feeling of our infirmities," the meaning is, We have an high priest who *can* be touched with the feeling of our infirmities."

Let us, then, plunge into the subject; and there are three things which we must regard. The first concerns His official character; the second regards His personal disposition; and the third the use we are to make of so interesting an announcement. For, brethren, when we come to examine, we shall find much depends upon our high priest being "touched with the feeling of our infirmities."

I. We have to notice His OFFICIAL CHARACTER. "An high priest."

In general, this is the substance of the gospel. "God so loved the world, that He gave His only begotten Son, that whosoever believeth in Him should not perish but have everlasting life." He is the Mediator of the new covenant, in the execution of which He sustains three offices—that of a Prophet, Priest, and King. His priestly office is the principal theme of this epistle. It is of unspeakable importance, and enters into every article of our creed. As a Prophet we rejoice in His instructions; and as a King we bow to His authority. But neither of these offices deeply affects the experience of a Christian. His Priesthood gives the vitality and efficiency to the other offices He sustains. Hence it has always been principally opposed by the enemies of the gospel, and therefore it becomes you to hold it the more tenaciously, and endeavour to get clear conceptions of it.

In order to obtain proper notions of His Priesthood, we may go back and consider the law, which was "a shadow of good things to come," while the body was Christ. The high priest was the principal person in the Jewish religion. All the worship of God was under His direction. He was the medium of God's communications to the people, and of the approach of His people to God. There were three things which peculiarly belonged to His functions.

First, *Sacrifices.* "Hence," says the Apostle, "every high priest is ordained to offer gifts and sacrifices. Wherefore it is of necessity that this man have somewhat also to offer." And He had "somewhat also to offer"; and it was nothing less than His own precious blood. "He made peace by the blood of His cross." "He hath put away sin by the sacrifice of Himself."

> "His precious blood did once atone,
> And now it pleads before the throne."

"It was an offering and a sacrifice to God for a sweet smelling savour," that is, it is infinitely acceptable to God, and delightful on our behalf. It is a mercy that a truth like this is so plainly revealed. "Surely He hath borne our griefs and carried our sorrows; yet we did esteem Him stricken, smitten of God, and afflicted. But He was wounded for our transgressions, He was bruised for our iniquities, the chastisement of our peace was upon Him, and by His stripes we are healed." Here the broken spirit is bound up; here the eyes wet with the tears of penitential grief wiped dry; and a voice is heard, saying, "Go in peace, thy sins are forgiven thee."

Secondly, *Intercession.* On the day of Atonement, the high priest took the blood of the slain victim in a basin, and entered with this into the most holy place, and sprinkled it upon the mercy-seat; and he burnt incense upon the golden altar, as prefigurative of the intercession of our Saviour for us. So says the Apostle, "Christ is become a High Priest for us; by a greater and more perfect tabernacle, not made with hands, that is to say, not of this building; neither by the blood of goats and calves, but by His own blood He entered in once into the holy place, having obtained redemption for us." It is not necessary to inquire whether this intercession be verbal; it is enough for us to know that it is real and effectual, for "the Father heareth Him always." His very appearance before God there is a proof that He hath finished the work that was given Him to do. There He shows the tokens of His sufferings; there He pleads His sacrifice on our behalf, and thus secures the acceptance of His people's persons and services, and obtains for all the redeemed the advantages derivable from His death.

Thirdly, *Benediction;* for after the sacrifice was offered, and intercession made by the burning of incense, He came forth from the divine presence and blessed the people who were now considered as reconciled. We have the form of words used on this occasion by Aaron and his sons, " On this wise ye shall bless the children of Israel, saying, the Lord bless thee and keep thee; the Lord make His face to shine upon thee, and be gracious unto thee; the Lord lift up His countenance upon thee, and give thee peace." But in all things Christ has the pre-eminence, for the priests under the law could only bless the people verbally. But Jesus can do more than this. He looks down and commands the blessing, even life for evermore. It is through Him that we "are blessed with all spiritual blessings."

II. We now pass to consider a very momentous article, HIS PERSONAL DISPOSITION. "For we have not an High Priest who cannot be touched with the feeling of our infirmities." Corporeally considered, I know not whether Christ was tall or short, stout or slender, plain or fair, but I perfectly know what His temper was—

> " His heart is made of tenderness,
> His bowels melt with love."

Before His Incarnation, it was prophesied concerning Him, " A bruised reed shall He not break, and the smoking flax shall He not quench: He shall bring forth judgment unto truth." " He shall save the souls of the needy." " He shall gather the lambs in His arms, and carry them in His bosom." Is it possible for us to read through His history while He was here, and not see all this exemplified? Who was it that wept at the grave of Lazarus? Who was it that wept over Jerusalem? Who was it that fed the hungry multitude on the grass, lest in returning home they should faint by the way? Who was it that stood still on His journey to hear the cry of the poor blind beggar? Who was it that said to a widow, " Weep not," and raising her son to life gave him back to her arms? Where shall we end? Who was it that " took our infirmities and bore our sicknesses"? It is He who was "touched with the feeling of our infirmities" while here. But is He so now? This is the question. Yes, " We have not an high priest who cannot be touched with the feeling of our infirmities" now. The Apostle employs the same word, where he says, "If one member suffer all the members suffer with it." But we are not to look to a suffering fellow-creature for a full explanation of this. His suffering days are now all over. Nevertheless He is clothed with a body like our own. He did not lay aside His humanity when He arose from the dead, and never will. After His resurrection, He said to His disciples, "Handle me, and see, for a spirit hath not flesh and bones as ye see me have; and He showed them His hands and His feet. Then were the disciples glad when they saw the Lord." His ascension did not deprive them of His affections. Nay, it served to give His feelings more force and sensibility. How, then, are we to understand the Apostle in the expression before us? It may, I think, include these four things: knowledge, experience, sympathy, and assistance.

It includes *knowledge.* He cannot be "touched with the feeling of our infirmities" if He be ignorant of them. You have a child some miles off, and he may now be groaning under a fracture of the limb, or he may be in the agonies of death. Why does not your hand minister to him? You know it not. Jacob knew nothing of Joseph's being thrown into a pit, or of his being sold as a slave, or of his being imprisoned and bound; and in vain Joseph cried from time to time, "My father, my father," for Jacob could not hear him. But it is otherwise here. Jesus is "touched with a feeling of our infirmities." He is acquainted with them all. "He knows all your walking through this great wilderness"; "He knows your soul in adversity"; and you may address Him in the language of David, "Thou tellest all my wanderings; put Thou my tears into Thy bottle. Are they not in Thy book? All my desire is before Thee, and my groaning is not hid from Thee." "Behold I go forward," says Job, "but He is not there, and backward, but I cannot perceive Him: on the left hand, where He doth work, but I cannot behold Him: He hideth Himself on the right hand, that I cannot see Him: but He knoweth the way that I take: when He hath tried me I shall come forth as gold."

It takes in, secondly, *experience.* We may exemplify this in the whole of the Saviour's life. For what can any of His people feel, that He has not felt before them? Are any of you poor? What do princes and kings know of your poverty?

But He has tasted the bitter cup; He has drank thereof Himself. He was born in a stable, and laid in a manger, and as He grew up He had not where to lay His head; and after His death, He was buried in another's grave. Are you suffering from satanic influence?

> "He knows what sore temptations mean;
> For He has felt the same."

It is said of Lot, that "his righteous soul was vexed from day to day by the filthy conversation of the wicked." So will yours be, if you have any regard for the honour of God, and concern for the salvation of those around you; you cannot be a spectator of wickedness and crime without pain and sorrow; but if you were ten times more holy than you are, you would be ten times more affected than you now are. How then was it with Him who was perfectly holy, and whose abhorrence of evil was complete? With what infinite emphasis could He say, in the words of inspiration, "I beheld the transgressors, and was grieved. Rivers of waters run down mine eyes because men keep not Thy law;" for we see that "He came to His own, and His own received Him not," "neither did His brethren believe in Him." He was deemed an impostor; "despised and rejected of men." You sometimes complain of the insensibility of your fellow-creatures and connections, while you may be suffering distress and affliction; but He looked for some to take pity, and there was none, and for comforters, and He found none. One of His disciples denied Him, and another betrayed Him, and others of them slept in the garden; they could not watch one hour; and "they all forsook Him and fled." Paul mentions cruel mockings among other things which the martyrs endured; and you know who said in prophecy, "Reproach hath broken my heart, and I am full of heaviness." Everything that was vile was laid to His charge. He was "a drunkard, a winebibber, and a friend of publicans and sinners." "He hath," said they, "a devil and is mad." He was seditious, and an enemy to Cæsar. He was called a blasphemer, and reckoned an enemy to the people. And for your sakes, brethren, His Father hid His face from Him, amidst His expiring agony. Are any of you walking in darkness and have no light? Call Him to mind who said upon the cross, "My God, my God, why hast Thou forsaken me?" Do you ever think of dying? O yes, you do. It is a source of alarm. It is an awful thing to die, for you have not gone this way heretofore. It is all new to you. Henry says, Christians will need strength they never had, when they come to do a work they never did; your fellow Christians may then attend to comfort you, but they do not know what it is to die, and it must be comparatively poor comfort, coming from absence of experience. But there is One who will be near you, who actually knows what it is by experience. Thus you may say, however you may reflect upon your condition, that your Saviour is "touched with the feeling of your infirmities."

Thirdly, it comprehends *sympathy.* If this does not entirely grow out of the former article, it is increased by it. You cannot sympathise with an individual properly without something of his experience. Here thought meets thought, and soul touches soul, and there is a passage open for grief to pass from one to the other. And what is it we most admire in our fellow-creatures? Is it a fine dress, or their large house, or their great wealth, or even their talents? Oh, no, but it is those fine feelings which render them tender, social, and useful. It is pity for the wretched, and compassion for the helpless; it is the softened heart, the melting eye, the sympathising countenance, the soothing voice. And where are those best learned but in the school of affliction? We expect therefore always that those who have been much in trouble will be the most humane. He who can say "I am the man who hath seen affliction," "He hath brought me into darkness and not into light," will never be able to hear with carelessness the moaning of a fellow-creature, whose poignancy of distress is so great as to induce him to say, "Pity me, pity me, O ye my friends, for the hand of God hath touched me." What said God to the Jews: "Be you kind to strangers." Why? "Ye were strangers in a strange land." Now we can apply all this to Our Lord and Saviour. "In that He Himself hath suffered being tempted, He is able to succour them that are tempted" —which reminds us of the article we have yet to notice,—

Assistance. Sympathy will lead to this; and some are relieved from no better principle than for the sake of relieving themselves of the uneasiness they feel at the sight of a fellow-creature in distress. "The eye of pity feedeth the heart;" but there may be persons who feel sincerely and deeply, but their sympathy can do very little, however generous they may be; and though the "ear is not heavy that it cannot hear," yet the hand is shortened that it cannot save," and they are constrained to say from sheer inability, "Go in peace, be ye warmed and be ye filled." But where there is power, we cannot believe your sympathy to be sincere unless it leads you to assist and relieve. Now, my brethren, you know with regard to our Saviour that "all power is given unto Him, in heaven and in earth," and "nothing is too hard for the Lord." He has the most ample resources, and can and will supply all your needs.

III. We are to glance at THE USE WE ARE TO MAKE OF THIS INTERESTING ANNOUNCEMENT. There is no truth in the Bible that is merely speculative. When it is examined, it will always be found to have a bearing upon experience. Hence we read of walking in the truth, and of walking "in all the commandments and ordinances blameless."

"We have not an high priest which can be touched with the feeling of our infirmities." There are here four results which we will just mention, and leave to your own meditation, if, indeed, you do ever meditate.

The first we mention is *love.* Love begets love. Surely we ought to love Him who hath so loved us; who, "because the children were partakers of flesh and blood, likewise Himself took part of the same, that through death He might destroy him that had the power of death, that is, the devil, and deliver them who through fear of death were all their lifetime subject to bondage;" "who, though He was rich, for our sakes became poor, that we through His poverty might be made rich;" "who died for us, that we might live for ever;" "who remembered us in our low estate;" and who is now "touched with the feeling of our infirmities." But how are you to show your love to Him? You are to show it by keeping Him in your thoughts, by talking of Him with your lips, by recommending Him in your lives, by denying yourselves, by taking up your cross, and by exerting all your influence and resources to promote His cause and advance His glory. "If ye love Me," said He, "keep My commandments." And if there is one command issued by His dying breath which requires but little sacrifice, and which is attended by but little self-denial, it is where He enjoins you to approach His table, saying, "Do this in remembrance of Me;" and, surely, you will peculiarly regard this, and attend to it with cheerfulness, gratitude and joy.

The record is *resemblance.* Admiration of Him is nothing unless you imitate Him. He is infinitely more, indeed, than an example, but then He is nothing less. "He that saith he abideth in Him, ought himself also to walk even as He walked." "If any man have not the Spirit of Christ, he is none of His." "Let the same mind, therefore, be in you, which was also in Christ Jesus." If He was "meek and lowly in heart," you should also seek to be "meek and lowly in heart." If He could say, "I delight to do Thy will, O God: Thy law is within my heart;" surely you should say, in your measure and degree, "My meat is to do the will of my Father which is in Heaven." And if He is "touched with the feeling of your infirmities," surely you ought to be touched with the infirmities of your fellow-creatures. "Bear ye one another's burdens, and so fulfil the law of Christ." This, surely, is the improvement of the subject: "We that are strong ought to bear the infirmities of the weak, and not to please ourselves."

Consolation is another result. How consoling it is to find those who have rejoiced in our prosperity weeping with us in adverse circumstances. Such friends are ministering spirits, sent to minister to the heart of salvation. O Christians, you may be greatly afflicted, but you are not alone. You have friends to feel for you, real friends. You have One especially "who sticketh closer than a brother." Oh, think of Him; He knows all your desires and all your distresses. "He will not suffer you to be tempted above that you are able to bear." Think of Him, who "does not afflict willingly, nor grieve the children of men." He has a gracious design in it. Think of Him who has said, "I will never leave thee, nor forsake thee." Are you pressed by the infirmities of old age? Think of Him who hath said, "Even to your old age, I am He; and even to hoar hairs will I carry you: I have made, and I will bear; even I will carry, and will deliver you." Are you called to suffer bodily disease? He will "strengthen you upon the bed of languishing." Are you bereaved? Who has not been bereaved? Who has not lost a friend? What says the language of prophecy concerning the Saviour? "The Spirit of the Lord God is upon me; because the Lord hath anointed me to preach good tidings unto the meek. He hath sent me to bind up the broken-hearted, to proclaim liberty to the captives, and the opening of the prison to them that are bound; to proclaim the acceptable year of the Lord, and the day of vengeance of our God; to comfort all that mourn; to appoint unto them that mourn in Zion, to give unto them beauty for ashes, the oil of joy for mourning, the garment of praise for the spirit of heaviness; that they might be called trees of righteousness, the planting of the Lord, that He might be glorified."

Lastly, *prayer.* You see what encouragement we have for this. This is the Apostle's own improvement of the thing, therefore we ought not to pass it by; for, says he, "LET US THEREFORE COME BOLDLY TO THE THRONE OF GRACE, THAT WE MAY OBTAIN MERCY, AND FIND GRACE TO HELP IN TIME OF NEED."

Other Solid Ground Titles

In addition to *Withhold Not Thine Hand* which you hold in your hand, Solid Ground is honored to offer many other uncovered treasure, many for the first time in more than a century:

LET THE CANNON BLAZE AWAY by Joseph P. Thompson
THE STILL HOUR: *Communion with God in Prayer* by Austin Phelps
COLLECTED WORKS of James Henley Thornwell (4 vols.)
CALVINISM IN HISTORY *by Nathaniel S. McFetridge*
OPENING SCRIPTURE: *Hermeneutical Manual* *by Patrick Fairbairn*
THE ASSURANCE OF FAITH *by Louis Berkhof*
THE PASTOR IN THE SICK ROOM *by John D. Wells*
THE BUNYAN OF BROOKLYN: *Life & Sermons of I.S. Spencer*
THE NATIONAL PREACHER: S*ermons from 2nd Great Awakening*
FIRST THINGS: F*irst Lessons God Taught Mankind* *Gardiner Spring*
BIBLICAL & THEOLOGICAL STUDIES *by 1912 Faculty of Princeton*
THE POWER OF GOD UNTO SALVATION *by B.B. Warfield*
THE LORD OF GLORY *by B.B. Warfield*
A GENTLEMAN & A SCHOLAR: *Memoir of J.P. Boyce* *by J. Broadus*
SERMONS TO THE NATURAL MAN *by W.G.T. Shedd*
SERMONS TO THE SPIRITUAL MAN *by W.G.T. Shedd*
HOMILETICS AND PASTORAL THEOLOGY *by W.G.T. Shedd*
A PASTOR'S SKETCHES 1 & 2 *by Ichabod S. Spencer*
THE PREACHER AND HIS MODELS *by James Stalker*
IMAGO CHRISTI *by James Stalker*
A HISTORY OF PREACHING *by Edwin C. Dargan*
LECTURES ON THE HISTORY OF PREACHING *by J. A. Broadus*
THE SCOTTISH PULPIT *by William Taylor*
THE SHORTER CATECHISM ILLUSTRATED *by John Whitecross*
THE CHURCH MEMBER'S GUIDE *by John Angell James*
THE SUNDAY SCHOOL TEACHER'S GUIDE *by John A. James*
CHRIST IN SONG: *Hymns of Immanuel from All Ages* *by Philip Schaff*
COME YE APART: *Daily Words from the Four Gospels* *by J.R. Miller*
DEVOTIONAL LIFE OF THE S.S. TEACHER *by J.R. Miller*

Printed in the United States
45570LVS00003B/1-3